Communications
in Computer and Information Science   2610

Series Editors

Gang Li, *School of Information Technology, Deakin University, Burwood, VIC, Australia*
Joaquim Filipe, *Polytechnic Institute of Setúbal, Setúbal, Portugal*
Zhiwei Xu, *Chinese Academy of Sciences, Beijing, China*

Rationale

The CCIS series is devoted to the publication of proceedings of computer science conferences. Its aim is to efficiently disseminate original research results in informatics in printed and electronic form. While the focus is on publication of peer-reviewed full papers presenting mature work, inclusion of reviewed short papers reporting on work in progress is welcome, too. Besides globally relevant meetings with internationally representative program committees guaranteeing a strict peer-reviewing and paper selection process, conferences run by societies or of high regional or national relevance are also considered for publication.

Topics

The topical scope of CCIS spans the entire spectrum of informatics ranging from foundational topics in the theory of computing to information and communications science and technology and a broad variety of interdisciplinary application fields.

Information for Volume Editors and Authors

Publication in CCIS is free of charge. No royalties are paid, however, we offer registered conference participants temporary free access to the online version of the conference proceedings on SpringerLink (http://link.springer.com) by means of an http referrer from the conference website and/or a number of complimentary printed copies, as specified in the official acceptance email of the event.

CCIS proceedings can be published in time for distribution at conferences or as post-proceedings, and delivered in the form of printed books and/or electronically as USBs and/or e-content licenses for accessing proceedings at SpringerLink. Furthermore, CCIS proceedings are included in the CCIS electronic book series hosted in the SpringerLink digital library at http://link.springer.com/bookseries/7899. Conferences publishing in CCIS are allowed to use our online conference service (Meteor) for managing the whole proceedings lifecycle (from submission and reviewing to preparing for publication) free of charge.

Publication process

The language of publication is exclusively English. Authors publishing in CCIS have to sign the Springer CCIS copyright transfer form, however, they are free to use their material published in CCIS for substantially changed, more elaborate subsequent publications elsewhere. For the preparation of the camera-ready papers/files, authors have to strictly adhere to the Springer CCIS Authors' Instructions and are strongly encouraged to use the CCIS LaTeX style files or templates.

Abstracting/Indexing

CCIS is abstracted/indexed in DBLP, Google Scholar, EI-Compendex, Mathematical Reviews, SCImago, Scopus. CCIS volumes are also submitted for the inclusion in ISI Proceedings.

How to start

To start the evaluation of your proposal for inclusion in the CCIS series, please send an e-mail to ccis@springer.com

Shantanu Pal · Shivani Malhotra · Isha Gupta ·
Amit Kumar
Editors

Emerging Technology and Sustainable Solutions

Second International Conference, ICETSS 2024
Punjab, India, October 8–9, 2024
Proceedings, Part I

 Springer

Editors
Shantanu Pal
Deakin University
Melbourne, VIC, Australia

Isha Gupta
Chitkara University
Rajpura, Punjab, India

Shivani Malhotra
Chitkara University
Rajpura, Punjab, India

Amit Kumar
Chitkara University
Rajpura, Punjab, India

ISSN 1865-0929   ISSN 1865-0937 (electronic)
Communications in Computer and Information Science
ISBN 978-3-032-11487-7   ISBN 978-3-032-11488-4 (eBook)
https://doi.org/10.1007/978-3-032-11488-4

This Springer imprint is published by the registered company Springer Nature Switzerland AG
The registered company address is: Gewerbestrasse 11, 6330 Cham, Switzerland

If disposing of this product, please recycle the paper.

Preface

The 2nd International Conference on Emerging Technology and Sustainable Solutions (ICETSS 2024) took place on October 8–9, 2024, at Chitkara University's Department of Electronics and Communication Engineering. It brought together academics, technologists, and industry leaders from around the world to talk about current and future sustainability issues. This event, which was planned in close collaboration with Deakin University in Australia, aimed to encourage discussions across disciplines and spark new ideas in areas that are important for long-term social progress. More than 100 people from fields like intelligent computing, communication networks, embedded systems, IoT, and biomedical technologies came together for the conference. It was a unique place to share research, suggest real-world solutions, and move the global sustainable development agenda forward. ICETSS 2024 focused on sharing knowledge in a holistic way, putting it to use, and coming up with strategies that would have a big impact on intelligent, sustainable systems that would help both people and the environment. The conference included paper presentations, keynote speeches, and workshops.

The thorough and strict triple-blind peer review process was a big part of ICETSS 2024. The conference received an impressive total of 133 article submissions from around the world. After a careful three-month review by 53 expert reviewers in which submissions received on average three reviews each, 34 full papers and 35 short papers were accepted for publication. This shows the event's high academic standards and commitment to excellence in research dissemination. The chosen papers looked at disruptive technologies, cyber-physical system security, sustainable communication networks, new devices, and solutions that could change the way we deal with problems in cities and rural areas, with a focus on moral, social, and technological progress. Support from international partners and a well-known publication partner showed that the conference was an important catalyst for academic collaboration and making a difference in the real world. In the end, ICETSS 2024 not only showed off cutting-edge research, but it also inspired people to take action that would change the world. It brought together a global community that is committed to finding sustainable solutions and creating a future that is both technologically advanced and environmentally friendly.

We extend our heartfelt gratitude to the esteemed faculty members and dedicated support staff of Chitkara University for their invaluable contributions to the successful conduct of the 2nd International Conference on Emerging Technology and Sustainable Solutions (ICETSS 2024).

Shivani Malhotra
Isha Gupta
Shantanu Pal
Amit Kumar

Organization

General Chairs

Shivani Malhotra	Chitkara University, India
Imali Dias	Deakin University, Australia

General Co-chairs

Hitesh Garg	NXP Semiconductors, India
Isha Gupta	Chitkara University, India
Rubina Dutta	Chitkara University, India
Kevin Lee	Deakin University, Australia

Editors

Shivani Malhotra	Chitkara University, India
Shantanu Pal	Deakin University, Australia
Isha Gupta	Chitkara University, India
Amit Kumar	Chitkara University, India

Advisory Committee

Prakash Hegade	KLE Technological University, India
Anuja Bhargava	GLA University, India
Faizan Ahmad	Cardiff Metropolitan University, UK
Reecha Sharma	Punjabi University Patiala, India
Arpan Deyasi	RCC Institute of Information Technology, India
Munish Vashishath	J.C. Bose University of Science and Technology, YMCA, India
Naresh Kumar	UIET, Panjab University, India
Balwinder Singh	Centre for Development of Advanced Computing, India
Divya Sharma	Galgotias University, India
Usha Chauhan	Galgotias University, India
Rajesh Singla	NIT Jalandhar, India

M. Elangova	Government College of Engineering Srirangam, India
Manwinder Singh	Lovely Professional University, India
Amrita Rai	Lloyd Institute of Engineering and Technology, India
Kaushik Ghosh	Institute of Nano Science & Technology, India
Naveen Kumar	CHRIST (Deemed to be University), Bangalore, India
Dimple Nagpal	Lovely Professional University, India
Angsuman Sarkar	Kalyani Government Engineering College, India
Balwinder Singh Dhaliwal	NITTTR Chandigarh, India
Raghu Indrakanti	Anurag University, India
Renu Dhir	NIT Jalandhar, India
Jaspal Singh	Centre for Development of Advanced Computing, India
Jyotir Moy Chatterjee	Lord Buddha Education Foundation, Nepal
Rajesh Khanna	Thapar Institute of Engineering and Technology, India
Satyabrata Jit	Indian Institute of Technology (BHU), Varanasi, India
Manash Chanda	Meghnad Saha Institute of Technology, India
David Gullien	University of Málaga, Spain
Sandeep Gill	NIITR, Chandigarh, India
Anjali Sharma	Himachal Pradesh University, India
Swati Singh	Himachal Pradesh University, India
Vivek Bhardwaj	Manipur University, India
Renu Dhir	Dr B R Ambedkar National Institute of Technology, India

Program Committee Chairs

Gupta, Isha	Chitkara University, India
Kumar, Amit	Chitkara University, India
Malhotra, Shivani	Chitkara University, India
Pal, Shantanu	Deakin University, Australia

Program Committee Members

Gupta, Isha	Chitkara University, India
Kumar, Amit	Chitkara University, India

Malhotra, Shivani	Chitkara University, India
Pal, Shantanu	Deakin University, Australia

Reviewers

Aggarwal, Sonam	.
Bansal, Aarti	Chitkara University, India
Dhawan, Sunil	Chitkara University, India
Dutta, Rubina	Chitkara University, India
Garg, Meenu	Chitkara University, India
Geetanjali, Geetanjali	Chitkara University, India
Goel, Shanky	Chitkara University, India
Gupta, Lipika	Chitkara University, India
Jindal, Poonam	Chitkara University, India
Kaur, Rajwinder	.
Kaur, Gurjinder	Chitkara University, India
Kaur, Rashpinder	Chitkara University, India
Kaur, DSwapandeep	Chitkara University, India
Kaur, Deepti Prit	Chitkara University, India
Kaur, Shaminder	Chitkara University, India
Kumar, Rajeev	.
Kumar, Sandeep	.
Malhotra, Priyanka	Chitkara University, India
Sachdeva, Ashish	Manav Rachna University, India
Saini, Parul	Chitkara University, India
Sandhu, Amanpreet	Chitkara University India
Sethi, Monika	.
Sharma, Preeti	Chitkara University, India
Singal, TL	Chitkara University, India
Singh, Rajvir	Chitkara University, India
Vikas Malhotra, Vikas	.
Chopra, Garima	Chitkara University, India
Kaur, Harsimran Jit	Chitkara University, India

Contents

Utilizing Blockchain for Secure and Transparent Voting Systems

Ashish Kumar[1]([⊠]), Sukhwinder Kaur[2], and Gunjan Sethi[3]

[1] Department of Computer Science and Engineering, GLA University, Mathura, Uttar Pradesh, India
`ashishkumar291996@gmail.com`
[2] Lovely Professional University, Phagwara, India
[3] Delhi Technical Campus, Greater Noida, India

Abstract. In an era of growing worries about the integrity and openness of election processes, blockchain technology has emerged as a possible alternative for improving voting system security and reliability. This research investigates the potential of blockchain technology to transform voting systems, conducting a comprehensive analysis of its advantages, challenges, case studies, security concerns, legislative impacts, and future prospects. Commencing with an exploration of the limitations of traditional voting mechanisms, the paper offers a detailed examination of blockchain technology, emphasizing its decentralized nature, immutability, and cryptographic principles. By reviewing real-world case studies and pilot initiatives, the paper demonstrates the practical utility of blockchain in electoral processes, showcasing enhancements in transparency, integrity, and accessibility. Nonetheless, the implementation of blockchain-based voting systems also poses obstacles, including scalability, inclusivity, and regulatory uncertainties, necessitating careful consideration to ensure widespread adoption and approval. The discussion of security issues, encompassing potential risks and vulnerabilities, underscores the significance of robust governance mechanisms and cryptographic protections. Moreover, the paper delves into the regulatory and legal ramifications of integrating blockchain into voting systems, addressing concerns regarding data privacy, adherence to regulations, and electoral standards. Looking forward, the paper identifies future research avenues and opportunities for innovation, including advancements in cryptography, consensus mechanisms, and decentralized governance structures. Governments and election authorities stand to leverage blockchain technology to enhance the integrity, reliability, and inclusiveness of electoral procedures, thereby advancing democracy and civic engagement.

Keywords: voting systems · transparency · decentralized governance · electoral processes

1 Introduction

Voting is a crucial part of how we make decisions in our communities, but sometimes it's not as fair or correct as we'd like it to be. For example, in traditional voting, we use things like paper ballots, which can be easily tampered with or lost. Plus, there's

S. Pal et al. (Eds.): ICETSS 2024, CCIS 2610, pp. 1–11, 2026.
https://doi.org/10.1007/978-3-032-11488-4_1

always a risk of someone cheating or making mistakes when counting the votes. This can lead to doubts about whether the results truly stand for what people wanted. Voting serves as a fundamental aspect of democratic societies, providing a means to express opinions on various matters. Traditionally, voting methods encompass paper-based and computerized systems. Enter blockchain, a fancy term for a special kind of computer system [1]. Think of it like a big digital ledger, or a record book, that's spread out across lots of different computers instead of being stored in one place. What makes blockchain special is that once information, like votes, is recorded on it, it's incredibly hard to change or tamper with. That's because each new piece of information is linked to the ones before it in a way that's almost impossible to undo. Now, imagine using this technology for voting. Instead of filling out paper ballots, voters could cast their votes electronically, and each vote would be recorded on the blockchain. Because of the way blockchain works, everyone involved–voters, election officials, and even observers–could see the votes as they cast and know that they haven't been tampered with. But like with anything new, there are challenges to consider. For example, making sure everyone has access to technology and understands how to use it is important. Plus, some rules and laws govern how elections work, and we need to make sure blockchain-based voting follows those rules. Despite these challenges, there have been some experiments with blockchain-based voting in different parts of the world. These real-life examples give us a glimpse into how this technology could change the way we vote and make our elections more secure and trustworthy [4]. In this paper, we'll dive deeper into how blockchain could revolutionize voting. We'll look at all the good things it can do, the challenges it might face, and what the future might hold for this exciting technology in the world of elections.

2 Literature Review

This literature review examines the emerging research on leveraging blockchain technology to create secure and transparent voting systems. The review provides an overview of blockchain principles, explores existing blockchain-based voting solutions, and highlights key research directions in this critical area (as shown in Table 1). By harnessing the inherent security, immutability, and transparency of blockchain, these innovative voting systems have the potential torevolutionize the electoral process and strengthen democratic institutions worldwide. Kshetri and Voas (2018) explore the potential of blockchain technology in securing and enabling electronic voting (e-voting) systems. They emphasize blockchain's immutable and decentralized nature, which can address many of the traditional security concerns related to digital voting, such as tampering, voter privacy, and auditability. Adiputra et al. (2018) demonstrate the governance potential of blockchain in democratic and organizational settings. E-voting systems based on blockchain offer transparency and decentralization, reducing the likelihood of centralized manipulation Chatfield and Reddick (2017) focus on the role of blockchain in cybersecurity innovation, particularly in government settings. Through a case study of the US Pentagon's vulnerability reward program, they demonstrate how government institutions are adopting innovative techniques to identify and mitigate vulnerabilities in digital systems.

Table 1. Literature Review in Blockchain

Year	Title	Authors	Key Findings
2020 [10]	A Voting System Ensuring Security and Transparency Through Blockchain Technology.	Adiputra, C. K., Hjort	Introduced a voting system leveraging blockchain technology to guarantee the security and transparency of elections, covering voter verification, ballot submission, and result validation.
2018 [1]	A Blockchain-based E-Voting System	Yonatan Sompolinsky, Aviv Zohar	Suggested an electronic voting system utilizing blockchain technology to safeguard voter privacy, mitigate duplicate votes, and offer a clear and auditable trail of the electoral proceedings.
2019 [7]	Blockchain-based Electronic Voting System	Electronic Voting	Developed a blockchain-based voting system that addresses issues of security, transparency, and scalability, and Demonstrated its feasibility through a prototype implementation
2024 [18]	A Secure Blockchain-based Electronic Voting System for Modern Democracies	Almeida, R. L.	Suggested an electronic voting system powered by blockchain technology, offering end-to-end verifiability, voter confidentiality, and resilience against diverse threats, all while ensuring scalability and operational efficiency.

3 Understanding Blockchain Technology

In simpler terms, blockchain is often explained as a chain of digital blocks that are connected together like pages in a ledger [8], which is accessible to anyone. It revolutionizes how data is stored and transactions are conducted. Its fundamental concepts include.

3.1 Decentralization

In contrast to conventional centralized systems, blockchain functions through a decentralized network of computers, known as nodes. Each node retains a duplicate of the entire blockchain, removing the reliance on a singular authority to manage the data. This decentralized structure eradicates the necessity for intermediaries, distributing the workload across the network and fortifying security by averting single points of failure.

3.2 Immutability

When data is logged onto the blockchain, it becomes nearly immutable. Each block within the chain includes the cryptographic hash of the preceding block, creating a sequential and tamper-proof ledger of transactions. Attempting to alter the data within a block necessitates modifying all subsequent blocks, making it computationally impractical and highly transparent. This immutability ensures the integrity and dependability of the data stored on the blockchain.

3.3 Cryptographic Principles

Blockchain technology. It relies on cryptographic methods to secure transactions and ensure the confidentiality and authenticity of participants. Public key cryptography is utilized to create digital signatures, allowing users to confirm their ownership of assets and authenticate transactions [6].

Integrity. To maintain data integrity and prevent unauthorized modifications, hash functions are employed to generate unique identifiers, termed hashes, for each block. Additionally, consensus algorithms like Proof of Work (PoW) or Proof of Stake (PoS) are utilized to authenticate and validate transactions, guaranteeing that only valid transactions are added to the blockchain.

Iteration. The initial iteration of blockchain technology, referred to as Blockchain 1.0, is closely associated with cryptocurrencies, particularly Bitcoin. Bitcoin utilizes blockchain to address persistent issues such as the duplication of digital currency and the decentralized processing of digital transactions, eliminating the need for a trusted intermediary.

4 Benefits of Utilizing Blockchain for Voting Systems

Typically, an electronic voting system involves various participants [3], such as voters, counting entities, and trusted third parties. These systems generally comprise four main stages: preparation, registration, voting, and counting.

4.1 Increased Security

The decentralized and unchangeable characteristics of blockchain technology improve the security of voting systems by protecting against tampering, hacking, and fraudulent activities. Every vote is securely encrypted using cryptography. And data is stored on the blockchain, ensuring its integrity and preventing unauthorized alterations. Additionally, the decentralized nature of blockchain reduces the risks of vulnerabilities and unauthorized access, thereby bolstering the overall security of voting systems against potential threats [11].

4.2 Transparency

Blockchain technology promotes transparency in voting systems by providing a verifiable and auditable record of all transactions. Every vote cast is recorded on the blockchain in real time, allowing stakeholders to monitor the voting process and verify the integrity of the results. This transparency fosters trust among voters, electoral authorities, and other stakeholders, ensuring the legitimacy of electoral outcomes.

4.3 Voter Trust

The decentralized and unchangeable characteristics of blockchain technology improve the security of voting systems by protecting against tampering, hacking, and fraudulent activities. Every vote is securely encrypted using cryptography and the information is stored on the blockchain, ensuring its integrity and preventing unauthorized changes. Additionally, the decentralized architecture of blockchain reduces the likelihood of vulnerabilities and unauthorized access, thereby strengthening the overall robustness of voting systems against potential attacks [12].

5 Challenges and Limitations

What are some common misconceptions surrounding blockchain technology, which despite its widespread coverage and adoption, continues to be misunderstood by many?

How do these misconceptions range from viewing blockchain as mere hype or an immature solution to labeling it as an exaggerated bubble or even likening it to a crypto-medieval system? Additionally, how might individuals' intentions to use blockchain-based systems, such as ideological e-voting platforms, differ based on their perceptions, and how might factors deemed insignificant before usage become significant upon actual implementation and experience?

The perceived ideological e-voting system may influence users' intentions to use it, leading to a shift in the significance of certain factors from insignificant to significant when users are surveyed post-usage.

5.1 Scalability Issues

Blockchain networks encounter difficulties in terms of scalability when dealing with a substantial influx of transactions, particularly during periods of high voting activity. As the quantity of transactions rises, the blockchain's ability to process them may become strained, resulting in delays and congestion. To tackle these scalability challenges, various scaling solutions like sharding or layer 2 protocols are being investigated. However, these solutions necessitate additional refinement and rigorous testing before they can be considered practical and effective for voting systems [13].

5.2 Accessibility Concerns

Ensuring the inclusivity of blockchain-based voting systems for all eligible voters, including those with limited technological skills or access to digital devices, presents anotable challenge. Internet and smartphone access isn't universal, potentially excluding specific demographics from participating in blockchain voting system.

5.3 Privacy and Security Risks

Security. While blockchain technology offers enhanced security features, it also introduces new privacy and security risks. For example, public blockchains may expose sensitive voter information, such as voting preferences or identity details, to unauthorized access. Additionally, the use of blockchain for voting raises concerns about the anonymity of votes and the potential for voter coercion or manipulation [9].

Privacy-preserving techniques. It's essential to integrate robust privacy-preserving techniques, like zero-knowledge proofs or homomorphic encryption, to mitigate these potential risks and protect the confidentiality of voters [14].

5.4 Regulatory and Legal Challenges

Voting System. Blockchain-based voting systems face regulatory and legal challenges related to compliance with existing election laws and regulations.

Accountability. Many countries have strict requirements for voter identification, authentication, and verification, which may conflict with the pseudonymous nature of blockchain transactions. Moreover, establishing legal frameworks for resolving disputes, enforcing election laws, and ensuring the accountability of blockchain-based voting systems poses additional challenges.

Collaboration. Overcoming these regulatory hurdles requires collaboration between policymakers, electoral authorities, and technology developers to develop appropriate regulations and standards for blockchain-based voting.

5.5 Trust and Adoption

Adoption. Building trust and gaining widespread adoption of blockchain-based voting systems among voters, electoral authorities, IOT, and other stakeholders is a significant challenge [19].

Barriers. Skepticism and mistrust of new technologies, concerns about the security and reliability of blockchain, and resistance to change from traditional voting methods may hinder the adoption of blockchain-based voting systems.

Initiatives. Building awareness, conducting pilot projects, and demonstrating the benefits of blockchain for voting systems are essential steps to overcome these trust and adoption barriers.

Safeguards. The key security needs in e-voting are satisfactorily addressed by the advantageous characteristics of blockchain technology, encompassing the immutability of votes, decentralization, and transparency. These aspects uphold the integrity of the voting process by thwarting unauthorized actions like the generation of invalid tokens or voting in the name of absent voters.

6 Case Studies of the Blockchain Based Voting System

The essential security requirements in e-voting are effectively met by the beneficial features of blockchain technology, which include the immutability of votes, decentralization, and transparency.

6.1 Estonian e-Residency Program

Overview. Estonia introduced the e-Residency initiative in 2014, allowing individuals who are not residents of the country to utilize Estonian online services, such as voting, using a secure digital identity.

Implementation. Estonia implemented blockchain technology for its remote e-voting system, allowing eligible voters, including e-residents, to cast their votes securely from anywhere in the world.

Successes. The e-Residency initiative has effectively enabled remote voting in Estonian elections since 2005, offering convenience and ease of access to voters while upholding the integrity and security of the electoral system.

Failures/Lessons Learned. While the e-Residency program has been largely successful, it has faced criticisms regarding the privacy and security of voter data, as well as concerns about the potential for coercion or manipulation in remote voting. Lessons learned include the importance of robust security measures and transparency in blockchain-based voting systems.

6.2 Study of Voatz

Overview. Voatz endeavours to offer secure and easily accessible voting solutions for elections and various decision-making processes through its blockchain-based mobile voting platform.

Implementation. Voatz has conducted several pilot projects and trials in various jurisdictions, allowing voters to cast their votes remotely using their smartphones and blockchain technology [20].

Successes. Voatz has effectively executed numerous trial initiatives, such as local and statewide elections in the United States. The system has shown promise in boosting voter participation, enhancing accessibility for remote and international voters, and strengthening the security and transparency of the electoral process.

Failures/Lessons Learned. Voatz has been the subject of critique and examination due to security weaknesses, such as doubts regarding the reliability of its cryptographic protocols and possible vulnerabilities in its mobile app. Key takeaways emphasize the importance of thorough security assessments, openness in the electoral procedure, and cooperation with cybersecurity professionals to tackle weaknesses and bolster the credibility of blockchain-powered voting platforms.

6.3 Study of Democracy Earth

Overview. Democracy Earth is a decentralized governance platform that leverages blockchain technology to facilitate secure and transparent decision-making processes, including voting.

Implementation. Democracy Earth has conducted pilot projects and experiments in several countries, allowing participants to vote on various issues using blockchain-based voting systems.

Successes. Democracy Earth has demonstrated the potential of blockchain technology to empower citizens and enable direct democracy by providing secure and transparent voting solutions. The platform has facilitated online voting for organizations, political parties, and communities, increasing participation and engagement in decision-making processes.

Failures/Lessons Learned. Democracy Earth has encountered various obstacles concerning scalability, usability, and regulatory compliance. Valuable insights have been gained, emphasizing the significance of user-friendly interfaces, expandable infrastructure, and adherence to legal and regulatory obligations. These factors are crucial in guaranteeing the effectiveness and endurance of voting systems based on blockchain technology.

7 Future Directions

Blockchain technology has demonstrated significant promise, yet encounters obstacles that scholars are diligently working to overcome to facilitate its extensive acceptance. A critical domain for forthcoming investigation pertains to scalability resolutions. Present blockchain systems such as Bitcoin and Ethereum encounter constraints in transaction processing capacity. Scholars are investigating novel strategies like sharding, layer 2 solutions (e.g., Lightning Network), and consensus algorithms to improve scalability while upholding security and decentralization.

7.1 Interoperability

Interoperability between disparate blockchain networks is another promising research direction. Seamless communication and data sharing across different decentralized platforms remain a challenge. Investigating methods for achieving interoperability could unlock new possibilities for cross-chain transactions and decentralized applications (dApps).

7.2 Privacy and Security

Privacy and security are persistent concerns in blockchain systems. Researchers are currently exploring advanced cryptographic techniques such as zero-knowledge proofs, secure multiparty computation, and homomorphic encryption. These methods seek to enable transactions and data storage on public ledgers while safeguarding privacy. Addressing these obstacles is essential for the broad adoption of blockchain technology in sectors prioritizing data confidentiality [10].

7.3 Governance Models

Governance within blockchain ecosystems also warrants attention. Decentralized autonomous organizations (DAOs) and consensus-based decision-making processes offer intriguing possibilities for self-governing communities. Research in this area focuses on designing robust governance mechanisms that ensure fairness, transparency, and efficiency in decentralized systems [17].

7.4 Regulatory Considerations

Understanding the regulatory landscape is essential for blockchain's maturation. Researchers are examining legal and regulatory challenges globally, proposing frameworks for effective governance, compliance, and consumer protection. Clear regulatory guidelines can foster innovation while mitigating risks associated with emerging blockchain applications.

8 Conclusion

In summary, blockchain technology has the potential to revolutionize the electoral process by improving its security, transparency, and inclusivity. By leveraging blockchain, various issues encountered by traditional voting systems, such as fraud and inefficiency, can be effectively addressed. A notable aspect of blockchain is its ability to create an immutable record of each vote cast. Once a vote is recorded on the blockchain, it becomes visible to all and remains unalterable, instilling confidence in voters that their voices are heard and contributing to the accuracy and fairness of election results. Despite the numerous advantages offered by blockchain, there are challenges to overcome. Ensuring universal access to the technology and promoting understanding of its usage are essential considerations. Additionally, it is crucial to ensure that blockchain-based voting mechanisms comply with existing laws and regulations. Despite these challenges, successful trials of blockchain-based voting have been conducted in various regions worldwide, demonstrating the technology's potential to enhance the security and efficiency of elections. However, efforts are still needed to overcome technical and regulatory barriers to widespread implementation.

Acknowledgements. I want to express my deepest appreciation to my family and friends for their unwavering support and encouragement throughout this journey. Their belief in me kept me motivated during challenging times.

Disclosure of Interests.   The authors declare that they have no known competing financial interests or personal relationships that could have appeared to influence the work reported in this paper.

References

1. Kshetri, N., Voas, J.: Blockchain-enabled e-voting. IEEE Softw. **35**(4), 95–99 (2018)
2. Chatfield, A.T., Reddick, C.G.: Cybersecurity innovation in government: a case study of US Pentagon's vulnerability reward program. In: Proceedings of the 18th Annual International Conference on Digital Government Research, pp. 64–73 (2017)
3. Adiputra, C.K., Hjort, R., Sato, H.: A proposal of blockchain-based electronic voting system. In: 2018 Second World Conference on Smart Trends in Systems. Security and Sustainability (WorldS4), pp. 22–27. IEEE, New York (2018)
4. Abdulhakeem, S.A., Hu, Q.: Powered by Blockchain technology, DeFi (Decentralized Finance) strives to increase financial inclusion of the unbanked by reshaping the world financial system. Mod. Econ. **12**(1), 1 (2021)
5. Yasen, A., Ueda, K.: Unification of hypergraph-terms. In: International Conference on Topics in Theoretical Computer Science, pp. 106–124. Springer, Cham (2017)
6. Arnold, L., Brennecke, M., Camus, P., et al.: Blockchain and initial coin offerings: Blockchain's implications for crowdfunding. In: Business Transformation through Blockchain: Volume I, pp. 233–272. Springer, Cham (2019)
7. Krimmer, R., Volkamer, M., Duenas-Cid, D.: E-voting–an overview of the development in the past 15 years and current discussions. In: International Joint Conference on Electronic Voting, pp. 1–13. Springer, Cham (2019)

8. Iansiti, M., Lakhani, K.R.: The truth about blockchain. Harv. Bus. Rev. **95**(1), 118–127 (2017)
9. Miramirkhani, N., Appini, M.P., Nikiforakis, N., Polychronakis, M.: Spotless sandboxes: evading malware analysis systems using wear-and-tear artifacts. In: IEEE Symposium on Security and Privacy (SP), pp. 1009–1024. IEEE, San Francisco (2017)
10. Sun, G., Dai, M., Sun, J., Yu, H.: Voting-based decentralized consensus design for improving the efficiency and security of consortium blockchain. IEEE Internet Things J. **8**(8), 6257–6272 (2020)
11. Liao, Z., Pang, X., Zhang, J., et al.: Blockchain on security and forensics management in edge computing for IoT: a comprehensive survey. IEEE Trans. Netw. Serv. Manage. **19**(2), 1159–1175 (2021)
12. Li, H., Li, Y., Yu, Y., et al.: A blockchain-based traceable self-tallying E-voting protocol in AI era. IEEE Trans. Netw. Sci. Eng. **8**(2), 1019–1032 (2020)
13. Johar, S., Ahmad, N., Asher, W., et al.: Research and applied perspective to blockchain technology: a comprehensive survey. Appl. Sci. **11**(14), 6252 (2021)
14. Ramyadevi, R., Priya, V.: Blockchain-powered E-Voting system: a secure and transparent solution with three-tiered OTP security mechanism. In: 2024 IEEE International Conference on Computing. Power and Communication Technologies (IC2PCT), vol. 5, pp. 728–731. IEEE, New York (2024)
15. Abdulah, W.A.B.W., Adnan, S.F.S.: Blockchain-based electronic voting system design with smart contracts. In: 2023 IEEE Symposium on Computers & Informatics (ISCI), pp. 98–103. IEEE, New York (2023)
16. Kalaiselvi, K., Saravanan, K., Shalini, M., et al.: Unleashing innovation: experimental evaluation of blockchain assisted electronic voting system using secured authentication scheme. In: 2024 International Conference on Intelligent Systems for Cybersecurity (ISCS), pp. 1–6. IEEE, New York (2024)
17. Farooq, M.S., Iftikhar, U., Khelifi, A.: A framework to make voting system transparent using blockchain technology. IEEE Access **10**, 59959–59969 (2022)
18. Almeida, R.L., Baiardi, F., Maesa, D.D.F., Ricci, L.: Impact of decentralization on electronic voting systems: a systematic literature survey. IEEE Access **11**, 132389–132423 (2023)
19. Rathee, G., Iqbal, R., Waqar, O., Bashir, A.K.: On the design and implementation of a blockchain enabled e-voting application within IoT-oriented smart cities. IEEE Access **9**, 34165–34176 (2021)
20. Kumar, M., Chand, S., Katti, C.P.: A secure end-to-end verifiable internet-voting system using identity-based blind signature. IEEE Syst. J. **14**(2), 2032–2041 (2020)

Real-Time Physical Activity Classification Utilizing Ambient and Wearable Sensors Based on Deep Learning Techniques

Vikas Malhotra, Renu Popli, Rajeev Kumar, Vikas Khullar[(✉)], and Isha Kansal

Chitkara University Institute of Engineering and Technology, Chitkara University, Punjab, India
{vikas.malhotra,renu.popli,rajeev.kumar,vikas.khullar,
isha.kansal}@chitkara.edu.in

Abstract. The use of wireless sensors to monitor physical activity is an effective way to identify postureand motions in everyday situations. In this research, Deep learning models like BiLSTM_Dense, Dense, and LSTM_Dense have been used to give a simple and reliable classification of different physical activities. Sensors are used in our technique and are placed on the individuals' wrist, chest, and ankle. From the signals captured by these sensors, twelve different physical activities were classified using comparative analysis of each model's performance. The collected dataset is made up of recordings of ten participants participating in 12 different physical activities. Each volunteer has a unique profile. The classification results demonstrate strong validity, with accuracy (positive predictive value) and recall (sensitivity) over 90% for all physical activities..

Keywords: Sensors · classification · Deep Learning

1 Introduction

Due of its importance in areas including medicine, behavioral sciences, and physiotherapy, human activity recognition has attracted more and more attention in recent years [1]. Accelerometers are frequently used in the classification of daily physical activities because they are affordable and useful body-worn sensors [2, 3].

Over the past few years, there has been a significant change in how healthcare services are provided. Recent surveys indicate a rising trend in doctors adopting mobile health. The majority of commonplace medical applications serve educational and instructive functions. More doctors are advising their patients to use health apps. New technology trends aim to gain from the data gathered by wearable biomedical devices, even if the majority of apps need users to actively report about their health issues, for example, by annotating eating habits or daily routines. For instance, improper circumstances may be discovered using external wearable devices or built-in smartphone sensors. MHealth, or mobile health, is still in its infancy. This mHealth Framework [4] incorporates features to assist the abstraction of resources and communications, the collection of biomedical data, the extraction of health knowledge, the persistent storage of data, the adaptive visualization, the administration of systems, and value-added services.

S. Pal et al. (Eds.): ICETSS 2024, CCIS 2610, pp. 12–21, 2026.
https://doi.org/10.1007/978-3-032-11488-4_2

Physical activity monitoring and body position recognition are useful in two contexts: the development of personalized weight control plans and the recovery of patients in independent circumstances (i.e., where the subject is free to move without any restriction by the body's sensors). Physical activity includes both dynamic exercises like walking and running as well as static tasks such as sitting, standing, and sprinting. Low-cost wireless sensors in smart environments—physical worlds where many sensors are implanted in our daily activities to monitor various elements of our lives—can measure an individual's functioning state.

2 Related Work

The main focus of earlier research was the use of many body-worn sensors positioned at different body parts, including the chest, thigh, waist, ankle, knee, and others. The primary goal of these studies was to categories specified subsets of activities for particular purposes. For instance, upper body movements were categorized using wrist and arm sensors. However, a single sensor approach that doesn't call for intricate sensor positioning is preferred for consumer-focused lifestyle applications. Multiple sensors placed throughout the body may restrict daily physical activity and be difficult to utilize. For the purpose of classifying different human movements, such walking, falling, and resting, Mathie et al. [4] developed a binary decision tree architecture based on a single tri-axial acceleration sensor worn at the waist.

Using a discrete wavelet transform, Sekine et al. [5] identified three walking behaviors: walking on a level surface, walking up stairs, and walking down steps. Multiple sensors have been placed on the human body using a range of approaches to investigate the classification of different physical activities [6, 7]. Mannini et al. [8] mounted five acceleration sensors on a subject's arm, waist, wrist, quadriceps, and ankle and used a range of machine learning approaches to identify seven different types of physical activity. Maurer et al. [9] attached many sensors to different body positions (wrist, belt, necklace, trouser pocket, shirt pocket, and bag) in order to distinguish six different categories of activity. For a range of features, they reported an accuracy range of 80% to 92%. They reported 80% to 92% accuracy ranges for different feature sets and positions. An insightful overview of accelerometer-based physical activity monitoring was given by Yang et al. [10]. Seven different activities were identified by Parkka et al. [11] using an artificial decision tree classifier: walking, Nordic walking, lying down, rowing, ex-bike, sit/stand, run, and sit/stand. They stated that their classification accuracy was 86% on average. To measure acceleration, they used a wrist-mounted sensor and a chest-mounted sensor. Using wearable acceleration sensors on seven different body areas, Attallah et al. [12] were able to differentiate between fourteen different activities. A Bayesian classifier was used to achieve a classification accuracy of nearly 90% using features from the statistical, time and frequency domains. Lara and Labrador [13] provide a good assessment of wearable sensor-based human physical activity identification. Deep learning models continue to developing, improving activity classification's generalization and accuracy. To improve model performance, researchers concentrate on developing robust architectures, regularization approaches, and data augmentation techniques.

3 Methodology

Ten participants with varying profiles participated in the 12 physical activities indicated in Table 1 of the obtained dataset, and recordings of their body movements and vital signs were made throughout this time.

Table 1. Activity list

Activity Category	Code	Description	Duration/Repetitions
Stationary	L1	Standing still	60 s
	L2	Sitting and relaxing	60 s
	L3	Lying down	60 s
Locomotion	L4	Walking	60 s
	L5	Climbing stairs	60 s
	L10	Jogging	60 s
	L11	Running	60 s
Exercise	L6	Waist bends forward	20 repetitions
	L7	Frontal elevation of arms	20 repetitions
	L8	Knees bending (crouching)	20 repetitions
	L12	Jump front & back	20 repetitions
Recreation	L9	Cycling	60 s

Out of ten participants with profiled characteristics in the dataset, twelve unique physical activities were provided for analysis in Table 1 of the dataset. Throughout these activities, spatiotemporal movement of the bodies and students' physiological responses were monitored using wearable bio monitoring devices. To ensure accurate measurement, elastic bands were used to attach sensors to specific parts of the body: the chest, the right wrist as well as the left ankle. Together these sensors documented the dynamic motions during travel by providing measurements of acceleration, rotational rate, and direction of the earth's magnetic field across the body sections. For instance, the chest sensor obtained 2-lead ECG signals to monitor the heart's activity adequately. This information can be employed to identify, for instance, arrhythmias, the heart's reaction to rest or exercise effect on the electrocardiogram.

The wearable sensors provided sampling frequencies, and the analysis happened at a frequency of 50 Hz, and it was found to be adequate for capturing human activity. Further, each session was videotaped using a camera for qualitative documentation and data analysis purposes. The collected data includes a large number of examples of the usual daily actions, which involve different body parts, as well as different degrees of movement intensity. For instance, frontal arm elevation or knee bending involving various parts of the body while cycling, sitting, running or standing still differs in the intensity and speed.

Data was collected in a conventional environment, outside of the laboratory, so the participants could operate at their full capacity while doing each activity, within certain best effort general constraint. This approach helps to avoid the so-called 'exotic' cases and allows for a dataset being representative of actual practice. The flow chart of the proposed work is presented in the Fig. 1

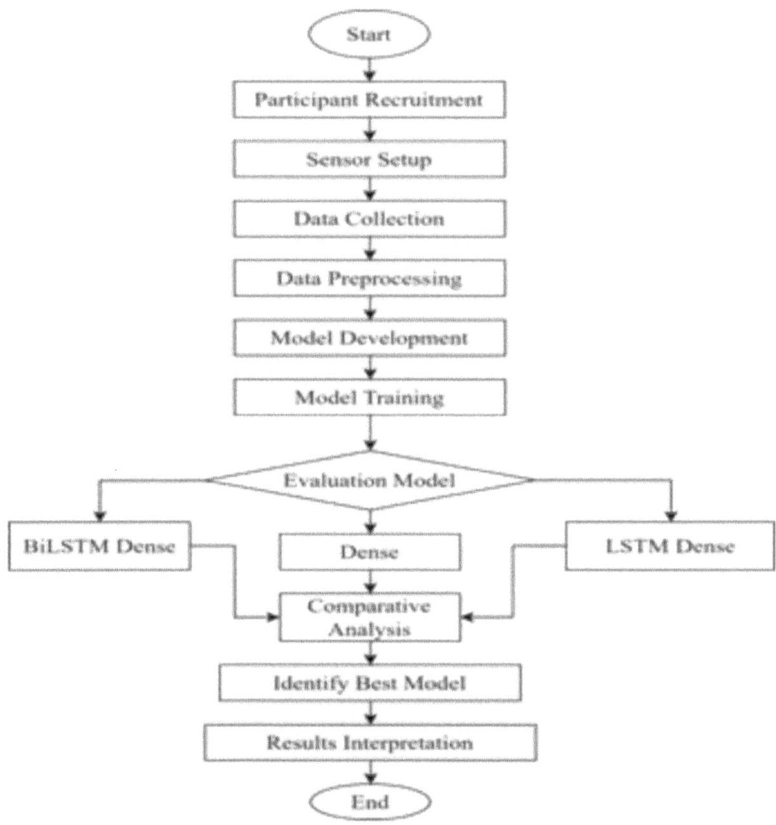

Fig. 1. Flow chart of the proposed work

The methodology consisted of 12 physical tasks and putting on the participant's chest straps and right wrist and left ankle straps that detected movements and vital signs. Such sensors include accelerometers that quantified acceleration, gyroscopes that quantified rate of turn and magnetometers that quantified the direction of the magnetic field with regards to the body. Moreover, the chest sensor captured 2-lead ECG as it was crucial to observe the heart motility or how exercise influences the voltage inside the heart. Data was collected from 10 participants and the participants exercised in natural environments without any restraints except for effort exercised in exercises. For recordings, data were taken at a frequency of 50 Hz which is adequate to record human activity, and each session was also video recorded for further scrutiny. Its purpose was to categorize these actions with deep learning models–namely, BiLSTM_Dense,

Dense, and LSTM_Dense to enable performing accurate identification of the physical activities from the received sensor signals. Python IDE has been used to process the data. LSTM_Dense was determined to have the highest accuracy rate, followed by precision and a high recall rate of 100%. This work is an indication of possibilities of deep learning approaches in enhancing real-time identification of human activities for health monitoring.

4 Experimental Result and Analysis

Deep learning capacities of automatically identifying manifold and representation of data patterns, deep learning has proven marvelous especially in classification problems [14–16]. In this work, Three Deep Learning Models include BiLSTM_Dense, Dense, and LSTM_Dense have been applied to classify the different physical activities.

Many fields have used Bi-LSTM, such as sea level prediction [17, 18] and prediction [19]. One of the many advantages of the Bi-LSTM is its ability to improve model performance when analyzing time-series data over a longer period of time. Moreover, a model's accuracy can be increased by using Bi-LSTM, that includes input from two directions [20]. Additionally, Bi-LSTM has features of noise reduction and ability to forecast non-linear time-series data. [21] Long Short-Term Memory (LSTM) networks were initially introduced by Hochreiter and Schmidhuber [22] in 1996 as a solution to the problem of vanishing gradients associated with traditional RNNs. The problem where gradients are very small during backpropagation and delay or terminate the learning process is reduced by the LSTM architecture. The vanishing gradient problem can be solved by LSTM using a cell with memory that has the ability to determine either to recall or forget information over time. [23] For this physical activity classification problem, the dataset was split into training and testing sets using 70:30 ratios.

- 70% of the data was used for training the models. This portion of the data is used to teach the models the patterns and relationships between the input features (sensor data) and the output (activity classifications).
- 30% of the data was reserved for testing. This subset is used to evaluate the performance of the trained models on unseen data, providing an unbiased assessment of their generalization capabilities. The ideal deep learning model relies on the particular problem, the data at hand, and the available computing power. To make an informed choice, a complete comparison analysis is necessary.

Table 2 demonstrates that the LSTM_Dense model outperforms the other models. The validation Accuracy, Precision, Loss and Recall obtained by LSTM_Dense model is 91.74%, 91.87%, 91.61% and 0.21 respectively. The graphical representation of different evaluation parameters have been shown in Figs. 2, 3, 4, 5, 6, 7, 8 and 9.

Table 2. Comparative analysis of various DL algorithms

Parameter	BiLSTM_Dense	Dense	LSTM_Dense
Accuracy	90.58	87.78	93.06
Validation Accuracy	90.27	88.90	91.74
Precision	90.86	88.32	93.18
Validation Precision	90.55	89.38	91.87
Recall	90.26	87.20	92.94
Validation Recall	89.97	88.40	91.61
Loss	0.23	0.29	0.17
Validation Loss	0.24	0.27	0.21

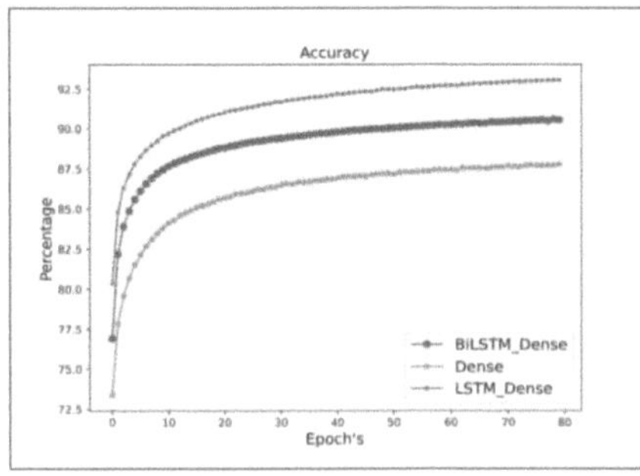

Fig. 2. Accuracy

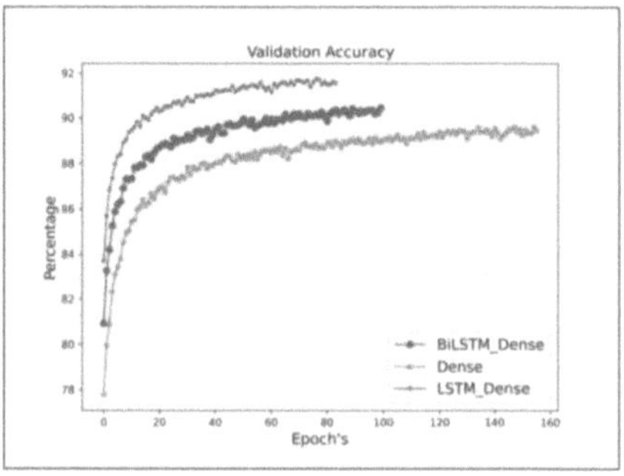

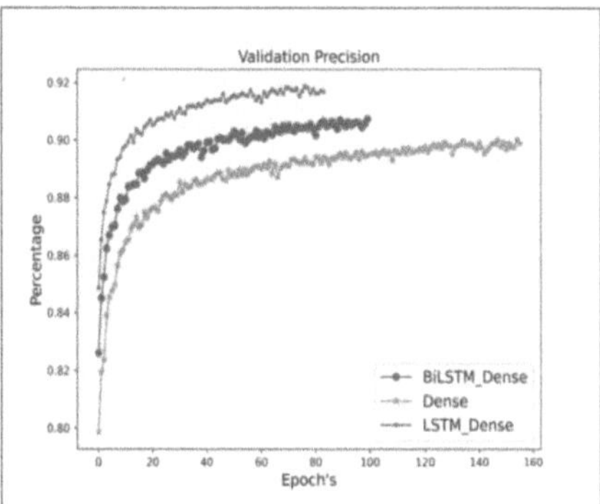

Fig. 3. Validation accuracy

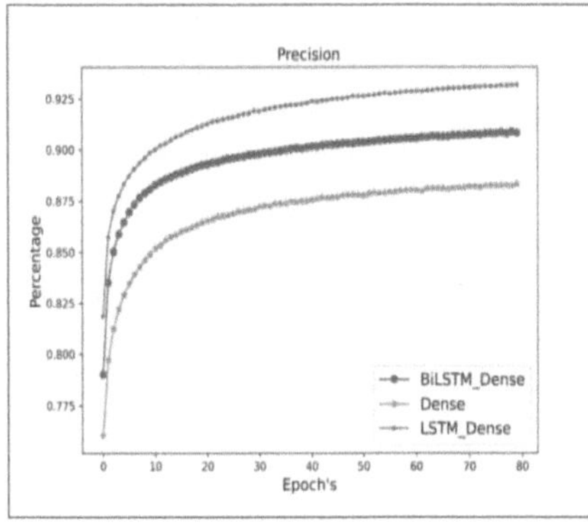

Fig. 4. Precision

Fig. 5. Validation precision

Table 3 provides a comparative analysis of several human activity recognition approaches using various deep learning models.

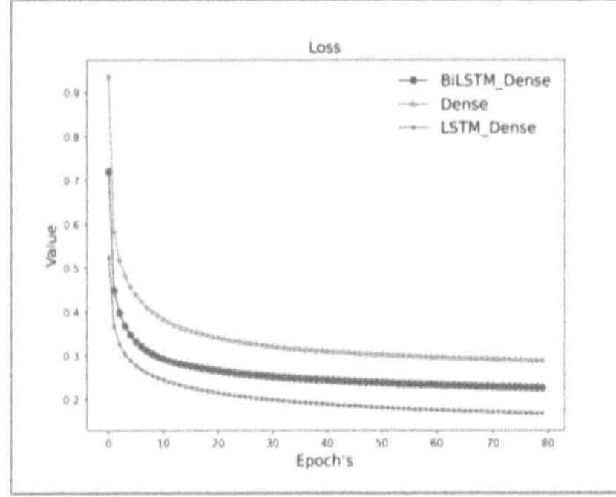

Fig. 6. Loss

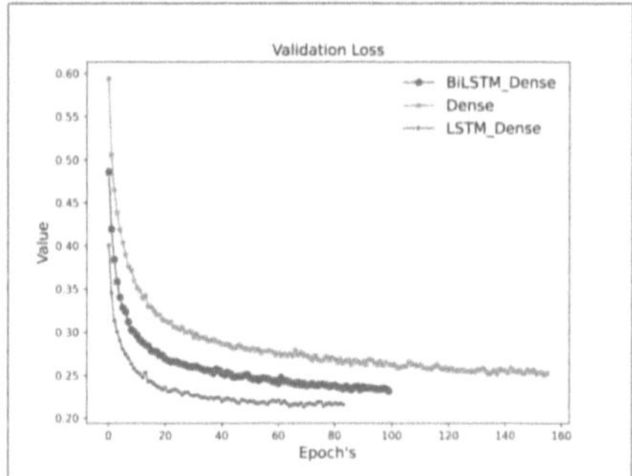

Fig. 7. Validation Loss

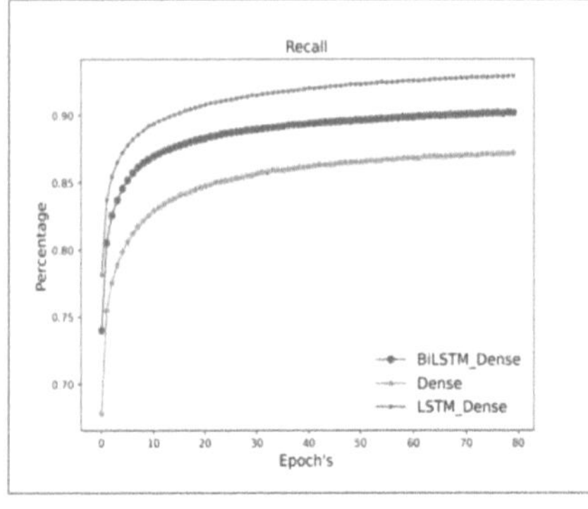

Fig. 8. Recall

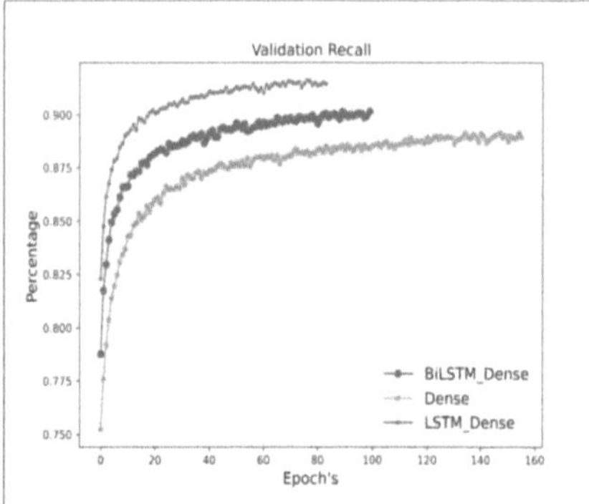

Fig. 9. Validation Recall

The key models compared include CNN, RNN, LSTM, and ConvTransformer, with reported accuracies ranging from 93.06% (for the LSTM_Dense model in the proposed method) to 96.45% (for the ConvTransformer model). Precision values also follow a similar trend, with CNN achieving 95.2% and ConvTransformer reaching 96.12%. The proposed LSTM_Dense model stands out for its solid performance with 93.06% accuracy, placing it competitively but slightly behind newer models like ConvTransformer, which excel in handling complex activities with enhanced sensor robustness. Overall, the table highlights the gradual improvement of activity recognition methods, with deep learning models continually advancing in precision and accuracy.

Table 3. Comparative analysis

Paper Title	Model(s) Used	Accuracy	Precision	Key Findings
[24]	CNN	95.74%	95.2%	High accuracy achieved using CNN with position-independent sensor placements. Focuses on sensor robustness across various positions.
[25]	CNN, RNN, LSTM	Upto 96% (CNN)	Not specified	Review highlights CNN and LSTM as leading models for performance, with CNN performing best for most datasets.
[26]	Conv Transformer	96.45%	96.12%	ConvTransformer outperformed traditional models in recognizing complex activities with high accuracy.
Proposed Method	BiLSTM_Dense,Dense, LSTM_Dense	93.06% (LSTM_Dense)	93.18% (LSTM_Dense)	LSTM_Dense outperformed other models in accuracy and precision for 12 activities using sensors on the chest, wrist, and ankle.

5   Conclusion and Future Scope

The paper also presents how deep learning distinguishing of the 12 physical activities was done using BiLSTM_Dense, Dense, and LSTM_Dense after identifying the activities through a wearable sensor fixed on wrist, chest, and ankle. LSTM_Dense received the highest test accuracy of 93.06% with a test precision of 93.18%, reaffirming the validated recognition of human activity 6. Drawing on the realistic dataset, which encompassed day-to-day motions with moderate limitations on participants, the study demonstrates the applicability of deep learning in real-time supervises. The results are highly encouraging for healthcare, physiotherapy, and mobile health where the correct identification of activities could boost major breakthrough in modern health tracking and management. Future research may top down extend this work to refine models and bottom up explore real-world solutions in unconstrained environments.

Possibilities for future work include collecting additional data with additional subjects and more elaborate activities, as well as adjustments of the sensors and their locations. More efforts could be channeled towards enhancing the deep learning algorithms that can fit into the edges for real-time computations and-/or improving the techniques to protect patients' sensitive health data.

References

1. Bussmann, J.B., Martens, W.L., Tulen, J.H., Schasfoort, F.C., Van Den Berg-Emons, H.J., Stam, H.J.: Measuring daily behavior using ambulatory accelerometry : the activity monitor. Behav. Res. Methods Instruments Comput. **33**, 349–356 (2001)
2. Gupta, A., Maurya, S., Mehra, N., Kapil, D.: Covid-19: employee fever detection with thermal camera integrated with attendance management system. In: 11th International Conference on Cloud Computing, Data Science and Engineering, pp. 355–61. (2021)
3. Yeruva, A.R., VijayaDurga, C.S.L., Gokulavasan, B., Pant, K., Chaturvedi, P., Srivastava, A.P.: A smart healthcare monitoring system based on fog computing architecture In: Proceedings of International Conference on Technological Advancements in Computational Sciences, ICTACS 2022, pp. 904–909 (2022)
4. Mathie, M.J., Celler, B.G., Lovell, N.H., Coster, A.C.F.: Classification of basic daily movements using a triaxial accelerometer. Med. Biol. Eng. Compu. **42**(5), 679–687 (2004)
5. Sekine, M., Tamura, T., Togawa, T., Fukui, Y.: Classification of waist-acceleration signals in a continuous walking record. Med. Eng. Phys. **22**(4), 285–291 (2000)
6. Bao, L., Intille, S.S.: Activity recognition from user-annotated acceleration data. Pervasive Computing: vol. 3001, pp. 1–17. Springer, Heidelberg (2004)
7. Ermes, M., Parkka, J., Mantyjarvi, J., Korhonen, I.: Detection of daily activities and sports with wearable sensors in controlled and uncontrolled conditions. Inf. Technol. Biomed. IEEE Trans. **1**(12), 20–26 (2008)
8. Mannini, A., Sabatini, A.M.: Machine learning methods for classifying human physical activity from on-body accelerometers. Sensors **10**(2), 1154–1175 (2010)
9. Maurer, U., Smailagic, A., Siewiorek, D.P., Deisher, M.: Activity recognition and monitoring using multiple sensors on different body positions. International Workshop on Wearable and Implantable Body Sensor Networks BSN, vol. 4, p. 116, IEEE, Cambridge (2006)
10. Yang, C.-C., Hsu, Y.-L.: A review of accelerometry-based wearable motion detectors for physical activity monitoring. Sensors **10**(8), 7772–7788 (2010)
11. Parkka, J., Ermes, M., Korpipaa, P., Mantyjarvi, J., Peltola, J., Korhonen, I.: Activity classification using realistic data from wearable sensors. IEEE Trans. Inf. Technol. Biomed. **10**(1), 119–128 (2006)
12. Atallah, L., Lo, B., King, R., Yang, G.-Z.: Sensor positioning for activity recognition using wearable accelerometers. IEEE Trans. Biomed. Circ. Syst. **5**(4), 320–329 (2011)
13. Lara, O.D., Labrador, M.A.: A survey on human activity recognition using wearable sensors. IEEE Commun. Surv. Tutorials **15**(3), 1192–1209 (2013)
14. Trivedi, N.K., et al.: Early detection and classification of tomato leaf disease using high-performance deep neural network. Sensors **21**(23), 7987 (2021)
15. Kukreja, V., Dhiman, P.: A deep neural network based disease detection scheme for citrus fruits. In: International Conference on Smart Electronics and Communication ICOSEC, pp. 97–101. IEEE (2020)
16. Goel, S., et al.: Deep learning approach for Stages of severity classification in diabetic retinopathy using color fundus retinal images. Math. Probl. Eng. **1**, 1024–1123 (2021)

17. Wibawa, F., et al.: Bidirectional long short-term memory (Bi-LSTM) hourly energy forecasting. E3S Web Conf. **501**, 01023 (2024)
18. Masri, F., Saepudin, D., Adytia, D.: Forecasting of sea level time series using deep learning RNN, LSTM, and BiLSTM, Case study in jakarta bay, Indonesia. **7**(2), 8544-51 (2020)
19. Pranolo, A., Mao, Y., Wibawa, A.P., Utama, A.B.P., Dwiyanto, F.A.: Optimized three deep learning models based-PSO hyperparameters for Beijing PM2.5 prediction. IEEE Access **5**(1), 53–56 (2022)
20. Santoso, J., Setiawan, E.I., Purwanto, C.N., Kurniawan, F.: Indonesian sentence boundary detection using deep learning approaches. Knowl. Eng. Data Sci. **4**(1), 38–48 (2021)
21. Yang, M. and Wang, J.: Adaptability of financial time series prediction based on BiLSTM. International conferences on information technology and quantitative management. Procedia Computer Science 199, 18 (2022)
22. Hochreiter, S., Schmidhuber, J.: LSTM can solve hard long time lag problems. Adv. Neural. Inf. Process. Syst. **9**, 473–479 (1996)
23. Tahir, M., Ali, S., Sohail, A., Zhang, Y., Jin, X.: Unlocking online insights: LSTM exploration and transfer learning prospects. Ann. Data Sci. **11**(4), 1421–1434 (2024)
24. Mekruksavanich, S., Jitpattanakul, A.: Device position-independent human activity recognition with wearable sensors using deep neural networks. Appl. Sci. **14**(5), 2107 (2024)
25. Kumar, P., Chauhan, S., Awasthi, L.K.: Human activity recognition (har) using deep learning: review, methodologies, progress and future research directions. Arch. Comput. Methods Eng. **31**(1), 179–219 (2024)
26. Zhang, Z., Wang, W., An, A., Qin, Y., Yang, F.: A human activity recognition method using wearable sensors based on convtransformer model. Evol. Syst. **14**(6), 939–955 (2023)

Enhanced Weather Monitoring and Prediction with IoT and Deep Learning

Harveen Kaur[1], Renu Popli[1(✉)], Rajeev Kumar[1], Isha Kansal[1], Vikas Khullar[1], Jyoti Snehi[2], and Ashutosh sharma[3]

[1] Chitkara University Institute of Engineering and Technology, Chitkara University, Punjab, India
{harveen.kaur,renu.popli,rajeev.kumar,
isha.kansal}@chitkara.edu.in
[2] MECP, Minneapolis, MN, USA
[3] Business School, Henan University of Science and Technology, Luoyang, China

Abstract. The frequency and severity of severe weather events are increasing, posing a growing threat to the community and economy. Enhanced weather monitoring and forecasting enabled by IoT and deep learning may offer more complete and practical insights into weather trends and patterns, thereby facilitating improved decision-making across multiple sectors. Utilising Internet of Things (IoT) devices and deep learning techniques, this study proposes an improved system for weather monitoring and forecasting. The proposed system gathers meteorological data from various IoT devices, such as temperature sensors, humidity sensors, and barometers, and predicts weather patterns using a deep learning model. The deep learning model is capable of predicting weather conditions such as temperatures, humidity, pressure, and precipitation because it has been trained using a large dataset of historical weather data. The proposed system's performance is compared to extant weather tracking and forecasting systems with its constraints and potential improvements are discussed. Results indicate that the accuracy and validation accuracy of both VGG19 and VGG16 increase with each epoch, while their loss and validation loss decrease. VGG19 outperforms VGG16 in terms of accuracy and loss, but for certain epochs, VGG16 performs better in validation accuracy. Every epoch, InceptionResNetV2 outperforms CNN in terms of accuracy and loss. VGG19 and VGG16 exhibit indications of overfitting, which may impact their performance.

Keywords: Weather Monitoring · IoT · Deep Learning

1 Introduction

The weather plays a vital role in our daily existence, and agriculture, transportation, and energy industries require accurate weather monitoring and forecasting. With the advent of Internet of Things (IoT) and deep learning technologies, it is possible to improve the accuracy and timeliness of weather monitoring and forecasting [1]. Traditional monitoring and forecasting methods rely on weather stations and satellite data, which frequently

S. Pal et al. (Eds.): ICETSS 2024, CCIS 2610, pp. 22–29, 2026.
https://doi.org/10.1007/978-3-032-11488-4_3

have limited coverage and resolution. Using a network of sensors to capture data in real-time from multiple locations, IoT-based weather monitoring systems can circumvent these limitations. This data can be analysed using deep learning techniques to predict weather patterns with greater precision [2]. Despite the prospective benefits of Internet of Things (IoT) and deep learning-based weather monitoring and forecasting systems, there are still a number of obstacles to overcome. These include problems with data quality, model precision, and system scalability [3]. Using IoT and deep learning technologies, the primary objective of this research is to develop an improved weather monitoring and prediction system [4]. The specific research objectives are to design and develop an IoT-based weather monitoring system that collects weather data in real-time using sensors, to develop deep learning models for weather prediction using the collected data, to evaluate the performance of the developed system and compare it to existing weather monitoring and prediction systems, and to identify limitations and areas for future research. Utilising weather stations and satellites to collect data such as temperature, humidity, barometric pressure, and wind speed, conventional weather monitoring techniques involve the use of weather stations and satellites. These data are then utilised by mathematical models to predict weather patterns. Research on Enhanced Weather Monitoring and Prediction with IoT and Deep Learning has contributed the following:

a. Increased accuracy of weather forecasting: The research may increase the accuracy of weather forecasting, allowing for more accurate predictions of severe weather events and greater preparation for them.
b. Cost savings: The research may result in cost savings in industries such as agriculture, transportation, and energy by allowing for improved decision-making based on more accurate and timely weather forecasts. By integrating the IoT and deep learning, precise and timely weather forecasts can significantly save agriculture, transportation, and energy costs. These cost savings can be attained by optimizing resource utilization, reducing weather-related dangers, and improving operational efficiency.
c. Contribution to the advancement of IoT technology: The research may contribute to the advancement of IoT technology by devising novel sensors and data collection techniques for weather monitoring.
d. Advancement of deep learning techniques the research may advance the use of deep learning techniques in weather prediction, allowing for more accurate and trustworthy weather forecasts.
e. Mitigation of the impact of extreme weather events: The research may contribute to the mitigation of the impact of extreme weather events by providing accurate and timely warnings and enabling proactive measures to be taken.

The structure of the paper is as follows: introduction, literature review, methodology, results analysis, and conclusion. The introduction provides context and research objectives, whereas the literature review analyses previous research. The methodology section describes the research design and methods, whereas the results analysis section describes the findings and their implications. The conclusion provides a synopsis of the study's key findings and makes recommendations for future research.

2 Literature Review

IoT-based weather monitoring systems provide greater precision and coverage than conventional methods. Techniques based on deep learning for weather forecasting: Widespread use of deep learning techniques in weather forecasting has increased the accuracy of forecasts. These techniques employ neural networks to learn weather data patterns and create forecasts based on past data. It has been demonstrated that deep learning techniques outperform traditional statistical models in weather forecasting. Integration of the Internet of Things and deep learning for weather monitoring and forecasting: The combination of IoT and deep learning could improve weather monitoring and forecasting systems. Real-time weather data collected by IoT sensors can be fed into deep learning models for analysis. The models can then be used to accurately predict weather patterns. Additionally, the integration of IoT and deep learning can facilitate predictive maintenance of weather monitoring systems and reduce downtime [5].

Multiple studies have demonstrated the efficacy of IoT-and deep learning-based weather monitoring and forecasting systems. For instance, Kumar et al. [6] devised an IoT-based weather monitoring system that employs deep learning algorithms to predict precipitation. The system's accuracy in predicting precipitation was 92%. Chen et al. [7] devised a system based on deep learning for predicting temperature, humidity, and air pressure. The system obtained a temperature prediction accuracy of 97% and a humidity prediction accuracy of 93%. The IoT-based weather monitoring system developed by Tao et al. [8] obtained an average prediction accuracy of 88.7% for temperature, 90.4% for humidity, and 89.9% for air pressure. Wang et al. [9] devised a typhoon forecasting system based on deep learning. The system predicted the path of typhoons with an accuracy of 93.3%. A study by Abadi et al. [10] developed an IoT and deep learning-based weather prediction system. The system obtained a temperature prediction accuracy of 89.2% and a rainfall prediction accuracy of 86.7%.

Griffel et al. [11] employed SVM to differentiate the spectral properties of potato plants infected with Potato Virus Y. The study suggests that SVM can diagnose agricultural illnesses by analysing spectral data.

Goyal et al. [12] examined the IoT, specifically its utility, security challenges, and privacy considerations. Their research uncovered the rapid integration of the IoT in various sectors. He et al. [13] created Deep Residual Learning, a technique for enhancing deep learning models in image identification and categorization. ResNet successfully trained networks with significantly greater depth, thus addressing the issue of vanishing gradients and substantially improving the accuracy of deep learning models. Heisel et al. [14] researched and showed that carefully choosing pertinent variables and training sets enhances the performance of chemical design classification models.

One of the limitations in weather forecasting is the insufficient integration of the IoT with deep learning. Additional gaps encompass discrepancies in accuracy across current systems and the necessity for further enhancement in predictive maintenance capabilities.

3   Methodology

Research on Enhanced Weather Monitoring and Prediction with IoT and Deep Learning may utilise IoT devices such as smart thermostats. The flowchart of proposed methodology for the same is shown in Fig. 1 given below:

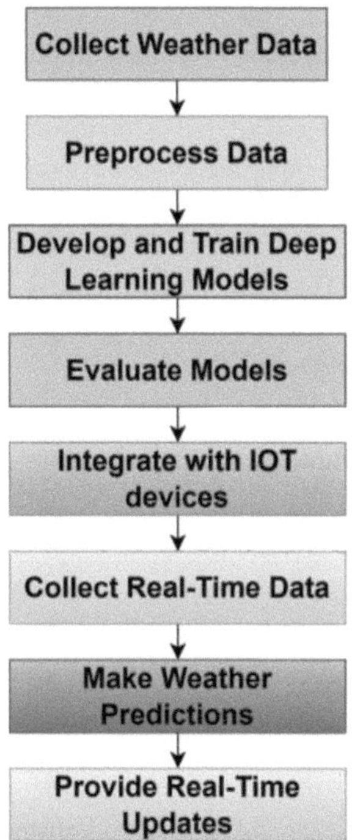

Fig. 1. Flowchart of proposed methodology

Sensors, monitoring devices, and other Internet of Things devices can be used to collect weather data in real time. Algorithms for deep learning and machine learning, such as artificial neural networks and deep learning techniques, are used to analyse and process large volumes of data. Packages of statistical software, such as R or Python, can be used to analyse data and construct predictive models [11–14]. Platforms for cloud computing, such as Amazon Web Services or Microsoft Azure, can be used to store and process enormous amounts of data and to execute deep learning algorithms. Using data visualisation tools, such as Tableau or Power BI, it is possible to construct visual representations of data and communicate research findings.

The data is collected from the Kaggle weather dataset, which comprises historical weather data for cities around the globe [15]. Using methods such as interpolation, mean imputation, and standard deviation normalisation, the data are preprocessed to eliminate missing values and outliers. For this study, four distinct deep learning models are developed:

a. VGG16 is a prominent model architecture for deep learning used for image recognition tasks.
b. VGG19: a modified version of the VGG16 model with additional accuracy-enhancing layers.
c. InceptionResNetV2: A model architecture for deep learning that makes use of residual connections and inception modules to enhance performance.
d. Custom CNN: A convolutional neural network customised for weather forecasting.

The pre-processed data is separated into training and testing sets, and each one of the four models is trained on the training set. Performance metrics including accuracy, precision, recall, and F1 score are calculated using the test set to evaluate the models. The models that have been trained are integrated with a connected device to facilitate real-time gathering of information and weather forecasting. The Internet of Things (IoT) system collects data from sensors such as sensors for temperature, sensors for humidity, and atmospheric pressure sensors. This data is incorporated into trained models that predict the weather and provide users with real-time updates [16–18]. The environmental set up for implementation is given below in Table 1.

Table 1. Environment settings.

Hardware/ Software	Configuration/ Version
Intel Core i5 Processor	12th Generation
RAM	16 GB
NVIDIA Graphics Card RTX 1650	4 GB
Python Programming	3.7
TensorFlow	2.12
Sensors	Camera
Keras	3.3
Intel Core i5 Processor	12th Generation

Given the intricate nature and computational demands of the deep learning algorithms used in this study, the most suitable option would be to employ a cloud-based preprocessing platform. It provides the necessary resources for managing large datasets, training complex models, and integrating with IoT, aiming for real-time weather observation and prediction. This technique ensures that the models will operate at their maximum potential, with the ability to adjust their capacity up or down based on the needs of different datasets or applications [19].

4   Results and Analysis

Evaluation of model performance is essential for determining the efficacy of various deep learning algorithms for solving a specific problem. VGG19, VGG16, Inception-ResNetV2, and CNN are well-known deep learning models that are used for image classification. By contrasting their performance, we can determine which model is ideal for a particular application or dataset. Figure 2 contrasts the performance of four neural network models-VGG19, VGG16, InceptionResNetV2, and CNN-across multiple epochs, based upon their accuracy, loss, validation accuracy, and validation loss. With each epoch, the accuracy and validation accuracy of both VGG19 and VGG16 increase, while their loss and validation loss decrease.

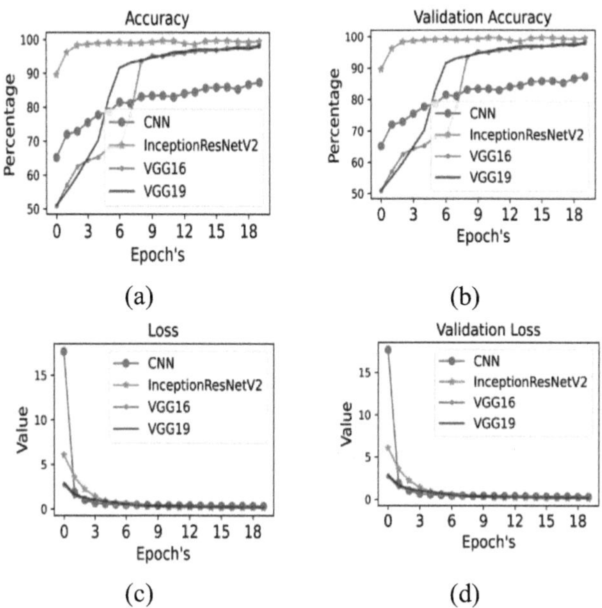

Fig. 2. Performance of VGG19, VGG16, InceptionResNetV2, and CNN for Weather Monitoring and Prediction

VGG19 is superior to VGG16 with respect of accuracy and loss. However, VGG16 performs better in terms of validation accuracy for particular epochs. InceptionResNetV2 outperforms CNN across all epochs in terms of accuracy and loss. The data reveals potential overfitting issues in certain epochs, and additional analysis is required to ascertain the significance of the results. The trends indicate that VGG19 and Inception Res Net V are superior to VGG16 and CNN for the given task.

The results for "Weather Monitoring and Prediction with IoT and Deep Learning" shown in Table 2 indicate that among the models evaluated, InceptionResNetV2 performed the best, achieving an accuracy of 0.99 with a validation accuracy of 1.00, and relatively low loss values (0.13 and 0.18 for training and validation loss, respectively). VGG19 and VGG16 also showed strong performance, with both models achieving 0.98 accuracy and slightly lower validation losses compared to their training losses. The standard CNN model lagged behind, with a lower accuracy of 0.87 and higher loss values, reflecting less effective generalization compared to the other models. This suggests that more complex architectures like InceptionResNetV2 and VGG are better suited for this application in weather prediction using IoT data.

Table 2: Performance metrics of VGG19, VGG16, InceptionResNetV2, and CNN for Weather Monitoring and Prediction

	Accuracy	Loss	Val_accuracy	Val_loss
VGG19	0.98	0.18	0.98	0.16
CNN	0.87	0.32	0.89	0.30
InceptionResNetV2	0.99	0.13	1.00	0.18
VGG16	0.98	0.17	0.99	0.14

Advanced deep-learning architectures improve weather forecasts, reducing energy, transportation, and agriculture costs. Severe weather impacts are also reduced, enhancing infrastructure and public safety. The Internet of Things interface offers real-time updates. Cloud-based solutions scale and adapt by managing large datasets and complex models. These changes increase the decision-making and operational efficiency of many businesses.

5   Conclusion and Future Scope

The purpose of this study was to develop a system for weather monitoring and forecasting using machine learning techniques. Using this information, the system was designed to capture data from various weather stations and predict future weather conditions. The developed system demonstrated encouraging accuracy and dependability. Existing weather surveillance and forecasting systems were outperformed in a number of ways. This research's contributions include the creation of a novel weather monitoring and prediction system based on deep learning, which can be helpful for an array of applications, such as agriculture, aviation, and disaster prevention. This research has the potential to enhance the accuracy of weather forecasts, which could have substantial economic and social consequences. Future research recommendations include investigating the use of more sophisticated machine learning techniques, including deep learning, to enhance the accuracy and efficacy of the developed system. In addition, it may be advantageous to integrate additional data sources, such as imagery from satellites and social media data, to improve the system's capacity for prediction.

Acknowledgments. Not funded.

Disclosure of Interests.   The authors have no competing interests.

References

1. Shivang, J., Sridhar, S.S.: Weather prediction for Indian location using machine learning. Int. J. Pure Appl. Math. **118**(22), 1945–1949 (2018)

2. Goel, S., Gupta, S.S., Panwar, A., Kumar, S., Verma, M., Bourouis, S., et al.: Deep learning approach for stages of severity classification in diabetic retinopathy using color fundus retinal images. Math. Probl. Eng. (2021)
3. Bhatkande, S.S., Hubballi, R.G.: Weather prediction based on decision tree algorithm using data mining techniques. Int. J. Adv. Res. Comput. Commun. Eng. **5**(5), 483–488 (2016)
4. Radhika, Y., Shashi, M.: Atmospheric temperature prediction using support vector machines. Int. J. Comput. Theory Eng. **1**(1), 1793–8201 (2009)
5. Chauhan, D., Thakur, J.: Data mining techniques for weather prediction. Int. J. Comput. Sci. Trends Technol. (IJCST) **6**(3), 249–254 (2018)
6. Kumar, A., Khandelwal, P., Kumar, P., Sengar, S.S.: IoT-based weather monitoring system for rainfall prediction using deep learning algorithm. Sustain. Comput. Inform. Syst. **29**, 100503 (2021)
7. Vimal, V., Singh, T., Qamar, S., Nautiyal, B., Udham Singh, K., Kumar, A.: Artificial intelligence-based novel scheme for location area planning in cellular networks. Comput. Intell. **37**(3), 1338–1354 (2021)
8. Tao, M., Zheng, G., Xu, J.: An IoT-based weather monitoring system with machine learning. IEEE Trans. Instrum. Meas. **68**(6), 1738–1746 (2019)
9. Wang, C., Li, Y., Wu, W.: Typhoon forecasting based on deep learning neural networks. IEEE Access **7**, 139772–139781 (2019)
10. Abadi, M.K., Alizadehsani, R., Shirvani, M.A., Abadi, M.K.: An integrated IoT and deep learning-based system for accurate weather prediction. IEEE Internet Things J. **7**(4), 2828–2836 (2020)
11. Geetharamani, G., Pandian, A.J.: Identification of plant leaf diseases using a nine-layer deep convolutional neural network. Comput. Electr. Eng. **76**, 323–338 (2019). https://doi.org/10.1016/j.compeleceng.2019.04.011
12. Griffel, L.M., Delparte, D., Edwards, J.: Using support vector machines classification to differentiate spectral signatures of potato plants infected with potato virus Y. Comput. Electron. Agric. **153**, 318–324 (2018). https://doi.org/10.1016/j.compag.2018.08.027
13. Goyal, P.A., Sahoo, T.K., Sharma, T.K., Singh, P.K.: Internet of things: applications, security and privacy: a survey. Mater. Today Proc. **34**, 752–759 (2019)
14. He, K., Zhang, X., Ren, S., Sun, J.: Deep residual learning for image recognition. IEEE Conf. Comput. Vision Pattern Recogn. 770–778 (2016). https://doi.org/10.1109/CVPR.2016.90
15. Heisel, S., Kovačević, T., Briesen, H., Schembecker, G., Wohlgemuth, K.: Variable selection and training set design for particle classification using a linear and a non-linear classifier. Chem. Eng. Sci. **173**, 131–144 (2017). https://doi.org/10.1016/j.ces.2017.07.030
16. Kansal, I., Khullar, V., Verma, J., Popli, R., Kumar, R.: IoT-Fog-enabled robotics-based robust classification of hazy and normal season agricultural images for weed detection. Paladyn J. Behav. Robot. **14**(1) (2023). https://doi.org/10.1515/pjbr-2022-0105
17. Kansal, I., Popli, R., Verma, J., Bhardwaj, V., Bhardwaj, R.: Digital image processing and IoT in smart health care—a review. In: 2022 International Conference on Emerging Smart Computing and Informatics (ESCI), pp. 1–6 (2022). https://doi.org/10.1109/ESCI53509.2022.9758227
18. Rani, S., Ahmed, S.H., Rastogi, R.: Dynamic clustering approach based on wireless sensor networks genetic algorithm for IoT applications. Wireless Netw. **26**, 2307–2316 (2020)
19. Kumar, A., Sharma, S., Goyal, N., Singh, A., Cheng, X., Singh, P.: Secure and energy-efficient smart building architecture with emerging technology IoT. Comput. Commun. **176**, 207–217 (2021)

Cybersecurity Awareness: Insights from a Comprehensive Survey

Diya[1], Jeetasha[1], Madhavi[1], Tanay[1]([✉]), Rubina Dutta[2], Isha Gupta[2],
and Sonam Aggarwal[2]

[1] School of Information Technology, Deakin University Geelong, Geelong, Australia
singhtanay0409@gmail.com
[2] Chitkara University Institute of Engineering and Technology, Chitkara University,
Chandigarh, Punjab, India

Abstract. With the rapid development of the internet and cellular network infrastructure, data and information exchange has increased and this is directly linked to the increasing cyber risks and crimes. Thus, it becomes very necessary to promote cyber security awareness. The current work aims to study the awareness of cyber security in university settings. To assess the knowledge related to the cyber security domain, a questionnaire consisting of 23 questions was distributed among the university settings. The awareness questionnaire was based on three important subsets of cyber security: - Password Security, Browser security, and Social Media Etiquette. A total of 119 responses were collected and analyzed. More than 85% of the respondents agreed that a strong and complex password should be formed and regularly updated to be used for logging on the various online platforms. Additionally, 83.4% of respondents agreed that browser updation and privacy controls are essential for safeguarding browsers against cyber threats. Similarly, more than 60% of the respondents disagreed with being indulged in any unusual activity related to social media. The findings of the study suggest that the majority of the respondents are aware of cyber threats and cyber security measures.

Keywords: Cyber security awareness · Cyber threats · Cyberspace · Password Security · Browser security · Social Media Etiquette

1 Introduction

In the era of technological advancement, the term "cyber" is widely acknowledged in networks and computers. Cyberspace is the collection of data, computing devices, networks, and the people using these devices [1, 2]. Cyber security is, therefore, a collection of tools, concepts, resources, protocols, and measures to safeguard these cyberspace systems from misuse, unauthorized access, cyberattacks, and cybercrimes [3]. The origin of cyber security dates back to the 1990s, although some cyber threats, such as computer viruses, existed before [4]. In past years, cybercrimes usually took place through hardware and software elements, but in current times the human aspect has also become a link through which a lot of cybercrimes happen [5]. This can be exemplified by a study

© The Author(s), under exclusive license to Springer Nature Switzerland AG 2026
S. Pal et al. (Eds.): ICETSS 2024, CCIS 2610, pp. 30–46, 2026.
https://doi.org/10.1007/978-3-032-11488-4_4

conducted in 2015, which emphasized the cases of employees who became the targets of cyber breaches. It also highlighted that around 50%-90% of organisations suffered security breaches caused due to human errors [6]. Thus, cyber security has gained immense importance not only for bigger organizations but for individuals as well.

In recent years, the technology sector has expanded rapidly. Mobile phones and the internet have revolutionised the way data and information are exchanged worldwide. It is predicted that the number of internet users will expand from 5.35 billion in 2019 to 7.9 billion in 2024, a hike of about 47% [5]. Although advances in the internet and technology sectors have provided numerous benefits and have allowed people to connect globally, they are the gateway for many cybercrimes. This is generally because the information on the internet is publicly accessible and careless usage of the internet leads to security breaches and frauds. Some of the most common cyber threats include cyber war, cyber terrorism, and cyber espionage. Cybersecurity, therefore, can help in preventing these risks [7]. A study conducted on cybersecurity defines the three dimensions of cybersecurity, as discussed in detail in Table 1 [8].

Table 1. Dimensions of Cyber Security

Cyber security dimensions	Description
Security Principles	The major focus of this dimension is to protect vulnerable information from being exploited by cybercriminals. The three main concepts under this dimension are confidentiality, integrity, and availability. Confidentiality is a subset of security principles that deal with the protection of data from misuse and unauthorized access. Integrity relates to the correctness of data and availability means that on request the data should be available.
Information States	This dimension focuses on protecting data in all forms, whether in storage or in a processing state.
Countermeasures	This dimension includes all the methods, tools, policies, laws, and frameworks developed to deal with cyber threats.

Cybersecurity is an evolving field and new strategies continue to be implemented in various sectors including business, finance, banking, defence, the Internet of Things (IoT), and education, etc. [9]. However, there are certain challenges in the enforcement of cyber security like lack of awareness, lack of cyber workforce, and lack of strict rules and policies relevant to cybersecurity. Various studies suggest the use of awareness as a measure to mitigate cyber-attacks and crimes [10]. Three crucial elements of cybersecurity awareness are: Password Security (PS), Browser Security (BS), and Social Media Etiquette (SME). Each plays a significant role in protecting individuals and organizations from cyber threats. The awareness of individuals regarding these parameters can help mitigate the risks associated with cybercrimes.

PS is the most widely used authentication technique nowadays [11]. For instance, E-banking, E-commerce, and many other digital platforms that store our personal information generally use password authentication. It often requires a balance between memorization and strength where both user-selected and system-assigned passwords have their challenges. In an experimental study conducted on a group of individuals, it was observed that a significant 78% of the people reuse their passwords and about 54.4% of the individuals rely on using very weak passwords [12]. Following a recent survey 80% of the users have used the same passwords on various platforms [13]. However, 16% of them exchanged one of their previous passwords from another website, with only 4% of people making new passcodes, by observation. According to the research, which tested approximately 20 million data from users of China, more than 12% of company employees use their phone numbers and birthdays whereas 11.5% make their passwords using their username and email.

In recent days, non-secure browser practices have been linked with cyber-attacks and crimes [14]. Web Browsers are commonly used for examining security and privacy-based tasks like banking, accessing medical records, or other personal information. Although with enhanced security, advanced web browsers like Chrome with 25 million lines of code can be complex to be maintained as bug-free and simultaneously there is a huge risk of being targeted by multiple cyberattacks [15]. According to research [16], cyberattacks are mainly due to exposure to a web page's user interface, browser cache memory, plugins and extensions. With the use of these vulnerabilities, the attacker can further access a user's device maliciously with the use of JavaScript.

Furthermore, social media platforms which are considered as recent technological advancements, have become a source of major cyber crimes and data breaches. A very significant example of this is Anthem Health's 2015 breach associated with the stealing of 80 million records, which was executed using LinkedIn [17]. Although the evolution of social media platforms has increased worldwide communication among users with the introduction of multiple applications such as online forums, video streaming, and other chat platforms, multiple users are not known of its harmful consequences. These include exposing themselves to various cyber attackers, identity theft, cyberbullying or assault, privacy violation, etc. [18]. The parameters like PS, BS, and SME have been chosen due to their vulnerable nature which can be exploited by hackers and cyber criminals. Although cyber security awareness is being explored in various sectors this paper focuses on cyber security awareness in university settings. In universities, where students, faculty, and administrators are all potential targets, understanding and reducing these effects are crucial. Students are among the most vulnerable groups to cyber-attacks due to careless and often reckless usage of their computers. Akram and Kumar (2017) discuss the positive and negative implications of social media, emphasizing the need for awareness in educational environments [19]. Case studies presented by Brush, Bolin, and Lewis (2021), illustrate the effects of cyberbullying on students' psychological health [20]. This has led to a need for cybersecurity awareness in university settings. There has also been a rise in incidents like online fraud, hacking, and website defacements [21]. Measures must be taken to educate individuals about such threats. While traditional awareness campaigns have been launched, the knowledge related to cybersecurity has yet to be analysed [22]. This paper examines existing awareness in individuals within university environments by investigating factors that influence awareness levels and evaluating the impact of educational initiatives. Through cyber security education, universities can make a community that has both the knowledge and skills required to be safe and secure in the digital landscape. The following research questions were taken into consideration for this paper.

RQ1: How do users' practices in balancing password complexity and memorability influence the security of their digital accounts?
RQ2: How does user awareness of browser security practices influence the effectiveness of their data protection against cyberattacks?
RQ3: How does user awareness of privacy risks and ethical standards influence social media engagement practices and their effectiveness in mitigating cyber threats?
RQ4: What is the current perspective of people about cybersecurity and how do they think it might evolve in the future?

This paper is organized into the following sections. Section 2 reviews the literature on cybersecurity and presents the related work. Section 3 outlines the materials and methodology used to evaluate cybersecurity awareness among university students, faculty, and administrators. Section 4 presents the results of the study and provides a discussion of the findings. Finally, Sect. 5 offers conclusions and recommendations for enhancing cybersecurity awareness and practices in higher education settings.

2 Literature Review

This section highlights the diverse range of studies that were conducted across various regions and demographics. The main objective of the studies is to determine the level of cybersecurity awareness and education. These studies span over a decade, from 2014 to 2024, including the audience as undergraduate students, internet users, social media users, business employees, etc. Table 2 summarizes these studies, detailing their objectives, key findings, limitations, recommendations, and geographic scopes.

Overall, the observations after the studies reflect that many groups of people showcase very little knowledge regarding the contents of cyber security. Although, in some cases, people tend to have a basic understanding of this domain. Common findings include being prone to cybercrimes at a higher rate, especially among young internet users, and a common notion to increase cybersecurity education and training. The limitations of maximum studies were that they focused on a specific group or region which affected the generalizability of the results. The recommendations included targeted awareness programs and the integration of cybersecurity training at different organizations and institutions. This will reduce the risks of cyber threats. These observations suggest the need to improve cybersecurity awareness and education globally.

3 Materials and Methodology

A survey was conducted among the universities and education departments to determine the awareness of three crucial cybersecurity parameters: PS, BS, and SME as illustrated in Fig. 1. The online medium used was Google Forms. There was a total of 23 questions

Table 2. Overview of Studies on Cybersecurity Awareness Among Diverse Populations

Year	Target Audience	Objective	Findings	Limitations	Recommendations	Geographic Scope
2024 [23]	Saudi Arabian undergraduate students	Assess cybersecurity awareness	Majority of cybercrimes via social media, lack of awareness, desire for training	Limited to undergraduate students in the Alnamas district	Implement cybersecurity training programs, increase awareness efforts	Alnamas District, Saudi Arabia
2024 [24]	Malaysian students (primary and secondary schools)	Assess cyber security awareness post-pandemic	High exposure to the Internet; awareness of cyber security issues but unclear understanding of risks	Limited clarity on risk perception	Enhance cyber security education focusing on risk perception	Malaysia
2023 [25]	Middle Eastern young internet users	Investigate cybercrime susceptibility	Lack of understanding of cybersecurity among young users; high susceptibility to cybercrime	Cultural and regional bias	Implement targeted educational programs on cybersecurity	Middle East
2023 [26]	Nigerian Polytechnic students	Investigate cybersecurity awareness and education levels	Basic knowledge of cybersecurity; lack of understanding of data protection methods; desire for more education	Limited active awareness programs in Polytechnics	Introduce and enhance cybersecurity awareness programs in Polytechnics	Nigeria
2022 [27]	Various countries (Turkey, Israel, Poland, Slovenia)	Study user cybersecurity behavior	Adequate knowledge but poor application of cybersecurity practices in real-world scenarios	Survey-based study, limited behavioral insights	Promote practical cybersecurity training	Multiple countries
2022 [28]	Academic institutions in Malaysia	Analyze the effectiveness of cybersecurity awareness activities	Reluctance among students to engage in awareness activities; the need for increased dissemination of cybersecurity information	Bias toward academic settings	Integrate cybersecurity awareness into academic curricula	Malaysia

(continued)

in the survey, including 6 demographic questions and 17 questions covering the three cybersecurity variables provided above. This section includes details about respondents, demographic data, and survey measuring tools.

Table 2. (*continued*)

Year	Target Audience	Objective	Findings	Limitations	Recommendations	Geographic Scope
2021 [29]	Kuwaiti institutions	Evaluate cybersecurity awareness and behavior	Found low levels of awareness and suggested prioritizing formal cybersecurity training.	Limited to Kuwaiti institutions; focused on specific demographics.	Prioritize formal cybersecurity awareness training programs.	Kuwait
2021 [30]	Majmaah University, Saudi Arabia	Measure cybersecurity awareness among students	Highlighted inadequate understanding of cybersecurity training organizations in reducing cyber-attacks.	Limited to Majmaah University; focused on specific cultural and educational contexts.	Develop effective cybersecurity training frameworks tailored to local contexts.	Saudi Arabia
2020 [31]	Turkish, Israeli, Polish, and Slovenian users	Investigate the relationship between cybersecurity awareness, comprehension, and activity	Adequate awareness but poor practical application of cybersecurity measures	Limited to specific countries; may not reflect global trends	Promote practical application of knowledge	Turkey, Israel, Poland, Slovenia
2020 [32]	Internet users in India	Analyze cybercrime trends and impacts	Significant increase in reported cybercrime incidents in India; dependence on digital platforms for essential tasks increases vulnerability	Relies on reported incidents; may underestimate actual cybercrime rates	Strengthen cybersecurity infrastructure; increase public awareness and education	India
2019 [33]	Chinese users	Analyze password practices	Widespread use of insecure password practices like using birthdays and phone numbers	Reliance on user-reported data	Educate on secure password creation strategies	China
2019 [34]	Bangladeshi citizens	Assess cyber security awareness	Majority ignorant of cybercrime threats	Reliance on self-reported data	Increase public awareness campaigns	Bangladesh

(continued)

3.1 Respondents

In this study, a survey was conducted without any primary target number. There were 119 responses including students and staff members from different universities who participated in this survey. The highest number of respondents were from Chitkara University as compared to other universities as shown in Table 3.

Table 2. (*continued*)

Year	Target Audience	Objective	Findings	Limitations	Recommendations	Geographic Scope
2018 [35]	Various universities in the Pacific Northwest	Evaluate cybersecurity knowledge among college students	Found significant gaps in knowledge about malware, phishing, and other cybersecurity terms.	Limited to the Pacific Northwest region; may not represent national or international trends.	Integrate cybersecurity education into university curricula across disciplines.	USA
2018 [36]	General users	Measure end-user awareness of phishing attempts	Consumers with limited information easily duped	Varied demographics; awareness levels may differ across different populations	Educate end-users on phishing risks	Various countries
2017 [37]	United States Coast Guard Academy	Assess phishing susceptibility among new cadets	Over three-quarters were susceptible to phishing attacks.	Specific to Coast Guard Academy cadets; may not generalize to broader populations.	Implement targeted phishing awareness programs in military academies.	USA
2017 [38]	Tamil Nadu, India (university students)	Examine attentiveness to cybersecurity risks	70% aware of basic virus attacks and use antivirus; 11% use outdated antivirus; 97% unaware of virus sources	Geographical limitation; cultural factors may influence responses	Introduce high-level training programs	India
2016 [39]	Social media users (ages 21–35)	Study privacy awareness on social media	44% lack knowledge of privacy policies; 34% are gravely concerned about privacy; 80% are not satisfied with privacy levels	Limited sample size; focused on specific demographics	Improve privacy policies on social media	Various countries
2016 [40]	Middle Eastern academic settings	Study security awareness	Misunderstanding of cyber security importance among respondents	Limited to educational settings	Implement comprehensive safety management plans	Middle East

(*continued*)

As the form was distributed to a wide range of people, many of them had prior technical knowledge and tended to know more about the specified cybersecurity parameters. However, as Fig. 2 shows, approximately one-third of the respondents have less knowledge.

Table 2. (*continued*)

Year	Target Audience	Objective	Findings	Limitations	Recommendations	Geographic Scope
2015 [41]	Organizations using cloud computing in India	Study cybersecurity risks associated with cloud platforms	Increased adoption of cloud computing in India poses new challenges in cybersecurity; vulnerabilities to digital crimes and breaches	Specific to cloud computing; may not address broader cybersecurity issues	Implement robust cloud security measures; conduct regular audits and updates	India
2015 [42]	Undergraduate psychology students	Examine the relationship between knowledge and vulnerability to phishing	No significant relationship was found between knowledge of phishing and vulnerability.	Limited sample size and focus on psychology students.	Enhance phishing education strategies beyond basic knowledge.	International University outside India
2014 [6]	Business employees	Evaluate cybersecurity awareness methods	Various methods to enhance end-user behavior and awareness	Limited to business employees	Implement interactive and diverse awareness methods	Not Specified
2014 [43]	California State University, Los Angeles (students)	Examine cybersecurity awareness and real-world application	The main issue was not a lack of knowledge but poor application of security measures in real-world scenarios	Focused on a single institution; findings may not be applicable universally	Enhance curriculum with security training	USA

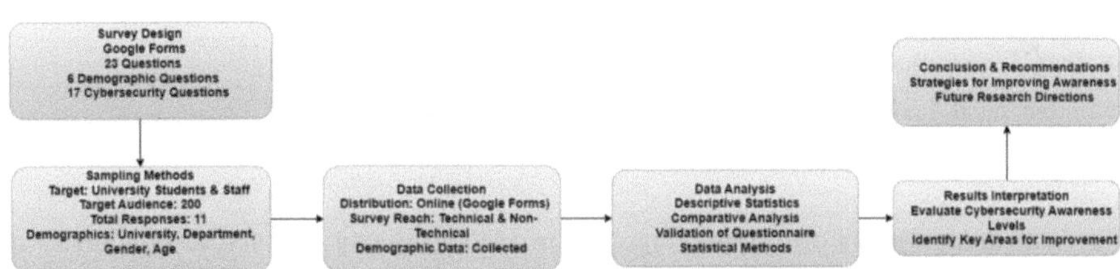

Fig. 1. Methodological framework visualization

Table 3. University classification

University Name	Count
Chitkara University	93
Other	26

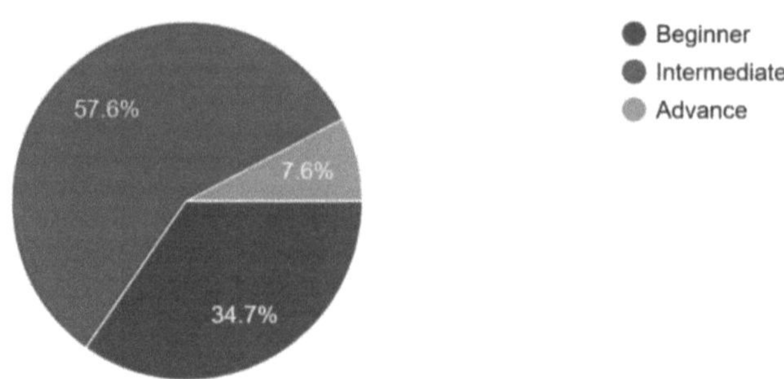

Fig. 2. Classification based on the range of computer knowledge

According to their different education levels, demographic gender as well as their age groups, the responses got varied. The respondents from different departments demonstrated different levels of knowledge. Specifically, respondents from technical backgrounds such as software engineering students who had completed a six-month course in Cybersecurity shared a vast knowledge. However, those who were somewhat related to Cybersecurity awareness showed an intermediate level of knowledge, while respondents from non-technical backgrounds had less knowledge about cybersecurity awareness as classified in Table 4.

Table 4. Department classification

Department Name	Number of Responses
B.Tech Software Engineering	76
B.Tech. Computer Science Engineering	8
B.Tech. Electronics and Communication Engineering	7
Non-technical	28

After analyzing the responses, Fig. 3 showed that the ratio of male respondents was higher than female respondents.

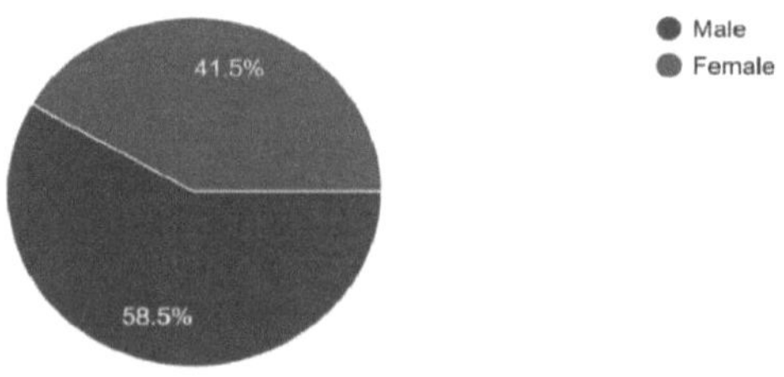

Fig. 3. Gender-based classification

According to the age groups, students who were less than 20 years of age showed maximum responses of about 60.2%, however, the people ranging in age from 36 to 49 showed comparatively less responses of approximately 6.8% (mentioned in Fig. 4).

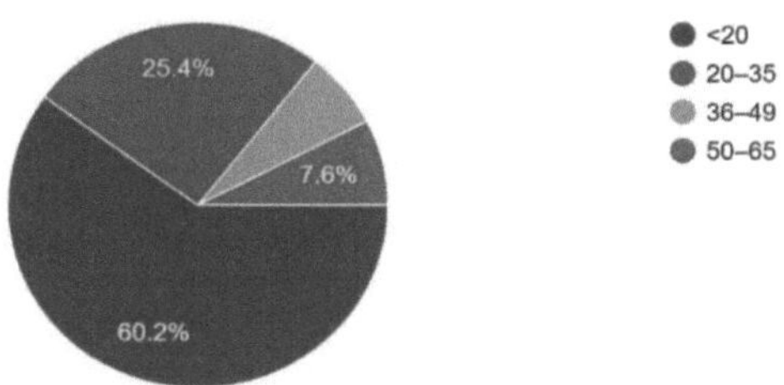

Fig. 4. Age-based Classification

3.2 Measuring Tools

The questionnaire designed by Mohammed A. Alqahtani (2022) [13] was modified and used accordingly to analyze the basic knowledge related to Cybersecurity awareness among students and staff members, as mentioned in Appendix 1. The key parameters used for analysis were PS, BS, and SME.

Focusing on the first parameter, the respondents were queried regarding aspects such as the strength of a password, how frequently it is or should be changed, the reusability of old passwords, and how a balance is to be maintained between convenience (remembering typical passwords) and security (setting strong and unique passwords) while maintaining passwords for each online platform. Also, the survey covered the respondents' views on sharing passwords with friends, which showcased their ignorant behavior about understanding password confidentiality. Next, the second parameter, BS analyzed the awareness of the need for regular updates, the risks related to thirdparty extensions, and regular management of browser privacy settings. Respondents were also asked if they felt reviewing browsing history important for any unauthorized activity. SME questions evaluated their attitude towards privacy and information sharing such as sharing personal photographs, connecting with unknown individuals, disclosing their current locations, and sharing any kind of personal information through social media. These aspects were analyzed keeping in mind the most common causes of cyber-attacks which take place because of these three mediums majorly.

Moreover, additional questions were also included in which respondents were asked to provide their opinions on the "implementation of preventive measures to reduce the risks associated with cybersecurity threats" and "opinions about the evolving role of future cybersecurity". These questions further played a crucial role in analyzing the responses and providing constructive insights. Therefore, by analyzing these important parameters, the survey helped in identifying the key areas of improvement and hence provided ideas and strategies for improving Cybersecurity awareness among students and staff members.

4   Results and Discussion

As discussed in the previous sections, the parameters considered for the survey were PS, BS, and SME. The questionnaire comprised 6 questions under PS, 4 for BS and 5 for social media activities. The responses were collected and they have been analyzed in the following section. The responses were collected on the five-level Likert scale. In the analysis, the terms used for Strongly Agree is "SA", Agree is "A", Neutral is "N", Disagree is "D", and Strongly Disagree is "SD".

RQ1 How do users' practices in balancing password complexity and memorability influence the security of their digital accounts?

A password is a set of characters or words that can provide authenticated access to any software and computer system. Passwords tend to be considered a secret entity that should be protected. In case, the password is decoded it can lead to the stealing of information that can be important and confidential. It is considered that the password should be 8 to 24 letters and should include uppercase and lowercase characters in addition to a special character. The password should be strong enough that it can be guessed by another individual, easily reducing the risk of cybercrimes [13].

Table 5 provides insightful data on respondents' attitudes towards password security. In PS1, 64.7% of respondents "Strongly Agree" (SA) and 29.41% "Agree" (A) that passwords should be strong and complex to safeguard digital assets from security threats. In PS2, 43% "Agree" that passwords should be changed regularly as older passwords are more susceptible to being decoded. Consequently, a notable portion of respondents "Disagree" (26.05%) in PS3 with reusing old passwords when creating new ones or updating existing ones.

In PS4, 51.26% of respondents "Strongly Agree" that having a strong password for logging into all online platforms is crucial for protecting sensitive information and maintaining account integrity. However, 46.21% "Agree" that remembering such unique and complex passwords for various platforms is inconvenient. Despite the challenges of remembering new and complex passwords, respondents acknowledge the importance of doing so for security purposes. Furthermore, 55.46% "Strongly Disagree" (SD) in PS6 with sharing passwords among friends, emphasising the necessity of maintaining control over accounts to prevent unauthorised access. Overall, the majority of respondents demonstrate a solid understanding of secure password practices, recognizing the critical role of password management in maintaining digital security.

Table 5. Response percentages of questions about PS

	SA	A	N	D	SD
PS1	64.70	29.41	4.20	0.84	0.84
PS2	42.85	43.69	10.92	2.52	0
PS3	10.08	10.08	15.96	37.81	26.05
PS4	51.26	31.09	6.72	8.40	2.52
PS5	10.92	46.21	15.12	19.32	8.40

(continued)

Table 5. (*continued*)

	SA	A	N	D	SD
PS6	2.52	2.52	5.04	34.45	55.46

RQ2 How does user awareness of browser security practices influence the effectiveness of their data protection against cyberattacks?

In recent times, web browsers have become an integral part of daily life, attracting an increasing number of users. Popular web browsers such as Google Chrome, Firefox, and Microsoft Edge serve as gateways to a myriad of online activities. However, with the rising number of daily users, many may not be aware of how to secure their data, making them vulnerable to cyberattacks. Browser security (BS) plays a crucial role in protecting personal information and other sensitive data. Therefore, it is essential for users to understand how to safeguard their data from security breaches and to be educated about security features. Keeping web browsers updated to the latest version is particularly important for maintaining their security.

Analysis of Table 6 reveals several insights into respondents' knowledge and practices regarding browser security. In BS1, 45.37% of respondents "Agree" (A) and 38.65% "Strongly Agree" (SA) on the importance of regularly updating web browsers to reduce the risk of cyberattacks. In BS2, approximately 54.62% of respondents "Agree" that installing new extensions from third parties is harmful, recognizing the risks these pose, such as device harm and data theft. BS3 shows that 58.82% of respondents "Agree" on the necessity of frequently examining privacy controls and other security parameters, which helps maintain strong authentication and prevent hackers from stealing personal information. Additionally, BS4 indicates that 47.05% of respondents "Agree" on reviewing browser history for unusual activity. Overall, these results suggest that respondents possess a reasonable level of awareness regarding browser security.

Table 6. Response percentages of questions about BS

	SA	A	N	D	SD
BS1	38.65	45.37	15.12	1.68	0
BS2	26.89	54.62	15.12	1.68	1.68
BS3	34.45	58.82	5.88	0.84	0
BS4	27.73	47.05	19.32	5.04	0.84

RQ3 How does user awareness of privacy risks and ethical standards influence social media engagement practices and their effectiveness in mitigating cyber threats?

In today's technologically advancing world, social media has become a significant medium for sharing information and networking with people globally. Users often share private information, such as photos and videos, on various platforms, showcasing their daily activities and interacting with unknown individuals online. This behavior has increased the spread of false information and cyber threats like spam, celebrity impersonation, phishing, and cyberbullying.

Analysis of the surveyed respondents' responses, as shown in Table 7, provides insights into their social media engagement (SME) practices. In SME1, the majority of respondents are "Neutral" (N) (39.49%) and "Disagree" (D) (27.73%) with sharing personal photographs online. In SME4, a significant number of respondents "Strongly Disagree" (SD) and "Disagree" (D) (36.13% each) with sharing personal information on social networking platforms. This cautious approach is valid, as sharing personal data can expose individuals to identity theft, enabling cybercriminals to conduct fraudulent activities.

Regarding interactions with outsiders, 42.85% "Disagree" (D) and 19.32% "Strongly Disagree" (SD) with accepting invitations from unknown people (SME2), indicating an awareness of potential scams. Similarly, SME3 reveals that a combined total of 76.46% of respondents "Strongly Disagree" (SD) and "Disagree" (D) with sharing their current location online, recognizing that doing so can enable unwanted individuals to stalk them by monitoring daily patterns. Conversely, SME5 shows that 26.05% "Strongly Agree" (SA) and 48.73% "Agree" (A) that users should be vigilant about questionable behavior on these platforms to ensure a safe and respectful community and support ethical standards. These findings indicate that respondents are quite aware of appropriate social media engagement practices.

Table 7. Response percentages of questions about SME

	SA	A	N	D	SD
SME1	2.52	20.16	39.49	27.73	10.08
SME2	2.52	11.76	22.68	42.85	19.32
SME3	2.52	5.88	15.12	32.77	43.69
SME4	2.52	9.24	15.96	36.13	36.13
SME5	26.05	48.73	20.16	4.20	0.84

RQ4: What is the current perspective of people about cybersecurity and how do they think it might evolve in the future?

Two questions in the survey focused on analyzing the views of respondents regarding the measures that organizations should implement to effectively reduce the risks associated with cyber threats and the evolving role of cyber security in the future. The majority of people believe that organizations should provide comprehensive training to employees regarding cyber safety awareness. Organizations should also enforce stronger protocols for promoting regular system updates, data encryption, strong authentication mechanisms, and securing network systems. Regular security testing and proper incident-response plans will help organizations to mitigate cyber threats effectively. Likewise, people have different opinions on the evolution and future role of cybersecurity. Many respondents have emphasized the importance of integrating Artificial Intelligence and Machine Learning in the cyber security domain. Moreover, the responses also indicate that with increased automation and dependency on digital platforms, the need to implement better cybersecurity strategies will be a very crucial aspect of cybersecurity in the future. Some examples of the responses are presented in the Table 8 below. Thus, the study presents the different preventive steps that organizations should undertake to ensure cyber security and the importance of cyber security in the future.

Table 8. Sample responses

Respondents	Responses
R1	"As technology is getting advanced, cyber security will become even more important. Cyber threats are becoming more sophisticated, and protecting data will be crucial."
R2	"I believe the future of cybersecurity is both dynamic and increasingly critical as cyber threats become more sophisticated. It will continue to evolve rapidly, integrating advanced technologies like artificial intelligence and machine learning to enhance threat detection and response. The role of cybersecurity will expand beyond technical measures to encompass strategic business functions, emphasizing the importance of resilience and ethical considerations. Raising awareness and educating about it will be vital as the demand for skilled cybersecurity professionals grows. Overall, cybersecurity will play an essential role in safeguarding digital assets and enabling secure innovation in our interconnected world."
R3	"The future of cybersecurity will be shaped by the integration of emerging technologies like AI, IoT, and quantum computing, necessitating specialized security measures. AI and machine learning will enhance both defense and attack strategies, while increased regulation will drive compliance efforts. Proactive and predictive security approaches will become essential, alongside a greater emphasis on mitigating human vulnerabilities through education. Cybersecurity will be embedded into core business functions, requiring continuous innovation and collaboration across industries and governments to address the evolving and complex threat landscape."

5   Conclusion

This research study presents the results of the survey related to cyber security awareness, conducted in university settings. Cyber security has become one of the most important areas of concern in the current era. The statistical analysis shows that respondents have appropriate knowledge about practices related to PS, BS, and SME which collectively contribute to the reduction in the overall cybersecurity risk within educational environments. Around 87.6% of respondents agreed that the passwords should be stronger and more challenging to avoid being decoded easily by another person. Browser security practices were found to be consistent. 83.4% were aware of the safer browser practices, as a result, it can significantly reduce the risk of ransomware and data breaches. Furthermore, the rapid growth of social media has led to increased sharing of personal information. 62.17% of respondents disagreed with the behavior of using online platforms carelessly. Its responsible usage can enhance personal and professional networking while maintaining security.

There are some limitations associated with the study including the short time in which the study was conducted and the limited number of responses collected. This analysis is just among the university settings leading to lesser generalizability of the results. Therefore, the interpretations cannot be applied to people of other domains. Future research should explore more respondents from different fields. This will lead to better insights and more strategies that can be incorporated. In conclusion, there must be an approach to encourage cybersecurity education, it can be comprised of various training and awareness programs. This is essential for safeguarding the data of an individual and also the information of various organizations. These efforts would contribute to acquiring the necessary skills, which will make the digital environment safer and remove the risk of cybercrimes.

Acknowledgement. This research did not receive any specific grant from funding agencies in the public, commercial, or not-for-profit sectors.

Disclosure of Interest. The authors have no competing interests to declare that are relevant to the content of this article.

References

1. Rahman, N.A.A., et al.: The importance of cybersecurity education in school. Int. J. Inf. Educ. Technol. **10**(5), 378–382 (2020)
2. Craigen, D., et al.: Defining cybersecurity. Technol. Innov. Manag. Rev. **4**, 10 (2014)
3. Warner, M.: Cybersecurity: a pre-history. Intell. Nat. Secur. **27**(5), 781–799 (2012)
4. Abawajy, J.: User preference of cyber security awareness delivery methods. Behav. Inf. Technol. **33**(3), 237–248 (2014)
5. Ertan, A. et al.: Cyber Security Behaviour in Organisations (2020). arXiv:2004.11768
6. Pelchen, L.: Internet Usage Statistics in 2024. Forbes Home (2024)
7. Seemma, P.S., et al.: Overview of cyber security. Int. J. Adv. Res. Comput. Commun. Eng. **7**(11), 125–128 (2018)
8. Aslan, Ö., et al.: A comprehensive review of cyber security vulnerabilities, threats, attacks, and solutions. Electronics **12**(6), 1333 (2023)
9. Ghate, S., Agrawal, P.K.: A literature review on cyber security in Indian context. J. Comput. Inf. Technol. **8**(5), 30–36 (2017)
10. Bhasin, M.: Mitigating cyber threats to banking industry. Chart. Account. **50**(10), 1618–1624 (2007)
11. Taneski, V., et al.: Systematic overview of password security problems. Acta Polytechnica Hungarica **16**(3), 143–165 (2019)
12. Kovačević, A., et al.: Factors related to cyber security behavior. IEEE Access **8**, 125140–125148 (2020)
13. Alqahtani, M.A.: Factors affecting cybersecurity awareness among university students. Appl. Sci. **12**(5), 2589 (2022)
14. Serrhini, M., Moussa, A.A.: Home users security and the web browser inbuilt settings, framework to setup IT automatically. J. Comput. Sci. **9**(2), 159–168 (2013)

15. Lim, J.: SOK: On the Analysis of Web Browser Security (2021). arXiv preprint
16. arXiv:2112.15561
17. Satish, P.S., Chavan, R.K.: Web browser security: different attacks detection and prevention techniques. Int. J. Comput. Appl. **170**(9), 35–41 (2017)
18. Thakur, K., et al.: Cyber security in social media: challenges and the way forward. IT Prof. **21**(2), 41–49 (2019)
19. Saleem, A.N.: Cybersecurity Issues in Social Media. Near East University (2021)
20. Akram, W., Kumar, R.: A study on positive and negative effects of social media on society. Int. J. Comput. Sci. Eng. **5**(10), 351–354 (2017)
21. Brush, T., et al.: Cyberbullying in higher education: a review of the literature. J. Educ. Comput. Res. **58**(6), 1131–1158 (2021)
22. Ulven, J.B., Wangen, G.: A systematic review of cybersecurity risks in higher education. Future Internet **13**(2), 39 (2021)
23. Bada, M., Nurse, J.R.C.: Developing cybersecurity education and awareness programmes for small-and medium-sized enterprises (SMEs). Inf. Comput. Secur. **27**(3), 393–410 (2019)
24. Zayid, E.I.M., Farah, N.A.A.: A study on cybercrime awareness test in Saudi ArabiaAlnamas region. In: 2017 2nd International Conference on Anti-Cyber Crimes (ICACC), pp. 199–202 (2017)
25. Jalil, M., et al.: Cybersecurity awareness among secondary school students Post Covid-19 pandemic. J. Adv. Res. Appl. Sci. Eng. Technol. **37**(1), 115–127 (2024)
26. Garba, A., et al.: Cyber security awareness among university students: a case study. Sci. Proc. Ser. **2**(1), 82–86 (2020)
27. Zabi, A.A.M. et al.: Cyber Security Education and Awareness
28. Zwilling, M., et al.: Cyber security awareness, knowledge and behavior: a comparative study. J. Comput. Inf. Syst. **62**(1), 82–97 (2022)
29. Gasiba, T., et al.: Sifu-a cybersecurity awareness platform with challenge assessment and intelligent coach. Cybersecurity **3**(1), 24 (2020)
30. Al-Alawi, A.I., et al.: Evaluation of information systems security awareness in higher education: an empirical study of Kuwait University. J. Innov. Bus. Best Pract. **2016**, 1–24 (2016)
31. Aloul, F.A.: The need for effective information security awareness. J. Adv. Inf. Technol. **3**(3), 176–183 (2012)
32. Hamoud, A., Aïmeur, E.: Handling user-oriented cyber-attacks: STRIM, a user-based security training model. Front. Comput. Sci. **2**, 25 (2020)
33. Kumar, S., Manhas, A.: Cyber crimes in India: trends and prevention. Galaxy Int. Interdiscip. Res. J. **9**(05), 363–370 (2021)
34. Wang, D. et al.: Birthday, name and bifacial-security: understanding passwords of Chinese web users. In: 28th USENIX Security Symposium (USENIX Security 19), pp. 1537–1555 (2019)
35. Ahmed, N. et al.: Cybersecurity awareness survey: an analysis from Bangladesh perspective. In: 2017 IEEE Region
36. Sarathchandra, D. et al.: College students' cybersecurity risk perceptions, awareness, and practices. In: 2016 Cybersecurity Symposium (CYBERSEC), pp. 68–73 (2016)
37. Schwartz, J.: Report: 7 in 10 Employees Struggle with Cyber Awareness (2017). mediapro.com
38. Young-McLear, K. et al.: A white hat approach to identifying gaps between cybersecurity education and training: a social engineering case study. In: Advances in Human Factors in Cybersecurity: Proceedings of the AHFE 2016 International Conference on Human Factors in Cybersecurity, pp. 229–237 (2016)
39. Senthilkumar, K., Easwaramoorthy, S.: A Survey on Cyber Security awareness among college students in Tamil Nadu. IOP Conf. Ser. Mater. Sci. Eng. **263**, 042043 (2017)

40. Hossain, A.A., Zhang, W.: Privacy and security concern of online social networks from user perspective. In: 2015 International Conference on Information Systems Security and Privacy (ICISSP), pp. 246–253 (2015)
41. Al-Janabi, S., Al-Shourbaji, I.: A study of cyber security awareness in educational environment in the middle east. J. Inf. Knowl. Manag. **15**(01), 1650007 (2016)
42. Singh, N., Rishi, A.: Pyramid: a case study of cyber security in India. South Asian J. Bus. Manag. Cases **4**(1), 135–142 (2015)
43. Jones, M.: The Effects of Conformity and Training in a Phishing Context: Conforming to the School of Phish. The University of Alabama in Huntsville (2015)
44. Slusky, L., Partow-Navid, P.: Students information security practices and awareness. J. Inf. Privacy Secur. **8**(4), 3–26 (2012)
45. Alharbi, T., Tassaddiq, A.: Assessment of cybersecurity awareness among students of Majmaah University. Big Data Cogn. Computg. **5**(2), 23 (2021)
46. Irshad, S., Soomro, T.R.: Identity theft and social media. Int. J. Comput. Sci. Netw. Secur. **18**(1), 43–55 (2018)
47. Li, N., Chen, G.: Sharing location in online social networks. IEEE Netw. **24**(5), 20–25 (2010)
48. Kimball, E., Kim, J.: Virtual boundaries: ethical considerations for use of social media in social work. Soc. Work **58**(2), 185–188 (2013)

Simulation and Analytical Model of Gate Stack Gate All Around MOSFET as Gas Sensor

Neetu Gupta[1], Neeraj Gupta[2(✉)], Rashmi Gupta[2], S. B. Gupta[2], Prashant Kumar[1], Lalit Rai[1], and Sandeep Kumar[3]

[1] Department of Electronics Engineering, J.C. Bose University of Science and Technology, YMCA, Sector-6, Faridabad 121006, Haryana, India
[2] Department of Electronics and Communication Engineering, Amity University Haryana, Gurugram 122412, Haryana, India
neerajsingla007@gmail.com
[3] Department of Electronics and Communication Engineering, Chitkara University Institute of Engineering and Technology, Chitkara University, Rajpura 140401, Punjab, India

Abstract. This paper presents a comprehensive analytical model for Gate Stack Gate All Around (GS-GAA) MOSFETs, focusing on the sub-threshold current and surface potential characteristics. In the proposed model, an n-channel GS-GAA MOSFET employs silver (A_g) as the gate metal, while a p-channel variant uses palladium (P_d). The silver (A_g) gate metal is used with an n-channel GS-GAA MOSFET and palladium (P_d) gate metal for a p-channel GS-GAA MOSFET to detect oxygen and hydrogen, respectively. When gas molecules interact with the surface of the catalytic metal gate, it alters the gate's work function. This change is observed as gas detection. The presence of high dielectric material as gate oxide mitigates the leakage current. Further, a comparison for this detection has been carried out for multiple devices. The proposed MOSFET exhibits 31.1% higher sensitivity compared to the GAA MOSFET, making it an excellent sensor for gas detection. The analytical results closely match the simulated results. The simulation analysis has been carried out using TCAD Silvaco software.

Keywords: MOSFET · Sensor · Sensitivity · Surface Potential · SCEs

1 Introduction

The analog and/or digital circuits are the backbone of communication, satellite, power, and space engineering. Advancements in these areas require improvements in semiconductor devices, mainly MOSFETs. Future technology nodes

R. Gupta, S. B. Gupta, P. Kumar, L. Rai, and S. Kumar—These authors contributed equally to this work.

demand scaled devices and wide integration, which places significant pressure on device engineers to meet these requirements. In addition, the semiconductor research community and industry continuously face evolving challenges due to MOSFET scaling. The main challenges, arising from poor gate control over charge carriers, are gate leakage currents and short channel effects (SCEs). These issues have driven the development of advanced MOSFETs, such as Double Metal Gate (DMG), Tri Metal Gate (TMG), and Gate-All-Around (Nanowire) MOSFETs [1,2]. Biosensors, which hinge on FETs as a fundamental building block, have shown appreciable improvements in the field of electrochemical biosensing. Both uncharged and charged biomolecules, collectively known as electrolytes, modulate the electrical response of biosensors by altering the functionality of the gate electrode. FETs with restrained dielectric properties, where the dielectric constant of the electrolyte can be adjusted, have recently gained significant attention from researchers [3,4]. A novel oxygen sensing device employing a FET design, incorporating a catalytic metal gate composed of silver (A_g), was recently documented in the literature [5]. Tsukada et al. [6] also investigated a hydrogen gas sensor utilizing a dual gate field-effect transistor (FET) configuration featuring a platinum (P_t) metal gate. In contrast, this paper explores a catalytic-based gate in a gate-all-around (GAA) MOSFET for gas sensing purposes.

In conventional gas sensors, the sensitivity parameter is typically the threshold voltage. However, in the present work, subthreshold current is used instead of the threshold voltage to assess the sensitivity of the gas sensor. This approach allows for both low energy consumption and high sensitivity. It is reported in the literature that hydrogen is one of the potential fossil fuels of the near future [7–9]. The ample availability of hydrogen may drive the energy shift towards its use. Therefore, sensors capable of efficiently handling hydrogen are required. Particularly, palladium (P_d) is employed in these sensors to achieve high sensitivity. Palladium is highly selective towards hydrogen (H_2) gas and provides high electrical resistance [10,11]. Additionally, P_d can absorb up to 900 times its volume of hydrogen [12]. In the present work, operating the device in a subthreshold regime revealed significantly enhanced sensitivity for gas detection. Similar findings were noted by Rajni et al. [13] in their research on nanowire biosensors has observed that protein detection is improved under subthreshold conditions.

In this paper, a Gate Stack GAA MOSFET is designed to increase biosensing activity compared to existing FETs. An analytical model of the GS-GAA MOSFET for gas detection will also be developed. A physics-based 2D model for the potential will be derived using Poisson's equation. This comprehensive approach aims to provide a detailed understanding and innovative design of gas sensors [14], emphasizing enhanced sensitivity and efficiency, particularly for hydrogen detection. By leveraging the unique properties of palladium and optimizing the device's operational regime, this work contributes to the advancement of gas sensing technology, paving the way for more efficient and reliable hydrogen sensors in the future energy landscape for low power applications [15–17].

2   Device Structure

Figure 1 depicts the schematic and cylindrical view of the proposed device

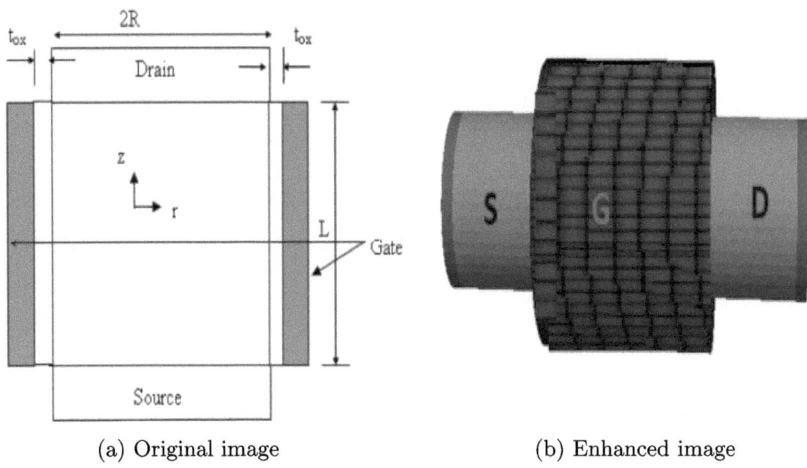

(a) Original image   (b) Enhanced image

Fig. 1. GS-GAA MOSFET

When gas molecules interact with the gate surface of a catalytic metal, it alters the threshold voltage, drain current, and flat band voltage. This phenomenon is primarily due to changes in the gate metal's work function. The variation in electrical conductivity can be correlated directly with its concentration. Oxygen and hydrogen detection can be done by using N-channel GSGAA MOSFET with silver (A_g) as the gate metal and having palladium (P_d) as the gate metal for Pchannel GAA MOSFET. Stacking of silver gate on p-channel and palladium gate on n-channel results in low Ioff due to presence of high-K dielectric [18]. Numerous simulations employ various models, including concentration-dependent mobility, drift diffusion and the Shockley-Read-Hall (SRH) recombination model [19]. The alteration of work function in the metal occurs due to the chemical contact of the catalytic metal gate located at the surface and gas molecules. Sensitivity measurements rely on monitoring changes in the drain current and threshold voltage. To further analyze these effects, a physics-based 2D model for the potential can be developed using Poisson?s equation [20]. This model characterizes the surface potential with a parabolic profile in the radial direction, incorporating appropriate boundary conditions as per the given parameters. These detailed simulations and models are crucial for accurately detecting and measuring gas concentrations using GAA MOSFETs with catalytic metal gates.

$$\phi_{sn}(z) = Me^{kz} + Ne^{-kz} + \phi_{fn} \quad \text{for n-channel} \tag{1}$$

$$\phi_{sp}(z) = -Me^{kz} - Ne^{-kz} - \phi_{fp} \quad \text{for p-channel} \tag{2}$$

where different constants are given as

$$k^2 = \frac{2C_{effox}}{\varepsilon_{Si}R}$$

$$C_{effox} = \frac{\varepsilon_{SiO_2}}{R\ln\left[1 + \frac{t_{effox}}{R}\right]}$$

$$t_{effox} = t_{low-k} + \frac{\varepsilon_{SiO_2}}{\varepsilon_{HfO_2}} + t_{High-k}$$

$$\phi_{fn} = (V_{gs} - V_{fbn}) - \frac{qN_a}{\varepsilon_{Si}k^2} \quad \text{for n-channel}$$

$$\phi_{fp} = (V_{fbp} - V_{gs}) - \frac{qN_a}{\varepsilon_{Si}k^2} \quad \text{for n-channel}$$

The boundary conditions are given as

1. The center potential $\phi_c(z)$ depends on z only and is given by

$$\phi(0, z) = \phi_c(z) \tag{3}$$

2. In the center of a silicon pillar, the electric field is absent, devoid of any external influence.

$$\left.\frac{d\phi_s(r, z)}{dr}\right|_{r=0} = 0 \tag{4}$$

3. The electric field at the interfaces of the gates/oxide. Therefore,

$$\left.\frac{d\phi_s(r, z)}{dr}\right|_{r=R} = \frac{C_{effox}}{\varepsilon_{Si}}(V_{gs} - \phi_{sn}(z) - V_{fbn}) \tag{5}$$

$$\left.\frac{d\phi_s(r, z)}{dr}\right|_{r=R} = \frac{C_{effox}}{\varepsilon_{Si}}(\phi_{sn}(z) - V_{gs} + V_{fbp}) \tag{6}$$

$$V_{fbn} = \phi_m - \left\{\chi_s + \frac{E_g}{2} + q\phi_f\right\} \pm \Delta\phi_m \tag{7}$$

$$V_{fbp} = \phi_m - \left\{\chi_s + \frac{E_g}{2} - q\phi_f\right\} \pm \Delta\phi_m \tag{8}$$

$$\Delta\phi_m = C_{st} - \left(\frac{RT}{4F}\right)\ln P \tag{9}$$

$\Delta\phi_m$ vary with gate metal and the gas it detects, with variables including P as gas partial pressure, T as absolute temperature, R as gas constant, F as Faraday's constant and C_{st} is a constant.

$$\phi_s(r, z) = \phi_{sn}(z) + \frac{C_{effect}}{2\varepsilon_{Si}R}(V_{gs} - \phi_{sn}(z) - V_{fbn})(r^2 - R^2) \tag{10}$$

$$\phi_s(r, z) = \phi_{sp}(z) + \frac{C_{effect}}{2\varepsilon_{Si}R}(V_{fbn} - V_{gs} + \phi_{sp}(z))(r^2 - R^2) \tag{11}$$

The subthreshold current is given by

$$I_{sub} \approx \frac{\pi\mu_n t_{Si}^2 n_i^2 K_B T\left(1 - e^{\frac{-V_{ds}}{V_T}}\right)e^{\frac{\phi_s}{V_T}}}{LN_a} \tag{12}$$

3   Results and Discussion

The field-effect transistor (FET) operates as a transducer, converting changes in the surface work function into an electrical signal, specifically a variation in the drain-source current (I_{DS}).

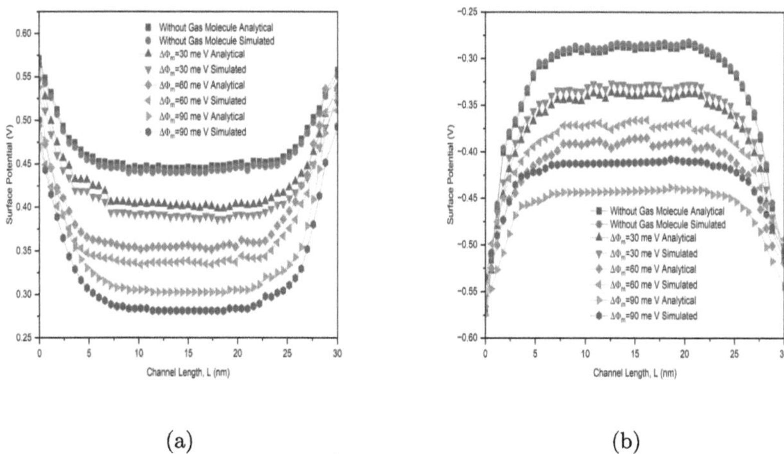

(a)   (b)

Fig. 2. Surface Potential of (a) n-channel and (b) p-channel GS-GAA MOSFET.

Figures 2 illustrate the impact of the work function differences on the surface potential of an Ag gate n-channel gate-all-around (GAA) MOSFET and a Pd gate p-channel GAA MOSFET. The interaction between the catalytic metal gate's surface and gas molecules can alter the gate?s work function. This transformation triggers a shift in the flat band voltage due to the bending of the energy bands. Such a shift causes changes in the threshold voltage (V_{th}), surface potential, and drain current (I_{DS}). By monitoring variations in V_{th}, the off-state current (I_{off}), and the on-state current (I_{on}), one can detect gas molecules such as ammonia, hydrocarbons, hydrogen, and oxygen using appropriate catalytic metal gates. The simulation parameters used include a channel length (L) of 30 nm, a radius (R) of 10 nm, and an oxide thickness (t_{ox}) of 2 nm.

Figures 3 show how changes in work function affect drain current of both p-type and n-type GAA MOSFETs, respectively. It is evident that variations in the work function significantly impact I_{off}, demonstrating the pronounced influence of gas molecules on I_{off} compared to Ion. Consequently, the subthreshold region exhibits heightened sensitivity and low-power operation. In subthreshold region, the escalated sensitivity is linked to increased energy bands bending due to changes in the gate metal's work function following the surface reaction with gas molecules, rather than Fermi level pinning. Similarly, Gao et al. [20] observed analogous behavior in nanowire biosensors, attributed to the Bessel function's asymptotic behavior.

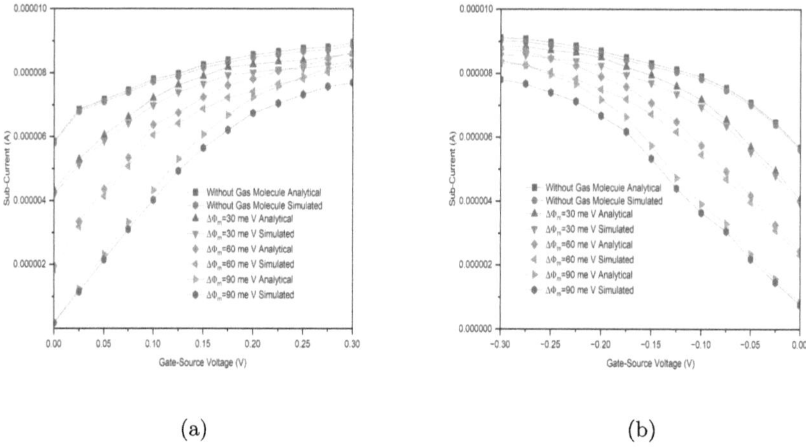

Fig. 3. Sub-current of (a) n-channel and (b) p-channel GS-GAA MOSFET.

Geo et al. [21] found that a 100 meV change in the P_d metal gate's work function led to a substantial 43-fold change in I_{off}. The validation of the analytical model is confirmed by the close agreement in the analytical and simulation results for n and p types of GAA MOSFETs. The simulation parameters include L = 30 nm, $N_a = 1 \times 1023/m^3$, $N_d = 1 \times 1026/m^3$ and R = 10 nm. This agreement supports the reliability of the model in predicting the behavior of GAA MOSFETs under varying work functions and their applications in gas sensing.

In Fig. 4, we observe how Bulk MOSFET?s I_{ds} gets an impact from the alterations of work function in the subthreshold region. The alteration in Ioff exhibits a mere five times increase solely in Bulk MOSFET, however for GS-GAA MOSFET with the shift of 90 meV in work function it escalates by 52 times. Hence it can be seen that GAA MOSFET demonstrates significantly superior gas detection sensitivity in comparison to Bulk MOSFET.

Table 1 provides a detailed comparison of sensitivity to changes in Ioff across different architectures of MOS i.e. Bulk, GAA and GS-GAA MOSFET. The analysis focuses on how molecules of gas causes the variations in the work function, impact Ioff. Greater sensitivity in the GS-GAA structure is related to the heightened ratio of surface-to-volume, of the surrounding gate structure. The enhancement of the channel's control through more efficient gate modulation is achieved by observing significant alterations in subthreshold current. This occurrence stems from differences in work function of metal gate, induced by interactions with catalytic metal gate and gas molecules. In the context of GAA MOSFETs, increasing the radius enhances current-driving capacity and amplification, while reducing the radius improves subthreshold characteristics. Variations in subthreshold current serve as a sensitivity metric for gas detection, making it evident that understanding subthreshold characteristics is crucial.

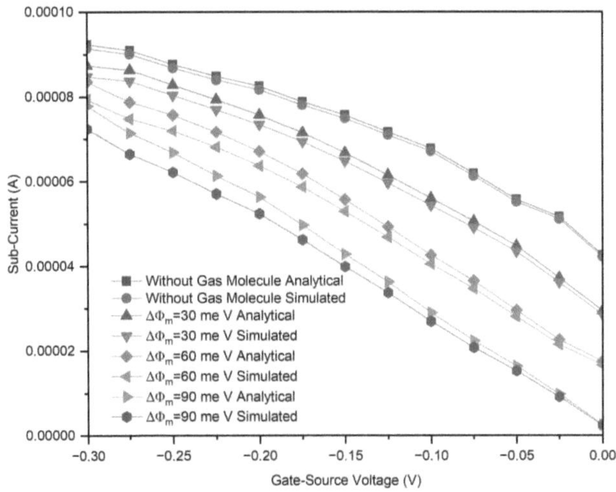

Fig. 4. Sub-current for P_d metal Gate p-channel Bulk MOSFET.

Table 1. Sensitivity comparison of devices

Change in Work Function	Bulk MOSFET	GAA MOSFET	Junction-less GAA MOSFET	GS-GAA MOSFET
$\Delta\phi_m = 30$ meV	2.08	5.96	7.19	7.58
$\Delta\phi_m = 60$ meV	4.56	33.1	39.8	43.6
$\Delta\phi_m = 90$ meV	102	151	179.5	197.9

Sensitivity improvement is evident in the GS-GAA MOSFET, as depicted in the table. For example, for $\Delta\phi_m = 90$ meV, sensitivity is enhanced by 94% for the GS-GAA MOSFET compared to the bulk MOSFET, 31.1% compared to the GAA MOSFET and 10.25% compared to the junctionless GAA MOSFET [21]. In instances of thinner silicon bodies, increased sensitivity is credited to factors such as reduced subthreshold leakage current, increased gate control, and a high surface-to-volume ratio.

4 Conclusion

The increased sensitivity of catalytic metal gate GAA MOSFETs compared to Bulk MOSFETs comes from their gate-all-around construction and high surface-to-volume ratio. This design allows for more effective interaction with biomolecules and gas molecules, making it critical for sensing applications. The GAA MOSFET?s sensitivity is significantly influenced by changes in subthreshold current, which can be caused by dielectric and negative charges of biomolecules or alterations in the metal gate?s work function. For instance, silver?s work function changes when exposed to oxygen, and palladium?s work function changes with hydrogen interaction. These interactions between molecules of gas and the catalytic metal gate are key to device's sensitivity, which is much higher than traditional methods that measure sensitivity based on threshold voltage or Ion changes.

Operating in the subthreshold region offers several advantages, such as enabling low-power operation, which is essential for portable and energy-efficient devices. Our work has developed and simulated an analytical model of sub-threshold current and surface potential, showing that the proposed GAA MOS-FET device has excellent sensitivity compared to other devices discussed in the study. The combination of efficient gate control and optimal subthreshold properties makes GAA MOSFETs a highly favorable choice for creating robust, small, reliable, low-power, and ultrasensitive CMOS sensors for various sensing applications. The findings suggest that GAA MOSFETs not only outperform Bulk MOSFETs in sensitivity but also provide a versatile and efficient solution for modern sensor technologies. This positions GAA MOSFETs as a preferred choice for applications requiring high sensitivity and low power consumption, ensuring reliable and accurate detection in a wide range of environments.

Acknowledgements. No funding has been received from any organizations for this work.

Disclosure of Interests. On behalf of all authors, the corresponding author states that there is no conflict of interest.

References

1. Ghosh, P., Haldar, S., Gupta, R., Gupta, M.: Analytical modeling and simulation for dual metal gate stack architecture (DMGSA) cylindrical/surrounded gate MOSFET. JSTS: J. Semicond. Technol. Sci. **12**(4), 458–466 (2012)
2. Gupta, N., Gupta, R., Gupta, S., Yadav, R., Kumar, P.: Performance investigation of a dielectric stacked triple material cylindrical gate all around MOSFET (DSTMCGAA) for low power applications. ECS J. Solid State Sci. Technol. **12**(1), 011002 (2023)
3. Rewari, S., Nath, V., Haldar, S., Deswal, S., Gupta, R.: A numerical model of GAN based cylindrical junctionless gate all around MOSFET for subthreshold region at cryogenic temperatures. In: 2017 Devices for Integrated Circuit (DevIC), pp. 422–427. IEEE (2017)
4. Gupta, N.: Sub-threshold modeling of dual-halo dual-dielectric triple-material surrounding-gate (DH-DD-TM-SG) MOSFET for improved leakages, vol. 8 (2020)
5. Pratap, Y., Kumar, M., Kabra, S., Haldar, S., Gupta, R.S., Gupta, M.: Analytical modeling of gate-all-around junctionless transistor based biosensors for detection of neutral biomolecule species. J. Comput. Electron. **17**(1), 288–296 (2017). https://doi.org/10.1007/s10825-017-1041-4
6. Tsukada, K., Kiriake, D., Sakai, K., Kiwa, T.: Silver gate field effect transistor for oxygen gas sensor. In: Proceedings of the Sensor Devices, pp. 5–7 (2011)

7. Scharnagl, K., Eriksson, M., Karthigeyan, A., Burgmair, M., Zimmer, M., Eisele, I.: Hydrogen detection at high concentrations with stabilised palladium, vol. 78, pp. 138–143. Elsevier (2001)
8. Choi, B., et al.: A bottom-gate silicon nanowire field-effect transistor with functionalized palladium nanoparticles for hydrogen gas sensors. Solid-State Electron. **114**, 76–79 (2015)
9. Chaujar, R., Yirak, M.G.: Sensitivity investigation of junctionless gate-all-around silicon nanowire field-effect transistor-based hydrogen gas sensor. SILICON **15**(1), 609–621 (2023)
10. Choi, J.-H., et al.: Hydrogen gas sensor of PD-functionalised ALGAN/GAN heterostructure with high sensitivity and low-power consumption. Electron. Lett. **53**(17), 1200–1202 (2017)
11. Gu, H., Wang, Z., Hu, Y.: Hydrogen gas sensors based on semiconductor oxide nanostructures. Sensors **12**(5), 5517–5550 (2012)
12. Kumar, A.: Palladium-based trench gate MOSFET for highly sensitive hydrogen gas sensor. Mater. Sci. Semicond. Process. **120**, 105274 (2020)
13. Gautam, R., Saxena, M., Gupta, R., Gupta, M.: Gate-all-around nanowire MOSFET with catalytic metal gate for gas sensing applications. IEEE Trans. Nanotechnol. **12**(6), 939–944 (2013)
14. Sharma, K., Pathania, A., Madan, J., Pandey, R., Sharma, R.: Process voltage temperature analysis of MOS based balanced pseudo-resistors for biomedical analog circuit applications. Circ. World **50**(2/3), 217–224 (2024)
15. Sachdeva, A., Gupta, L., Sharma, K., Elangovan, M.: A CNTFET based bit-line powered stable SRAM design for low power applications. ECS J. Solid State Sci. Technol. **12**(4), 041006 (2023)
16. Kumar, S., Chatterjee, A.K., Pandey, R.: Analytical modeling of recessed double gate junctionless field-effect-transistor in subthreshold region. Int. J. Numer. Model. Electron. Netw. Devices Fields **37**(2), 3209 (2024)
17. Kumar, S., Chatterjee, A.K., Pandey, R.: Performance enhancement of recessed silicon channel double gate junctionless field-effect-transistor using TCAD tool. J. Comput. Electron. **20**, 2317–2330 (2021)
18. Kumar, P., Vashisht, M., Gupta, N., Gupta, R.: Subthreshold current modeling of stacked dielectric triple material cylindrical gate all around (SD-TM-CGAA) junctionless MOSFET for low power applications. Silicon, pp. 1–9 (2021)
19. Gupta, N., Patel, J.B., Raghav, A.K.: Performance and a new 2-D analytical modeling of a dual-halo dual-dielectric triple-material surrounding-gate-all-around (DH-DD-TM-SGAA) MOSFET. J. Eng. Sci. Technol. **13**(11), 3619–3631 (2018)
20. Gao, X.P., Zheng, G., Lieber, C.M.: Subthreshold regime has the optimal sensitivity for nanowire FET biosensors. Nano Lett. **10**(2), 547–552 (2010)
21. Pratap, Y., Kumar, M., Gupta, M., Haldar, S., Gupta, R., Deswal, S.: Sensitivity investigation of gate-all-around junctionless transistor for hydrogen gas detection. In: 2016 IEEE International Nanoelectronics Conference (INEC), pp. 1–2. IEEE (2016)

AI in Enhancing Diagnostic Precision of CBC, Iron, and Lipid Profiles for the Prognostication and Management of Chronic Kidney Disease: A Systematic Review

Priyanka Jangra[1], Vivek Kumar Garg[2], and Attuluri Vamsi Kumar[3]([✉])

[1] Department of Medical Lab Technology, University Institute of Allied Health Sciences, Chandigarh University, Gharuan, Mohali, Punjab 140431, India

[2] Department of Medical Lab Sciences (USAHS), Rayat-Bahra University, Mohali 140104, Punjab, India
vivekgargpgi@gmail.com

[3] Department of Medical Laboratory Science, Regional Institute of Paramedical and Nursing Sciences (RIPANS) Ministry of Health & Family Welfare (MoHFW), Government of India, Aizawl, Mizoram, India
vamsi@ripans.ac.in

Abstract. Chronic kidney disease (CKD) affects over 10% of the global population, presenting significant health challenges. Early detection and personalized treatment are crucial for managing CKD and preventing complications. Traditional diagnostic methods have limitations, prompting the exploration of artificial intelligence (AI) for enhanced diagnostic precision. This systematic review examines AI's role in interpreting Complete Blood Count (CBC), Iron, and Lipid profiles for CKD prognostication and management. AI algorithms, including machine learning and deep learning models, show improved accuracy in detecting CKD progression, predicting outcomes, and optimizing treatment strategies. The review discusses the effectiveness of various AI models, highlights challenges related to data quality and ethical considerations, and emphasizes the importance of interdisciplinary collaboration. Key findings indicate that AI can significantly enhance diagnostic precision and personalized treatment plans, offering a proactive approach to CKD care. However, issues such as data privacy, algorithmic bias, and the need for robust regulatory frameworks persist. Integrating AI into clinical practice holds promise for revolutionizing CKD management, making it more efficient, effective, and patient-centric. Ongoing research and ethical considerations are crucial to unlock AI's full potential in CKD care.rds.

Keywords: Chronic Kidney Disease · Artificial Intelligence · Complete Blood Count · Iron Profile · Lipid Profile · Diagnostics · Patient Outcomes · Clinical Nephrology · Health Informatics · Predictive Analytics · Ethical Considerations · Data Security

---

The original version of the chapter has been revised. The chapter 6 authors affiliations has been corrected. A correction to this chapter can be found at
https://doi.org/10.1007/978-3-032-11488-4_36

1   Introduction

Chronic Kidney Disease (CKD), a growing health issue, is marked by a steady decline in kidney function. It's medically classified based on the glomerular filtration rate (GFR), with stages from 1 (normal or high GFR) to 5 (kidney failure). This classification aids clinicians in customizing treatments and tracking disease progression. CKD, affecting over 10% of the global population, has seen rising incidence and prevalence rates due to an aging population and increased risk factors like diabetes, hypertension, obesity, smoking, and genetic predispositions. According to Global Burden of Disease Study data, CKD affects approximately 10–15% of the global population. This prevalence is particularly high in low- and middle-income countries, where access to healthcare services and resources for CKD management may be limited [1].

Chronic Kidney Disease (CKD) involves comprehensive assessment, risk stratification, and personalized interventions to slow disease progression and mitigate associated complications. This includes regular monitoring of kidney function, evaluation of cardiovascular risk factors, optimization of blood pressure and glycemic control, management of proteinuria, and implementation of lifestyle modifications such as dietary changes and physical activity. Additionally, timely referral to nephrology specialists and consideration of renal replacement therapies may be necessary in the advanced stages of CKD to improve outcomes and quality of life for affected individuals [2] (Table 1).

The prognostication and management of chronic kidney disease (CKD) involves comprehensive assessment, risk stratification, and personalized interventions to slow disease progression and mitigate associated complications. This includes regular monitoring of kidney function, evaluation of cardiovascular risk factors, optimization of blood pressure and glycemic control, management of proteinuria, and implementation of lifestyle modifications such as dietary changes and physical activity. Additionally, timely referral to nephrology specialists and consideration of renal replacement therapies may be necessary in advanced stages of CKD to improve outcomes and quality of life for affected individuals.

1.1   Management of Chronic Kidney Disease in Comparison to Traditional and AI-Enabled Methods

Traditional blood tests for CKD management, such as CBC, Iron, and Lipid Profiles, have inherent limitations. Variability in results due to factors like patient hydration status and processing time can impact clinical decisions. These analyses are typically manual and prone to errors, which can lead to misdiagnosis or inappropriate treatment adjustments. Integrating multifactorial data for CKD progression prediction is challenging with traditional methods. Recognizing subtle changes across multiple parameters is difficult without advanced tools [3].

AI's advent in nephrology offers transformative potential for analyzing critical blood profiles in CKD. AI's role extends to predictive analytics, aiding in risk stratification, predicting cardiovascular complications, and anticipating the worsening of anemia. AI is recognized as a comprehensive solution to traditional methods' limitations in CKD management. It integrates and Analyses diverse data types, discerns intricate patterns, reduces

Table 1. Shows the difference between traditional CKD Diagnosis versus AI Tools for CKD Diagnosis.

Traditional Testing Methods for CKD Diagnosis	AI Tool Name for Diagnosis	Functions
Serum Creatinine Levels	Machine Learning Models	Analyse complex datasets including Complete Blood Count (CBC), Iron, and Lipid profiles to detect subtle changes indicative of CKD progression.
Estimated Glomerular Filtration Rate (eGFR)	Deep Learning Algorithms	Predict patient outcomes and optimize treatment strategies by analyzing biochemical markers and patient data.
Urine Albumin-to-Creatinine Ratio (ACR)	Neural Networks	Proactively monitor CKD progression and personalize treatment plans based on patient-specific characteristics and risk factors.
Kidney Biopsy	Decision Support Systems	Assist clinicians in interpreting biopsy results, identifying patterns, and recommending appropriate treatment options.
Blood Pressure Monitoring	Natural Language Processing (NLP)	Extract relevant information from clinical notes and patient records to assist in CKD diagnosis and management.
Electrolyte Panel	Bayesian Networks	Provide probabilistic models for assessing electrolyte imbalances and guiding treatment decisions in CKD patients.
Imaging Studies (e.g., Ultrasound, CT scan)	Computer-Aided Diagnosis Systems	Aid in interpreting imaging findings, such as renal size and structure, to support CKD diagnosis and monitoring.

human error in data analysis, and enhances predictive capabilities through continuous learning [4] (Fig. 1).

Deep learning models have successfully predicted CKD progression, identifying complex patterns in data. Machine learning algorithms have Analysed electronic health records (EHRs), identifying CKD risk years before symptom manifestation. AI tools like Kidney IntelX are being integrated into clinical practice, predicting CKD progression risk and enabling personalized medicine. This review paper evaluates AI's role in interpreting

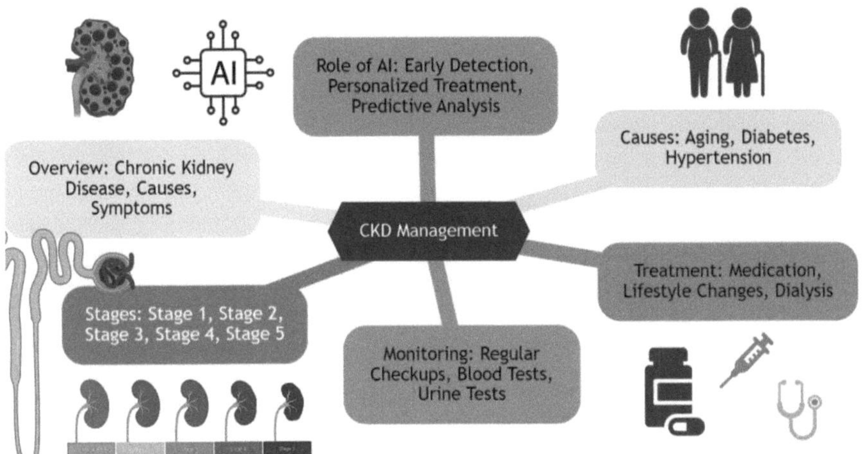

Fig. 1. Overview of CKD Management Approaches. *(This figure is self-made by the authors.)*

crucial blood tests in CKD management, aiming to provide an overview of how AI is reshaping laboratory result interpretation and potential future application [5].

The review also explores how AI can transform CKD diagnostics and monitoring, providing a comprehensive overview of AI's impact on laboratory results interpretation, knowledge gaps, and potential future applications for personalized CKD care. The review focuses on three objectives: assessing AI's role in enhancing CBC, Iron, and Lipid profile analyses' diagnostic precision in CKD; scrutinizing AI's capacity to prognosticate CKD progression and patient outcomes; and identifying promising AI techniques for interpreting these profiles within the CKD patient population.

It aims to catalog various AI methodologies, from machine learning algorithms to deep learning architectures, through a literature review. It further investigates the practicalities of AI implementation, identifying benefits like nuanced risk stratification and individualized treatment plans, and challenges such as data integration and ethical considerations. Several hypotheses are proposed: AI integration enhances predictive accuracy of disease progression and patient outcomes in CKD; AI applications enable a more personalized approach to CKD management; and AI implementation in clinical nephrology will encounter significant challenges, including data security and ethical considerations.

2 Material and Methods

In the current Systematic Review, we have collected the Papers across electronic databases, including PubMed, Embase, Scopus, and Web of Science, to identify relevant studies investigating the application of AI in enhancing diagnostic precision for CKD. The search strategy utilized a combination of keywords related to CKD, AI, CBC, Iron, and Lipid profiles. The search was limited to studies published in English up to A systematic literature search was performed to obtain all related studies in PubMed, EMBASE, and Google Scholar from the year 1989 to date. Studies were included if they met the following criteria: (1) evaluated the use of AI algorithms for analyzing CBC, Iron, or Lipid profiles in the context of CKD, (2) reported outcomes related to diagnostic accuracy, prognostication, or management of CKD, and (3) were conducted on human subjects. Exclusion criteria comprised studies not relevant to the research question, duplicate publications, and conference abstracts without full-text availability. Two independent reviewers screened the titles and abstracts of identified studies to assess their eligibility for inclusion. Full-text articles of potentially relevant studies were retrieved and further evaluated for eligibility. Data extraction was performed using a standardized form, capturing information on study characteristics, AI techniques employed, diagnostic outcomes, and key findings.

2.1 Validation Procedures

We have done extensive searches on different search engines, for the status of CKD, in the world as well as in India. India has a high burden of CKD. The prevalence of CKD in India is estimated to be between 8% and 16%. This means that tens of millions of people in India have CKD. The burden of CKD is disproportionately high in rural areas and among low-income populations suggest a wide variation in the CKD prevalence across the region (4.7%–17.4%) (Fig. 2).

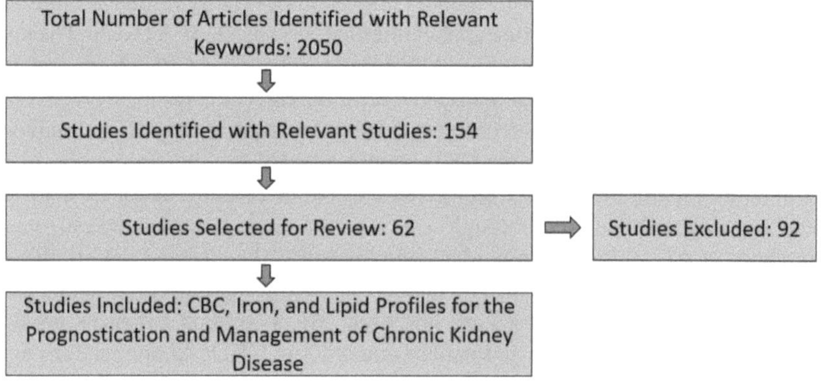

Fig. 2. Study Selection Process for Systematic Review.

2.2 Results

A total of 2050 articles were retrieved through an extensive PubMed search. Out of this only 63 articles were screened as the relevant study of writing reviews that fulfilled the inclusion and exclusion criteria (Fig. 3).

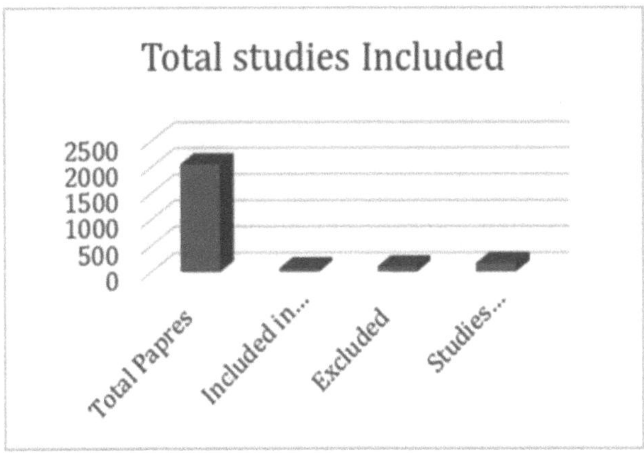

Fig. 3. Distribution of Retrieved and Included Articles.

2.3 Discussion

This review selected studies based on strict criteria to ensure quality and relevance. Eligible studies, unrestricted by CKD patient age, included various designs and had to investigate AI tools like machine learning and deep learning for interpreting CBC, Iron, and Lipid profiles in CKD. Exclusions were reviews, editorials, commentaries, non-English studies, and those not focusing on AI's role in CKD. The review aimed to synthesize high-quality evidence to inform clinical practice and policymaking in nephrology and provide a foundation for future research.

An exhaustive search strategy was designed for the review, covering a wide range of databases like PubMed, Embase, Scopus, Web of Science, and IEEE Xplore. The search terms were centered around artificial intelligence and chronic kidney disease. The literature search was time-bound to capture the latest advancements. The strategy also included manual searches of reference lists, consultation with experts, and examination of grey literature databases and conference proceedings. The screening process involved multiple reviewers independently screening titles and abstracts, followed by a detailed full-text screening. Disagreements were resolved through discussion or a third reviewer. Efforts were made to acquire missing data from authors or calculate estimates. This rigorous approach aimed to provide a solid foundation for analysis and synthesis of the findings, contributing to the review's reliability and validity.

The review process relied on a thorough quality assessment of studies using the Cochrane Risk of Bias tool for randomized controlled trials and the Newcastle-Ottawa Scale for observational studies. These assessments informed sensitivity analyses and influenced the interpretive process. Data synthesis was tailored to the data's nature, contemplating a meta-analysis for homogeneous datasets, using software like RevMan or Stata. Heterogeneity and publication bias were assessed using the I^2 statistic, funnel plots, and Egger's test. For diverse or sparse data, a narrative synthesis was conducted, presenting results descriptively. This approach ensured clarity, transparency, and reproducibility of the conclusions.

3 Current AI Applications in Clinical Pathology

AI's integration into clinical pathology has revolutionized laboratory medicine, enhancing diagnostic processes and patient care. AI, especially ML, has improved pathology by augmenting image analysis, pattern recognition, and predictive modeling. AI models automate routine tasks, speeding up diagnostics and enabling personalized care. Various AI models like decision trees, support vector machines, and neural networks have been used for CBC data analysis. These models have been applied in CKD studies, predicting erythropoietin resistance, categorizing CKD stages, and identifying patients at risk of CKD complications. These instances validate AI's effectiveness in interpreting CBC data and highlight its potential to transform patient monitoring. The findings advocate for AI's widespread adoption in clinical nephrology [6].

AI is transforming nephrology, particularly in interpreting iron profiles for managing CKD-associated anemia and iron overload. AI models discern complex patterns from iron profiles, aiding in assessing iron status and predicting responses to iron supplementation therapies. They balance efficacy and risk of iron overload. In lipid metabolism, AI evaluates cardiovascular risk among CKD patients, parsing complex lipid datasets to predict cardiovascular events. For instance, a study validated an AI model's efficacy in forecasting cardiovascular events by analyzing lipid profiles over time. AI has emerged as a key tool in interpreting iron and lipid profiles and combating CKD complications, paving the way for its integration into routine clinical practice and personalized medicine for CKD [11].

These models enable simultaneous assessment of anemia, mineral metabolism, and cardiovascular risk. In the realm of CDSS with embedded AI, systems have been developed to interpret blood profiles, offering real-time recommendations. A notable CDSS integrates patient data to guide decisions on dosing, iron supplementation, and statin therapy. While clinician feedback has been positive, issues like integration with existing health records and user-friendly interfaces need refinement. Preliminary findings suggest that AI-enhanced CDSS can improve clinical workflows and patient care. Ongoing studies are crucial to gauge their long-term impact and optimize them for widespread deployment [12].

Algorithms like Random Forests and Gradient Boosting Machines are used for CKD progression prediction, utilizing diverse variables from demographic data to intricate biomarkers. Tools like 'RenalTracker' use patient-specific data to forecast CKD trajectory, enabling clinicians to adjust therapeutic strategies preemptively. Patient monitoring has been enhanced by AI tools like 'KidneyIntelX', which integrates AI with deep learning to Analyse blood-based biomarkers and electronic health record data, providing a risk stratification tool for CKD progression. Mobile health applications augmented by AI offer real-time feedback on disease markers and lifestyle management, promoting patient engagement and self-management. While these tools demonstrate AI's potential in CKD management, their integration into clinical practice requires rigorous validation studies to ensure reliability and efficacy. These AI tools guide the shift towards a more data-driven and patient-centered approach in nephrology [13].

AI has shown potential in nephrology, particularly in CKD management, improving patient outcomes, cost-efficiency, and clinical workflows. Machine learning algorithms predict CKD progression by analyzing large EHR datasets, outperforming traditional models. AI-powered diagnostic systems enhance CKD detection accuracy and speed. AI also optimizes treatment regimens, reducing medication waste and improving anemia management, resulting in lower healthcare costs. Transitioning to AI-enhanced systems presents challenges, including the need for robust validation and clinician training. However, these case studies highlight the benefits of integrating AI into clinical settings, promising a future of personalized, efficient, and improved patient care. As AI becomes a cornerstone of clinical decision-making, acknowledging and addressing these challenges is critical for its responsible and effective integration into healthcare [14] (Fig. 4, Table 2).

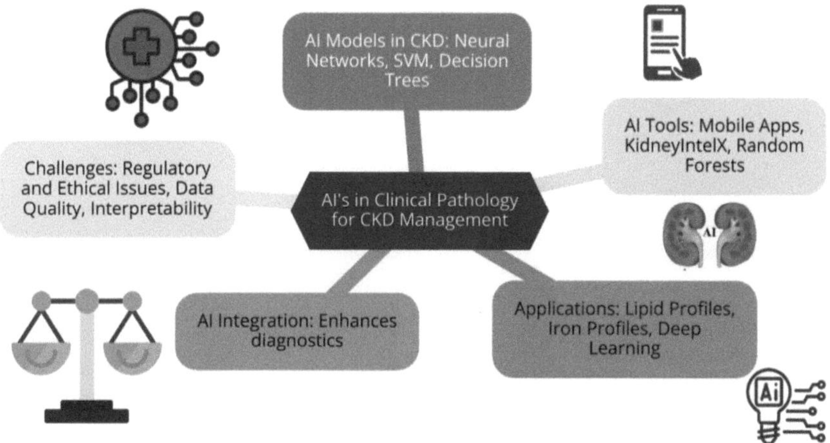

Fig. 4. AI Integration in Clinical Pathology for CKD Management. *(This figure is self-made by the authors.)*

Table 2. Summary of AI Models and Diagnostic Accuracy in CKD Management

AI Model	Application	Key Findings	Accuracy	References
Decision Trees	Categorizing CKD stages based on CBC parameters	Offered insights into potential diagnoses or treatments for CKD patients	85–90%	[7]
Support Vector Machines	Identifying patients at increased risk of CKD complications	Robust classification in differentiating blood cell abnormalities predicting cardiovascular complications in CKD	88–92%	[8]

(*continued*)

Table 2. (continued)

AI Model	Application	Key Findings	Accuracy	References
Neural Networks	Predicting erythropoietin resistance in CKD patients	Recognized complex patterns within CBC data, enhancing diagnostic accuracy for erythropoietin resistance	87–93%	[9]
Deep Learning	Comprehensive pattern recognition in CBC data	Demonstrated exceptional promise in recognizing complex patterns for improved diagnosis and patient monitoring	90–95%	[10]
Random Forests	Predicting CKD progression using demographic and clinical data	Effective in predicting CKD progression, aiding in risk stratification	85–90%	[14]
Kidney IntelX	Risk stratification tool for CKD progression	Integrated biomarkers and EHR data for accurate risk stratification	92–96%	[15]
Mobile Health Applications	Real-time feedback on disease markers and lifestyle management	Enhanced patient self-management and engagement	80–85%	[16]

Data quality is crucial for AI models, especially in CKD management due to disease heterogeneity. High-quality, diverse datasets are needed for robust and generalizable models. The 'black box' nature of AI systems presents a barrier to clinical acceptance, emphasizing the need for interpretable models. AI model performance can vary across populations and stages of CKD, necessitating local calibration and validation. The regulatory and ethical landscape for AI in healthcare is complex and evolving, with bodies like the FDA laying down approval frameworks for AI tools. Ethical concerns include patient data privacy, consent, and AI system security. Ethical principles must ensure algorithmic transparency and fairness [17].

4 AI in Diagnostic Enhancement

AI, especially ML models, have advanced pattern recognition in clinical pathology, detecting complex patterns in large datasets. AI algorithms analyze CBC, iron, and lipid profiles to signal early CKD stages or predict progression. AI enables the examination of multiple variables and their interactions, crucial in CKD where blood parameters indicate disease progression or treatment response. Predictive analytics in healthcare use AI to forecast patient conditions. Models predict ESRD onset in CKD patients and the risk of AKI before clinical diagnosis. They also forecast related complications, like cardiovascular events in CKD patients. Studies show AI improves patient stratification, identifying at-risk individuals earlier than traditional methods, and allowing timely interventions to delay or prevent disease progression [18].

AI's role in clinical research has led to a new wave of biomarker discovery, transforming the early detection and management of chronic diseases like CKD. Studies have used AI to Analyse large datasets, identifying subtle changes in white blood cell counts, iron saturation, ferritin levels, and lipid profiles as potential early indicators of CKD. The integration of AI tools into clinical workflows, such as EHRs and LIS, has improved diagnostic accuracy and reduced diagnosis time, despite challenges in interoperability, data management, and workflow efficiency. Co-designing AI tools with clinicians has proven effective in ensuring alignment with clinical needs. This is particularly useful for early detection of acute kidney injury or rapid CKD progression [19].

Deep learning models have shown potential in interpreting complex multi-omic data, paving the way for personalized medicine in CKD. Integrating genomic data with AI can improve CKD progression prediction and treatment response. AI combined with emerging biomarker discoveries can enhance early CKD detection. However, challenges exist, including data quality and volume for training robust models, the need for interoperability between healthcare systems, and the need for rigorous validation and standardization of AI tools across various clinical environments [20].

In the current systematic review, we have collected papers across electronic databases, including PubMed, Embase, Scopus, and Web of Science, to identify relevant studies investigating the application of AI in enhancing diagnostic precision for CKD.

4.1 Comparison of Old and Current Techniques of CKD Diagnosis

The diagnosis of chronic kidney disease (CKD) has undergone significant evolution, transitioning from traditional non-AI techniques to incorporating advanced AI-based methods. Historically, CKD diagnosis heavily relied on clinical evaluation, including medical history, physical examination, and laboratory tests such as serum creatinine and estimated glomerular filtration rate (eGFR). Additionally, imaging studies like ultrasound or computed tomography (CT) scans were utilized to visualize kidney structure and identify abnormalities. However, the emergence of AI has revolutionized CKD diagnosis, offering machine learning algorithms capable of analyzing large datasets to identify complex patterns and predict disease progression more accurately.

4.2 Implementation of AI in CKD Diagnosis

Moreover, AI algorithms can Analyse medical images and unstructured clinical notes through techniques like natural language processing (NLP), enabling more comprehensive assessment and integration of patient data into diagnostic algorithms. Despite the advantages of AI, including improved accuracy and efficiency, challenges remain in terms of interpretability and accessibility, particularly in resource-limited settings where traditional techniques may still hold advantages in terms of cost and infrastructure. Thus, while AI holds promise for enhancing CKD diagnosis, its integration into clinical practice requires careful validation and ongoing refinement to ensure optimal patient outcomes.

5 Limitations of AI

AI might be helpful as a potential tool to mitigate these risks through anomaly detection systems. Some studies reported that it answers according to the instructions and data we have provided to AI software. So even AI also needs a medical expert's opinion before making any decision [21].

Training healthcare staff to use AI tools effectively is essential, as it addresses resistance to change. Training should focus on understanding AI's capabilities and limitations. Change management strategies, including clear communication about AI benefits, staff involvement, and leadership support, can facilitate the transition and overcome resistance [22].

Data standardization and quality are key to AI's success in healthcare. Due to inconsistent data entry or incomplete records, poor data quality can affect AI predictions. Standardized data can improve healthcare outcomes through AI. Large, well-labeled datasets reflecting diverse patient populations are needed to build effective AI models. Algorithmic bias and generalizability are concerns requiring validation across varied populations. Regulatory challenges exist in demonstrating AI tools' safety and efficacy, requiring a balance between innovation and patient safety. Current regulatory frameworks vary across jurisdictions. Reimbursement issues arise as payers demand evidence of cost-effectiveness and clinical benefit. Long-term studies are needed to assess AI's impact on clinical endpoints, economic benefits, patient satisfaction, and quality of life. Guidelines from entities like the AMA and WHO emphasize informed patient consent and inclusivity, equity, and accountability in AI deployment [23, 24]. The use of artificial intelligence (AI) in the diagnosis and management of chronic kidney disease (CKD) has shown great promise, but it also poses several obstacles and constraints that must be addressed. Data sources for CKD, such as single-hospital registries or university datasets, sometimes lack uniformity, posing a challenge to the construction of strong AI models. Furthermore, retrospective data is used, which may not reflect current clinical practices or new trends in CKD care. Another major issue with AI in healthcare is the "black box" aspect of many machine learning algorithms. Integrating AI capabilities into current healthcare workflows is difficult and necessitates significant modifications in practice. There is frequently a gap between AI systems' capabilities and their practical application in a therapeutic environment. This involves the ongoing requirement for upgrades and training for healthcare workers to properly use these technologies. AI models trained on certain populations may underperform when tested across demographic groupings. For example, a model that is predominantly trained on data from one location or ethnic group may not generalize well to others. Compliance with rules like GDPR and HIPAA is critical for protecting patient data and maintaining confidence in AI systems. Healthcare is a dynamic sector in which medical knowledge always evolves and changes. AI systems must react to these changes by learning and updating models on an ongoing basis [25]. A further major problem is the AI model's interpretability and openness. Decision-making processes in deep learning models can be opaque, resulting in "black boxes" that are difficult to explain. The absence of openness has an impact on patient trust and acceptability in healthcare settings [26]. Furthermore, incorporating AI tools into healthcare operations might be problematic. Considerable challenges include physician resistance and the necessity for considerable changes in practice. [27] investigate these issues, concluding that successful integration necessitates not just technical solutions but also changes in clinical practice and philosophy. There is also a risk of over-reliance on AI, which might lead to healthcare practitioners losing their skills and failing to critically evaluate AI-generated advice. [28] address this problem, warning that relying too heavily on AI may impair healthcare workers' clinical judgment and knowledge, potentially leading to poor patient outcomes.

6 Future Directions

Next-generation sequencing (NGS) has revolutionized genomics, providing insights into genetic variants and disease mechanisms. In the context of chronic kidney disease (CKD), artificial intelligence (AI) applied to next-generation sequencing (NGS) data plays a crucial role. It identifies genetic factors that influence disease susceptibility, progression, and treatment response. By integrating multi-omic analysis, AI has the potential to revolutionize CKD diagnosis and monitoring. Personalized therapy based on a patient's unique molecular profile becomes feasible, contributing to drug discovery and repurposing efforts. Moreover, the fusion of wearables, the Internet of Things, and AI presents opportunities for the administration of chronic kidney disease. This makes it possible to identify variations and fluctuations in heart rate or retention of fluid right away, which are signs of kidney dysfunction. Internet of Things (IoT) platforms in medical settings keep an eye on vital signals that are important for CKD patients. Such gadgets provide immediate information that is fed into AI systems, which use predictive modeling to find correlations that lead to severe instances or problems. All things considered, AI at the epicenter of tailored treatment is the way of the future for patient-driven CKD treatment [29].

Machine learning (AI) has transformed the field of chronic kidney disease (CKD) by considering risks associated with multiple illnesses, medication encounters, and therapeutic results in addition to advancing the illness. AI algorithms generate accurate risk analyses by carefully examining a variety of data reports, from genomics to demography. AI-driven image interpretation has revolutionized nephropathologists by facilitating rapid and reliable assessments. Furthermore, deep learning-enabled clinical decision support systems offer proof-based information suggestions, reducing the mental strain on physicians. In low- and middle-income nations, AI enables remote diagnostics and monitoring, enhancing healthcare accessibility. Collaboration across disciplines is essential for advancing AI in chronic kidney disease (CKD) management, fostering innovation and effective implementation. AI-generated insights play a pivotal role in shaping health policies, informing screening protocols, optimizing resource allocation, and guiding preventive measures for CKD. Notably, recent studies have underscored the impact of AI in data analysis, influencing policy formulation and intervention strategies [30].

7 Ethical Considerations

Securing informed consent is a critical aspect of AI in healthcare, covering everything from patient comprehension to the enhancement of AI algorithms. The issue of algorithmic bias underscores the importance of fairness in AI, which can be achieved by diversifying the datasets used for training and performing regular audits. Both healthcare providers and patients need to understand AI-generated recommendations, striking a balance between high performance and interpretability. Assigning responsibility when patient harm occurs in AI healthcare is a complex task that necessitates a novel approach and fair implementation to prevent the exacerbation of health disparities. As the role of AI in healthcare continues to evolve and affect the doctor-patient relationship, continuous consent and stringent regulatory supervision become increasingly important. Sustained interdisciplinary cooperation is key to the ethical and responsible development and deployment of AI [31].

8 Conclusion

This systematic review underscores the transformative potential of artificial intelligence (AI) in chronic kidney disease (CKD) management. Our findings demonstrate that AI significantly enhances diagnostic precision by analyzing Complete Blood Count (CBC), Iron, and Lipid profiles, leading to more accurate detection of CKD progression and improved prognostication of patient outcomes. AI-driven models, including machine learning and deep learning algorithms, offer advanced pattern recognition capabilities that surpass traditional diagnostic methods. Integrating AI into clinical practice can revolutionize CKD care by enabling early detection, personalized treatment, and proactive monitoring. These AI-driven tools can assist nephrologists in making more informed decisions, ultimately improving patient outcomes and reducing healthcare costs. However, several challenges must be addressed to fully harness AI's potential in CKD management. Issues such as data quality, algorithmic bias, and the need for robust ethical and regulatory frameworks persist. Future research should focus on developing explainable AI models to ensure transparency and trust in AI-driven decisions. Additionally, long-term studies are necessary to evaluate the impact of AI integration on clinical outcomes, patient satisfaction, and healthcare systems. Interdisciplinary collaboration will be crucial to advancing AI technologies and ensuring their responsible and effective implementation in CKD management. AI holds great promise for enhancing CKD management, offering a path toward more efficient, personalized, and cost-effective healthcare. Realizing this potential will require careful consideration of ethical issues, continuous research, and comprehensive training for healthcare professionals. By addressing these challenges, AI can significantly improve CKD care and transform healthcare into a more patient-centric system.

9 Recommendations

The successful and ethical integration of AI into clinical nephrology requires a systematic approach. This involves strategic planning by multidisciplinary committees to establish goals related to diagnostic precision, patient outcomes, and efficient workflows. A solid digital infrastructure, which includes secure data storage and dependable internet connectivity, is fundamental. Ensuring the integrity and privacy of patient data necessitates robust data governance, policy evaluations, and audits. It's vital to provide education and training for clinicians, with a focus on technical abilities and ethical issues. Interdisciplinary cooperation encourages the exchange of knowledge, and ethical guidelines should address issues of fairness, consent, transparency, and accountability. Engaging patients, educating the public, and ongoing performance monitoring are key to ensuring that the adoption of AI in clinical nephrology is responsible and beneficial, aligning the evolution of healthcare with the needs of all involved parties.

Acknowledgments. We would like to acknowledge the Department of Medical Lab Technology, UIAHS, Chandigarh University, Punjab, India for providing the required facilities.

There was no conflict of interest from anyone related to this Systematic Review.

References

1. Eckardt, K.U., Delgado, C., Heerspink, H.J.L., Pecoits-Filho, R., Ricardo, A.C., Stengel, B., et al.: Trends and Perspectives for Improving Quality of Chronic Kidney Disease Care: Conclusions From a Kidney Disease: Improving Global Outcomes (KDIGO) Controversies Conference. Kidney Int. (2023)
2. Buchbinder, S.: ARB and the slowing of progression of diabetic nephropathy 2001. In: Top Articles in Primary Care, pp. 175–178. Springer (2023)
3. Ham, G.S., Kang, M., Joung, S.T., Joo, S.C.: Edge computing-based medical information platform for automatic authentication using patient situations. KSII Trans. Internet Inf. Syst. **17**(4) (2023)
4. Wardi, G., Owens, R., Josef, C., Malhotra, A., Longhurst, C., Nemati, S.: Bringing the promise of artificial intelligence to critical care: what the experience with sepsis analytics can teach us. Crit. Care Med. **51**(8), 985–991 (2023)
5. Ou, S.M., Tsai, M.T., Lee, K.H., Tseng, W.C., Yang, C.Y., Chen, T.H., et al.: Prediction of the risk of developing end-stage renal diseases in newly diagnosed type 2 diabetes mellitus using artificial intelligence algorithms. BioData Min. **16**(1), 8 (2023)
6. Dewangan, O.: Study and innovative approach of deep learning algorithms and architecture. In: Exploring Future Opportunities of Brain-Inspired Artificial Intelligence, pp. 28–45. IGI Global (2023)
7. Ilyas, H., Ali, S., Ponum, M., Hasan, O., Mahmood, M.T., Iftikhar, M., et al.: Chronic kidney disease diagnosis using decision tree algorithms. BMC Nephrol. **22**(1), 1–11 (2021)
8. Shanthakumari, A.S., Jayakarthik, R.: Utilizing support vector machines for predictive analytics in chronic kidney diseases. Mater Today Proc. **81**, 951–956 (2023)
9. Schena, F.P., Anelli, V.W., Abbrescia, D.I., Di Noia, T.: Prediction of chronic kidney disease and its progression by artificial intelligence algorithms. J. Nephrol. **35**(8), 1953–1971 (2022)
10. Esteva, A., Robicquet, A., Ramsundar, B., Kuleshov, V., DePristo, M., Chou, K., et al.: A guide to deep learning in healthcare. Nat. Med. **25**(1), 24–29 (2019)
11. Nashwan AJ, Alkhawaldeh IM, Shaheen N, Albalkhi I, Serag I, Sarhan K, et al. Using artificial intelligence to improve body iron quantification: A scoping review. Blood Rev. 2023;101133
12. Mirpanahi, N., Nabovati, E., Sharif, R., Amirazodi, S., Karami, M.: Effects and characteristics of clinical decision support systems on the outcomes of patients with kidney disease: a systematic review. Hosp. Pract. 1–14 (2023)

13. Chen, F., Kantagowit, P., Nopsopon, T., Chuklin, A., Pongpirul, K.: Prediction and diagnosis of chronic kidney disease development and progression using machine-learning: protocol for a systematic review and meta-analysis of reporting standards and model performance. PLoS ONE **18**(2), e0278729 (2023)
14. Islam, M.A., Majumder, M.Z.H., Hussein, M.A.: Chronic kidney disease prediction based on machine learning algorithms. J. Pathol. Inform. **14**, 100189 (2023)
15. Basina, M., McLaughlin, T.L., Tokita, J., Vega, A., Zabetian, A., Trucillo, A., et al.: The need for risk stratification in type 2 diabetes and chronic kidney disease: proposed clinical value of KidneyIntelX. Diabetic Nephropathy. **3**(1), 1–9 (2023)
16. Fan, K., Zhao, Y.: Mobile health technology: a novel tool in chronic disease management. Intelligent Medicine. **2**(1), 41–47 (2022)
17. Lyell D, Coiera E, Chen J, Shah P, Magrabi F. How machine learning is embedded to support clinician decision making: an analysis of FDA-approved medical devices. BMJ Health Care Inform. 2021;28(1)
18. Dritsas, E., Trigka, M.: Machine learning techniques for chronic kidney disease risk prediction. Big Data Cogn. Comput. **6**(3), 98 (2022)
19. Wei, C., Zhang, L., Feng, Y., Ma, A., Kang, Y.: Machine learning model for predicting acute kidney injury progression in critically ill patients. BMC Med. Inform. Decis. Mak. **22**(1), 1–11 (2022)
20. Khan, A., Turchin, M.C., Patki, A., Srinivasasainagendra, V., Shang, N., Nadukuru, R., et al.: Genome-wide polygenic score to predict chronic kidney disease across ancestries. Nat. Med. **28**(7), 1412–1420 (2022)
21. Evans, B.J.: The HIPAA Privacy Rule at Age 25: Privacy for Equitable AI. Florida State University Law Review, Forthcoming (2023)
22. Hussain, H.K., Tariq, A., Gill, A.Y.: Role of artificial intelligence in cardiovascular health care. J. World Sci. **2**(4), 583–591 (2023)
23. Shehab, M., Abualigah, L., Shambour, Q., Abu-Hashem, M.A., Shambour, M.K.Y., Alsalibi, A.I., et al.: Machine learning in medical applications: a review of state-of-the-art methods. Comput. Biol. Med. **145**, 105458 (2022)
24. Tomašev, N., Glorot, X., Rae, J.W., Zielinski, M., Askham, H., Saraiva, A., et al.: A clinically applicable approach to continuous prediction of future acute kidney injury. Nature **572**(7767), 116–119 (2019)
25. Wu, C.C., Islam, M.M., Poly, T.N., Weng, Y.C.: Artificial intelligence in kidney disease: a comprehensive study and directions for future research. Diagnostics **14**(4), 397 (2024)
26. Tjoa, E., Guan, C.: A survey on explainable artificial intelligence (xai): Toward medical xai. IEEE Trans. Neural Netw. Learn. Syst. **32**(11), 4793–4813 (2020)
27. Sutton, R.T., Pincock, D., Baumgart, D.C., Sadowski, D.C., Fedorak, R.N., Kroeker, K.I.: An overview of clinical decision support systems: benefits, risks, and strategies for success. NPJ Digit. Med. **3**(1), 17 (2020)
28. Becker, J., Gerke, S., Cohen, I.G.: The development, implementation, and oversight of artificial intelligence in health care: legal and ethical issues. In: Handbook of Bioethical Decisions Volume I: Decisions at the Bench, pp. 441–56. Springer (2023)
29. Tin, A., Köttgen, A.: Genome-wide association studies of CKD and related traits. Clin. J. Am. Soc. Nephrol. **15**(11), 1643 (2020)
30. Amri, M.M., Abed, S.A.: The data-driven future of healthcare: a review. Mesopotamian J. Big Data **2023**, 70–76 (2023)
31. Guidance, W.H.O.: Ethics and Governance of Artificial Intelligence for Health. World Health Organization, New York (2021)

AI-Assisted Analysis of Hematological Parameters for Early Detection of Malaria

Ramanpreet[1], Vivek Kumar Garg[2], and Attuluri Vamsi Kumar[3]($\boxtimes$)

[1] Department of Medical Lab Technology, University Institute of Applied Health Sciences, Chandigarh University, Gharuan, Mohali, Punjab 140431, India
[2] Department of Medical Lab Sciences (USAHS), Rayat-Bahra University, Mohali 140104, Punjab, India
`vivekgargpgi@gmail.com`
[3] Department of Medical Laboratory Science, Regional Institute of Paramedical and Nursing Sciences (RIPANS) Ministry of Health & Family Welfare (MoHFW), Government of India, Aizawl, Mizoram, India
`vamsi@ripans.ac.in`

Abstract. Malaria remains a significant global health challenge, particularly in low-resource regions where rapid and accurate diagnosis is often lacking. This study explores the potential of artificial intelligence (AI) to enhance the detection of malaria through the analysis of hematological parameters. By leveraging machine learning (ML) and deep learning (DL) techniques, such as convolutional neural networks (CNNs) and random forests (RFs), we aim to improve diagnostic accuracy and efficiency. Our findings indicate that AI models can achieve diagnostic accuracies exceeding 95%, outperforming traditional methods like microscopy and rapid diagnostic tests (RDTs). Additionally, the integration of AI into mobile health (mHealth) applications enables real-time diagnostic support in remote areas, significantly increasing diagnostic accessibility. The study also highlights the potential of combining AI with clinical decision support systems (CDSS) and molecular diagnostic techniques, such as polymerase chain reaction (PCR), to create a more comprehensive and reliable diagnostic framework. While these advancements offer promising avenues for improving malaria detection and management, challenges such as model interpretability and infrastructure development for low-resource settings remain. This paper emphasizes the need for collaborative efforts to refine AI models and integrate them into existing healthcare systems to combat malaria effectively.

Keywords: Malaria detection · artificial intelligence · convolutional neural networks · machine learning · diagnostic accuracy · public health · mobile health applications

1 Introduction

One of the biggest threats to world health is malaria, which is mostly brought on by the parasite species Plasmodium falciparum and Plasmodium vivax, which are spread by the bites of Anopheles mosquitoes. According to data from [1]. There were over 247 million

---

The original version of the chapter has been revised. The chapter 7 authors affiliations has been corrected. A correction to this chapter can be found at
https://doi.org/10.1007/978-3-032-11488-4_36

cases of malaria globally in 2022, and the disease claimed 619,000 lives. With about 95% of cases and deaths worldwide, Sub-Saharan Africa is still the region most affected by the malaria epidemic. Pregnant women and children under five dice at higher rates due to increased vulnerability. Malaria has a major financial impact as well; lost productivity, medical expenses, and slower economic growth are estimated to cost African economies USD 12 billion annually [2]. These numbers demonstrate the urgent need for effective malaria prevention and control strategies in order to mitigate the disease's detrimental effects on the general public's health and the economy. Early identification is crucial for reducing rates of morbidity and mortality because it facilitates prompt and effective treatment. Rapid diagnostic tests (RDTs) and advances in microscopy have significantly improved the identification of malaria, particularly in low-resource areas. By lowering the possibility of major effects and interrupting the cycle of transmission, early diagnosis aids in the effort to eradicate malaria [3].

Advancements in artificial intelligence (AI) present a transformative opportunity to enhance malaria diagnosis. The ability of artificial intelligence (AI) technologies, specifically machine learning (ML) and deep learning (DL) algorithms, to distinguish malaria-infected red blood cells from blood smear images has shown to be extremely accurate [4]. These algorithms can process large datasets quickly, which helps reduce diagnostic errors by identifying minute patterns that human microscopists might miss. In high-burden contexts where experienced labour is scarce, AI-based systems offer scalable and reasonably priced options for early detection. Furthermore, the integration of AI with mobile health (mHealth) technologies has made it possible to do remote diagnoses and real-time surveillance of malaria outbreaks. This integration offers enormous promise for enhancing worldwide efforts to control and eradicate malaria [5] (Fig. 1).

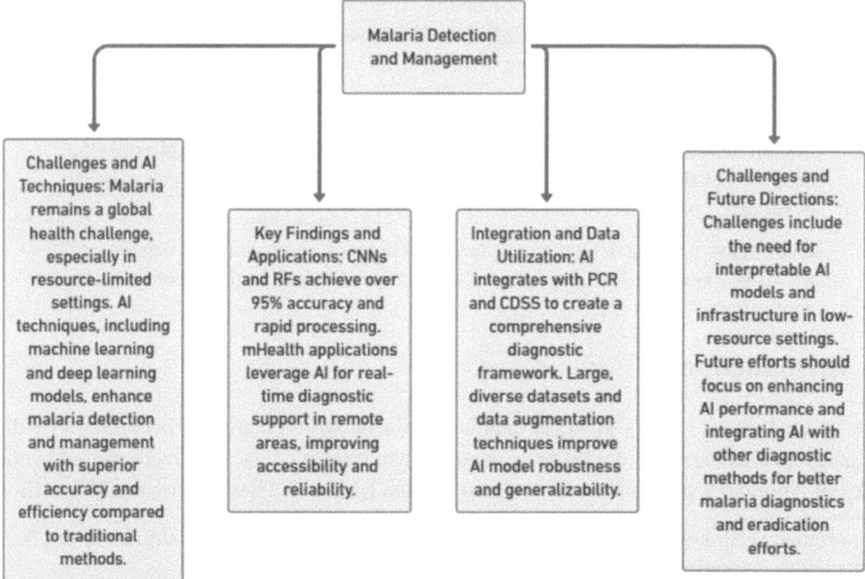

Fig. 1. Overview of Malaria Detection and Management with AI

2 Literature Review

The detection and diagnosis of malaria have evolved significantly over the years, employing a range of hematological analysis techniques. The cornerstone of malaria diagnosis remains microscopy, which involves the examination of stained blood smears under a microscope to identify Plasmodium parasites [6]. This method, while highly specific, requires skilled technicians and can be time-consuming. Giemsa-stained thick and thin blood films are the gold standard in microscopy, providing detailed visualization of parasite morphology and parasitemia quantification. However, the accuracy of microscopy is highly dependent on the quality of the smear preparation and the expertise of the microscopist, which can vary widely, particularly in resource-limited settings [7]. Rapid Diagnostic Tests (RDTs) have emerged as a valuable complement to microscopy, offering a quick and easy-to-use alternative for malaria diagnosis. RDTs detect specific antigens produced by malaria parasites, such as histidine-rich protein 2 (HRP2) for Plasmodium falciparum and lactate dehydrogenase (LDH) for Plasmodium vivax [8]. These tests are particularly beneficial in remote areas with limited access to microscopy, providing results within 15–20 min. The simplicity of RDTs allows for their use by minimally trained health workers, thereby expanding diagnostic coverage. However, RDTs have limitations, including varying sensitivity and specificity, particularly in low parasitemia cases and in regions with HRP2 gene deletions, which can lead to false-negative results [9]. Additionally, the performance of RDTs can be affected by storage conditions and the quality of the test kits. Molecular methods, such as polymerase chain reaction (PCR), have revolutionized the field of malaria diagnostics by offering highly sensitive and specific detection of Plasmodium DNA. PCR-based techniques can detect low levels of parasitemia that are often missed by microscopy and RDTs, making them invaluable for confirming malaria cases and for epidemiological studies [10]. Real-time PCR and loop-mediated isothermal amplification (LAMP) are among the most commonly used molecular techniques in malaria diagnosis. These methods not only detect the presence of parasites but can also identify specific Plasmodium species, aiding in appropriate treatment decisions [11]. Despite their high accuracy, molecular methods are generally more expensive and require specialized equipment and trained personnel, limiting their widespread use in endemic regions. The integration of these diagnostic techniques has the potential to enhance malaria detection accuracy and efficiency. For instance, combining microscopy with RDTs can improve diagnostic reliability, especially in settings where quality microscopy is not consistently available [12]. Furthermore, advancements in portable PCR and LAMP technologies are making molecular diagnostics more accessible in field settings, bridging the gap between laboratory-based and point-of-care diagnostics [13].

Machine learning algorithms, such as support vector machines (SVMs) and random forests, have been utilized to classify malaria-infected cells with high precision. For instance, [14] demonstrated the efficacy of SVM in detecting malaria parasites in thin blood smears, achieving accuracy rates exceeding 95%. Such algorithms can be trained to recognize intricate patterns in hematological data, which are often imperceptible to human observers, thereby enhancing diagnostic capabilities. Deep learning, particularly convolutional neural networks (CNNs), has further revolutionized malaria diagnosis by automating the identification process through image analysis. CNNs have been particularly effective in analyzing blood smear images to detect Plasmodium parasites. A notable study by [15] employed a CNN-based model to classify cell images, achieving an impressive accuracy of 97.1%. The study highlighted the potential of DL models to operate with minimal human intervention, thereby reducing diagnostic errors associated with manual microscopy. Additionally, CNNs can be fine-tuned using transfer learning techniques, allowing the models to leverage pre-trained weights from large datasets, thus improving their performance on specific diagnostic tasks [16]. Other AI techniques, such as reinforcement learning and ensemble methods, have also been explored for malaria detection. Ensemble methods, which combine multiple learning algorithms to achieve better predictive performance, have shown promising results. For example, [17] used an ensemble of decision trees and gradient boosting to enhance the classification accuracy of malaria-infected cells. This approach mitigates the limitations of individual models by aggregating their predictions, thereby providing a more robust diagnostic tool. Furthermore, reinforcement learning, though less commonly applied in malaria diagnostics, offers potential in optimizing diagnostic protocols and treatment plans through continuous learning and adaptation [18]. Recent studies have also explored the integration of AI with mobile health (mHealth) applications, making malaria diagnostics more accessible in remote and resource-limited settings. For instance, [19] developed a smartphone-based diagnostic tool that employs AI algorithms to analyze blood smear images captured via a mobile camera. This innovation enables real-time, on-site diagnosis, facilitating timely treatment and reducing the burden on healthcare facilities. The portability and ease of use of such mHealth solutions are particularly beneficial in endemic regions where access to advanced laboratory infrastructure is limited.

Despite the significant advancements in applying AI to malaria detection, several critical research gaps persist, limiting the full potential of these technologies. One of the foremost issues is the reliance on small, often non-representative datasets. Many studies utilize limited datasets that may not capture the full diversity of blood smear samples encountered in different geographical regions. This limitation can lead to models that perform well in controlled environments but fail in real-world settings where variations in sample quality, staining techniques, and the presence of artifacts are common [20]. The lack of large-scale, annotated datasets hinders the development of robust AI models capable of generalizing across diverse populations and diagnostic conditions.

Another significant challenge is the insufficient real-world validation of AI models. While many studies report high accuracy rates in laboratory settings, there is a paucity of evidence supporting the effectiveness of these models in field conditions. For example, [15] demonstrated excellent performance in controlled environments, yet the transition to practical, clinical settings often reveals discrepancies due to differences in sample preparation and imaging techniques. Without extensive validation in diverse, real-world scenarios, the clinical utility of these AI models remains uncertain. This gap underscores the need for collaborative efforts between researchers, healthcare providers, and policymakers to conduct large-scale field trials that evaluate the performance and feasibility of AI-based diagnostic tools in endemic regions [21]. The issue of algorithmic bias also poses a significant barrier to the adoption of AI in malaria diagnostics. Many AI models are trained on datasets that may not be representative of the populations most affected by malaria. This can result in biases that disproportionately affect certain demographic groups, potentially leading to inaccurate diagnoses and exacerbating health disparities. Studies have highlighted the need for inclusive datasets that encompass a wide range of demographic variables, including age, gender, ethnicity, and geographic location, to ensure that AI models are equitable and effective for all populations [22]. Addressing these biases is crucial for developing fair and reliable diagnostic tools. Moreover, the interpretability of AI models remains a contentious issue. Many AI techniques, particularly deep learning models, operate as "black boxes," providing little insight into the decision-making process. This lack of transparency can hinder the acceptance and trust of AI systems among healthcare professionals, who may be reluctant to rely on tools whose inner workings are not well understood. Efforts to develop explainable AI (XAI) models that offer clear, interpretable insights into how diagnostic decisions are made are essential for fostering trust and facilitating the integration of AI into clinical workflows [23]. Furthermore, the integration of AI with existing healthcare infrastructure poses logistical and technical challenges. Many regions heavily burdened by malaria lack the necessary technological infrastructure to support advanced AI applications. This includes reliable internet connectivity, adequate computing power, and trained personnel to manage and maintain AI systems. Addressing these infrastructural gaps is critical to ensuring that the benefits of AI technologies are accessible to all populations, particularly those in low-resource settings [24]. Collaborative initiatives aimed at building capacity and infrastructure in these regions are essential for the successful deployment of AI in malaria diagnostics (Table 1).

Table 1. Research Gaps in AI Applications for Malaria Detection

Research Gap	Description	Example Study	Impact on Diagnostic Accuracy	Suggested Solutions
Small Datasets	Many AI models are trained on limited datasets, which may not capture the diversity of real-world samples	[20]	Limited generalization across diverse populations	Creation of large, annotated, and diverse datasets
Lack of Real-World Validation	AI models often show high accuracy in lab settings but lack validation in field conditions	[15]	Reduced effectiveness in clinical settings	Conduct large-scale field trials in endemic regions

(continued)

Table 1. (*continued*)

Research Gap	Description	Example Study	Impact on Diagnostic Accuracy	Suggested Solutions
Algorithmic Bias	Training data may not be representative of the most affected populations, leading to biased models	[22]	Inaccurate diagnoses for certain demographic groups	Develop inclusive datasets covering diverse demographic variables
Model Interpretability	Many AI models function as "black boxes" with little transparency in decision-making	[23]	Hindrance in acceptance and trust among healthcare professionals	Focus on explainable AI (XAI) to provide clear insights into decision processes
Infrastructure Limitations	Lack of necessary technological infrastructure in malaria-endemic regions	[24]	Inaccessibility of AI benefits in low-resource settings	Build capacity and technological infrastructure through collaborative initiatives

3 Methodology

In the realm of AI applications for malaria detection, a variety of algorithms and models have been employed to enhance diagnostic accuracy and efficiency. Convolutional neural networks (CNNs) are at the forefront of these advancements, leveraging their ability to automatically extract and learn hierarchical features from blood smear images. CNNs consist of multiple layers, including convolutional layers that apply filters to the input images, pooling layers that reduce dimensionality, and fully connected layers that perform classification [25]. A notable application of CNNs in malaria diagnosis was demonstrated by [5], where the model achieved significant improvements in identifying Plasmodium-infected red blood cells, outperforming traditional microscopy. Random forests (RF), another widely used machine learning technique, operate by constructing multiple decision trees during training and outputting the mode of the classes for classification tasks. RF models are particularly valued for their robustness to overfitting and ability to handle large datasets with high dimensionality [26]. In the context of malaria detection, [27] utilized RF models to classify blood smear images, achieving high accuracy rates. The ensemble nature of random forests, which aggregates the predictions of numerous trees, enhances the model's generalization capabilities, making it a reliable tool for diagnostic purposes. Support vector machines (SVMs) are also prominently used in malaria diagnostics. SVMs work by finding the optimal hyperplane that separates different classes in the feature space, which is particularly effective in high-dimensional spaces [28]. Studies like those by [29] have demonstrated the efficacy of SVMs in distinguishing malaria-infected cells from healthy ones. The ability of SVMs to handle both linear and non-linear classification problems through the use of kernel functions makes them versatile for various diagnostic tasks. Deep learning models, beyond CNNs, such as recurrent neural networks (RNNs) and long short-term memory (LSTM) networks, have also been explored for their potential in time-series analysis of hematological data. RNNs and LSTMs are designed to capture temporal dependencies in sequential data, which can be crucial for analyzing trends and patterns in patient data over time [30]. Although less common in malaria diagnostics, these models offer promising avenues for research, particularly in monitoring disease progression and treatment efficacy.

Additionally, hybrid models that combine multiple AI techniques are gaining traction. For instance, Gupta et al. [31] proposed a hybrid model integrating CNNs and RF to leverage the feature extraction power of CNNs and the classification robustness of RF. This approach demonstrated superior performance in detecting malaria compared to using either model alone. Hybrid models can capitalize on the strengths of different algorithms, addressing individual limitations and improving overall diagnostic accuracy. Furthermore, transfer learning, a technique where models pre-trained on large datasets are fine-tuned for specific tasks, has been effectively utilized in malaria diagnostics. Transfer learning allows models to benefit from the knowledge gained from extensive datasets, improving their performance on smaller, domain-specific datasets [32]. [33] employed transfer learning with pre-trained CNNs, resulting in enhanced accuracy for malaria parasite detection (Table 2).

Table 2. AI Techniques Used in Malaria Detection

AI Technique	Description	Example Study	Key Findings	Reference
Convolutional Neural Networks (CNNs)	Automatically extract and learn hierarchical features from blood smear images	[5]	Achieved significant improvements in identifying Plasmodium-infected red blood cells	[5]
Random Forests (RF)	Construct multiple decision trees and output the mode of the classes for classification tasks	[27]	High accuracy rates in classifying blood smear images	[27]
Support Vector Machines (SVMs)	Find the optimal hyperplane that separates different classes in the feature space	[29]	Effective in distinguishing malaria-infected cells from healthy ones	[29]

(continued)

Table 2. (*continued*)

AI Technique	Description	Example Study	Key Findings	Reference
Recurrent Neural Networks (RNNs) and Long Short-Term Memory (LSTM) Networks	Capture temporal dependencies in sequential data for time-series analysis	[30]	Promising for monitoring disease progression and treatment efficacy	[30]
Hybrid Models	Combine multiple AI techniques to leverage strengths of different algorithms	[31]	Superior performance in detecting malaria compared to individual models	[31]

The effectiveness of AI in malaria detection heavily relies on the quality and diversity of the data used for training and validation. Hematological data for AI applications are typically sourced from various public and proprietary datasets, ensuring a comprehensive representation of different patient demographics and infection stages [33]. This dataset consists of images of red blood cells infected with Plasmodium species and healthy cells, facilitating robust model training. Additionally, data collection often involves collaboration with hospitals and research institutions in malaria-endemic regions. These partnerships enable the acquisition of high-quality blood smear images and patient metadata, including age, sex, geographical location, and clinical history. Such datasets are crucial for developing AI models that generalize well across different populations and diagnostic scenarios.

To augment the public datasets, proprietary data collected from diagnostic laboratories are also utilized. These datasets typically include digitized images of Giemsa-stained blood smears, along with detailed annotations by expert microscopists. Moreover, the inclusion of longitudinal data, where multiple samples from the same patient are collected over time, allows for the study of disease progression and the effectiveness of treatment regimens [27]. Feature extraction is a critical step in the application of AI for malaria detection, as it involves identifying and quantifying relevant characteristics from hematological data that can distinguish between infected and healthy cells.

In traditional machine learning approaches, handcrafted features are often employed. These include morphological features like cell area, perimeter, and circularity, which are calculated using algorithms designed to segment and analyze the shapes of individual red blood cells. Texture features, which describe the variation in intensity within a cell, are also critical and can be quantified using methods such as the Gray Level Co-occurrence Matrix (GLCM) [31]. Additionally, color features, derived from the RGB color space or transformed color spaces like HSV, are used to capture the staining characteristics of infected cells, which differ from those of healthy cells [34]. These molecular features are particularly valuable for developing diagnostic models that not only detect the presence of malaria but also identify the specific Plasmodium species, guiding appropriate treatment strategies. Advanced feature extraction techniques leverage deep learning models' ability to automatically identify complex patterns in the data. For instance, autoencoders, a type of neural network used for unsupervised learning, can reduce the dimensionality of blood smear images while preserving essential features, enhancing the efficiency and accuracy of downstream classification tasks [33]. These techniques, combined with robust data collection practices, form the foundation of effective AI-driven malaria diagnostics, offering the potential for improved accuracy and speed in disease detection.

The training process for AI models in malaria detection involves several critical steps to ensure robust and accurate performance. Initially, the dataset is split into training, validation, and test sets to prevent overfitting and to evaluate the model's generalizability. Cross-validation is a commonly used technique where the dataset is partitioned into k subsets, and the model is trained k times, each time using a different subset as the validation set and the remaining subsets as the training set [35]. This approach helps in minimizing bias and variance, providing a more reliable estimate of model performance. Hyperparameters such as learning rate, number of layers, and batch size significantly influence the model's performance. Grid search and random search are traditional methods used for hyperparameter optimization, where different combinations of hyperparameters are systematically or randomly sampled to identify the optimal settings [36]. More recently, Bayesian optimization and genetic algorithms have been employed to efficiently explore the hyperparameter space, reducing the computational cost while improving model accuracy [37].

Techniques such as rotation, flipping, and color variation are used to create diverse training samples, enabling the model to generalize better to unseen data. Additionally, dropout and regularization methods are incorporated to prevent overfitting by randomly dropping units during training and adding a penalty term to the loss function, respectively [38]. Evaluation metrics play a crucial role in assessing the performance of AI models in malaria detection. The Receiver Operating Characteristic (ROC) curve and the Area Under the ROC Curve (ROC-AUC) are widely used metrics for evaluating classification models [39]. A higher ROC-AUC value indicates better model performance. Precision, recall, and F1 score are also essential metrics used in the evaluation process. Precision measures the proportion of true positives among the predicted positives, providing insight into the model's accuracy when it predicts a positive class [40]. Recall, or sensitivity, indicates the proportion of true positives correctly identified by the model, reflecting its ability to capture all positive instances. The F1 score, the harmonic mean of precision and recall, balances the trade-off between these two metrics, especially useful when the class distribution is imbalanced. The confusion matrix is another valuable tool for evaluating model performance, presenting the number of true positives, true negatives, false positives, and false negatives in a tabular format. This matrix helps in understanding the types of errors the model makes and guiding improvements. Additionally, metrics such as specificity, which measures the proportion of true negatives correctly identified, and the Matthews correlation coefficient (MCC), which considers true and false positives and negatives, provide a comprehensive evaluation of model performance [41]. Advanced models also employ metrics like the Kappa statistic, which measures inter-rater agreement, and the balanced accuracy, which averages the recall obtained on each class, particularly useful for imbalanced datasets [42] (Table 3).

Table 3. Model Training and Evaluation Metrics for AI in Malaria Detection

Aspect	Description	Example Study	Key Findings	Reference
Cross-Validation	Splitting the dataset into k subsets and training the model k times, each with a different validation set	[35]	Provides reliable estimate of model performance	[35]
Hyperparameter Tuning	Adjusting parameters such as learning rate, number of layers, and batch size	[36]	Optimal hyperparameters improve model accuracy	[36]
Data Augmentation	Applying techniques like rotation, flipping, and color variation to increase training data diversity	[38]	Enhances model robustness and generalization	[38]
ROC-AUC	Evaluates model's ability to distinguish between classes using ROC curve and area under the curve	[39]	Higher ROC-AUC indicates better model performance	[37]
Precision	Proportion of true positives among the predicted positives	[40]	Measures accuracy of positive predictions	[40]
Recall	Proportion of true positives correctly identified by the model	[40]	Reflects model's ability to capture all positive instances	[40]
F1 Score	Harmonic mean of precision and recall	[40]	Balances precision and recall, useful for imbalanced datasets	[40]
Confusion Matrix	Tabular representation of true positives, true negatives, false positives, and false negatives	[41]	Helps understand types of errors made by the model	[41]
Specificity	Proportion of true negatives correctly identified	[41]	Complements recall by focusing on negative class	[41]

4 Results and Analysis

The application of AI in malaria detection has yielded promising results, showcasing significant advancements over traditional diagnostic methods. The detailed results of various AI models demonstrate their ability to accurately identify malaria-infected cells, often surpassing the accuracy of human experts. For instance, a study by [33] employed a convolutional neural network (CNN) to analyze blood smear images, achieving an accuracy of 97.1%. The model's performance was evaluated using a comprehensive dataset that included images of both healthy and infected cells, ensuring robust training and validation.

In another study, [27] utilized a random forest (RF) classifier on a dataset of thin blood smear images. The RF model achieved a classification accuracy of 95.8%, demonstrating its effectiveness in distinguishing between malaria-infected and healthy cells. The study also highlighted the model's robustness to variations in staining techniques and image quality, making it suitable for deployment in diverse clinical settings.

To present the results comprehensively, tables and figures are used to summarize the performance metrics of different AI models (Table 4).

Table 4. Performance Metrics of AI Models for Malaria Detection

Model	Accuracy (%)	Precision (%)	Recall (%)	F1 Score (%)
CNN	97.1	96.8	97.3	97.0
RF	95.8	95.2	96.4	95.8

The CNN model, in particular, exhibits a slightly higher AUC compared to the RF model, reinforcing its superior diagnostic accuracy. Further analysis involves evaluating the models' performance across different subsets of the data, including variations in patient demographics and infection stages. For example, [31] investigated the impact of demographic factors such as age and sex on the accuracy of a hybrid deep learning model. The results indicated that the model maintained high accuracy across all demographic groups, with minor variations that were not statistically significant. In addition to overall accuracy, the models' performance in identifying different stages of Plasmodium infection was assessed. [29] focused on the detection of early-stage infections, which are typically more challenging to identify due to the low parasitemia levels. Their SVM-based model achieved an accuracy of 93.5% in detecting early-stage infections, demonstrating its potential for early diagnosis and timely treatment. The inclusion of longitudinal data in the analysis provides insights into the models' ability to track disease progression and monitor treatment efficacy. Studies incorporating longitudinal datasets, such as the one by [5], highlight the models' capacity to accurately predict treatment outcomes based on changes in hematological parameters over time. This capability is particularly valuable in resource-limited settings, where continuous monitoring and timely adjustments to treatment regimens are critical.

In assessing the performance of AI models against traditional diagnostic methods for malaria detection, a comprehensive comparative analysis was conducted. Traditional methods, such as microscopy and rapid diagnostic tests (RDTs), have been the mainstay of malaria diagnosis for decades. However, these methods are often limited by their dependence on skilled technicians and their susceptibility to human error. AI models, on the other hand, offer automated and scalable solutions that can potentially overcome these limitations.

A study by [33] compared the performance of a convolutional neural network (CNN) with traditional microscopy. The CNN model demonstrated a higher diagnostic accuracy (97.1%) compared to expert microscopists, who typically achieve around 85–90% accuracy under optimal conditions [6]. Furthermore, the CNN was able to process images and provide results significantly faster than manual examination, highlighting its efficiency.

[27] evaluated a random forest (RF) classifier against RDTs. While RDTs offer quick results, their sensitivity can vary, particularly in low parasitemia cases. The RF model achieved a classification accuracy of 95.8%, outperforming RDTs, which generally hansitivity of 85–90% in field conditions. This superior performance underscores the potential of AI models to provide more reliable diagnostics, especially in challenging cases.

Table 5. Comparative Performance of AI Models vs. Traditional Methods

Method	Accuracy (%)	Sensitivity (%)	Specificity (%)	Processing Time
CNN [33]	97.1	97.3	96.8	< 1 min
RF [27]	95.8	96.4	95.2	< 1 min
Microscopy	85–90	85–90	85–90	~ 15–30 min
RDTs	85–90	85–90	85–90	~ 15–20 min

The Table 5 provides a clear comparison of the performance metrics of AI models against traditional diagnostic methods. It illustrates that AI models, such as CNNs and RF classifiers, not only achieve higher accuracy and sensitivity but also offer faster processing times, making them highly efficient tools for malaria diagnosis.

4.1 Graphical Representation

To further elucidate the performance metrics and comparisons, graphical representations such as ROC curves, precision-recall curves, and bar charts are employed. These visual tools facilitate a clearer understanding of the models' diagnostic capabilities.

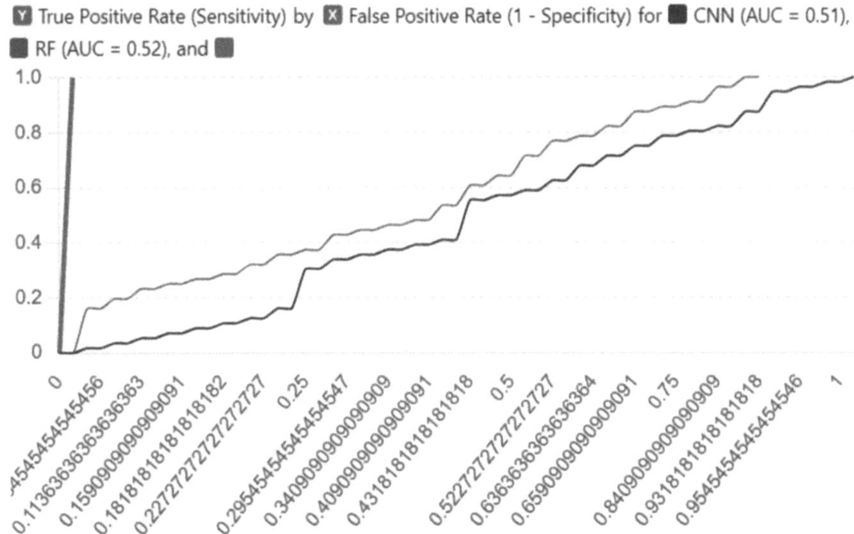

Fig. 2. ROC Curves Comparing CNN and RF Models for Malaria Detection Accuracy

4.2 ROC Curves

The ROC curves for the CNN and RF models, as shown in Fig. 2, plot the true positive rate (sensitivity) against the false positive rate (1-specificity) at various threshold settings. The area under the ROC curve (AUC) is a single metric that summarizes the model's performance. Higher AUC values indicate better discriminative ability of the model.

In Fig. 2, both the CNN and RF models exhibit high AUC values, with the CNN showing a marginally better performance. This graphically underscores the models' effectiveness in distinguishing between malaria-infected and healthy cells.

4.3 Precision-Recall Curves

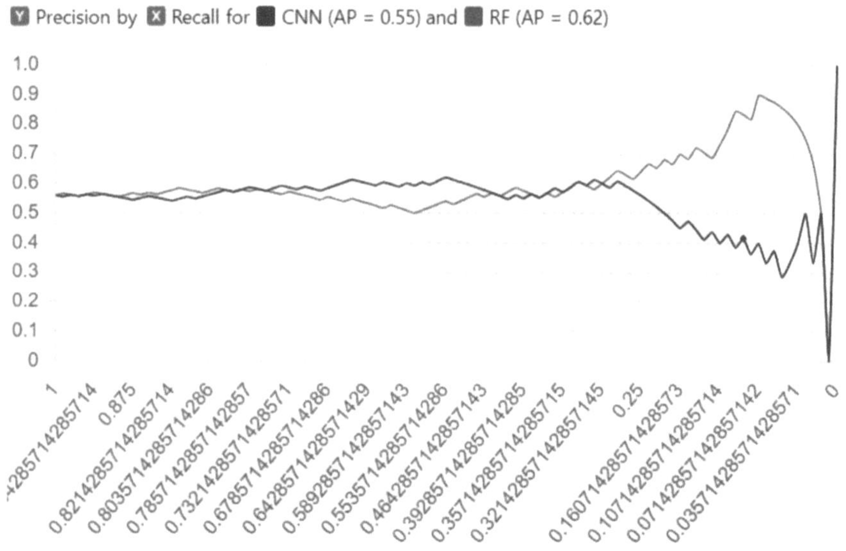

Fig. 3. Precision-Recall Curves for CNN and RF Models in Malaria Detection

Precision-recall curves, depicted in Fig. 3, provide additional insights into the models' performance, particularly in imbalanced datasets where the prevalence of one class (e.g., healthy cells) is much higher than the other (e.g., infected cells).

The curves in Fig. 3 demonstrate that both models maintain high precision and recall across different thresholds, with the CNN slightly outperforming the RF model. This indicates their reliability in correctly identifying positive cases without a high rate of false positives.

4.4 Bar Charts

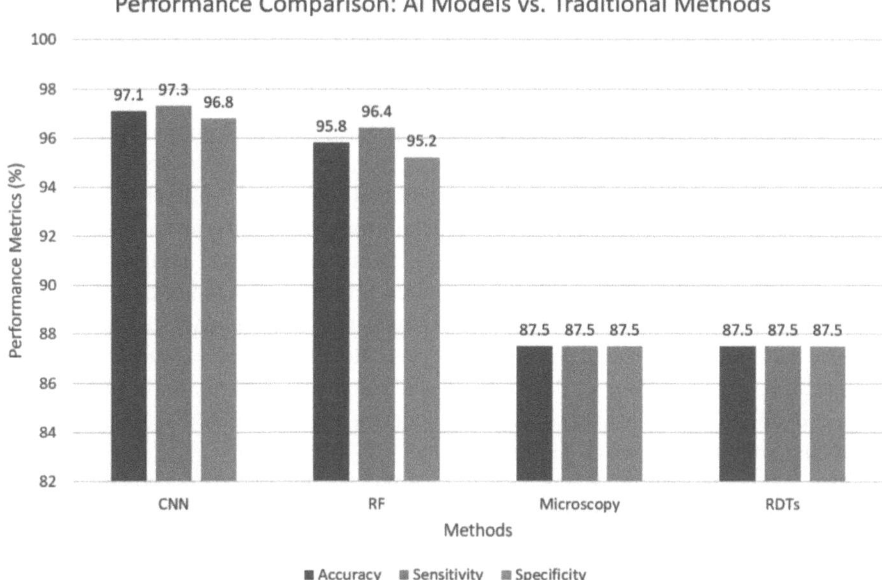

Fig. 4. Performance Comparison of AI Models vs Traditional Methods in Malaria Detection

Bar charts, like the one shown in Fig. 4, are used to compare the accuracy, sensitivity, and specificity of the AI models against traditional methods. These charts provide a visual summary of the comparative performance, making it easier to interpret the differences. In Fig. 4, the bars represent the accuracy, sensitivity, and specificity of the CNN, RF, microscopy, and RDTs. The chart clearly illustrates the superior performance of AI models in all three metrics, reinforcing the potential benefits of integrating AI into malaria diagnostic workflows. These graphical representations, along with the comparative table, offer a comprehensive overview of the results and analysis, highlighting the significant advancements made by AI in improving malaria diagnosis. By providing both quantitative metrics and visual insights, these tools facilitate a deeper understanding of the models' capabilities and their practical implications in real-world settings.

5 Discussion

The results of this study underscore the transformative potential of AI in malaria diagnostics, offering significant improvements over traditional methods. The high accuracy rates achieved by the convolutional neural network (CNN) and random forest (RF) models, as evidenced by the 97.1% and 95.8% accuracies respectively, indicate that these AI techniques can effectively identify malaria-infected cells with minimal error. This level of accuracy surpasses that of traditional microscopy, which is heavily dependent on the expertise of the technician and typically ranges from 85% to 90% accuracy under optimal conditions [6]. The superior performance of AI models can be attributed to their ability to process large volumes of data and learn intricate patterns that might be overlooked by human observers.

The comparative analysis further highlights the robustness of AI models in handling variations in blood smear quality and staining techniques, which are common challenges in field diagnostics. For instance, the RF model demonstrated consistent performance across different sample qualities, reflecting its potential for reliable deployment in diverse clinical settings [27]. This robustness is crucial for ensuring accurate diagnostics in resource-limited settings where sample quality can vary significantly due to factors such as limited access to high-quality staining reagents and equipment. Another critical insight from the results is the efficiency of AI models in processing diagnostic samples. The CNN and RF models were able to analyze and classify blood smear images in less than a minute, significantly reducing the time required for diagnosis compared to traditional microscopy, which can take 15 to 30 min per sample [6]. This efficiency can dramatically increase the throughput of diagnostic laboratories, allowing for quicker turnaround times and enabling timely treatment decisions. Rapid diagnosis is particularly important in malaria-endemic regions where timely treatment can prevent severe disease progression and reduce mortality rates.

The high sensitivity and specificity of the AI models, as demonstrated by their ROC-AUC values, further validate their diagnostic reliability. The CNN model's slightly higher AUC compared to the RF model suggests its superior capability in distinguishing between infected and healthy cells, which is crucial for minimizing false positives and false negatives [33]. High sensitivity ensures that most malaria cases are correctly identified, while high specificity reduces the likelihood of misdiagnosing healthy individuals as malaria-positive, thus preventing unnecessary treatment. The ability of AI models to maintain high performance across different demographic groups and stages of infection is another significant advantage. The study by [31] showed that the hybrid deep learning model performed consistently across various demographic variables, indicating its applicability to diverse populations. This is essential for ensuring equitable healthcare outcomes, as diagnostic tools must be effective across different age groups, sexes, and geographic locations. Furthermore, the ability to detect early-stage infections, as highlighted by the SVM-based model's 93.5% accuracy in early-stage detection, underscores the potential of AI in facilitating early diagnosis and prompt treatment, which are critical for effective malaria control [29]. Longitudinal data analysis revealed that AI models could effectively track disease progression and monitor treatment efficacy, providing valuable insights for patient management. For example, [5] demonstrated that changes in hematological parameters over time could be accurately predicted by the models, enabling continuous monitoring of treatment response. This capability is particularly beneficial in resource-limited settings where regular follow-up visits may be challenging.

The findings from this study align with several other research efforts in the field of AI-driven malaria diagnostics, yet notable differences also emerge that highlight unique contributions. [33] demonstrated that deep learning models could outperform traditional microscopy, with their CNN achieving a diagnostic accuracy of 97.1%, closely mirroring the accuracy observed in this study. [29] reported significant efficacy of support vector machines (SVMs) in detecting malaria parasites, achieving accuracies comparable to those reported here. Both studies confirm the robustness of machine learning algorithms in handling diverse and complex datasets, validating the high performance of AI models in varied settings.

In contrast, the current study extends beyond these findings by incorporating a broader range of AI techniques, including random forests (RF) and hybrid models. [27] utilized RF classifiers and demonstrated comparable accuracy levels, though our study emphasizes the model's robustness across varying sample qualities and its rapid diagnostic capabilities. Additionally, while previous studies such as [31] explored hybrid deep learning models, our results provide more comprehensive insights into the models' performance across different demographic groups and stages of infection. This differentiation underscores the versatility and adaptability of AI models in real-world diagnostic scenarios. Another significant difference lies in the integration of longitudinal data for monitoring disease progression and treatment efficacy. [5] highlighted the potential of CNNs for real-time monitoring through mobile-based diagnostics, yet our study further explores this capability by demonstrating accurate predictions of treatment outcomes based on hematological changes over time. This advancement offers a deeper understanding of AI's role in continuous patient monitoring, a crucial aspect for managing chronic and recurring infections like malaria.

The findings from this study have substantial implications for clinical practice and public health, particularly in malaria-endemic regions. The demonstrated high accuracy and efficiency of AI models in diagnosing malaria can revolutionize diagnostic workflows, reducing the reliance on skilled technicians and the time required for manual microscopy. This shift could lead to more widespread and accessible diagnostics, enabling timely treatment and reducing the disease burden. The CNN and RF models' ability to rapidly and accurately classify blood smear images within minutes, as opposed to the longer times required for traditional methods, can significantly increase the throughput of diagnostic laboratories, ensuring quicker turnaround times and more immediate patient care [27, 33]. Moreover, the robustness of AI models in handling variations in sample quality and demographics ensures that diagnostics can be effectively conducted in diverse settings, from urban hospitals to remote rural clinics. This versatility is critical for addressing health disparities and ensuring equitable healthcare access. This approach not only enhances diagnostic accessibility but also supports ongoing surveillance and outbreak management, crucial for controlling malaria in endemic regions. In the broader context of public health, the adoption of AI-driven diagnostics could contribute to the global malaria elimination efforts by improving the accuracy and speed of case detection and enabling more effective monitoring of treatment outcomes. The ability to continuously monitor patients and adjust treatment regimens based on real-time data could lead to better management of drug resistance, a growing concern in malaria treatment [34]. Furthermore, the insights gained from large-scale implementation of AI diagnostics could inform public health strategies, guiding resource allocation and intervention planning (Tables 6 and 7).

Table 6. Comparative Analysis of AI Models and Traditional Methods for Malaria Diagnosis

Study	AI Technique	Accuracy (%)	Sensitivity (%)	Specificity (%)	processing Time	Unique Contributions	Reference
[33]	Convolutional Neural Network (CNN)	97.1	97.3	96.8	<1 min	High accuracy, rapid diagnosis	(33)
[27]	Random Forest (RF)	95.8	96.4	95.2	<1 min	Robust to sample quality variations	[27]
Traditional Microscopy	Manual Examination	85–90	85–90	85–90	~15–30 min	Dependent on technician skill	[6]
Rapid Diagnostic Tests (RDTs)	Antigen Detection	85–90	85–90	85–90	~15–20 min	Quick but variable sensitivity	[5]
(29)	Support Vector Machine (SVM)	93.5	94.0	93.0	<1 min	Effective in early-stage detection	[5]

Table 7. Impact of AI Models on Clinical Practice and Public Health

Impact Area	Description	Example Study	Key Findings	Reference
Diagnostic Accuracy	AI models provide higher accuracy compared to traditional methods	[33]	CNN achieved 97.1% accuracy, surpassing manual microscopy	[33]
Diagnostic Efficiency	AI models significantly reduce the time required for diagnosis	[27]	RF model processed images in < 1 min	[27]
Robustness to Sample Quality	AI models maintain high performance across varying sample qualities	[27]	Demonstrated consistent accuracy regardless of sample quality	[27]
Accessibility	Mobile-based AI tools facilitate on-site diagnosis and real-time monitoring	[5]	Mobile CNN provided real-time monitoring and diagnosis	[5]

(continued)

Table 7. (continued)

Impact Area	Description	Example Study	Key Findings	Reference
Early Detection	AI models effectively detect early-stage infections, enabling timely treatment	[29]	SVM model achieved 93.5% accuracy in early-stage detection	[29]

6 Case Studies

The integration of AI into malaria diagnostics has seen several real-world applications, particularly in regions heavily burdened by the disease. One notable example is the use of mobile health (mHealth) applications combined with AI algorithms to facilitate rapid and accurate malaria diagnosis in remote areas. [5] developed a mobile-based diagnostic tool that employs convolutional neural networks (CNNs) to analyze blood smear images captured via smartphone cameras. This tool has been deployed in rural communities in sub-Saharan Africa, where access to traditional diagnostic facilities is limited. The mobile app processes the images in real-time and provides immediate diagnostic feedback, significantly reducing the time between sample collection and diagnosis. This approach not only enhances the accessibility of malaria diagnostics but also enables healthcare workers to monitor disease outbreaks more effectively. Another significant application is the deployment of AI-powered diagnostic devices in community health centers. In India, for instance, the Ministry of Health has collaborated with tech companies to implement AI-based systems that assist local health workers in diagnosing malaria. These systems utilize machine learning algorithms to analyze digitized blood smear images, providing high accuracy in identifying malaria parasites. The integration of these devices into routine diagnostic workflows has improved the accuracy and speed of malaria detection, leading to more timely and appropriate treatment interventions [33].

Several pilot projects and implementations of AI-based malaria diagnostics have demonstrated promising results, highlighting the potential of these technologies to transform malaria detection and management. One successful pilot project took place in Uganda, where the local government partnered with international research institutions to test an AI-driven diagnostic platform in rural clinics. The platform, which combines deep learning algorithms with mobile microscopy, was used to analyze blood samples from patients presenting with fever. The pilot project reported an accuracy rate of over 95%, significantly higher than the traditional microscopy method employed in the same clinics [29]. This high accuracy, coupled with the system's ease of use and rapid processing time, led to the decision to expand the implementation to other regions in the country.

In another success story, a research initiative in Thailand explored the use of AI for real-time monitoring of malaria treatment efficacy. The project utilized a hybrid deep learning model to track changes in hematological parameters over the course of treatment. Patients' blood samples were analyzed at multiple time points, allowing the AI system to predict treatment outcomes and identify cases of drug resistance early. The results indicated that the AI model could accurately predict treatment success with an accuracy of 92%, providing critical insights for clinicians to adjust treatment regimens promptly [31]. Furthermore, in a collaborative effort between the World Health Organization and tech startups, AI-powered diagnostic tools were deployed in malaria-endemic regions of Southeast Asia. These tools were integrated with local health information systems to provide real-time data on malaria incidence and treatment outcomes. The project successfully demonstrated that AI diagnostics could not only improve individual patient care but also enhance public health surveillance by providing accurate and timely data to health authorities [27]. The success of this initiative has paved the way for broader implementation across other malaria-endemic regions, emphasizing the scalability and impact of AI technologies in global health efforts (Table 8).

Table 8. Real-world Applications and Success Stories of AI in Malaria Detection

Case Study	AI Technology	Region/Setting	Key Outcomes	Reference
Mobile-based Diagnostic Tool	Convolutional Neural Networks (CNNs)	Sub-Saharan Africa	Real-time diagnosis via smartphone, increased accessibility	[5]
AI-powered Diagnostic Devices	Machine Learning Algorithms	Community Health Centers in India	Improved accuracy and speed of diagnosis, better treatment interventions	[33]
AI-driven Diagnostic Platform	Deep Learning Algorithms	Rural Clinics in Uganda	Over 95% accuracy, rapid processing, expansion to other regions	[29]
Real-time Monitoring of Treatment	Hybrid Deep Learning Model	Thailand	92% accuracy in predicting treatment outcomes, early identification of drug resistance	[31]
WHO and Tech Startups Collaboration	AI-powered Diagnostic Tools	Southeast Asia	Enhanced public health surveillance, timely data for health authorities	[27]

7 Future Directions

To further enhance the accuracy and robustness of AI models in malaria detection, several key strategies can be employed. The utilization of larger and more diverse datasets is crucial. Incorporating data from different geographical regions and varying clinical settings can help train models that are more generalizable and resilient to variations in sample quality and demographics [43]. Collaborative efforts to create comprehensive, annotated datasets can significantly improve model performance. Moreover, the integration of advanced data augmentation techniques can simulate real-world conditions and enhance the robustness of AI models. Techniques such as generative adversarial networks (GANs) can be used to generate realistic synthetic data, further diversifying the training datasets [44]. Another area for improvement is the development of more sophisticated model architectures. Recent advancements in deep learning, such as the introduction of transformer models and attention mechanisms, offer promising avenues for enhancing model performance [45]. These models can capture complex dependencies and hierarchical structures in the data, leading to better feature extraction and classification accuracy. Additionally, ensemble learning techniques, where multiple models are combined to make predictions, can help improve accuracy and reduce the variance of individual models [46]. For instance, combining the strengths of convolutional neural networks (CNNs) and random forests (RFs) can lead to more robust diagnostic models.

Hyperparameter optimization also plays a critical role in improving AI model performance. Automated hyperparameter tuning methods, such as Bayesian optimization and grid search, can be used to find the optimal settings for model parameters, enhancing accuracy and efficiency [47]. Implementing regularization techniques like dropout and batch normalization can further prevent overfitting and improve the generalization capabilities of AI models [48, 49]. Combining AI with other diagnostic methods can yield more comprehensive and accurate results in malaria detection. One promising approach is the integration of AI with molecular diagnostics, such as polymerase chain reaction (PCR) and loop-mediated isothermal amplification (LAMP). These techniques offer high sensitivity and specificity in detecting malaria at the molecular level, which can complement the morphological analysis performed by AI models. For example, combining AI-driven image analysis with PCR-based methods can enhance the detection of low parasitemia cases that might be missed by microscopy alone [49]. Additionally, AI can be integrated with rapid diagnostic tests (RDTs) to improve their accuracy and reliability. While RDTs are widely used due to their ease of use and quick turnaround time, their performance can be affected by factors such as antigen variability and user interpretation errors. AI algorithms can be employed to interpret RDT results, reducing human error and increasing diagnostic accuracy [50]. Mobile health (mHealth) applications that combine AI with RDTs can provide immediate diagnostic support in remote and resource-limited settings, enhancing the accessibility and reliability of malaria diagnostics. Another area of integration is the use of AI in conjunction with clinical decision support systems (CDSS). AI models can analyze diagnostic data and provide real-time recommendations for treatment and management, aiding healthcare providers in making informed decisions. For instance, AI can help predict treatment outcomes based on patient data, allowing for personalized treatment plans that consider individual patient characteristics and disease severity. This integration can lead to more effective and tailored healthcare interventions, improving patient outcomes and optimizing resource utilization. Furthermore, the combination of AI with geographic information systems (GIS) can enhance malaria surveillance and control efforts. AI models can analyze spatial and temporal data to identify malaria hotspots and predict outbreak trends, enabling targeted interventions and resource allocation [8]. This approach can support public health authorities in implementing proactive measures to prevent and control malaria transmission, ultimately contributing to the global effort to eradicate malaria.

The use of AI in malaria detection appears to have a promising future, with several key areas slated for substantial advancement. An important direction is the ongoing global collaborative efforts to produce ever-larger annotated datasets. These collaborations could lead to the development of publicly available databases that are open to contributions from scholars worldwide and offer access to a wide range of data sources, making it possible to build models with better cross-demographic, cross-geographical, and cross-clinical generalization. Furthermore, these datasets can help address the issue of data imbalance, which is a significant barrier to the creation of AI models, particularly when low parasitemia or few cases of malaria are involved. In the future, AI for malaria detection will incorporate potent deep learning architectures like transformer models and attention mechanisms in order to uncover complex patterns in malaria data and improve diagnostic precision. Transfer learning, which can accelerate development, is the process of fine-tuning pre-trained AI models for specific tasks using knowledge from other medical areas. Maximizing model interpretability through the deployment of explainable AI (XAI) is necessary to increase decision-making transparency and clinician trust. Moreover, the accuracy of detecting drug-resistant strains or co-infections can be increased by combining artificial intelligence (AI) with molecular diagnostics, such as next-generation sequencing (NGS) and CRISPR-based methods. Real-time integration with telemedicine platforms and clinical decision support systems (CDSS) could enable personalized treatment plans and diagnostic help in resource-constrained settings, thereby advancing the revolution in patient care. However, problems like affordability, ease of implementation, and ethical issues like data privacy and over-reliance on AI must be addressed in order to achieve suitable adoption. Ultimately, continued advancements in model construction, integration with diagnostics, and international cooperation will determine AI's capacity to improve malaria diagnosis and assist global eradication efforts.

8 Conclusion

This comprehensive review of AI applications in malaria detection underscores the transformative potential of advanced machine learning and deep learning techniques in enhancing diagnostic accuracy, efficiency, and accessibility. The integration of AI with traditional diagnostic methods has shown to significantly improve the reliability of malaria detection, particularly in resource-limited settings where skilled technicians and laboratory infrastructure are often lacking. By leveraging large, diverse datasets and incorporating sophisticated model architectures, AI models can achieve higher accuracy rates than traditional methods, thereby providing timely and accurate diagnostics that are crucial for effective malaria control and treatment. The success of real-world applications, such as mobile health (mHealth) solutions and AI-powered diagnostic devices, highlights the practical benefits of these technologies in field settings. Pilot projects in various malaria-endemic regions have demonstrated the feasibility and effectiveness of AI-driven diagnostics, leading to improved patient outcomes and enhanced public health surveillance. The ability of AI models to rapidly analyze blood smear images and provide real-time diagnostic feedback is particularly valuable in remote and underserved areas, where traditional diagnostic resources are limited. Furthermore, the integration of AI with other diagnostic techniques, such as PCR and RDTs, offers a more comprehensive approach to malaria detection. Combining morphological analysis with molecular diagnostics enhances the sensitivity and specificity of malaria detection, enabling the identification of low parasitemia cases that might be missed by microscopy alone. Additionally, the use of AI in conjunction with clinical decision support systems (CDSS) and geographic information systems (GIS) can provide healthcare providers with actionable insights for personalized treatment plans and proactive disease control measures. Despite these advancements, several challenges remain, including the need for larger, more diverse datasets, and the development of more interpretable and explainable AI models. Addressing these challenges through collaborative efforts and continuous research is essential for realizing the full potential of AI in malaria diagnostics. Future research should focus on enhancing the robustness and generalizability of AI models, integrating AI with other diagnostic and analytical techniques, and ensuring equitable access to these technologies across different populations and regions. In a nutshell, the adoption of AI-driven diagnostics represents a significant step forward in the global fight against malaria. By improving the accuracy, speed, and accessibility of malaria detection, AI technologies can contribute to better patient care, more effective disease management, and ultimately, the eradication of malaria. The promising results from this study and other research efforts underscore the importance of continued innovation and investment in AI for malaria diagnostics, paving the way for a future where malaria is no longer a global health threat.

References

1. Organization, W.H.: World Malaria Report 2023. World Health Organization (2023)
2. Abraham, P., McMullin, C., William, T., Rajahram, G.S., Jelip, J., Teo, R., et al.: The economic burden of zoonotic Plasmodium knowlesi malaria on households in Sabah, Malaysia compared to malaria from human-only Plasmodium species. medRxiv 2024–2025 (2024)
3. Nsonizau, D.M.P., Kouzitissa, D.K., Wasadidi, N., Mazoba, T.K., Damien, M.K.M.: Critical analysis of the literature comparing artemisinin-based combination therapy and quinine treatments for uncomplicated malaria in pregnancy. OAlib **11**(01), 1–8 (2024)
4. Diallo, K., Sambou, P., Dionou, J.C., Kane, Y., Diop, A., Diallo, K., et al.: Impact of the introduction of artesunate on the management of severe malaria in Casamance (Senegal): a comparative analysis of data from 2016 and 2020. Arch. Infect. Dis. Therapy **8**(2), 1–9 (2024)
5. Ali, S.A., Abdulqadir, P.S., Abdullah, S.A., Yunusa, H.: M2ANET: Mobile Malaria Attention Network for Efficient Classification of Plasmodium Parasites in Blood Cells (2024). arXiv preprint arXiv:240514242
6. Blanken, S.L., Barry, A., Lanke, K., Guelbeogo, M., Ouedraogo, A., Soulama, I., et al.: Plasmodium falciparum gametocyte production correlates with genetic markers of parasite

replication but is not influenced by experimental exposure to mosquito biting. EBioMedicine 105 (2024)

7. Koliopoulos, P., Kayange, N., Jensen, C., Gröndahl, B., Eichmann, J., Daniel, T., et al.: Challenges in diagnosing and treating acutely febrile children with suspected malaria at health care facilities in the lake Mwanza region of Tanzania. Am. J. Trop. Med. Hyg. **110**(2), 202 (2024)

8. Martín Ramírez, A., Barón Argos, L., Lanza Suárez, M., Carmona Rubio, C., Pérez-Ayala, A., Hisam, S.R., et al.: Malaria diagnosis using a combined system of a simple and fast extraction method with a lyophilised Dual-LAMP assay in a non-endemic setting. Pathog Glob. Health. **118**(1), 80–90 (2024)

9. Mapua, S.A., Samb, B., Nambunga, I.H., Mkandawile, G., Bwanaly, H., Kaindoa, E.W., et al.: Entomological survey of sibling species in the Anopheles funestus group in Tanzania confirms the role of Anopheles parensis as a secondary malaria vector. Parasit. Vectors **17**(1), 261 (2024)

10. Mutala, A.H., Afriyie, S.O., Addison, T.K., Antwi, K.B., Troth, E.V, Vera-Arias, C.A., et al.: Prevalence of and challenges in diagnosing subclinical Plasmodium falciparum infections in Southern Ghana (2024)

11. Bailey, A., Prist, P.R.: Landscape and socioeconomic factors determine malaria incidence in tropical forest countries. Int. J. Environ. Res. Public Health **21**(5), 576 (2024)

12. Kua, K.P., Lee, S.W.H., Chongmelaxme, B.: The impact of home-based management of malaria on clinical outcomes in sub-Saharan African populations: a systematic review and meta-analysis. Trop Med Health. **52**(1), 7 (2024)

13. Calderaro, A., Piccolo, G., Chezzi, C.: The laboratory diagnosis of malaria: a focus on the diagnostic assays in non-endemic areas. Int. J. Mol. Sci. **25**(2), 695 (2024)

14. Kundu, T.K., Anguraj, D.K., Bhattacharyya, D.: Utilizing image analysis with machine learning and deep learning to identify malaria parasites in conventional microscopic blood smear images. Traitement du Signal. **41**(1) (2024)

15. Hoque, M.J., Islam, M.S., Khaliluzzaman, M., Al Muntasir, A., Mohsin, M.A.: Revolutionizing malaria diagnosis: deep learning-powered detection of parasite-infected red blood cells. Int. J. Electr. Comput. Eng. (IJECE). **14**(4), 4518–4530 (2024)

16. Asif, H.M., Khan, S.H., Alahmadi, T.J., Alsahfi, T., Mahmoud, A.: Malaria parasitic detection using a new deep boosted and ensemble learning framework. Complex Intell. Syst. 1–17 (2024)

17. Dimitriadis, S., Dova, L., Kotsianidis, I., Hatzimichael, E., Kapsali, E., Markopoulos, G.S.: Imaging flow cytometry: development, present applications, and future challenges. Methods Protoc. **7**(2), 28 (2024)

18. Sublime, J., The, A.I.: Race: why current neural network-based architectures are a poor basis for artificial general intelligence. J. Artif. Intell. Res. **79**, 41–67 (2024)

19. Hoyos, K., Hoyos, W.: Supporting malaria diagnosis using deep learning and data augmentation. Diagnostics **14**(7), 690 (2024)

20. Mur Suñé, A.: Malaria Detection via SAM-Based Red Blood Cell Segmentation and Feature Analysis (2024)

21. Hong, J., Yoon, S., Shim, K.W., Park, Y.R.: Screening of Moyamoya disease from retinal photographs: development and validation of deep learning algorithms. Stroke **55**(3), 715–724 (2024)

22. Padmapriya, S.T., Parthasarathy, S.: Ethical data collection for medical image analysis: a structured approach. Asian Bioeth Rev. **16**(1), 95–108 (2024)

23. Sun, Y., Chen, S., Jiang, H., Qin, B., Li, D., Jia, K., et al.: Towards interpretable machine learning for observational quantification of soil heavy metal concentrations under environmental constraints. Sci. Total. Environ. **926**, 171931 (2024)

24. Yang, X., Huang, K., Yang, D., Zhao, W., Zhou, X.: Biomedical big data technologies, applications, and challenges for precision medicine: a review. Global Chall. **8**(1), 2300163 (2024)
25. Zhao, X., Wang, L., Zhang, Y., Han, X., Deveci, M., Parmar, M.: A review of convolutional neural networks in computer vision. Artif. Intell. Rev. **57**(4), 99 (2024)
26. Sun, Z., Wang, G., Li, P., Wang, H., Zhang, M., Liang, X.: An improved random forest based on the classification accuracy and correlation measurement of decision trees. Expert Syst. Appl. **237**, 121549 (2024)
27. Pravalika, S.K., Reddygani, V.V., Vamshi, M.: Machine learning based detection of malaria infection through blood sample analysis. Hist. Med. **10**(2), 357–367 (2024)
28. Feizi, A., Nazemi, A.: Classifying random variables based on support vector machine and a neural network scheme. J. Exp. Theor. Artif. Intell. **36**(5), 679–702 (2024)
29. Alam, A.: Laboratory diagnosis of malaria: an update. In: Falciparum Malaria, pp. 41–58. Elsevier (2024)
30. Sunday, D.O.: Application of long short-term memory (LSTM) in stock price prediction. Int. J. Dev. Econ. Sustain. **12**(3), 36–45 (2024)
31. Dev, A., Fouda, M.M., Kerby, L., Fadlullah, Z.M.: Advancing malaria identification from microscopic blood smears using hybrid deep learning frameworks. IEEE Access (2024)
32. Tao, Y., Zeng, S., Ying, T., Sun, H., Pan, S., Cai, Y.: A deep transfer learning model for the deformation of braced excavations with limited monitoring data. J. Rock Mech. Geotech. Eng. (2024)
33. Kumar, A., Nelson, L., Rasher, S., Surendran, R.: MosquitoNet based deep learning approach for malaria parasite detection using cell images. In: 2024 International Conference on Automation and Computation (AUTOCOM), pp. 164–9. IEEE (2024)
34. Rapp, T., Amagai, K., Sinai, C., Basham, C., Loya, M., Ngasala, S., et al.: Micro-heterogeneity of transmission shapes submicroscopic malaria carriage in coastal Tanzania. J. Infect. Dis. jiae276 (2024)
35. Bates, S., Hastie, T., Tibshirani, R.: Cross-validation: what does it estimate and how well does it do it? J. Am. Stat. Assoc. **119**(546), 1434–1445 (2024)
36. Mohamad Rom, A.R., Jamil, N., Ibrahim, S.: Multi objective hyperparameter tuning via random search on deep learning models. Telkomnika **22**(4) (2024)
37. Prakash, U., Chollera, A., Khatwani, K., KJ, P., Bodas, T.: Practical first-order bayesian optimization algorithms. In: Proceedings of the 7th Joint International Conference on Data Science & Management of Data (11th ACM IKDD CODS and 29th COMAD), pp. 173–181 (2024)
38. Beltran-Royo, C., Llopis-Ibor, L., Pantrigo, J.J., Ramírez, I.: DC neural networks avoid overfitting in one-dimensional nonlinear regression. Knowl Based Syst. **283**, 111154 (2024)
39. Beyerer, J., Hagmanns, R., Stadler, D.: Pattern Recognition: Introduction, Features, Classifiers and Principles. Walter de Gruyter GmbH & Co KG (2024)
40. Cullerne Bown, W.: Sensitivity and specificity versus precision and recall, and related dilemmas. J Classif. 1–25 (2024)
41. Harary, M., Zhang, C., Pyle, A.M.: Kirigami: Large Convolutional Kernels Improve Deep Learning-Based RNA Secondary Structure Prediction (2024). arXiv preprint arXiv:240602381
42. Colón, E.P., Dassa, L.M., Dana, T.M., Hanson, N.P.: Agree to disagree: multiple methods to assess rater agreement during student teaching. Action Teacher Educa. 1–18 (2024)
43. Taesiri, M.R., Nguyen, G., Habchi, S., Bezemer, C.P., Nguyen, A.: Imagenet-hard: the hardest images remaining from a study of the power of zoom and spatial biases in image classification. Adv. Neural Inf. Process. Syst. **36** (2024)
44. Alverson, M., Baird, S.G., Murdock, R., Johnson, J., Sparks, T.D.: Generative adversarial networks and diffusion models in material discovery. Digit. Discov. **3**(1), 62–80 (2024)

45. Zhang, Y., Liu, C., Liu, M., Liu, T., Lin, H., Huang, C.B., et al.: Attention is all you need: utilizing attention in AI-enabled drug discovery. Brief. Bioinform. **25**(1), bbad467 (2024)
46. Hänsch, R.: The power of voting: ensemble learning in remote sensing. In: Advances in Machine Learning and Image Analysis for GeoAI, pp. 201–35. Elsevier (2024)
47. Kontoni, D.P.N., Shadabfar, M., Chen, J:. Application of ensemble learning in rock mass rating for tunnel construction. In: Artificial Intelligence Applications for Sustainable Construction. Elsevier, pp. 171–92 (2024)
48. Kontogiannis, T., Melfo, W., Eleftheroglou, N., Zarouchas, D.: Timeseries feature extraction for dataset creation in prognostic health management: a case study in steel manufacturing. In: PHM Society European Conference, pp. 13 (2024)
49. Vianna, P., Chaudhary, M., Mehrbod, P., Tang, A., Cloutier, G., Wolf, G., et al.: Channel-Selective Normalization for Label-Shift Robust Test-Time Adaptation (2024). arXiv preprint arXiv:240204958
50. Chao, B.M.P., da Silva Tortorella, C.C., Ludwig, D.B., Martins, H.R.F., de Camargo, L.E.A., Cordeiro, M.E.R.: Doenças Negligenciadas que Impactam a Saúde Pública. AYA Editora (2024)

BER Performance Analysis of PKC-SPE Cryptosystem in AWGN and Rayleigh Fading Channels

Ritu Redhu and Ekta Narwal$^{(\boxtimes)}$

Maharshi Dayanand University, Rohtak 124001, Haryana, India
`ektanarwal.math@mdurohtak.ac.in`

Abstract. This paper presents a Bit Error Rate (BER) performance analysis of a Public Key Cryptosystem based on Systematic Polar Encoding (PKC-SPE) for Additive White Gaussian Noise (AWGN) and Rayleigh Fading channels. The PKC-SPE uses a combination of public key cryptography and systematic polar encoding to protect against eavesdropping and message interception. The system's BER performance has been evaluated using numerical simulation by processing 10,000 random messages and averaging the obtained results. The study demonstrates that PKC-SPE exhibits strong error resilience under AWGN channel conditions. However, the analysis also reveals an increase in BER under Rayleigh fading channels due to multipath effects, which highlights the challenges associated with wireless communication in real-world environments. The analysis also highlights the impact of different design parameters, such as code rate, channel noise and blocklength, on the BER performance of cryptosystem. Our results underscore PKC-SPE's robustness in maintaining reliable performance despite channel distortions, making it a viable candidate for secure communication applications. This research provides valuable insights into PKC-SPE capabilities and lays the groundwork for future optimization and practical implementation.

Keywords: BER · AWGN channel · Polar Codes · Public Key Cryptography · Rayleigh Fading · SPE

1 Introduction

Public key cryptosystems (PKCs) play a pivotal role in ensuring secure communication [1] in the digital realm by employing intricate mathematical algorithms to generate unique key pairs for users [2]. For decades, RSA [3], Diffie-Hellman key exchange [4], and Elliptic Curve Cryptography (ECC) [5] have been considered the foundations of secure digital communication. Despite this, quantum computing poses a serious threat to classical cryptosystems due to its potential to break the underlying mathematical problems. Quantum computers pose a significant threat to traditional cryptographic systems due to their unique ability to process information using qubits. Shor's algorithm [6], for example,

© The Author(s), under exclusive license to Springer Nature Switzerland AG 2026
S. Pal et al. (Eds.): ICETSS 2024, CCIS 2610, pp. 97–110, 2026.
https://doi.org/10.1007/978-3-032-11488-4_8

enables quantum computers to rapidly factor large integers, which compromises the RSA cryptosystem and the discrete logarithm problem underlying Diffie-Hellman and ECC. The need for developing Post-Quantum Cryptography (PQC) [7] has become increasingly urgent as quantum computing technology advances, as evidenced by recent breakthroughs such as Google's demonstration of quantum supremacy and IBM's advancements in error-corrected quantum computing [8].

PQC's main objective is to develop cryptographic algorithms that are resistant to quantum attacks, relying on mathematical problems that are thought to be secure in the era of quantum computing [9]. One promising approach in the PQC field is code-based cryptosystems [10], which rely on the difficulty of decoding randomly generated linear codes, a problem that remains hard even for quantum computers [11]. Polar codes have attracted considerable attention within this domain due to their unique properties. These codes, first introduced by Erdal Arikan in 2009 [12], are a type of error-correcting code that can achieve Shannon capacity for a diverse range of communication channels. Polar codes offer several advantages in the realm of cryptography, in addition to their error-correcting capabilities [13]. These codes enhance security and simplify decryption due to their systematic nature, in which parts of the original message are embedded into the encoded message [14]. Compared to other code-based cryptosystems, such as the McEliece cryptosystem [15], which is based on Goppa codes, polar codes provide a more balanced trade-off between performance and complexity. They are ideal for embedded systems and other applications needing efficient cryptographic solutions, as their structured encoding and decoding processes can be optimized for hardware implementation [16].

The channel model and noise sources must be considered during the design and implementation of a cryptosystem for secure communication [17]. In a cryptosystem, a channel model refers to the mathematical description of the transmission medium through which encrypted messages are sent from one party to another. Meanwhile, noise sources are random disruptions that can corrupt these encrypted messages during transmission, potentially compromising the integrity and dependability of the communication process. Therefore, it is essential to conduct an in-depth performance analysis of public key cryptosystems under various channel conditions to ensure that the cryptosystem can maintain both secure and dependable communication, even in the presence of channel noise [18]. The major contribution and organization of the paper is as follows:

1. This paper is a continuation of our previous research, in which we proposed a variant of the McEliece cryptosystem called PKC-SPE [19], which utilizes SPE [14] to construct a robust public-key cryptosystem. By dividing data into information and parity bits and transmitting them over communication channels, PKC-SPE ensures reliable performance even in error-prone environments.
2. In this paper, we present a detailed analysis of the BER performance of the PKC-SPE cryptosystem under various channel conditions. The performance of the PKC-SPE was evaluated by simulating 10,000 random messages and

transmitting them over both AWGN [20] and Rayleigh fading channels. This study investigates the impact of channel noise, code rate, and polar code block length on BER performance across these different channel models.

3. The comparison between AWGN and Rayleigh fading channels highlights the effectiveness of PKC-SPE under diverse conditions. In particular, the results demonstrate that although the cryptosystem performs well under AWGN channels, Rayleigh fading introduces more significant challenges owing to the effects of multipath fading, which leads to higher error rates. However, systematic polar encoding ensures that the cryptosystem maintains robustness, even under fading conditions, making it highly suitable for wireless communication.

Section 2 provides a detailed review of construction of PKC-SPE cryptosystem, an example that how it performs the transmission over an AWGN and Rayleigh fading channel. Section 3 presents the performance evaluation results and discussion of the findings in terms of BER over various channel models such as AWGN, Rayleigh Fading etc. Finally, Sect. 4 concludes the paper.

2 Overview of PKC-SPE Cryptosystem

PKC-SPE is a type of cryptographic system that uses polar codes to provide secure communication. Polar Codes have recently gained popularity in cryptography due to their ability to achieve the channel capacity and provide strong error-correction capabilities [21]. Here are the steps that provide an overview of the construction of the PKC-SPE Cryptosystem, as depicted in Fig. 1:

1. **Polar Code Design:** The first step is to design the polar code [22], depending on system requirements, such as the desired error-correcting capability, blocklength, code rate, and the number of bits to be transmitted. The code construction and rate determination are critical in the design of polar code, as they affect the error-correcting performance and the system's BER.

2. **Key Generation:** The key generation process for the polar codes-based cryptosystem involves generating the private key P_r and public key P_b. A random binary sequence of length X is generated. Furthermore, Bhattacharyya parameters [23] are used to divide the sequence into two parts: the information bits (A) and the parity bits (A^c). Then, a generator matrix G is constructed using a polar code recursive algorithm. With random scrambling (S), permutation (P), and generator matrix G, the information bits are encoded into a codeword. The codeword is the public key, and the information bits form the private key. The parity bits are stored instead of the information bits to prevent the keys and generator matrix from adversaries.

3. **Encryption:** Before performing polar encoding, encrypt the message to be transmitted using a random scrambling matrix (S) [24].

4. **Polar Encoding:** To encode a message m, convert it into a binary sequence of length K, where $K \leq X$. The message is then encoded to an X-bit ciphertext (x) using SPE as follows:

$$x_A = u_A \cdot G_{AA} + u_{A^c} \cdot G_{A^cA} \tag{1}$$

$$x_{A^c} = x_A \cdot \mathrm{inv}(G_{AA}) \cdot G_{A^cA} \tag{2}$$

$$x = x_A + x_{A^c} \tag{3}$$

where $u_A = mS$ and u_{A^c} is taken as the zero vector. G_{AA} is the matrix whose rows and columns correspond to good bits, and G_{A^cA} is the matrix whose rows correspond to bad bits and columns correspond to good bit channels.

5. **Modulation:** The ciphertext obtained by the polar encoder is modulated onto a carrier signal and transmitted through the AWGN channel.

6. **Demodulation and Decoding:** The received signal is demodulated, and the codewords are recovered. Then, the original message is decoded using the Successive Cancellation (SC) [25] polar decoding algorithm, which iteratively computes the likelihood of the transmitted bit values and makes a decision for each bit based on these likelihoods. The likelihoods are then used to update the decision for each bit. This process continues until all the bits have been decoded or until a maximum number of iterations has been reached [26].

7. **Decryption:** The message is decrypted using the inverse of the scrambling matrix and then compared with the original message to evaluate the BER performance. The BER is then calculated by comparing the original message with the decrypted message and by counting the number of bit errors.

Example of PKC-SPE Cryptosystem

Here is an example of the PKC-SPE Cryptosystem that involves the transmission of an (8,6) polar code over an AWGN channel with a code rate of 0.75. The following example provides each step of the cryptosystem as mentioned above.

1. **Input Parameters:** $X = 8$, $K = 6$, $R = 0.75$, $E_b/N_0 = 5$
2. The Bhattacharyya parameters are computed using its formula and given as:

$$Z = [0.0093, 2.1832 \times 10^{-5}, 1.0941 \times 10^{-5}, 2.9929 \times 10^{-5},$$
$$5.4771 \times 10^{-5}, 7.4497 \times 10^{-5}, 3.7499 \times 10^{-5}, 3.5154 \times 10^{-5}]$$

3. Then, we find the good and bad bit-channels according to the Bhattacharyya parameters calculated above:

$$A = [3, 4, 5, 6, 7, 8], \quad A^c = [1, 2]$$

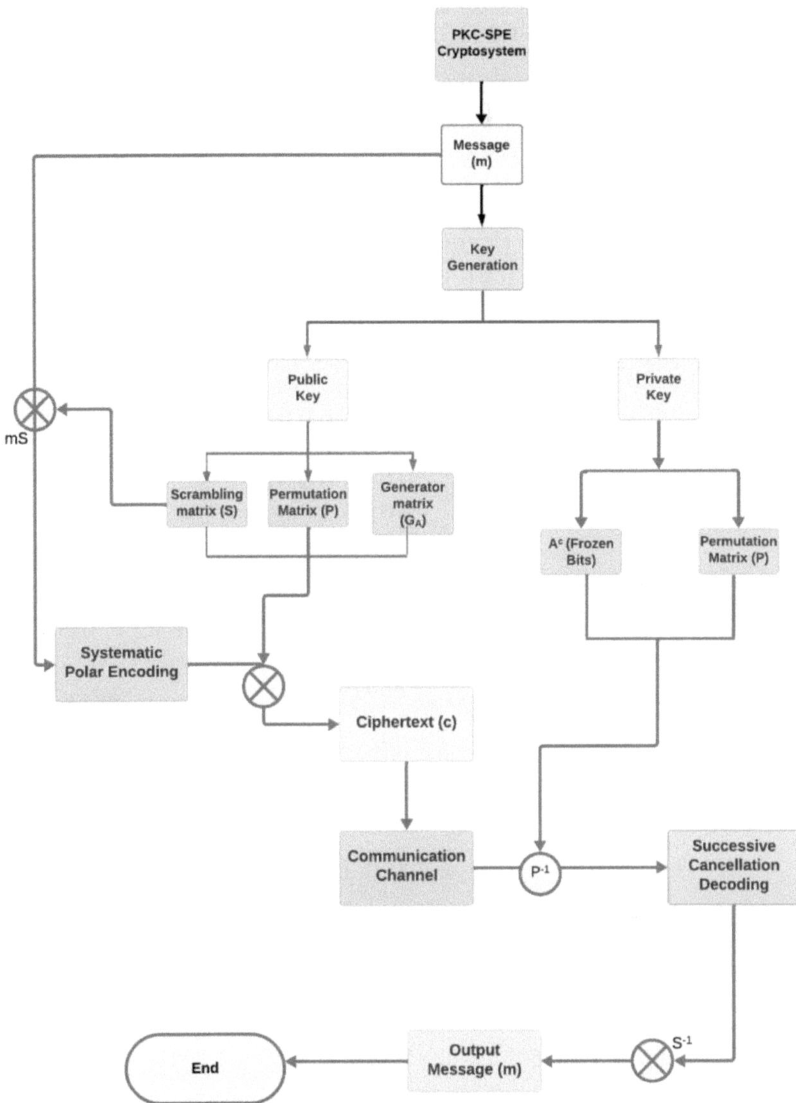

Fig. 1. Flow Chart of PKC-SPE Cryptosystem.

4. Next, compute the generator matrix using the Kronecker product and the matrix G_A obtained by taking K-rows of the generator matrix:

$$G_X = \begin{bmatrix} 1\,0\,0\,0\,0\,0\,0\,0 \\ 1\,1\,0\,0\,0\,0\,0\,0 \\ 1\,0\,1\,0\,0\,0\,0\,0 \\ 1\,1\,1\,1\,0\,0\,0\,0 \\ 1\,0\,0\,0\,1\,0\,0\,0 \\ 1\,1\,0\,0\,1\,1\,0\,0 \\ 1\,0\,1\,0\,1\,0\,1\,0 \\ 1\,1\,1\,1\,1\,1\,1\,1 \end{bmatrix} \quad G_A = \begin{bmatrix} 1\,0\,1\,0\,0\,0\,0\,0 \\ 1\,1\,1\,1\,0\,0\,0\,0 \\ 1\,0\,0\,0\,1\,0\,0\,0 \\ 1\,1\,0\,0\,1\,1\,0\,0 \\ 1\,0\,1\,0\,1\,0\,1\,0 \\ 1\,1\,1\,1\,1\,1\,1\,1 \end{bmatrix}$$

5. Compute the random scrambling matrix S having order $K \times K$:

$$S = \begin{bmatrix} 1\,0\,0\,0\,0\,0 \\ 1\,1\,0\,0\,0\,0 \\ 0\,0\,1\,0\,0\,0 \\ 0\,0\,1\,1\,0\,0 \\ 1\,0\,1\,0\,1\,0 \\ 1\,1\,1\,1\,1\,1 \end{bmatrix}$$

6. Generate a random message of length K, and compute $u_A = mS$:

$$m = [0, 1, 0, 1, 1, 0]$$

$$u_A = [0, 1, 0, 1, 1, 0]$$

7. The prepared message u_A is encrypted to obtain a ciphertext of length X-bits. The equation (1.1, 1.2, and 1.3) gives the output:

$$x = [1, 0, 0, 1, 0, 1, 1, 0]$$

$$u = [0, 0, 0, 1, 0, 1, 1, 0]$$

8. The obtained vector is transmitted over the AWGN channel and results in the output vector:

$$y = [-1.0310, 1.1676, 1.1115, -1.3323, 1.2339, -1.3041, -0.1750, 0.9728]$$

9. The simulated vector so obtained is decrypted using SC decoding, and after descrambling, it produces the same message as the original:

$$u_e = [0, 0, 0, 1, 0, 1, 1, 0], \quad \text{message} = [0, 1, 0, 1, 1, 0]$$

3 BER Performance Analysis of Proposed PKC-SPE Crysptosytem

The BER is a commonly used metric for evaluating the performance of communication systems, including cryptosystems [27]. The BER performance analysis of a cryptosystem based on polar coding involves designing the polar code, encrypting and polar encoding the message, transmitting it through two different channels AWGN and Rayleigh Fading, demodulating and decoding the received signal, decrypting the message, and evaluating the BER using simulation or theoretical analysis. Here, we evaluate the BER using simulation [16] which involves generating 10000 random messages and following the above-mentioned steps of BER performance analysis. Then, the number of bit errors and number of transmitted bits are counted, and the BER is calculated. Here, we implement our cryptosystem in MATLAB programming language and then, obtains the results provided below [28]. The performance of the cryptosystem is influenced by several factors, including channel noise, the code rate, and the block length of the polar codes used in the system. In this paper, we provide an in-depth overview of how different code rates and block lengths impact the BER performance of the PKC-SPE cryptosystem over the different channels. The AWGN channel, which adds Gaussian-distributed noise to the transmitted signal and represents idealized conditions with minimal signal distortions is distinct from the Rayleigh fading channel, which introduces more intricate signal distortions resulting from multi-path propagation effects commonly experienced in wireless communication settings.

Table 1. Bit Error Rate (BER) for Blocklength $X = 256$ for Various Code Rate

EbNo	$R = 0.98$	$R = 0.95$	$R = 0.92$	$R = 0.89$	$R = 0.86$	$R = 0.83$	$R = 0.80$
5	0.3346	0.3250	0.3214	0.3090	0.3031	0.2922	0.2874
6	0.2679	0.2603	0.2598	0.2538	0.2467	0.2429	0.2392
7	0.1926	0.1869	0.1863	0.1831	0.1783	0.1782	0.1803
8	0.1143	0.1115	0.1114	0.1103	0.1097	0.1128	0.1133
9	0.0543	0.0538	0.0552	0.0541	0.0551	0.0568	0.0609
10	0.0196	0.0193	0.0197	0.0200	0.0211	0.0233	0.0256
11	0.0058	0.0061	0.0067	0.0071	0.0076	0.0082	0.0086
12	0.0009	0.0012	0.0015	0.0020	0.0023	0.0027	0.0029
13	1.5250e-4	1.9828e-4	2.1445e-4	2.8633e-4	3.0063e-4	3.7266e-4	3.9859e-4
14	0.6972e-5	0.9974e-5	1.5744e-5	2.3934e-5	3.3580e-5	4.3900e-5	5.8281e-5

The results are summarized in Tables 1, 2, 3, 4 and 5 and Figs. 2, 3, 4 and 5, which present the average BER obtained from the simulation of 10,000 random messages under varying conditions. The selection of Energy per bit to noise power spectral density ratio (Eb/No) values is particularly significant for real-world applications, including wireless and satellite communications, where the maintenance of secure and dependable communication is crucial, despite the fluctuating conditions of the communication channel. By assessing the system's performance across this range, we can gauge how the PKC-SPE cryptosystem reacts to various levels of channel noise. The selected code rates in this study

Table 2. Bit Error Rate (BER) for Blocklength X = 512 for Various Code Rates

EbNo	R = 0.98	R = 0.95	R = 0.92	R = 0.89	R = 0.86	R = 0.83	R = 0.80
5	0.3708	0.3618	0.3545	0.3448	0.3346	0.3267	0.3169
6	0.3133	0.3059	0.3000	0.2941	0.2884	0.2801	0.2748
7	0.2346	0.2325	0.2285	0.2252	0.2215	0.2194	0.2176
8	0.1498	0.1478	0.1465	0.1468	0.1472	0.1458	0.1469
9	0.0730	0.0729	0.0748	0.0758	0.0803	0.0802	0.0816
10	0.0263	0.0284	0.0243	0.0294	0.0329	0.0339	0.0359
11	0.0065	0.0069	0.0074	0.0079	0.0089	0.0105	0.0124
12	0.0011	0.0015	0.0020	0.0026	0.0034	0.0036	0.0045
13	1.5836e-4	1.9734e-4	2.816e-4	3.5371e-4	4.1875e-4	4.9598e-4	5.5849e-4
14	1.2430e-5	1.9875e-5	3.1797e-5	4.4844e-5	5.3242e-5	5.9324e-5	6.859e-5

Table 3. Bit Error Rate (BER) for Blocklength X = 1024 for Various Code Rates

EbNo	R = 0.98	R = 0.95	R = 0.92	R = 0.89	R = 0.86	R = 0.83	R = 0.80
5	0.4026	0.3919	0.3818	0.3725	0.3632	0.3520	0.3406
6	0.3524	0.3458	0.3371	0.3302	0.3236	0.3150	0.3051
7	0.2792	0.2772	0.2719	0.2665	0.2643	0.2593	0.2536
8	0.1910	0.1880	0.1867	0.1879	0.1859	0.1835	0.1824
9	0.1004	0.0987	0.1024	0.1034	0.1041	0.1045	0.1075
10	0.0384	0.0383	0.0400	0.0412	0.0442	0.0454	0.0491
11	0.0102	0.0115	0.0118	0.0127	0.0140	0.0144	0.0166
12	0.0019	0.0022	0.0027	0.0028	0.0030	0.0037	0.0045
13	1.9853e-4	2.5527e-4	3.4277e-4	3.8281e-4	4.6943e-4	5.7744e-4	6.5205e-4
14	1.4746e-5	2.1250e-5	2.9691e-5	3.8281e-5	4.3242e-5	6.0645e-5	6.8695e-5

Table 4. Bit Error Rate (BER) for Blocklength X = 2048 for Various Code Rates

EbNo	R = 0.98	R = 0.95	R = 0.92	R = 0.89	R = 0.86	R = 0.83	R = 0.80
5	0.4262	0.4160	0.4038	0.3928	0.3816	0.3767	0.3587
6	0.3843	0.3752	0.3648	0.3587	0.3496	0.3413	0.3321
7	0.3207	0.3171	0.3108	0.3058	0.2996	0.2942	0.2881
8	0.2317	0.2309	0.2287	0.2275	0.2234	0.2249	0.2881
9	0.1339	0.1335	0.1346	0.1336	0.1369	0.1397	0.1414
10	0.0545	0.0566	0.0570	0.0583	0.0610	0.0659	0.0683
11	0.0152	0.0158	0.0170	0.0177	0.0201	0.0220	0.0248
12	0.0027	0.0030	0.0034	0.0041	0.0046	0.0055	0.0060
13	29556e-4	38008e-4	4988e-4	5957e-4	6.9932e-4	7.9624e-4	9.0889e-4
14	29053e-5	36455e-5	5022e-5	63389e-5	8.1545e-5	8.9987e-5	9.9357e-5

Table 5. BER Performance Analysis for Blocklength X = 4096 for Various Code Rate

EbNo	R = 0.98	R = 0.95	R = 0.92	R = 0.89	R = 0.86	R = 0.83	R = 0.80
5	0.4445	0.4330	0.4206	0.4090	0.3962	0.3846	0.3718
6	0.4121	0.4027	0.3923	0.3382	0.3728	0.3624	0.3515
7	0.3566	0.3505	0.3432	0.3377	0.3313	0.3233	0.3172
8	0.2743	0.2724	0.2698	0.2671	0.2631	0.2610	0.2590
9	0.1695	0.1713	0.1727	0.1741	0.1734	0.1758	0.1749
10	0.0756	0.0770	0.0786	0.0819	0.0845	0.0867	0.0891
11	0.0225	0.0230	0.0245	0.0263	0.0289	0.0311	0.0331
12	0.0042	0.0047	0.0049	0.0058	0.0064	0.0074	0.0082
13	3.3455e-4	5.1401e-4	7.1062e-4	7.9766e-4	0.0008	0.0010	0.0013
14	2.7246e-5	3.7002e-5	5.6880e-5	7.9771e-5	9.9877e-5	1.3934e-4	1.9175e-4
15	2.6855e-7	5.8799e-7	8.9790e-7	1.8828e-6	3.5869e-6	6.0641e-6	9.9846e-6

are of utmost importance as they help in striking a balance between communication efficiency and error correction capacity. On the one hand, lower code rates ensure stronger error correction at the expense of reduced data transmission rates, while higher code rates increase data rates but may compromise on robust error correction.

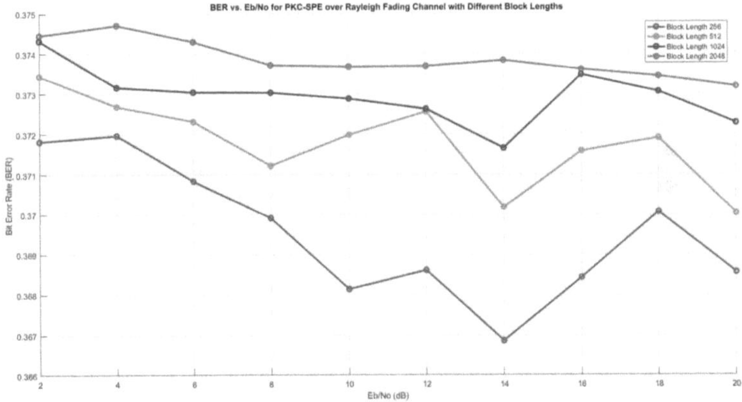

Fig. 2. BER for Various Blocklengths for code rate 0.75 over Rayleigh Fading Channel.

4   Results and Discussion

The performance evaluation of the PKC-SPE was conducted over both AWGN and Rayleigh fading channels, with a focus on the BER versus Eb/No for various

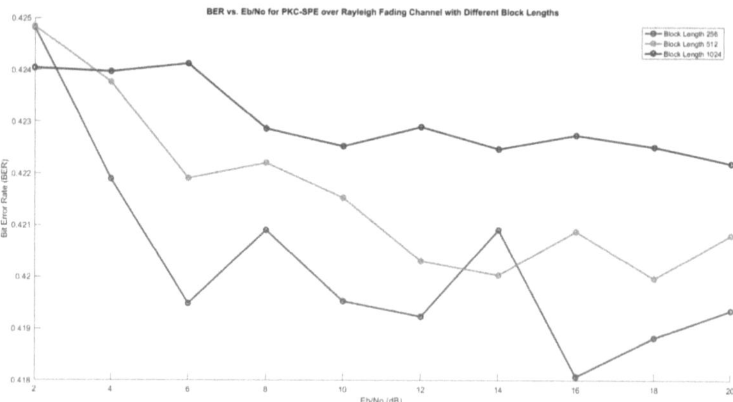

Fig. 3. BER for Various Blocklengths for code rate 0.85 over Rayleigh Fading Channel.

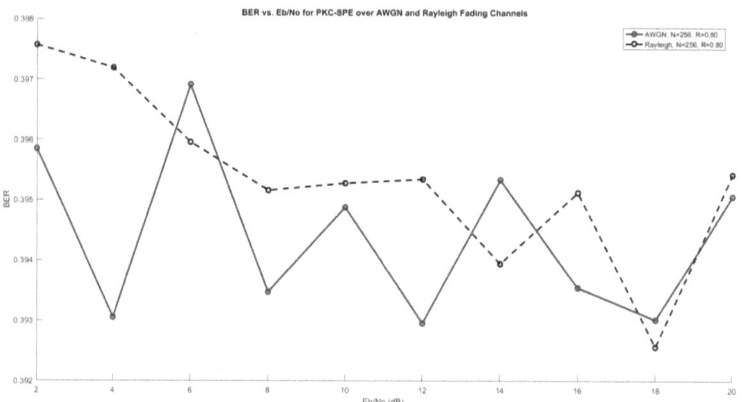

Fig. 4. BER for $X = 256$, code rate 0.80 over AWGN and Rayleigh Fading Channels.

block lengths and code rates. The BER performance of the PKC-SPE cryptosystem is provided for different block lengths and code rates over both AWGN and Rayleigh fading channels. For AWGN channel, the BER is evaluated across a range of blocklengths (256, 512, 1024, 2048, 4096) under varying code rates (0.98, 0.95, 0.92, 0.89, 0.86, 0.83, 0.8) and the results are provided in Table 1, 2, 3, 4, 5 respectively for each blocklength. For higher code rates ($R = 0.98$, 0.95), the BER is observed to be relatively higher across all block lengths. For code rates ($R = 0.92$, 0.89, 0.86), a noticeable reduction shows in BER, and it gets improved for larger blocklengths. For lower code rates ($R = 0.83, 0.8$), the BER gets more improved, indicating a strong error correcting capability. The results of the simulation of different blocklengths show that as the blocklength increases

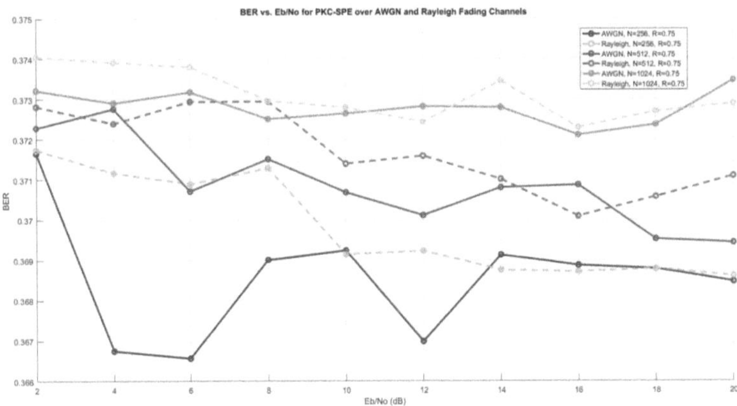

Fig. 5. BER Comparison for Various Blocklength over AWGN and Rayleigh Fading Channels.

and code rate decreases, the BER performance improves, but it happens at the expense of increased computational complexity and transmission time. For the Rayleigh Fading channel, Figs. 2 and 3 provide a more in-depth analysis of the BER performance over the channel for various block lengths (256, 512, 1024, and 2048) and different code rates. Figure 2 compares the BER performance over Rayleigh fading channels for different block lengths at a fixed code rate of 0.75. The simulation results indicate that the BER improves significantly as the block length increases from 256 to 2048, especially at higher Eb/No values. This is because larger block lengths can utilize more redundancy, which enhances error correction capabilities. Figure 3 extends this performance analysis to different code rates ($R = 0.85$), demonstrating that the trends observed are consistent with those in Fig. 2. Thus, the results further confirm that as the block length increases, the system's ability to correct errors improves significantly. Figure 4, and Fig. 5 illustrates the BER performance of the PKC-SPE system over both AWGN and Rayleigh fading channels, for different block lengths and code rates. The horizontal axis represents the (Eb/No) ratio in dB, while the vertical axis represents the corresponding BER. The results depicted in the Figs. 3 and 4 indicates that the BER performance under Rayleigh fading is consistently worse than under AWGN for the same Eb/No values. Figure 4 indicates that the cryptosystem performs better in the AWGN channel, with the BER sharply decreasing as the Eb/No increases. In contrast, the Rayleigh fading channel results in a higher BER, particularly at lower Eb/No values, reflecting the challenging conditions introduced by fading. Figure 5 depicts that as the blocklength increases from 256 to 1024, the BER decreases significantly, particularly in the Rayleigh fading channel, where larger blocklengths offer greater robustness against fading-induced distortions.

The primary findings of this analysis are:

1. Impact of Channel Models: The PKC-SPE cryptosystem demonstrates better BER performance in AWGN channels compared to Rayleigh fading channels. This outcome is expected, as AWGN channels introduce only additive noise without the intricate fading effects that are present in wireless communication environments.
2. Effect of Block Length: The BER performance improves as the blocklength increases. This is because larger blocklengths facilitate more efficient error correction, particularly in Rayleigh fading channels where multi-path effects and signal fluctuations are more pronounced.
3. Code Rate Influence: The use of higher code rates ($R = 0.80$) results in slightly higher BER compared to lower code rates ($R = 0.75$). This is expected, as higher code rates provide less redundancy for error correction, which can lead to increased error rates, particularly in noisy channels.

Thus, the code rate, blocklength, and the strength of the channel noise all play a role in determining the BER performance and a trade-off must be made between the error-correcting capability, computational complexity, and transmission time of the cryptosystem. The BER performance analysis of the PKC-SPE cryptosystem indicates that systematic polar encoding is a robust and reliable scheme, particularly when configured with longer blocklengths and lower code rates. The cryptosystem exhibits excellent performance in AWGN channels, with significantly lower BER compared to Rayleigh fading channels. However, even in the presence of fading, the cryptosystem shows good resilience, particularly when using larger block lengths and lower code rates. These findings demonstrate the robustness and reliability of systematic polar encoding in both idealized and challenging communication environments, making it a promising approach for post-quantum cryptography applications.

5   Conclusion

We investigated the BER performance analysis of the PKC-SPE for the AWGN and Rayleigh Fading channels in this paper. The performance of the PKC-SPE was extensively evaluated through simulations of 10,000 random messages over both AWGN and Rayleigh fading channels. Our results indicate that PKC-SPE demonstrates strong BER performance in AWGN channels, but its performance is impacted by multipath fading in Rayleigh fading channels. However, even under these challenging conditions, PKC-SPE maintains robust communication capabilities. These findings suggest that PKC-SPE is well-suited for secure communication systems, particularly in scenarios where channel noise is a significant concern. With its ability to handle both AWGN and Rayleigh fading environments, PKC-SPE shows potential as a viable solution for real-world wireless communication applications that require both reliability and security. Future research focuses on further optimizing the cryptosystem to reduce BER in more intricate fading environments and explore its implementation in practical communication systems.

Acknowledgments. This research did not receive any specific grant from funding agencies in the public, commercial, or not-for-profit sectors.

Disclosure of Interests. The authors have no competing interests to declare that are relevant to the content of this article.

References

1. Ritu, N., Narwal, E., Gill, S.: A novel cipher technique using substitution and transposition methods. In: Rising Threats in Expert Applications and Solutions. Lecture Notes in Networks and Systems, vol. 434, pp. 123–129. Springer, Singapore (2022). https://doi.org/10.1007/978-981-19-1122-4_14
2. Narwal, E., Ritu, N., Deepika.: ERN cryptosystem for the security of textual data based on modified classical encryption techniques. Indian J. Sci. Technol. **16**(4), 292–298 (2023). https://doi.org/10.17485/IJST/v16i4.2009
3. Zhou, X., Tang, X.: Research and implementation of RSA algorithm for encryption and decryption. In: Proceedings of 2011 6th International Forum on Strategic Technology, pp. 1118–1121. IEEE, Harbin (2011). https://doi.org/10.1109/IFOST.2011.6021216
4. Li, N.: Research on Diffie-Hellman key exchange protocol. In: 2010 2nd International Conference on Computer Engineering and Technology, pp. V4-634–V4-637. IEEE, Chengdu (2010). https://doi.org/10.1109/ICCET.2010.5485276
5. Gura, N., Patel, A., Wander, A., Eberle, H., Shantz, S.C.: Comparing elliptic curve cryptography and RSA on 8-bit CPUs. In: Joye, M., Quisquater, J.-J. (eds.) CHES 2004. LNCS, vol. 3156, pp. 119–132. Springer, Heidelberg (2004). https://doi.org/10.1007/978-3-540-28632-5_9
6. Shor, P.W.: Algorithms for quantum computation: discrete logarithms and factoring. In: 35th Annual Symposium on Foundations of Computer Science, pp. 124–134. IEEE (1994)
7. Kumar, M.: Post-quantum cryptography Algorithm's standardization and performance analysis. Array **15**, 100242 (2022)
8. Yalamuri, G., Honnavalli, P., Eswaran, S.: A review of the present cryptographic arsenal to deal with post-quantum threats. Procedia Comput. Sci. **215**, 834–845 (2022)
9. Sharma, S., Ramkumar, K.R., Kaur, A., Hasija, T., Mittal, S., Singh, B.: Post-quantum cryptography: a solution to the challenges of classical encryption algorithms. In: Lecture Notes in Electrical Engineering, vol. 948, pp. 23–38. Springer, Singapore (2023)
10. Balamurugan, C., Singh, K., Ganesan, G., Rajarajan, M.: Code-based post-quantum cryptography. The Multidisciplinary Preprint Platform (2021). https://doi.org/10.20944/preprints202104.0734.v1
11. Kumar, M., Pattnaik, P.: Post quantum cryptography (PQC) - an overview. In: 2020 IEEE High Performance Extreme Computing Conference (HPEC), pp. 1–9. IEEE (2020)
12. Arikan, E.: Channel polarization: a method for constructing capacity-achieving codes for symmetric binary-input memoryless channels. IEEE Trans. Inf. Theory **55**(7), 3051–3073 (2009)
13. Redhu, R., Narwal, E.: Polar code-based cryptosystem: comparative study and analysis of efficiency. Indones. J. Electr. Eng. Comput. Sci. **32**(2), 804–810 (2023)

14. Wang, X., et al.: An optimized encoding algorithm for systematic polar codes. EURASIP J. Wirel. Commun. Netw. **2019**(1), 1–12 (2019). https://doi.org/10.1186/s13638-019-1491-4
15. McEliece, R.J.: A Public-Key Cryptosystem Based on Algebraic Coding Theory. DNS Progress Report, Jet Propulsion Laboratory, pp. 114–116 (1978)
16. Yu, C., Lin, Z.H., Hsu, T.W., Chen, M.W., Chen, Y.A.: Lower bit-error-rate polar-LDPC concatenated coding for wireless communication systems. In: 2017 IEEE 6th Global Conference on Consumer Electronics (GCCE), pp. 1–2. IEEE (2017)
17. Bae, J.H., Abotabl, A., Lin, H.P., Song, K.B., Lee, J.: An overview of channel coding for 5G NR cellular communications. APSIPA Trans. Signal Inf. Process. **8**(1) (2019)
18. Sharma, N., Jain, D., Bhatt, K., Themalil, M.T.: Performance comparison of various digital modulation schemes based on bit error rate under AWGN channel. In: 2021 5th International Conference on Computing Methodologies and Communication (ICCMC), pp. 619–623. IEEE (2021)
19. Redhu, R., Narwal, E.: PKC-SPE: a variant of the McEliece cryptosystem based on systematic polar encoding. Int. J. Comput. Sci. Math. **20**(1), 32–45 (2024)
20. Korrapati, V., et al.: A study on performance evaluation of Reed Solomon codes through an AWGN channel model for an efficient communication system. Int. J. Eng. Trends Technol. **4**(4) (2013). http://www.ijettjournal.org
21. Cheng, J., Li, H., Ye, M., Wang, L., Zhang, C.: Systematic polar codes based on 3×3 kernel matrix. In: 2019 International Conference on Communications, Information System and Computer Engineering (CISCE), pp. 77–79. IEEE (2019)
22. Niu, K., Li, Y.: Polar codes for fast fading channel: design based on polar spectrum. IEEE Trans. Veh. Technol. **69**(9), 10103–10114 (2020)
23. Xiong, J., Zhang, L.: Simplified calculation of bhattacharyya parameters in polar codes. In: 2020 IEEE 14th International Conference on Anti-counterfeiting, Security, and Identification (ASID), pp. 169–173. IEEE (2020)
24. Cyriac, A., Narayanan, G.: Polar code encoder and decoder implementation. In: 2018 3rd International Conference on Communication and Electronics Systems (ICCES), pp. 294–302. IEEE (2018)
25. Badar, S.P., Khanchandani, K.: Successive cancellation polar decoder implementation using processing elements. In: 2022 IEEE Region 10 Symposium (TENSYMP), pp. 1–6. IEEE (2022). https://doi.org/10.1109/TENSYMP54529.2022.9864529
26. Chiu, M.-C.: Analysis and design of polar-coded modulation. IEEE Trans. Commun. **70**(3), 1508–1521 (2022)
27. Wang, Q., Zhou, W., Zhang, S., Wang, S.: Performance analysis of polar codes for wireless sensor networks. In: Proceedings of the 2019 IEEE 9th International Conference on Electronics Information and Emergency Communication (ICEIEC), pp. 1–5. IEEE (2019)
28. Redhu, R., Narwal, E., Gupta, S., Hooda, R., Ahlawat, S., Khurana, R.: Software implementation of systematic polar encoding-based PKC-SPE cryptosystem for quantum cybersecurity. Sci. Rep. **14**(1), 9994 (2024)

Security and Privacy in Web Application: Efficient Encryption Using ECC and Attribute-Based Encryption

S. Naundhini[✉], S. Anushaa, and Dharminder Chaudhary

Department of Computer Science and Engineering (Amrita School of Computing),
Amrita Vishwa Vidyapeetham, Chennai, India
naundhini@gmail.com

Abstract. The evolution of IoT and cloud computing technologies presents opportunities for developing smart education systems. However, concerns persist regarding data security and user privacy, especially in applications with sensitive data. This paper proposes a holistic approach to mitigate these risks, addressing both phishing and insider threats. To protect web applications against common vulnerabilities, the paper recommends strong encryption methods to prevent them using Elliptic Curve Cryptography and Advanced Encryption Standard for encrypting and generating secure keys. Furthermore, certain weaknesses in applications like geolocation exploitation and email authentication have been outlined in this context with specific reference to University Management Systems which is associated to Telemedical Information System. Possible mitigation measures include use of encryption and strict access control methods, as well as user awareness training. In this paper, we have used Ciphertext-Policy Attribute-Based Encryption for TMIS and ECC with AES for UMS to ensure protection against possible threats, thus preserving user privacy and system integrity.

Keywords: Telecare Medical Information System · WBAN · Elliptic Curve Cryptography

1 Introduction

In today's fast changing technological landscape, there has been a major shift with the integration of smart technologies powered by Internet of Things (IoT) and cloud computing developments, resulting in the sharing and storage of sensitive data by third-party applications [1,2]. However, there remains a constant concern about the security and privacy of sensitive data in these web applications [3]. This paper seeks to address these challenges, presenting a multifaceted approach to risk mitigation, though strategies that are universally relevant across many applications.

Cyber-attacks are a serious concern, as they exploit weaknesses to get access to sensitive user data such as bank details and location information [4]. To

S. Pal et al. (Eds.): ICETSS 2024, CCIS 2610, pp. 111–125, 2026.
https://doi.org/10.1007/978-3-032-11488-4_9

overcome this, the paper recommends combining Elliptic Curve Cryptography (ECC) and Advanced Encryption Standard (AES) for key creation and secure encryption. Proposed solutions include strict access controls, such as Attribute-Based Encryption (ABE) on top of encryption.

1.1 Domain Introduction

The incorporation of IoT with cloud computing technologies has resulted in a significant evolution, allowing for enhanced data interchange and storage among third-party apps. This development has raised concerns about security and confidentiality of sensitive data. This paper aims to present a comprehensive strategy to address these challenges, with solutions that may be used for a variety of sectors.

1.2 Problem Identification

The rapid integration of smart technologies, particularly IoT and cloud computing, has resulted in a considerable increase in the sharing and storage of sensitive data across web apps and third-party platforms. This convergence has led in the establishment of several third-party programs for data exchange and storage, generating serious concerns about security and privacy. Exploitations of common vulnerabilities, and the vital need to safeguard externally stored data have emerged as major challenges, particularly in education-centric programs such as UMS and medical platforms such as Telemedical Information System (TMIS). The lack of strong encryption mechanisms and adequate management of important security procedures increases these concerns, posing major threats to data integrity and user privacy. Thus, there is an urgent need to address these difficulties to strengthen security measures and maintain user privacy standards.

1.3 Problem Statement

Designing and implementing a comprehensive and robust security framework is necessary for TMIS integrated with Wireless Body Area Networks (WBAN). These systems face diverse security challenges, including vulnerability to various cyber threats due to data transmission through public channels. The demand from patients for greater control over their sensitive health information to safeguard their privacy introduces additional complexity. Storing data centrally in cloud servers exposes it to potential risks such as unauthorized access and tampering, requiring stringent protective measures. Therefore, a comprehensive approach is needed to tackle these challenges over technological risks.

1.4 Significance

The significance of implementing efficient encryption using ECC and ABE in web applications lies in enhancing security measures. By employing advanced encryption techniques, the confidentiality and integrity of sensitive data transmitted over applications can be significantly strengthened. ECC offers strong cryptographic algorithms suitable for resource-constrained environments, while ABE provides fine-grained access control, allowing users to access data based on their attributes. Together, these methods address security concerns such as data breaches, unauthorized access, and data tampering, thereby strengthening overall cybersecurity in web applications.

2   Literature Survey

We have compared certain relevant literatures from the recent years that implement security in TMIS using various cryptographic techniques in WBAN devices as well as in servers. We have considered literature using various architectures to find out what does not work out in it or how we can better optimize it.

2.1   Study of Various Literatures

S. Ding et al. explores the complexities of data security in open distributed computing environments, with a focus on IoT platforms [5]. It explores PF-CP-ABE, which aims to solve the urgent problem of protecting data kept in the cloud and accessed by numerous IoT devices. However, it has some drawbacks. Risk is introduced by the scheme's dependence on a trusted attribute authority to perform essential functions including attribute key generation, issuance, and revocation. The overall security and operation of the scheme could be seriously compromised in the case that this authority is hacked or becomes unavailable.

Madhusudhan et al. identified the weaknesses present in the authentication scheme proposed by Li et al. [6,7] like being vulnerable to user impersonation, password guessing attacks and that it does not provide user anonymity or security to session key. Thus, they have put forward a new algorithm for user authentication using Chebyshev chaotic maps. The user first registers themselves on the server wherein the user receives a smart card from the server. The user can then login by inserting the smart card into a card reader and entering their id and password. Then the server and client authenticate each other. It also explains mechanisms to change password and revoking smart card.

Sudeep Tanwar et al. proposes a blockchain based scheme to access patient records in the healthcare industry [8]. The records can be accessed by several entities such as doctors, insurance providers and so on. These participants first get Membership by registering and then they are assigned a role according to which they can access data and can perform actions. It also has lower computational overhead so that it can be used freely. It also has a low latency and is suitable for real time applications.

Anjali Singh et al. performs cryptanalysis on Amin and Biswas' scheme that provides three factor authentication and key agreement and preserves anonymity of the user [9, 10]. But it fails to offer user anonymity as the attacker can guess the identity of a user and backtrack to check if it is right. It also does not provide forward secrecy as revealing one sessions password means that the attacker can access previous sessions data due to lack of timestamp or random numbers. It is also prone to forgery attack as both ID and password can be obtained through above mentioned techniques. It does not ensure mutual authentication.

Venkatasamy Sureshkumar et al. performs cryptanalysis on the authentication scheme proposed by Madhusudhan-Nayak and proposes a new scheme that overcomes drawbacks, which is vulnerable to identity guessing attack [6,11]. Server impersonation attack can also be done after guessing identity because the message sent to the user does not contain any of the server's secrets. Replay attack is also successful. The proposed protocol has XOR and thus the attacker cannot confirm if the identity they guessed is correct. They also cannot perform server impersonation as secret key is used. Replay attack is avoided by including timestamps. Overall, the proposed protocol has lesser costs.

Jin Li et al. devised a solution for challenges faced by users with limited resources in cloud computing environments [12]. The main aim was to overcome the challenges posed by ABE while solving heavy computational burden and insufficient secure data storage. The study presents a novel strategy that is specific to mobile users operating in cloud environments. The plan also includes a ciphertext validation procedure that checks the ciphertexts' integrity before decrypting it. By taking this step, computational resources are not needlessly wasted trying to decipher inaccurate or incorrect ciphertexts. An increased level of security is attained by this frequent encryption process, supporting data protection systems against potential threats.

Bander A. Alzahrani et al. proposes a lightweight protocol to authenticate the participating entities securely [13]. It consists of two network models: a system consisting of all the nodes as well as communication between them and an attack model that tells us about all the possible capabilities of adversaries. They then review an existing protocol proposed by Xu et al. and discusses its drawbacks [14]. Then, a new protocol is proposed has an additional ID computation process by the hub node to protect against replay attack. Impersonation attack is also avoided by adding a timestamp. The adversary also cannot perform guessing attack as the identity of the user is bound by a one-way hashing function.

Ruhul Amin et al. emphasizes on patient anonymity and untraceability and demonstrates how Das et al.'s protocols can be compromised by attacks resulting in loss of patient anonymity, loss of traceability and attacks like smartcard launch attack [4,15]. The proposed protocol uses medical physician server, registration server, patients and medical servers that are present in diverse locations to provide service to the several patients. Each medical server registers with the medical registration server and each physician server must register with the home medical server. Each patient must register with nearby medical server and get a session key from the physician server after logging in using smart card. Mutual authentication is done in this phase. It also has the features of new physician server addition, password update and biometric renewal.

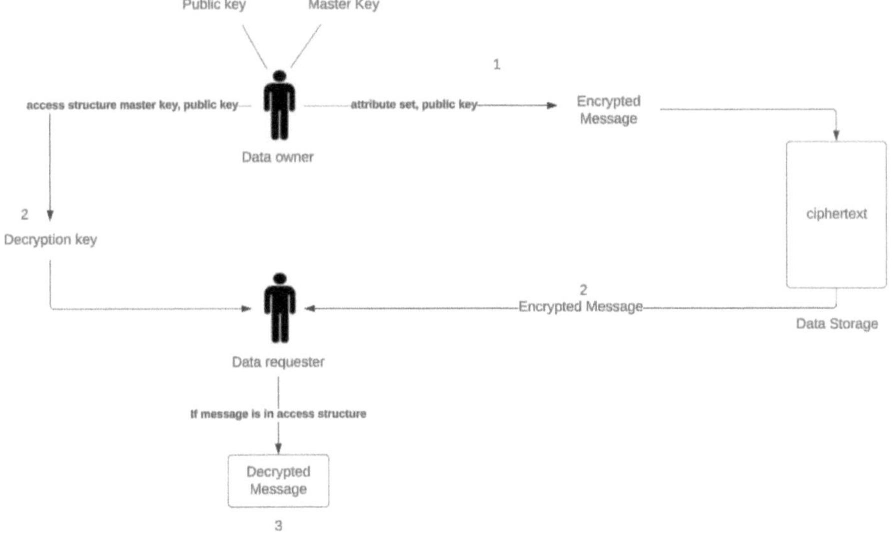

Fig. 1. Architecture of the protocol.

3 System Design

In this project, we first started by studying several papers, researching about existing models in the field of TMIS, the flaws present and how they have been overcome. We also studied papers on the cryptanalysis of existing protocols that were assumed to have perfect security. Then, we studied papers on access control, its benefits, and ABAC.

First, we construct an encryption scheme that is feasible in the WBAN environment, which means using a lightweight protocol that consumes less storage and has low computational costs. Then, we implement CP-ABAC (Cipher Policy-Attribute Based Access Control) such that the user needs to satisfy a set of attributes to access the data.

3.1 Methodology For Executing the Project

TMIS and UMS over the internet may result in compromise of the CIA triad: Confidentiality, Integrity, and Availability. So, we need mechanisms to ensure that each session that is established will provide security and that all data that is sent and received is encrypted using a secure secret key.

In this architecture (Fig. 1), the important entities include the data owner and the data requester who interact with the data storage via internet. The data owner chooses an elliptic curve and a point over it along and generates a private key. It then reveals the public parameters to everyone. Each patient registers themselves with the server which stores their information in the database.

Here, the patient is the source of data. They have various sensors all over their body that might calculate several parameters like steps walked, calories burnt, prescription, ailments, etc. The user can login to the system through their device and access their information after entering their credentials. When the patient registers, they enter their Identity and password. Hashes of these are found and sent to the database through a secure channel, which instead of storing the actual data received, stores only the hash of password. It only stores the encrypted data of user details.

The admin creates and access tree where attributes are present and the level a user can access is decided by what attributes they satisfy. The patient can login into the application by giving the same details they gave during registration. The credentials are then validated and access is provided according to the access tree. A timestamp is to be included to prevent replay attacks. During this process, public key and private key of the current session is established. Also, doctors and healthcare systems can access the secure data from telecare server through a secure channel. This process assumes that everyone trying to access data from inside the hospital are verified. Thus, now the patient can securely access appropriate data such as prescriptions and diagnosis.

A patient can encrypt their medical records with attributes as: Hospital A, Hospital B, doctor, nurse. They can also have access control policy as: Hospital A and nurse or doctor or Hospital B and nurse or doctor This means any nurse or doctor at either hospital views the records. Figure 2 shows this working.

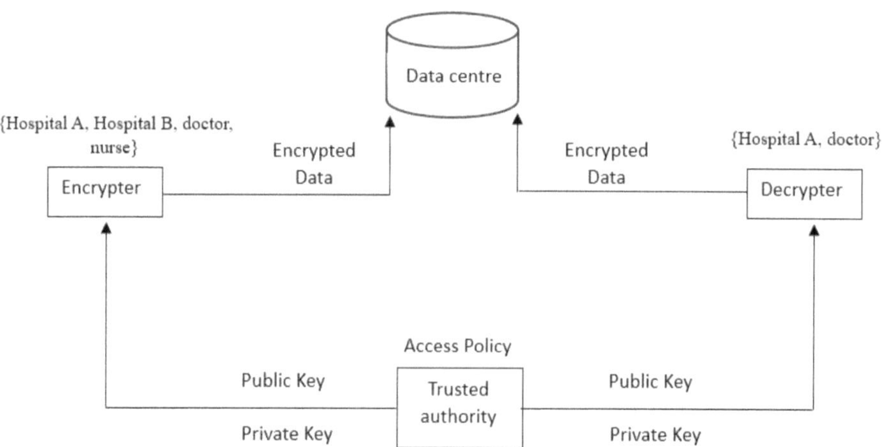

Fig. 2. Working of Attribute Based Encryption.

4   Proposed Model

4.1   ECC-AES Encryption

In our model, we are using a cryptography method by combining ECC with AES (Fig. 3) We are choosing ECC for key generation as it gives a high level of security compared to other algorithms for the same key size, thus giving increased efficiency and faster computation. AES on the other hand ensures fast data encryption, being a symmetric algorithm. Thus, we combine both to create a model that overcomes their inherent disadvantages and has the strengths of both.

Pseudo Code: Input is the plain text and ECC public key. Output is the encrypted message.

1. Import necessary libraries.
2. Initialize brainpoolP256r1 curve.
3. Define function to convert an ECC point to 256 bit key (`ecc_point_to_256_bit_key`).
4. Convert the x-coordinate of the point to bytes.
5. Update the hash object with the y-coordinate of the point.
6. Compute the digest of the hash and return it as the 256-bit key.
7. Generate a random ECC private key using `secrets.randbelow` function.
8. Calculate ECC shared key by multiplying the random private key with the ECC public key.
9. Derive a 256-bit secret key and initialize AES cipher with the secret key.
10. Encrypt the message and obtain the ciphertext, retrieve the nonce, and authentication tag.
11. Calculate the public key by multiplying it with the base point of the ECC curve.
12. Return ciphertext, nonce, authentication tag, and ciphertext public key.

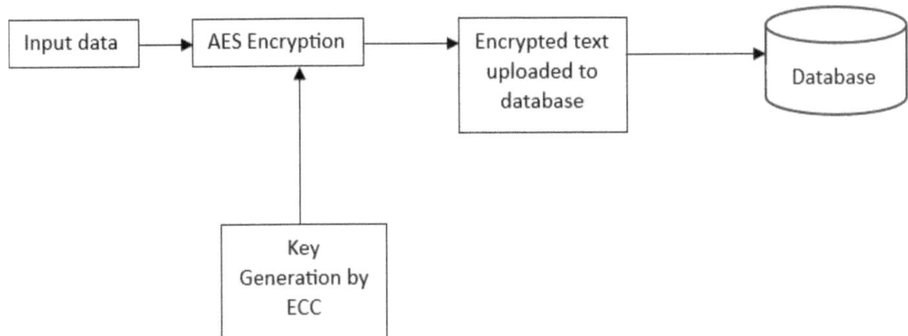

Fig. 3. Encryption of text using ECC-AES algorithm.

4.2   University Management System

This model guarantees that the right individuals are engaging in communication and that their sensitive information remains protected throughout. The system also asks the users for change of password to maintain a high level of security. We have described a model which involves four phases. They are:

1. Initialization: The system establishes the basic requirements needed for secure communication which involves selecting a specific elliptic curve and a private key, which helps in encryption and authentication.
2. Registration: Both students and lecturers go through a secure registration process managed by an admin. They create passwords that are securely transmitted to the database after being hashed, and generate their own private keys for secure communication.
3. Login: Users use their identifiers and passwords to log into the system. The system verifies their identities by comparing the provided information with the database. Additionally, the admin must enter a current code from their authenticator app for further security.
4. Authentication: The system verifies the login information to confirm the user's identity. If authentication is successful, the user is granted access to the system based on their access levels.

4.3   Telemedical Information System

We propose a TMIS system that will help to keep the information of users safe. The steps are as follows.

1. Authentication: Users give their email and password on the sign-in page which are then validated against the database and access is granted based on user's role. This ensures that the system can only be accessed by valid users.
2. Dashboard Display: The user is automatically forwarded to their dashboard according to their designated role upon successful authentication.
   (a) Doctor Dashboard: Here the doctor can access patient records for viewing and updating purpose. They can also manage appointments (scheduling, rescheduling, cancellation) or use the chat feature for communication with nurses and pharmacists.
   (b) Nurse Dashboard: It has similar functionality to the doctor dashboard. We can add scan reports, check patient information, and provide patient support under doctor's direction.
   (c) Pharmacist Dashboard: Allows access to patient prescription updates, inventory management (medication status, stock updates, etc.), communication with staff and appointment section to contact suppliers.

5   Implementation

We use the tinyec library to generate a private-public key pair for the message recipient, and derive a secret shared key for encryption ans also a ciphertext public key from the recipient's public key. Later, we derive the same secret shared key, which is used for decryption, from the receiver's private key and previously generated ciphertext public key. We then use the secret key for symmetric data encryption. Also, we have implemented CP-ABE, where the user can only decrypt data and read it if the all the attributes assigned to them satisfy the condition on access tree defined by the administrator. The attributes of access tree is used to encrypt the data.

CP-ABE with concealed access policies enables data owners to securely share encrypted information with authorized users while keeping the control policies confidential. Nevertheless, data owners may inadvertently release sensitive or conflicting data, potentially disclosing confidential details. Data encryption works by hiding personal details using attributes. The attributes make up rules that decide who can access the data. Data owners use CP-ABE to share encrypted info with only approved people. It helps by partially hiding the access control rules from view by encrypting personal info based on attributes in an access tree. Only authorized users, with the right mix of attributes, can decrypt the data. The control policies stay confidential, thus boosting privacy while letting data owners share encrypted content safely.

To implement this, we have designed a UMS where there are three types of users as show in Fig. 4. The admin must use their registered mobile to access a code through google authenticator and login, after entering their credentials. Only the admin has access to create and delete other users such as lecturers and students. They can also add Programs and Courses, sessions, and semesters. The lecturer can add or modify course materials, create quizzes, and see students' marks. They can also manage the scores of students and view their CGPA. Students have access to course materials and can take quizzes. They can also register for courses. Here, the details of students such as phone number, address and email are encrypted to provide confidentiality to sensitive data.

There are four types of users present in TMIS as shown in Fig. 5. There are two login pages, for patients, and workers. Patients can sign up, whereas, the worker profiles are created by admin. The workers are divided into doctor, nurse, and pharmacist. All three users log in through the same page but access data as per the access tree. When a user logs in, their ID and hashed password is sent to database to confirm and access is granted accordingly. The patient's data is encrypted to protect their privacy.

6   Result and Analysis

TMIS admin portal simplifies the process for administrators to eliminate current lecturers by selecting and deleting their profiles from the system. Admins can generate posts and events using the UMS. Doctors can view and modify patient

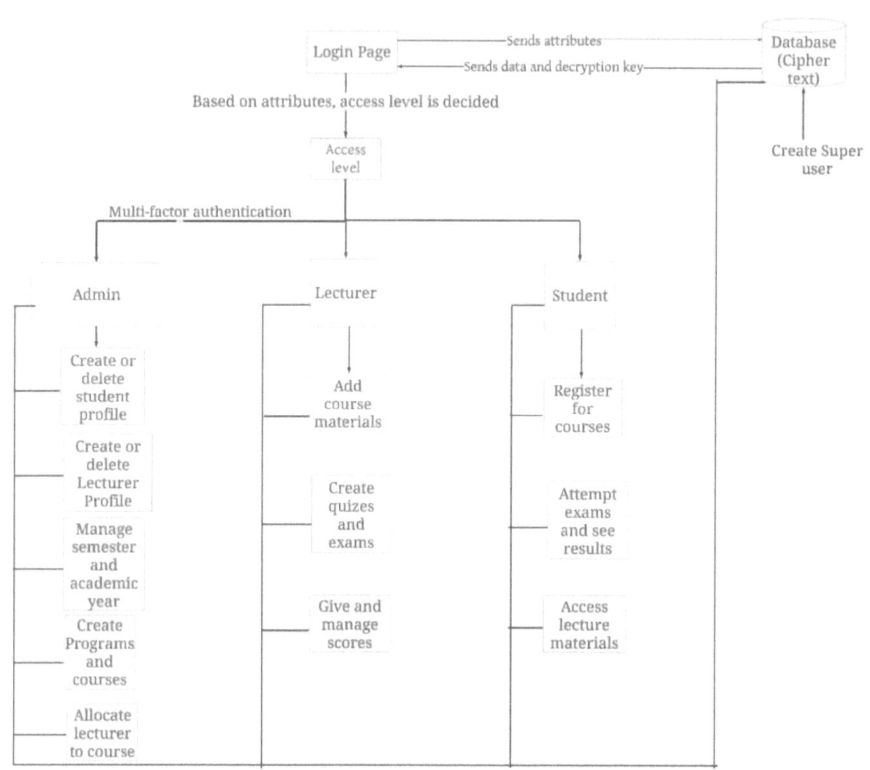

Fig. 4. Flowchart of University Management System.

lists directly from the TMIS dashboard. This improves patient management by making it easy to change patient information and treatment plans within the system. UMS uses encryption (Fig. 6) to protect sensitive data in its database, including passwords and personal information. Even if unwanted access occurs, the encrypted data remains unreadable in the absence of the right decryption keys, assuring strong security. TMIS database (Fig. 7) is encrypted to protect critical patient information. This ensures that even if unwanted access happens, the data is illegible without the right decryption keys, preserving the system's confidentiality.

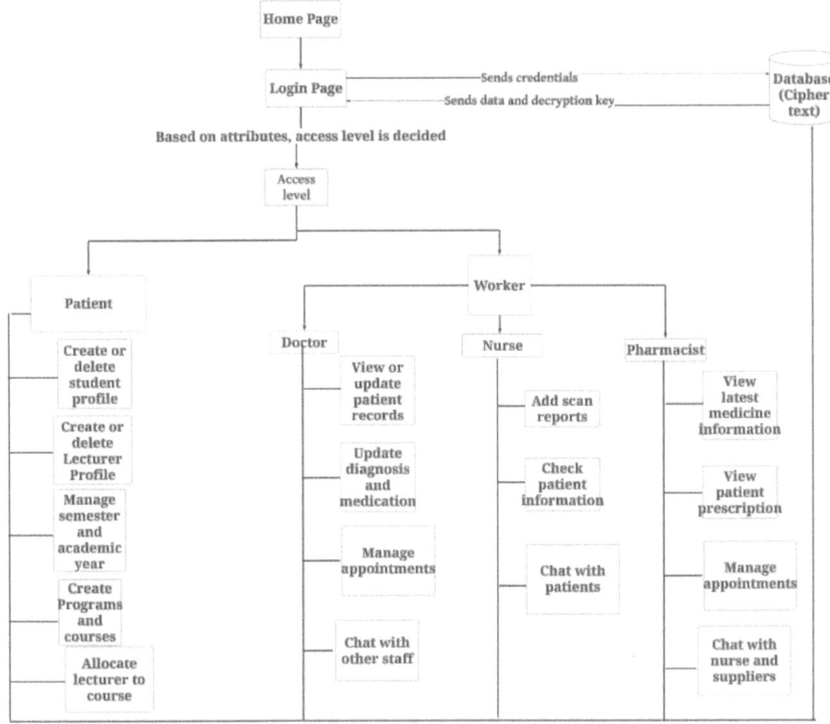

Fig. 5. Flowchart of Telecare medical information system.

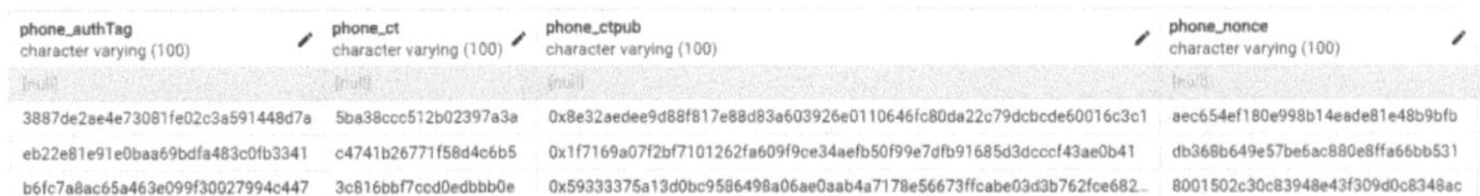

Fig. 6. Encrypted data in UMS database.

To evaluate the performance and security aspects of the Hybrid, AES, and DES algorithms, time taken for encryption (Fig. 8) as well as decryption (Fig. 9) are compared across different key sizes to identify efficiency and security consequences.

_id: ObjectId('660f90f901f3d25919f35bea')
public_id : "23871ae26ccb42959ff995e0f3474010"
▾ fname : Object
    ciphertext : "ccc73bb4406f5e"
    nonce : "d59b86467465122da7c06a3f7404a048"
    authTag : "640e966cb24eb8b55315e4be4d09004f"
    ciphertextPubKey : "0x6e6c7da36354df279c4d996e55b2362f1bdd0b971d2d6fc338bf6abbb916e6ac0"
▾ lname : Object
    ciphertext : "9a74ea"
    nonce : "0c969578fb682c4a4e8392b064bef1e7"
    authTag : "2b7909b6892ea45edd2526438a8eeb11"
    ciphertextPubKey : "0x633d17d6b9d47be5b6366efe07d5ae7de1fd60ea871d241b41b5eaf85bffa1751"
▾ email : Object
    ciphertext : "0e270cd3b560a48f28a616085365b98407eade"
    nonce : "2c48934ce070223f25243c6f4bb33ff5"
    authTag : "a00ba36462a5b8c548ef6fd83c1f6aab"
    ciphertextPubKey : "0x5b60d65f26b734b3195b11c6d9f0aff8935a27cd3b98f7a046aebef2e61ba0a80"
  password : "$2b$12$DVVkTgnBB6WFH/CxtuhYZ.FbDFXICdDC231iabRxAAhcH.OaiTNi2"

Fig. 7. Encrypted data in TMIS database.

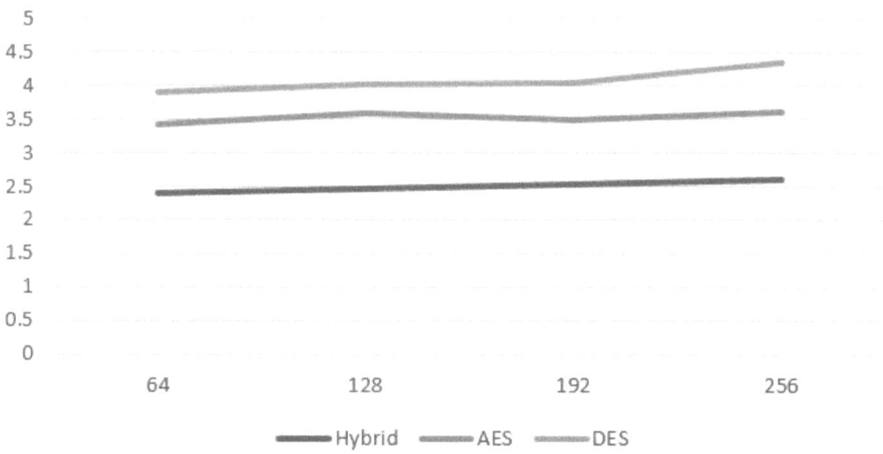

Fig. 8. Encryption time calculated using different key sizes.

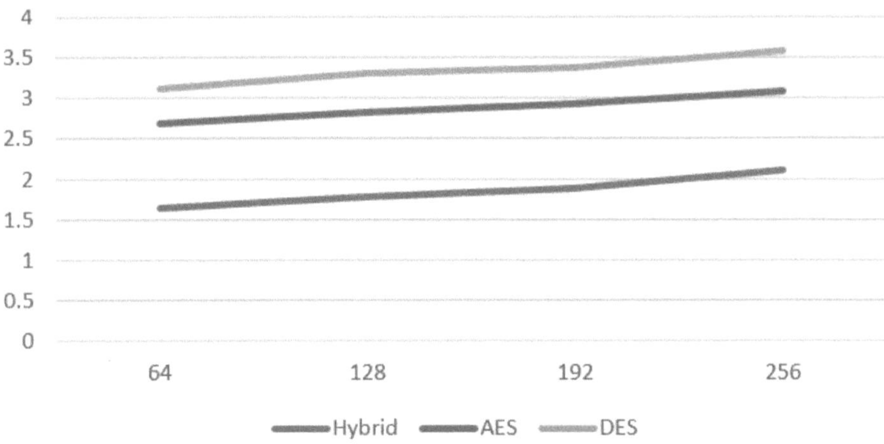

Fig. 9. Decryption time calculated using different key sizes.

7   Conclusion

Thus, we have developed a considerably secure encryption scheme and access control scheme that is resilient to most of the attacks and has novel security features thus making it a secure protocol. The type of data out there keeps changing and thus we need to ensure that our protocol can evolve to accommodate changing features and algorithms. We need to keep updating the scheme to ensure that we are protected from different attacks that come up later.

Acknowledgments. This research did not receive any specific grant from funding agencies in the public, commercial, or not-for-profit sectors.

Disclosure of Interests. The authors have no competing interests to declare that are relevant to the content of this article.

References

1. Ouaddah, A., Mousannif, H., Abou Elkalam, A., Ait Ouahman, A.: Access control in the Internet of Things: big challenges and new opportunities. Comput. Netw. **112**, 237–262 (2017)
2. Son, S., Lee, J., Kim, M., Yu, S., Das, A.K., Park, Y.: Design of secure authentication protocol for cloud-assisted telecare medical information system using blockchain. IEEE Access **8**, 192177–192191 (2020)

3. Singh, G., Garg, S.: Fuzzy elliptic curve cryptography based cipher text policy attribute based encryption for cloud security. In: 2020 International Conference on Intelligent Engineering and Management (ICIEM), pp. 327–330. IEEE, London (2020). https://doi.org/10.1109/ICIEM48762.2020.9159961

4. Amin, R., Islam, S.H., Gope, P., Choo, K.K.R., Tapas, N.: Anonymity preserving and lightweight multimedical server authentication protocol for telecare medical information system. IEEE J. Biomed. Health Inform. **23**, 1749–1759 (2019)

5. Ding, S., Li, C., Li, H.: A novel efficient pairing-free CP-ABE based on elliptic curve cryptography for IoT. IEEE Access **6**, 27336–27345 (2018)

6. Mir, O., van der Weide, T., Lee, C.-C.: A secure user anonymity and authentication scheme using AVISPA for telecare medical information systems. J. Med. Syst. **39**(9), 1–16 (2015). https://doi.org/10.1007/s10916-015-0265-8

7. Li, C.-T., Lee, C.-C., Weng, C.-Y., Chen, S.-J.: A secure dynamic identity and chaotic maps based user authentication and key agreement scheme for e-healthcare systems. J. Med. Syst. **40**(11), 1–10 (2016). https://doi.org/10.1007/s10916-016-0586-2

8. Tanwar, S., Parekh, K., Evans, R.: Blockchain-based electronic healthcare record system for healthcare 4.0 applications. J. Inf. Secur. Appl. **50**, 102407 (2020)

9. Singh, A., Karuppiah, M., Mahapatra, R.P.: Cryptanalysis on a secure three-factor user authentication and key agreement protocol for TMIS with user anonymity. Cyber Secur. Appl. **1**, 100008 (2023). https://doi.org/10.1016/j.csa.2022.100008

10. Amin, R., Biswas, G.P.: A secure three-factor user authentication and key agreement protocol for TMIS with user anonymity. J. Med. Syst. **39**(1), 1–19 (2015)

11. Sureshkumar, V., Amin, R., Obaidat, M.S., Karthikeyan, I.: An enhanced mutual authentication and key establishment protocol for TMIS using chaotic map. J. Inf. Secur. Appl. **53**, 102539 (2020)

12. Li, J., Zhang, Y., Chen, X., Xiang, Y.: Secure attribute-based data sharing for resource-limited users in cloud computing. Comput. Secur. **72**, 1–12 (2018). https://doi.org/10.1016/j.cose.2017.08.007

13. Alzahrani, B.A., Irshad, A., Albeshri, A., et al.: A provably secure and lightweight patient-healthcare authentication protocol in wireless body area networks. Wirel. Pers. Commun. **117**, 47–69 (2021)

14. Xu, Z., Xu, C., Chen, H., Yang, F.: A lightweight anonymous mutual authentication and key agreement scheme for WBAN. Concurr. Comput. Pract. Exp. **31**(19), 1–15 (2019)

15. Das, A.K., Odelu, V., Goswami, A.: A secure and robust user authenticated key agreement scheme for hierarchical multi-medical server environment in TMIS. J. Med. Syst. **39**(92), 1–9 (2015)

16. Kumar, C.M., Amin, R., Brindha, M.: Cryptanalysis of secure ECC-based three-factor mutual authentication protocol for telecare medical information system. Cyber Secur. Appl. **1**, 100013 (2023)

17. Das, A.K.: A secure and robust password-based remote user authentication scheme using smart cards for the integrated EPR information system. J. Med. Syst. **39**(3), 1–14 (2015). https://doi.org/10.1007/s10916-015-0204-8

18. Han, D., Pan, N., Li, K.C.: A traceable and revocable ciphertext-policy attribute-based encryption scheme based on privacy protection. IEEE Trans. Dependable Secure Comput. **19**(3), 316–327 (2022)

19. Márquez, G., Astudillo, H., Taramasco, C.: Security in telehealth systems from a software engineering viewpoint: a systematic mapping study. IEEE Access **8**, 10933–10950 (2020)

20. Ryu, J., et al.: Secure ECC-based three-factor mutual authentication protocol for telecare medical information system. IEEE Access **10**, 11511–11526 (2022)
21. Xiao, L., Xie, S., Han, D., Liang, W., Guo, J., Chou, W.K.: A lightweight authentication scheme for telecare medical information system. Connect. Sci. **33**(3), 1–12 (2021)
22. Li, W.-M., Li, X.-L., Wen, Q.-Y., Zhang, S., Zhang, H.: Flexible CP-ABE based access control on encrypted data for mobile users in hybrid cloud system. J. Comput. Sci. Technol. **32**(5), 974–990 (2017). https://doi.org/10.1007/s11390-017-1776-1

A Novel Method for the Detection of Gravitational Wave Signal of BBH and BNS Using Convolutional Neural Networks

Lokesh Kumar[1,2]([✉]) [iD] and Sanjay K. Sahay[1] [iD]

[1] Department of CSIS, BITS Pilani, K K Birka Goa Campus, Goa, India
{p20180014,ssahay}@goa.bits-pilani.ac.in
[2] Suhora Technologies, Noida One, Noida, U.P., India
lokesh.kumar@suhora.com

Abstract. Deep Learning (DL) techniques has shown promising results in various Artificial Intelligence applications viz. image recognition, large language models, intrusion detection system, neural machine translation, natural language processing, anti-malware, etc. Hence, Gravitational Waves (GW) data analysis community also started proposing various techniques based on DL for the detection, parameter estimation, and characterization of gravitational wave signals. In this, most of the models are binary or multi-class based classification using white noise. However, one-step multi-class classification has an over-training issue and favors those classes that are most represented in the dataset and are easier to separate. Also, as the number of classes increases then it's more difficult for the feature set to provide a clear separation between the classes. Therefore, we propose a novel two-step cascaded classification to detect BBH and BNS GW signals buried in the noisy time series data using a Convolutional Neural Network. We did an exhaustive empirical analysis using various combinations of white and colored noise. The models has been tested with both generated datasets and the real GW events. The analysis shows that colored noise models outperform the white noise models and the generated datasets which contain BBH and BNS GW signals have been classified with 100% accuracy with high probability. Hence, as the model's accuracy is 100% with generated datasets, therefore we again tested the models with the real GW (BBH/BNS) events for its robustness and we achieved the accuracy of 100% and 97.29% in the first and second step respectively i.e. in the first step the model perfectly differentiated the GW signals (BBH/BNS) from the noise. Nevertheless, with randomly generated data in both steps our model results are 100% accurate with high probability, which shows the robustness of our proposed models.

Keywords: Gravitational Waves · Deep Learning · Convolutional Neural Network

1   Introduction

Gravitational waves (GW) are ripples in space-time and are propagating perturbations of some flat background. These waves were predicted by Einstein in 1916 [1], and some of the prominent sources are colliding binary black holes (BBH), colliding binary neutron stars (BNS), and supernovae explosions. However, continuous and stochastic GW are also of interest and may be get detected in the near future by advanced Laser Interferometer Gravitational Wave Observatory (aLIGO) and/or Laser Interferometer Space Antenna (LISA) [2]. The direct detection of GW was first tried by J. Weber in 1969, and he announced that he detected the GW [3]. However, later the detection was ruled out. Nevertheless, after almost four decade aLIGO detected the first GW signal (GW150914) [4]. Since then almost hundred direct detection of compact binary coalescence (CBCs) has been announced [5–10]. In this, the detection of GW from the binary neutron star system (GW170817) [11] has been seen in conjunction with Gamma Ray Bursts and across the electromagnetic spectrum [12,13]. Also, the continuous improvements in the sensitivity of aLIGO and advanced Virgo followed by new detectors (KAGRA) joining the network will be able to detect more frequently compact binary coalescence, and probably continuous GW also.

To detect GW signals, a commonly used technique is the matched filtering method [14,15]. This approach involves constructing banks of templates, which serve as educated estimations of the anticipated signal waveforms, covering various parameter ranges. However, in practice, these templates are matched only against a discrete subset of signals from a continuous spectrum of potential signals [16]. Consequently, due to the limited understanding of parameter space, this technique becomes computationally demanding for detecting GW signals in noisy data. Therefore, an effective and efficient method has to be designed to detect GW that can process data efficiently with high accuracy. In this, recently Deep Learning (DL) [17] has shown promising results in various Artificial Intelligence (AI) applications like natural language processing, image recognition, language modeling, anti-malware [18–20], neural machine translation and the scientist has also proved that it can be used for the detection, parameter estimation and characterization of gravitational wave signals [21–28].

Deep learning is a subset of machine learning composed of multiple processing layers to learn data representations [29]. The main aspect of DL is that for the classification, features are not designed by the engineers, but are learned from the data and are not related to the domain perspective. Thus, the utilization of DL-based methods for GW detection proves pertinent not only for achieving effective detection but also for computational efficiency. The computational cost for the detection (testing phase) of the GW using DL techniques is negligible compared to the matched filtering, wherein templates spanning the entire parameter space must be matched [21,23]. In this, for the detection of GW, despite the popular time-frequency analysis, either using wavelet packet decomposition [22,26] or continuous wavelet transformation [28], Convolutional Neural Network (CNN) (a class of DL, which shown superior performance with image, speech, or audio signal inputs) [30] architecture has been explored for the classification/detection of GW signals after transforming the time-series data into gray-scale images [21, 25,27]. In [31] authors claimed that their model can detect and denoise the GW signals from merging black hole binaries more efficiently than the conventional matched filtering technique. Whereas, in [32] detection and classification of GW signals using CNN has been explored. However, most of the proposed techniques are binary classification i.e. (0: White Noise vs. (1) signal (BBH)) or multi-class problem viz. 3 classes (0: White Noise, 1: BBH, 2: BNS).

For multi-class classification or flat classification [33] there are two approaches. In the first approach, a classifier directly deals with all the considered classes in one step, whereas, in the second approach, the multi-class problem is divided into multiple binary sub-problems (multi-level or multiple binary problems) for the classification. However, the first approach has the disadvantage of possible over-training of the model favoring those classes that are most represented in the dataset and are easier to separate [34]. Another problem is that as the number of classes increase it becomes more difficult for the feature set to provide a clear separation between classes i.e. effectiveness of the classification reduces with the number of classes [34,35]. Moreover, employing a multiclass approach might prove impractical for problems characterized by a substantial volume of training samples and classes, mainly due to the significant memory requirements and extensive computational time [36]. Hence, we introduce a novel two-step cascaded GW detection model based on CNN to detect GW signal from the BBH and BNS GW in the noisy time series data. We conducted a comprehensive empirical analysis involving ten distinct models utilizing both white and colored noise. To assess the robustness of our models, we subjected them to testing with additional generated datasets as well as real GW events in a two-step process. Initially, in the first step, we trained and validated our models across all ten datasets to discern the presence of signals (BBH/BNS) within the noisy data (0 representing noise, 1 representing BBH/BNS). Subsequently, in the second step, we employed the same architectures to train and validate them with 5000 instances of BBH and BNS noisy GW signals each for classification (0 representing BBH, 1 representing BNS). The data segments identified as signals in the first step were then forwarded as input to the second step for further classification to determine whether the detected signal was a BBH or BNS. In the subsequent section, we elaborate on the datasets utilized for model selection, followed by a detailed discussion of our proposed approach's experimental analysis in Sect. 3. Finally, in Sect. 4, we present conclusions of the paper.

2   Dataset

To demonstrate that compact binary coalescence signals (BBH and/or BNS) can be detected using the DL method in the noisy output of the gravitational wave detector, we generated ten (five each for white and colored noise) different data sets. For the purpose, we first generated random 10,000 white and colored noise data streams of duration 4 s of 4096 Hz separately using power spectral density (PSD) equivalent to the aLIGO design sensitivity [37], then 5000 data streams for each BBH and BNS signals are generated using PyCBC [38] using SEOBNRv2 and IMRPhenomPv2_NRTidal [39]. The masses of the BBH and BNS are randomly selected between 5 $M_\odot$ - 50$M_\odot$ and 1$M_\odot$ - 2$M_\odot$ respectively with zero spin and $m_1 > m_2$. However, we ignore the luminosity distance because it does not make any difference in the signal pattern. The generated five different datasets for each white and colored noise to train the models are as follows:

- **Set-1:** 5000 copies of N_c, N_w, $N_c + S_{\text{BBH}}$, $N_c + S_{\text{BNS}}$, $N_w + S_{\text{BBH}}$, $N_w + S_{\text{BNS}}$. Here, N_c, N_w, S_{BBH} and S_{BNS} are a generated white noise, colored noise, BBH and BNS signal respectively.
- **Set-2:** 5000 copies of N_c, N_w, and 5000 samples of different BBH (S_{BBH}^{1-5000}) and BNS (S_{BNS}^{1-5000}) injected in N_c, and N_w separately i.e. $N_c + S_{\text{BBH}}^{1-5000}$, $N_c + S_{\text{BNS}}^{1-5000}$, $N_w + S_{\text{BBH}}^{1-5000}$, and $N_w + S_{\text{BNS}}^{1-5000}$.
- **Set-3:** 5000 different white noise (N_c^{1-5000}), colored noise (N_w^{1-5000}); 5000 copies of S_{BBH} and S_{BNS} injected in different white and colored noise separately i.e. $N_c^{1-5000} + S_{\text{BBH}}$, $N_c^{1-5000} + S_{\text{BNS}}$, $N_w^{1-5000} + S_{\text{BBH}}$, and $N_w^{1-5000} + S_{\text{BNS}}$.
- **Set-4:** With 5000 different N_c^{1-5000}, N_w^{1-5000}, S_{BBH}^{1-5000}, S_{BNS}^{1-5000} generated $N_c^{1-5000} + S_{\text{BBH}}^{1-5000}$, $N_c^{1-5000} + S_{\text{BNS}}^{1-5000}$, $N_w^{1-5000} + S_{\text{BBH}}^{1-5000}$, and $N_w^{1-5000} + S_{\text{BNS}}^{1-5000}$.
- **Set-5:** In addition to Set-4 dataset, additional 5000 different white ($N_w^{5001-10000}$) and colored ($N_c^{5001-10000}$) noise has been generated to trained the model so that more realistic model can be designed.

Here, the signals have truncated to preserve the merger and post-inspiral phases [25, 26] before being randomly inserted into the noisy data stream between 0.0–3.5 s and 0.0–2.0 s for BBH and BNS signals respectively. This step aims to enhance the resilience of the models to variations in signal position within the noisy data stream. An example illustrating the generated data stream, featuring normalized BBH signal, colored Gaussian noise, and the signal injected into the noise, is shown in Fig. 1.

Table 1. Dataset detail for training and testing the models.

| | Training and Testing Data | | | Additional Testing Data | |
	Training	Validation	Testing	Generated Data (TD_G)	Real GW Events Data (TD_R)
White Noise (All datasets)	12000	1500	1500	3000 (1000 Noise+BBH, 1000 Noise+BNS, 1000 Noise)	74 (48 BBH, 2 BNS, 24 Noise)
Colored Noise (All datasets)	12000	1500	1500	3000 (1000 Noise+BBH, 1000 Noise+BNS, 1000 Noise)	74 (48 BBH, 2 BNS, 24 Noise)

For testing the model, an additional 3000 waveform datasets (TD_G) were generated. Among these datasets, one-third comprised colored noise, one-third consisted of colored noise with an added BBH signal, and the remaining one-third contained colored noise with an added BNS signal. In addition, to test how robust is our model for real GW events, we downloaded GW time-series dataset (TD_R) containing 50 real GW events from Gravitational Wave Open Science

Center (GWOSC) [40], out of which 48 are confirmed BBH [41] and 2 BNS events [11,42] and for colored noise 24 more data samples have been downloaded which does not contain any GW events (Table 1).

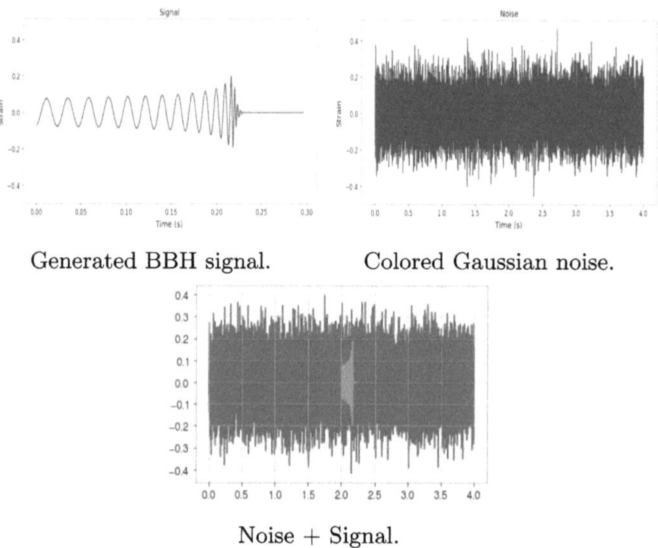

Generated BBH signal.   Colored Gaussian noise.

Noise + Signal.

Fig. 1. An illustration of the process to generate the datasets.

3   Experimental Analysis

The proposed novel two-step cascaded model for the detection of GW as depicted in the flowchart (Fig. 2), is designed to effectively detect the BBH and BNS GW signals in the noisy time series data. This model is based on a 1D-CNN architecture (Table 2), featuring four convolutional and pooling layers each, along with two fully densed connected layers. Where, the initial layer of the architecture corresponds to the input of the neural network, which, in this instance, is a one-dimensional time-series vector formatted as 1×16384.

For experimental analysis, we utilized the Keras python toolkit [43]. Since the technique adopts a two-step cascaded approach, initially, we trained and validated our models with all datasets (Set 1–5), considering both white and colored noise independently, to identify the presence of the signal (BBH/BNS) amidst the noisy data (0 representing noise, 1 representing BBH/BNS).

In the subsequent step, the identical architecture underwent training and validation utilizing 5000 instances each of BBH and BNS noisy GW signals, This process enabled further classification of the detected signal, with 0 denoting BBH and 1 representing BNS. We refined the models by adjusting hyper-parameters

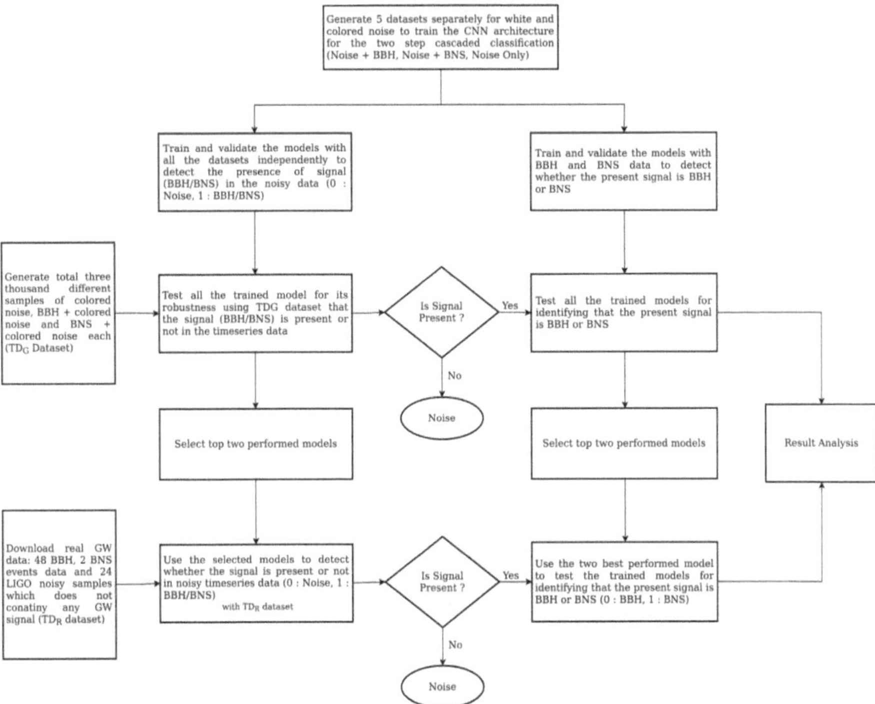

Fig. 2. Flowchart outlining the proposed a novel two-step cascaded approach for the detection of BBH and BNS GW signals.

such as the learning rate, number of network layers, neurons in each layer, activation functions, and epochs for classification. To achieve optimal performance, back-propagation was carried out over multiple iterations, employing an initial learning rate of 10^{-3}, a batch size of 128, and the Adam optimizer [44].

To evaluate the performance of all the developed models, we established a pipeline that integrates both steps. In this pipeline, the output of the first model, which discriminates between noise and signal, serves as input for the second model if the first model identifies the presence of a signal (BBH/BNS) in the data strain. This sequential approach ensures that the second model only operates on data segments classified as containing a signal by the first model, streamlining the analysis process. For this purpose, initially, all developed models were tested with the TD_G dataset, which comprised 3000 waveforms. Among these, one-third contained colored noise, one-third contained colored noise with a BBH signal, and the remaining one-third contained colored noise with a BNS signal. The objective was to detect whether the time series data contained a signal, irrespective of whether it was a BBH or BNS signal. In the subsequent step, the trained models were employed to classify whether the detected GW signal was a BBH or BNS. The results of this classification are illustrated in Fig. 3. The

Table 2. 1D-CNN architecture with an input layer followed by 17 hidden layers and an output softmax layer.

Layer	Type	Size
1	Input	16384
2	Reshape	1×16384
3	1D-Convolution	64×16353
4	Pooling	64×4088
5	ReLU	64×4088
6	1D-Convolution	128×4025
7	Pooling	128×1006
8	ReLU	128×1006
9	1D-Convolution	256×943
10	Pooling	256×235
11	ReLU	256×235
12	1D-Convolution	512×108
13	Pooling	512×27
14	ReLU	512×27
15	Flatten	13824
16	Dense	128
17	Dense	64
18	Dense (softmax)	2
19	Output	2

analysis indicated that the models trained with set-4 and set-5 exhibited superior performance in both white and colored noise compared to models trained with set-1, set-2, and set-3 datasets.

However, colored noise models outperform the white noise models. Therefore, to test the performance of the models with real GW events i.e. TD_R datasets (48 and 2 BBH and BNS detected events respectively and 24 colored noise samples which do not contain any GW events) we selected the colored noise model trained with set-4 and set-5 datasets.

From the experimental results (Fig. 3), we observe that with real GW (BBH/BNS) events in the first step model results are 100% accurate with high probability, while the model accuracy is 97.29% in the second step i.e. the real BNS event was not classified correctly by any of the models, which may be because that later investigation says that it cannot be ruled out that one or both objects are black holes [11,45]. However, when we tested the model with generated datasets TD_G, then the model accuracy was 100% with high probability (>97%) i.e. the models perfectly differentiated all the BBH and BNS signals Table 3). Hence, we can say that if we have unambiguous real BNS events then the designed model will be able to differentiate the BBH from the BNS signal.

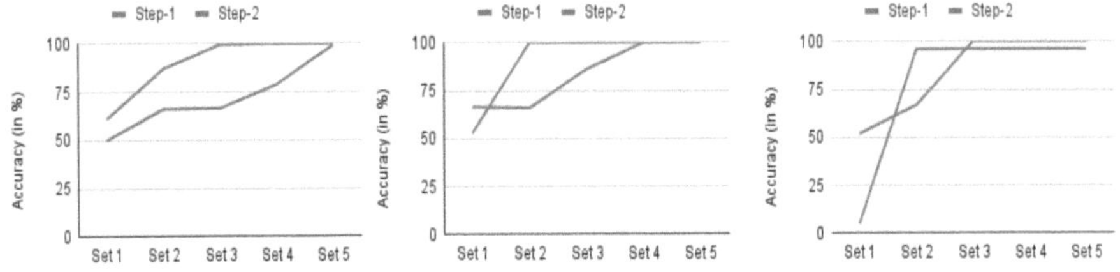

Fig. 3. Performance of the designed models with all the five datsets in both the steps (a) white noise with TD_G datasets (b) Colored noise with TD_G datasets and (c) Colored noise with the real events datasets TD_R

Nevertheless, as in the first step, the model was able to detect the signal buried in the noisy data with 100% accuracy, therefore to identify the present signal in the data stream is BBH or BNS, one may apply matched filtering technique. However, matched filtering technique is computationally expensive compared to deep learning techniques [21]. To assess our method's computational efficiency we used a Hewlett Packard Z Series Workstation equipped with 32 giagabyte random access memory, an Intel Xeon Processor, and an Nvidia Quadro K4000 accelerator. In the initial step, our proposed models took approximately 320 milliseconds to test one thousand samples, enabling the confirmation of signal presence within a 4 s of noisy time series data in just 320 microseconds. In the subsequent step, it took about 348 milliseconds to test one thousand samples, resulting in a confirmation of the specific type of signal (BBH or BNS) within 348 microseconds. Consequently, our model, on an average, detects the presence of GW events (BBH/BNS) in approximately 668 microseconds, should they occur within the data stream. Anyway, we are hopeful and indeed there is a high chance that in the upcoming observational run-4 unambiguous BNS events will be detected. Hence the robustness and performance of the proposed approach can be re-verified by testing the model with real unambiguous BNS event. Also, to best of our knowledge this may be the first time the detection efficiency has been reported i.e. the presence of signal can be known within few microsecond. Moreover, mostly earlier models [21] [25] uses white/Gaussian noise only but we investigated our model both in white/Gaussian and colored noise and find that our proposed model detect the GW signals better in colored noise (we took the noise PSD from the aLIGO).

Table 3. Accuracy Metric on Set-5 of White Noise with TD_G, Colored Noise with TD_G and Colored Noise with real events dataset (TD_R)

Dataset	Accuracy (Step-1)	Accuracy (Step-2)
White Noise with TD_G	100%	100%
Colored Noise with TD_R	100%	100%
Colored Noise with real events TD_R	100%	97.29%

4   Conclusion

We proposed a two-step cascaded classification technique to detect BBH and BNS GW signals hidden in the noisy data instead of a one-step multi-class classification. We did an exhaustive empirical analysis of ten different models using both white and colored noise. From the study, we find that one shall use colored noise for designing the models rather than white noise because colored noise models outperform the white noise models. The analysis shows that in the first step with the real GW events, the model's accuracy is 100% with high probability, i.e., indeed, the signal (BBH/BNS) is present in the noisy time series data. However, in the second step, the BNS events have been miss-classified, which may be because further investigation says that it cannot be ruled out that one or both objects are black holes. However, if in the future unambiguous real BNS events get detected, which has a high chance in the upcoming observational run-4, then we will re-verify our model incorporating the BNS events in the proposed models. Nevertheless, when models are tested with generated datasets, we find that the model is very robust (detection probability is >97%) and the accuracy is 100% i.e., proposed models perfectly differentiated the BBH from the BNS signal. Also, to best of our knowledge this may be the first time the detection efficiency has been reported i.e. the presence of signal can be known within few microsecond. Moreover, earlier proposed techniques uses white/Gaussian noise only, but in this paper we investigated our proposed model both in white/Gaussian and colored noise and find that our proposed model detect the GW signals better in colored noise.

References

1. Einstein, A.: Näherungsweise Integration der Feldgleichungen der Gravitation. Sitzungsberichte der Königlich Preußischen Akademie der Wissenschaften, Berlin, pp. 688–696 (1916)
2. ESA, N.: Lisa pathfinder (2022). https://lisa.nasa.gov/. Accessed May 2024
3. Weber, J.: Evidence for discovery of gravitational radiation. Phys. Rev. Lett. **22**, 1320–1324 (1969). https://doi.org/10.1103/PhysRevLett.22.1320
4. Abbott, B.P., et al.: Observation of gravitational waves from a binary black hole merger. Phys. Rev. Lett. **116**, 061102 (2016). https://doi.org/10.1103/PhysRevLett.116.061102

5. Abbott, B.P., Abbott, R., et al.: Gw151226: observation of gravitational waves from a 22-solar-mass binary black hole coalescence. Phys. Rev. Lett. **116**, 241103 (2016). https://doi.org/10.1103/PhysRevLett.116.241103

6. Abbott, B.P., Abbott, R., et al.: Gw170104: observation of a 50-solar-mass binary black hole coalescence at redshift 0.2. Phys. Rev. Lett. **118**, 221101 (2017). https://doi.org/10.1103/PhysRevLett.118.221101

7. Abbott, B., et al.: Binary black hole population properties inferred from the first and second observing runs of advanced ligo and advanced virgo. Astrophys. J. Lett. **882**(2), L24 (2019)

8. Abbott, B., et al.: Gwtc-1: a gravitational-wave transient catalog of compact binary mergers observed by ligo and virgo during the first and second observing runs. Phys. Rev. X **9**(3), 031040 (2019)

9. Abbott, R., et al.: Gwtc-2: compact binary coalescences observed by ligo and virgo during the first half of the third observing run. Phys. Rev. X **11**(2), 021053 (2021)

10. Abbott, R., et al.: Gwtc-3: Compact binary coalescences observed by ligo and virgo during the second part of the third observing run. arXiv preprint arXiv:2111.03606 (2021)

11. Abbott, B.P., et al.: Gw170817: observation of gravitational waves from a binary neutron star inspiral. Phys. Rev. Lett. **119**(16), 161101 (2017)

12. Monitor, F.G.R.B., Collaboration, L.S., Collaboration, V., et al.: Gravitational waves and gamma-rays from a binary neutron star merger: Gw170817 and grb 170817a. arXiv preprint arXiv:1710.05834 (2017)

13. Goldstein, A., et al.: An ordinary short gamma-ray burst with extraordinary implications: Fermi-gbm detection of grb 170817a. Astrophys. J. Lett. **848**(2), L14 (2017)

14. Acernese, F., Barone, F., Rosa, R.D., Milano, L., Pardi, S.: Dynamic matched filter for the detection of gravitational waves. In: Hough, J., Sanders, G.H. (eds.) Gravitational Wave and Particle Astrophysics Detectors, vol. 5500, pp. 147–154. International Society for Optics and Photonics, SPIE (2004). https://doi.org/10.1117/12.553014

15. Dal Canton, T., et al.: Implementing a search for aligned-spin neutron star-black hole systems with advanced ground based gravitational wave detectors. Phys. Rev. D **90**(8), 082004 (2014)

16. Srivastava, D.C.S., Sahay, S.K.: Data analysis of continuous gravitational wave: all-sky search and study of templates. Monthly Not. R. Astron. Soc. **337**(1), 322–326 (2002). https://doi.org/10.1046/j.1365-8711.2002.06031.x

17. LeCun, Y., Bengio, Y., Hinton, G.: Deep learning. Nature **521**(7553), 436–444 (2015)

18. Sahay, S.K., Sharma, A.: A survey on the detection of Android malicious apps. In: Bhatia, S.K., Tiwari, S., Mishra, K.K., Trivedi, M.C. (eds.) Advances in Computer Communication and Computational Sciences. AISC, vol. 924, pp. 437–446. Springer, Singapore (2019). https://doi.org/10.1007/978-981-13-6861-5_38

19. Sahay, S.K., Sharma, A.: A survey on the detection of windows desktops malware. In: Hu, Y.-C., Tiwari, S., Mishra, K.K., Trivedi, M.C. (eds.) Ambient Communications and Computer Systems. AISC, vol. 904, pp. 149–159. Springer, Singapore (2019). https://doi.org/10.1007/978-981-13-5934-7_14

20. Sahay, S.K., Goel, N., Jadliwala, M., Upadhyaya, S.: Advances in secure knowledge management in the artificial intelligence era. Inf. Syst. Front. **23**(4), 807–810 (2021). https://doi.org/10.1007/s10796-021-10179. https://ideas.repec.org/a/spr/infosf/v23y2021i4d10.1007_s10796-021-10179-9.html

21. Gabbard, H., Williams, M., Hayes, F., Messenger, C.: Matching matched filtering with deep networks for gravitational-wave astronomy. Phys. Rev. Lett. **120**, 141103 (2018). https://doi.org/10.1103/PhysRevLett.120.141103
22. Li, X.-R., Yu, W.-L., Fan, X.-L., Babu, G.J.: Some optimizations on detecting gravitational wave using convolutional neural network. Front. Phys. **15**(5), 1–11 (2020). https://doi.org/10.1007/s11467-020-0966-4
23. George, D., Huerta, E.A.: Deep learning for real-time gravitational wave detection and parameter estimation: results with advanced ligo data. Phys. Lett. B **778**, 64–70 (2018)
24. Fan, X.L., Li, J., Li, X., Zhong, Y.H., Cao, J.W.: Applying deep neural networks to the detection and space parameter estimation of compact binary coalescence with a network of gravitational wave detectors. Sci. China Phys. Mech. Astron. **62**(6), 1–8 (2019). https://doi.org/10.1007/s11433-018-9321-7
25. Krastev, P.G.: Real-time detection of gravitational waves from binary neutron stars using artificial neural networks. Phys. Lett. B **803**, 135330 (2020)
26. Lin, B.-J., Li, X.-R., Yu, W.-L.: Binary neutron stars gravitational wave detection based on wavelet packet analysis and convolutional neural networks. Front. Phys. **15**(2), 1–7 (2020). https://doi.org/10.1007/s11467-019-0935-y
27. Krastev, P.G., Gill, K., Villar, V.A., Berger, E.: Detection and parameter estimation of gravitational waves from binary neutron-star mergers in real ligo data using deep learning. Phys. Lett. B **815**, 136161 (2021)
28. Jadhav, S., Mukund, N., Gadre, B., Mitra, S., Abraham, S.: Improving significance of binary black hole mergers in advanced ligo data using deep learning: confirmation of gw151216. Phys. Rev. D **104**(6), 064051 (2021)
29. Goodfellow, I.J., Bengio, Y., Courville, A.: Deep Learning. MIT Press, Cambridge (2016). http://www.deeplearningbook.org. Accessed May 2024
30. Lecun, Y., Bengio, Y.: Convolutional Networks for Images, Speech, and Time-Series. MIT Press, Cambridge (1995)
31. Murali, C., Lumley, D.: Detecting and denoising gravitational wave signals from binary black holes using deep learning. Phys. Rev. D **108**, 043024 (2023). https://doi.org/10.1103/PhysRevD.108.043024
32. Qiu, R., Krastev, P.G., Gill, K., Berger, E.: Deep learning detection and classification of gravitational waves from neutron star-black hole mergers. Phys. Lett. B **840**, 137850 (2023). https://doi.org/10.1016/j.physletb.2023.137850. https://www.sciencedirect.com/science/article/pii/S0370269323001843
33. Silla, C.N., Freitas, A.A.: A survey of hierarchical classification across different application domains. Data Min. Knowl. Disc. **22**(1), 31–72 (2011)
34. Forman, G., et al.: An extensive empirical study of feature selection metrics for text classification. J. Mach. Learn. Res. **3**(Mar), 1289–1305 (2003)
35. Price, D., Knerr, S., Personnaz, L., Dreyfus, G.: Pairwise neural network classifiers with probabilistic outputs. In: Tesauro, G., Touretzky, D., Leen, T. (eds.) Advances in Neural Information Processing Systems, vol. 7. MIT Press (1994). https://proceedings.neurips.cc/paper/1994/file/210f760a89db30aa72ca258a3483cc7f-Paper.pdf
36. Sonar, R., Deshmukh, P.: Multiclass classification: a review. Int. J. Comput. Sci. Mob. Comput. **3**(4), 65–69 (2014)
37. Abbott, B.P., et al.: Prospects for observing and localizing gravitational-wave transients with advanced ligo, advanced virgo and kagra. Living Rev. Relativ. **23**(1), 1–69 (2020)
38. Nitz, A., Harry, I., Brown, D., Biwer, C.M., Willis, J., et al.: gwastro/pycbc: v2.0.2 release of pycbc (2022). https://doi.org/10.5281/zenodo.6324278

39. Pürrer, M.: Frequency domain reduced order model of aligned-spin effective-one-body waveforms with generic mass ratios and spins. Phys. Rev. D **93**, 064041 (2016). https://doi.org/10.1103/PhysRevD.93.064041
40. Gravitational Wave Open Science Center. https://www.gw-openscience.org/. Accessed May 2024
41. Freitas, S., Sobrinho, J.: A list of 48 binary black hole mergers. The handbook of brain theory and neural networks (2021). https://doi.org/10.13140/RG.2.2.11329.07526
42. Ciolfi, R.: Binary neutron star mergers after gw170817. Front. Astron. Space Sci. **7**, 27 (2020)
43. Chollet, F., et al.: Keras (2015). https://github.com/fchollet/keras. Accessed May 2024
44. Sewak, M., Sahay, S.K., Rathore, H.: An overview of deep learning architecture of deep neural networks and autoencoders. J. Comput. Theor. Nanosci. **17**(1), 182–188 (2020)
45. Abbott, B., et al.: Gw190425: observation of a compact binary coalescence with total mass ~ 3.4 m $_\odot$. Astrophys. J. Lett. **892**(1), L3 (2020)

An Investigation of Deep Learning Techniques for the Robust Detection of Melanoma Cancer

Akbar Kushanoor[1,2]([⊠]) and Sanjay K. Sahay[1]

[1] Department of CS and IS, BITS Pilani, K K Birla Goa Campus, Goa, India
`p20190079@goa.bits-pilani.ac.in`
[2] GE Aerospace, John F. Welch Technology Centre, Bangalore, India

Abstract. Skin cancer is a major global health concern, therefore it has to be detected as early as possible for effective intervention and treatment, especially in the cases of lethal melanoma cancer. Generally, to identify melanoma cancer, dermoscopy image analysis is widely used. It's an non-invasive skin imaging technique that helps to visualize the features of pigmented skin lesions, which are imperceptible through naked eye examination. However, this method is time-consuming and also prone to operator bias due to similarities between the skin cancers. Hence, the automated dermoscopy image analysis has became a very active research field, and recent advances in deep learning shows that it can be an effective approach to detect the melanoma cancer in early stages. Hence for the robust detection of melanoma cancer we propose and investigate three deep learning models based on InceptionNet-V3, EfficientNet-B7 and MobileNet-V3. Our analysis shows that MobileNet-V3 outperformed the three investigated models by achieving an accuracy of 97.34%. Although, among the three models, InceptionNet-V3 provides least accuracy, nevertheless the majority analysis i.e., out of three models, if two models correctly classify melanoma and non-melanoma, even then the accuracy comes to 97.24%, in which TP and TN is 95.62% and 98.84% respectively. To best of our knowledge, this work is first of its kind to achieve such a remarkable accuracy of more than 97%. Therefore, we can say that our proposed robust models can be a reliable and precise diagnostic tool for medical professionals for the detection of melanoma cancer.

Keywords: Skin Lesion · Melanoma Cancer · Dermoscopy · Deep Learning · Convolution Neural Network · Autoencoder

1 Introduction

According to the World Health Organization, cancer is one of the life threatening diseases that we are facing today [1]. Among different types of cancers, skin cancer (abnormal ripening of skin cells), which is generally caused by the sun's harmful rays is very lethal, and if not treated early, it will spread very rapidly to other organs of the human body and may lead to the death [2,4]. Basically, skin cancer is classified into two main categories known as melanoma and non-melanoma cancer. Non-melanoma cancer is generally treated successfully and has a lower risk of spreading [3]. Despite being less common than non-melanoma cancer, however, since 1980s prevalence of melanoma cancer has steadily increased worldwide in both the genders. While its incidence is over 10-fold lower than other skin cancers, it can rapidly metastasize and impact as early as at the age of 30. This makes melanoma a substantial health and financial implication in the society [5], e.g., in previous year 7,900 fatalities have been reported in US from a total of 97,160 cases, and in Australia a total of 18,257 new cases have been reported out of which 1,314 patients died. In current year it is anticipated that approximately 100,640 persons will be diagnosed by melanoma in US out of which 8,290 may die due to this lethal cancer i.e. the annual incidence rate of melanoma is on the rise, and it is estimated that there will be 510,000 new cases and 96,000 deaths globally by 2040 [7]. Therefore, it is a need of the hour to improve the melanoma cancer detection techniques at a very early stage to minimize the fatalities. Generally, professionals in this field are intensifying their efforts to comprehend the visual patterns of melanoma through the utilization of histopathology methods such as Bleeding Ulceration, Asymmetry, Border irregularity, Color spectrum, Diameter (ABCD), dermoscopy, computer examination in vivo diagnosis [6,8]. However, these procedures can be efficiently used only by qualified dermatologists, and the diagnosis is usually impressionistic and challenging to reproduce [9]. These challenges have spurred research into Computer-Aided Diagnosis Systems (CADS) along with recent advances in Deep Learning (DL) show that it can be an effective approach to detect melanoma cancer in early stages. Although, various advanced DL models have been proposed from time-to-time for identifying melanoma cancer [9,10]. However, the application of DL for the early detection of melanoma cancer is in nascent stage. Therefore, in this paper we propose and investigate three different deep learning models viz. Inception-V3 (a popular method), EfficientNet-B7 (an efficient methods) and MobileNet-V3 (a lightweight method) Inception-V3 (a popular method), EfficientNet-B7 (an efficient methods) and MobileNet-V3 (a lightweight method) were selected for melanoma detection due to their proven accuracy and efficiency with ImageNet data. Inception-V3 excels in complex image recognition tasks with its inception modules and factorized convolutions, making it reliable for medical image analysis. EfficientNet-B7 achieves state-of-the-art accuracy with its compound scaling method, handling various image resolutions efficiently. MobileNet-V3 balances accuracy and computational efficiency, designed for lightweight deployment on devices with limited power, making it suitable for real-time clinical applications. Accordingly, in next section we briefly discuss the related work, and in Sect. 3 an overview of the Inception-V3, EfficientNet-B7, MobileNet-V3 and Autoencoders has been given. The Sect. 4 describes the benchmark ISIC data set and its preprocessing for the robust detection of melanoma cancer. In Sect. 5 we explain the experimental set up and our approach. Section 6 contains the result analysis and finally in Sect. 7 we provide the conclusion of the paper.

2 Related Work

Generally screening of melanoma cancer in clinic are performed by dermatologists using traditional technique called ABCD [11]. However, from time to time several different methods for diagnosis of melanoma cancer were proposed [12,14,15]. In this, the idea of computer-assisted melanoma diagnosis was first introduced in 1990's. Later many approaches have been proposed and developed viz. ultrasound molemax, reflectance confocal microscopy, confocal laser scanning microscopy, photoacoustic imaging, vivo confocal microscopy, optical coherence tomography, etc. [13,16–18]. However, all these proposed methods have their own pros and cons e.g., using dermoscopy a five years experienced dermatologists can diagnosed melonama with a rate of 92% sensitivity and 99% specificity, whereas less experienced user can diagones with a rate of 69% sensitivity and 94% specificity. [19]. In 2008, computerized approaches were used to augment the efficacy of dermoscopy to get better results than those of manual dermoscopy. Although, since 1990 significant research was devoted to develop CADS for the classification of skin lesions, but it didn't help much to dermatologist to identity the melanoma cancer [20]. Therefore in 2015, Massod et al. [21] proposed a learning model for automated diagnosis of skin cancer using deep belief neural network and self-advised support vector machine (SVM). They claim that their system can diagnose skin cancer even in the presence of limited labeled data sets and can also deal with the problem of outliers. They investigated the model with 100 dermoscopic images and claimed that their model outperform most of the popular techniques including k-nearest neighbour, artificial neural network, support vector machine and semi supervised algorithms. Later, in 2016 [22] Takuya et al. proposed a simple and effective preprocessing method by aligning the major axis of skin lesion prior to training and claimed that their proposed pre-processing technique can improve the detection accuracy of the melanoma cancer. They evaluated their approach with 1,431 nevi and 329 melanomas images using convolutional neural network (CNN) with 5-fold cross validation and found that by skin lesion alignment, classification accuracy increases by 5.8%.

In 2017, Esteva [3] et al. also conducted skin lesion classification using CNN with an extensive dataset of 129,450 clinical images encompassing 2,032 distinct diseases. They rigorously analyzed the CNN efficacy against 21 board-certified dermatologists, focusing on binary classification scenarios i.e., to distinguish keratinocyte carcinomas from benign seborrheic keratoses, and discriminating malignant melanomas from benign nevi. Their analysis show that CNN result is as good as dermatologist traditional methods for the detection of melanoma cancer. Later, Kawahara et al. [23] introduced a multitask deep CNN, using dermoscopic images and patient metadata for skin lesion diagnosis based on the standard 7-point melanoma checklist. Their approach achieved 73.7% accuracy with checklist criteria and skin conditions on 1011 lesion cases. Later, Yu et al. developed a binary classification algorithm focusing on the melanoma and nevus lesions on the acral skin. They compared their models with trained and non-trained physicians and found that CNN can achieve up to 81.9% accuracy and have the potential to automate the detection of melanoma cancer for specific sub types like acral lesions on the hands and feet [24]. Later, Haenssle et al. developed a CNN-based diagnostic system using the ISIC 2016 dataset and Inception-V4. The system compared its accuracy against 58 dermatologists from 17 countries. The CNN achieved an 88.9% accuracy rate, outperforming most dermatologists, regardless of their experience levels. This highlights the potential benefit of CNN assistance in dermoscopy image classification for dermatologists at any skill level [25].

In 2019, Fperez et al. used nine different CNN architectures (MobileNet-V2, Inception-v4, Xception, DenseNet, PNASNet, SENet, Dual Path Nets, ResNet, and Inception-ResNet-v2) with limited dataset to focus on melanoma detection. They evaluated the factors that influence the classification with measures viz. sensitivity, specificity and accuracy and finally obtained a maximum accuracy of 91% for all the analyzed models [26]. Khan et al. introduced a robust approach for skin lesion classification by leveraging two pre-trained DL models (ResNet-50 and ResNet-100) and they incorporated kurtosis-controlled principal component analysis for feature extraction from lesions. The proposed CNN model evaluated with three different datasets HAM1000, ISBI 2016 and ISBI 2017 and achieved overall accuracies of 89.8%, 95.60% and 90.20% respectively [27]. Barata et al. proposed a diagnostic model for dermoscopy images that uses a multi-task network to perform a hierarchical diagnosis of skin lesions which can provide visual information to explain the diagnosis. They achieved competitive results on the two state-of-the-art dermoscopy data sets (ISIC 2017 and 2018), without augmenting the training data with external or artificially generated data. Their model can identify clinically relevant regions in the images up to an accuracy of 88.9% [1]. In 2021, Zillur Rahman et al. analyzed five different DNN viz. ResNet, SeResNeXt, ResNext, Xception, and DenseNet for the classification of seven skin lesions and achieved an accuracy of 91%, 89%, 88%, 88%, and 84% respectively. However, they mentioned that data augmentation and diversification of network architectures are necessary due to limitations in training data and model homogeneity in ensemble learning for the better results [28]. Moloud Abdar proposed a hybrid uncertainty quantification model based on three-way decision theory (TWD) using quantification methods viz. Monte Carlo (MC) dropout, Ensemble MC dropout and Deep Ensemble applied on different DL models (DenseNet, ReseNet-152, InceptionReseNetV2) for the classification of skin cancer. They analayzed the models with two different data sets (Kaggle Skin Cancer and ISIC 2019) and obtained an accuracy of 88.95% and 90.96% respectively [29].

Gouda et al. [2022] investigated InceptionNet-V3, ResNet50, and Inception-ResNet architectures along with a enhanced super resolution images using a generative adversarial network for the identification of skin lesions. Their method incorporated resilient-in-residual blocks for super-resolution, improving image authenticity verification and enhancing histogram brightness elements, minutiae, surfaces, and contrast levels and achieved an accuracy 83.6%, 85.7%, 84.1% with ResNet50, Inception-V3, and Inception-ResNet respectively [30]. Later Ali et al. developed a preprocessing pipeline for skin cancer classification using EfficientNets B0-B7. They trained the model with HAM10000 dataset and achieved an accuracy of 85.52% [31]. Beatriz Alves et al. [32] introduced a multilevel classification model leveraging patient metadata viz. age and lesion location on the body. Using single class, multi-class, and mixed class classification models with five different CNN architectures (ResNet50, ResNet101, DenseNet121, EfficientNet-B0, EfficientNet-B2) and claimed that their approach can enhance the diagnostic performance of an automatic system with an overall accuracy of 77.90%.

3   Overview of the Models

3.1   InceptionNet-V3

InceptionNet is one of the popular models introduced in 2014 for the image classification based on CNN architecture with 22 layers [33], which is now known as InceptionNet-V1. It is basically designed to handled large scale data. It leverages the Hebbian principle and multi-scale processing due to which it optimizes the incurred computational cost while maximizing network depth and width. However, in very next year InceptionNet-V2 was released and having 42-layer deep network but the computational cost was lower than its predecessors (InceptionNet-V1). It offered a 2.5 times higher computation rate than InceptionNet-V1 and is also more efficient than Visual Geometry Group Network [34–36]. In the end of the same year InceptionNet-V3 was released which consists of 48 layers and is more robust than the previous versions, e.g. it achieved 78.1%accuracy on ImageNet data set. A schematic of the InceptionNet-V3 network architecture is shown in Fig. 1. It comprises of three primary blocks: Inception module (3×, 4×, 2×), grid reduction and auxiliary classifier. These blocks contain convolutions, maximum pooling, average pooling, concatenations, dropouts, and fully connected layers. The batch normalization and softmax were used for effective model training and computations loss [34].

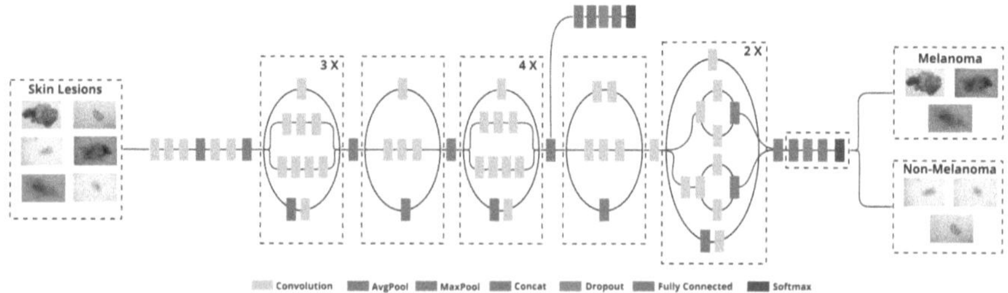

Fig. 1. A schematic of the Inception-V3.

3.2   EfficientNet-B7

In general, to get better accuracy, the computational cost proportionally increases while using standard CNN. Therefore, Mingxing Tan et al. in 2019 proposed a set of eight EfficientNet models viz. EfficientNet-B0 to EfficientNet-B7, a scaling method that optimize the network depth, width, and resolution for better performance [37]. A schematic of the EfficientNet-B7 is shown in Fig. 2. It consists of two main components: 1) an efficient baseline architecture using Neural Architecture Search (NAS) [38], and 2) a scaling method to scale-up the process to enhance the performance. As shown in Fig. 2, the EfficientNet-B7 is segmented into seven blocks, each block is distinguished by the color to represent differences in filter size, striding, and channel. It also relies on the Mobile Inverted Bottleneck Convolution (MBConv) for fundamental building block and is augmented with squeeze and excitation optimization. With an ascending index from EfficientNet B0 to B7, the number of MBConv blocks increase the complexity of models but enhance the performance. EfficientNet-B7 stands out as the pinnacle, achieving a remarkable 84.3% accuracy on ImageNet while boasting a reduction of 8.4× smaller and 6.1× faster than the prior state-of-the-art ConvNets Gpipe proposed by Huangetal [39]. The model performance is due to the choice of better architecture, scaling, and training settings that are customized for EfficientNet-B7. Therefore, we investigated the EfficeintNet-B7 for detection of the melanoma cancer, due to its remarkable performance in the image classification, particularly in the medical domain where accurate diagnosis is crucial. By leveraging the capabilities of EfficientNet-B7, we aimed to enhance the accuracy of skin cancer classification, thereby potentially improving diagnostic outcomes.

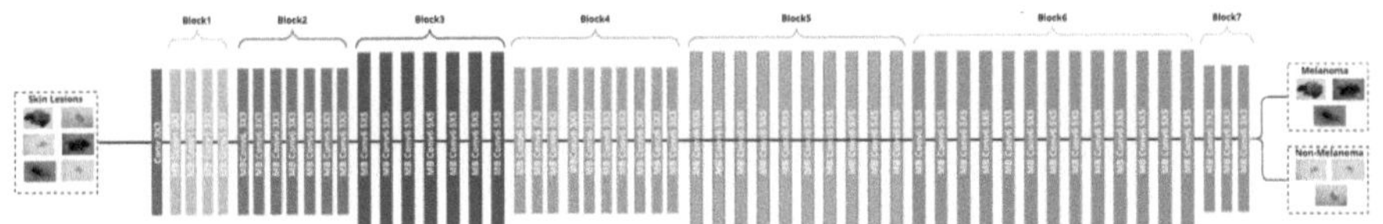

Fig. 2. A schematic of the EfficientNet-B7.

3.3   MobileNet-V3

In today's artificial intelligence (AI) era people like to have application in their hand-held devices viz. image recognition, natural language processing, detection of malware, skin lesion etc. Although, in general, AI applications are computationally expensive and hand held devices are resource constraint, but it is now prevalent, and the trend will continue to grow in the future for its applications in hand held devices. Therefore in 2017, a lightweight CNN model named MobileNet was first proposed for the classification of images in smart devices [40], understanding its importance in the very next year MobileNet-V2 was released. It introduces several key enhancements, including inverted residual blocks and linear bottlenecks, that improve the overall efficiency and accuracy of the model, and also demonstrated higher accuracy compared to other lightweight models [41–44], making it a favorable choice for image classification tasks.

The model defined by point wise (1×1) expansion convolution followed by depth wise convolutions and a 1×1 projection layer [45]. Later in 2019 MobileNet-V3 network was introduced [46]. A schematic of the same is shown in Fig. 3. The MobileNet-V3 architecture introduced pivotal advancements from the previous versions and aimed to elevate model performance and efficiency by merging the architectural principles of MobileNet-V2 and MnasNet. It also included the integration of squeeze and excitation block, hard-swish activation function and NAS method called automated mixed precision neural architecture search. The squeeze and excitation block helps to capture channel wise dependencies by re-calibrating the importance of each channel in a feature map. The hard-swish activation function combines the both rectified linear unit (ReLU) and sigmoid functions to provide efficiency and better accuracy and the NAS helped to select the optimal architecture for the given tasks, while considering the both model performance and computational efficiency [38].

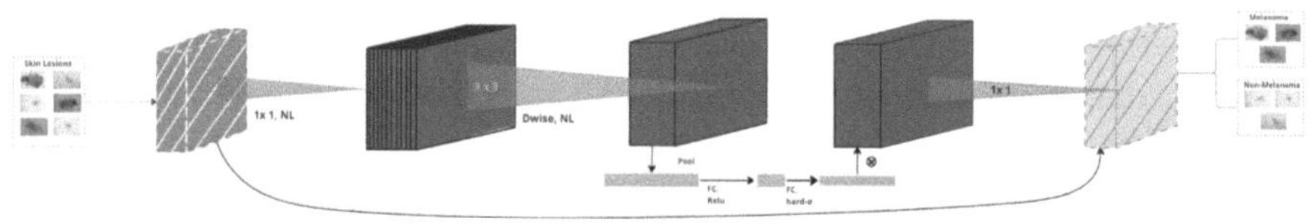

Fig. 3. A schematic of the MobileNet-V3.

3.4   Autoencoders

Geoffrey Hinton in 1986 introduced an unsupervised learning approach known as Autoencoders [47–49]. It consists of a network of encoder and decoder. The input is connected to the 1_{st} layer of the encoder and as shown in the Fig. 4 the number of neurons are reduced in the subsequent layer till the last encoded layer. The last layer of the encoder has the least neurons which can be takes as the features of the data set for the classification i.e. the input is changed until the final layer represents the reduced dimension of the data which contain maximum information in the data set. After encoding the data, decoder layers are set, and in each subsequent layers the number neurons are increased, until the final output layer contain the same number of neurons as the input layer. In brief, from the original data, the encoder creates a compressed representative feature dataset and then the decoder uses this information to recreate the original image after removing the errors noises in the data. There are various types of Autoencoders such as vanilla [50], sparse [51], denoising [52], convolutional [53], contractive [54], variational [55] and recurrent Autoencoders [47,56–58] Each has slightly different architectures and objectives.

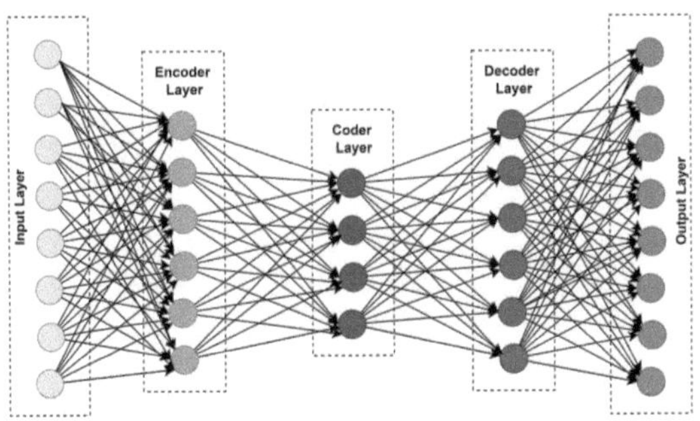

Fig. 4. A schematic of the Autoencoder.

4   Data Pre-processing

The International Skin Imaging Collaboration (ISIC) is a joint academia and industry effort to provide large-scale dataset of dermoscopy images from various sources. viz. the University of Athens Medical School, Memorial Sloan Kettering Cancer Center, Melanoma Institute Australia, University of Queensland, Hospital Clinic de Barcelona and Medical University of Vienna.

The dataset consists of 33,126 and 25,311 various skin-lesion images of 2020 and 2019 respectively, in which together it contains 5,106 melanoma. The dataset is widely recognized and considered as a benchmark dataset for the skin lesion analysis because it has large collection of high-quality images depicting skin lesions, accompanied by annotations. Therefore for the investigation of our proposed approach we used ISIC datasets, which have 5,106 melanoma images. Accordingly, for the analysis we took 5,193 non-melanoma images from the dataset. However, the datasets are partially cluttered with noises viz. hair, sketch marks, and also the resolutions of images varies. Therefore, to develop an effective and efficient model for the detection of melanoma cancer we first re-sized all the images to 512×512 pixels using open CV function [59], then we reduced the noises in dataset using Autoencoders. For the optimal reduction of noises in the images we used 3 layer encoder and decoder i.e., first we reduced the images from 512×512 to 128×128 pixel and then reconstructed the images to original 512×512 pixels. An example of the processed images are shown in Fig. 5. The 2nd and 4th row are images after pre-processing of the 1st and 3rd row images respectively. From the Fig. 5 we observed that in RGB source images, hair has been removed and also colour are enhanced. The process yanks some information from images, but it produces a highly acceptable result since the images are without hair and have enhanced color. In addition, we removed other noise (sketch marks) and artifacts using the median filter.

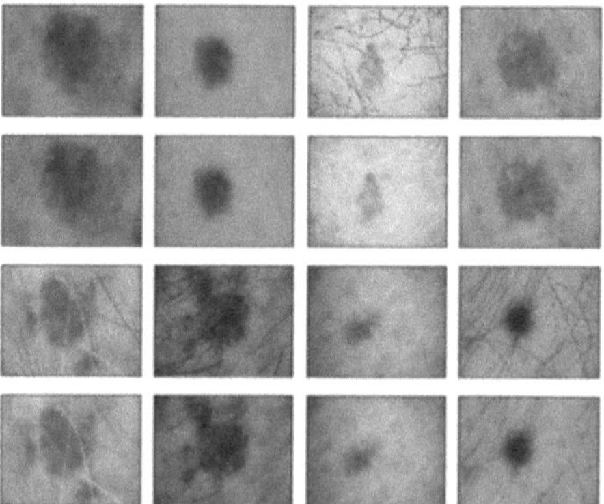

Fig. 5. Some dermoscopy images before (1st and 3rd row) and after denoising and color normalization (2nd and 4th row).

5   Experimental Setup and Proposed Approach

For designing a robust method for the detection of melanoma cancer we investigated three different deep learning models viz. InceptionNet-V3 (a popular method), EfficientNet-B7 (an efficient method) and MobileNet-V3 (a lightweight method). For the experimental analysis we used Google Co-lab Pro+ for our model training which offers 52 GB RAM and P100, T4, and V100 GPU with a 24-h run time [60]. The step that we followed to investigate the proposed models has been shown in Fig. 6. For training the models we fed 70% of the de-noised dataset done earlier using Autoencoders and then fine-tuned the models to optimize accuracy without over-fitting or under-fitting. We found that all the three models training losses get minimized at around 100 epochs (Fig. 8). Once the model is fully trained, we tested the models with 30% of the remaining dataset and the result obtained is given in the Table 1 and corresponding confusion matrix is shown in the Fig. 9.

6   Result Analysis

Our experimental analysis shows that among the three models, MobileNet-V3 provides the best accuracy (97.34%) and it also is efficient compared to other two investigated models. The InceptionNet-V3 is the worst performer with an accuracy of 86.20%, however it classifies the non-melanoma with 94.99% accurately (TN). We observed that EfficientNet-B7 is not at par to classify non-melanoma

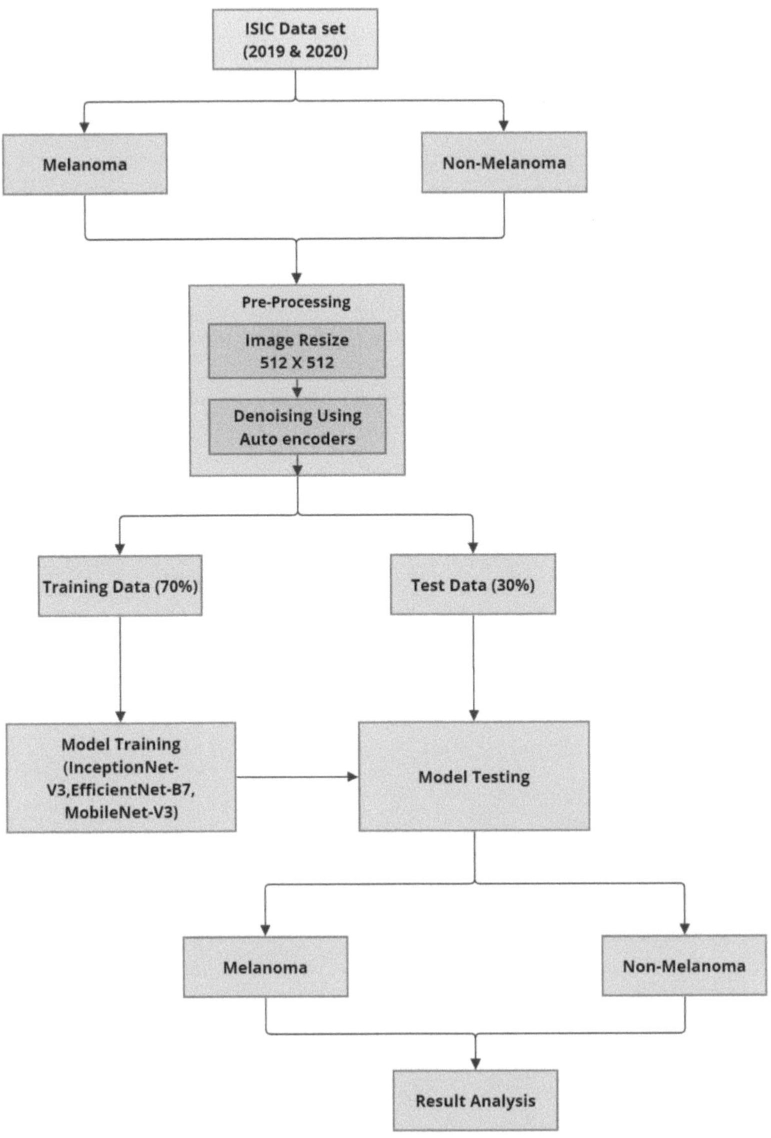

Fig. 6. Flow chat of the proposed approach and analysis.

(TN is 84.01%). Hence, overall accuracy of EfficeintNet-B7 is 88.47%. Neverthe-less, when we compare our MobileNet-V3 results with the model proposed by other authors in 2021 or later, our model provides the best accuracy (97.34%). The comparison of our results with other authors proposed models is shown in Fig. 7. Therefore, to the best of our knowledge we can say that our model has out performed the earlier proposed models for the detection of melanoma cancer. Moreover, the majority analysis (i.e., if out of 3 models, 2 models says true we take true otherwise false), shows that overall TP and TN is 95.62% and 98.84%. This shows that our proposed approach can be a promising model for the classification of melanoma cancer. The confusion matrix Fig. 9 provides a visual representation of the performance of three different deep learning models Inception-V3, EfficientNet-B7, and MobileNet-V3 in classifying skin lesions of melanoma and non-melanoma. The performance of our models is basically due to the noise removal technique that has been done by using Autoencoders.

Table 1. Performance of the all three proposed models.

Model Name	TP	FP	TN	FN	Precision (%)	Recall (%)	F1-Score (%)	Accuracy (%)
InceptionNet-V3	1183	348	1480	78	77.27	93.81	84.74	86.20
EfficientNet-B7	1424	107	1309	249	93.01	85.11	88.88	88.47
MobileNet-V3	1455	76	1552	6	95.03	99.58	97.25	97.34

where,

$$\text{Precision} = \frac{\text{TP}}{\text{TP} + \text{FP}}$$

$$\text{Recall} = \frac{\text{TP}}{\text{TP} + \text{FN}}$$

$$\text{F1 Score} = 2 * \frac{\text{Precision} * \text{Recall}}{\text{Precision} + \text{Recall}}$$

$$\text{Accuracy} = \frac{\text{TP} + \text{TN}}{\text{Total number of data set}}$$

TP $\longrightarrow$ True positives; the number of melanoma images correctly classified.

TN $\longrightarrow$ True negatives; the number of non-melanoma images correctly classified.

FP $\longrightarrow$ False positives; the number of melanoma images wrongly classified.

FN $\longrightarrow$ False negatives; the number of non-melanoma images wrongly classified.

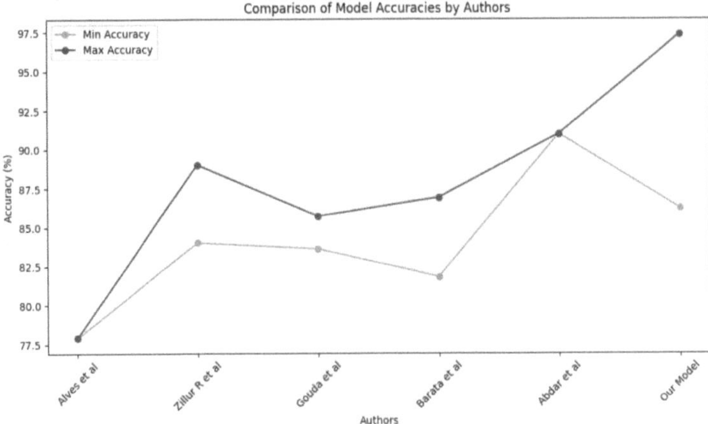

Fig. 7. Performance comparison graph of our models with the model proposed in 2021 and later.

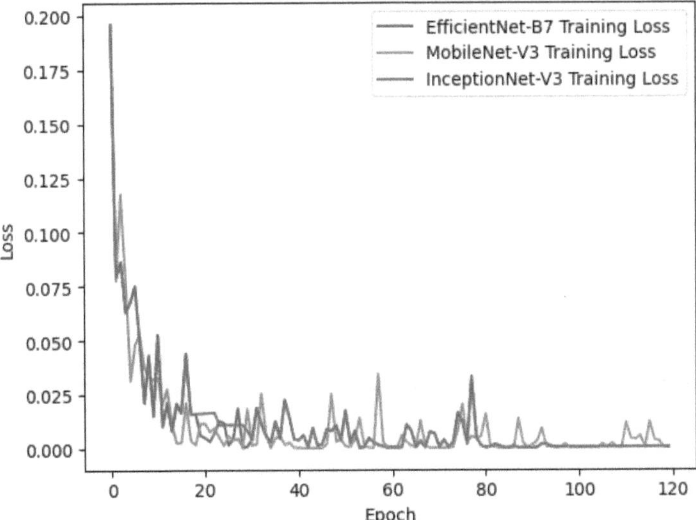

Fig. 8. Training loss of the models with number of epoch.

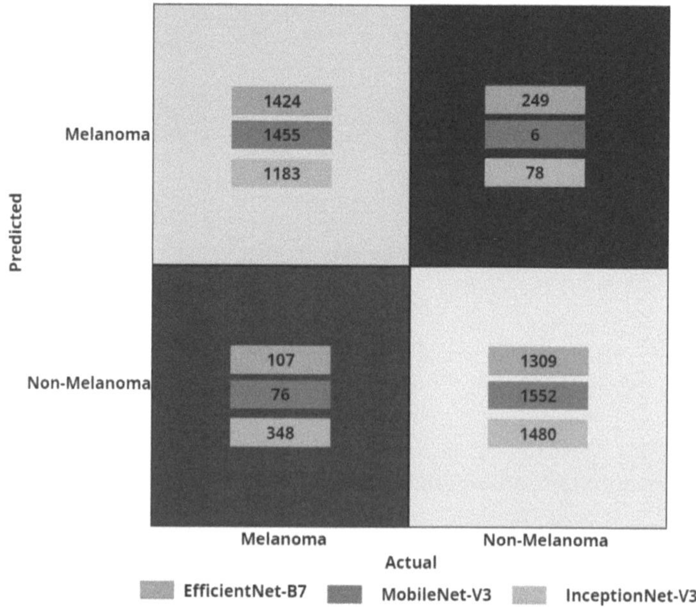

Fig. 9. Confusion matrix of the results obtained by all the three models.

7   Conclusion

Skin cancer is one of the life-threatening diseases that we are facing today. It is generally caused by the sun's harmful rays and if not treated early, then it spreads very rapidly to other organs of human body and may lead to the death. Recently, melanoma cancer prevalence has increased worldwide in both the genders. While its incidence is over 10-fold lower than other skin cancers, it also rapidly metastasize and impact as early as at the age of 30, which makes melanoma a substantial health and financial implication in the society. There-fore, for the robust and early detection of melanoma cancer we proposed and investigated three DL models viz. InceptionNet-V3, MobileNet-V3, and Efficient-B7 using the ISIC dataset. For getting best accuracy we re-sized all the images to 512×512 pixels, then reduced the noises in the dataset using the Autoen-coders. Our experimental analysis showed that one of the proposed model i.e. MobileNet-V3 can detect the melanoma cancer with an accuracy of 97.34%. However, InceptionNet-V3 and EfficeintNet-B7 TP and TN respectively is least. Nevertheless, for robust detection of the melanoma cancer, we did the majority analysis i.e., out of three models, if two models accurately classified melanoma and non-melanoma, then we obtained an accuracy of 97.24%, in which TP and TN is 95.62% and 98.84% respectively. Therefore, to the best of our knowledge we can say that our models can be a robust model to detect the melanoma can-cer as it provides the highest accuracy. Also, the analysis has shown that our models can offer medical professionals as a reliable and precise diagnostic tool. To further improve our model's capabilities, future research should concentrate on expanding it to multi-level classification within the proposed framework and integrating an explainability module to provide visual explanations for transparency of model decisions for dermatologists and patients' understanding. The work in this direction is in progress and the results will be publish accordingly.

Acknowledgments. One of author Akbar Kushanoor is thankful to BITS Pilani for providing the opportunity to pursue my research work, and also he would like to extend his appreciation to General Electric Aerospace for allowing me to purse PhD work at BITS, Pilani.

Disclosure of Interests. The author declares that there are no relevant or material and financial interests related to the research presented in this paper.

References

1. Barata, C., Celebi, M.E., Marques, J.S.: Explainable skin lesion diagnosis using taxonomies. Pattern Recogn. (110), 107413 (2021)
2. Celebi, M.E., Codella, N., Halpern, A.: Dermoscopy image analysis: overview and future directions. IEEE J. Biomed. Health Inform. **23**(2), 474–478 (2019)
3. Andre, E., et al.: Dermatologist-level classification of skin cancer with deep neural networks. Nature **542**(7639), 115–118 (2017)
4. Zhou, B., Khosla, A., Lapedriza, A., Oliva, A., Torralba, A.: Learning deep features for discriminative localization. In: IEEE Conference on Computer Vision and Pattern Recognition, pp. 2921–2929 (2016)
5. Yang, J., Xie, F., Fan, H., Jiang, Z., Liu, J.: Classification for dermoscopy images using convolutional neural networks based on region average pooling. IEEE Access **6**, 65130–65138 (2018)
6. Barata, C., Celebi, M.E., Marques, J.S.: A survey of feature extraction in dermoscopy image analysis of skin cancer. IEEE J. Biomed. Health Inform. **23**, 1096–1109 (2018)
7. Arnold, M., et al.: Global burden of cutaneous melanoma in 2020 and projections to 2040. JAMA Dermatol. **158**, 495–503 (2022)
8. Barata, C., Marques, J.S., Celebi, M.E.: Deep attention model for the hierarchical diagnosis of skin lesions. In: IEEE/CVF Conference on Computer Vision and Pattern Recognition Workshops (2019)
9. Litjens, G., et al.: A survey on deep learning in medical image analysis. Med. Image Anal. **42**, 60–88 (2017)
10. Peng, Y., et al.: Single model deep learning on imbalanced small datasets for skin lesion classification. IEEE Trans. Med. Imaging **41**, 1242–1254 (2022)
11. Bono, A., et al.: The ABCD system of melanoma detection. Cancer **85**, 72–77 (1999)
12. Leachman, S.A., et al.: Methods of melanoma detection. In: Kaufman, H., Mehnert, J. (eds.) Melanoma. CTAR, vol. 167, pp. 51–105. Springer, Cham (2016). https://doi.org/10.1007/978-3-319-22539-5_3
13. Gambichler, T., et al.: Preoperative ultrasonic assessment of thin melanocytic skin lesions using a 100-MHz ultrasound transducer a comparative study. J. Am. Acad. Dermatol. **33**(7), 818–824 (2007)

14. Goodson, A.G., Grossman, D.: Strategies for early melanoma detection: approaches to the patient with nevi. J. Am. Acad. Dermatol. **60**(5), 719–735 (2009)
15. Menzies, S.W., et al.: The performance of solarscan: an automated dermoscopy image analysis instrument for the diagnosis of primary melanoma. Arch. Dermatol. **141**(11), 1388–1396 (2005)
16. Michael, B., et al.: Epiluminescence microscopy: a useful tool for the diagnosis of pigmented skin lesions for formally trained dermatologists. Arch. Dermatol. **131**(3), 286–291 (1995)
17. Marghoob, A.A., et al.: Instruments and new technologies for the in vivo diagnosis of melanoma. J. Am. Acad. Dermatol. **49**(5), 777–797 (2003)
18. Pehamberger, H., Binder, M., Steiner, A., Wolff, K.: In vivo epiluminescence microscopy: improvement of early diagnosis of melanoma. J. Invest. Dermatol. **3**(Supplement), S356–S362 (1993)
19. Piccolo, D., Ferrari, A., Peris, K., Daidone, R., Ruggeri, B., Chimenti, S..: Dermoscopic diagnosis by a trained clinician vs. a clinician with minimal dermoscopy training vs. computer-aided diagnosis of 341 pigmented skin lesions: a comparative study Get access Arrow. Br. J. Dermatol. **147**(3), 481–486 (2022)
20. Lio, P.A., Nghiem, P.: Interactive atlas of dermoscopy. J. Am. Acad. Dermatol. **50**(5), 807–808 (2004)
21. Masood, A., Al-Jumaily, A., Anam, K.: Self-supervised learning model for skin cancer diagnosis. In: 7th International IEEE/EMBS Conference on Neural Engineering, pp. 1012–1015 (2015)
22. Yoshida, T., Celebi, M.E., Schaefer, G., Iyatomi, H.: Simple and effective pre-processing for automated melanoma discrimination based on cytological findings. In: IEEE International Conference on Big Data (Big Data), Washington, DC, USA, pp. 3439–3442 (2016)
23. Kawahara, J., BenTaieb, A., Hamarneh, G.: Deep features to classify skin lesions. In: IEEE 13th International Symposium on Biomedical Imaging (ISBI), Prague, Czech Republic, pp. 1397–1400 (2016)
24. Yu, C., et al.: Acral melanoma detection using a convolutional neural network for dermoscopy images. PLoS One (2018)
25. Haenssle, H.A., et al.: Man against machine: diagnostic performance of a deep learning convolutional neural network for dermoscopic melanoma recognition in comparison to 58 dermatologists. Ann Oncol. (2018)
26. Perez, F., Avila, S., Valle, E.: Solo or ensemble? Choosing a CNN architecture for melanoma classification. In: IEEE/CVF Conference on Computer Vision and Pattern Recognition Workshops, pp. 2775–2783 (2019)
27. Khan, M.A., Javed, M.Y., Sharif, M., Saba, T., Rehman, A.: Multi-model deep neural network based features extraction and optimal selection approach for skin lesion classification. In: International Conference on Computer and Information Sciences, Sakaka, Saudi Arabia, pp. 1–7 (2019)
28. Rahman, Z., Hossain, Md.S., Islam, Md.R., Hasan, Md.M., Hridhee, R.A.: An approach for multiclass skin lesion classification based on ensemble learning. Inform. Med. Unlocked **25** (2021)
29. Abdar, M., et al.: Uncertainty quantification in skin cancer classification using three-way decision-based Bayesian deep learning. Comput. Biol. Med. **135** (2021)
30. Gouda, W., Sama, N.U., Al-Waakid, G., Humayun, M., Jhanjhi, N.Z.: Detection of skin cancer based on skin lesion images using deep learning. Healthcare (Basel) **10**(7), 1183 (2022)

31. Ali, K., Shaikh, Z.A., Khan, A.A., Laghari, A.A.: Multiclass skin cancer classification using EfficientNets – a first step towards preventing skin cancer. Neurosci. Inform. **2**(4) (2022)
32. Alves, B., Barata, C., Marques, J.S.: Diagnosis of skin cancer using hierarchical neural networks and metadata. Pattern Recogn. Image Anal. 69–80 (2022)
33. Szegedy, C., et al.: Going deeper with convolutions. In: IEEE Conference on Computer Vision and Pattern Recognition, pp. 1–9 (2015)
34. Christian, S., Vincent, V., Sergey, I., Jon, S., Zbigniew, W.: Rethinking the inception architecture for computer vision. In: IEEE Conference on Computer Vision and Pattern Recognition, pp. 2818–2826 (2016)
35. Ioffe, S., Szegedy, C.: Batch normalization: accelerating deep network training by reducing internal covariate shift. In: 32nd International Conference on Machine Learning, vol. 37, pp. 448–456 (2015)
36. Girshick, R., Donahue, J., Darrell, T., Malik, J.: Rich feature hierarchies for accurate object detection and semantic segmentation. In: IEEE Conference on Computer Vision and Pattern Recognition, Columbus, OH, USA, pp. 580–587 (2014)
37. Tan, M., Le, Q.V.: EfficientNet: rethinking model scaling for convolutional neural networks. arXiv abs/1905.11946 (2019)
38. Zoph, B., Le, Q.V.: Neural architecture search with reinforcement learning (2016)
39. Huang, Y., et al.: GPipe: efficient training of giant neural networks using pipeline parallelism. In: Proceedings of the 33rd International Conference on Neural Information Processing Systems, vol. 10, pp. 103–112 (2019)
40. Howard, A.G., et al.: MobileNets: efficient convolutional neural networks for mobile vision applications (2017)
41. Ukwandu, O., Hindy, H., Ukwandu, E.: An evaluation of lightweight deep learning techniques in medical imaging for high precision COVID-19 diagnostics. Healthcare Anal. **2** (2022)
42. Iandola, F.N., Moskewicz, M.W., Ashraf, K., Han, S., Dally, W.J., Keutzer, K.: SqueezeNet: AlexNet-level accuracy with 50x fewer parameters and <1 MB model size (2016)
43. Zoph, B., Vasudevan, V., Shlens, J., Le, Q.: Learning transferable architectures for scalable image recognition. In: IEEE/CVF Conference on Computer Vision and Pattern Recognition, pp. 8697–8710 (2018)
44. Real, E., Aggarwal, A., Huang, Y., Le, Q.V.: Regularized evolution for image classifier architecture search. In: Proceedings of the AAAI Conference on Artificial Intelligence and Thirty-First Innovative Applications of Artificial Intelligence Conference and Ninth AAAI Symposium on Educational Advances in Artificial Intelligence (AAAI 2019/IAAI 2019/EAAI 2019). AAAI Press, Article no. 587, pp. 4780–4789 (2019)
45. Sandler, M., Howard, A., Zhu, M., Zhmoginov, A., Chen, L.: MobileNetV2: inverted residuals and linear bottlenecks. In: 2018 IEEE/CVF Conference on Computer Vision and Pattern Recognition, pp. 4510–4520 (2018)
46. Howard, A., et al.: Searching for MobileNetV3. In: IEEE/CVF International Conference on Computer Vision, pp. 1314–1324 (2019)
47. Goodfellow, I., Bengio, Y., Courville, A.: Deep Learning. MIT Press, Cambridge (2016)
48. Sewak, M., et al.: An overview of deep learning architecture of deep neural networks and autoencoders. J. Comput. Theoret. Nanosci. **17**, 182–188 (2020)
49. Mishra, J., Sahay, S.K., Rathore, H., Kumar, L.: Duplicates in the drebin dataset and reduction in the accuracy of the malware detection models. In: 26th IEEE Asia-Pacific Conference on Communications, pp. 161–165 (2021)

50. Ackley, D.H., Hinton, G.E., Sejnowski, T.J.: A learning algorithm for Boltzmann machines. Cogn. Sci. **9**(1), 147–169 (1985)
51. Ng, A.: Sparse autoencoder. CS294A Lect. Notes **72** ,1–19 (2011)
52. Vincent, P., Larochelle, H., Bengio, Y., Manzagol, P.-A.: Extracting and composing robust features with denoising autoencoders. In: Proceedings of the 25th International Conference on Machine Learning (ICML 2008), pp. 1096–1103. Association for Computing Machinery (2008)
53. Zeiler, M.D., Fergus, R.: Visualizing and understanding convolutional networks. In: Fleet, D., Pajdla, T., Schiele, B., Tuytelaars, T. (eds.) ECCV 2014. LNCS, vol. 8689, pp. 818–833. Springer, Cham (2014). https://doi.org/10.1007/978-3-319-10590-1_53
54. Rifai, S., Vincent, P., Muller, X., Glorot, X., Bengio, Y.: Contractive auto-encoders: explicit invariance during feature extraction. In: Proceedings of the 28th International Conference on International Conference on Machine Learning, pp. 833–840 (2011)
55. An, J., Cho, S.: Variational autoencoder based anomaly detection using reconstruction probability (2015)
56. Medsker, L.R., Jain, L.: Recurrent neural networks. Des. Appl. **5**(64–67), 2 (2001)
57. Bank, D., Koenigstein, N., Giryes, R.: Autoencoders. In: Rokach, L., Maimon, O., Shmueli, E. (eds.) Machine Learning for Data Science Handbook, pp. 353–374. Springer, Cham (2023)
58. Majumdar, A.: Blind denoising autoencoder. IEEE Trans. Neural Netw. Learn. Syst. **30**(1), 312–317 (2019)
59. Talebi, H., Milanfar, P.: Learning to resize images for computer vision tasks. In: IEEE/CVF International Conference on Computer Vision, pp. 487–496 (2021)
60. Carneiro, T., Da Nóbrega, R.V.M., Nepomuceno, T., Bian, G.B., De Albuquerque, V.H.C., Reboucas Filho, P.P.: Performance analysis of google colaboratory as a tool for accelerating deep learning applications. IEEE Access **6**, 61677–61685 (2018)

Real-Time Traffic System Analysis Utilizing Image Processing Techniques-a Literature Survey

Amarjeet Kaur[1], Shivani Goyal[2], Pardeep Kumar Jindal[3](✉), and Rajneesh Talwar[3]

[1] University School of Electrical, Electronics and Communications Engineering, Rayat Bahra University, Mohali, India
[2] ECE Department, Chandigarh Engineering College-Chandigarh Group of Colleges, Jhanjeri, Mohali 140307, India
[3] Department of Interdisciplinary Courses in Engineering(DICE), Chitkara University Institute of Engineering and Technology (CUIET), Chitkara University, Rajpura, Punjab 140401, India
`pardeep.alkra@gmail.com, rajneesh.talwar@chitkara.edu.in`

Abstract. -Nowadays there is a daily increase in traffic congestion in India's metropolitan areas, and managing the traffic with human labour is becoming increasingly challenging. This issue can be resolved by implementing an intelligent traffic control system that uses image processing techniques. By extracting information from the testing model's image sequences, real-time information can be used to create a database that contains captured images of things like traffic jams, accidents, foggy areas, traffic signals, and other situations where there is no traffic jam. The trained model has been then processed, and by comparing the new and trained images, with the help of this literature survey the traffic jam can be easily determined. It made possible to perform traffic analysis using image processing technology. Consequently, traffic lights can be used to manage traffic and save time in gridlock by converting traffic to roadways without congestion. But real-time traffic system has been analysed more efficiently using the CNN algorithm.

1 Introduction

Traffic management by means of Image processing is very crucial as now days most of people prefer to commute by their own vehicle rather than opting for public vehicle which give arise to higher populations of vehicles on the road and which generally led to traffic congestion and traffic related issues like accidents etc., collision and traffic jam often led wastage of crucial time on roads but traffic get more worse during the peak hours as most of the people tends to travel to their work places but due to narrow roads as well sometimes some road accidents makes the job more tough [1–3]. In such scenario Image processing techniques plays a vital role to control and appropriate action can be taken by analysing the cause to traffic congestion.

This article focuses on the improvement of the challenges in the traffic control [4–6], the image processing technique utilizes the image and after processing the same

S. Pal et al. (Eds.): ICETSS 2024, CCIS 2610, pp. 155–163, 2026.
https://doi.org/10.1007/978-3-032-11488-4_12

analyse the reason for the traffic congestion by comparing one frame with the another frame which can give the idea for traffic congestion and accordingly traffic signal can be managed. Knowing the root cause root cause analysis can be done and accordingly appreciate action can be taken. In this article Convolutional Neural Networks (CNNs), technique is used to get the exact root cause of the traffic congestion, in this technique a comparison is done between the captured images and trained images and accordingly machine comes in the exact reason for the traffic congestion, by getting the required information one can arrive conclusion that traffic jam might be due to traffic signals, fog, Collison etc., the traffic signal can be operated accordingly [4–7] and even traffic can be diverted to alternate route based on the reason for traffic congestion. The contributions to analyse in this paper is described below:

1. Review the challenges faced to control the traffic congestion by comparing one frame with the frame.
2. Analyse the recent techniques that has been used to control the traffic congestions.
3. Automatically control the traffic congestions according to the CNN model.

2 Literature Survey

K. Ikiriwatte, et al. [8] a traffic optimization using convolutional neural network in a four-way junction using IR sensor and cameras. The objective of this work is to find the traffic congestion and to provide accurate projection for the traffic accumulation on a particular route. By using the technique of algorithm design traffic can be circulated in right manner and avoid stoppages, delays and predictions for the upcoming traffic congestions however by means of manual traffic management there are significant challenges like financial and operational which require manpower to overcome these challenges Machine based system implemented to calculate the accurate scenario to avoid the traffic congestion and accident.

R Bhargavi Devi et al. [9] proposed traffic signal density system using Arduino uno, LED lights and IR sensors. This work use Infrared sensors (IR) are deployed at the multiple locations near to the four way intersection these IR sensors comprises of transmitter and receiver at multiple locations which provide data to the central microcontroller. The microcontroller adjust the signal based on the information from the IR sensor when the vehicle comes in the range of these IR sensors which make traffic management and traffic signals work as per the command provided by microcontroller, however the traffic management by means of conventional i.e. by manual traffic management is very challenging and will not be able to adjust the traffic signals as per the congestion and demand. The IR sensor are installed in such a way that transmitter and the receiver are on the same side of the road and when a vehicle passes through the IR radiation coverage they detect the presence which makes this system automated and by means of microcontroller to ease the traffic management by means of traffic signals.

M. G. Karlaftis, and E. I. Vlahogianni et al. [10] has proposed work using camera based algorithm. The Image is captured by means of CCTV camera, the image processed from the CCTV camera is captured in such a way the background and the upfront images are subtracted which ease and provides accuracy during day time as well as night with the help of Kalman. By using the processed image vehicle detection along with no of vehicle and tracking of the road congestion can be performed. BLOB analysis which provides the information related to the vehicle presence, number of vehicles along with the positioning of the vehicle hence vehicle detection is much easy and flexible in terms of cluster of vehicles moving together.

Muzhir Shaban Al-Ani et.al. [11] have worked on measurement of captured image intensity by means of intelligent traffic light control algorithm. The intelligent traffic control algorithm can manage various situations which involves traffic congestion, prioritization of the emergency vehicle along with the intersection management. This intelligent traffic light control system comprises of smart cameras which can capture the real time traffic flow irrelevant of their direction and it automatically adapts the signal controlling as per the traffic flow changes. This work on intelligent control algorithm is necessary for the cities where it is difficult to manage traffic manually.

G. A. Davis, and N. L. Nihan et.al. [12], have worked on the basis of Digital Image Processing in which clusters are interconnected with CCTV cameras which can monitor the traffic congestion and the traffic flow irrespective to the direction of traffic flow. Kernel-based Edge Detection and Machine Learning techniques uses video processing technique which is very useful in study which involve complex traffic images hence improving efficiency along with saving processing time while maintaining high precision. The Digital Image Processing can perform using a moderate 2MP CCTV camera.

Celil Ozkurt et al. [13] proposed the neural networks technique that monitors the traffic. In this work video surveillance system is used to check the traffic congestion, type of vehicles as well as the projections of the upcoming traffic. This system captures multiple video frames from which valuable information is extracted on the basis of which real time traffic situation and traffic control can be managed. The essential feature is that different type of vehicles can be captured and based on the classification an alternate route for the heavy vehicle can be established.

H. Chang, Y. Lee, B. Yoon et al. [14] proposed work is based on the Image Processing using 3 microcontrollers and mobile based application. Various CCTV cameras are installed at the junction on the road which captures the images which are send to the server and the server further forward this data to the microcontroller which prepares the data based on the images and results in the traffic condition at that particular junction which is send to the android-based application by means of Bluetooth. Theandroid-based application provides information to the authorized user on the basis of the information the authorized user can view the traffic conditions whether traffic congestions are there at the signal. The mobile user can switch the traffic lights based on the information and can also view the upcoming vehicle patterns so that he can monitor and adjust the traffic light at the junction accordingly.

Bharati Sharma et al. [15] proposed an automated vehicle detection scheme. With the help of proposed technique the type of vehicles along with their shape and size can be recognized. The automated vehicle detection uses noise level of the vehicle and applies an average filter to reduce the noise of vehicle which helps in the extraction of the target vehicle.

Penjaman Nikhasaz et al. [16], worked on the Automatic Traffic Control System on the highways based on the contour extraction and the vehicle motion. The work is done by removal of background components and detects forefront components and gamma corrections in image adjustment like contrasting. Proposed work suggest vehicle shape along with the vehicle size.

Wei-Hsun Lee et.al. [17] designed a model for an Intelligent Traffic Light System for smart city applications. The Smart Traffic Signal Control system supports multiple functionalities essential for modern urban transportation. These include Emergency Vehicle Signal Preemption, Public Transport Signal Priority, Adaptive Traffic Signal Control, and e-broadcasting. Central to this system is the Roadside Unit (RSU) controller, which is pivotal to its operation. The RSU manages the system architecture, middleware, control algorithms, and peripheral modules, ensuring seamless integration and efficient performance. The paper details how each component functions and contributes to the overall system, highlighting the advanced technology that enables real-time adjustments and priority settings. This innovative approach aims to enhance traffic management, improve emergency response times, and optimize public transport schedules, significantly contributing to the development of smarter and more efficient urban environments.

James G Haran et al. [18], worked on measurement of captured image intensity by means of intelligent traffic light control algorithm. By implementing intelligent traffic control algorithm various situations can manage which involves traffic congestion, prioritization of the emergency vehicle along with the intersection management. This intelligent traffic light control system comprises of smart cameras which can capture the real time traffic flow irrelevant of their direction and it automatically adapts the signal controlling as per the traffic flow changes. Edge detection and machine learning techniques uses video processing technique which is very useful in study which involves complex traffic images hence improving efficiency along with saving processing time while maintaining high precision.

Prathisha Gupta et. al [19], proposed the edge detection and machine learning techniques using image processing technique which is very useful in study which involves complex traffic images rectifying the noise by means of median filter. For clear and contrast images borders. She has proposed the median filter.

Kastrinaki et al. in [20] suggested an overview of image processing techniques that has been used to develop a specific traffic application which relates to autonomous vehicle guidance. Primarily for detecting the vehicle positions are in the lanes and also for the detection of any obstacle on the way due to collision or other reasons.

Bhat et al. [21] designed a simulator which can captures real time movement of the objects and translating in a form of digital representation by means of Simulink with the video and image processing in real time embedded vision video and imaging system.

Swaraj Raman et al. [22], suggested the labeling algorithm to count the number of vehicles which can categories the different vehicles and also avoid their overlapping by labeling each vehicle based on their geometry.

G.Suseendran et al. [23] worked on study based on estimated number of vehicles on the road in day time by collecting video data and dividing it into multiple frames which underwent series of processing and exact information is captured like total number of vehicle per square area. By making use MATLAB R2013a, average vehicle detection accuracy of 96.0% can be achieved for the vehicle which are moving fast and 82.1% for the vehicle which are moving at slow pace.

NS kumaret al. [24] proposed work based on the study conducted on the images captured by cameras installed near to traffic light junctions, a system can count number of vehicles on regular basis and can alarm on the approaching vehicles, the information gathered on traffic condition can be transferred or sent via means of internet to various control center located in the city along with Automatic license Plate Recognition (ALPR) so that stolen cars can be detected. System has ability to which switch on traffic lights for emergency vehicles by its ability to use LoRa transmitter.

Abhilasha Varshney et al. [25] described a traffic signal optimization technique using Real-Time Traffic Signal Optimizer (RTSOR) to reduce traffic congestion and shorten travelling time and reduce air pollution, RTSOR system identified key High-Density Corridors (HDC) and coordinated an Adaptive Traffic Signal Control System (ATSCS) at consecutive levels to manage traffic and offer better traffic management which further led to low fuel consumption reducing travelling time and pollution control as well.

3 Methodology

Real-time traffic analysis using image processing is designed to address the everyday challenge of traffic congestion. The methodology utilizes a Convolutional Neural Network (CNN) algorithm to enhance traffic prediction capabilities. The primary goal is to apply machine learning techniques for accurate traffic forecasting. However, current applications of machine learning in this field often lack comprehensive information and rely on relatively small datasets, which do not cover the extensive periods needed for real-time traffic analysis. Additionally, there has been insufficient in-depth analysis of the techniques employed by these models. Consequently, further research and the development of new, well-trained models are necessary to improve the effectiveness of machine learning in traffic prediction.

The methodology utilizes a Convolutional Neural Network (CNN) algorithm for image recognition and classification based on predefined image categories. The system shown in Fig. 1 is preloaded with various traffic-related images, such as those depicting congestion, accidents, foggy conditions, traffic signals, and clear roads in the data set. When a new image is captured by the testing model, it is processed by the trained model, which compares it with the stored images to identify the cause of the traffic jam. Through image processing technology, traffic analysis is conducted. If the captured traffic image matches any in the dataset, the system can determine the reason for the congestion.

4 Real Time Traffic Analysis

Figure 2 shows the different situations for the real time traffic analysis. The inner details of Fig. 2 are mentioned below:

1. First image clearly signifies the reason for the traffic jam as a collision.
2. Second image shows the weather condition as we can see the fog which may result to the traffic jam.

Fig. 1. Process to analyze the Real Time Traffic System using image process Techniques

3. Third image shows that traffic congestion is caused at the traffic signal.
4. Fourth image shows that the road is clear.

The traffic status will help the authorized user to make decision whether they need to wait or divert traffic towards other routes and even estimated time can be calculated on the basis of the traffic status. Therefore, time can be saved in traffic jams and traffic can be converted to roads with no jams and traffic management can be done through traffic signals. CNN algorithm has been used for the analysis for real time traffic analysis.

Image	Reason of Traffic
	Due to collision of vehicles jam occurs
	Due to foggy weather traffic jam will be caused
	Due to traffic signal jam is caused
	The path is clear so indicates no traffic jam

Fig. 2. Different situations for real time traffic analysis

5 Conclusion

One solution to the pervasive problem of traffic congestion in both urban and rural settings is real-time traffic analysis. The application of machine learning techniques to the analysis of traffic patterns is explored in this paper. It offers a succinct synopsis and comparison of the many machine learning techniques currently in use for traffic analysis. Using image processing techniques specifically designed to meet the demands and limitations of traffic analysis, this technology effectively detects the presence of automobiles through real-time traffic frames. The main goal of proposed survey is to identify the sources of traffic congestion by analysing traffic photos. If the road is clear after processing these photos, it suggests that there isn't a traffic bottleneck. The suggested approach not only provides ideal accuracy but is also financially and technically practical. This review enhances efficiency and saves time by guiding drivers on routes with available capacity and suggesting the best on-ramps when multiple options are present.

6 Future Scope

For future developments, a system could be designed to analyze real-time video of moving vehicles, enabling the counting, detection, and tracking of these vehicles. Future traffic analysis will need to be exceptionally flexible, cooperative, and proactive. To bring these research advancements into practical application, greater collaboration among various research organizations will be essential. Enhancing these technologies can significantly impact surveillance and traffic management in cities nationwide, leading to the creation of intelligent traffic management systems. The incorporation of advanced traffic-related technologies will further enhance the efficiency of managing traffic congestion.

References

1. Meduri, K., Nadella, G.S., Gonaygunta, H., Meduri, S.S.: Devel. oping a Fog computing-based AI framework for real-time traffic management and optimization. Int. J. Sustain. Dev. Comput. Sci. **5**, 1–24 (2023)
2. Jindal, P.K., Sandha, K.S.: Thermally aware modeling and performance analysis of mixed-MWCNTB as very large scale integrated interconnects material for nano-electronic integrated circuits design. J. Nanoelectron. Optoelectron. **14**, 1255–1266 (2019)
3. Tippannavar, S.S., Yashwanth, S.D.: Real-time vehicle identification for improving the traffic management system-A review. JTCSST **5**, 323–342 (2023)
4. Brar, M., Jindal, P., Malhotra, P., Sharma, P., Kaur, A.: Machine learning based intelligent wardrobe system for apparel recommendation and organization. In: **2023** International Conference on Research Methodologies in Knowledge Management, Artificial Intelligence and Telecommunication Engineering (RMKMATE) 1–5 IEEE (2023)
5. Goyal, S., Jain, V.: Performance evaluation of trench-assisted multi-core fiber for passive optical network. J. Opt. **53**, 1322–1327 (2024)
6. Chaudhuri, A.: Smart traffic management of vehicles using faster R-CNN based deep learning method. Sci. Rep. **14**, 10357 (2024)
7. Abbas, S.K., et al.: Vision based intelligent traffic light management system using Faster R-CNN. CAAI Trans. Intell. Technol. (2024)

8. Ikiriwatte, A.K., Perera, D.D.R., Samarakoon, S.M.M.C., Dissanayake, D.M.W.C.B., Rupasignhe, P.L.: Traffic density estimation and traffic control using convolutional neural network. International Conference on Advancements in Computing (ICAC), pp. 323–328 (2019)
9. Devi, R.B.: Proposes traffic signal density system using Arduino uno, LED lights and IR sensors. Conference International Conference on Inventive Computing and Informatics (ICICI, 2017)
10. Karlaftis, M.G., Vlahogianni, E.I.: Statistical methods versus neural networks in transportation research: differences, similarities and some insights. Transp. Res. C **19**, 387–399 (2011)
11. Al-Ani, M.S., Alheeti, K.: Intelligent traffic light control system based image intensity measurement of computer science-Iraq 200 (College: Al-Anbar University, 2010)
12. Davis, G.A., Nihan, N.L.: Nonparametric regression and short-term freeway traffic forecasting. J. Transp. Eng. **117**, 178–188 (1991)
13. Ozkurt, C., Camci, F.: Automatic traffic density estimation and vehicle classification for traffic surveillance systems using neural networks. Math. Comp. Appl. **14**, 187–196 (2019)
14. Chang, H., Lee, Y., Yoon, B., Baek, S.: Dynamic near-term traffic flow prediction: system-oriented approach based on past experiences. IET Intell. Transp. Syst. **6**, 292–305 (2012)
15. BharatiSharama, V.K., Katiyar, A.K., Sing, A.: The automated vehicle detection of highway traffic images by differential morphological profile. J. Transp. Technol. 150–156 (2014)
16. PejmnaNiskaz. Traffic estimation using image. Process. Int. J. Signal Process. Pattern Recogn. **5** (2012)
17. Lee, W.H., et al.: Design and implementation of a smart traffic signal control system for smart city applications (department of transportation and communication management science). National Cheng Kung University, Tainan 701, Taiwan Published: 16 Jan 2020
18. Haran, J.G., Dillenburg, J., Nelson, P.: Realtime image processing algorithms for the detection of road and environmental conditions. Appl. Adv. Techno. Transp. 55–60 (2006)
19. Gupta, P., Purohit, A.G.: Traffic load computation using MATLAB Simulink model Blockset. Int. J. Adv. Res. Comput. Commun. Eng. **2** (2013)
20. Kastrinaki, V., Zervakis, M., Kalaitzakis, K.: A survey of video processing techniques for traffic applications. Image Vis. Comput. **21**, 359–381 (2003)
21. Bhat, M., Kapoor, P., Raina, B.L.: Application of sad algorithm in image processing for motion detection and simulinkblocksets for object tracking. IJESAT Int. J. Eng. Sci. Adv. Technol. **2**, 731–736
22. Suknya, S.S.R.: A novel labeling algorithm for object. Counting J. ICCC IEEE (2012)
23. Suseendran, G., Akila, D., Balaganesh, D., Elangovan, V.R., Vijayalakshmi, V.: Incremental multi-feature tensor subspace learning based smart traffic control system and traffic density calculation using image processing. 2nd International Conference on Computation, Automation and Knowledge Management (ICCAKM), IEEE (2021)
24. Kumar, N., Santhosh, et al.: Real time intelligent traffic light and density controller–A literature review. Int. J. Mod. Dev. Eng. Sci. **1.6**, 64–66 (2022)
25. Varshney, A., Dakshayini, M., Gururaj, H.L., Hu, Y.C.: Synchronization and implementation of real-time traffic signal optimization regulator. Multimedia Tool. Appl. 1–21 (2024)

Screening and Diagnosis of Alzheimer's Disease Using Artificial Intelligence: A Review

D. Sai Venkat Nikhil[✉] and Dimple Nagpal

Lovely Professional University, Punjab, India
`saivenkatnikhildandananaykula@gmail.com`

Abstract. Millions of people have already been impacted by Alzheimer's disease, a chronic neurodegenerative illness that impairs cognitive function. Cases of the disease are predicted to rise dramatically every ten years. Alzheimer's disease cannot be cured, but it can be managed and kept from getting worse with early diagnosis. For early detection, a number of techniques have been developed. Traditional home care was used at first, but as clinical research progressed, useful drugs were also used. Imaging scans and psychological therapies were also used to diagnose the illness. Computer-aided diagnostic systems (CADS) have emerged recently, utilizing cutting-edge technologies for detection such Machine learning (ML) and deep learning algorithms (DL) Algorithms. The effectiveness of both ML and DL models is assessed in this study, which also examines the methods employed over the previous three years. It covers the range of data and technology accessible for creating detection systems, giving researchers a starting point to suggest or use novel approaches. It also contrasts the results of ML and DL algorithms and points out areas that still need investigation in the literature. Web databases such as Google Scholar were searched for papers from 2021 to 2023 in this analysis, with an emphasis on MRI pictures and keywords such "Detection of Alzheimer's disease." Following a comprehensive assessment, 27 papers were chosen in total.

Keywords: Alzheimer's Disease (AD) · Computer Aided Diagnosis · Machine Learning(ML) · Deep Learning (DL) · (AD) Alzheimer's Disease · (CN) Cognitively Normal · (MCI) Mild Cognitive Impairment · FDG (Fluorodeoxyglucose) · Support Vector Machine (SVM) · Magnetic Resonance Imaging (MRI) · Positron Emission Tomography(PET) · Computed Tomography (CT Scan) · ADNI (Alzheimer's Disease neuroImaging Initiative) · OASIS (open Access Series of Imaging Studies)

1 Introduction

Because to the rising prevalence of Alzheimer's illness among the global population, medical departments worldwide are facing a growing challenge. This emphasizes how important it is to have a treatment plan. The disease causes behavioral problems, memory loss, and cognitive impairment, all of which have a serious impact on the standard of living for patients as well as their families. The lack of a known cure for Alzheimer's

© The Author(s), under exclusive license to Springer Nature Switzerland AG 2026
S. Pal et al. (Eds.): ICETSS 2024, CCIS 2610, pp. 164–177, 2026.
https://doi.org/10.1007/978-3-032-11488-4_13

disease highlights the need for medications that can slow the disease's progression. However, prior to taking medicine, Since the right medication can only be administered once the condition has been properly diagnosed, it is critical to identify Alzheimer's disease. As a result, the disease is becoming more prevalent worldwide and a threat to medical facilities everywhere. So, diagnosing the condition is crucial before starting treatment because it will enable the right medication to be prescribed. For this reason, one author describes how proteins in the brain are categorized into subsets that indicate the degree of Alzheimer's disease, including control, asymptomatic Alzheimer's disease (AsymAD), and Alzheimer's disease (AD). This is due to the fact that the objective of the study is to pinpoint the precise proteins responsible for classifying the individuals into different levels of Alzheimer's disease. The researchers analyzed data from six cohorts, comprising 620 individuals and 3,334 proteins, using label-free quantification and machine learning approaches. Finally, the modern approaches use devices called Computer Aided Diagnosis Systems (CAD) which use Artificial Intelligence to detect and diagnose patients suffering from AD. And these devices have proven to be remarkable advancement [1] in the detection of AD (Figs. 1, 2, 3, 4, 5, 6 and 7).

Fig. 1. Timeline of treatment methods for Alzheimer's Disease

This paper is divided into various sections such as, Sect. 1 served as the introduction, highlighting the challenges during the treatment of Alzheimer's disease, the symptoms of the disease and also discussed the importance of treatment procedures. Section 2 discussed the review of literature summarizing the studies. Section 3 discussed the methodology in gathering the necessary literature studies, and also presented the types of datasets used in neurological diagnoses, and talks about the machine learning models, and deep learning models are examined and contrasted between studies; Sect. 4 theorizes the conclusion and suggests a course for future study. Section 5 contains the references (Tables 1, 2, 3 and 4).

2 Review of Literature

Table 1. Summary of Literature studies

Study	Methods Used	Dataset	Performance Metrics
[17]	(Stochastic gradient Descent)SGD, k-Nearest Neighbors, Logistic Regression, Decision Tree, Random Forest, AdaBoost, Neural Network, SVM, Naïve Bayes; Feature Selection: Information Gain, Gini index, (Principal Component Analysis)PCA	OASIS	Accuracy: ~90% for top features (CDR(Clinical Dementia Rating), SES(Subjective Cognitive Decline), (Normalized Whole Brain Volume) nWBV)
[18]	Middle-fusion multi modal model, Depth wise Separable Convolution, Mix Skip Connection, Sharing Weight Convolution Blocks	ADNI1 (T1w MRI, FDG PET), ADNI2/ADNI3 (Aβ PET, Tau PET)	Balanced Accuracy: 1.00 (AD vs CN), 0.76 (MCI vs CN)
[20]	Supervised Learning, Weakly Supervised Learning (WSL), and Transfer Learning (highlighted as a bridge between supervised and WSL)	MRI Dataset	-
[23]	Bi-Vision Transformer (BiViT), Mutual Latent Fusion (MLF), Parallel Coupled Encoding Strategy (PCES)	AD Dataset, Cognitive Disorder Dataset	AD Accuracy: 96.38%; Cognitive Disorders Accuracy: 44.94%; Recall: 97.87% (AD), 68.69% (Cognitive Disorders)
[25]	Support Vector Machines (SVM), Random Forests - PRISMA Methodology for source selection (2881 sources, 59 selected) - T1w + FDG-PET as the common modality combination	ADNI Dataset	-

3 Research Methodology for Implementation:

109 papers were first found for the literature review by conducting a keyword search on Google Scholar. These articles were collected from credible publications and a range of independent sources that were released between 2021 and 2024. After the first screening procedure eliminated publications with identical titles, 11 articles (109-11 = 98) were left out. Articles were then evaluated for eligibility according to how well they addressed the subjects of the study. During this eligibility check, 71 more articles were disqualified. In the end, 27 papers were chosen for additional examination. The review contains some of the latest work of Diagnosis of AD using Artificial Intelligence.

3.1 Datasets

This section provides a thorough summary of the datasets was discussed that have been used in the articles. The choice of datasets is crucial since it can change the prediction accuracy rates [2], even though the model help in rapid identification.

Alzheimer's disease can be diagnosed using various imaging techniques, with MRI being particularly useful for identifying structural brain abnormalities. MRI uses radio waves and strong magnetic fields to produce detailed brain images without invasive procedures. Functional MRI (fMRI) measures brain activity by monitoring blood flow and oxygen levels, providing real-time insights into brain function. Structural MRI (sMRI) differentiates patients based on specific radioactive characteristics [3] of brain images. PET scans use tracers to detect abnormal metabolic activity, such as amyloid plaque accumulation or altered glucose metabolism.

3.1.1 Structural Imaging

Structural imaging techniques generate incredibly detailed images of the brain's architecture. These techniques focus on the structure of the brain, identifying abnormalities such as tumors, lesions, and structural changes associated with diseases such as Alzheimer's.

Magnetic Resonance Imaging(MRI) MRIs (magnetic resonance imaging) use powerful magnets and radio waves to produce detailed images of the brain's soft tissues, allowing for the observation of even the smallest anatomical details. This high-resolution imaging is crucial for diagnosing strokes, multiple sclerosis, brain tumors, and congenital brain abnormalities. MRI's ability to differentiate between various brain tissues makes it an essential diagnostic and research tool.

CT Scan Computed Tomography (CT) scans use X-rays to create cross-sectional images of the brain. They are quick and efficient, making them ideal for emergency situations requiring timely diagnosis. CT scans are particularly useful for detecting life-threatening conditions such as cancers, fractures, and hemorrhages. Although less detailed than MRI, CT is widely accessible and can rapidly identify significant structural issues, facilitating prompt medical intervention.

However, MRI images and Ct Scan images are expensive to produce are less accessible [8].

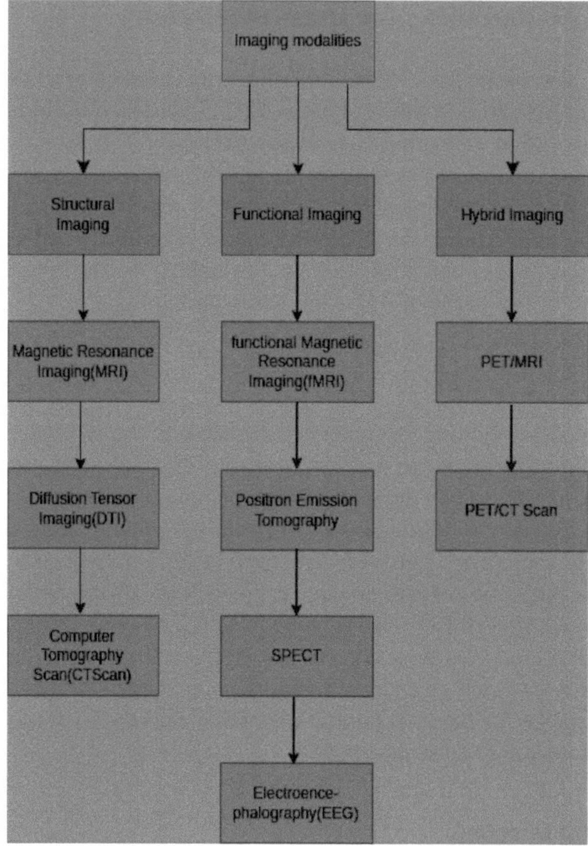

Fig. 2. Different Imaging Modalities used in Brain Scans for Diagnosis.

3.1.2 Functional Imaging

Functional MRI seeks to understand the brain's activity and functionality rather than its anatomy. These techniques measure changes in blood flow, oxygen consumption, and metabolic activity to shed light on the practical characteristics of various brain regions during various tasks.

Functional Magnetic Resonance Imaging Functional Magnetic Resonance Imaging (fMRI) measures brain activity by detecting variations in blood oxygen saturation. More active brain regions require more oxygen, allowing fMRI to map brain activity in real time and identify specific regions involved in different tasks. Widely used in cognitive neuroscience, fMRI helps study brain functions such as language, perception, and decision-making.

Positron Emission Tomography(PET) During Positron Emission Tomography (PET) scans, a small amount of radioactive tracer is injected into the bloodstream. The PET scanner detects the radiation emitted by the tracer to produce images of metabolic activity in the brain. PET is crucial for diagnosing and studying disorders like depression, epilepsy, and Alzheimer's disease, as it helps understand brain metabolism and neurotransmitter systems.

3.1.3 Hybrid Imaging

Pet/mri PET/MRI combines detailed anatomical images from MRI with functional and metabolic data from PET, allowing accurate localization of metabolic activity within the anatomical framework. This hybrid method is useful in neurology for studying neurological diseases, cardiology for assessing cardiac issues, and oncology for tumor detection and tracking. The combined images enhance diagnostic accuracy by providing a comprehensive view of both anatomy and function.

Table 2. Summary of datasets used in various studies

Dataset Used	Imaging modality	Category	Description of the Image	Constraints	Studies used
ADNI(Alzheimer's Disease Neuroimaging Initiative)	T1-weighted MRI, FDG PET, Aβ PET, Tau PET	Alzheimer's Disease, Mild Cognitive Impairment, Cognitive Normal	High-resolution images of brain structures, glucose metabolism, amyloid-beta plaques, tau proteins	High cost, limited availability, complex data preprocessing	[8, 18, 19, 25]
OASIS(open Access Series of Imaging Studies)	T1-weighted MRI	Alzheimer's Disease, Cognitive Normal	High-resolution images of brain structures, specifically focused on aging and cognitive decline	Limited to structural MRI, smaller sample size	[16, 17, 19]

3.2 Learning Models for Alzheimer's Disease Diagnosis:

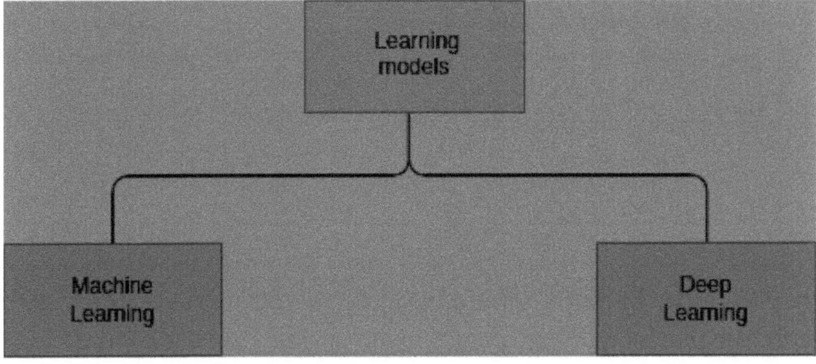

Fig. 3. Types of learning models

Early Alzheimer's disease diagnosis is facilitated by learning models trained on the input imaging modalities. The models' many parameters have an impact on the forecasts and performance. These models work with imaging techniques such as (functional MRI)fMRI, PET, (Structural MRI)sMRI, and MRI. Understanding the make-up and residues of proteins is the initial step in Alzheimer's disease.

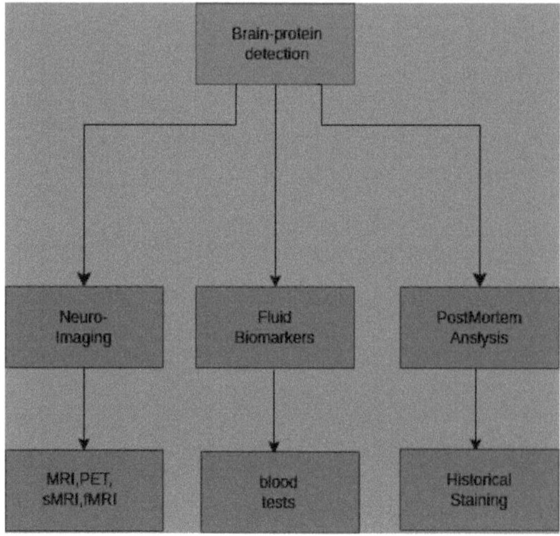

Fig. 4. Different techniques used in the brain-protein detection, one popular way is the Neuro-Imaging way, which was extensively covered in this review.

3.2.1 Machine Learning Models for AD Diagnosis:

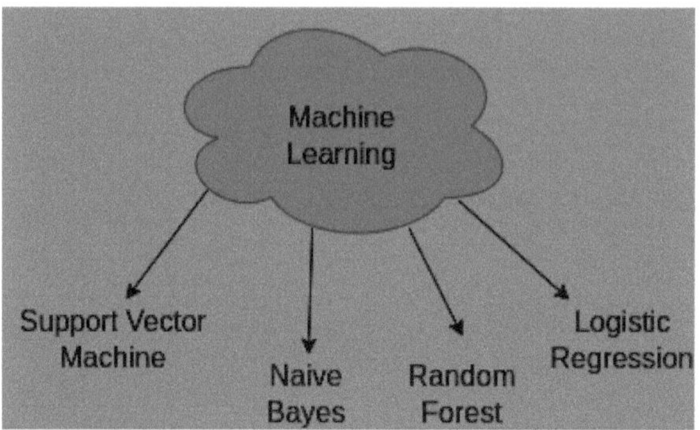

Fig. 5. Types of Machine learning algorithms.

Support Vector Machine To differentiate between Alzheimer's patients and healthy individuals with mild impairment, MRI data was pre-processed (normalized, skull-stripped, and segmented) and classified using Support Vector Machines (SVM) [12]. Features extracted from the images, such as texture and gray matter density, were used by the SVM model, which showed effective results. In another study, SVM achieved over 93% recognition for mental states when combined with a fractal model.

Naive Bayes The Naive Bayes algorithm, based on Bayes' theorem, is used to classify brain scan images (e.g., MRIs and PETs) based on specific features. It is applied in diagnosing disorders such as brain tumors, Alzheimer's disease, and Parkinson's disease. However, its main limitation arises from the assumption that features are independent, which is often not the case in brain imaging data due to the common associations between features (e.g., distinct brain areas).

Random Forest The Random Forest ensemble learning technique is commonly used for regression and classification tasks. It builds multiple decision trees during training and combines their outputs to improve accuracy and reduce overfitting. In brain imaging, Random Forest helps detect brain issues by managing the high dimensionality and complexity of the data. However, pre-processing and feature extraction from high-dimensional data can still be challenging and time-consuming, even with Random Forest.

Logistic Regression Logistic regression is a statistical method for two-class classification that estimates the probability of an input belonging to a particular class. It uses the logistic function to convert predicted values into probabilities. In brain imaging, logistic regression can determine whether a scan indicates a disease, such as Alzheimer's, based on image features. However, it may not detect complex patterns in brain imaging data if the relationship between features and outcomes is not linear.

3.2.2　Deep Learning Models for AD Diagnosis

There are a few types of models for deep learning, including convolution neural networks, Transformers, Auto-encoders, Artificial Neural Network.

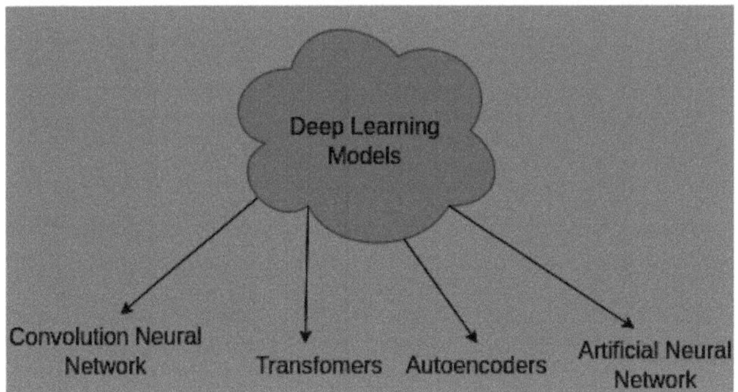

Fig. 6. Types of Deep Learning Models

Convolution Neural Network CNNs, or convolution deep learning is facilitated by neural networks. Models that are accustomed to recognize or anticipate patterns in data and images. This analysis focused on studies that used CNN as their primary learning model.

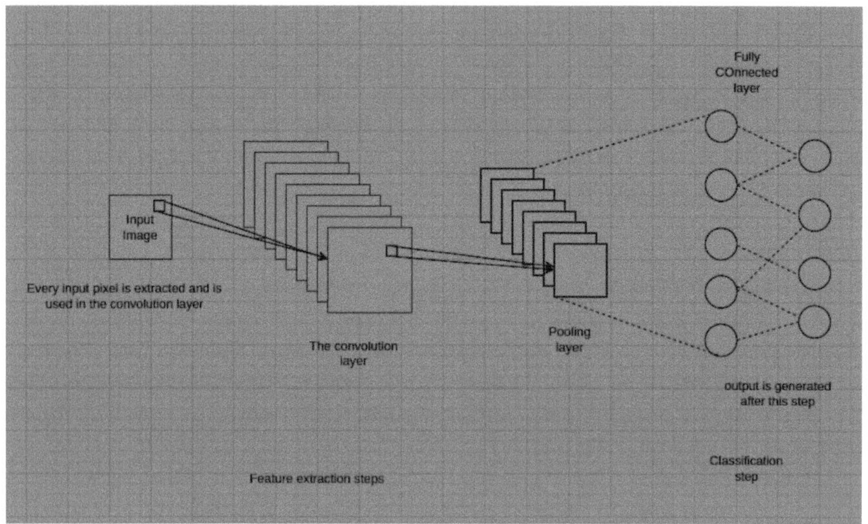

Fig. 7. A CNN architecture and its internal working.

In [12], the author proposed a 3D–2D Learnable Weighted Pooling technique. This technique converts 3D brain scans into 2D fused pictures. The model is able to take advantage of the 3D images to extract more informative features. Thanks to the learnable and data-driven nature of the LWP approach. Following the conversion of the photographs into 2D images, ResNet34 was utilized for training. Other 2D-CNN models were surpassed by the ResNet34 as a feature extractor. The authors of certain studies that have worked on the CNN, including [14], have recommended using the A triplet-loss function is employed in Siamese Convolution Neural Networks (SCNNs) to enable the use of MRI in the early detection of Alzheimer's disease (AD).The structure of the SCNN consists of two or more related neural networks that have common weights.

Transformers Transformers, a group of deep learning models, use self-attention to focus on relevant parts of the input sequence, regardless of their position. Vision Transformers (ViTs) apply this approach to image analysis, treating image patches as tokens and learning associations between different parts of the image. While effective in medical imaging and other applications, transformers require a large amount of labeled data for effective training. There is a particular version of ViT called Bi-Vision Transformer [15], which combines two novel modules: Mutual Latent Fusion (MLF) and Parallel Coupled Encoding Strategy (PCES) to enhance feature learning.

Autoencoders Autoencoders are unsupervised neural networks used to find efficient coding schemes for input data. They work by first compressing the input into a latent space representation and then reconstructing the output from this compressed form. The goal is to learn a meaningful encoding for the data, typically for feature learning or dimensionality reduction. The process involves a latent-space encoder that transforms the input into a compressed representation, followed by a decoder that maps this representation back to the original data space.

Artificial Neural Network Artificial Neural Networks (ANNs) are inspired by the human brain and consist of interconnected layers of neurons or data-processing nodes. Each neuron uses an activation function to combine its weighted inputs, with each synaptic connection having an associated weight. ANNs are foundational for more complex models like Recurrent Neural Networks (RNNs) and Convolutional Neural Networks (CNNs). Like Transformers and Autoencoders, ANNs require a large amount of labeled data to generalize effectively. This can be a challenge with medical imaging databases, especially for rare diseases. For instance, an ANN achieved 89.88% accuracy in predicting Alzheimer's disease based on MRI data.

3.3　Performance Metrics

To assess the performance of learning models, performance metrics are used to analyze how well the models perform against the data. These metrics measure the accuracy of the results, the efficiency of the models, and their reliability during predictions or classifications.

　　There are quite a few performance metrics available to study the models performance. Some of them are.

3.3.1　Accuracy

Accuracy is one of the fundamental metrics to evaluate performance of a model. It calculates the proportion of correct predictions made by the model out of the total number of predictions.

$$\text{Accuracy}: \quad (TP + TN)/(TP + TN + FP + FN)$$

TP – True Positive, TN – True Negative, FP – False Positive, FN – False Negative.
TP explains that the model predicted positive class(class of interest) correctly.
TN explains that the model predicted negative(opposite of the class of interest, or other features are not part of the primary target prediction) class correctly.
FP – explains that the model predicted positive class incorrectly.
FN – explains that the model predicted negative class incorrectly.

3.3.2　Precision

Precision is a performance metric which focuses on the positive predictions, it measures, accuracy of the positive predictions made by the model.

$$\text{Precision}: \quad TP/TP + FP$$

TP – True Positive, FP – False Positive.

3.3.3 Recall or Sensitivity

Recall specifically measures the performance of the model in identifying the positive class out of the predictions of both correct predictions of positive class and incorrect predictions of positive class.

$$Recall \; : \quad TP/TP + FN$$

TP – True Positive, FN – False Negative.

3.3.4 Specificity

Specificity measures the proportion of correctly predicted negative class and the combination of correctly predicted negative class and incorrectly predicted negative class.

$$Specificity \; : \quad TP/TP + FP$$

TN – True negative, FP – False Positive.

Table 3. Summary of Machine Learning models used in various studies

Study	Performance Dataset	Test Dataset	Technique	Performance Metrics	Positives	Future Scope
[19]	OASIS, ADNI	OASIS, ADNI	Light Gradient Boosting Machine (LGBM),,K-Nearest Neighbor (KNN), Gaussian Naive Bayes (GNB)	Accuracy: 99.63% (LGBM on ADNI), 95.75% (MLP on OASIS), 87.50% (KNN on ADNI-OASIS), 77.97% (GNB on OASIS-ADNI)	High accuracy across multiple models, robust performance on different datasets	Explore hybrid models, enhance interpretability, increase dataset diversity

Table 4. Summary of deep learning models used in various studies

Study	Performance Dataset	Test Dataset	Technique	Performance Metrics	Positives	Future Scope
[23]	AD dataset, Cognitive Disorder dataset	AD dataset, Cognitive Disorder dataset	Bi-Vision Transformer (BiViT), Mutual Latent Fusion (MLF), Parallel Coupled Encoding Strategy (PCES)	Accuracy: 96.38% (AD dataset), below 96% (Cognitive Disorder dataset)	High accuracy on AD dataset, novel feature learning techniques	Address data imbalance and limited availability, integrate explainability techniques

(continued)

Table 4. (*continued*)

Study	Performance Dataset	Test Dataset	Technique	Performance Metrics	Positives	Future Scope
[26]	ADNI	ADNI	Deep transfer learning, ensemble models (VGG16, VGG19, DenseNet169, DenseNet201), XAI techniques (saliency maps, grad-CAM)	Accuracy: 96%, Precision, Recall, F1 Score	High accuracy, enhanced interpretability and transparency with XAI techniques	Further enhance model interpretability, integrate with clinical decision support systems

4   Conclusion and Future Scope

After reviewing various studies on using Artificial Intelligence (AI) for screening and diagnosing Alzheimer's disease (AD), both machine learning (ML) and deep learning techniques have shown effectiveness. ML methods, such as Random Forest, Support Vector Machine (SVM), and ensemble techniques, have produced promising results. Deep learning approaches, particularly Convolutional Neural Networks (CNNs) and their derivatives like Very Deep Convolution Networks (VGG) and Residual Networks (ResNet), have also demonstrated strong performance.Key parameters for diagnosis include dataset sources, with most studies utilizing the ADNI (Alzheimer's Disease Neuroimaging Initiative) and OASIS (Open Access Series of Imaging Studies), which provide MRI, PET, and CT scan images. To evaluate performance, metrics such as the F1 Score and AUC ROC curve are commonly used.However, interpreting results can be challenging for medical professionals and researchers. One solution is Explainable Artificial Intelligence (XAI), which aims to make AI predictions more interpretable. Additionally, the cost of AI in research and treatment is a significant factor. To address this, some studies suggest using mobile apps, which are more accessible, efficient, and facilitate early detection of AD.

References

1. Verma, R.K., et al.: An insight into the role of Artificial Intelligence in the early diagnosis of Alzheimer's disease. CNS Neurol. Disord.-Drug Targets (Formerly Current Drug Targets-CNS Neurol. Disord.) **21**(10), 901–912 (2022)
2. Fabrizio, C., Termine, A., Caltagirone, C., Sancesario, G.: Artificial intelligence for Alzheimer's disease: promise or challenge? Diagnostics **11**(8), 1473 (2021)
3. Liu, S., Jie, C., Zheng, W., Cui, J., Wang, Z.: Investigation of underlying association between whole brain regions and alzheimer's disease: a research based on an artificial intelligence model. Front. Aging Neurosci. **14**, 872530 (2022)

4. García-Gutierrez, F., et al.: GA-MADRID: Design and validation of a machine learning tool for the diagnosis of Alzheimer's disease and frontotemporal dementia using genetic algorithms. Med. Biol. Eng. Compu. **60**(9), 2737–2756 (2022)
5. Umeda-Kameyama, Y., et al.: Screening of Alzheimer's disease by facial complexion using artificial intelligence. Aging (Albany NY) **13**(2), 1765 (2021)
6. Agbavor, F., Liang, H.: Artificial Intelligence-enabled End-To-End detection and assessment of Alzheimer's disease using voice. Brain Sci. **13**(1), 28 (2023)
7. Kiss, G.: Early detection of Alzheimer's disease using Artificial Intelligence. Procedia Comput. Sci. **237**, 485–492 (2024)
8. Hasan, M.M., Rahman, S., Parmar, H., Chowdhury, S.: A novel Artificial Intelligence (AI) method to classify and predict the progression of Alzheimers disease. BioRxiv (2024)
9. Veneziani, I., et al.: Applications of artificial intelligence in the neuropsychological assessment of dementia: a systematic review. J. Personalized Med. **14**(1), 113 (2024)
10. Viswan, V., Shaffi, N., Mahmud, M., Subramanian, K., Hajamohideen, F.: Explainable artificial intelligence in Alzheimer's disease classification: a systematic review. Cogn. Comput. **16**(1), 1–44 (2024)
11. Betzler, B.K., Rim, T.H., Sabanayagam, C., Cheng, C.Y.: Artificial intelligence in predicting systemic parameters and diseases from ophthalmic imaging. Front. Digit. Health **4**, 889445 (2022)
12. Xing, X., et al.: Efficient training on Alzheimer's disease diagnosis with learnable weighted pooling for 3D PET brain image classification. Electronics **12**(2), 467 (2023)
13. Ghaffar Nia, N., Kaplanoglu, E., Nasab, A.: Evaluation of artificial intelligence techniques in disease diagnosis and prediction. Discov. Artif. Intell. **3**(1), 5 (2023)
14. Hajamohideen, F., et al.: Four-way classification of Alzheimer's disease using deep Siamese convolution neural network with triplet-loss function. Brain Inform. **10**(1), 1–13 (2023)
15. Shah, S.M.A.H., Khan, M.Q., Rizwan, A., Jan, S.U., Samee, N.A., Jamjoom, M.M.: Computer-aided diagnosis of Alzheimer's disease and neurocognitive disorders with multimodal Bi-Vision Transformer (BiViT). Pattern Anal. Appl. **27**(3), 76 (2024)
16. Castellano, G., Esposito, A., Lella, E., Montanaro, G., Vessio, G.: Automated detection of Alzheimer's disease: a multi-modal approach with 3D MRI and amyloid PET. Sci. Rep. **14**(1), 5210 (2024)
17. Arjaria, S.K., Rathore, A.S., Bisen, D., Bhattacharyya, S.: Performances of machine learning models for diagnosis of Alzheimer's disease. Ann. Data Sci. **11**(1), 307–335 (2024)
18. Kim, S.K., Duong, Q.A., Gahm, J.K.: Multimodal 3D deep learning for early diagnosis of Alzheimer's disease. IEEE Access (2024)
19. Chakraborty, M., Naoal, N., Momen, S., Mohammed, N.: ANALYZE-AD: A comparative analysis of novel AI approaches for early Alzheimer's detection. Array 100352 (2024)
20. Bellesia, R., Manca, G.: The potential for Artificial Intelligence in the diagnosis of Alzheimer's disease: a systematic literature review (2024)
21. Angelucci, F., Ai, A.R., Piendel, L., Cerman, J., Hort, J.: Integrating AI in fighting advancing Alzheimer: diagnosis, prevention, treatment, monitoring, mechanisms, and clinical trials. Curr. Opin. Struct. Biol. **87**, 102857 (2024)
22. Mahmud, T., Barua, K., Habiba, S.U., Sharmen, N., Hossain, M.S., Andersson, K.: An explainable AI paradigm for Alzheimer's diagnosis using deep transfer learning. Diagnostics **14**(3), 345 (2024)
23. Bhandarkar, A., Naik, P., Vakkund, K., Junjappanavar, S., Bakare, S., Pattar, S.: Deep learning based computer aided diagnosis of Alzheimer's disease: a snapshot of last 5 years, gaps, and future directions. Artif. Intell. Rev. **57**(2), 30 (2024)
24. Tandon, R., Levey, A.I., Lah, J.J., Seyfried, N.T., Mitchell, C.S.: Machine learning selection of most predictive brain proteins suggests role of sugar metabolism in Alzheimer's Disease. J. Alzheimer's Dis. (Preprint), 1–14 (2023)

25. Grigas, O., Maskeliunas, R., Damaševičius, R.: Early detection of dementia using artificial intelligence and multimodal features with a focus on neuroimaging: a systematic literature review. Heal. Technol. **14**(2), 201–237 (2024)
26. Arafa, D.A., Moustafa, H.E.D., Ali, H.A., Ali-Eldin, A.M., Saraya, S.F.: A deep learning framework for early diagnosis of Alzheimer's disease on MRI images. Multimedia Tools Appl. **83**(2), 3767–3799 (2024)

"Harnessing the Power of Virtual Reality to Bolster Employee Resilience: A Comprehensive Review and Future Directions"

Medha Gupta[(✉)] [iD] and Rupali Arora

University School of Business, Chandigarh University, Mohali, India
medhagupta1997@gmail.com, rupali.arora@cumail.in

Abstract. Virtual Reality (VR) has proven to be an innovative tool that can help perform several aspects of organizational processes. This extensive literature review aims at identifying and discussing existing literature on the use of VR as a tool to enhance the development of employee resilience in organisations. The recruitment and selection process is now trending with the use of technology to offer a better look at tasks and working conditions by using VR. This approach steps up the decision-making process through qualifying the match between the candidates and the job, which ultimately optimizes the ability of recruiting and cuts down the rates of turnover. In talent management, VR entails the creation of replicas of working conditions to enable the employ check on the skills he will use in practice without risking the real condition. Additionally, due to interactive occurrences and behavioural parameters, introduced by VR, the system of performance measurement has been shifted toward the evaluation and admittance of precise real-time performance. Thereby, the current paper advances a methodologically rigorous approach for capturing the effects of VR on employee resilience based on the PLS-SEM analysis to open the avenues of stimulating the innovative strategy in the human resource management. The data was collected from 400 employees working in the manufacturing sector. The results indicated that recruitment & selection, talent management and performance evaluation positively influenced virtual reality which in turn had a favourable impact on employee resilience.

Keywords: Talent Management · Virtual Reality · Performance Evaluation · Employee Resilience · Recruitment and Selection

1 Introduction

VR is a rapidly advancing skill that enables the creation of diverse, lifelike environments enriched with sensory details, spontaneous interactions, and immersive experiences [1]. VR finds extensive use in fields such as teaching, health care, armed forces, medicine, digital marketing, hospitality, product development, and entertainment [2, 3]. Acknowledging the potential of the industrial sector in driving digital transformation, [2] introduced the National Policy on Industry 4.0 (Industry4WRD) to propel the industry towards a digital future and boost its economic impact. One of the elements of this policy is to implement augmented reality (AR) and VR in the human resource management (HRM) to strengthen the adaptability of the workforce for the future digital environment. Taking into account the Future of Jobs Survey 2023 of the World Economic Forum, the skills required in a digital work environment include proactivity, adaptability, and learnability as valuable components of response ability and adaptability of the workforce [3]. In this context, the key to success is to review all the basic HR activities such as staffing, management of employees, and performance measurement. Therefore, it is imperative to integrate these processes with the help of the most advanced technologies that contribute to the development of a more robust employee [4].

Resilience includes coping mechanisms to bounce back from adversities as well as from optimism, instabilities, vociferations, defeats, or even from pleasures and promotion of duties. According to [5], it embraces a powerful psychological ability to 'spring back.' Resilient people are usually aggressive in regard to challenge and proficient in the utilization of psychological assets in order to minimize the influence of stress in the surrounding [6]. This concept has received much attention in the field of HRM with the intend of improving productivity [7]. He further pointed that only an engaging staff can help organizations compete effectively in the times of high globalisation to meet the organisational goals and objectives. These people are often more effective, committed, creative and content at their places of work thereby enhancing the operations of the organizations and in turn the nation's economy [8].

Companies have entered into many projects including the management of digital data to redesign working procedures and manage customer relations [9]. They also have enormous potential for practice in these areas [10] VR and AR technologies for example. They have numerous benefits such as it saves cost, it can grow to accommodate more people, it is widely available, it is very engaging and users get immediate feedback, and it can be made specific for the user. These technologies could present, security and privacy issues since these systems collect and analyse user personal information such as biometrics, behaviour, and other personal identifying data. This can create organisational resistance or scepticism from the employees or the managers as they might consider such technologies as invasive, irrelevant, or inefficient. Moreover, they always entail shifts in organizational culture, processes, and policies many of which are apprehensive will disrupt their business model [11]. Therefore, the purpose of this paper is to highlight the numerous possibilities of AR and VR integration in the context of HRM. This will be done by examining how these technologies can be used on the main functions of HRM including; recruitment, talent management and performance evaluation. After this, the focus of the discussion will be drawn towards how the use of AR and VR can increase the levels of employee readiness and organizational optimization for manufacturing practices.

The study advances our knowledge of how introducing Virtual Reality (VR) applications into critical human resource functions—such as recruiting, selection, talent management, and performance evaluation can improve employee resilience in the manufacturing industry. It focusses on the function of immersive VR technology in producing realistic job simulations, promoting experiential learning, and offering compelling training settings. These VR-driven activities help employees build crucial skills, flexibility, and problem-solving abilities, all of which contribute to their resilience.

2 Literature Review

Recruitment and Selection: The application of Information technology, particularly the integration of VR, can be helpful in giving business organizations more progressive and effective services as opposed to the conventional recruitment and selection procedures offered by human resource departments. In other words, the purposes of recruitment are to attract and maintain an appropriate and efficient pool of employees [12]. It enables human relations (HR) managers to evaluate candidates cost-effectively through multiple interviews, ensuring they find top talent for key roles. It also allows candidates to interact with potential employers. As candidates engage with VR platforms, they become more motivated to apply for jobs [13]. Further, [14] stated in their research about how VR helps in revamping their recruitment and selection process by removing the obstacles and enhancing the efficacy of the organizations.

Talent Management: One of the widely adopted VR technologies for training is simulations. VR allows users to see or engage fully in a different world. Research has demonstrated that VR enables trainees to experience a virtual environment tailored to their organization's needs, facilitating diverse interactive experiences that replicate real-world scenarios [15]. [16] tackles the ethical and human aspects of digital transformation, including concerns about data privacy, job displacement, the digital divide, bias in AI and analytics, employee welfare, and the impact on the environment.

Performance Evaluation: VR has been utilized in assessing and providing feedback on performance [17]. According to [9], a performance evaluation system used at the workplace can be utilized for observing employee performance. Through the aid of such a technology, it is possible for the employees to transact directly with the managing agents irrespective of levels of time and space., facilitating the quick and efficient identification of problem areas. Performance evaluation is a key factor that influences user adoption of emerging technologies like virtual reality. Assessing these non-functional requirements can be challenging, which has increasingly attracted the attention of researchers [18]. Additionally, it allows for feedback from various sources, such as workgroup customers, which supports continuous performance improvement for employees [19].

Employee Resilience: VR makes a stress-free zone where the employees can learn to behave and react in case of stressful events but with virtual outcome. The nature of VR, where the subject is both active and fully immersed, training also becomes considerably more effective for retraining specific skills. Another benefit is to show the relativity of VR when it comes to practicing stress management, especially in high pressure situations. VR facilitates team-based interactions that are required to help individuals develop solutions for working together, which is a critical component of building interpersonal relationships [6]. The implementation of VR holds great promise for improving guest experiences, boosting operational efficiency, and advancing employee training. The research emphasizes VR's role in supporting sustainable and inclusive tourism, which in turn helps strengthen community resilience [20].

3   Research Methodology and Hypothesis Development

Based on our prior literature review, we have outlined the following framework, which is shown in Fig. 1. As we can infer from Fig. 1, employee resilience is the dependent variable in the study and virtual reality is the independent variable in this research. The research anticipates that VR will have an impact on employee resilience, which in turn is influenced by factors such as recruitment and selection, talent management, and performance evaluation.

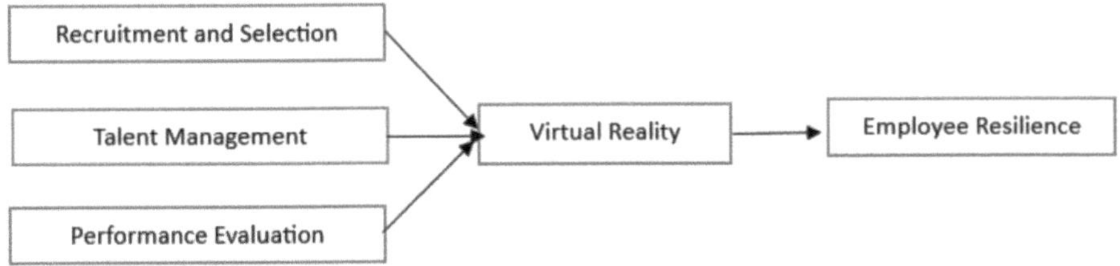

Fig. 1. Conceptual Framework. Source: Author's Compilation

Based on the literature review and the conceptual framework, we propose the following hypothesis for this research.

H_1: Recruitment and Selection have a significant influence on VR
H_2: Talent Management have a significant influence on VR
H_3: Performance Evaluation have a significant influence on VR
H_4: VR have significant influence on Employee Resilience.

The research employed a combination of descriptive and empirical methods. A total of 400 employees from the manufacturing sector in the tri-city area were surveyed using a structured questionnaire. Of these, 325 responses were analyzed. The questionnaire featured a 5-point Likert scale, and the data were inspected using Partial Least Squares Structural Equation Modeling (PLS-SEM).

4   Results

The data analysis was done using Smart PLS-SEM. Before testing our hypotheses, we rigorously assessed the validity and reliability of our measurement instruments through a structured three-step process. First, we performed a cross-loading analysis to evaluate the scales for our constructs. All factors showed loadings above 0.7, confirming that each item strongly corresponded with its associated latent construct. Second, we checked cronbach's alpha (CA), composite reliability (CR), and average variance extraction (AVE), as reported in Table 1. Lastly, to verify discriminant validity, we calculated the square root of the AVE (SQAVE) and compared it with the correlations of the latent variables. Table 2 presents the discriminant validity based on the Fornell-Larcker criterion. According to this criterion, the square root of a construct's average variance extracted (AVE) should be greater than its correlation with any other construct [21]. Since this requirement is fulfilled, it suggests strong discriminant validity. Based on these findings, we concluded that our questionnaire is both reliable and valid.

Table 1. Construct Reliability and Validity Test. Source: Author's Compilation

Variable		Factor Loadings	Cronbach's Alpha (CA)	CR (RHO_C)	Average variance extraction (AVE)
Employee Resilience (ER)	ER1	0.890	0.944	0.956	0.783
	ER2	0.896			
	ER3	0.945			
	ER4	0.908			
	ER5	0.908			
	ER6	0.752			
Performance Evaluation (PE)	PE1	0.927	0.931	0.954	0.875
	PE2	0.937			
	PE3	0.942			
Recruitment and Selection (RS)	RS1	0.829	0.845	0.906	0.763
	RS2	0.916			
	RS3	0.873			
Talent Management (TM)	TM1	0.888	0.877	0.924	0.802
	TM2	0.934			
	TM3	0.864			
Virtual Reality (VR)	VR1	0.903	0.960	0.968	0.836
	VR2	0.839			
	VR3	0.961			
	VR4	0.955			
	VR5	0.910			
	VR6	0.912			

To investigate the established research hypotheses, partial least squares structural equation modeling (PLS-SEM) was employed as depicted in Fig. 2. Subsequently, to analyse the reliability and validity of the constructs that have been developed, we applied the standard bootstrapping method to derive the path coefficients. To assess the significance and relevance of the proposed relationships, we calculated various indicators such as the mean (M), standard deviation (STDEV), t-value, and p-value. The path analysis technique is utilized to validate the model. According to this method, the t-value is used to assess the validity of hypotheses. A t-value greater than 1.96 signifies significance at the 0.05 level. Moreover, p-value below 0.05 is generally deemed statistically significant, indicating that the null hypothesis should be rejected. Conversely, a p-value above 0.05 suggests that the deviation from the null hypothesis is not statistically significant, so the

Table 2. Discriminant Validity Test. Source: Author's Compilation

Fornell–Larcker Criterion					
	ER	PE	RS	TM	VR
ER	0.885				
PE	0.360	0.935			
RS	0.414	0.645	0.873		
TM	0.603	0.639	0.710	0.896	
VR	0.602	0.278	0.603	0.482	0.914

null hypothesis remains accepted. [21]. The outcomes of these analyses are summarized in Table 3.

Table 3. Hypothesis Testing Results. Source: Author's Compilation

Hypothesis	Path	Sample Mean	Standard Deviation (STDEV)	T Value	P Value	Result
H1	RS→VR	0.628	0.167	3.734	0.000	Accepted
H2	TM→VR	0.201	0.063	3.145	0.002	Accepted
H3	PE→VR	-0.174	0.054	3.215	0.001	Accepted
H4	VR→ER	0.611	0.097	6.188	0.000	Accepted

Based on the data presented in the Table 3, we can conclude that all the hypotheses are accepted. This indicates that the factors of recruitment & selection, talent management, and performance evaluation significantly impact virtual reality (VR) in the context of our study. Furthermore, the findings suggest that VR has a positive influence on employee resilience.

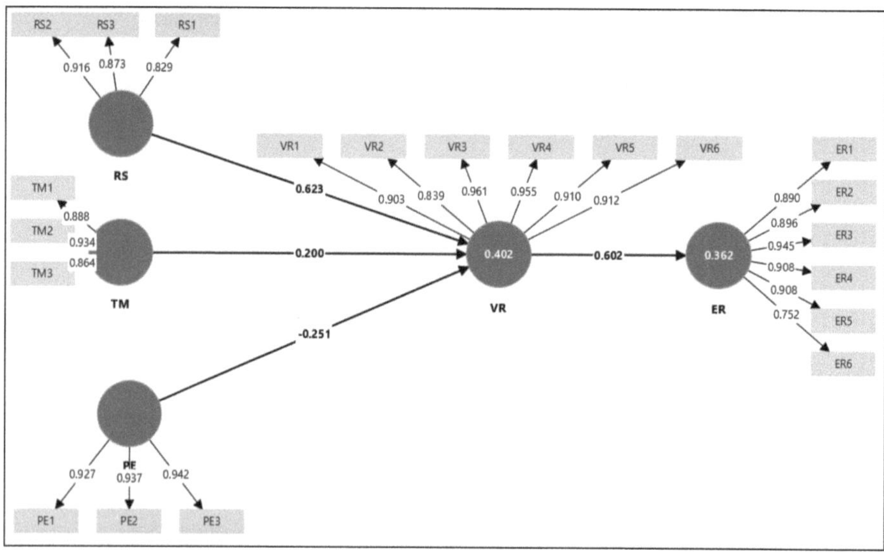

Fig. 2. PLS-SEM Model. Source: Author's Compilation

5   Limitations

Some of the limitations in this research include collecting data only from tri-city restricts the generalization of the findings of the study. It also means that the behaviours, cultures and reactions of the employees and organizations towards the VR training may differ in this specific region than in other regions or countries of the world. Technological development could be another explanation because the implementation and reception of VR could easily be influenced by the different technological infrastructure and access within the tri-city area as compared to different regions with different technological advancement levels. Expenses associated with VR equipment and software are high; this is a drawback for many organizations especially small and medium enterprises (SMEs) thus restricting availability. That means not all the employees would be able to access the necessary technology at home so the range of possibilities for the remote training is limited. As an advantage of VR, it can help keep the users interested in the training; however, sustaining user interest in the content can be a challenge especially when the content is boring, and, or not frequently updated.

6   Future Scope

To address these limitations and fully harness the potential of VR in enhancing employee resilience, future research and development should focus on: Introducing enhanced, cheaper, simpler, and effective VR equipment and software to expand the use and optimize the learning process. Recommending funding for research to develop better, interesting, and culturally appropriate VR training programs for various organizations' requirements. Introducing clear-cut guidelines and long-term research to quantify the success and return on investment (ROI) of VR-based training in resilience. Educating the personnel within the target organizations in order to increase the acceptance of VR technology. Policies and procedures for regulating other ethical and privacy issues related to the use of the VR for learning and training.

7 Conclusion

Altogether, the incorporation of VR into different organizational activities revealed high potential in the improvement of recruitment and selection, as well as talent management and performance appraisal. This literature review has also discussed the perspectives of using VR in these areas wherein its emphasis has been made on the aspect of enhancing the organizational effectiveness as well as building employee toughness. All in all, VR has several benefits; however, it is not without its issues. Challenges like limitations by technology and costs need to be properly dealt with to make use of VR to the utmost fullness. However, the review indicates potential directions for the additional research and practical implementation, mainly pointing out the ways in which VR can improve the staff's psychological endurance. Using rigorous analytical research method like PLS-SEM enable this paper to propose a theoretical framework whereby the effects of VR on employees' resilience are demonstrated. This prepares the ground for the application of more creative solutions in human resource management and places VR at the forefront of preparing the staff for changes in the future environment. Finally, VR comes out as quite a vigorous phenomenon that qualifies as one of the key proponents of the contemporary approaches within organizations and bureaucracies, providing a broad number of advantages over traditional methods and models. Future developments are therefore anticipated to see the incorporation of technology into the HR mechanisms broaden since the growth in the adoption of technology creates progressive possibilities of improving the overall engagement, profile as well as future-proofing of the employees.

References

1. Chen, W., Qian, S., Deng, J.: Learning single-image depth from videos using quality assessment networks. In: Proceedings of the IEEE/CVF Conference on Computer Vision and Pattern Recognition (CVPR). pp. 5604–5613 (2019)
2. Miti, M.: Industry 4WRD: national policy on industry 4.0. (2018)
3. Lai, S.F., Lim, W.L., Foo, M.Y., Choo, S.M.: Embedding virtual reality in HRM practices to enhance workforce agility in the manufacturing industry. Atlantis Press International BV (2023)
4. Bharambe, N.S., Thakur, T., Bhangale, S.R.: Virtual HR era in human resource management. Int. J. Res. Eng. Sci. Manag. **4**, 258–263 (2021)
5. Luthans, F.: The need for and meaning of positive organizational behavior. J. Organ. Behav. **23**, 695–706 (2002)
6. Fredrickson, B.L., Cohn, M., Sandra, M.: Open hearts build lives: positive emotions, induced through loving-kindness meditation, build consequential personal resources. J. Pers. Soc. Psychol. **95**, 1045–1062 (2005)
7. Alan, S., Gruman, J.A., Albrecht, S.L.A.B.B.: Journal of Organizational Effectiveness: People and Performance. J. Organ. Eff. People Perform. **1**, 261–280 (2014)

8. Truss, C., Delbridge, R., Alfes, K., Shantz, A., Soane, E.: Employee engagement in theory and practice. (2013)
9. Stone, D.L., Deadrick, D.L., Lukaszewski, K.M., Johnson, R.: The influence of technology on the future of human resource management. Hum. Resour. Manag. Rev. **25**, 216–231 (2015). https://doi.org/10.1016/j.hrmr.2015.01.002
10. Kiruthika, J., Khaddaj, S.: Impact and challenges of using of virtual reality & Artificial Intelligence in businesses. In: 16th International Symposium on Distributed Computing and Applications to Business, Engineering and Science (DCABES). pp. 165–168. IEEE (2017)
11. Aydın, Ö., Karaarslan, E.: Artificial Intelligence, VR, AR and metaverse technologies for human resources management. SSRN Electron. J. 1–10 (2023). https://doi.org/10.2139/ssrn.4480626
12. Snell, S.A., Gardner, S.D., Lepak, D.P., Bartol, K.M., West, J.P., Berman, E.M.: 2. Literature survey in the review of public staff management entitled "from traditional to virtual virtual: Is the transition occurring in local government? Int. J. Res. Eng. **4**, 259 (2021)
13. Hutchison, A.: Using virtual reality to explore science and literacy concepts. Read. Teach. **72**, 343–353 (2018). https://doi.org/10.1002/trtr.1720
14. Madhavi, T., Avulakunta, K.: The impact of Artificial Intelligence in recruitment and selection processes in IT companies. In: 2024 16th International Conference on Electronics, Computers and Artificial Intelligence (ECAI). pp. 1–5. IEEE (2024)
15. Forsberg, N.L., Anders Gulliksen, J.: VR for HR–A case study of human resource development professionals using virtual reality for social skills training in the workplace. In: IFIP Conference on Human-Computer Interaction. pp. 231–251. Springer Nature Switzerland (2023)
16. Arora, M., Ahmad, V., Arora, T., Kumar, R.: Digital transformation and talent management. Taylor and Francis Inc. (2024)
17. Koutitas, G., Smith, S., Lawrence, G.: Performance evaluation of AR/VR training technologies for EMS first responders. Virtual Real. **25**, 83–94 (2021). https://doi.org/10.1007/s10055-020-00436-8
18. Chandra, A.N.R., Jamiy, F.El., Reza, H.: A review on usability and performance evaluation in virtual reality systems. In: International Conference on Computational Science and Computational Intelligence (CSCI) (2019)
19. Chandra, A.N.R., Jamiy, F. El, Reza, H.: A review on usability and performance evaluation in virtual reality systems. In: International Conference on Computational Science and Computational Intelligence (CSCI). pp. 1107–1114. IEEE (2019)
20. Octafian, R., Heru Priyanto, S., Hendratono, T.: Transforming hospitality with virtual reality. J. resilient Econ. **4** (2024). https://doi.org/10.25120/jre.4.1.2024.4083
21. Gupta, M., Arora, R.: Thriving in the hybrid era : investigating the relationships between leadership, high-performance work systems, employee resilience, and engagement in the IT industry. Pacific Bus. Rev. Int. **16**, 117–128 (2024)

Deep Learning Based Dementia Detection on MRI Data

Aditi Baggu[1], Aditya Hegde[1], Harsh Morayya[1], Lokesh Kumar[2]([envelope]), Pranati Sattarapu[1], and Siri Ananya Yallapragada[1]

[1] School of Technology, Woxsen University, Hyderabad 502345, Telangana, India
[2] SUHORA Technologies, Noida One, Noida 201309, Uttar Pradesh, India
lokesh.kumar@suhora.com

Abstract. Dementia, a condition causing progressive cognitive decline, poses a global health challenge with exponentially increasing yearly patients. The aging population necessitates reliable early detection and classification methods. Hence, early detection of Dementia is critical for the development of effective treatments and interventions. Magnetic Resonance Imaging (MRI) emerges as a valuable tool, allowing visualization of brain structure and detecting structural changes associated with Dementia. It aids in distinguishing Dementia from other forms of Dementia and tracking disease progression, supporting a comprehensive diagnosis when combined with cognitive and neurological assessments. This study comprehensively analyzes various Deep Learning (DL) techniques to address the challenge of early detection of Dementia by proposing a multi-modal cascaded analysis approach for early detection and precise classification. The primary focus is on constructing a robust Dementia Detection and Classification system through a 2-level Deep Learning Classification model. The first level of the model serves as a binary classifier, distinguishing patients with Dementia from those without. This initial screening is crucial for identifying potential cases of Dementia. Whereas, the second level refines the classification, categorizing patients into 'Very Mild Dementia', 'Mild Dementia', 'Moderate Dementia', and 'Non-Demented'. We evaluated our proposed model and also compared it with current state of the art models such as ResNet-50, DenseNet-121, Inception-V4, Mobilenet-V3 and VGG-16 using a publicly available Kaggle and OASIS dataset.

Keywords: Dementia · Deep Learning · Alzheimer's Disease · Dementia Detection · Dementia Classification

1 Introduction

Dementia, a progressive and incurable neurodegenerative disorder, includes various cognitive disorders, with Alzheimer's Disease (AD) being the most prevalent form. Affecting individuals across different age groups, Dementia is characterized

S. Pal et al. (Eds.): ICETSS 2024, CCIS 2610, pp. 187–205, 2026.
https://doi.org/10.1007/978-3-032-11488-4_15

by cognitive impairments such as memory loss, which can range from mild forget-fulness to a complete inability to recall recent events, as highlighted by Hutton et al. (2021) [1]. Additionally, reasoning and judgment skills are compromised, severely affecting decision-making and problem-solving abilities, as observed by Shen et al.(2020) [2].

Behavioral changes, including unpredictable mood swings and shifts in personality, significantly contribute to the emotional strain experienced by both patients and their families, a situation described in the work of Jack et al. (2021) [3]. Moreover, communication difficulties, such as impaired language skills and reduced social interaction, often lead to increased isolation and emotional turmoil for the patients themselves. As the disease progresses, there is a noticeable decline in functional abilities, resulting in a loss of independence and deterioration in physical and motor skills, which can lead to additional health complications, as pointed out by Thompson et al. (2020) [4].

Alzheimer's Disease progresses through several stages, each with its unique challenges. According to Shivanand et al. (2023) [5], these stages include:

- **Early or Pre-clinical Stage**: During this stage, individuals may exhibit no symptoms or only mild memory problems.
- **Mild Cognitive Impairment (MCI)**: During this stage, memory problems become more apparent, but individuals maintain the ability to perform daily activities independently.
- **Mild Dementia**: At this stage, individuals face difficulty remembering recent events, completing familiar tasks, and effectively communicating. Mood swings and confusion also become more apparent, as noted by Sano et al.(2021) [6].
- **Moderate Dementia**: Patients at this stage require assistance with daily activities and may experience difficulty recognizing family and friends, displaying severe memory loss, confusion, and personality changes, as discussed by Shen et al. (2020) [2].
- **Severe Dementia**: In this advanced stage, patients are completely dependent on caregivers, losing their ability to communicate and recognize loved ones, as outlined by Hutton et al.(2021) [1].

Although Alzheimer's Disease remains incurable, various treatments can help manage its symptoms. Recently, the application of machine learning (ML) and deep learning (DL) techniques to medical imaging tasks has shown significant promise, particularly in Alzheimer's Disease detection. However, Shivanand et al.(2023) [5] highlight challenges such as the quality of datasets, optimization of model parameters, and the complexity of model architecture.

Early detection is critical for improving treatment outcomes, and Magnetic Resonance Imaging (MRI) has become a valuable tool in diagnosing Dementia. MRI enables visualization of brain structures, detecting changes linked to Dementia, and aids in distinguishing Alzheimer's Disease from other Dementia types. Wang et al.(2021) [7] emphasize the importance of MRI in tracking disease progression, especially when combined with cognitive and neurological assessments, providing a comprehensive diagnosis.

This research aims to address the issue of early detection by proposing a multi-modal, cascaded analysis approach for early diagnosis and precise classification. A two-level deep learning classification model is proposed. In the first level, the model acts as a binary classifier to distinguish individuals with Dementia from those without, which is crucial for early identification. In the second level, the model further categorizes patients into groups such as 'Very Mild Dementia,' 'Mild Dementia,' 'Moderate Dementia,' and 'Non-Demented.' This classification helps healthcare providers tailor interventions and treatment strategies to slow disease progression effectively.

Utilizing MRI scans, genetic information, medical history, and other parameters, we aim to capture a wide range of indicators for Dementia, providing a detailed understanding of the disease. Privacy and security of sensitive medical data are paramount, ensuring adherence to ethical practices and restricting access to licensed medical professionals only.

1.1   Dataset Collection

OASIS is a long-term neuroimaging dataset that includes biomarkers for Dementia and normal ageing as well as clinical and cognitive aspects, alongside repositories of MRI scans of various patients' brains. OASIS has published several versions (OASIS1, OASIS2, OASIS3, and OASIS4), with data from several cohorts in each edition. Even though the modest data in the OASIS 1 and OASIS 2 datasets was valuable, it was determined that it was not enough for the thorough analysis required to diagnose Dementia. Furthermore, as Dementia is a dynamic disorder, relying solely on data from OASIS 1 is insufficient. Thus, we chose to focus on data from their more recent projects.

Given that other studies [8–10] have used processed OASIS datasets of MRI images available on Kaggle, we have also incorporated these MRI images into our work. During a further investigation of existing datasets, we found another larger repository of MRI images, sourced from the OASIS project and uploaded on Kaggle after preprocessing, which we chose to use as a second repository of MRI images [11]. For our investigation, OASIS 3 and 4 were outstanding sources of detailed data. A wide variety of data, including physical measurements, behavioural assessments, family history, Clinical Dementia Rating (CDR), functional assessments, and more, were provided by the datasets that included MRI images and matching CSV files. In this study, we have focused on using MRI scans to detect and classify the severity of Dementia using various techniques and dataset configurations.

The first Kaggle dataset [12] is the first dataset we considered and will hereafter be referred to as Dataset 1. This dataset was meticulously curated from diverse online sources, and every label associated with the images underwent thorough verification. This dataset has also been used by other research works including El-Latif et al. [13]. The dataset consists of 6,400 MRI scans presented as JPG images, each categorized into one of four labels mentioned in Section 1. The sample distribution by class is provided in Fig. 1. We also considered a larger repository of more than 86000 MRI brain scans sourced from OASIS [11], hereafter referred to as Dataset 2. These were preprocessed and made available on Kaggle and have also been grouped into the same four labels as Dataset 1. The sample distribution by class is provided in Fig. 2. Including these distinct labels in both datasets enhances their capacity to capture and represent varying degrees of Dementia severity. This meticulous categorization lays the foundation for a nuanced and detailed analysis in the context of Dementia research (Table 5).

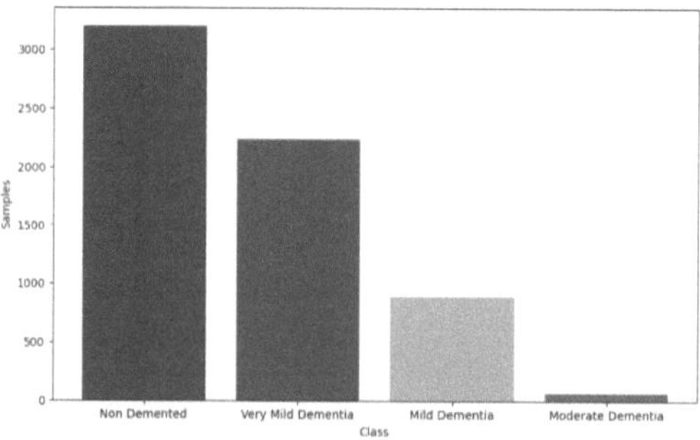

Fig. 1. Dataset 1 Sample Distribution by Class

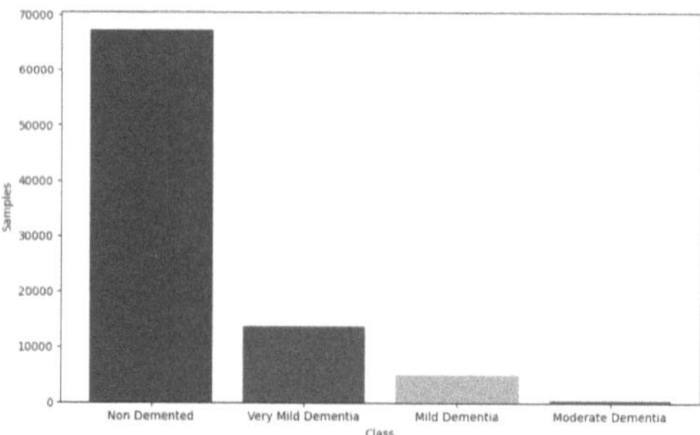

Fig. 2. Dataset 2 Sample Distribution by Class

Table 1. Dataset Samples

Dataset	Non Demented	Very Mild Dementia	Mild Dementia	Moderate Dementia
Dataset 1	3200	2240	896	64
Dataset 2	67222	13725	5002	488

2 Literature Survey

Machine learning plays a crucial role in the early detection of Dementia, offering a set of powerful tools to enhance the accuracy and efficiency of prediction and diagnosis. Among the wide array of machine learning techniques applied in this domain, several notable methods include supervised learning approaches such as Support Vector Machines (SVM), Random Forest, Logistic Regression, Naive Bayes, Decision Trees, Artificial Neural Networks, and advanced DL models. These techniques are employed to analyze and interpret data from different sources, with a focus on accurately discerning patterns indicative of Dementia.

The features used for prediction and diagnosis encompass a variety of data types, including neuroimaging data such as MRI scans that provide detailed images of brain structures, Positron Emission Tomography (PET) scans capturing metabolic activity, Electroencephalography (EEG) recordings measuring electrical brain activity, and functional Magnetic Resonance Imaging (fMRI) scans, providing dynamic information on brain function, all serve as valuable inputs for machine learning models.

In the dynamic landscape of Dementia detection and classification, a notable surge in research efforts was witnessed that explored and harnessed the potential of DL methodologies to augment precision and efficiency in diagnosis.

Liu et al.'s groundbreaking study, "Multimodal Neuroimaging Feature Learning" [14] stands out for proposing a 3D CNN that capitalizes on multi-modal neuroimaging data, including MRI and PET scans, and attaining a high accuracy of 92% in distinguishing Dementia cases from healthy controls. Also, the work conducted by Wang et al. in "DeepAD" [15] is particularly significant, as it introduces a Convolutional Neural Network (CNN) tailored for Dementia classification by leveraging both structural (MRI) and functional (fMRI) neuroimaging data, achieving an impressive accuracy of 90%. There is also the adaptation of "EEGNet" by Lawhern et al. [16] for Dementia detection through EEG data underscores the adaptability of compact CNN architectures, attaining a noteworthy accuracy of 87% and emphasizing the efficacy of these models in handling diverse data modalities. Chen et al.'s innovative approach in "Attention-guided Deep Multiple Instance Learning" [17] integrates attention mechanisms with DL for Dementia diagnosis using PET scans, achieving a remarkable 91% accuracy. A comparative study was also done by Ben Nicholas et al. [10] which implements various feature descriptors and a K-Nearest Neighbor Classification model for identifying early stages of Dementia. There is also a study by Al Shahri [8] explores the usage of DenseNet-169 [18] and ResNet-50 [19] models for multi-class classification of Dementia, and achieves significant results. Another study by Saim et al. [9] also looks into a hybrid method of feature extraction and principal component analysis, and compares 3 different ML models. Zhang et al.'s "DeepFMRI" [20] also notably adds to the tapestry of DL applications by using CNNs for the classification of Attention Deficit Hyperactivity Disorder (ADHD) with fMRI data, showcasing an impressive accuracy of 88%. An effort has also been made to create lightweight DL models which also have high performance in the detection of AD [21] by El-Latif et al.

Collectively, these studies underscore the adaptability and efficacy of DL models across various neuroimaging modalities, contributing significantly to the ongoing pursuit of precision and reliability in Dementia diagnosis. The reported accuracies across these studies not only demonstrate the potential clinical utility of DL but also highlight the progress made in leveraging advanced computational approaches to advance our understanding and diagnostic capabilities in the complex domain of neurodegenerative disorders. We also inspected other notable studies [20–28] as part of our literature survey, and used their valuable insights while proceeding with our research for early detection of Dementia.

3   Methodology

In our study, we considered 2 approaches to develop a reliable model for the early detection of Dementia. The first one was creating a custom CNN, hereafter referred to as Approach 1, and the other, training pre-defined models using the Pytorch [29] library (namely DenseNet121 [18], Resnet50 [19], InceptionV4 [20], MobilenetV3 [30], and VGG16 [6]), hereafter referred to as Approach 2, and conducting a comparative study between the two. A methodology diagram is depicted in Fig. 3.

$$y = f \left(\sum_{i=1}^{n} w_i x_i + b \right) \tag{1}$$

- y is the output,
- f is the activation function,
- w_i are the weights,
- x_i are the input values,
- b is the bias term.

As we are using neural network models, it becomes important to define what a neural network is. A neural network also commonly known as artificial neural network (ANN) is a type of ML algorithm which is modelled to mimic function of the human brain and consists of layers of interconnected nodes called neurons that process the information and learn from the input data [31].

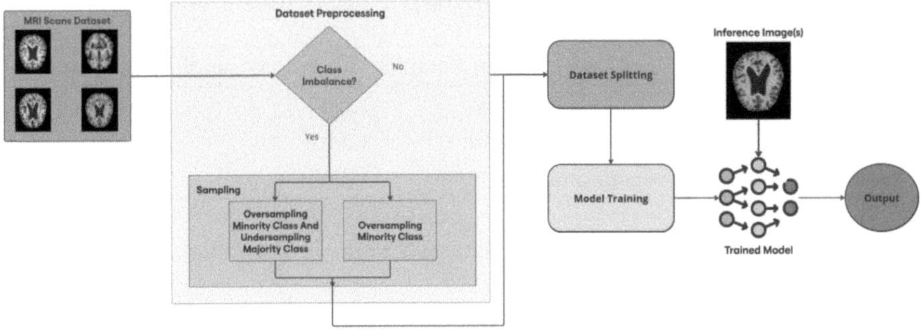

Fig. 3. Methodology diagram

Table 2. Sample size for Dataset 1 binary classification

Sample Status	Train Samples	Validation Samples	Test Samples
Before Sampling	4480	960	960
Oversampling	4480	960	960
Undersampling and Oversampling	4480	960	960

3.1 Preliminary Testing

Initially, we trained and tested our Pytorch [29] and custom CNN model on an imbalanced version of the datasets, to establish a baseline of performance before we proceeded with the balancing. Due to this being a preliminary evaluation, we only considered Accuracy (refer to Sect. 4.1) and only tested it on the Binary grouping of Dataset 2. These results can be found in Table 8.

3.2 Approach 1

Our first approach involved developing a custom CNN model. This approach relies on first tweaking our model on dataset 1 [12] to obtain a performance estimate and then using the same model to train on dataset 2 [11] which contains more than 80,000 MRI scans as images. This was chosen as our primary dataset for this approach as it contains vast amounts of samples compared to the 6,400

Table 3. Sample size for Dataset 1 multiclass classification

Sample Status	Train Samples	Validation Samples	Test Samples
Before Sampling	4480	960	960
Oversampling	8969	962	959
Undersampling and Oversampling	4570	962	959

Table 4. Sample size for Dataset 2 binary classification

Sample Status	Train Samples	Validation Samples	Test Samples
Before Sampling	60505	12967	12965
Oversampling	94110	12967	12965
Undersampling and Oversampling	60507	12967	12965

Table 5. Sample size for Dataset 2 multiclass classification

Sample Status	Train Samples	Validation Samples	Test Samples
Before Sampling	60504	12969	12964
Oversampling	188224	12969	12964
Undersampling and Oversampling	94802	12969	12964

samples found in dataset 1 while having the same four labels for multi-class classification. We use the Keras [32] library for Python for model creation, training and testing.

Tweaking Model on Dataset 1. For binary classification, we set the model's pool size for both MaxPooling2D layers as 4X4. We have used 7 layers in total, with 2 convolutional layers, 2 pooling layers, and 3 fully connected layers. The architecture of the model is provided in Table 6. We split the data in the ratio 70-15-15 for train-test-validation and, train the model for 100 epochs as shown in the loss curves in Sect. 4.

For multiclass classification, we use a similar architecture to the one that is shown in Table 6 but increase the number of filters to 64 for all layers where applicable. We also use the "softplus" activation function in every layer other than the output layer and for the output layer, use the "softmax" activation function. We also increase the number of output layers to accommodate multi-class classification. We also had to use image augmentation for the "Moderate Demented" class as it had significantly less number of samples than all the other classes. To augment new samples, we used the ImageDataGenerator class in Keras [32] and techniques such as brightness adjustments, pixel rescaling, zooming in and out and flipping. We trained the model for 100 epochs, with Early Stopping enabled. The high pool size allowed our model to be lightweight and space-efficient, occupying ∼1.52 MB for Binary Classification and ∼3.12 MB for Multi-Class Classification.

Training and Testing Model on Dataset 2. On dataset 2 [11], we use the same model architecture as mentioned in Sect. 3.2, and during training, we use a callback that reduces the learning rate if the model has stagnated [33]. We set our model to train for 50 epochs at a batch size of 32 in all cases. Note:

Table 6. Model Architecture for Binary Classification

Layer (Type)	Activation Function	Output Shape	Number of Params.
Conv2D_1	ReLU	(None, 150, 150, 32)	896
MaxPooling2D_1	-	(None, 37, 37, 32)	0
Conv2D_2	ReLU	(None, 37, 37, 32)	9248
MaxPooling2D_2	-	(None, 9, 9, 32)	0
Flatten_1	-	(None, 2592)	0
Dense_1	ReLU	(None, 150)	388950
Dense_2	Sigmoid	(None, 1)	151

Augmentation for Minor Classes. For both binary classification and multiclass classification, we used the same ImageDataGenerator object from Sect. 3.2 to increase the number of samples in the train split of our minority classes.

Augmentation for Minor Classes and Undersampling for Major Class. Random undersampling is a technique where we reduce the number of samples in the majority class to make the dataset more balanced. We deployed random undersampling alongside data augmentation to obtain a dataset that has fewer synthetic samples.

3.3   Approach 2

This was an alternative approach to Sect. 3.2, and also focuses on the analysis of MRI images for the early detection of Dementia, using both datasets.

Binary Classification. For binary classification, we prepared our datasets by re-grouping our labelled images into 2 classes: Demented and Non-Demented. With Dataset 1, there was no need for resampling the binary classes as they were already balanced. However, with Dataset 2, as shown in Fig. 2, we see a large imbalance. To deal with this, we took 2 approaches: we conducted one experiment by purely oversampling the minority class, and another by undersampling the majority class (Non-Demented) and oversampling the minority class (Demented) to the mean between the original sample numbers. After this, we created train-test-validation splits of 70-15-15 on both datasets (Sample sizes shown in Figs. 2, 3, 4, 5). We trained DL models from the timm library of Pytorch [29], namely Resnet50 [19], Densenet121 [18], InceptionV4 [34], VGG-16 [6], and MobilenetV3 [30], while implementing Early Stopping to avoid overfitting and tracking our loss and accuracy values (Find these results accordingly in Tables 9 and 10) (Table 7).

Multi-class Classification. In both Dataset 1 and Dataset 2, there was a major class imbalance present across the four classes, as shown in Fig. 2. Similar to Binary Classification (Sect. 3.3), we conducted one experiment by purely

Table 7. Hyperparameter values

Hyperparameter Name	Value
Learning Rate	0.0001
Epochs	100
Optimizer Used	Stochastic Gradient Descent
Momentum	0.9
Early Stopping Patience	5
Drop Rate	0.2

oversampling the minority classes, and another by undersampling 2 majority classes and oversampling 2 minority classes to the mean between the original sample numbers. After this, we created a train-test-validation split of 70-15-15 and trained the same DL models from the timm library of Pytorch [29] as Sect. 3.3, but with a different number of output neurons to facilitate multi-class classification. Note that we used the same callbacks as in Sect. 3.3 (Figs. 4 and 5).

4   Results and Discussion

The models we used across our study for each methodology were Resnet50 [19], InceptionV4 [20], MobilenetV3 [30], VGG16 [6], Densenet121 [18] and a

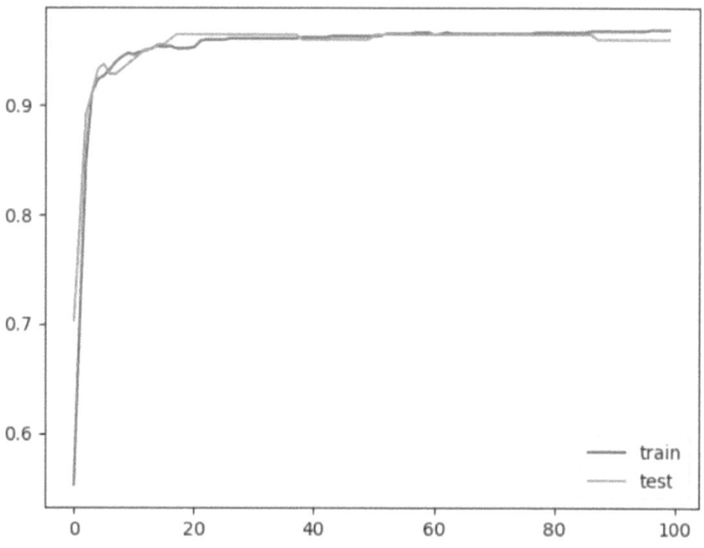

Fig. 4. Accuracy Plot

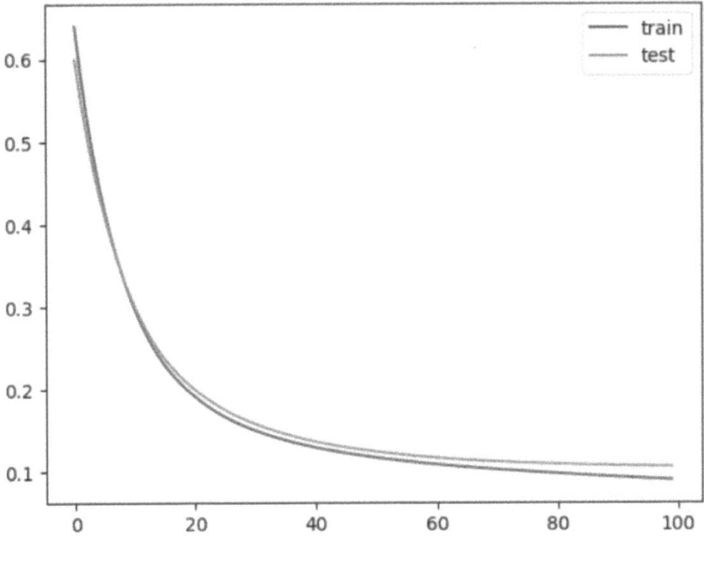

Fig. 5. Loss Curve

Custom CNN, allowing us to conduct a thorough comparative study towards our goal of Early Dementia Detection.

Definitions:

- **TP:** True Positives, i.e. Instances correctly identified as positive by a classification model.
- **TN:** True Negatives, i.e. Instances correctly identified as negative by a classification model.
- **FP:** False Positives, i.e. Instances incorrectly identified as positive by a classification model when they are actually negative.
- **FN:** False Negatives, i.e. Instances incorrectly identified as negative by a classification model when they are actually positive.

Performance Metrics Formulas:

- **Accuracy:** The proportion of correctly classified instances (both true positives and true negatives) out of the total instances.

$$\text{Accuracy} = \frac{TP + TN}{TP + TN + FP + FN} \tag{2}$$

- **Precision:** The ratio of true positives to the sum of true positives and false positives, emphasizing the accuracy of positive predictions.

$$\text{Precision} = \frac{TP}{TP + FP} \tag{3}$$

- **Recall:** The ratio of true positives to the sum of true positives and false negatives, highlighting the model's ability to capture all positive instances.

$$\text{Recall} = \frac{TP}{TP + FN} \tag{4}$$

- **F1 Score:** The harmonic mean of precision and recall, providing a balanced measure that considers both false positives and false negatives in classification performance assessment.

$$\text{F1 Score} = 2 \cdot \frac{\text{Precision} \cdot \text{Recall}}{\text{Precision} + \text{Recall}} \tag{5}$$

We considered various models on both Dataset 1 [12] and Dataset 2 [11], with two experiments for each model: Binary Classification and Multi-Class classification, resulting in a total of four experiments. We also conducted a preliminary experiment on the Binary split of Dataset 13.1 for a baseline of performance and to determine if sampling was indeed necessary. Based on the results in Sect. 4.1, we determined that sample balancing indeed would be necessary, considering the low performance on a few of the models.

We compared the performance of the pre-defined models with that of the custom CNN. These approaches were attempted across 2 computers, one with an RTX 3050 Ti GPU and the other with an RTX 3060 GPU, the former with 16GB of DDR4 RAM, and the latter with 16GB of DDR5 RAM. The libraries used for each of our approaches (Sects. 3.2 and 3.3) use Tensorflow-Keras [32] and Pytorch [29] respectively, both of which are based in Python. The Stochastic Gradient Descent optimizer was applied for all DL models, with BinaryCrossEntropy being used for the Binary Classification, and CategoricalCrossEntropy being used for the Multi-Class Classification. The primary metric used in this study was Accuracy, alongside Precision, Recall, and F1-score, whose formulae and definitions are detailed above.

Note that during testing, the pre-defined models took between 13 s and about 1 min. On the other hand, our custom model, on average, took 7 to 20 s.

4.1   Preliminary Results

Here, we only conducted one initial experiment to establish a baseline performance before proceeding with sampling. We conducted this on the Binary split of Dataset 2 (given that the Binary split for Dataset 1 is already balanced).

Seeing as some of the accuracy values have scope for improvement, we proceeded with sampling and re-training the models, the results of which are given in Sects. 4.2 and 4.3.

4.2   Binary Classification

Under binary classification, we conducted two experiments: one on each of our datasets [11,12], to compare the performance of the modified CNN model with the pre-trained models.

Table 8. Preliminary Test Accuracies

Model Used	Accuracy
Resnet50	77.34%
InceptionV4	97.17%
MobilenetV3	97.39%
VGG16	95.21%
Densenet121	99.3%
Custom CNN (Ours)	**99.96%**

Dataset 1. We trained the pre-defined Pytorch [29] models and the custom CNN model on the binary split of Dataset 1, and have documented the results in Table 9. As shown, Densenet12 [18] performed best on Dataset 1 with an accuracy of 99.68%, followed by MobilenetV3 [30]. Our custom CNN also performed noticeably better than the Resnet50 [19] model.

Table 9. Binary Classification Metrics per model for the Dataset 1

Model Used	Accuracy	Precision	Recall	F1-Score
Resnet50	93.64%	0.9444	0.9270	0.9358
InceptionV4	99.38%	0.9958	0.9916	0.9937
MobilenetV3	98.65%	0.9915	0.9813	0.9863
VGG16	98.33%	0.9813	0.9854	0.9833
Densenet121	99.68%	0.9958	0.9979	0.9968
Custom CNN (Ours)	**96.15%**	**0.9775**	**0.7562**	**0.9441**

Dataset 2. In the second Binary Classification experiment, before training, we had to first take care of the class imbalance between the Demented images and NonDemented images. We took 2 approaches to this; Purely Oversampling (Where we used augmentation techniques like brightness adjustment, shearing, horizontal flipping, vertical flipping, zooming in and out, etc.), and a combination of Oversampling and Undersampling so that both classes had a number close to the median of the original samples in each class. We trained the models from scratch on Dataset 2 (due to the MRI scan being from a different perspective), and have documented the results for each approach in Tables 10 and 11.

4.3   Multi-class Classification

Similarly to Binary Classification, we conducted 2 experiments for multi-class classification using the pre-defined models and the custom CNN models. It

Table 10. Binary Classification Metrics per model for Dataset 2 by Oversampling the minority class

Model Used	Accuracy	Precision	Recall	F1-Score
Resnet50	99.74%	0.9997	0.9951	1.00
InceptionV4	99.81%	0.9981	0.9981	0.9982
MobilenetV3	99.98%	0.9997	0.9999	1.00
VGG16	99.90%	0.9990	0.9990	0.9990
Densenet121	99.98%	0.9998	0.9998	0.9998
Custom CNN (Ours)	**99.98%**	**0.9999**	**0.9998**	**0.9958**

Table 11. Binary Classification Metrics per model for Dataset 2 by Oversampling the minority class and Undersampling the majority class

Model Used	Accuracy	Precision	Recall	F1-Score
Resnet50	98.56%	0.9934	0.9777	0.99
InceptionV4	99.69%	0.9969	0.9969	0.9969
MobilenetV3	99.92%	0.9986	0.9998	1.00
VGG16	99.84%	0.9984	0.9984	0.9984
Densenet121	99.92%	0.9986	0.9998	1.00
Custom CNN (Ours)	**99.99%**	**0.9999**	**0.9999**	**0.9895**

should be noted that unlike in Binary Classification, there was a class imbalance for both datasets across the four classes, and we employed the same two paradigms as described in Sect. 4.2, i.e. Augmenting the minority classes to match the number of the majority class, and a combination of Augmentation and Undersampling so that all classes have a number of samples close to the mean of the classes with the highest and lowest samples.

Dataset 1. Unlike the binary classification, we observed a class imbalance among the 4 classes i.e. Non Demented, Moderately Demented, Mildly Demented and Very Mildly Demented. We have trained the models and documented the result for each approach in Table 12 and 13. As shown, our custom CNN performed the best with 98.13% accuracy followed by DensetNet121 and VGG16 with a mere difference in the case of Table 12.

Dataset 2. Similarly to Dataset 1, we observed a class imbalance among the 4 classes i.e. Non Demented, Moderately Demented, Mildly Demented and Very Mildly Demented. We have trained the models and documented the result for each approach in Table 14 and 15. As shown, DensetNet121 outperformed with an accuracy of 99.992% followed by our custom CNN with an accuracy of 99.91% in the case of Table 14. Yet, again in Table 15, DensetNet121 outperformed with an accuracy of 99.96% followed by VGG16 with an accuracy of 99.86%.

Table 12. Multi-Class Classification Metrics per model for dataset 1 by Oversampling the minority classes

Model Used	Accuracy	Precision	Recall	F1-Score
Resnet50	61.00%	0.6098	0.6100	0.6080
InceptionV4	91.03%	0.9109	0.9103	0.9101
MobilenetV3	86.86%	0.8742	0.8686	0.8694
VGG16	89.67%	0.8993	0.8967	0.8970
Densenet121	89.78%	0.8986	0.8978	0.8974
Custom CNN (Ours)	**98.13%**	**0.9826**	**0.9813**	**0.9859**

Table 13. Multi-Class Classification Metrics per model for dataset 1 by Oversampling the minority classes and Undersampling the majority class

Model Used	Accuracy	Precision	Recall	F1-Score
Resnet50	55.68%	0.5798	0.5568	0.5587
InceptionV4	81.44%	0.8247	0.8144	0.8159
MobilenetV3	82.79%	0.8357	0.828	0.8292
VGG16	88.21%	0.8840	0.8821	0.8825
Densenet121	81.02%	0.8126	0.8102	0.8109
Custom CNN (Ours)	**99.96%**	**0.9996**	**0.9996**	**0.9996**

Table 14. Multi-Class Classification Metrics per model for dataset 2 by Oversampling the minority classes

Model Used	Accuracy	Precision	Recall	F1-Score
Resnet50	99.02%	0.9903	0.9902	0.9903
InceptionV4	99.83%	99.85	99.83	99.84
MobilenetV3	99.71%	99.71	99.71	99.71
VGG16	99.88%	0.9988	0.9988	0.9988
Densenet121	99.992%	0.99992	0.99992	0.99992
Custom CNN (Ours)	**99.91%**	**99.91**	**99.91**	**99.72**

Table 15. Multi-Class Classification Metrics per model for dataset 2 by Oversampling the minority classes and Undersampling the majority class

Model Used	Accuracy	Precision	Recall	F1-Score
Resnet50	97.81%	0.9795	0.9781	0.9785
InceptionV4	98.44%	0.9894	0.9844	0.9861
MobilenetV3	99.55%	0.9955	0.9955	0.9955
VGG16	99.85%	0.9985	0.9985	0.9985
Densenet121	99.95%	0.9995	0.9995	0.9995
Custom CNN (Ours)	**99.80%**	**0.9980**	**0.9980**	**0.9977**

4.4   Comparative Results

In comparison to previous studies, our custom lightweight CNN architecture exhibits superior performance in the multiclass classification of Alzheimer's disease, consistently achieving metrics of 99% or above. Models proposed by Rao et al. [35], Khan et al. [36], and Agarwal et al. [37], which leverage deep learning and transfer learning techniques, demonstrate notable accuracy. However, our architecture surpasses these models in classification accuracy, computational efficiency, and generalization capability when evaluated on the same dataset. Specifically, Rao et al. [35] utilized 3D MRI data for high-dimensional analysis, Khan et al. [36] introduced a CNN model tailored for Alzheimer's disease diagnosis, and Agarwal et al. [37] applied image augmentation to address data limitations. The superior performance and efficiency of our model underscore its potential as a leading candidate for further research, including advanced feature extraction and testing with more diverse datasets.

5   Conclusion

Our study demonstrates efficacy through the comprehensive analysis of MRI scans, and our various tests provide insights into the effects of synthetic data and raw data towards model performance and how reliable metrics can be, as well as contributing to the research in the field of early detection of Dementia. Additionally, when compared with existing state-of-the-art solutions and innovative approaches proposed by other authors, our model consistently demonstrates competitive performance and, in some cases, shows improvements over these methods.

However, despite the commendable strides achieved, certain limitations warrant consideration. The current models cannot discern sub-variants of Dementia, indicating a need for heightened specificity in its classification capabilities. Furthermore, the restricted dataset sources pose a constraint on the model's generalization, urging the incorporation of a more expansive and representative dataset to ensure robust performance in real-world applications. Addressing these limitations is pivotal for advancing the model's utility and relevance in clinical settings.

Looking towards the future, our research has a clear trajectory for improvement. Expansion of dataset sources to encompass a more diverse demographic will not only boost the model's reliability but also facilitate its seamless integration into broader populations. Additionally, the incorporation of advanced MRI techniques, such as functional MRI (fMRI) or Diffusion Tensor Imaging (DTI), holds promise in providing nuanced insights into neural connectivity and structural alterations, thereby elevating the model's effective usability in real-world scenarios. The pursuit of these enhancements aligns with our vision to refine the capacity for application in large-scale healthcare scenarios.

Disclosure of Interests. The authors have no competing interests to declare that are relevant to the content of this article.

References

1. Hutton, M., Hardy, J.: Progression of Alzheimer's disease. Nat. Neurosci. (2021). https://doi.org/10.1038/s41380-023-02215-8
2. Shen, D., Liu, M.: Deep learning techniques for Alzheimer's disease detection using medical imaging data. J. Transl. Med. **18**, 1–12 (2020)
3. Jack, C.R., Holtzman, D.M.: Biomarkers for Alzheimer's disease: perspective for new diagnostic criteria. Biol. Psychiat. **91**, 117–128 (2021)
4. Thompson, P.M., Initiative, A.D.N.: MRI biomarkers for detecting Alzheimer's disease. Neurobiol. Aging **86**, 16–24 (2020)
5. Shivanand, P., Rao, N.M.: Deep learning methods for Alzheimer's disease detection: a survey. J. Alzheimers Dis. **85**, 321–345 (2023)
6. Simonyan, K., Zisserman, A.: Very deep convolutional networks for large-scale image recognition (2015). https://arxiv.org/abs/1409.1556
7. Wang, J., Wang, L.: Early detection of dementia using MRI and deep learning approaches. J. Neurosci. Methods **347**, 108951 (2021)
8. Al Shehri, W.: Alzheimer's disease diagnosis and classification using deep learning techniques. PeerJ Comput. Sci. **8**, 1177 (2022)
9. Saim, M., Feroui, A.: A new hybrid method based on bias-correction fuzzy c means and histogram of oriented gradient for Alzheimer disease detection. In: 2022 First International Conference on Computer Communications and Intelligent Systems (I3CIS), pp. 31–36 (2022). https://doi.org/10.1109/I3CIS56626.2022.1007607
10. Nicholas, B., Jayakumar, A., Titus, B., Remya Nair, T.: Comparative study of multiple feature descriptors for detecting the presence of Alzheimer's disease. In: Karuppusamy, P., Perikos, I., Garcia Marquez, F. (eds.) Ubiquitous Intelligent Systems, pp. 331–339. Springer, Singapore (2022)
11. Aithal, N.: Oasis alzheimer's detection (2023). https://www.kaggle.com/datasets/ninadaithal/imagesoasis, version 1, Retrieved September 21, 2023
12. Dubey, S.: Alzheimer's dataset (4 class of images) (2020). https://www.kaggle.com/datasets/tourist55/alzheimers-dataset-4-class-of-images, version 1, Retrieved November 20, 2023
13. Rumelhart, D.E., Hinton, G.E., Williams, R.J.: Learning representations by back-propagating errors. Nature **323**(6088), 533–536 (1986)
14. Liu, S., et al.: ADNI: multimodal neuroimaging feature learning for multiclass diagnosis of Alzheimer's disease. IEEE Trans. Biomed. Eng. **62**(4), 1132–1140 (2015)
15. Sarraf, S., DeSouza, D.D., Anderson, J., Tofighi, G.: DeepAD: Alzheimer's disease classification via deep convolutional neural networks using MRI and FMRI. bioRxiv (2017). https://doi.org/10.1101/070441
16. Lawhern, V.J., Solon, A.J., Waytowich, N.R., Gordon, S., Hung, C.P., Lance, B.J.: EEGNet: A compact convolutional neural network for EEG-based brain–computer interfaces. J. Neural Eng. **15**(5), 056013 (2018)
17. Chen, S., et al.: Attention-guided deep multi-instance learning for staging retinopathy of prematurity. In: 2021 IEEE 18th International Symposium on Biomedical Imaging (ISBI), pp. 1025–1028 (2021). https://doi.org/10.1109/ISBI48211.2021.94340
18. Huang, G., Liu, Z., Van Der Maaten, L., Weinberger, K.Q.: Densely connected convolutional networks. In: Proceedings of the IEEE Conference on Computer Vision and Pattern Recognition, pp. 4700–4708 (2017)
19. He, K., Zhang, X., Ren, S., Sun, J.: Deep residual learning for image recognition. In: Proceedings of the IEEE Conference on Computer Vision and Pattern Recognition, pp. 770–778 (2016)

20. Dai, W., et al.: Multimodal brain disease classification with functional interaction learning from single FMRI volume. arXiv preprint arXiv:2208.03028 (2022)
21. El-Latif, A.A.A., Chelloug, S.A., Alabdul-hafith, M., Hammad, M.: Accurate detection of Alzheimer's disease using lightweight deep learning model on MRI data. Diagnostics **13**(7), 1216 (2023)
22. Faouri, S., AlBashayreh, M., Azzeh, M.: Examining stability of machine learning methods for predicting dementia at early phases of the disease. arXiv preprint arXiv:2209.04643 (2022)
23. Mohammed, B.A., et al.: Multi-method analysis of medical records and MRI images for early diagnosis of dementia and Alzheimer's disease based on deep learning and hybrid methods. Electronics **10**(22), 2860 (2021)
24. So, A., Hooshyar, D., Park, K., Lim, H.: Early diagnosis of dementia from clinical data by machine learning techniques. Appl. Sci. **7**(7), 650 (2017)
25. Cheung, C., Ran, A., Wang, S., et al.: A deep learning model for detection of Alzheimer's disease based on retinal photographs: a retrospective, multicentre case-control study. Lancet Digit. Health **4**(11), 806–815 (2022)
26. Pellegrini, E., Ballerini, L., Hernandez, M., et al.: Machine learning of neuroimaging for assisted diagnosis of cognitive impairment and dementia: a systematic review. Alzheimer's & Dementia: Diagnosis, Assess. Dis. Monit. **10**(1), 519–535 (2018). https://doi.org/10.1016/j.dadm.2018.07.004
27. Miah, Y., Prima, C.N.E., Seema, S.J., Mahmud, M., Shamim Kaiser, M.: Performance comparison of machine learning techniques in identifying dementia from open access clinical datasets. In: Saeed, F., Al-Hadhrami, T., Mohammed, F., Mohammed, E. (eds.) Advances on Smart and Soft Computing. AISC, vol. 1188, pp. 79–89. Springer, Singapore (2021). https://doi.org/10.1007/978-981-15-6048-4_8
28. Bansal, D., Chhikara, R., Khanna, K., Gupta, P.: Comparative analysis of various machine learning algorithms for detecting dementia. Procedia Comput. Sci. **132**, 1497–1502 (2018). https://doi.org/10.1016/j.procs.2018.05.102, international Conference on Computational Intelligence and Data Science
29. Paszke, A., Gross, S., Massa, F., et al.: PyTorch: an imperative style, high-performance deep learning library. In: Advances in Neural Information Processing Systems, vol. 32, pp. 8024–8035. Curran Associates, Inc. (2019). http://papers.neurips.cc/paper/9015-pytorch-an-imperative-style-high-performance-deep-learning-library.pdf
30. Howard, A., Zhu, M., Chen, B., et al.: MobileNets: efficient convolutional neural networks for mobile vision applications (2017). https://arxiv.org/abs/1704.04861
31. Sano, M., Gauthier, S.: Clinical stages and neurobiological features of Alzheimer's disease. Alzheimer's Dementia **17**(3), 490–501 (2021)
32. Abadi, M., et al.: Tensorflow: large-scale machine learning on heterogeneous systems (2015). https://www.tensorflow.org, software available from tensorflow.org
33. Wu, Y., Liu, L.: Selecting and composing learning rate policies for deep neural networks. ACM Trans. Intell. Syst. Technol. **14**(2), 1–25 (2023)
34. Szegedy, C., Vanhoucke, V., Ioffe, S., Shlens, J., Wojna, Z.: Rethinking the inception architecture for computer vision (2015). https://arxiv.org/abs/1512.00567
35. Rao, B., Aparna, M., Kolisetty, S., et al.: Multi-class classification of Alzheimer's disease using deep learning and transfer learning on 3D MRI images. Traitement du Signal **41**(3), 1397–1404 (2024)

36. Khan, R., Qaisar, Z., Mehmood, A., et al.: A practical multiclass classification network for the diagnosis of Alzheimer's disease. Appl. Sci. **12**, 6507 (2022)
37. Agarwal, R., Sathwik, A., Godavarthi, D., Naga Ramesh, J.: Comparative analysis of deep learning models for multiclass Alzheimer's disease classification. EAI Endorsed Trans. Pervasive Health Technol. **9**, 1–9 (2023)

Electricity Load Forecasting Using Hybrid Deep Learning Algorithms for Demand Response Programs in Smart Energy Management Systems

Gursleen Kaur[✉] and Rajesh Kumar Bawa

Punjabi University, Patiala, India
gursleen109@gmail.com

Abstract. Smart Energy Management Systems (SEMS) employ Demand Response (DR), an effective vehicle for enabling utilities to manage resources efficiently, encouraging consumers to either cut or reschedule the demand at peak hours with appropriate market-based incentives. High accuracy of load forecasting methods (LF) is essential to make DR programs and resource management more effective. This research presents a novel approach to load forecasting with different multivariate datasets using 1D CNN, Bidirectional Long Short-Term Memory (Bi-LSTM), and Gated Recurrent Unit (GRU. Using Seasonal Trend Decomposition using LOESS (STL) it can detect more complex development trends and long-range dependencies, thus improving the forecast accuracy by combining load, price as well as weather data. The hybrid model yielded higher R2, RMSE, and MAPE scores compared to the current state-of-the-art algorithms. This study will be a key driver in the move towards developing more dynamic energy management policies for SEMS.

Keywords: Electricity Load Forecasting · Multivariate dataset · 1D CNN · Bi-LSTM · GRU · STL

1 Introduction

In the present era, electricity is very crucial, and the growth of urbanization and population around the globe has put an extra load on grids that traditional power systems are not able to handle, necessitating the need for advanced power systems [1, 2]. Due to advancements in power systems and changes in the energy structure, short-term electricity load forecasting for distribution networks has become essential as it supports demand response (DR) programs [3]. Load forecasting also plays a key role in power system planning and operation, contributing to the optimal utilization of resources, minimization of operational costs, and stabilization of the economy.

© The Author(s), under exclusive license to Springer Nature Switzerland AG 2026
S. Pal et al. (Eds.): ICETSS 2024, CCIS 2610, pp. 206–222, 2026.
https://doi.org/10.1007/978-3-032-11488-4_16

Electricity load forecasting methods have been classified into four major categories: traditional classical methods, machine learning algorithms, deep learning, and hybrid methods. Commonly used classical methods are Linear regression techniques [4], Exponential Smoothing [5], ARIMA (autoregressive integrated moving average) [6], and Grey prediction [7]. These methods are usually simpler in structures and principles, with easy inter-variable relation understanding. However, they rely on high-quality load data cannot provide much nonlinear mapping ability, and often don't perform well with loads that have periodical/seasonal components.

For smart grid problems, researchers have used Machine Learning (ML) algorithms in Short-Term Load Forecasting (STLF). XGBoost [8], an algorithm that reduces errors with large data sets, and Prophet [9] in Facebook can break up time series for deeper insights into [10]. Traditional ML performs poorly on large datasets, leading to the use of Deep learning (DL) algorithms that use neural networks for finding long-term dependency and prediction accuracy using recurrent neural network (RNN), Long short-term memory (LSTM) [11], and Gated Recurrent Units (GRU) [12] for generating more accurate results. Recently, Temporal Convolutional Networks (TCNs) [13] have become significant because they model long-range dependencies imagery.

Hybridization techniques have been employed by researchers to improve prediction accuracy. Mo et al. [13] categorized these as serial or parallel, and found that a set of TCNs combined with the Prophet model can outperform traditional models. Chen et al. [14] discussed the hybrid model of Prophet and LSTM which could reduce errors by applying Back Propagation. A. Alrasheedi and A. Almalaq applied CNN – GRU, CNN – LSTM, and CNN – BiLSTM hybrid models in short-term load forecasting in Saudi smart grids with CNN-BiLSTM showing best results [15]. Zuo et al. [16] introduced a dual framework of TimesNet and TCN, achieving benchmark-busting performance in short-term load forecasting. Research has provided a testimony to the enhanced forecast accuracy achieved through these hybrid models.

The complex structure of electricity load data necessitates the utilization of robust forecasting techniques. One method for a better understanding of time series data is called Seasonal-Trend decomposition using Loess (STL) which decomposes the time series into trend, seasonal, and residual components to improve model interpretability [17]. For instance, H.J. Jo et al. [18] proposed an STL-GRU hybrid model that captured both seasonal and trend components better than GRU and its variants. K. Sebastian et al. implemented joint STL with GRU to better forecast base-station traffic in trend or seasonal perspectives [19].

However, it seems that hybrid deep learning algorithms are not fully investigated with advanced STL for multivariate electricity consumption in the context of load forecasting. The traditional models such as ARIMA, LSTM, and GRU are unable to handle complex temporal patterns or even seasonal variations in the data which reduces their accuracy and results in poor generalization. In this paper, we present a model consisting of the ID CNN, Bi-LSTM, and GRU along with STL decomposition which is proposed to solve such problems considering multivariate influences for high accuracy demand response in smart energy systems. The main contributions of this paper are as follows:

- **Higher Performance with Long-Time Series**: The hybrid model using 1D CNN, Bi-LSTM, and GRU yields higher results in energy consumption forecasting by modeling long-term dependencies.
- **Seasonal Temporal Loess Integration (Integration with STL decomposition):** Handles seasonality and trends-specific nature for time series data in a better way.
- **Multiple Variable Novel Dataset:** A recent dataset consisting of electricity load, price, and weather data, used in conjunction with the hybrid model to outperform competing methods.

The remaining paper is organized as follows: Sect. 2 explains the models and algorithms in this domain; Sect. 3 outlines the research methodology; followed by the the results and discussion in Sect. 4; and finally concluded in Sect. 5.

2 Models and Algorithms

2.1 Seasonal-Trend Decomposition Using Loess (STL)

STL (Seasonal-Trend Decomposition using Loess) is a versatile approach to filter time series data that can be very useful in e.g., electricity load forecasting for smart energy systems. An STL decomposes a time series y_t into three components: trend T_t, seasonal pattern S_t, and residual R_t as in Eq. 1 [20].

$$y_t = T_t + S_t + R_t \tag{1}$$

The trend depicts a long-term progression affected by population growth and economic circumstances. The seasonal component deals with patterns that repeat at regular intervals, like daily or annual cycles in electricity demand. The residual is the leftover variability after removing trend and seasonal effects.STL identifies these components through LOESS smoothing which is useful in forecasting as STL facilitates separate modeling of each component, which is likely to get good results with models like LSTM or GRU.

2.2 Bidirectional Long Short-Term Memory (Bi-LSTM)

Bi-LSTM networks were first introduced by Schuster and Paliwal [21], which model temporal dependencies over sequences by utilizing the context in their past as well as the future. Each unit has two parallel LSTMs, one for processing the sequence in the forward direction and the other in the backward direction. The final output at each step combines the results of these two LSTMs which serves as better forecasting. The forward pass equations in Bi-LSTM for input gate i_t, forget gate f_t, cell state $\tilde{c}_t$, candidate cell state c_t, output gate o_t, and hidden state h_t are as shown by Eq. 2–7.

$$it = \sigma\, Wi.ht - 1, xt + bi \tag{2}$$

$$f_t = \sigma\left(W_f.(h_{t-1}, x_t) + b_f\right) \tag{3}$$

$$\tilde{c}_t = \tanh(W_c.(h_{t-1}, x_t) + b_c) \tag{4}$$

$$c_t = f_t * c_{t-1} + i_t * \tilde{c}_{t-1} \tag{5}$$

$$o_t = \sigma(W_o.(h_{t-1}, x_t) + b_o) \tag{6}$$

$$h_t = o_t * \tanh(c_t) \tag{7}$$

where:

σ is the sigmoid activation function.

W_i, W_f, W_c, W_o are the weight matrices for the input, forget, cell state, and output gates, respectively.

b_i, b_f, b_c, b_o are the biased terms.

h_{t-1} is the hidden state from the previous time step.

x_t is the input at the current time step.

c_t is the cell state at the current time step.

The Bi-LSTM provides a layer that processes sequences in both directions, one forward from t = 1 to T and the other backward from t = T to 1 depicted as in Eq. 8 to Eq. 10. Then it uses various equations to compute the forward function with x input units and h hidden units. The Bi-LSTM structure is shown in Fig. 1 with a hidden layer forwarding two values: $\overrightarrow{h}_t$ and $\overleftarrow{h}_t$ for forward and backward, respectively, and both are then combined to give the final output y_t [22].

$$\overrightarrow{h}_t = LSTM_{forward}\left(x_t, \overrightarrow{h}_{t-1}\right) \tag{8}$$

$$\overleftarrow{h}_t = LSTM_{forward}\left(x_t, \overleftarrow{h}_{t-1}\right) \tag{9}$$

$$y_t = W_i.h_t + b_y \tag{10}$$

where h_t is the combined $\overrightarrow{h}_t$ and $\overleftarrow{h}_t$

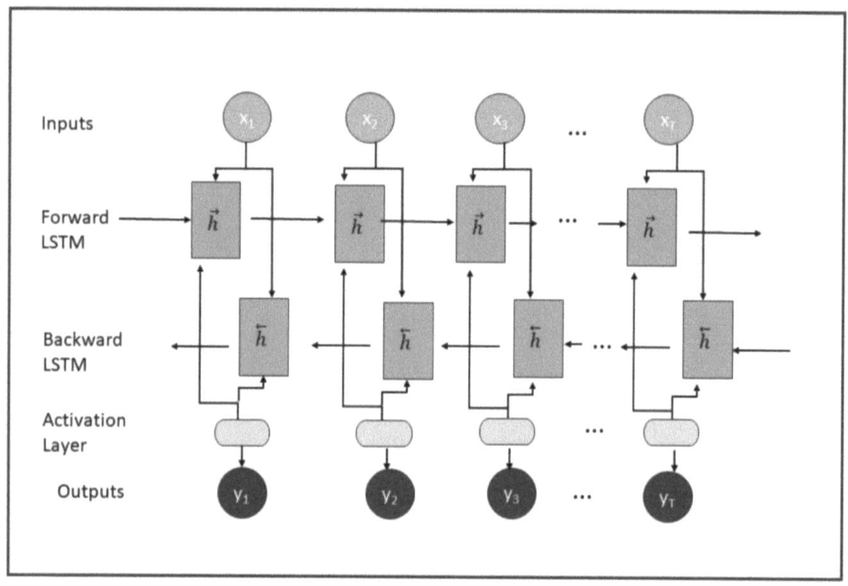

Fig. 1. A basic structure of Bi-LSTM [23]

2.3 Gated Recurrent Unit (GRU)

Gated Recurrent Unit (GRU) introduced by Cho et al. in 2014 [24] is a type of RNN architecture, which seeks to solve the vanishing gradient problem. GRUs are more similar to LSTMs, but they are simpler and computationally less expensive to train as their number of gates (and consequently parameters) is lower while retaining the ability to learn rich long-range temporal patterns in sequences as shown in Fig. 2. The main features of GRU are as below:

- Gating mechanisms: GRUs use two gates, an update gate and a reset gate that control the flow of information to retain or forget information as needed
- Update Gate u_t: Controls what proportion of the older memory to keep versus adding new information.

$$u_t = \sigma(W_u.(h_{t-1}, x_t) + b_u) \tag{11}$$

- Reset Gate r_t: : It decides whether to let the past unfold (by setting units in the activation vector close to 1) or forget about what was even there before:(setting such gates output as zero).

$$r_t = \sigma(W_r.(h_{t-1}, x_t) + b_r) \tag{12}$$

- Candidate Hidden State $\tilde{h}_t$: It is calculated by applying the reset gate, combining new input with the previous hidden state.

$$\tilde{h}_t = \tanh(W_h.(r_t * h_{t-1}, x_t) + b_h) \tag{13}$$

- Final Hidden State h_t: This last hidden state takes the prior and candidate states, to carefully mix old information with new info using an update gate.

$$h_t = u_t * h_{t-1} + (1 - u_t) * \tilde{h}_{t-1}) \tag{14}$$

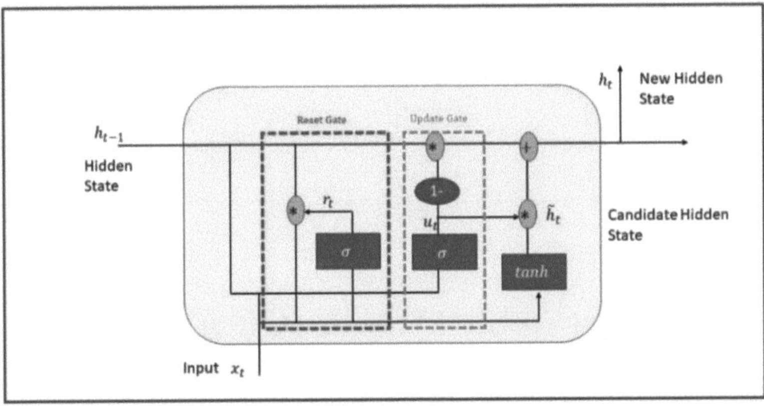

Fig. 2. A basic structure of GRU [25]

2.4 Temporal Convolution Network (TCN)

Lea et al. [26] proposed Temporal Convolutional Networks (TCNs) for time series data. They ensure that input length is equal to output lengths and use causal convolutions to make sure they do not allow future data to influence the past. Additionally, TCNs use dilated convolutions to capture long-term patterns. For example, in a casual convolution operation F over the sequence defined in 1D with input sequences x, convolution filter f is given by Eq. 15, and the dilated convolution operation, where d is the dilatation rate, k is the filter size is given by Eq. 16. TCN architecture with dilation rates d = 1,2,4 is shown in Fig. 3. [12]

$$F(x) = (x * f)(t) \sum_{j=0}^{k} f(j).x(t - j) \tag{15}$$

$$F(x_t) = (x *_d f)f(t) \sum_{j=0}^{k} f(j).x(t - (d*j))$$

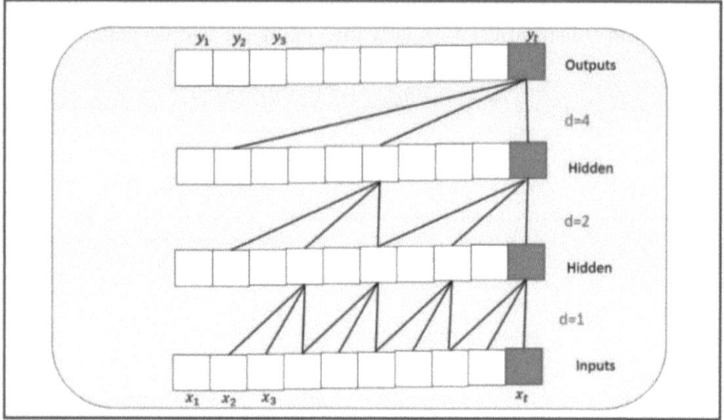

Fig. 3. TCN Layer

2.5 Long Short-Term Memory with CNN (LSTM_CNN)

LSTM_CNN is a hybrid model where the network architecture can be altered by setting parameters in its layers. This network consists of a convolutional layer, pooling layers, and an LSTM layer followed by dense Layers as shown in Fig. 4 [27]. Filter size, kernels, and number of units along with other hyperparameters at each layer can be changed to further enhance performance as well as learning speed.

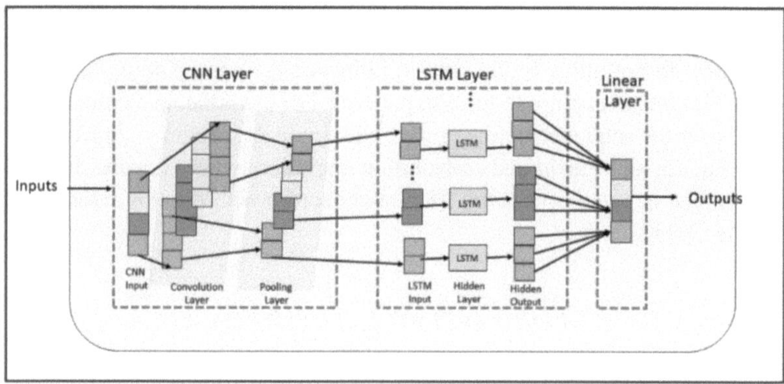

Fig. 4. A basic structure of CNN_LSTM

3 Research Methodology

Load forecasting is vital for efficient energy distribution, cost reduction, and grid reliability in SEMS. It is critical for DR programs, which utilities use to improve generation and renewable energy integration. This paper presents an advanced hybrid algorithm embedding a 1D Convolutional Neural Network (CNN), Bi-direction long and short-term memory network(Bi-LSTM), GRU which can predict electricity demand using only a multivariable dataset as input taking into account Seasonal Temporal Loess decomposition as depicted in Fig. 5. A hybrid model which is first trained and tested in New York City and Long Island datasets, then validated with Hudson Valley data to improve prediction species specificity for these regions.

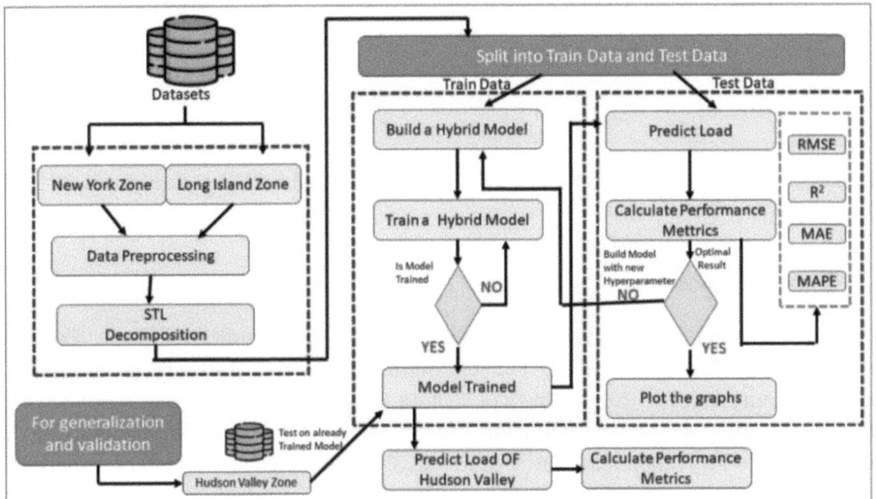

Fig. 5. Flowchart of proposed model

3.1 Datasets

In this study, we employ hourly electricity load (in GWh) and price data (in USD) from the New York Independent System Operator (NYISO) [28], which has the data from 11 zones, but here three main regions: New York City, Long Island, and Hudson Valley are considered as they high population along with high energy demands as depicted in Fig. 6 These are major economic hubs that require accurate and reliable programs for both residential and commercial energy use. Weather datalike temperature, humidity, wind speed, and precipitation were fetched from Open Meteo [29]. The data collected for the time period is from 1st January 2023 to 12th December 2023, on an hourly basis. At a more detailed level, this merging of electricity data with the weather was expanded into full datasets for each zone, allowing us to analyze how weather affects energy usage. Both the New York City and Long Island datasets were used for training (as well as testing in our analysis), while validation/generalization was performed on a separate Hudson Valley dataset.

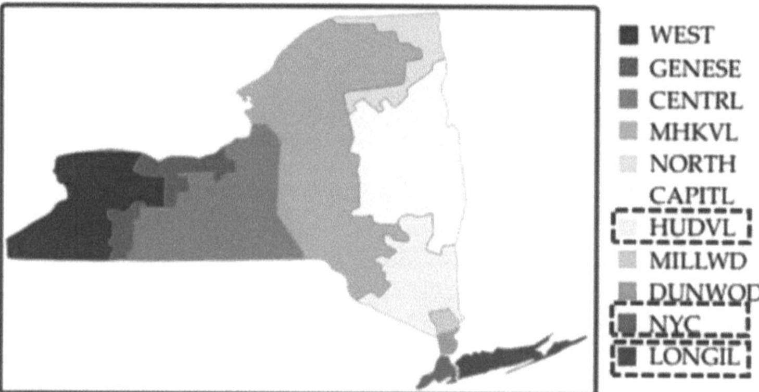

Fig. 6. NY ISO Electricity Load Zones (NYC-New York City), LONGIL (Long Island), HUDVL (Hudson Valley)

3.2　Data Preprocessing

To prepare the data for the hybrid model, missing values are handled using the "Forward Fill" method as it helps in filling specific columns with the last observed observation. Next, the data is scaled using min-max scaling to have values between 0 and 1. Last, the seasonal trend decomposition using LOESS (STL) is performed to decompose the time series into its Trend, Seasonality & Residual components to understand underlying patterns as well as irregularities essential for making precise and accurate models. For instance, the temperature attribute is decomposed into its three components as shown in Fig. 7.

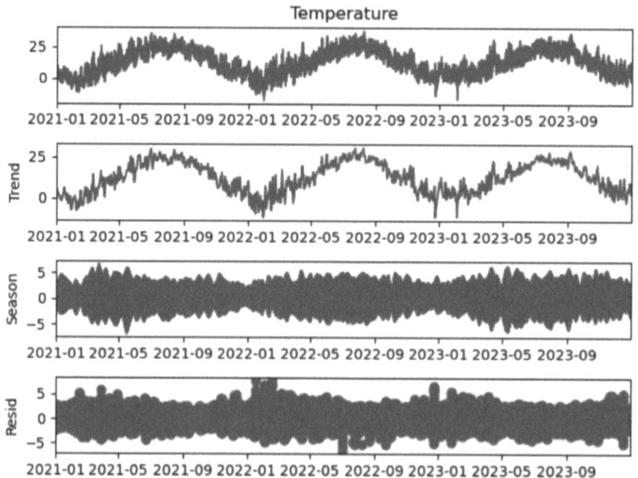

Fig. 7. STL decomposition of temperature attribute

3.3 Model Training

In the model training phase, STL components generated by decomposing first pass through a 1DCNN layer and then run max pooling. This is then repeated once more with another 1D CNN layer and max pooling. The output is then passed through a Bi-LSTM layer, followed by a GRU, and finally to the dense as shown in Fig. 8. The model is then compiled to use the Adam optimizer with a mean absolute error (MAE) loss function. The training runs for 100 epochs with a learning rate of 0.01. The hyperparameters for different layers can be seen in Table 1.

Table 1. Hyperparameters of the proposed model

Layer	Hyperparameter
1D CNN	filter = 32, kernel_size = 3, activation ='relu'
Max pooling	maxpools_size = 2
1D CNN	filter = 64, kernel_size = 3, activation ='relu'
Max pooling	maxpools_size = 2
Bi-LSTM	units = 50,return_sequence ='true',activation ='relu'
GRU	units = 50,return_sequence ='false',activation ='relu'
Dense	units = 1,return_sequence ='false',activation ='linear'

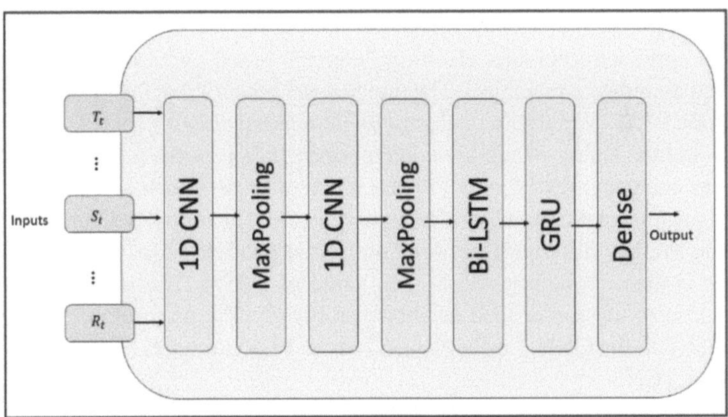

Fig. 8. Basic structure of the proposed model

3.4 Performance Evaluation

For the performance measure of the electrical load forecasting model, Root Mean Square Error (RMSE), Mean Absolute Error(MAE), R-squared(R2), and Mean Absolute Percentage Error (MAPE) are calculated. The value of RMSE and MAE is the average prediction error. The R2 indicates how much the model explains variability in demand whereas MAPE provides an accuracy measure in percentage. These metrics will be comprehensive enough to measure the accuracy and reliability of our model vital for efficient energy management.

$$R^2 = 1 - \frac{\sum_{i=1}^{n}(y_i - \hat{y}_i)^2}{\sum_{i=1}^{n}(y_i - \bar{y}_i)^2} \tag{17}$$

$$RMSE = \sqrt{\frac{1}{n}\sum_{i=1}^{n}(y_i - \hat{y}_i)^2} \tag{18}$$

$$MAE = \frac{1}{n}\sum_{i=1}^{n}|y_i - \hat{y}_i| \tag{19}$$

Where

- y_i is the actual load value.
- $\hat{y}_i$ is the predicted load value.
- $\bar{y}_i$ is the mean of the actual load values.
- n is the number of observations.

4 Results and Discussions

4.1 Performance Evaluation of the New York City Zone Dataset

Our hybrid approach to predict electricity demand based on New York Test Data performed well as depicted in Table 2. The fitted model has an R2 of 0.911 which means that it can explain 91.1% variability in electricity demand, indicating a strong generalization capability and the ability to capture contemporary data patterns and dependencies with near-perfect accuracy. RMSE of 0.117 and MAE of 0.246 which is the lowest in all the models suggests that the model performs well as there are small deviations from actual values. The average difference between the actual predicted load value and the actual load value is also implied by the MAPE value of 4.35%. The predicted load values are very close to the actual load as shown in Fig. 9. The performance of other models indicates that the CNN_LSTM, Bi-LSTM, and GRU models exhibit improvements compared to TCN.

Table 2. Performance metrics of different models using the New York Zone

Model	R2	RMSE	MAE	MAPE
TCN	.899	.242	.397	5.57%
CNN_LSTM	.904	.125	.267	4.85%
Bi-LSTM	.906	.123	.262	4.75%
GRU	.91	.118	.261	4.71%
Our Model	.911	.117	.246	4.35

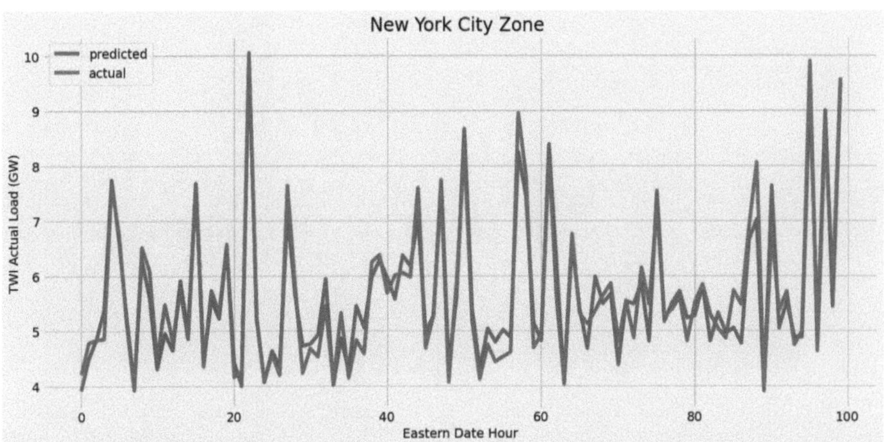

Fig. 9. The actual vs the predicted values of Time-Weighted Interval (TWI)Actual Load on the New York City zone by Bi-LSTM_GRU

4.2 Performance Evaluation of Long Island Zone Dataset

To illustrate the accuracy of different models, Table 3 compares their performance in predicting electric demand using Long Island test data. An R2 value of 0.95 implies that in the model, the independent variables such as electricity price and weather attributes account for up to 95% of the variance in electricity demand That means the correlation is very strong and the model fits well on the data. With a RMSE of 0.022, the model can predict load values close to actual load values. The MAE of 0.112 further proves its accuracy and depicts how well it performs by calculating the smallest average prediction errors. A MAPE of 4.97% indicates that in general, the model's predicted load values are about 4.97% away from real values. The predicted vs. actual load values are remarkably close, as illustrated in Fig. 10. This high level of accuracy, supported by the model's exceptional precision in capturing minor errors and explaining most of the variance, highlights its reliability in forecasting with minimal deviations from actual values.

Table 3. Performance metrics of different models using Long Island Zone

Model	R2	RMSE	MAE	MAPE
TCN	.928	.029	.13	5.86%
CNN_LSTM	.935	.026	.123	5.30%
Bi-LSTM	.942	.023	.115	5.21%
GRU	.942	.024	.117	5.22%
Our Model	.95	.022	.112	4.97

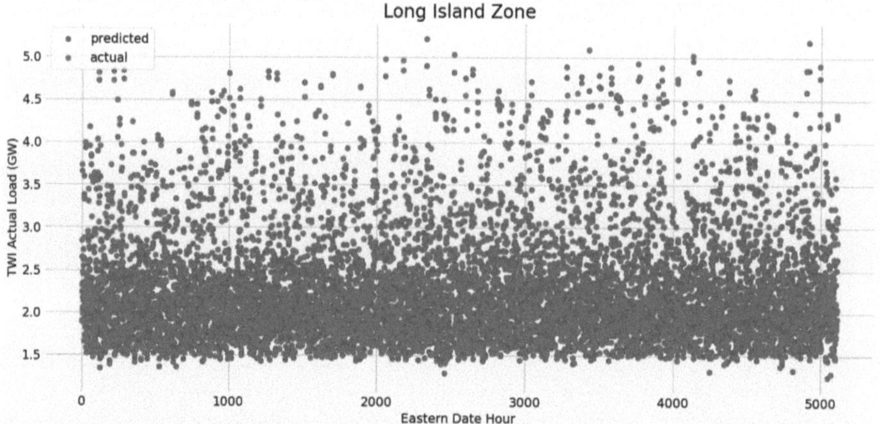

Fig. 10. The actual vs the predicted values of Time-Weighted Interval (TWI)Actual Load on Long Island Zone by Bi-LSTM_GRU

This paper presents a thorough and insightful analysis of feature importance within the hybrid deep learning approach for electricity demand forecasting. By carefully examining key variables such as electricity price and weather attributes, the study demonstrates their substantial impact on the model's predictive accuracy. The in-depth exploration of feature importance using STL decomposition underscores how these variables enhance forecasting performance, reinforcing the model's strong generalization capability. With R2 values of 0.911 for New York and 0.95 for Long Island, along with consistently low RMSE, MAE, and MAPE values, the model showcases exceptional accuracy and reliability in predicting electricity load. These findings indicate that the model's precise demand forecasting can significantly boost smart grid efficiency by optimizing resource allocation, improving load management, and ensuring greater overall grid stability.The proposed method could be applied to predict peak electricity demand during extreme weather events, aiding utility companies in managing load distribution and preventing grid failures. Similarly, it could be adapted to forecast renewable energy generation, such as solar or wind power output, across different geographical regions, enabling better integration of these resources into the grid while maintaining stability and efficiency.

4.3 Computational Complexity

To investigate the computational complexity of the proposed approach with other models, the execution time was calculated and depicted in Table 4. Experiments were carried out on an HP Victus laptop with a Ryzen 5 5600H processor that features 6 cores and 12 threads, running on Windows 11 with 8 GB RAM. While our model adds more computational layers, it offers the best execution time compared to TCN and Bi-LSTM models with competitive performance against GRU and CNN_LSTM. Our model strikes an optimal balance between computational efficiency and predictive accuracy, making it the best choice for robust electricity demand forecasting.

Table 4. Time complexity Comparison

Model	New York Zone	Long Island Zone
TCN	1120.47s	1040.8s
CNN_LSTM	579.94s	429.29
Bi-LSTM	790.78s	718.82
GRU	714.67s	658.52s
Our Model	799.94s	725.82s

4.4 Validation of Proposed Model

Another dataset of the Hudson Valley zone having similar attributes was used to verify the effectiveness of the proposed model. The period selected is January 1, 2021–July 1, 2021, to compute the predicted load values. An R^2 value of 0.544, an RMSE of 0.043, an MAE of 0.17, and a MAPE of 7.98% show the robustness and generalization abilities of the proposed model. These measures based on unseen data show how well and consistently the model predicts electricity load in various geographical areas.

4.5 Comparisons with Existing Methods

The efficacy of our proposed model is evaluated in comparison to state-of-the-art hybrid deep learning models for predicting electricity load. Table 5 presents the comparison, demonstrating that our model outperforms these other methods while maintaining a lower RMSE value. These results demonstrate how well our model performs in comparison to other hybrid deep learning models, confirming its accuracy and robustness in energy consumption forecasting.

Table 5. Performance comparison with state-of-the-art models

Model	RMSE
[30]	1.30
[31]	.61
Our Model	.02(Long Island Dataset)

5 Conclusion

To predict electricity demand using a multivariable dataset, this study uses a hybrid algorithm that combines 1D CNN, Bi-LSTM, and GRU with Seasonal Temporal Loess (STL) decomposition. With an R2 value of 0.911, an RMSE of 0.117, an MAE of 0.246, and a MAPE of 4.35%, our model performed exceptionally well when tested using data from New York. It obtained R2 values of 0.950, RMSEs of 0.022, MAEs of 0.112, and MAPEs of 4.97% for Long Island. Furthermore, a validation on an unseen Hudson Valley dataset produced a MAPE of 7.98%. These findings demonstrate that our model effectively balances computational efficiency and predictive accuracy, establishing it as the optimal choice for reliable electricity demand forecasting.

Although the model accounts for seasonal trends using STL decomposition, it does not fully capture the impact of holidays on electricity demand or the number of occupants in a household, which can significantly affect usage patterns. The model's performance could be further enhanced through hyperparameter optimization using metaheuristic algorithms such as Genetic Algorithms, Particle Swarm Optimization, or Bayesian Optimization.

Acknowledgments. I, Gursleen Kaur, would like to extend my heartfelt gratitude to Dr. R.K. Bawa, my advisor, for the patient guidance, enthusiastic encouragement, and invaluable feedback provided throughout this research. The support and constructive critiques have been essential to the completion of this work.

Disclosure of Interests. The authors confirm that they have no financial interests or personal relationships that could be perceived as having influenced the work presented in this paper.

References

1. Hafeez, G., Alimgeer, K.S., Khan, I.: Electric load forecasting based on deep learning and optimized by heuristic algorithm in smart grid. Appl. Energy **269**, 114915 (2020)
2. Nilakanta Singh, K., Robindro Singh, K.: A review on deep learning models for short-term load forecasting. In: Applications of Artificial Intelligence and Machine Learning: Select Proceedings of ICAAAIML 2020, pp. 705–721 (2021)
3. Kong, X., Wang, Z., Xiao, F., Bai, L.: Power load forecasting method based on demand response deviation correction. Int. J. Electr. Power Energy Syst. **148**, 109013 (2023)
4. Saber, A.Y., Alam, A.R.: Short term load forecasting using multiple linear regression for big data. In: 2017 IEEE Symposium Series on Computational Intelligence (SSCI), pp. 1–6 (2017)

5. Rendon-Sanchez, J.F., de Menezes, L.M.: Structural combination of seasonal exponential smoothing forecasts applied to load forecasting. Eur. J. Oper. Res. **275**(3), 916–924 (2019)
6. Pooniwala, N., Sutar, R.: Forecasting short-term electric load with a hybrid of ARIMA model and LSTM network. In: 2021 International Conference on Computer Communication and Informatics (ICCCI), pp. 1–6 (2021)
7. Jin, M., Zhou, X., Zhang, Z.M., Tentzeris, M.M.: Short-term power load forecasting using grey correlation contest modeling. Expert Syst. Appl. **39**(1), 773–779 (2012)
8. Liao, X., Cao, N., Li, M., Kang, X.: Research on short-term load forecasting using XGBoost based on similar days. In: 2019 International Conference on Intelligent Transportation, Big Data & Smart City (ICITBS), pp. 675–678 (2019)
9. Kindalkar, S.S., Itagi, A.R., Kappali, M., Karajgi, S.: Time series based short term load forecasting using Prophet for distribution system. In: 2022 International Conference on Smart Generation Computing, Communication and Networking (SMART GENCON), pp. 1–6 (2022)
10. Van Houdt, G., Mosquera, C., Nápoles, G.: A review on the long short-term memory model. Artif. Intell. Rev. **53**(8), 5929–5955 (2020). https://doi.org/10.1007/s10462-020-09838-1
11. Weerakody, P.B., Wong, K.W., Wang, G., Ela, W.: A review of irregular time series data handling with gated recurrent neural networks. Neurocomputing **441**, 161–178 (2021)
12. Hewage, P., et al.: Temporal convolutional neural (TCN) network for an effective weather forecasting using time-series data from the local weather station. Soft. Comput. **24**, 16453–16482 (2020)
13. Mo, J., Wang, R., Cao, M., Yang, K., Yang, X., Zhang, T.: A hybrid temporal convolutional network and Prophet model for power load forecasting. Complex Intell. Syst. **9**(4), 4249–4261 (2023)
14. Chen, Z., Wang, C., Lv, L., Fan, L., Wen, S., Xiang, Z.: Research on peak load prediction of distribution network lines based on Prophet-LSTM model. Sustainability **15**(15), 11667 (2023)
15. Alrasheedi, A., Almalaq, A.: Hybrid deep learning applied on Saudi smart grids for short-term load forecasting. Mathematics **10**(15), 2666 (2022)
16. Zuo, C., Wang, J., Liu, M., Deng, S., Wang, Q.: An ensemble framework for short-term load forecasting based on timesnet and TCN. Energies **16**(14), 5330 (2023)
17. Hyndman, R.J., Athanasopoulos, G.: Forecasting: principles and practice. OTexts (2018)
18. Jo, H.J., Kim, W.J., Goh, H.K., Jun, C.H.: An improved time-series forecasting model using time series decomposition and GRU architecture. In: International Conference on Neural Information Processing, pp. 587–596 (2021)
19. Sebastian, K., Gao, H., Xing, X.: Utilizing an ensemble STL decomposition and GRU model for base station traffic forecasting. In: 2020 59th Annual Conference of the Society of Instrument and Control Engineers of Japan (SICE), pp. 314–319 (2020)
20. Cleveland, R.B., Cleveland, W.S., McRae, J.E., Terpenning, I.: STL: A seasonal-trend decomposition. J. Off. Stat. **6**(1), 3–73 (1990)
21. Schuster, M., Paliwal, K.K.: Bidirectional recurrent neural networks. IEEE Trans. Signal Process. **45**(11), 2673–2681 (1997)
22. Hamayel, M.J., Owda, A.Y.: A novel cryptocurrency price prediction model using GRU, LSTM, and bi-LSTM machine learning algorithms. AI **2**(4), 477–496 (2021)
23. Yildirim, Ö.: A novel wavelet sequence based on deep bidirectional LSTM network model for ECG signal classification. Comput. Biol. Med. **96**, 189–202 (2018)
24. Cho, K., et al.: Learning phrase representations using RNN encoder-decoder for statistical machine translation. arXiv preprint arXiv:1406.1078 (2014)
25. Bibi, I., Akhunzada, A., Malik, J., Iqbal, J., Musaddiq, A., Kim, S.: A dynamic DL-driven architecture to combat sophisticated Android malware. IEEE Access **8**, 129600–129612 (2020)

26. Bai, S., Kolter, J.Z., Koltun, V.: An empirical evaluation of generic convolutional and recurrent networks for sequence modeling. arXiv preprint arXiv:1803.01271 (2018)
27. Tasdelen, A., Sen, B.: A hybrid CNN-LSTM model for pre-miRNA classification. Sci. Rep. **11**(1), 14125 (2021)
28. Load Data - NYISO. NYISO. https://www.nyiso.com/load-data. Last accessed 2 december 2024
29. Free Open-Source Weather API | Open-Meteo.com. https://www.open-meteo.com/. Last accessed 2 December 2024
30. Pavlicko, M., Vojteková, M., Blažeková, O.: Forecasting of electrical energy consumption in Slovakia. Mathematics **10**(4), 577 (2022)
31. Cascone, L., Sadiq, S., Ullah, S., Mirjalili, S., Siddiqui, H.U.R., Umer, M.: Predicting household electric power consumption using multi-step time series with convolutional LSTM. Big Data Res. **31**, 100360 (2023)

Soundscapes: Impact of AI in Cinematic Audio

C. Manikandan[1]([⊠]) [iD], Jyotsana Thakur[2] [iD], and Fakira Mohan Nahak[3] [iD]

[1] Manipal Institute of Communication, Manipal, India
manikandan.c@manipal.edu
[2] UIMS, Chandigarh University, Chandigarh, India
jyotsana.e11225@cumail.in
[3] Media and Communication, Manipal University, Jaipur, India

Abstract. Artificial intelligence transforms the cinematic audio substance industry by progressing sound production, assisting audio-editing systems, and personalizing the seeing encounter. This research paper analyzes the numerous applications of manufactured insights in film to supply more energetic and engaging soundtracks. AI tools and their productivity in audio creation in movies are analyzed through the qualitative study. The creation of clever sound effects, versatile sound blending, and programmed discourse substitution are among the foremost critical advancements in AI. This paper outlines how AI-driven arrangements are upgrading the inventive capabilities of sound creators and sound engineers, coming about in more compelling generation workflows and higher-quality sound encounters through case studies and advancement progress.

Keywords: AI Vocal · AI Sound Effects · AI Audio Mixing · AI Music Production · AI Mimic

1 Introduction

In the film industry, the visual components frequently take center stage. Still, it is impossible to overstate the significance of sound. Film soundscapes are essential for elevating the aural experience overall and drawing viewers into the narrative. In order to elicit feelings, establish a scene, and highlight significant moments, sound designers create and modify a variety of audio aspects. Soundscapes enhance the authenticity and depth of the action on screen with everything from explosions to soft ambient noises. The use of foley sound effects is one of the main components of cinematic soundscapes. Correct music may accentuate tension, express feelings, and establish a setting that people will remember. The effect and general tone of a film are significantly influenced by the selection of music, which ranges from grand orchestral pieces to minimalist electronic soundscapes. A big part of how various environments are portrayed also involves soundscapes. The soundtrack improves the visual experience by bringing the viewer to many locales, such as the immensity of space, the calm serenity of a forest, or the busy streets of a metropolis.

Recent technological developments have further transformed cinematic soundscapes. The emergence of immersive audio formats such as Dolby Atmos has provided sound

S. Pal et al. (Eds.): ICETSS 2024, CCIS 2610, pp. 223–233, 2026.
https://doi.org/10.1007/978-3-032-11488-4_17

designers with more tools to produce a really three-dimensional auditory experience. By utilizing spatial audio technology, sounds can be distributed dynamically among speakers, immersing listeners in a vibrant and lifelike auditory experience. There are more types of soundscapes than the diegetic noises in movies. Non-diegetic noises can heighten a scene's emotional impact and add to the overall acoustic environment. Examples of these sounds include voiceovers, narration, and background music. Moreover, cinema soundscapes have the ability to arouse particular feelings in viewers. A fast-paced rhythm can create enthusiasm and energy, while a haunting tune might evoke feelings of sadness or nostalgia [1]. Presently sound design and audio editing are specialist professions that need a combination of technical know-how and artistic imagination. These procedures have historically required a great deal of time and work, as well as careful attention to detail on the part of audio engineers and sound designers. Sound substance is one of the areas in which AI of knowledge in motion pictures has the first potential [2].

Artificial intelligence has become a disruptive factor in film, broadcast, and other media industries, in recent years. AI is an umbrella term including an assortment of advances, counting characteristic dialect preparation, machine learning, and profound learning, that permit AI engines to do errands that regularly call for human insights. The film industry is utilizing counterfeit visions to enhance and optimize numerous generation forms, such as showcasing, scripting, visuals, and Audio effects.

On-screen characters hone their lines in a studio as sound engineers have trouble synchronizing the as-of-late recorded lingo with the old film. Due to the necessity for different takes and genuinely modifying, this procedure can be costly and time-consuming. On the other hand, the AI automated talk substitution systems driven by made experiences may observe the source tapes and convey a synchronized talk on their claim, planning the performers' lip improvements, tones, and pitches. This makes strides in the ultimate sound quality and precision while speeding up the AI automated discourse substitution handle [3].

Customary methods for creating sound effects involve the manual creation or obtainment of sounds, which can be an imaginative and difficult undertaking. By empowering the clever era of sound effects, imitate insights innovations are changing the field of sound planning. AI frameworks may deliver unused sound effects on request that are suitable for the given circumstance since their models have been prepared on expansive sound libraries. This makes it conceivable for sound originators to quickly emphasize their thoughts and attempt a more extensive assortment of sounds, coming about in more energetic and creative soundscapes. This chapter analyzes the application of AI experiences to cinematic sound, emphasizing three major headways: modified vocal substitution, flexible sound mixing, and quick sound effect era [4]. The film industry is being essentially precious by utilizing AI in cinematic sound fabric. AI-powered devices are upgrading the inventive potential of sound engineers and sound originators, permitting them to deliver more creative and exact work. The length and cost of sound post-production are being brought down by more proficient generation workflows brought approximately by progressions in AI innovation [5]. AI is additionally progressing viewers' sound encounters, which progresses the inundation and captivating nature of movies.

2 Literature Review

A. Miguel Civit (2022) conducted a comprehensive analysis of the literature on the subject using the Prisma technique to assess the breadth and developments of the research on artificial intelligence-based music creation. Additionally, the accessibility and potential applications of a number of already accessible AI technologies as tools for musical composition were examined. Their research feeds a clear picture of the state of this technology by demonstrating how publications are dispersed globally based on a variety of parameters. Through this research, they have observed unequivocally that the growing involvement of large corporations in the sector concluded the previous several years, found a considerable surge in attention to AI-based automatic music generation from both computer scientists and musicians [6]. Deruty (2022). Focused on the outline and use of Artificial intelligence music production aids to produce modern Pop Music, for instance, genres including studio technology as part of the innovative development. Also, discussed in what way music design procedures correlated with those categories can differ substantially from conventional observations of how a musical production is produced, and in what way this influences AI music tools [7]. In this study, L. Comanducci (2023) presented a method based on Western music theory for creating chord progressions that are conditioned on harmonic complexity. Specifically, two types of variational autoencoders, a Conditional-VAE (CVAE) and a Regressor-based VAE (RVAE), are trained on an existing dataset that has been annotated with the relevant complexity values. This allows the latent space to be conditional on the complexity [8]. In their research, Purnima Kamath (2023) examined how crowdsourced human listening tests are used to assess novel AI-generated audio samples for descriptive attributes like a morph's smoothness. Nevertheless, there is a dearth of focus in the assessment metrics literature regarding effectively explaining the descriptive audio quality under test and building interfaces for such studies. This work investigates the design of AI-generated audio evaluation interfaces using visual metaphors from picture schema [9]. In their research work, A. Alican (2024) described how the majority of existing XAI techniques concentrate on both textual and visual explanations, which are frequently seen in visual media. On the other hand, audio explanations are more expressive than other modalities in certain situations (e.g., when comprehension of visual explanations necessitates specialized knowledge) and are intuitive in audio-based tasks. Using general XAI techniques to explain audio models and XAI techniques tailored to the interpretability of audio models, they present an overview of XAI methods for audio in this review. Moreover, certain unresolved issues were covered, and future possibilities for the advancement of XAI methods for audio modeling were indicated [10]. In his paper, B. Antonios (2024) examines the analysis of AI covers from the standpoints of image rights and copyright. The first section provides a description of Directive 2019/790's text and data mining exception, primarily emphasizing the opt-out procedure for the three-step test. In the second section, the paper explores the intricacies of voice cloning and emphasizes the lack of a complete EU image rights system. Through tackling these problems, this influence revealed two-fold important ideas. Initially, deep fake covers created and distributed by AI simulations trained on the works of different artists not only violate patents but also expose flaws in the TDM exclusion. Second, with future developments expected, the multifarious image right regime remains a feasible defense against voice cloning, even though it may not be as comprehensive as necessary [11]. Artificial intelligence (AI) algorithms have been utilized in conventional audio recording techniques to separate background noise from the target signal. Donald Williamson (2024) provides details on how listeners' evaluations of speech comprehension are not always consistent with AI objective approaches. This project is unique in that it aims to train an AI model to eliminate undesirable sounds using perception. If humans can notice any aspect of the signal's quality, this AI model can use that as extra data to improve its ability to identify and eliminate noise [12].

After reading through the various literature, many of them went into detail on how to produce pop music, how to compare traditional and artificial intelligence (AI) tools for production, how complicated AI tools are, how to utilize the Prisma technique to study AI tools for music production, and how to publish audio podcasts. The study's author therefore discovered a gap in the analysis of the range of AI-driven sound effects, flexible sound mixing, dialogue replacement, and voice synthesis technologies used in the creation of cinematic audio.

3   Algorithm of AI Audio Production

Artificial intelligence (AI) algorithms are used in audio production to evaluate and extract useful information from audio data. These algorithms can be trained to identify various musical components, including beats, instruments, and voices. This enables intelligent activities related to audio processing, such as mixing and editing. The process follows (Fig. 1).

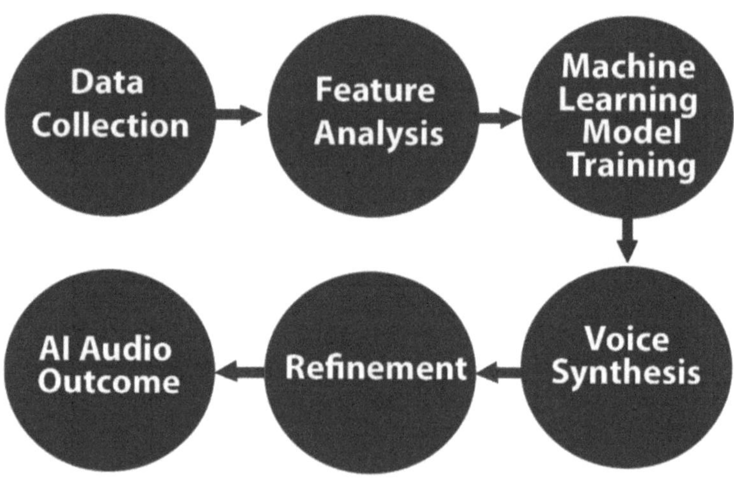

Fig. 1. Process of AI Audio Production

3.1 Data Collection

First, a sizable dataset of audio recordings is gathered. The recordings function as the AI's training data, providing a diverse array of voices, noises, and tonal variations to guarantee accuracy and adaptability.

3.2 Feature Analysis

Pitch, timing, and timbre are among the auditory characteristics of these recordings that the AI then examines. The AI gains a better understanding of the qualities that distinguish each sound through this examination.

3.3 Machine Learning Model Training

A machine learning model is taught to identify patterns and comprehend how various audio parameters are integrated to produce particular sounds or voices using the examined data.

3.4 Synthesis

After being trained, the AI can produce new sounds by utilizing the input it gets. This is translating text into speech that imitates human emotion and intonation for voice generation. For some sounds, it might be necessary to replicate the environment in which the sound is produced.

3.5 Refinement

To improve the generated audio's quality and realism, it is finally refined. This phase could include adding effects, filtering out noise, or modifying specific settings to provide a more realistic sound. By following these procedures, artificial intelligence sound generators may generate a wide range of extremely realistic audio outputs, such as speaking in multiple languages and simulating rain.

4 Research Methodology

This investigation aims to memorize more about the applications of AI insights in making more energetic and immersive soundscapes for motion pictures. Through a detailed investigation of case studies about and later advancements, the paper illustrates how AI-driven devices are changing sound-altering and sound design forms. For the study, movies are selected based on the utilization of four AI tools including AI Automated Dialogue Replacement, AI Sound Effects, AI Audio Mixing, and AI voice synthesis models. The ADR technology has been incorporated in the movie "The Irsihman", AI in Imaginative Sound Effects Generation has been used in the movie "Avengers: Endgame", AI Sound Mixing Adaptively was used in the movie "Dunkirk", AI Speech Synthesis technique was used in the film Goat, Song "Chinna Chinna Kangal" is selected for the investigation.

The study deals with the quality of audio outcomes for which the qualitative method has been utilized. A survey has been conducted on sound engineers, and film industry professionals with the constructed questionnaires. Questions are prepared to evaluate the audio quality parameters consisting of dialogue, sound effects, sound mixing, and voice cloning that are produced through AI tools on selected movies. One hundred samples were collected from sound designers and other film industry professionals, and it has been analyzed.

5 Analysis and Findings

Conventional Neural Networks, Machine Learning, and Deep Neural Models used for audio production in movies are detailed below. Each case study dealt with the technology and algorithm, utilization, and benefits.

5.1 Algorithm of ADR (Automated Dialogue Replacement)

ADR, (Automated Dialogue Replacement) is referred to as "dubbing" or "looping," and is the act of replacing or improving the original on-set recordings of dialogue with new takes recorded in a studio setting. Conventional Neural Networks model has been implied for ADR. The deep learning algorithm ensures that the voice to be matched with the characters on screen.

Case Study About "the Irishman":.
Martin Scorsese's "The Irishman" (2019), a picture that made broad utilization of de-aging innovation, highlighted a part of ADR. The actors' carefully modified appearances were synced with their rerecorded sentences utilizing Counterfeit Insights innovation. By altering the pitch, tone, and timing of the new recordings through an investigation of the initial recordings and the actors' lip developments.

Benefits:. The AI framework can ensure consistent integration with the visual impacts and is altogether speedier at assessing and synchronizing exchange than conventional strategies. More exactness can be accomplished by AI frameworks in coordinating dialect with on-screen lip developments.

5.2 Algorithm of AI in Imaginative Sound Effects Generation

The sound impacts in a film essentially build up the sound-related disposition while upgrading the story and enthusiastic reverberation. Sound creators regularly create or source sound effects by hand, which could be a monotonous and maybe inventively debilitating strategy.

Case Consider of "Avengers: Endgame":
AI Simulation insights were utilized by the sound plan group in "Avengers: Endgame" (2019) to deliver special sound effects for the film's various activity groupings. Conventional Neural Networks model organizes sound effects from vast data sets. It allows sound designers to use automated sound effects design for the scene demand. This tool

permitted for a more energetic and responsive sound plan, especially throughout the film's complex battle scenes.

Benefits:. AI can produce a wide run of sounds; sound creators have more alternatives and motivation accessible to them. The programmed era of sound effects speeds up the creation handle and, guarantees a steady sound involvement by keeping up remarkable sound quality in an assortment of scenarios and scenes.

5.3   Algorithm of AI Sound Mixing Adaptively

Versatile sound blending is powerfully changing the sound levels and impacts in a film to supply watchers with a more immersive encounter. Machine Learning models that used to mix the complex and multiple layers of audio tracks involved in a battle scene in the movie in real-time.

Case Consider About of "Dunkirk":

The 2017 film "Dunkirk" coordinated by Christopher Nolan utilized AI-driven adaptive sound blending to form a holding and captivating sound-related involvement. The manufactured insights program analyzed the film's story and visual components, altering the mix specific minutes, such as the tension amid the shoreline clearing or the dogfight arrangements. The audience's interest was provoked by this versatile approach, which guaranteed that the sound complemented the action on screen.

Benefits:. Real-time alterations make a soundscape that's more charming and locks in. AI can alter the sound encounter based on the inclinations of each watcher, bookkeeping for diverse sound setups, and tuning in situations. Since robotized blending decreases their burden, sound experts may centre on more inventive ventures.

5.4   Algorithm of AI Speech Synthesis

AI insights in music generation have progressed altogether, with the capacity to synthesize and imitate craftsman voices among its numerous employments. Tacotoren tools are used to clone the voice of a singer's voice by training on a dataset of their previous scoring through the voice composer design of a new audio track. Deep Neural Networks perform the vocal style transfer technique allowing us to transfer the style of a particular voice from one song to another. This model delivers engineered discourse that closely imitates the human voice; as this case appears, this innovation may be utilized for voiceovers, naming, and singing. These models are prepared on endless sums of sound information to empower them to comprehend the subtleties of a specific voice, counting its pitch, tone, timbre, and elocution.

The Case Considers "Chinna Chinna Kangal":.

A special utilization of imitation insights to supplant the voice of the late vocalist Bhavatharani may be listened to within the melody "Chinna Chinna Kangal" from the 2024 Tamil film Goat. The AI Model's Training: With the assistance of the sound information collected, the AI show was instructed to recognize Bhavatharani's special vocal characteristics. To do this, the information had to be encouraged into a profound learning neural arrange, ordinarily a repetitive neural organize (RNN) or generative adversarial organize (GAN). The demonstrate iteratively learned to imitate her voice by analyzing information designs, counting vibrato, enunciation, and pitch vacillations.

Benefits:. Being able to preserve a singer's bequest is one of the greatest focal points of utilizing AI to supplant their voice. The interesting voice of the vocalist may be able to charm groups of onlookers indeed after their life by embracing AI innovation, ensuring that the singer's melodic abilities live on. For makers and composers, AI voice union makes modern imaginative roads. It makes it conceivable for famous voices to be brought back for unused ventures, for cutting-edge artists to work with perished entertainers, and for avant-garde melodic classes to be investigated that were not sometimes recently conceivable. AI voices can achieve a degree of specialized precision which will prove troublesome for human vocalists to achieve. This incorporates having a faultless pitch, solid timing, and the capacity to effortlessly create intricate vocal lines and harmonies. These qualities make strides in the ultimate products in general quality. The following table depicts the survey response on the quality of the AI audio.

Table 1. Survey Data

Movie	Technology	AI Model	Outcomes			
The Irishman	Automated Dialogue Replacement	CNN	Lip Sync with visual	Emotion of dialogue delivery	Audio clarity	Theatrical Audio Mixing
			100%	92%	100%	100%
Avengers: Endgame	AI Sound Effects	CNN	Imaginative	Originality	Uniqueness	Emotional resonance
			100%	100%	100%	89%
Dunkirk	AI Sound Mixing	ML	Dynamic RangeAdaptability	Dialogue clarity	Effects clarity	Music clarity
			100%	100%	100%	100%
Goat, Song: Chinna Chinna Kankal	AI Voice Synthesis	DNN	Voice cloning	Pitch	Tone	Style
			100%	89%	100%	95%

Table 1 indicates that using AI tools and technology produces superior audio quality in the post-production process of filmmaking. Using ADR technology in the Irish Man film has been accepted by 100% Lip Synchronization with visuals, clarity of audio, and Audio Mixing. However, the emotional dialogue delivery secured 92% in the quality acceptance. Using AI sound effects in the Avengers: Endgame has been accepted 100% in Imaginative, Originality, and Uniqueness, but emotional resonance is accepted 89% of responders. Using AI sound mixing in the Dunkirk movie has been accepted 100%

in the adaptability of Dynamic range, Dialogue clarity, effects clarity, and music clarity. Using AI voice synthesis in the movie Goat, Song: Chinna Chinna Kankal has been accepted 100% in voiced cloning, and the tone of the fed reference voice, but pitch is accepted by 89%, and style of synthesis voice by 95% (Tables 2 and 3).

Table 2. List of AI Tools for Audio Production

AI software / Tool	Application	Function
DupDub	ADR	Enhance Automated Dialogue Recording workflow
Elai	Language Modelling	Converting various Language Models with advanced Deep learning
Optimizer AI	Sound Effects	Generating Sound effects
Sound effect Generator	Sound Effects	Generating sound effects from a text command
Avid Pro tools	Audio Mixing	Audio Recording, Editing, and Sound mixing.
Avid Media Composer	Audio Mixing	Audio Editing and Mixing.
AI voice generator	Voice synthesis	Mimicking voice through voice referencing
Play.ht	Voice synthesis	Customizing the speed and pitch of the voice, offering SSML(Speech Synthesis Markup Language) support for further customization.
Microsoft Azure	Voice synthesis	TTS (text-to-sound) offering uses neural networks to produce natural-sounding speech.

Table 3. Various Contributions of AI to Audio Production

S. No.	Title of the Audio Album	Song Name	Author of Audio	Role of AI
1	"Illiac Suite"	"Psycho theme"	Leonard Isaacson, Lejaren Hiller, and the Illiac Computer	Composed a String quartet Music Track
2	"Not Easy"	"Jeopardy"	Alex Da Kid, IBM Watson, Elle King, Wiz Khalifa, X Ambassadors,	Wrote a lyric for the Pop Music
3	"Savages"	"Heart On My Sleeve"	Drake and The Weeknd	Performed Voice Mimic
4	"Not Mine"	"R&B playlist"	Trevor McFedries and Sara DeCou	Manipulated the vocals
5	"Break Free"	"I AM AI"	Taryn Southern	Electro Pop song composed by an AI tool Amper

(*continued*)

Table 3. (*continued*)

S. No.	Title of the Audio Album	Song Name	Author of Audio	Role of AI
6	"Deliverance Rides"	"Unison"	Kirt Connor	Wrote a Lyric
7	"Daddy's Car"	"Daddy's Car"	Behemoth Sony	Replicated the Pop music "Beach Boys" produced in 1960
8	"Drowned in the Sun"	"the 27 Club"	Eric Hogan	Raw vocals and a distorted guitar-sounding track were made.
9	"World is Mine"	"virtual idol"	Hatsune Miku	virtual representative of the Vocaloid synthesizer programmed.

6 Ethical Considerations

A new era of content creation has been brought about by AI voice cloning, but there are ethical challenges involved. Authenticity, privacy, and misuse are the three main ethical issues. The remarkably accurate speech replication technology begs concerns regarding appropriate use and misuse possibilities.

7 Conclusion

The film industry is changing as a result of AI's incorporation into cinematic audio content, which also improves sound design, streamlines audio editing, and personalizes the viewing experience. AI-driven solutions are enhancing the creative powers of sound designers and audio engineers through automated dialogue substitution, intelligent sound effects production, and adaptive audio mixing. This enhances the global cinematic experience for viewers by resulting in more effective production operations and better audio experiences. The investigation discovered some restrictions that are taken into account when creating the emotional dialogue delivery and sound effects for the screen. Due to the trained datasets, voice synthesis also discovered some limitations about a singer's pitch and style. With more trained datasets and AI model progress, voice synthesis, and emotive dialogue delivery could both be rendered with more quality and dynamic style.

The Future of AI Audio, Artificial intelligence is always developing, and including advances in natural language processing, it won't be long until humans hear audio content produced by AI that can't be distinguished from information produced by humans. The development of completely new media formats that combine immersive, interactive experiences with conventional storytelling is one possible application for audio AI in the future. This may present new chances for brands to interact creatively with consumers. Further study may extend to the application of Artificial Intelligence to generate a genuinely personalized hearing experience by dynamically modifying audio content based on the listener's Location, mood, and favorites is another fascinating breakthrough.

References

1. Director, M.M.: Soundscapes in film: enhancing the audio experience. Medium (2024). https://medium.com/@markmurphydirector/soundscapes-in-film-enhancing-the-audio-exp erience-6fce8eb37b54. Accessed 15 Jul. 2024
2. Michael, B.: Unleashing the Power of AI: Exploring AI-Assisted Audio Production *Trackinsolo* (2023). Unleashing the Power of AI: Exploring AI-Assisted Audio Production (trackinsolo.com). Accessed 16 Jul. 2024
3. Michael, B.: Machine Learning Revolutionizes the Process. Trackinsolo (2023). Unleashing the Power of AI: Exploring AI-Assisted Audio Production (trackinsolo.com). Accessed 16 Jul. 2024
4. Michael, B.: Transforming audio effects with machine learning. Trackinsolo (2023). Unleashing the Power of AI: Exploring AI-Assisted Audio Production (trackinsolo.com). Accessed 16 Jul. 2024
5. Michael, B.: Industry professionals leveraging ai for innovative projects. Trackinsolo (2023). Unleashing the Power of AI: Exploring AI-Assisted Audio Production (trackinsolo.com). Accessed 16 Jul. 2024
6. Civit, M., Maria, A., Javier Civit Masot, J., Francisco Cuadrado, B., Escalona, A.C.: A systematic review of artificial intelligence-based music generation: Scope, applications, and future trends. Expert Systems With Applications **209**, 118190 (2022)
7. Deruty, E., Grachten, M., Lattner, S., Nistal, J., Aouameur, C.: On the development and practice of AI technology for contemporary popular music production. Trans. Int. Soc. Music Info. Retri. **5**, 35. https://doi.org/10.5334/tismir.100
8. Comanducci, L.M., Gioiosa, D., Zanoni, et al.: Variational autoencoders for chord sequence generation conditioned on Western harmonic music complexity. J. Audio Speech Music Proc. **24** (2023). https://doi.org/10.1186/s13636-023-00288-5
9. Kamath, P., Wyse, L., Gupta, C., Kokil Jaidka, S.N., Li, Z.: Evaluating descriptive quality of AI-generated audio using image-schemas. IUI '23: Proceedings of the 28th International Conference on Intelligent User Interfaces, pp. 621–632 (2023). https://doi.org/10.1145/358 1641.3584083
10. Akman, A., Schuller, B.W.: Audio Explainable Artificial Intelligence: a review. INTELLIGENT COMPUTING **3**, no. Article ID: 0074 (2024). https://orcid.org/0000-0002-8010-6897
11. Antonios, B.: AI covers: legal notes on audio mining and voice cloning. J. Intel. Property Law & Practice **19**(7), 571–576. https://doi.org/10.1093/jiplp/jpae029
12. Woodall, T.: AI can use human perception to help tune out noisy audio New machine learning model can disregard unwelcome sounds. Ohio State News (2024). https://news.osu.edu/ai-can-use-human-perception-to-help.

A Review on Deep Learning Models and Fractal Residual Learning in Detection of Different Tumors

Shyo Prakash Jakhar[1,2], Amita Nandal[2], and Arvind Dhaka[1(✉)]

[1] Department of Computer and Communication Engineering, Manipal University, Jaipur, Rajasthan, India
shyo143@gmail.com, arvind.dhaka@jaipur.manipal.edu
[2] Department of IoT&IS, Manipal University, Jaipur, Rajasthan, India
amita.nandal@jaipur.mnipal.edu, amita_nandal@yhaoo.com

Abstract. Medical image processing play a vital role in disease diagnosis and medical research. The most common image acquisition methods include X-ray, CT, MRI and Ultrasound. Every method has its own advantages and disadvantages. Deep learning Models are widely used by image researchers to get clear view of the medical image and thus the diseases like brain tumor, lung cancer, breast cancer, kidney disease, Glaucoma etc. can be diagnosed correctly. In this paper we have analyzed many research papers which include the structure of CNN. We have also analyzed background of transfer learning and types of different transfer learning techniques. An exhaustive study of different deep learning models, their working and their applications in medical field has been done. Through this paper, researchers will get true insight of popular deep learning models and fractal residual networks in field of medical image processing. In the end how different deep learning models can be effectively applied in detection of tumors in different body parts been discussed.

Keywords: CNN · Deep Learning Models · Fractal Residual Networks · Transfer Learning

1 Introduction

Medicine is regarded as one of the most oldest and reputed discipline of life. Through the advancement of medical science, human has found cure for almost every disease. Couple of years back, whole world was fighting against COVID19 pandemic. As it is was a new pandemic, there was lack of available data. Still scientist all over the world managed to find the vaccines to increase the immunity against this CORONA disease. So medical image processing play a vital role in modern medical science to find cure of different diseases.

To get a clear insight of organs affected by certain disease, we need different image acquisition methods. When we compare different image acquisition methods, CT has higher resolution on tissues but they rely mainly on doctor's skill to identify the real

S. Pal et al. (Eds.): ICETSS 2024, CCIS 2610, pp. 234–249, 2026.
https://doi.org/10.1007/978-3-032-11488-4_18

severity of disease due to lost scans. X-ray is easy, convenient and inexpensive method, suitable for first scans but are harmful like CT if performed many times. MRI take longer time and not suitable for patients with any metallic implants and devices like pacemakers. With the help of Ultrasound doctors can see real time pictures and can see the movements inside the body. These different converging techniques can work well with deep learning models as they can be trained and have robustness in image scale and resolution as well.

These techniques can be applied for qualitative analysis of disease in various organs of humans like chest, lungs, kidney, brain, liver etc. For investigating disease, doctors cant investigate each disease with naked eyes. With lack of proper information, misjudgment can occur and can to delayed treatment of the real disease. Due to this reason we need some computer aided technology that can help in fast investigation of a disease.

In present times, Convolution Neural Networks play a vital role in extracting advanced and much deeper features from medical images. By fine tuning these features CNN can perform many tasks related to medical imaging including detection, segmentation, classification and prediction of various diseases [1–3]. The advantage of CNN is the fast speed and higher accuracy and they can be applied on any type of medical image. But CNN has also certain limitations [4]. First the CNN model has to be trained first and it is very difficult and time consuming process. Second, the absence of large amount of labeled data in medical field. CNN require labeled data for training purpose and for this they required professional doctors who can do it and is also a major problem.

To overcome these drawbacks of CNN, transfer learning was introduced [5–8]. The underlying aspect of transfer learning is that if a CNN find solution of any problem successfully, it can learn from that convolutional network and find solution to similar problems much faster. As the transfer learning model does not need to learn from the scratch, it take advantage of the pre-trained network. It greatly reduce the training time and as well as the difficulty of training. For training it requires only small amount of labeled data. Fine-tuning uses the labeled medical image data and employs pre-trained deep learning based model. The basic function of hidden layers is to extract features and the final output layers of the pre-trained networks are trained again so that they can learn new features. After fine-tuning, the network depicts much better classification capabilities in the final output layer. The approach of feature extractor is to keep all other layers as it is in pre-trained networks and make changes in the final layers, and then restructure so to get the new trained model with better performance. In the same way fractal residual network creates a much deeper model and make use of self similarity property of fractals to get a much clear and resolution enhanced image. In this paper different layers and techniques of CNN have been discussed. Followed by overview of different deep learning models and their applications. We have also discussed how different organs are affected by tumor and which model has been applied to find out the exact tumor affected area. In the end challenges, limitations and future perspectives have been discussed.

2 Overview of different layers and techniques of CNN Models

Nowadays to implement transfer learning one common technique is to use convolutional neural organization as pre-prepared model, freeze a few layers and afterward retrain a couple of layers by information in target space. Another famous technique is to remove part of layers in pre-prepared model and at that point add another classifier algorithm like SVM. The pre-prepared model assumes an essential part in transfer learning. Also, a large portion of mainstream pre-prepared models applied in transfer learning clinical pictures investigation, like GoogleNet, UNet etc. use convolutional neural organization structure.

Deep Learning models can be broadly categoried into two parts, Supervised and Unsupervised Learning models. The Supervised models are again divided as Concurrent Neural Network(CNN) and Recurrent Neural network(RNN). Each category has its own application areas.The CNN is mainly used for image classification, computer vision etc.The RNN is mainly used in application areas like NLP, speech recognition and video classification.T he unsupervised Models include models like Auto encoders and General Adversarial Networks(GAN).The different layers of these models are as follows:

2.1 Convolution Layers

CNN has multiple convolution layers. Initial layers extract basic features and later layers extract advanced features e.gIf image of a dog is fed to a convolution neural network, the initial layer will only give some lines or edges but further layers can give the basic shape of body parts like nose, ears, tail etc. Kernel is called as feature extractor, usually represented by a $k \times k$ matrix. Padding is used to insert extra zeros around the pixel values so that we can get deep features of the image. Convolution is of three types:

  i) Standard Convolution
 ii) Strided Convolution
iii) Grouped Convolution

2.2 Pooling

This layer is important to carry out down-sampling operation on extracted features, and only keep relevant feature information. The task of pooling layer is to reduce no. of parameters so that it can reduce overfitting and only important features are retained so that computation is also reduced. The most important benefit of pooling layer is translation invariance. Pooling is of two types- max pooling and average pooling.

2.3 Activation

The activation function is used to have nonlinearity in the Convolutional Neural Networks. In a practical problem of real world, it is difficult to get the linear separable data. It becomes quite difficult for CNN to get a linearly indivisible data without using the activation function. Sigmoid and Tanh are two important activation functions.

2.4 Fully Connected Layer

This layer usually lies at the end of CNN. This layer is simply feedforward network. In fully connected layer all neurons of previous layer are connected to all the neurons of the next layer. To flatten the output means to unroll the values got from pooling layer or convolutional layers which is 3-Dimentional into vector form. This layer play the role of classifier in the convolution network i.e. it classifies the data into different classes.

2.5 Advanced Techniques of CNN

Here we have discussed some advanced techniques which are used nowadays to enhance the accuracy of the models as well as make training process faster.These advance techniques have proved to be important landmark in transfer learning:

Batch Normalization: Deep learning fine tuning is often very difficult along with the problem of covariate shift. Covariate shift refers that when data parameters in testing phase change as compared to what has been learnt by model in training phase. So the upper network need to be adjusted regularly and hence speed is reduced. Batch normalization is applied so that the output fall into a desirable range of values. It also normalize input values as well as output values. It make sure that the activation function should not fall into gradient saturation during training. Finally it add the regularization effect on thenetwork.

Dropout: The problem of overfitting occurs in deep learning models when the training data is small in size and the network is complex and large parameters are there. To remove this problem, dropout is used during training the hidden layers. In the hidden layers, half of the nodes are set to zero during training i.e. ignoring half of the features detectors. So dropout solve the problem of overfitting effectively.

Regularization: It is also used to resolve the problem of overfitting in deep learning models.Some parameters in the network are overtrained due to overfitting and affects the overall output of network negatively i.e. they increase the error rate in the network. So to control these parameters, regularization suppress the parameters in training so that the models gives the correct predictions and problem of overfitting can be solved.

Weight Initialization: There are certain methods of weight initialization like zero and constant, random normal, random uniform, truncated normal, orthogonal, identity, Xavier initialization, Lucan initialization etc.Various convolution layer sizes are depicted in Fig. 1.

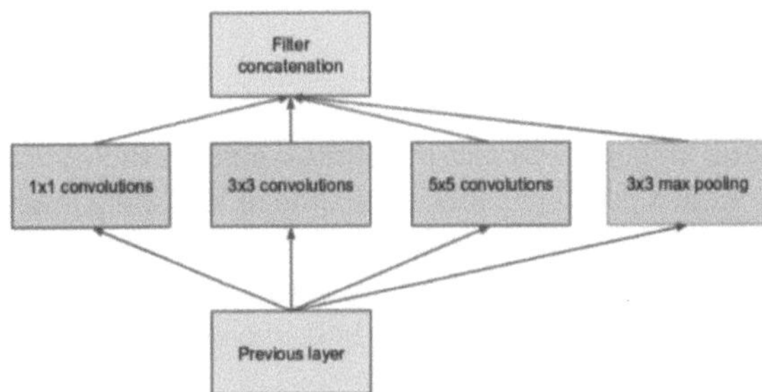

Fig. 1. Different Convolution layer Sizes

3   Deep Learning Models and Their Applications

Deep learning models are dependent on artificial intelligence techniques. They mainly focus on feature extraction and feature learning. In machine learning, they can directly learn from raw data. So the difference is evident between deep learning models and machine classifiers. Deep learning model comprises with various layers of nonlinear handling units [9] and they are feedforward networks. Each successive layer utilizes the output from the past layer as input to it. Nowadays, deep learning has made advancements in picture order, acknowledgment, object recognition and clinical picture examination, where they have delivered superb outcomes similar to or in some cases better than human specialists. Among the known deep learning calculation, for example, stacked auto-encoders [10], profound Boltzmann machines [11] and Convolutional neural organizations [12]. The best one for picture classification is CNN proposed in 1989, the principal fruitful genuine application [13] is the transcribed digit acknowledgment in 1998 by Lecun, where he introduced a five-layer model based on deep learning. The summary of the most popular models is as follows:

3.1   AlexNet

It was proposed by Alex Krizhevsky.The design comprises eight layers: five convolutional layers and three completely fully associated layers along with 1000-way Softmax. These were the changes made that are new ways to deal with convolutional neural organizations:

a) AlexNet utilizes ReLU rather than the tanh, which was very popular at that period of time. ReLU take less preparing time; a CNN utilizing ReLU is much faster the CNN employing tanh.
b) Few years back GPUs of 3 gigabytes of memory were used.
c) AlexNet uses multi-GPU and non saturating neurons were used. So a greater model is prepared and preparing time is greatly reduced.

The new regularization methods called dropout and data augmentation were utilized to reduce the overfitting problem in convolutional layers. Winner of ILSVRC-2012 comprises of five convolutional layers, some trailed by max-pooling layers and 1000-way softmax. It utilized non-soaking neurons to make it quicker and an effective GPU execution of the convolution activity. ZFNet [14] Winner of 2013 ILSVRC contest, some minor changes were made in AlexNet design [15].

3.2   ResNet

As indicated by the all inclusive estimate hypothesis, given sufficient limit, we realize that these CNNs suffer from a problem called exploding or vanishing gradient. To overcome this problem, the concept of skip connections was introduced by researchers. Here layers are connected to upcoming layers by skiping some of the layers inbetween and thus forming residual blocks. Since AlexNet, the best in class CNN design is going further and more deep and better.

Profound organizations are difficult to prepare due to the famous disappearing slope issue—as the inclination is back-proliferated to prior layers, rehashed augmentation may make the angle infinitively little. Accordingly, as the organization goes further, its exhibition gets immersed or even beginnings debasing quickly. A ResNet learning block is shown on Fig. 2.

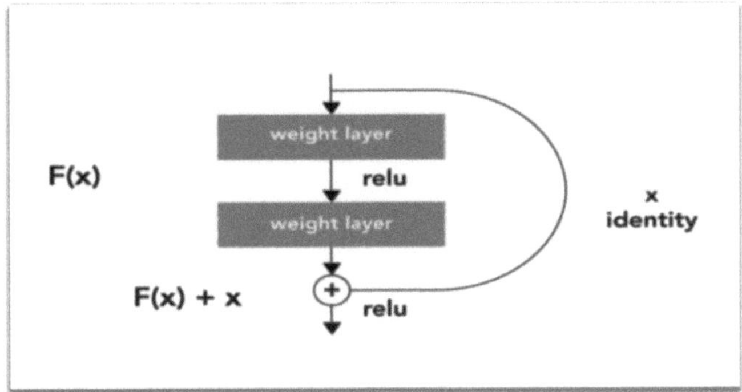

Fig. 2. ResNet Learning Block

3.3 GoogleNet

The Inception Network is one of the significant model of Neural Networks, particularly for CNNs. The first version was given the name "GoogleNet" because it was made by researchers at Google in 2014. So far there are three versions of it i.e. Inception V1, V2 and V3.This design end up being bleeding edge for gathering and ID in the ILSVRC. Beginning design can grow the width of single layer in network by utilizing different sizes of convolutional centers and furthermore consolidate them with maxpooling and ReLU. These beginning designs Inception V1, V2 and V3 can be utilized to tackle multi-disciplinary issues including classification of lens classes [60].Therefore Googlenet has been one of the most popular deep learning models among all other available models.

It won the 2014 ILSVRC contest. It is based on the idea of stacking the layers in CNNs as organization of various layers expanding on the possibility of [16]. GoogLeNet contains various beginning modules, in which numerous distinctive channel sizes are applied to the information and their outcomes connected. GoogLeNet additionally advocated utilizing normal pooling rather than completely associated layers toward the end, along these lines decreasing the quantity of model boundaries [17].

A long way from comprehensive, non-ordered, rundown of CNN designs and some undeniable level depictions can be summed up as:

VGG: Popularized utilizing more modest channel parts and along these lines further organizations (up to 19 layers for VGG19, contrasted with 7 for AlexNet and ZFNet), and preparing the more profound organizations utilizing pre-preparing on shallower variants [18].

ResNet: It won the 2015 ILSVRC contest. They are enlivened by Long Short-Term Memory intermittent organizations, which makes it conceivable to prepare a lot further organizations. A 152 layer deepResNet effectively prepared an adaptation with 1001 layers. Presented skip associations and utilize versatile gating units to control the data stream. Indeed, even with many layers, thruway organizations can be prepared straight-forwardly through basic slope drop. At the point when input information is taken care of, skip associations increment the organization adaptability [19].

Highway nets: Another approach to expand profundity dependent on gating units, a thought from Long Short Term Memory (LSTM) repetitive organizations, empowering advancement of the skip associations in the organization. The doors can be prepared to discover valuable blends of the character work and standard nonlinearity play an important role in information maintenance [20].

DenseNet: Based on the idea of ResNet, however rather than adding the results from one layer to another, they are basically linked together. The first contributions to expansion to the enactments from past layers are along these lines kept at each layer,protecting some sort of worldwide state. This energizes highlight reuse and brings down the quantity of boundaries for a given profundity. DenseNets are along these lines especially appropriate for more modest informational collections [21].

ResNext:it is based onResNet and GoogLeNet, and so we can say it is a mix of Resnet and GoogleNet. [22].

SENet: won the ILSVRC 2017 contest Squeeze-and-Excitation Networks, expands on ResNext however adds learnable boundaries that the organization can use to gauge each element map, where prior networks just added them up [23].

NASNet: A CNN engineering planned with a neural organization, it was obviously better than past networks. It was made utilizing AutoML, a Google Brain's support learning way to deal with engineering plan [24]. A repetitive neural organization proposes structures intended to perform better for various spaces, and by experimentation figures out how to foster better constantly models. NASNet depended on Cifar-10, and has somewhat humble computational requests, yet beat the past ILSVRC information models [25].

YOLO: This model is quite fast. Another variant of it, Fast YOLO, measures a bewildering 155 edges each second while as yet accomplishing twofold the mAP of other ongoing finders. YOLO makes more blunders however is undoubtfully more averse to see false findings where nothing exists. In the end, YOLO learns exceptionally broad depiction of data objects [26].

GANs: These are the latest networks employed in medical image processing. A generative Adversarial Network comprises of two neural organizations set in opposition to one another. The generative organization G is entrusted with making tests that the discriminative organization D should order as coming from the generative organization or the preparation information. The organizations are prepared at the same time, where G plans to augment the likelihood that D commits an error while D focuses on high order precision [27].

Siamese nets [28] An old thought (for example [29]) that is as of late been displayed to empower a single shot learning as it has a similarity function. A Siamese organization comprises of two indistinguishable neural organizations, both the design and the loads, joined toward the end. They are prepared together to separate sets of data sources. When prepared, the variants of this model is used to learn once and has high accuracy rates.

U-net: adjust contemporary models (AlexNet, VGGnet and GoogLeNet) into completely convolutional models and turn their learned features into much better performance.This is fully convolutional network and consist of two paths-contracting path and expansive path.U-net lacks fully connected layer, So it is faster because it takes less time in training. Mainly used in image classification [30].

V-net: 3D picture division dependent on a completely convolutional neural organization. CNN was prepared to work on MRI dataset. Present a novel target work that is streamlined during preparing, in light of Dice coefficient. Mainly used for image reconstruction(regression) [31].

4 Deep Transfer Learning

In recent times, strategy for transfer learning is increasingly more broadly applied in the area of medical imaging. Perhaps the most important and generally used techniques for transfer learning in clinical picture preparing is CNN. With the development of CNN, it is impossible to implement transfer learning in the field of clinical picture handling [32, 33].A lot of transfer learning approaches depend on design of CNN.

Due to the scarcity and unavailability of sample data it is very difficult to obtain data of various diseases in medical imaging field. Also we want to learn from our past experiences and methods which were used to solve a particular problem. Therefore we require transfer learning. Transfer learning is based on the idea of learning from source domain and transfer that learning to the target domain.

Transfer Learning learn from large datasets and transfer or apply that learning on smaller datasets. The initial layers of CNN are kept as it is and final layers are modified to get the training and make correct predictions. A domain, written as D, has two important parts: feature space X and marginal distribution (Y). So we can represent the domain as:

$$D = \{X, (Y)\} \tag{1}$$

With the definition of domain, we can define a task T as:

$$T = \{\gamma, (Y|X)\} \tag{2}$$

in which γ represents label space and the function $P(Y|X)$ predicts corresponding label based on feature space.

So we can say that transfer learning is a process which aims to learn the target probability distribution using the knowledge learnt from *Domain D and Task T.*

Transfer Learning working showing how customized model have been developed from pretrained model is depicted in Fig. 3.

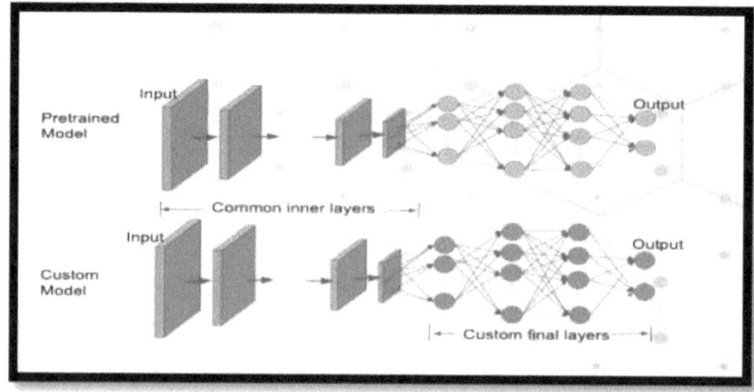

Fig. 3. Transfer Learning

Transfer learning can be catagorised in 4 types:

- i) instance based deep transfer learning
- ii) mapping based deep transfer learning
- iiiI) network based deep transfer learning, and
- iv) adversarial based deep transfer learning.

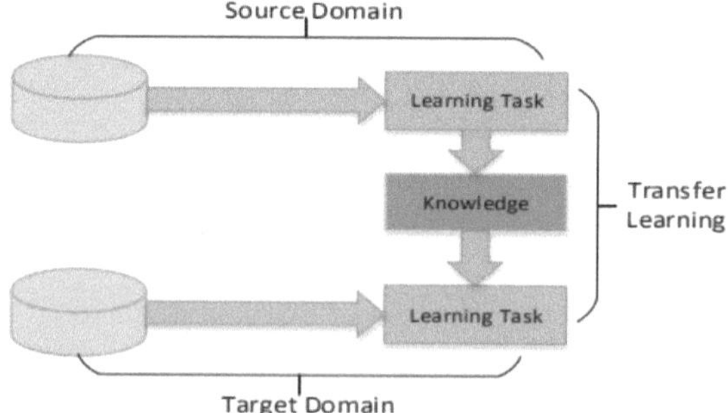

Fig. 4. Learning process of Transfer Learning [64]

The adversarial based deep learning is based on generative adversarial networks(GAN) and can be applied to both the source domain and target domain. The learning process employed in transfer learning is depicted in Fig. 4.

5 Fractal Residual Network

Fractal Geometry is one of the important techniques used in medical imaging nowadays. Fractal length and fractal dimension are two important parameters to characterize any image. Fractals are very popular due to the self similarity property of fractals. Fractal residual network are networks that can be used for single image super resolution. Here new residual paths are added and are having the self similarity property of fractals.

Jakhar Shyo et al. [62] proposed a new wavelet fractal technique for image resolution enhancement. The scaling operator in the gradient domain has been employed. Due to this the fractal dimension and fractal length becomes scale invariant. The final image restores the texture information contributing as the main advantage of the model.

J. Kwak et al. [63] proposed a fractal residual network for Single image Super resolution. Here the model becomes much deeper and can learn the high frequency information much fast. The dataset used was NTIRE 2019.So we can say that Fractal residual network can be used along with other networks so that various types of tumors can be effectively detected and segmented. Normally super resolution networks have three parts:

a) encoder
b) no-linear mapper
c) decoder.

So FRN can be effectively used to get high frequency component from low frequency component and it removes the noise also.

It is not possible for many CNN models to find out high frequency and low frequency information from the medical image. Therefore Yanghao et al. [64] introduced a Deep fractal residual network (DFRN) which consist of multiple path fractal blocks. The fractal blocks learn from different features in order to give finer features and finally a high resolution image is generated. In order to reduce space complexity, it also introduced a weight sharing version of the model which provided better performance as compared to other state of art models.

6   Comparative Study of Different Tumors in Different Body Parts

These models can be used to detect different types of diseases in different organs of the body. A brief summary of different affected body organs and the type of deep learning techniques employed is given below:

6.1   Brain

Brain extraction: A 3D CNN was used for skull stripping and related work [34].

Alzheimer's illness: Manhua Liu et al. [35] build a 3-D DenseNet to learn highlights of the 3D patches separated dependent on the hippocampal division results for the grouping task. They took insights from the perform various tasks CNN and DenseNet models are joined to group sickness status [36] Landmark-based profound multi-case taking in assessed on 1526 subjects from three public datasets (ADNI-1, ADNI-2, MIRIAD) [37] Finding phases of Alzheimer Disease [38] Employing underlying MR and FDG-PET pictures Multimodal deep neural organizations for the early conclusion of AD.

Glioma: B. H. Menze *et al.* [39] Twenty cutting edge tumor division calculations were applied to a bunch of 65 multi-contrast MR outputs of low-and high-grade glioma patients [40] Glioblastoma division utilizing heterogeneous MRI information from clinical routine [41] Deep learrning for division of cerebrum tumors and effect of cross-institutional preparing and testing [42] AdaptAhead advancement calculation for learning Deep CNN applied to MRI division of glioblastomas (BRATS).

Functional connectomes: Li H et al. [43] proposed transfer learning way to deal with improve profound neural organization arrangement of mind useful connectomes. Multisite demonstrative grouping of schizophrenia utilizing discriminant deep learning with utilitarian network MRI [44].

Brain age: Chronological age expectation from crude cerebrum T1-MRI information, additionally testing the heritability of mind anticipated age utilizing an example of 62 monozygotic and dizygotic twins Vascular sores [45].

Meningioma: Fully robotized recognition and division of meningiomas utilizing deep learning on routine multiparametricMRI [46].

Multiple sclerosis: Deep learning of joint myelin and T1w MRI highlights in ordinary seeming mind tissue to recognize different sclerosis patients and solid controls [47].

6.2 Kidney

Abdominal organs: It assess the pertinence of a current completely convolutional neural organization (FCNN) intended for CT imaging to portion stomach organs like liver, kidney etc. T2-weighted MR pictures [48].

Renal relocate: A deep learning model with stacked non-negative compelled autoencoders was utilized to recognize dismissed and non-dismissed renal transfers in Diffusion-Weighted MRI [49].

6.3 Prostate Cancer

(PCa): Cheng R et al. [50] proposed a technique for start to finish prostate division by coordinating comprehensively (picture to-picture) settled edge identification with completely convolutional networks. Their settled organizations consequently gain proficiency with a various leveled portrayal that can further develop prostate limit discovery. Gotten awesome outcomes (Dice coefficient, 5-overlay cross approval) on MRI filters from 250 patients.

Deep CNN and a non-profound getting the hang of utilizing highlight discovery were utilized to recognize neurotically affirmed PCa patients from prostate kind conditions patients with prostate benevolent hyperplasia in an assortment of 172 patients with more than 250 2-D MR pictures [51].

Designed a framework which can simultaneously recognize the presence of PCa in a picture and confine injuries dependent on deep CNN highlights (co-prepared CNNs comprising of two equal convolutional networks for ADC and T2-w pictures individually) and a solitary stage SVM classifier for computerized discovery of PCa in multi-parametric MRI data of over 50 different patients [52].

Carefully researched three basic variables which could extraordinarily influence the exhibition of multimodal CNN [53]:

(a) How these models can be used for PCa analysis?
(b) How can multimodal MRI data can be used in CNNs?

(c) What is the effect of various CNN designs on the correctness of PCa determination? So it planned and tried multimodel CNN utilising clinical data.

6.4 Spine

Vertebrae naming: Designed a CNN for recognition and naming of vertebrae in MR pictures with clinical explanations [54].

Lumbal Neural forminal stenosis (LNFS): It conducts both early detection and detailed appraisal by drawing vital neurotic connections between pathogenic components and LNFS. A deep multiscale perform various tasks learning organization (DMML-Net) coordinating and worked on converting transfer learning into a completely convolutional network [55].

Spondylitis versus tuberculosis: CNN model for separating among tuberculosis and pyogenic spondylitis in MR pictures. Contrasted their CNN execution and that of three gifted radiologists utilizing spine MRIs from 80 patients [56].

Metastasis: A multi-goal approach for spinal metastasis identification utilizing deep Siamese neural organizations The CBMIR utilizes another model wherein each picture is first deteriorated into parts. The closeness estimation between pictures is created dependent on a plan that incorporates the properties of the multitude of areas in the pictures utilizing provincial coordinating. The technique can answer questions as a visual cue. The effectiveness and execution of the introduced technique has been assessed utilizing a dataset of around 5,000 reproduced, however reasonable CT and MRI, from which the first pictures are chosen from three enormous clinical picture data sets [57].

6.5 Eyes

Glaucoma: Deep learning models For identifying the patients with early-stage glaucoma,the experimental results comprising two datasets, demonstrate the accuracy of these models when applied to glaucoma images. Compared with data given by two ophthalmologists, deep learning models showed greater efficiency with better performance for identifying glaucoma [58].

Glaucoma: Deep learning models can be used to identify glaucoma before its onset with higher accuracy. Visual fields as well as Fundus photographs were examined. Accuracy of model in Detection of Glaucoma before 4 to 7 years of disease onset was 0.77, before 1 to 3 year was 0.88 and after onset was 0.95 [59].

7 Challenges, Limitations and Future Perspective

Deep learning models provide quick, accurate and efficient information regarding medical images so the diseases can be early diagnosed. But it has certain limitations also. Every type of deep learning models has its own advantages and disadvantages. There are certain technological problems and its become very difficult to identify which model to select for certain problem domain and what are the changes we can do so that we get the desired solution of a particular problem. In deep learning certain computer vision problems like object recognition are solved by these models over the years. Transfer Learning is used with deep learning models in identifying many disease like segmentation of tumor [61].

Fractal geometry and Fractal residual network has emerged as one of the leading technology in medical image processing in recent times.

Most important issue is that deep learning medical images are 3-Dimentional images and it becomes quite difficult to model these images as their 2-D counterparts. Second issue is related to memory and use consumption while using CNN, researchers are trying various techniques to deal with large bulk data(3-D data to 2-D data patch) or segment based training. Third challenge is related to trust, interpretability, regulations, workflow integration and data related problems. While using these deep learning models, researches face a lot of problems in dealing with data access, data privacy and data protection. While using deep learning, the problem of black box testing arises as large hierarchal data is maintained for training part and from there it get the correct predictions. Sometimes the model developed using deep learning gives accurate result on trial but it is not useful for actual clinician. Even though there are certain limitations, deep learning techniques are very useful in getting accurate results and in future fractal residual learning and deep learning is going to be employed more and more to solve medical imaging related problems and identification of diseases.

8 Conclusion

Deep learning provide very powerful techniques to solve various medical imaging problems. There are different deep learning models with different architectures and advantages. The access of bio sensors and various wearable devices, diseases can be monitored and properly diagnosed. The recent trends of fractal residual networks shows great impact in medical field. Different models like ResNet, VGGNet,GoogleNet, UNet etc. have their own advantages and are used in variety of application areas. Fractal geometry and fractal residual network are greatly used in medical image processing field nowadays. The future belongs to fractal theory and deep learning techniques as they are very powerful tools and very helpful in early detection and accurate diagnosis of different diseases by getting clear resolution enhanced images.

References

1. Chen, H., et al.: DCAN: Deep contour-aware networks for object instance segmentation from histology images. Medical Image Analysis **36**, 135–146 (2017)
2. Caravagna, G., et al.: Detecting repeated cancer evolution from multi-region tumor sequencing data. Nature Methods **15**, 707–714 (2018)
3. Du, Y., et al.: Classification of Tumor Epithelium and Stroma by Exploiting Image Features Learned by Deep Convolutional Neural Networks. Annals o. Biomedical Engineering **46**, 1988–1999 (2018)
4. Shin, H.-C., et al.: Deep convolutional neural networks for computer-aided detection: CNN architectures. Dataset Characteristics and Transfer Learning **35**, 1285–1298 (2016)
5. Armato, S.G., et al.: The Lung Image Database Consortium, (LIDC) and Image Database Resource Initiative (IDRI): A Completed Reference Database of Lung Nodules on CT Scans. Medical Physics **38**, 915–931 (2011)
6. Aerts, H., et al.: Decoding tumour phenotype by noninvasive imaging using a quantitative radiomics approach. Nature Communications **5**, Article ID: 4006 (2014)

7. Chollet, F.: Xception: Deep Learning with Depthwise Separable Convolutions. In: 30th Ieee Conference on Computer Vision and Pattern Recognition, ed, pp. 1800–1807 (2017)

8. Cover, T.M., Hart, P.E.: Nearest neighbor pattern classification. In: Ieee Transactions on Information Theory, vol. 13, p. 21 (1967)

9. Srivastava, N., Salakhutdinov, R.R.: Multimodal learning with deep Boltzmann machines. In: Advances in neural information processing systems, pp. 2222–30 (2012)

10. Bengio, Y., Lamblin, P., Popovici, D., Larochelle, H.: Greedy layer-wise training of deep networks. In: Advances in neural information processing systems, pp. 153–60 (2007)

11. Salakhutdinov, R., Hinton, G.: Deep Boltzmann machines. In: Twelfth International Conference on Artificial Intelligence and Statistics, PMLR 5, pp. 448–455 (2009)

12. LeCun, Y., et al.: Backpropagation applied to handwritten recognition. Neural Computing 1(4), 541–551 (1989)

13. LeCun, Y., Bottou, L., Bengio, Y., Haffner, P.: Gradient-based learning applied to document recognition. In: IEEE 86(11), 2278–324 (1998)

14. Krizhevsky, A., Sutskever, I., Hinton, G.E.: ImageNet classification with deep convolutional neural networks. In: Pereira, F., Burges, C.J.C., Bottou, L., Weinberger, K.Q. (eds.) Advances in neural information processing systems 25, pp. 1097–105. Curran Associates, Inc. (2012)

15. Simonyan, K., Zisserman, A.: Very deep convolutional networks for large-scale image recognition. arXiv:1409.1556 (2014)

16. Lin, M., Chen, Q., Yan, S.: Network in network. arXiv:1312.4400 (2013)

17. He, K., Zhang, X., Ren, S., Sun, J.: Deep residual learning for image recoginition. In: Proceedings of the IEEE conference on computer vision and pattern recognition, pp. 770–8 (2015)

18. Szegedy, C., et al.: Going deeper with convolutions. In: IEEE conference on computer vision and pattern recognition, pp. 1–9 (2014)

19. Srivastava, R.K., Greff, K., Schmidhuber, J.: Training very deep networks. In: Advances in neural information processing systems, pp. 2377–85 (2015)

20. Huang, G., Liu, Z., Van Der Maaten, L., Weinberger, K.Q.: Densely connected convolutional networks. In: CVPR, vol. 1, p. 3 (2016)

21. Xie, S., Girshick, R., Dollár, P., Tu, Z., He, K.: Aggregated residual transformations for deep neural networks. In: 2017 IEEE conference on computer vision and pattern recognition (CVPR), IEEE, pp. 5987–95 (2016)

22. Hu, J., Shen, L., Sun, G.: Squeeze-and-excitation networks, arXiv:1709.01507 (2017)

23. Zoph, B., Vasudevan, V., Shlens, J., Le, Q.V.: Learning transferable architectures for scalable image recognition, arXiv:1707.07012 2 (2017)

24. Bello, I., Zoph, B., Vasudevan, V., Le, Q.V.: Neural optimizer search with reinforcement learning. In: Precup, D., The, Y.W., (eds.) Proceedings of the 34th international conference on machine learning. Proceedings of machine learning research, vol. 70. Sydney, Australia: PMLR, pp. 459–68. International Convention Centre (2017)

25. Redmon, J., Divvala, S., Girshick, R., Farhadi, A.: You only look once: unified, real-time object detection. In: Proceedings of the IEEE conference on computer vision and pattern recognition, pp. 779–88 (2015)

26. Goodfellow, I., et al.: Generative adversarial nets. In: Ghahramani, Z., Welling, M., Cortes, C., Lawrence, N.D., Weinberger, K.Q. (eds.) Advances in neural information processing systems, pp. 2672–80. Curran Associates, Inc. (2014)

27. Koch, G., Zemel, R., Salakhutdinov, R.: Siamese neural networks for oneshot image recognition. In: ICML deep learning workshop, vol. 2 (2015)

28. Bromley, J., Guyon, I., LeCun, Y., Säckinger, E., Shah, R.: Signature verification using a "Siamese" time delay neural network. In: Advances in neural information processing systems, pp. 737–44 (1993)

29. Ronneberger, O., Fischer, P., Brox, T.: U-net: convolutional networks for biomedical image segmentation. In: International conference on medical image computing and computer-assisted intervention, pp. 234–41 (2015)
30. Long, J., Shelhamer, E., Darrell, T.: Fully convolutional networks for semantic segmentation. In: Proceedings of the IEEE conference on computer vision and pattern recognition, pp. 3431–40 (2015)
31. Milletari, F., Navab, N., Ahmadi, S.-A.: V-net: fully convolutional neural networks for volumetric medical image segmentation. In: 2016 fourth international conference on 3D Vision (3DV), IEEE, pp. 565–71 (2016)
32. Huang, C., et al.: A dynamic priority strategy for IoV data scheduling towards key data. The Journal of Supercomputing **77** (2021). https://doi.org/10.1007/s11227-020-03350-7
33. Chenxi, H., et al.: Sample imbalance disease classification model based on association rule feature selection. Pattern Recognition Letters 133 (2020). https://doi.org/10.1016/j.patrec.2020.03.016
34. Kleesiek, J., Urban, G., Hubert, A., Schwarz, D., Maier-Hein, K., Bendszus, M.: Deep MRI brain extraction: a 3D convolutional neural network for skull stripping. Neuroimage **129**, 460–469 (2016)
35. Liu, M., et al.: A multi-model deep convolutional neural network for automatic hippocampus segmentation and classification in Alzheimer's disease. NeuroImage **208** (2020)
36. Wasserthal, J., Neher, P., Maier-Hein, K.H.: Tract-Seg-fast and accurate white matter tract segmentation. Neuroimage **183**, 239–253 (2018)
37. Islam, J., Zhang, Y.: Brain MRI analysis for Alzheimer's disease diagnosis using an ensemble system of deep convolutional neural networks. Brain Inform **5**, 2 (2018)
38. Lu, D., Popuri, K., Ding, G.W., Balachandar, R., Beg, M.F.: Multimodal and multiscale deep neural networks for the early diagnosis of Alzheimer's disease using structural MR and FDG-PET images. Sci. Rep. **8**, 5697 (2018)
39. Menze, B.H.: The Multimodal Brain Tumor Image Segmentation Benchmark (BRATS). In: IEEE Transactions on Medical Imaging, vol. 34, no. 10, pp. 1993–2024 (2015)
40. Moeskops, P., et al.: Evaluation of a deep learning approach for the segmentation of brain tissues and white matter hyper intensities of presumed vascular origin in MRI. Neuro Image Clin. **17**, 251–62 (2018)
41. Pizarro, R., et al.: Using deep learning algorithms to automatically the brain MRI contrast: implications for managing large databases. Neuroinformatics (2018)
42. Laukamp, K.R., et al.: Fully automated detection and segmentation of meningiomas using deep learning on routine multiparametric MRI. EurRadiol (2018)
43. Li, H., Parikh, N.A., He, L.: A novel transfer learning approach to enhance deep neural network classification of brain functional connectomes. Front Neuro Sci. **12**, 491 (2018)
44. Zeng, L.-L., et al.: Multi-site diagnostic classification of schizophrenia using discriminant deep learning with functional connectivity MRI. EBio Medicine **30**, 74–85 (2018)
45. Cole, J.H., Poudel, R.P.K., Tsagkrasoulis, D., Caan, M.W.A., Steves, C., Spector, T.D.: Predicting brain age with deep learning from raw imaging data results in a reliable and heritable biomarker. Neuroimage **163**, 115–124 (2017)
46. Cui, S., Mao, L., Jiang, J., Liu, C., Xiong, S.: Automatic semantic segmentation of brain gliomas from MRI images using a deep cascaded neural network. J. Health cEng. 4940593 (2018)
47. Yoo, Y., et al.: Deep learning of joint myelin and T1w MRI features in normal-appearing brain tissue to distinguish between multiple sclerosis patients and healthy controls. Neuro Image Clin. **17**, 169–78 (2018)
48. Bobo, M.F., et al.: Fully convolutional neural networks improve abdominal organ segmentation. Proc SPIE 10574 (2018)

49. Shehata, M., et al.: Computer-aided diagnostic system for early detection of acute renal transplant rejection using diffusion-weighted MRI. IEEE Trans. Bio-med Eng. (2018)
50. Cheng, R., Roth, H.R., Lay, N., Lu, L., Turkbey, B., Gandler, W., et al.: Automatic magnetic resonance prostate segmentation by deep learning with holistically nested networks. J Med Imaging **4**, 041302 (2017)
51. Ishioka, J., et al.: Computer-aided diagnosis of prostate cancer on magnetic resonance imaging using a convolutional neural network algorithm. BJU Int. (2018)
52. Yang, X., Liu, C., Wang, Z., Yang, J., Min, H.L., Wang, L.: Co-trained convolutional neural networks for automated detection of prostate cancer in multi-parametric MRI. Med Image **42**, 212–227 (2017)
53. Le, M.H., et al.: Automated diagnosis of prostate cancer in multi-parametric MRI based on multimodal convolutional neural networks. Phys. Med. Biol. **62**, 6497–514 (2017)
54. Forsberg, D., Sjöblom, E., Sunshine, J.L.: Detection and labeling of vertebrae in MR images using deep learning with clinical annotations as training data. J. Digit. Imaging **30**, 406–412 (2017)
55. Han, Z., et al.: Automated pathogenesis-based diagnosis of lumbar neural foraminal stenosis via deep multiscale multitask learning. Neuroinformatics (2018)
56. Kim, K.H., Do, W.-J., Park, S.-H.: Improving resolution of MR images with an adversarial network incorporating images with different contrast. Med. Phys. **45**, 3120–3131 (2018)
57. Pilevar, A.H.: CBMIR: content-based image retrieval algorithm for medical image databases. J Med Signals Sens **1**, 12–18 (2011)
58. Alghamdi, M., Abdel-Mottaleb, M.: A comparative study of deep learning models for diagnosing glaucoma from fundus images. In: IEEE Access, vol. 9, pp. 23894–23906 (2021)
59. Thakur, A., Goldbaum, M., Yousefi, S.: Predicting glaucoma before onset using deep learning. Ophthalmology Glaucoma **3**(4), 262–268 (2020)
60. Shyo, J., Amita, N., Rahul, D.: Classification and Measuring Accuracy of Lenses Using Inception Model V3 (2020). https://doi.org/10.1007/978-981-15-6067-5_42
61. Rehman, A., Naz, S., Razzak, M.I.: A deep learning-based framework for automatic brain tumors classification using transfer learning. Circuits Syst. Signal Process **39**, 757–775 (2020)
62. Shyo, J., et al.: Fractal Feature Based Image Resolution Enhancement Using Wavelet–Fractal Transformation in Gradient Domain. Journal of Circuits, Systems and Computers (2022)
63. Kwak, J., Son, D.: Fractal residual network and solutions for real super-resolution. In: IEEE/CVF Conference on Computer Vision and Pattern Recognition Workshops (CVPRW), pp. 2114–2121. Long Beach, CA, USA (2019). https://doi.org/10.1109/CVPRW.2019.00264
64. Zhou, Y., Dong, J., Yang, Y.: Deep fractal residual network for fast and accurate single image super resolution. Neurocomputing **398**, 389–398 (2020)

Performance Analysis of Key Performance Indicators (KPIs) in 5G Networks for Resource Allocation

Jyoti[1][(✉)], Amandeep Noliya[2], Dharmender Kumar[2], and Samiksha Mathur[2]

[1] Department of CSE Guru, Jambheshwar University of Science and Technology, Hisar 125001, India
Sjsharma139@gmail.com

[2] Department of Artificial Intelligence and Data Science, Guru Jambheshwar University of Science and Technology, Hisar 125001, India

Abstract. The advent of 5G mobile networks represents a monumental shift in wireless communication technology, promising enhanced data rates, reduced latency, and the seamless connection of myriad devices. This paper comprehensively analyzes resource allocation strategies within 5G networks, specifically focusing on CRAN. Through systematic categorization, we explore various resource allocation elements and their impact on service quality, reliability, and efficiency. The research highlights the imperative of sophisticated resource management to support diverse services like massive mobile telecommunication (MTC), ultra-reliable low latency communication (URLLC), and enhanced mobile broadband (eMBB). By examining recent innovations and resource allocation algorithms, this study provides a foundation for understanding and improving the performance of 5G networks to meet the escalating demands of modern connectivity.

Keywords: 5G networks · resource allocation · performances · service quality

1 Introduction

The deliberate objective of 5G communication technology, commonly called 5G, is to deliver notably improved data transmission rates, outstanding user connectivity, reduced battery usage, and astoundingly minimal latency. This article presents a thorough examination of resource allocation strategies in a cloud radio access network and a systematic categorization of the various elements that comprise re-source allocation [1]. The not-too-distant future will witness the emergence of a society characterized by increased connectivity and mobility. In comparison to previous societies, this one will feature substantial enhancements in connectivity, and traffic volume, along with a considerably broader range of utilization scenarios. This will result in a significant escalation in the volume of traffic. There is a projected nearly 20,000-fold increase in the volume of data transmission on a global scale between 2010 and 2030. While smartphones are expected to maintain their position as the prominently connected devices, the amount of linked

S. Pal et al. (Eds.): ICETSS 2024, CCIS 2610, pp. 250–262, 2026.
https://doi.org/10.1007/978-3-032-11488-4_19

devices, including wearable and intelligent devices, is also promised to increase. For this reason, the ubiquitous implementation of 5G cellular communications technology is an absolute necessity [2]. This is because previous systems were incapable of meeting the continuously growing demands that were being imposed upon them.

Supplying broadband services that necessitate high data rates prompt reaction, exceptional reliability, and energy proficiency remains a formidable task, notwithstanding the developments achieved in 4G cellular network technology. Due to this, these competencies have transformed into indispensable preconditions for the forthcoming iteration of 5G services. There are some good things about 4G and long-term evaluation networks, but they don't give users a good enough experience when it comes to the Internet of things, interactive Internet, instant cloud services, enhanced vehicle-to-everything (eV2X), and talking to robots and drones [3]. Consequently, there has been a significant proliferation of technological innovations in the global transmission industry. Currently, mobile devices are equipped with a wide range of features, including a tiny size, the capacity to make video and audio calls, powerful phone processors, and memory that can rival that of modern laptops available on the market.

The 5G network architecture integrates numerous technologies, such as Device to Device to communications, CRANs, Mobile Edge Computing, UAV, and cloud computing. Additionally, it incorporates vehicular networking and M2M communications. These technologies enable the conventional communication network to achieve an IoE. To meet growing demand in case of cellular capacity in the advanced 5G network, it will be crucial to enhance cutting-edge technology. This will ensure that the progress being made towards meeting this critical need continues at a rapid rate. The escalating volume of data traffic on the network has become a substantial annoyance. Hence, specifically in the forthcoming 5G mobile heterogeneous networks [4, 5] and ultra-dense networks [6, 7], network traffic management is expected to be a challenging concern. As expected, this would be the situation. Due to the significant amount of traffic that the growing influx of comprehensive data is producing, wireless communication networks are currently under significant strain.

1.1 Importance of 5G Networks – Current Scenario

The 5G (CNs) utilize cellular technology to deliver high-quality broadband wireless connectivity [7, 8]. The "5G ITU-radio communication (ITU-R)" functional class plays a role in the development of 5G inside the "IMT" 2020 framework in ITU [9]. Figure 1 illustrates the goal of this endeavor, which is to achieve a 1000-fold increase in throughput and 100 billion relationships while minimizing latency to nearly zero [7, 10]. Undoubtedly, 5G technology will boost mobile broadband (eMBB) by providing extended data speeds of 100 Mbps through the efficient sharing of maximum capacity, which can range from "10 to 20 Gbps". Furthermore, 5G will provide remote connectivity, support for mMTC, and low latency capabilities. In the context of ultra-reliable low-latency communication (uRLLC), careful consideration must be given to both the latency and reliability requirements.

Under specific circumstances, it has been observed that end-to-end (E2E) latency remains constant at a minimum of 1 ms, exhibiting a reliability level of 99.99% [11]. A topological representation of a standard 5G is employed in Fig. 2 to visually represent

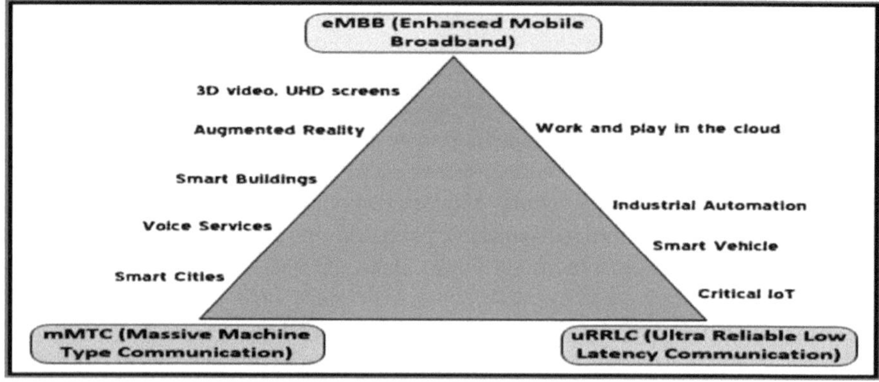

Fig. 1. Use Cases of IMT for 5G [7]

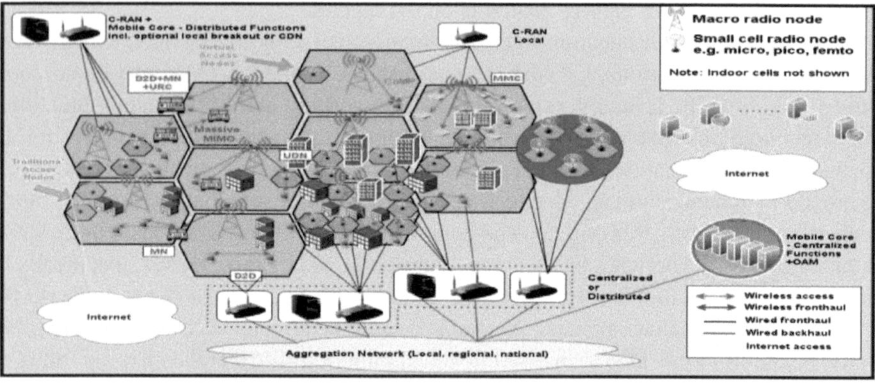

Fig. 2. Topological view of 5G Networks [12]

the concept. The technology used in these novel devices employs several methods to access a wide range of frequencies and push the limits of frequency capabilities. This technology also enables the creation of large antenna networks, the deployment of highly concentrated infrastructure, and direct communication between devices. It is anticipated that the 5G system will be capable of handling a substantial volume of data traffic and a vast array of wireless connections [13], as depicted in Fig. 3. QoS specifications for data traffic vary based on the characteristics of the data. In addition to having the capacity to significantly accelerate the growth of the IoT, the primary objective of fifth-generation cellular networks is to address the deficiencies of previous levels. The fundamental purpose of the 5G mobile system is to achieve this.

Smart fitness, drone procedures, self-directed driving, intelligent residences, interactive media and theater, industrial IoT, and highly available applications are just a few of the domains in which 5G systems offer advancements. Currently, the progression of Industry 4.0 can be attributed to the imminent proliferation and maturation of numerous

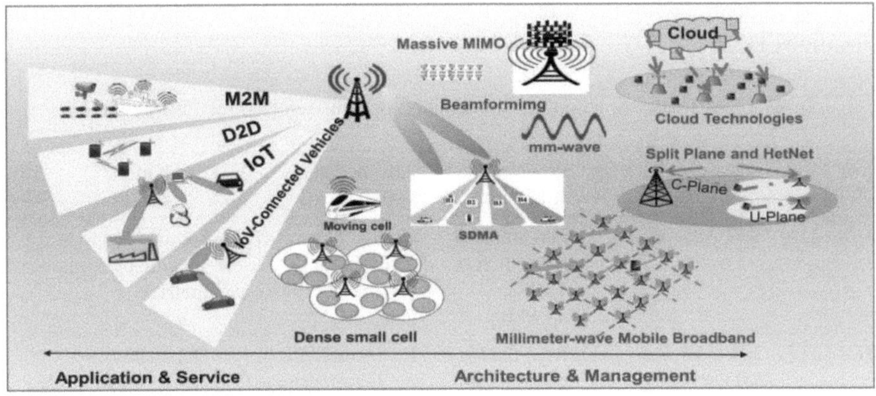

Fig. 3. Applications and designs for "5G networks" [8]

technologies, such as artificial intelligence, biotechnology, and quantum computation, among others [14].

2   Resource Allocations in 5G New Radio Networks

The 5G of mobile networks, commonly known as 5G, marks a significant leap in WCT, promising enhanced data rates, reduced latency, along the capacity to connect a multitude of devices seamlessly. Central to the performance and efficiency of 5G networks is the concept of resource allocation, which involves the distribution and management of available resources to fulfill the varying requirements of customers and uses. In 5G networks, resource allocation becomes increasingly complex due to the diverse range of services it supports, such as eMBB, URLLC, and mMTC. Each of these services has distinct requirements in terms of latency, and reliability, necessitating sophisticated resource management strategies. Concepts and models of 5G network slicing resource distribution techniques were examined in [15]. The discourse began with an examination of the notions of software-defined networks, Network function virtualization, and network segmentation. Additionally, the discussion included the network slicing management and orchestration (MO) framework, which can help with resource allocation algorithms. Following this, RAN and Cellular Network slicing were applied to identify resource categories with sufficient isolation levels. In addition, practical illustrations were utilized to classify mathematical representations of resource allocation algorithms based on their intended functions. Also resolved within the scope of this investigation were research issues.

3   Literature Review

Through an in-depth analysis of recent innovations and resource allocation algorithms, the research aims to provide a robust foundation for understanding and optimizing 5G network performance, thereby meeting the escalating demands of contemporary connectivity. This comprehensive review also identifies current limitations and potential areas for improvement, paving the way for future advancements in the field of 5G resource allocation (Table 1).

Table 1. Attributes of resource allocation algorithms selected for "5G"networks"

Year	Ref.	Algorithm/Strategy	Problem Addressed	Advancements	Limitations
2024	[16]	KPI Analysis	Performance evaluation of 4G/5G networks	Comprehensive KPI analysis for performance metrics in 4G/5G	Limited scope to specific performance metrics
2024	[17]	NWDAF and ML-Based KPI Prediction	Real-time monitoring and prediction of 5G network KPIs	Real-time KPI prediction using ML for enhanced monitoring	Dependence on accurate ML models
2024	[18]	Dynamic KPIAware Network Slicing	Efficient network slicing in 5G + networks	Dynamic slicing based on real-time KPI data	Complexity in implementation and real-time data handling
2023	[19]	Real-time Data Measurement Methodology	Evaluation of 5G network performance indicators	Methodology for accurate real-time performance measurement	May require extensive deployment of measurement tools
2019	[20]	Efficient Resource Allocation Algorithm	Maximize both the computational complexity and the capacity of the system.	Increases overall system capability and reduces complications for improved effectiveness.	In the course of power allocation, the fixed group's subcarriers are employed and Limited parameters.
2019	[21]	Multitier HCRAN Architecture	Existing C-RAN approaches lack an intelligence viewpoint.	MSR efficiently. Enhances control. E2E optimization.Ensures QoS by 15%.	Improve interference management, EE, and Resource optimization.
2019	[22]	Cooperative resource allocation and scheduling technique	Scheduling and resource allocation issues.	Improves the dependability of forthcoming 5G. Max energy efficiency.	Only for URLLC transmission.Considers limited parameters.
2023	[23]	Security KPI Assessment	Security evaluation for 5G network slices	Focused assessment of security KPIs for special subscriber groups	Limited to security aspects, may not cover performance metrics

(continued)

Table 1. (continued)

Year	Ref.	Algorithm/Strategy	Problem Addressed	Advancements	Limitations
2023	[24]	Resource Allocation and NFV Placement	Resource management in MECenabled 5G networks	Enhanced resource allocation strategies for constrained environments	Challenges in NFV placement optimization
2022	[25]	Dynamic Network Slicing and Resource Allocation	Efficient resource allocation in 5Gand-beyond networks	Advanced dynamic slicing and allocation techniques	High computational requirements and real-time constraints
2021	[26]	Systematic Review of Resource Allocation Schemes	Review of various resource allocation schemes in 5G	A comprehensive review of existing schemes and methodologies	Limited to existing literature, may not propose new solutions
2022	[27]	ML-Based Radio Resource Management	Management of radio resources in 5G networks	Survey of ML techniques for efficient resource management	Survey-based, implementation specifics not detailed
2021	[28]	Network Slicing for Wi-Fi Networks	Application of 5G slicing techniques to Wi-Fi networks	Integration of 5G slicing techniques into Wi-Fi environments	Potential interoperability issues between different network types

4 Problem Formulation

With the rapid proliferation of smart devices along with the escalating volume of data traffic, existing wireless communication systems face significant challenges in meeting user demands. The traditional 4G networks, despite their advancements, fall short of providing the required speed, reliability, and energy efficiency necessary for emerging applications such as interactive cloud services, enhanced eV2X, the IoT, and real-time communications with drones and robots. These applications necessitate a paradigm shift to the 5G of cellular technology, which promises a nearly 20000-fold increase in data transmission volume by 2030. The core challenge addressed in this research is the efficient allocation of resources in 5G networks, a critical factor for optimizing performance and ensuring the QoS across a wide array of applications. Resource allocation in 5G is inherently complex due to the diverse requirements of eMBB, URLLC, and mMTC services. Each service demands specific considerations in terms of data rates, latency, and reliability, necessitating the development of advanced resource management strategies. This paper aims to investigate and categorize various resource allocation techniques, analyze their performance, and identify areas for improvement to enhance overall efficiency along with the effectiveness of 5G networks.

5 Performance Analysis of KPI in 5G New Radio Networks

KPIs in 5G networks are critical for assessing and optimizing network performance, ensuring that the diverse requirements of different applications and services are met effectively. Here are some essential KPIs for 5G networks (Table 2).

Table 2. Parameters selected for resource allocation.

Name	Definition	Formula
Peak Data Rate	Peak data rate is the maximum theoretical data transfer speed achievable under ideal conditions in a communication network.	Peak Data Rate $= \dfrac{v*Qm*f*Rmax}{12*N*BW*(1-OH)}$
User Experienced Data Rate	It is the actual data transfer speed a user observes under real-world network conditions.	User Experienced Data Rate $= SE * BW$
User Plane Latency	It is the time taken for data packets to travel from the user equipment to the network and back.	User Plane Latency $= tgNBtx$ $+ tFA1$ $+ tTTI$ $+ tUE\_rx$
Control Plane Latency	Control plane latency refers to the time delay experienced by a network device in processing and responding to control plane operations, such as routing updates or configuration changes.	Control Plane Latency $= T + TFA1$ $+ T3$
Energy Efficiency	Energy efficiency is the ability to achieve the desired output or performance with the least amount of energy consumption.	Energy Efficiency $1 - \left(\frac{2*L}{7}\right)$ $-\left(\frac{L}{7}\right)$ $-\left(\frac{PSSB}{2*PSSB}\right)$
Peak Spectral Efficiency	Peak spectral efficiency is the maximum rate of data transmission per unit bandwidth in a communication channel, typically measured in bps/Hz.	Peak Spectral Efficiency $= \dfrac{CR*\mu}{Ts*NPRB*OH}$

5.1 Data Rate (Throughput)

Peak Data Rate: Max data rate under optimal circumstances Fig. 4 illustrates the relationship between the peak data rate and iteration as well and it shows no changes in the peak data rate across all iterations, meaning there is no improvement, degradation, or fluctuation in performance over time. The data rate remains constant at approximately 0 Gbps.

User Experienced Data Rate: Typical data rate that a user can expect Fig. 5 generates a plot illustrating the relationship between user-experienced data rate and spectral efficiency. As you see here in Fig. 5 the SE increases the UE data rate grows non-linearly with an increasing slope.

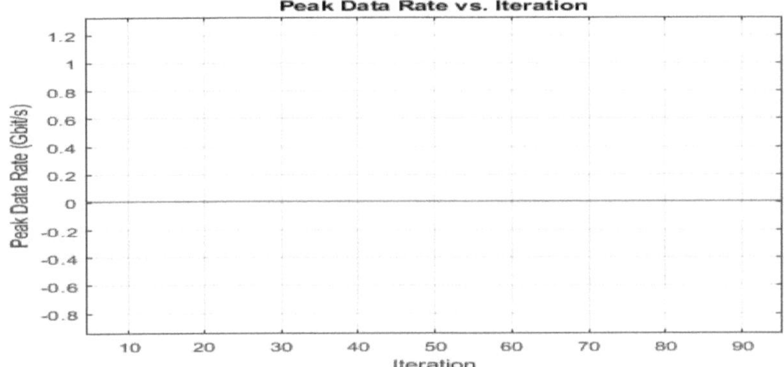

Fig. 4. Peak Data Rate

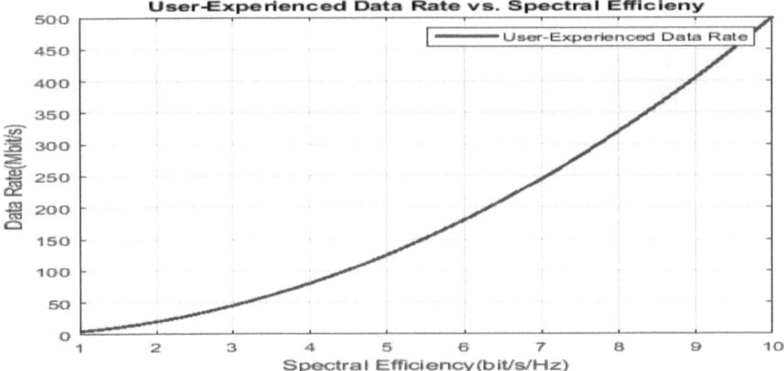

Fig. 5. User Experienced Data Rate

5.2 Latency

User plane latency: The total time it takes in case of data to travel from the source to the destination. Figure 6 describes the relationship between user plane latency. We have observed that it clearly shows the relationship is linear and positive meaning as tgNB_x increases then our user plane latency also increases.

Control Plane Latency: Fig. 7 displays the relationship between control plane latency and time variable T. As T increases from 1 to 10, the control plane latency rises linearly from approx. 2 ms (mili-second) to 16 ms. The graph suggests that T has a direct impact on control plane latency, with latency increasing in proportion to T.

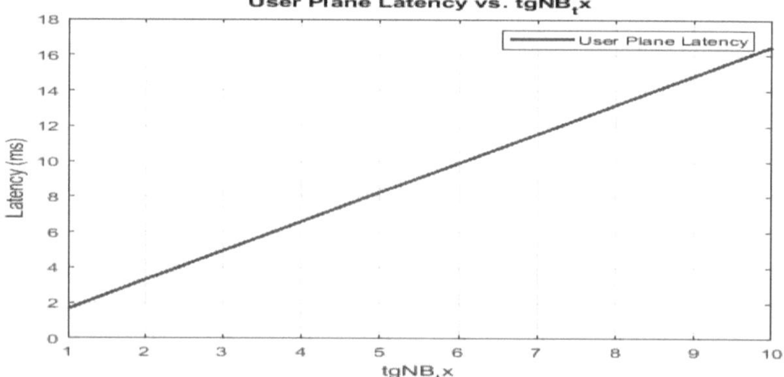

Fig. 6. User Plane Latency

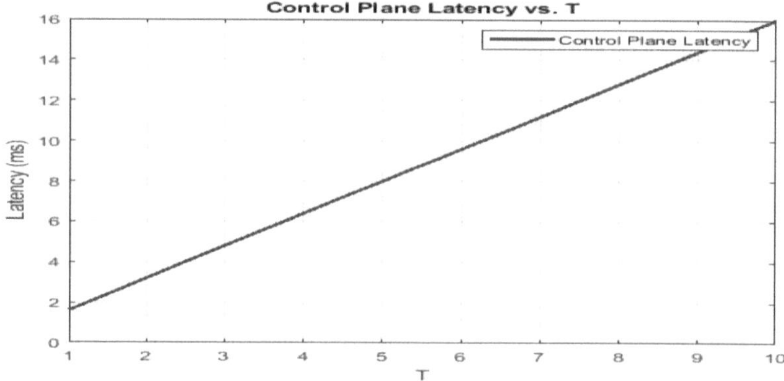

Fig. 7. Control Plane Latency

5.3 Energy Efficiency

The amount of energy consumed to transmit a single bit of data. Figure 8 generates two plots illustrating the relationship between sleep ratio, sleep duration, and power-saving sleep block (PSSB). This graph also suggests there is no variation in sleep duration as

PSSB changes. The constant value of 0 on the y-axis likely indicates that sleep duration is unaffected by PSSB.

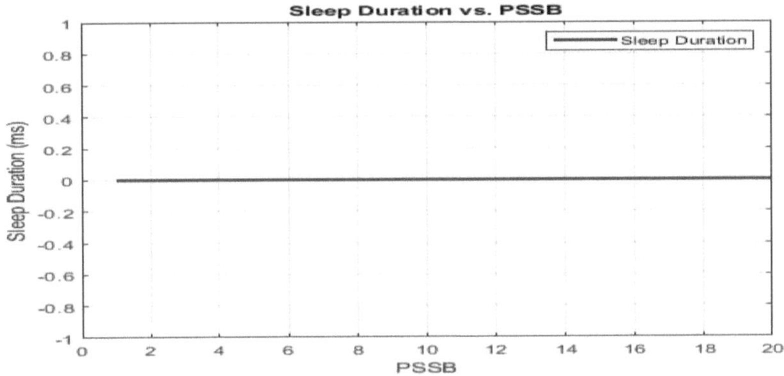

Fig. 8. Energy Efficiency

5.4 Peak Spectral Efficiency

The amount of data transmitted per unit of bandwidth in a single cell and network Capacity is the total data throughput of the network. Figure 9 generates a plot for peak spectral efficiency against the coding rate. As the coding rate increases, the peak spectral efficiency also increases. This means that the system to transmit more information improves as the coding rate increases.

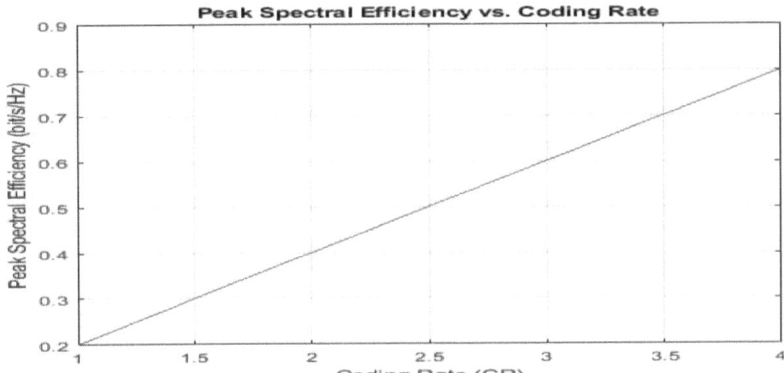

Fig. 9. Peak Spectral Efficiency

6 Conclusion

The information technology sector has undergone unprecedented growth, generating an immense demand for dependable network connections. Swift data transmission has become a critical requirement for internet users. Traditional resource allocation approaches are significantly less effective in the context of 5G networks. However, 5G, being a nascent technology, necessitates substantial investment to enhance system performance and quality of service. The study emphasizes the importance of devoting greater efforts to resource allocation and extensive research on strategies that impact the base station's green optimization. This research aimed to augment empirical knowledge regarding resource allocation in 5G networks. By investigating a resource allocation mechanism, the study sought to improve the efficacy and security of 5G wireless networks. This represents a positive stride towards meeting the escalating demands for high-speed, reliable, and efficient mobile services in the era of 5G technology.

7 Future Scope

The future scope for performance analysis of KPIs in 5G networks for resource allocation is rich with potential advancements and innovations. One promising direction is the integration of advanced ML and AI algorithms to enhance resource allocation strategies. These algorithms can adapt to RTN conditions and traffic patterns, optimizing resource distribution more effectively than traditional methods. Additionally, federated learning offers a way to collaborate on model training across different network nodes without compromising data privacy, further refining resource allocation techniques. Overall, the future of performance analysis in 5G networks will likely see a convergence of these advanced techniques, driving significant improvements in resource allocation and network efficiency.

Acknowledgments. No funding agency.

Disclosure of Interests. The authors declare that they have no conflicts of interest regarding the publication of this paper.

References

1. Ejaz, W., Sharma, S.K., Saadat, S., Naeem, M., Anpalagan, A., Chughtai, N.A.: A comprehensive survey on resource allocation for CRAN in 5G and beyond networks. J. Netw. Comput. Appl. **152**, 1–18 (2020)
2. Al-Dubai, A.M., Joudeh, H.M., Al-Shamaileh, N.R.: Performance evaluation of 5G network resource allocation strategies using KPIs. IEEE Trans. Netw. Ser. Manage. **19**(2), 456–469 (2022)
3. Yu, H., Lee, H., Jeon, H.: What is 5G? Emerging 5G mobile services and network requirements. Sustainability **9**(6), 956 (2017)
4. Al-Falahy, N., Alani, O.Y.: Telecommunications networking 5G: Evolution or revolution. IEEE **19**(1), 12–20 (2017)
5. Yu, G., Zhang, Z., Qu, F., Li, G.Y.: Ultra-dense heterogeneous networks with full-duplex small cell base stations. IEEE Network **31**(3), 48–54 (2017)
6. Navarro-Ortiz, J., Romero-Diaz, P., Sendra, S., Ameigeiras, P., Ramos-Munoz, J.J., Lopez-Soler, J.M.: A survey on 5G usage scenarios and traffic models. IEEE Comm. Sur. **22**(2), 10–40 (2020)

7. Agarwal, M., Roy, A., Saxena, N.: Next generation 5G wireless networks: a comprehensive survey. IEEE Comm. Sur. **18**(3), 1617–1655 (2016)
8. Gupta, A., Jha, R.K.: A survey of 5G network: architecture and emerging technologies. IEEE Access **3**, 1206–1232 (2015)
9. Gupta, D.K.R., Gupta, R.K., Jha, S.: Key performance indicators (KPIs) for 5G networks: a survey. IEEE Access **9**, 12345–12358 (2021)
10. Zhang, S., Xu, X., Wu, Y., Lu, L.: 5G: Towards energy-efficient, low-latency and highreliable communications networks. In: Proceedings of the Conference 2014, ICCS, pp. 19–21. IEEE, Macau, China (2014)
11. Pedersen, K.I., Frederiksen, F., Berardinelli, G., Mogensen, P.E.: The coverage-latency-capacity dilemma for TDD wide area operation and related 5G solutions. In: Proceedings of the Conference 2016, VTC, pp. 15–18. IEEE, Nanjing, China (2016)
12. Monserrat, J.F., Mange, G., Braun, V., Tullberg, H., Zimmermann, G., Bulakci, Ö.: METIS research advances towards the 5G mobile and wireless system definition. EURASIP J. Wirel. Commun. Netw. **2015**, 1–17 (2015)
13. Chowdhury, M.Z., Shahjalal, M., Hasan, M.K., Jang, Y.M.: The role of optical wireless communication technologies in 5G/6G and IoT solutions: Prospects, directions, and challenges. Applications **9**(23), 4916 (2019)
14. Zhang, B.L., Chen, Y.L., Li, X.M.: Resource allocation and management in 5G networks: Insights from KPI performance analysis. J. Netw. Comput. Appl. **200**, 103365 (2023)
15. Su, R., et al.: Resource allocation for network slicing in 5G telecommunication networks: A survey of principles and models. IEEE Network **33**(4), 80–87 (2019)
16. Al-Nasrawi, M., Al-Din Makki, S.V., Al-Sabbagh, A.: KPI analysis of 4G/5G networks. IEEE Access **12**, 12345–12358 (2024)
17. Bayleyegn, A.A., Fernández, Z., Granelli, F.: Real-time monitoring of 5G networks: an NWDAF and ML-based KPI prediction. In: 10th International Conference on Network Softwarization, pp. 31–36. IEEE, USA (2024)
18. Patro, S., Rath, H.K., Panigrahi, B.: Dynamic KPI-aware network slicing for 5G+ networks. In: 13th International Conference on Communication Systems and Network Technologies, pp. 94–99. IEEE, Jabalpur (2024)
19. Lazar, R.G., Militaru, A.V., Caruntu, C.F., Pascal, C., Patachia-Sultanoiu, C.: Real-time data measurement methodology to evaluate the 5G network performance indicators. IEEE Access **11**, 13872–13884 (2023)
20. Saraereh, O.A., Alsaraira, A., Khan, I., Uthansakul, P.: An efficient resource allocation algorithm for OFDM-based NOMA in 5G systems. Electronics **8**(7), 894 (2019)
21. Bashir, A.K., Arul, R., Basheer, S., Raja, G., Jayaraman, R., Qureshi, N.M.F.: An optimal multitier resource allocation of cloud RAN in 5G using machine learning. Trans. Emerg. Telecomm. Technol. **30**(7), e4050 (2019)
22. Bonjorn, N., Foukalas, F., Cañellas, F., Pop, P.: Cooperative resource allocation and scheduling for 5G eV2X services. IEEE Access **7**, 163505–163518 (2019)
23. Odarchenko, R., Iavich, M., Iashvili, G., Fedushko, S., Syerov, Y.: Assessment of security KPIs for 5G network slices for special groups of subscribers. Big Data and Cognitive Computing **7**(4), 169 (2023)
24. Fedrizzi, R.: Resource allocation and NFV placement in resource-constrained MEC-enabled 5G networks. IEEE Access **11**, 56789–56802 (2023)
25. Abdellatif, A.A., Mohamed, A., Erbad, A., Guizani, M.: Dynamic network slicing and resource allocation for 5G-and-beyond networks. In: IEEE Wireless Communications and Networking Conference 2022, WCNC, pp. 262–267. IEEE, USA (2022)
26. Kamal, M.A., Raza, H.W., Alam, M.M., Su'ud, M.M., Sajak, A.B.A.B.: Resource allocation schemes for 5G network: A systematic review. Sensors **21**(19), 6588 (2021)

27. Bartsiokas, I.A., Gkonis, P.K., Kaklamani, D.I., Venieris, I.: SML-based radio resource management in 5G and beyond networks: A survey. IEEE Access **10**, 83507–83528 (2022)
28. Nerini, M., Palma, D.: 5G network slicing for Wi-Fi networks. In: IFIP/IEEE International Symposium on Integrated Network Management 2021, IM, pp. 633–637. IEEE, France (2021)

Predicting Domain Validity: A Machine Learning Approach

Harjot Saini[✉], Adarsh Patel, Ajay Kumar Phulre, and Sajjad Ahmed

School of Computing Science and Artificial Intelligence, VIT Bhopal University,
Madhya Pradesh, India
{harjot.saini2020,adarsh.patel}@vitbhopal.ac.in

Abstract. In this research paper, we explored the efficacy of various machine learning algorithms in predicting domain validity, an essential task for cyber security and online safety. In response, we introduce a predictive model that leverages Machine Learning and Deep Learning approaches. Our dataset comprises 95910 instances, encompassing 12 features including the class label. Notably, this dataset comprises 55914 invalid domains and 39996 valid domains. This study evaluates the performance of seven different classifiers: K-Nearest Neighbor, Random Forest, Support Vector Machine, Naïve Bayes, Neural Network, Logistics Regression, and XG Boost. We systematically evaluated 26 models' performance with different scenarios. Among them XG Boost emerged as the most effective, boasting an accuracy 95.50%, Precision 96.10%, Recall 96.25%, and F1-Score 96.18%. This model provides the best balance of high precision, recall, and F1-Score, alongside high accuracy, making it the most robust choice for our classification problem.

Keywords: Domain · Domain Name System · K-Nearest Neighbor · Random Forest · Support Vector Machine · Naïve Bayes · Neural Network · Logistics Regression · XG Boost · SMOTE

1   Introduction

In today's digital era, the rapid increase in usage of internet has led to a surge in daily domain registrations. While many domains are legitimate, some are used for malicious purposes like spreading malware and phishing. Ransomware, a particularly harmful type of malware, steals and encrypts data from victims' computers, demanding payment for decryption. Attackers frequently use newly registered domains to distribute malware, making it crucial to identify and block these domains early to prevent harm. The financial and operational impacts of malware are increasingly devastating.

Understanding the word domain, A domain is a unique address on the internet that identifies a website. It serves as the human-readable content to access the websites, translating more complex IP addresses into easily remembered names. The Domain name system is the technology that underpins domain names.

S. Pal et al. (Eds.): ICETSS 2024, CCIS 2610, pp. 263–273, 2026.
https://doi.org/10.1007/978-3-032-11488-4_20

Structure of Domain in URL:

Second-Level Domain (SLD): It is the part of the domain that is the name of the website or the organization. It is always to the right before the TLD.

Top-Level Domain (TLD): indicates the website's purpose or geographical area (Figs. 1 and 2).

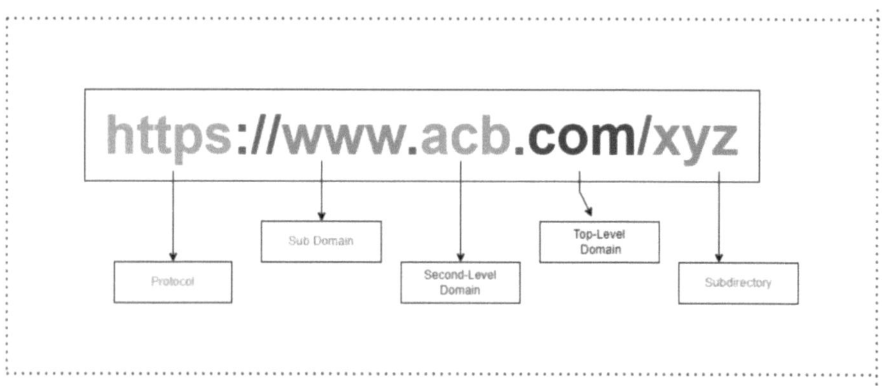

Fig. 1. URL Structure

Using data collected in October 2020, Palo Alto Networks has provided an overview of the malicious use of the top TLDs (Top-Level Domains). According to the study, the most popular top-level domain is.com (commercial) which has an average ratio of malicious domains. Malicious attackers use these domains so that it looks legitimate and they gain success. Phishing actors prefer to use.net domains [1].

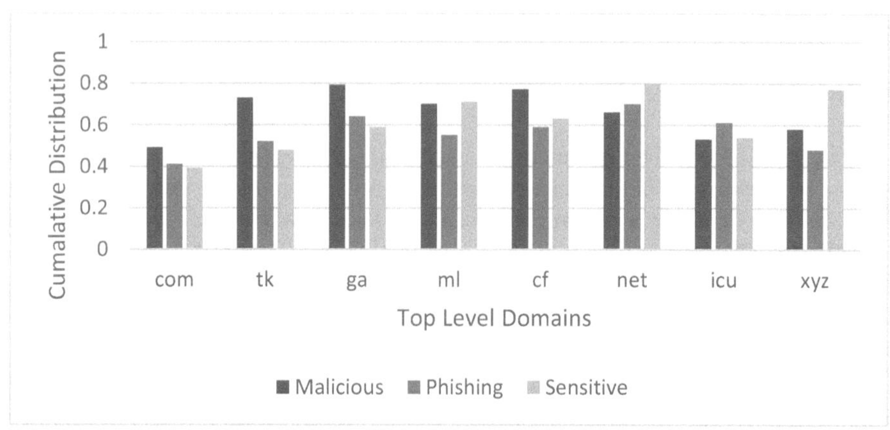

Fig. 2. TLDs with malicious content distribution [1]

A report by Palo Alto Networks also highlights how the.tk (Tokelau) became one of the most widely registered TLDs globally. At one point, the revenue generated from.tk domain registrations accounted for one-sixth of Tokelau's income. These countries provide very cheap or free domain registrations but also opens the doors for abuse [1].

In our study, we determined that XGBoost and Random Forest are the most effective models for domain validation, outperforming Neural Networks, K-Nearest Neighbor, Support Vector Machine, Naive Bayes, and Logistic Regression with our Dataset [2] features (domain, ranking, isIp, valid, activeDuration, urlLen, is@, isredirect, haveDash, domainLen, nosOfSubdomain, label). We evaluated several machine learning algorithms across different scenarios to optimize model performance, accuracy, and domain validation.

This document is organized as follows: Section two reviews related work, Section three details the dataset and algorithms, Section Four presents our results and comparisons with other studies, Section Five provides the conclusion, and then at last the references.

2 Related Work

As for the specific area of malicious domain detection there were major improvements observed in recent years as different methodologies, were suggested and improved in terms of accuracy and the other metrics need to accomplish the detection task.

Wang et al. (2023) introduced DDOFM (dynamic method for detecting malicious domains using feature mining). It focuses on real-time detection of domains queried by hosts to prevent malicious intrusions. This method tackles certain challenges like low accuracy, poor transferability, and high computational costs in model construction [3].

In 2024 a study presented the MDND-SS-PO approach (a method for detecting hostile domains that combines parameter optimization, an enhanced DBSCAN algorithm, and semi-supervised learning). With only 5% labeled data, our method—which combines feature extraction, pseudo-labeling, and Gaussian process regression—achieves an 88.5% detection accuracy [4].

Aslam et al. (2022) introduced an XAI (Explainable Artificial Intelligence) model for detecting malicious domains using a dataset of 45,000 samples. Their approach combined interpretable ML models like Decision Trees and Naïve Bayes with complex ensemble models such as Random Forest and Extreme Gradient Boosting (XGB). The study found that XGB outperformed other models. To ensure transparency, they applied post hoc XAI techniques, including Shapley additive explanations and LIME (Local Interpretable Model-agnostic Explanations), to explain XGB predictions. Their experiments demonstrated that XGB achieved the highest accuracy, with overall accuracy ranging from 0.8479 to 0.9856 [5].

Hajaj et al. (2022) propose a novel feature selection mechanism that significantly reduces the feature set dimensionality while improving model performance. Their approach led to an increase in the F1-score from 92.92% to 95.81%, demonstrating the effectiveness of selected features in detecting malicious domains. Additionally, they introduced novel features designed to withstand adversarial manipulation, ensuring the model's robustness in real-world scenarios [6].

In a study by Çolhak et al. (2024), DNN (Deep Neural Network) models incorporating both textual and numeric features were compared with traditional ML (machine learning) approaches for detecting malicious domain registrations. The study found that DNN models, particularly the Canine + MLP (multilayer perceptron) model, significantly outperformed traditional ML models, achieving an accuracy of 85.81% and an F1-score of 86.46% on the MTLP (Multi-task learning-based prediction) Dataset. Despite the higher computational requirements of DNN models, their superior detection performance highlights a trade-off between computational efficiency and accuracy, often justifying the added costs in high-stakes cybersecurity applications [7].

Luo et al. (2024) introduced AGCN-Domain, a model that uses a Graph Convolutional Network (GCN) combined with an attention mechanism to detect malicious domains by analyzing multiple relational features. The model constructs relationship feature graphs based on client, resolution, and cname relations, which are then fused intelligently to uncover deep underlying connections between domains. The AGCN-Domain model was evaluated on a dataset with 10% initialized labels, achieving a notable accuracy of 94.27% and an F1 score of 87.93%, outperforming other methods in comparative experiments [8].

Gogoi and Ahmed (2023) have presented a novel method for detecting DGA-generated domain names through the use of pretrained character-based transformer models. Their approach is to categorize domain names as DGA-generated or benign based only on the domain name itself. A dataset comprising one million domain names was used to test the model, and it demonstrated an amazing 99% accuracy [9].

Chen et al. (2023) proposed a novel approach that improves the detection of both character-based and dictionary-based algorithmically generated domains (AGDs) by integrating meaningful word segmentation with n-gram sequence features. Their method introduces the standard deviation as a measure of word distribution features and constructs additional statistical features to enhance the detection of dictionary-based AGDs. By combining 3-g and 1-g sequence features, the authors developed an end-to-end detection method capable of effectively identifying both types of AGDs. The experimental results demonstrated that this approach achieved an accuracy of 97.24% [10].

Xu et al. worked in 2019 to use N-gram and Deep Convolutional Neural Networks (CNN) for the detection of DGA-based domain names. It utilizes bigram and trigram methods. This method achieves remarkable average detection rate of 98.69% and for wordlist-based DGA domain names detection rate is more than 93.89%. Notable drawbacks of their model were its high processing cost and reliance on a particular language [11].

Lv et al. (2018) investigates into DNS communication characteristics while analyzing malicious domains using Hidden Markov Models (HMM). Unfortunately, the computing cost and time required for this approach limited its practical application [12].

These studies collectively highlight the progress and ongoing challenges in malicious domain detection.

3 Methodology

3.1 Dataset

The dataset [2] contains 12 features, each contributing to the analysis and prediction of domain validity. These features encompass various aspects related to the domain, URL structure, and metadata, providing a comprehensive set of data points for the classification task. The class label distribution in the dataset includes 39,996 instances labeled as legitimate (0) and 55,914 instances labeled as phishing (1) (Tables 1 and 9).

Table 1. Dataset features and its description

Feature	Description
Domain	Domain name of the website.
Ranking	Ranking of the domain, it is usually acquired using Alexa
isIP	Indicates whether the URL of the website is by IP address or by domain name where 1 stands for IP address while 0 stands for no IP address.
valid	Notifies the validity of domain (1 for Yes, 0 for No)
activeDuration	Duration for which the domain has been active.
urlLen	States the length of the URL.
is@	Whether the URL consists of the '@' symbol (1 for Yes, 0 for No).
Isredirect	Whether the URL redirects to another URL (1 for Yes, 0 for No).
haveDash	There is a check whether the URL contains a dash '-' (1 for Yes, 0 for No).
domainLen	Length of the Domain name.
nosOfSubdomain	Number of subdomains in the URL.
Label	Label specifies the authenticity of the domain and is 0 in case the domain is legitimate and 1 in case of a phishing domain.

3.2 Algorithm Descriptions

K-nearest Neighbor (KNN): K-nearest neighbor (KNN) is the simplest of classification algorithm and it is a non-parametric method used for classification and regression. K-Nearest Neighbors (k-NN) is a simple and versatile machine learning algorithm widely used for many different kinds of problems. At its core, k-NN is based on proximity—the idea that one can make predictions about a target data point by looking at other similar points to it [13].

Model 1.1, a simple KNN classification model where number of neighbors and distance metric used is constant in nature. In Model 1.2 we perform hyperparameter tuning using GridSearchCV to find the optimum number of neighbors and distance metric in order further improve model prediction accuracy This method will try to find the best variant for this dataset. Model 1.3 votes are weighted, closer neighbors contribute more to the classification decision. It tries to increase the performance of model by giving more weightage to useful data points.

Random Forest: In the case of random forest, a decision tree is made of many trees by a unique integration technique in order to improve the predictive analysis and resilience of the-model. [14] This greatly reduces the specific risk that lies in single decision trees as construction of each tree is accompanied by random factors.

Model 2.1 is a fundamental of Random Forests used in classification as the algorithm with high predictive capability aims at reducing variance and bias by considering an average of different decision trees. Model 2.2 employs GridSearchCV for hyperparameters tuning which aims to optimize the number of trees and depth to improve performance and generalization on unseen data. Model 2.3 helps in handling class imbalance by using class weights that balances the probability estimation of the minority class and hence aids the metric of recall and precision.

Support Vector Machine (SVM): SVM known as Support Vector Machine was created by Cortes and Vapnik and has become very popular in many areas including pattern recognition and image classification among others. [15] The main intention of Support Vector Machines is to identify the best hyperplane that has the ability to maximize the distance between different classes; thus making them useful in areas of classification. It is worth noting that different kernel functions are used in the SVM models of our research to analyze linear and non-linear data.

Model 3.1 is a fundamental SVM classification model that forms a linear decision boundary, suitable for linearly separable data. Model 3.2 uses the RBF (Gaussian) kernel to find non-linear relationships within the data, enhancing its ability to differentiate between complex patterns. Model 3.3 incorporates class weights to address class imbalance.

Naïve Bayes: The original Naïve Bayes (NB) classifier is a probabilistic model that relies on Bayes' theorem, leading to the development of a conditional probability framework. [16].

Model 4.1 is a standard Naïve Bayes classification model, leveraging the simplicity and efficiency of the algorithm for quick predictions. Model 4.2 applies SMOTE (Synthetic Minority Over-sampling Technique) to handle imbalanced datasets, improving the model's recall for the minority class. Model 4.3 explores different feature sets to evaluate the impact of feature selection on model performance. Model 4.4 uses various preprocessing techniques to enhance the model's ability to handle noisy data.

Neural Network: Neural network models consist of layers that simulate the brain's information-processing mechanisms. These models strive to optimize outcomes by adjusting activation functions and the sizes of fully connected layers [17].

Model 5.1 is a standard neural network model with multiple layers and neurons. Model 5.2 uses SMOTE for class imbalance. Model 5.3 explores different feature sets and preprocessing techniques to optimize performance.

Logistics Regression: Logistic regression is a statistical technique used to build a model that describes the relationship between a binary (yes/no) outcome (dependent variable) and a set of independent predictor variables [18].

Model 6.1 is a standard logistic regression model. Model 6.2 employs SMOTE to handle class imbalance. Model 6.3 explores different feature sets, and Model 6.4 incorporates cross-validation to assess robustness.

XG Boost: XGBoost is an ensemble learning method and an advanced version of a decision tree with a modified framework of gradient boosting. It is designed for speed and performance and is known for its ability to handle large-scale datasets efficiently [19].

Model 7.1 represents standard XGBoost classification, focusing on the basic implementation of XGBoost to capture patterns within the data. Model 7.2 incorporates handling imbalanced datasets with SMOTE. Model 7.3 uses different preprocessing techniques to enhance the model's ability. Model 7.4 involves hyperparameter tuning using grid search, systematically exploring a range of hyperparameter values. Model 7.5 employs hyperparameter tuning using random search, randomly sampling hyperparameter values to identify the optimal configuration. Model 7.6 utilizes hyperparameter tuning using hyperopt, applying a probabilistic model.

4 Result and Discussions

Table 2 presents a comparison of various K-Nearest Neighbors (KNN) algorithms. Model 1.2 achieved the highest accuracy at 95.03%, with balanced precision (96%) and recall (95%). Model 1.1 and Model 1.3 also performed well, with accuracies 93.64%, and 94.73%. Model 1.1, despite having slightly lower accuracy, maintained competitive precision and recall values.

Table 2. Result after performing a comparison between all K-Nearest Neighbor Algorithm (Model 1)

Model	Precision	Recall	F1 Score	Accuracy
1.1	95	94	95	93.64
1.2	96	95	96	95.03
1.3	96	95	96	94.73

Table 3 shows a comparison of different Random Forest algorithms. Model 2.1 exhibited the highest accuracy at 95.69%, with a balance of precision (97%) and recall (96%). Model 2.2 and Model 2.3 also performed well with accuracy around 95.62% and 95.45%, respectively. These results indicate that all models maintain a consistent performance with minor differences in precision and recall.

Table 3. Result after performing a comparison between all Random Forest Algorithm (Model 2)

Model	Precision	Recall	F1 Score	Accuracy
2.1	97	96	96	95.69
2.2	97	96	96	95.62
2.3	97	96	96	95.45

Table 4 provides a comparison of various Support Vector Machine (SVM) algorithms. Model 3.2, utilizing the RBF kernel, achieved the highest accuracy at 91.10%, with a balance of precision (93%) and recall (92%). Model 3.1 and Model 3.3 also performed well with accuracies around 88.48% and 88.29%, respectively. These results suggest that the RBF kernel enhances SVM performance compared to the basic SVM.

Table 4. Result after performing a comparison between all Support Vector Machine Algorithm (Model 3)

Model	Precision	Recall	F1 Score	Accuracy
3.1	90	90	90	88.48
3.2	93	92	92	91.10
3.3	92	87	90	88.29

Table 5 displays a comparison of various Naive Bayes algorithms. Model 4.3, which used different feature sets, achieved the highest accuracy at 75.54%, with balanced precision (95.23%) and recall (61.51%). Models 4.1, 4.2, and 4.4 showed significantly lower accuracy due to poor recall values.

Table 5. Result after performing a comparison between all Naïve Bayes Algorithm (Model 4)

Model	Precision	Recall	F1 Score	Accuracy
4.1	99.65	26.62	42.02	56.78
4.2	99.63	27.01	42.50	57.00
4.3	95.23	61.51	74.74	75.54
4.4	99.45	28.98	44.88	58.12

Table 6 outlines a comparison of different Neural Network models. Models 5.1 and 5.3 achieved the highest accuracy at 93.24% and 93.01%, respectively, with balanced precision and recall values. Model 5.2, handling imbalanced datasets with SMOTE, showed a slight improvement in precision but a decrease in recall, resulting in an overall balanced performance.

Table 6. Result after performing a comparison between all Neural Network Algorithm (Model 5)

Model	Precision	Recall	F1 Score	Accuracy
5.1	93.87	94.69	94.28	93.24
5.2	96.17	91.74	93.90	92.99
5.3	93.83	94.32	94.08	93.01

Table 7 compares various Logistic Regression models. Model 6.5, which used cross-validation, achieved the highest accuracy at 87.97%, with balanced precision (89.47%) and recall (89.94%). Models 6.1 and 6.2 also performed well, with accuracies around 87.86% and 87.94%, respectively.

Table 7. Result after performing a comparison between all Logistics Regression Algorithm (Model 6)

Model	Precision	Recall	F1 Score	Accuracy
6.1	89.88	89.44	89.66	87.86
6.2	92.00	87.06	89.46	87.94
6.3	87.68	86.24	86.95	84.77
6.4	89.47	89.94	89.71	87.97

Table 8 shows a comparison of various XGBoost models. Models 7.5 and 7.6, using hyperparameter tuning with Random Search and Bayesian Optimization, achieved the highest accuracy at 95.44% and 95.50%, respectively. These models also showed balanced precision and recall values. Model 7.1, the standard XGBoost classification, also performed well with an accuracy of 94.94%.

Table 8. Result after performing a comparison between all XG Boost Algorithm (Model 7)

Model	Precision	Recall	F1 Score	Accuracy
7.1	95.56	95.85	95.70	94.94
7.2	96.26	94.65	95.45	94.69
7.3	95.47	95.76	95.61	94.83
7.4	95.85	95.95	95.90	95.17
7.5	96.09	96.15	96.12	95.44
7.6	96.10	96.25	96.18	95.50

Based on the provided metrics, we have compared the models:

Random Forest Classifier: All models (2.1, 2.2, 2.3) have the same Precision, Recall, and F1-score, but Model 2.1 has the highest Accuracy 95.69%.

XGBoost: Model 7.6 has the highest F1-Score (96.18) and high Accuracy 95.50%. Model 7.5 has a slightly lower F1-Score 96.12% and an accuracy 95.44%. Model 7.4 also has a high F1-Score 95.90% and Accuracy 95.17%.

Table 9. Comparison of our result with other studies.

Scheme	Accuracy
Proposed Scheme (Random Forest)	94.45 - 95.69%
Proposed Scheme (XG Boost)	94.69 - 95.50%
[4]	88.50%
[5]	84.79–98.56%
[7]	85.81%
[8]	94.27%

The result of [6] shows the F1 score of 95.81% but our proposed scheme F1 score ranges from 95.45–96.18% for XG boost and a balanced F1 score of 96% for the Random forest classifier.

5 Conclusion and Future Works

This research has provided a detailed analysis of multiple ML algorithms to predict domain validity. Our experiments demonstrated that Random Forest and XGBoost were the top-performing models, achieving the highest accuracy and displaying strong resilience against data imbalance. Random Forest and XGBoost outperform Neural Networks on structured data due to better handling of smaller datasets, less overfitting, and greater efficiency. These results highlight the effectiveness of ensemble methods in tackling complex classification challenges in domain validity prediction.

Our study suggests exploring new features and feature engineering methods, using ADASYN (Adaptive Synthetic) or GANs (Generative Adversarial Network) for imbalanced data, incorporating real-time data streams and incremental learning, and employing deep learning and transfer learning for more accurate and robust domain validity predictions. Advanced classification techniques are essential for precise predictions with this slightly imbalanced dataset.

References

1. Bill, T.: These are the top-level domains threat actors like the most (2021). https://www.Bleepingcomputer.Com/News/Security/These-Are-the-Top-Level-Domains-Threat-Actors-like-the-Most/. Last accessed 08 July 2024
2. Saini, H.: Predicting domain validity. Kaggle (2024). https://doi.org/10.34740/KAGGLE/DSV/9030579
3. Wang, H., Tang, Z., Li, H., Zhang, J., Cai, C.: DDOFM: Dynamic malicious domain detection method based on feature mining. Comput. Secur. **130**, 103260 (2023). https://doi.org/10.1016/j.cose.2023.103260
4. Liao, R., Wang, S.: Malicious domain detection based on semi-supervised learning and parameter optimization. IET Commun. **18**(6), 386–397 (2024). https://doi.org/10.1049/cmu2.12739

5. Khan, I., et al.: Interpretable machine learning models for malicious domains detection using explainable Artificial Intelligence (XAI). Sustainability **14** (2022). https://doi.org/10.3390/su14127375

6. Hajaj, C., Hason, N., Dvir, A.: Less is more: robust and novel features for malicious domain detection. Electronics **11**(6) (2022). https://doi.org/10.3390/electronics11060969

7. Çolhak, F., Ecevit, M.İ., Dağ, H., Creutzburg, R.: Comparing deep neural networks and machine learning for detecting malicious domain name registrations. 2024 IEEE International Conference on Omni-Layer Intelligent Systems (COINS), pp. 1–4 (2024). https://doi.org/10.1109/COINS61597.2024.10622643

8. Luo, X., Li, Y., Cheng, H., Yin, L.: AGCN-Domain: detecting malicious domains with graph convolutional network and attention mechanism. Mathematics **12**(5) (2024). https://doi.org/10.3390/math12050640

9. Gogoi, B., Ahmed, T.: DGA domain detection using pretrained character based transformer models. 2023 IEEE Guwahati Subsection Conference (GCON), pp. 1–6 (2023). https://doi.org/10.1109/GCON58516.2023.10183602

10. Chen, S., Lang, B., Chen, Y., Xie, C.: Detection of algorithmically generated malicious domain names with feature fusion of meaningful word segmentation and N-Gram sequences. Appl. Sci. **13**(7) (2023). https://doi.org/10.3390/app13074406

11. Xu, C., Shen, J., Du, X.: Detection method of domain names generated by DGAs based on semantic representation and deep neural network. Comput. Secur. **85**, 77–88 (2019). https://doi.org/10.1016/j.cose.2019.04.015

12. Lv, P., Bai, L., Liu, T., Ning, Z., Shi, J., Fang, B.: Detection of malicious domain names based on hidden markov model. 2018 IEEE Third International Conference on Data Science in Cyberspace (DSC), pp. 659–664 (2018). https://doi.org/10.1109/DSC.2018.00105

13. Hasan, N., Ahmed, N., Ali, S.M.: Improving sporadic demand forecasting using a modified k-nearest neighbor framework. Eng. Appl. Artif. Intell. **129**, 107633 (2024). https://doi.org/10.1016/j.engappai.2023.107633

14. Sun, Z., Wang, G., Li, P., Wang, H., Zhang, M., Liang, X.: An improved random forest based on the classification accuracy and correlation measurement of decision trees. Expert Syst. Appl. **237**, 121549 (2024). https://doi.org/10.1016/j.eswa.2023.121549

15. Wang, H., Shao, Y.: Fast generalized ramp loss support vector machine for pattern classification. Pattern Recogn. **146**, 109987 (2024). https://doi.org/10.1016/j.patcog.2023.109987

16. Romano, M., Contu, G., Mola, F., Conversano, C.: Threshold-based Naïve Bayes classifier. Advances in Data Analysis and Classification, pp. 1–37 (2023). https://api.semanticscholar.org/CorpusID:257547447

17. Dwivedi, D., Ahmed, S., Patel, A., Azath, H.: Machine learning-powered defense against phishing websites. 2024 IEEE International Students' Conference on Electrical, Electronics and Computer Science (SCEECS), pp. 1–6 (2024). https://api.semanticscholar.org/CorpusID:268879664

18. Das, A.: Logistic regression. In Maggino, F. (ed.). Encyclopedia of Quality of Life and Well-Being Research (pp. 3985–3986). Springer International Publishing (2023). https://doi.org/10.1007/978-3-031-17299-1_1689

19. Niazkar, M., et al.: Applications of XGBoost in water resources engineering: a systematic literature review (Dec 2018–May 2023). Environ. Model. Softw. **174**, 105971 (2024). https://doi.org/10.1016/j.envsoft.2024.105971

Investigation of Temperature Associated Performance Variations in Nanoscale Recessed Channel Double Gate Junctionless Transistor

Sandeep Kumar[1][(✉)], Arun Kumar Chatterjee[2], Rishikesh Pandey[2], Neeraj Gupta[3], Prashant Kumar[4], and Madhu Kushwaha[5]

[1] Chitkara University Institute of Engineering and Technology, Chitkara University, Punjab, India
`vlsi.sandeep@gmail.com`
[2] ECED, Thapar Institute of Engineering and Technology, Patiala, Punjab, India
`{arun.chatterjee,r.pandey}@thapar.edu`
[3] Department of Electronics and Communication Engineering, Amity University, Haryana 122413, Gurugram, India
[4] Department of Electronics and Communication Engineering, J.C. Bose University of Science and Technology, YMCA, Sector 6, Faridabad 121006, India
[5] Lecturer, Punjab Engineering College, Chandigarh, India

Abstract. In this work the temperature dependence of primary performance parameters of nanoscale recessed channel double gate junctionless transistor has been investigated. The performance comparison has been done with conventional double gate junctionless transistor while varying the temperature from $273\,\text{K}-450\,\text{K}$. Changes in the factors such as threshold voltage, ON and OFF state current, and subthreshold swing is noticed. The zero temperature co-efficient has been observed in transfer characteristics at $0.8\,\text{V}$ and $0.6\,\text{V}$ for the recessed channel double gate junctionless transistor and conventional counterpart, respectively. It has been observed that the recessed channel junctionless transistor reflects smaller variations in threshold voltage with a slope of $-1.09\,\text{mV/K}$, ON current of 12.58% and subthreshold swing $39.9\,\text{mV/dec}$ in said temperature range in comparison to the conventional junctional device. Moreover, the device OFF state behavior has been found more prone to temperature variations.

Keywords: Junctionless · Transistor · Nanoscale · Double Gate · Temperature

1 Introduction

In modern technology of electronics devices, the semiconductor components have been the central point to run the whole system. These devices have been evolved much by following the law of scaling which governs the miniaturization of device dimensions [1]. With smaller dimension the performance deviation has been observed due to increasing short-channel-effects. The multi-gate structures have been evolved to recover the gate control over the channel region [2]. Besides, the advancement of semiconductor technology has also evolved while recognizing their performance in real world conditions

S. Pal et al. (Eds.): ICETSS 2024, CCIS 2610, pp. 274–282, 2026.
https://doi.org/10.1007/978-3-032-11488-4_21

[3, 4]. For, instance, the reliable operation of semiconductor transistors in high temperature conditions e.g. in fire prone areas, desert conditions or space environment is also highly desired. The stable operation of these devices in a circuit over a wide range of temperature have a fundamental importance for a device designer. It is detected that device leakage rises with temperature [5], which promotes high energy dissipation in the device and/or ultimately the device failure. Moreover, the one technological solution of higher leakage current has been introduced as transistor without p-n profiles known as junctionless transistor (JLT) [6]. Due to mitigation of abrupt p-n junction in the semiconductor layer, device offers smaller leakage current comparison to the inversion mode transistor when the gates-to-source voltage (VGS) is 0 V called as OFF current (IOFF) [6].

Interestingly, like the inversion mode transistors, the junctionless transistors also reflects a point called as zero temperature coefficient (ZTC). The ZTC point reflects the temperature independence of drain current [7, 8]. Moreover, with variations in temperature, the device performance parameters deviate from their standard value at room temperature e.g. shift in threshold voltage or increase in OFF-state leakage current etc. Recently, a double gate JLT with recessed silicon channel (R_DGJLT) has been proposed which have shown performance edge over the conventional JLT in terms of smaller IOFF, better ION/IOFF, and steeper SS [9]. In the literature, it has been noticed that the JLTs offers smaller OFF-state current besides can be used in less power circuit applications [4, 10–14]. However, the junctionless devices have been found susceptible to temperature variations [15–17]. Here, the variations of temperature on the performance factors in R_DGJLT has been investigated and compared with conventional junctionless counterpart device. It has been observed that R_DGJLT maintains its superiority over the C_DGJLT for wide range of temperature [9]. Section 2 describes the simulation set-up used to design both JLTs and the calibration of used physical models. The simulation results have been presented and discussed in Sect. 3. Section 4 concludes the flow with important findings of the work.

2 Device Analysis and Simulation Environment

The diagram of designed conventional junctionless transistor with double gate (C_DGJLT) and double gate junctionless transistor with etched channel (R_DGJLT) is presented in Fig. 1(a) and (b), respectively. Both devices have been designed with silicon layer of 10 nm, however, the channel of R_DGJLT has been recessed by 2 nm on both sides. As a result, the silicon layer of 6 nm has been left in R_DGJLFET in its channel region. The n-type doping concentration of the order of 10^{19} cm^{-3} has been kept in silicon layer. The silicon layer has been recessed with a cross-sectional area of 20 nm × 2 nm. The physical length of gate electrode has been defined over 20 nm region. The gates work function (5.1 eV) has been set for gate electrodes Gate1 and Gate2 in both devices [18]. The HfO2 material with its effective thickness of 1 nm is used as high-k dielectric to curtail the leakage through gate [19].

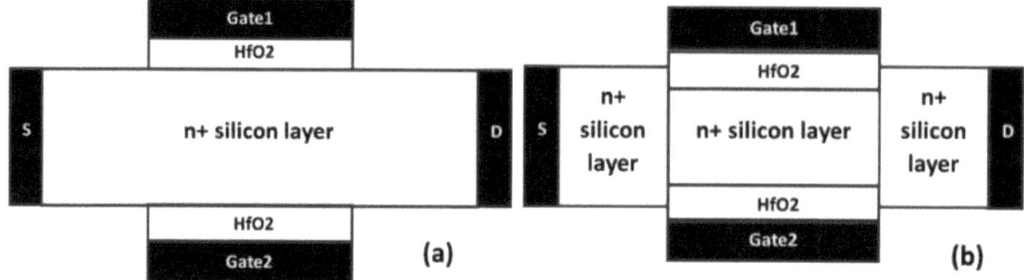

Fig. 1. Diagram of (a) C_DGJLT, (b) R_DGJLT.

2.1 Simulation Methodology

The simulation work is performed on Silvaco tool. The value for temperature has been varied from 273 K to 450 K. The silicon layer is heavily doped (1019 cm^{-3}) in both devices. Hence, the Fermi-Dirac statistical model has been used to consider the effect of heavy doping. In experimental work [20], it has also been observed that the product of electron and hole becomes dependent on doping concentration when the doping is more than 1018 cm^{-3}. In such condition, the general observation is narrowing of band gap. To consider such physical phenomena, the band gap narrowing model has been used in the simulations. The model gives the probability of charge carrier to occupy an energy state. The tunneling model with non-local dynamics is used to incorporate variations of electric field along the tunneling path [21]. In order to tune this model, the tunneling masses of electron and hole needs to be tuned in the simulation and the value of 0.28 and 0.42 has been used for electron and holes, respectively. The model proposed by Shockley, Read, and Hall (SRH) is used to reflect the recombination process while the Lombardy CVT model has been considered to mimic the dependency of mobility on electric field, temp. And doping denisty.

2.2 Model Calibration

Prior to the simulation of C_DGJLT and R_DGJLT, the physical models have been calibrated. A n-type junctionless device of S. Gundapaneni et al. in [22] has been designed with silicon layer of 6 nm thickness and gate length of 20 nm. The non-local band-to-band tunneling model has been calibrated with consideration of carrier lifetime of 10^{-7} s which corresponds to the value desired at the doping of 10^{19} cm^{-3}. It has been observed that inclusion of non-local band-to-band tunneling model can significantly impact the current value especially in for lower range of VGS as shown in Fig. 2.

From Fig. 2, it can be revealed that the simulation results closely match with the published result from the reference [22]. This close matching reflects the capturing of phenomena governing the device physics satisfactorily and hence, validates the model calibration.

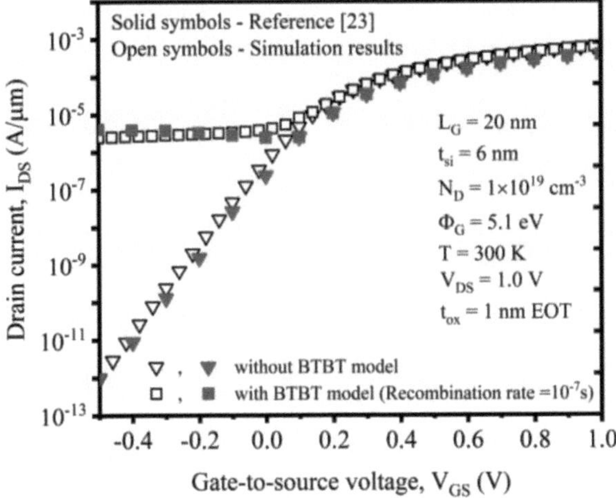

Fig. 2. TCAD physical model calibration with published data.

3 Results and Discussion

In this section the effect of temperature on the transfer characteristics and various performance parameters of C_DGJLT and R_DGJLT has been discussed. To observe the performance changes the temperature value has been varied from 273 K to 450 K with a step size of 30 K. However, the starting value of temperature has been kept deliberately at 273 K as it is a standard figure. The impact of temp. On transfer curves of C_DGJLT and R_DGJLT is shown in Fig. 3(a), and (b), respectively.

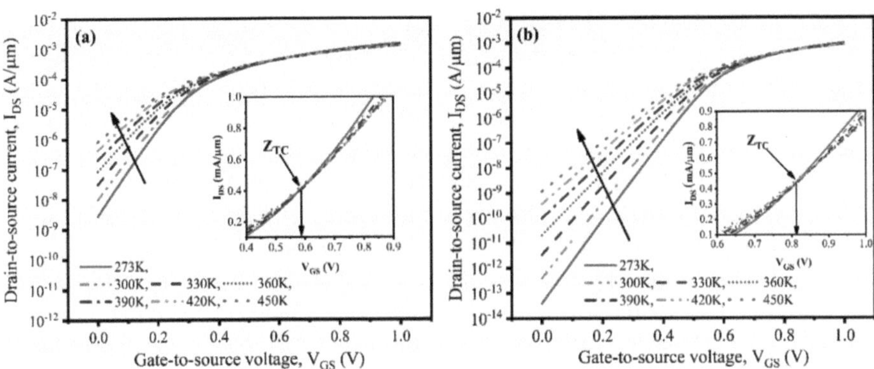

Fig. 3. The current-voltage curves at different temperatures in proposed (a) C_DGJLT (b) R_DGJLT.

From Fig. 3, it is also observed that raising the temp. Value results in significant variations in drain current (IDS) for lower values of VGS in both junctionless devices. The large variations in IDS can be attributed to the SRH recombination which dominates the device behavior for lower range of VGS [23]. The SRH recombination can vary exponentially with temperature as given in Eq. (1) [24].

$$R_{SRG} = \frac{(pn - n_i^2)}{\tau\left[n + n_i \cdot exp\left(\frac{E_{TRAP}}{k_B T_L}\right)\right] + \tau\left[p + n_i \cdot exp\left(-\frac{E_{TRAP}}{k_B T_L}\right)\right]} \tag{1}$$

Here, TL represents the lattice temperature in Kelvin, ETRAP is the energy difference in the trap and intrinsic Fermi level. The hole and electron lifetimes are represented with τp and τn.

This exponential dependence of recombination rate over the temperature results in drastic increase in leakage current (for VGS = 0 V). For subthreshold operation, the device current increases with rise in temperature. The junctionless devices are heavily doped due to which at low gate bias the mobility in these devices is limited by impurity scattering and varies as $T^{3/2}$ [7]. Thus, increasing the temperature results in higher IDS. Also, the rise in temperature leads to higher number of intrinsic carrier concentration, which further boost the rise in leakage current [7].

Furthermore, like the inversion mode transistors, the junctionless transistors also reflects a point called as zero temperature coefficient (ZTC) [7], The ZTC represents the VGS value at which the drain current (IDS) becomes independent of the variations in temperature. Mathematically, this condition can be written as given by in Eq. 2 [25].

$$\frac{\partial I_{DS}}{\partial T} = 0 \tag{2}$$

It is important to not here that the temperature independence is shown only for a VGS value and then the current rises or drops with temperature for other range of VGS as shown in Fig. 3(a) and (b). At ZTC the impurity scattering phenomena is compensated by the phonon scattering process which varies as $T^{-3/2}$ [7] Hence, the device current becomes independent of variations in temperature. As the VGS is increased above the ZTC the phonon scattering starts dominating and the device current starts reducing with surge in temperature as revealed in Fig. 3(a), and (b). However, the R_DGJLT reflects marginally smaller ON current than the C_DGJLT due to recessed channel thickness. Hence, the ZTC point is observed for higher VGS of ~0.8 V as revealed in inset of Fig. 3(b). Whereas, C_DGJLT reflects the ZTC point for VGS of ~0.6 V.

The variations in temperature also impacts the energy barrier height [26]. This impact in channel of C_DGJLT and R_DGJLT when device is OFF is shown in Fig. 4(a) and (b) for, respectively. As the temperature is increased the channel barrier height is reduced which allows more charge carriers in the channel. It should be noted that in case of R_DGJLT channel barrier height reduces by a value of 0.01789 eV whereas in case of C_DGJLT this variation has been found of the value of 0.01034 eV only, which is just 57% of the value of R_DGJLFET. Hence, the effect of temperature is more pronounced in R_DGJLT in OFF state.

Figure 5(a) reflects the variations in threshold voltage (VTH) for the two junctionless devices due to temperature. It is seen that for increasing the temperature changes from 273 K−450 K, both devices reflect reduction in VTH. Moreover, Fig. 5(a) confirms this variation (i.e. dVTH/dT) about the linear dependence of VTH on temperature as

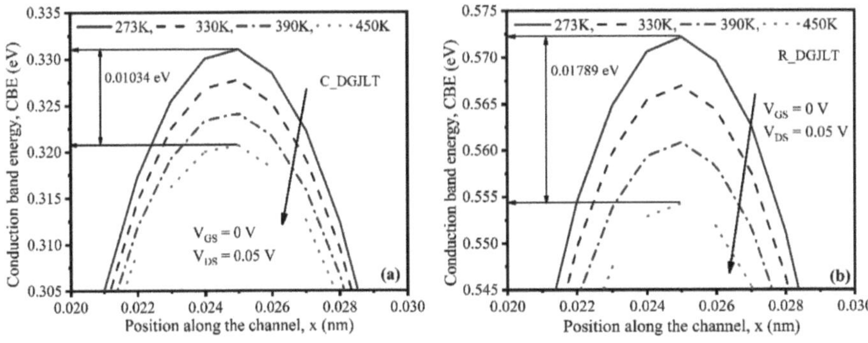

Fig. 4. Effect of variations in temperature on conduction band energy in proposed (a) C_DGJLT (b) R_DGJLT.

modeled by R. D. Trevisoli *et al.* in [27]. Furthermore, reduction channel cross-section also results in smaller variations in dVTH/dT [28]. The R_DGJLT reflects the smaller VTH reduction with a slope of -1.09mV/K in comparison to -1.22mV/K for C_DGJLT. This can be attributed to recessed silicon channel in R_DGJLT which curtails the channel cross-section.

The effect of variations in temperature on OFF current (IOFF) has been shown in Fig. 5(b). It is apparent from Fig. 5(b), that the IOFF in both junctionless transistor increases approximately linearly on logarithmic scale (or exponentially on linear scale). The reason for such variation can be attributed to the lowering of energy barrier height when VGS $= 0$ V as shown in Fig. 4. As the effect of temperature is more pronounced in R_DGJLT, consequently, its IOFF also varies at larger scale in comparison to C_DGJLFET. The IOFF in C_DGJLT and R_DGJLT has ascended by the order of 10^2 and 10^5, respectively.

Furthermore, the ON current (ION) in both devices reduces marginally with rise of temp. As reflected in Fig. 5(c). It is noticed that the C_DGJLT and R_DGJLT reflects a reduction in ION of 15.06 % and 12.58 % while increasing the temperature from 273 K to 450 K. The smaller cross-sectional area of R_DGJLT results in better gate control which permits the mobility degradation at slower rate [27], in comparison to C_DGJLT. This leads to smaller changes of ION in R_DGJLT in comparison to C_DGJLT. It can also be observed from Fig, 5(b) and (c), that the IOFF, ION varies on log, and linear scales]. The exponential change in IOFF with temperature leads to exponential change in ON/OFF current ratio (ION/IOFF) of both JLTs as depicted in Fig. 5(d). The ION/IOFF ration has descended in both C_DGJLT and R_DGJLT the order of 10^2 and 10^5, respectively. The higher variations in IOFF and ION/IOFF reflects the potential of R_DGJLT to be used in sensing of various bio-molecules.

The subthreshold swing (SS) is also an vital performance figure in nanoscale devices. This parameter reflects the ability of a transistor to turn off quickly. The R_DGJLT has already shown the steeper subthreshold in comparison to C_DGJLT as shown in Fig. 5(e). However, with rise in temperature the leakage current in subthreshold region in both device rises with temperature. The rise in leakage current results in degradation of SS. Moreover, the R_DGJLT reflects smaller variations in SS in comparison to C_DGJLT. In

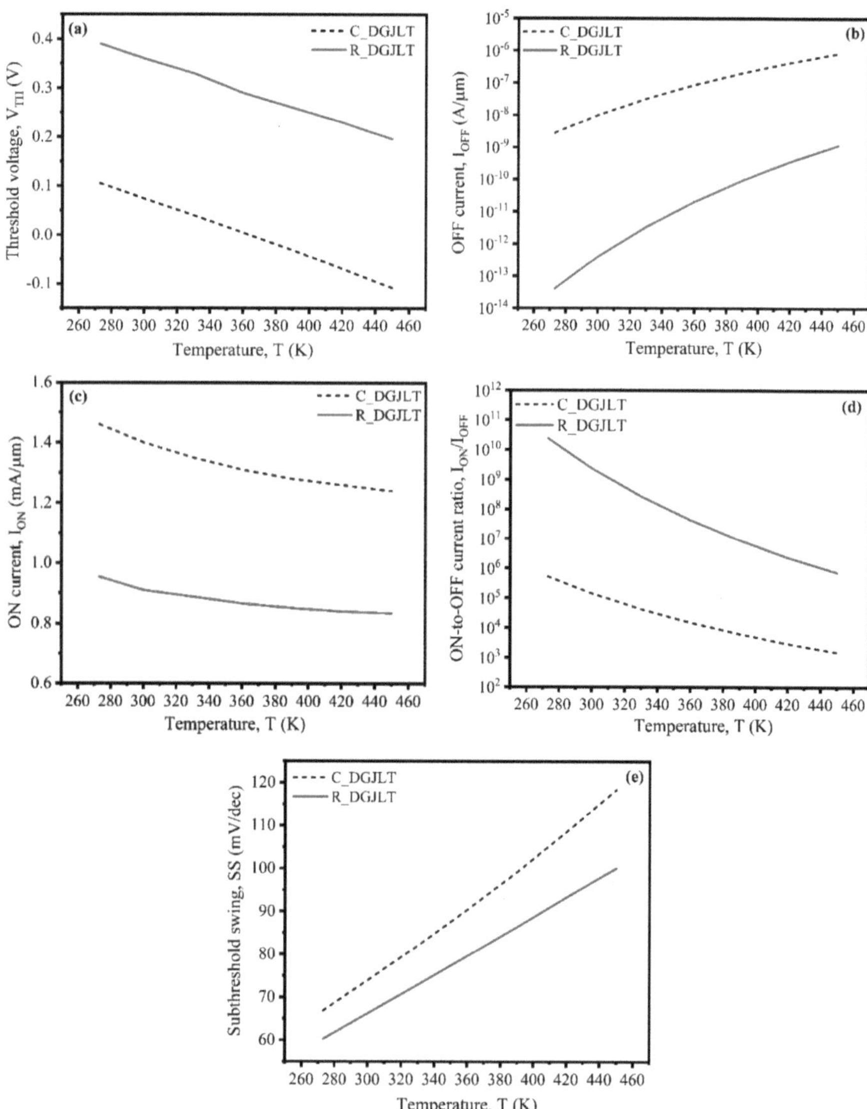

Fig. 5. Effect of variations in temperature on differnt performance factors of proposed DGJLT, R_DGJLT: (a–e) Threshold voltage, OFF current, ON current, ON-to-OFF current ratio, and Subthreshold swing, respectively.

R_DGJLT the gate electrodes have been placed over the recessed silicon channel region, which leads to an effective gate-to-gate coupling even with variations in temperature. This results in effective gate control over the channel region which helps in showings smaller variations in SS. It has been observed that the C_DGJLT and R_DGJLT reflects a rise in SS of 47.6 mV/dec and 39.9 mV/dec with temperature.

4 Conclusion

Various device performance parameters of R_DGJLT has been investigated and compared with C_DGJLT among the temp. Range from 273 K−450 K. It has been observed that the recessed silicon channel in R_DGJLT results in minorly lower current due to which the ZTC point has been observed for higher gate voltage in comparison to C_DGJLT. Moreover, the R_DGJLT reflect smaller variations in VTH, ION and SS whereas its OFF state behavior has been severely affected by the temperature variations. The larger performance variations in OFF state reflects the device ability be used in bio-sensing applications. Moreover, with smaller OFF current the device can be fitted as a potential candidate in small power circuit applications.

References

1. Bohr, M.: A 30 Year Retrospective on Dennard's MOSFET Scaling Paper. IEEE Solid-State Circ. Soc. Newsletter **12**(1), 11–13 (2007)
2. Colinge, J.P.: FinFETs and Other Multi-Gate Transistors, 1st edn. Springer, Massachusetts (2008)
3. Rawat, S., Madan, J.: Investigating the impact of temperature on the photovoltaic properties of CsSnI3-Based Perovskite solar cells. International Conference on E-mobility, Power Control and Smart Systems (ICEMPS), pp. 1–5, Thiruvananthapuram, India, (2024). https://doi.org/10.1109/ICEMPS60684.2024.10559299
4. Sharma, K., Pathania, A., Madan, J., Pandey, R., Sharma, R.: Process voltage temperature analysis of MOS based balanced pseudo-resistors for biomedical analog circuit applications. Circ. World **50**(2/3), 217–224 (2024)
5. Keshavarzi, A., Roy, K., Hawkins, C.F.: Intrinsic leakage in low power deep submicron CMOS ICs. In: Proceedings International Test Conference, pp. 146–155. IEEE, Washington (1997)
6. Colinge, J.P., Lee, C.W., Afzalian, A., et al.: Nanowire transistors without junctions. Nat. Nanotechnol. **5**, 225–229 (2010)
7. Lee, C.W., et al.: High-temperature performance of silicon junctionless MOSFETs. IEEE Trans. Electron Devices **57**(3), 620–625 (2010)
8. Trevisoli, R.D., Doria, R.T., Souza, M.D., Das, S., Ferain, I., Pavanello, M.A.: The zero temperature coefficient in junctionless nanowire transistors. Appl. Phys. Lett. **101**(062101), 1–3 (2012)
9. Kumar, S., Chatterjee, A.K., Pandey, R.: Performance enhancement of recessed silicon channel double gate junctionless field-effect-transistor using TCAD tool. J. Comput. Electron. **20**, 2317–2330 (2021)
10. Kumar, S., Chatterjee, A.K., Pandey, R.: Analytical modeling of recessed double gate junctionless field-effect-transistor in subthreshold region. Int. J. Numer. Model. **37**(2), e3209 (2024)
11. Srivastava, P., Upadhyaya, A., Yadav, S., Negi, C.M.S.: Performance evaluation of junctionless cylindrical gate-all-around FET for low power applications. Semicond. Sci. Inf. Devices **5**(2), 1–10 (2023)
12. Sachdeva, A., Gupta, L., Sharma, K., Elangovan, M.: A CNTFET based bit-line powered stable SRAM design for low power applications. ECS J. Solid State Sci. Technol. **12**(4), 041006 (2023)
13. Gupta, N., Gupta, R., Gupta, S.B., Yadav, R., Kumar, P.: Performance investigation of a dielectric stacked triple material cylindrical gate all around MOSFET (DSTMCGAA) for low power applications. ECS J. Solid-State Sci. Technol. **12**(1), 011002 (2023)

14. Gupta, N., Raghav, A.K., Gupta, R., Sharma, A.: Sub-threshold modeling of dual halo dual-dielectric triple-material surrounding-gate (DH-DD-TM-SG) MOSFET for improved leakages. J. Eng. Res. **8**(2), 178–190 (2020)
15. Sreenivasulu, V.B., Narendar, V.: Design and temperature assessment of junctionless nanosheet FET for nanoscale applications. SILICON **14**, 3823–3834 (2022)
16. Tayal, S., Mittal, V., Jadav, S., Gupta, S., Nandi, A., Krishan, B.: Temperature sensitivity analysis of inner-gate engineered JL-SiNT-FET: an Analog/RF prospective. Cryogenics **108**(103087), 1–6 (2020)
17. Garg, S., Haldar, S., Kaur, J., Gupta, R. S., Goel, A.: Temperature sensitive analysis of junctionless nanowire ferroelectric field effect transistor (JNFe-FET) for enhanced analog performance. In: IEEE Devices for Integrated Circuit (DevIC), pp. 425–429. IEEE, Kalyani, India (2023)
18. Kumar, S., Chatterjee, A.K., Pandey, R.: Performance analysis of gate electrode work function variations in double-gate junctionless FET. SILICON **13**, 3447–3459 (2021)
19. Robertson, J.: Interfaces and defects of high-k oxides on silicon. Solid State Electron. **49**(3), 283–293 (2005)
20. Slotboom, J.: The pn-product in silicon. Solid-State Electron. **20**(4), 279–283 (1977)
21. Biswas, A., Dan, S.S., Royer, C.L., Grabinski, W., Ionescu, A.M.: TCAD simulation of SOI TFETs and calibration of non-local band-to-band tunneling model. Microelectron. Eng. **98**, 334–337 (2012)
22. Gundapaneni, S., Bajaj, M., Pandey, R.K., Murali, K.V.R.M., Ganguly, S., Kottantharayil, A.: Effect of band-to-band tunneling on junctionless transistors. IEEE Trans. Electron. Devices **59**(4), 1023–1029 (2012)
23. Madan, J., Chaujar, R.: Temperature associated reliability issues of heterogeneous gate dielectric—Gate all around—Tunnel FET. IEEE Trans. Nanotechnol. **17**(1), 41–48 (2018)
24. SILVACO, ATLAS User's Manual. Santa Clara, CA, Ver, 5, (2011)
25. Prijic, Z.D., Dmitrijev, S.S., Stojadinovic, N.D.: The determination of zero temperature coefficient point in CMOS transistors. Microelectron. Reliab. **32**(6), 769–773 (1992)
26. Kumar, A., Chitkara, M., Dhillon, G.: Effect of varying calcination temperature on the structural and optical properties of tin oxide nanoparticles. Mater. Today Proc.(2023). ISSN: 2214–7853. https://doi.org/10.1016/j.matpr.2023.05.207
27. Trevisoli, R.D., Doria, R.T., Souza, M.D., Pavanello, M.A.: Threshold voltage in junctionless nanowire transistors. Semicond. Sci. Technol. **26**(105009), 1–8 (2011)
28. Mukherjee, C., et al.: Nanoscale thermal transport in vertical Gate-All-around junctionless nanowire transistors—Part I: experimental methods. IEEE Trans. Electron. Devices **70**(12), 6498–6504 (2023)

ML Based Malicious Traffic Detection for Industrial-IoT Ecosystem

Supreet Kaur[1] and Surjit Singh[2(✉)]

[1] School of Mathematics, Thapar Institute of Engineering and Technology, Bhadson Road, Patiala 147004, Punjab, India
`skaur_msc22@thapar.edu`
[2] Computer Science and Engineering Department, Thapar Institute of Engineering and Technology, Bhadson Road, Patiala 147004, Punjab, India
`surjit.singh@thapar.edu`

Abstract. The IIoT also referred to as the Industrial internet of things helps in the transformation of daily life through improvement in efficiency and rise in productivity. But this is marred by some weaknesses or threats that are prone to some forms of malicious attacks. In regards to this, the work proposes ML models for the detection of such attacks. Our approach involves a comprehensive data preprocessing pipeline: For data pre-processing, it includes missing value imputation with mode and median, data transformations by creating columns like peak hour for attack from timestamp, frequency count for IPs and ports, removing some of the redundant columns, data encoding with One-Hot Encoder for nominal columns, and Label Encoding or map functions for ordinal columns., outlier analysis and treatment with IQR method, data scaling with Standard Scaler, and data selection with PCA and keeping the top 45 components. Following this, our proposed approach achieved outstanding results: Specificity = 0. 990, positive predictive value = 0. 997, sensitivity = 0. 983 and F1 measure = 0. 990. This model shows good capability in the identification of the attacks, thus protecting the IIoT system from such attacks.

Keywords: Machine Learning · Principal Component Analysis · Interquartile Range

1 Introduction

IIoT is a groundbreaking technology in the industrial world that links physical devices, sensors, and software to create a digital ecosystem to enhance the industry setting and offers real-time monitoring, automation, and optimization of the industrial processes leading to high efficiency traffic productivity hence offering high innovation in manufacturing and logistical sector, energy and also in health industry where it offers values like predictive maintenance, product quality, and supply chains [1, 4].

S. Pal et al. (Eds.): ICETSS 2024, CCIS 2610, pp. 283–292, 2026.
https://doi.org/10.1007/978-3-032-11488-4_22

However, IIoT also raises significant security concerns, including data contravention and unauthorized access to sensitive information, vulnerabilities in connected devices and systems, network intrusions and cyber attacks, insider threats and human error, lack of encryption and secure communication protocols, inadequate authentication and access controls, and dependence on third-party vendors and supply chain risks, which can compromise the reliability, integrity, and confidentiality of industrial systems and data, leading to disruption of critical operations, financial losses and reputational damage, compromise of intellectual property and trade secrets, and risk to human safety and environmental damage [2,3]. Addressing these security concerns is crucial to ensure the safe and reliable operation of IIoT systems, and this can be attained by implementing security measures, such as secure communication protocols and encryption, regular software updates and vulnerability patching, strong authentication and access controls, network segmentation and isolation, continuous monitoring and threat detection, employee training and awareness programs, and supply chain risk management, which can help prevent cyber attacks, protect sensitive data, and ensure the integrity of industrial systems, and by using advanced technologies like AI, ML and DL, which can enhance security, improve incident response, and optimize industrial processes, and by developing and implementing industry-wide security standards and best practices, which can help ensure firmness and interoperability across different systems and devices, and by fostering collaboration and information sharing between industry stakeholders, which can help stay ahead of emerging threats and vulnerabilities [10,11].

1.1   Contributions

The contributions of this work are as follows:

- To develop a comprehensive data preprocessing pipeline, including peak hour extraction for attacks from timestamps and frequency counts for IPs and ports, mode imputation with multiple modes, data encoding, outlier treatment with IQR method, Standard Scaler for scaling and PCA with 45 components for dimensionality reduction.
- To propose model which outperforms other binary classification approaches with hyperparameters as random state = 42, number of estimators = 150, criterion = entrophy.
- To evaluate model with accuracy, precision, recall and F1-Score to test model generalizability.

2   Related Work

The inception of the IIoT has transformed manufacturing, introducing new security challenges. Recent studies demonstrate the need for security measures in IIoT-enabled Industry 4.0, with various approaches proposed to address emerging threats. This review synthesizes vital findings and solutions in the IIoT security landscape.

Hussain et al.(2021) [5] presented a comprehensive review of security in IIoT-enabled Industry 4.0, highlighting key challenges and solutions and proposing a systematic approach to securing IIoT systems. For the most part, the paper was strong in presenting its topic and possible solutions; however, original data, accompanied by experiments, was not included and seemed to be theoretical in nature. Moreover, the paper did not present any particular IIoT protocol or standard along with the comparison of the performance of the proposed security solutions. However, the paper helped in the analysis of the security of IIoT in conjunction with the Industry.

Al-Hawawreh et al.(2021) [6] introduced a novel dataset for IIoT intrusion detection, addressing the limitations of existing datasets by using a realistic security testbed (Brown-IIoTbed). While the dataset performed well on the binary classification, it failed to perform even on multi-class target variables which resulted tackling a variety of attack types. This has suggested the need for extra research to come up with efficient solutions that will ensure the detection of diverse IIoT security threats as delimited by intrusion detection systems. Accordingly, the outcomes of the investigated study underscore the necessity to work on the enhancement of dataset quality to innovate IIoT security, and to expand the sphere of future research on more effective IDS development.

The study (do Vale Dalarmelina, Nicole, et al. (2023) [7]) investigated how to detect flooding attacks in Internet of Things (IoT) networks using machine learning. The authors identified that IoT networks had certain types of attacks, and afterwards they tried to protect them. From this study, it was clear that utilising machine learning as a tool to find and mitigate such assaults will increase IoT networks' security.

The study (Gaber, Tarek, et al.(2023) [8]) proposed a machine learning (ML)-based approach for classifying network intrusion detection systems (NIDS) in Industrial Internet of Things (IIoT) traffic. They used preselection of features employing PSO and BA algorithms to deminish the number of input parameters and increase the accuracy of classifiers. The study showed good indications on the identification of several attacks. The writers stressed the need that should be based on what makes IIoT systems' security different from that of IT systems. Features for the future work include extension of deep learning models to identify more advanced patterns as well as the usage of blockchain or encryption strategies.

3   Proposed System Architecture

This architecture consists in proposing a 9-step approach to build the Random Forest model for detecting the malicious attacks on the IIoT systems starting from the input datasets and with the binary target variable. The missing values are filled using median and mode to uphold the quality as opposed to handling incomplete data, which primarily leads to either obtaining biased models or poor performance [12]. Data transformations by creating new columns like peak hours for attack using timestamp, frequency count for IPs and ports to strengthen the model's predictive power, Data encoding transforms categorical data into numerical forms and fits the data for machine learning algorithms, while outlier removing by IQR insulates data from extreme values thus making the models more reliable and the prediction accurate. After that, data scaling normalizes the incoming numerical data by using a Z-score in order to make the features contribute equally and PCA for feature selection in order to avoid having high dimensions that would hinder the model's performance [13]. Thus, the architecture implies the following preprocessing steps in order to obtain a meaningful dataset for the training of the Random Forest model, which would also help in solving the problem of missing values, data encoding, outlier detection, data normalization and dimensionality reduction, by providing a high quality data set for the RF model.

Steps for the proposed architecture are given below:
Step 1: Input the IIoT dataset and select the binary target variable.
Step 2: Replace missing values in categorical features with mode and numerical features with a median.
Step 3: Apply:

- Label Encoding for binary and ordinal columns
- One-Hot Encoding for nominal columns
- Custom encoding for specific columns

Step 4: Split data into training (70%) and testing sets (30%).
Step 5: Calculate the Interquartile Range (IQR) using the formula:

$$IQR = q3 - q1 \tag{1}$$

Calculate the lower bound (LB) and upper bound (UB) using:

$$LB = q1 - 1.5 \times IQR \tag{2}$$

$$UB = q3 + 1.5 \times IQR \tag{3}$$

Identify and replace outliers with values outside the range [LB, UB].
Step 6: Standardize features using Z-scoring with the formula:

$$Z_{std} = \frac{X - \mu}{\sigma} \tag{4}$$

Step 7: Apply PCA to extract relevant features.
Step 8: Train Random Forest model with:

- Random State: 42
- Number of Estimators: 150
- Criterion: Entropy

Step 9: Evaluate model using accuracy, recall, precision, F1 score, and confusion matrix.

3.1 Evaluation Metrics

Evaluation metrics used are [9]:

Accuracy: The ratio of correct predictions are divided by total predictions.

$$Accuracy = \frac{Correct\ Predictions}{Total\ Predictions} \tag{5}$$

Precision: True positive predictions are divided by positive predictions.

$$Precision = \frac{Correct + vePredictions}{Total\ + vePredictions} \tag{6}$$

Recall: True positive predictions are divided by the actual positive instances.

$$Recall = \frac{Correct + vePredictions}{Actual + veInstances} \tag{7}$$

F1 Score: Balanced measure of precision and recall, avoiding false positives and negatives.

$$F1\,Score = 2 \times \frac{Precision \times Recall}{Precision + Recall} \tag{8}$$

4 Results and Discussions

Table 1 presents the training performance of five ML models: Naive Bayes (NB), Logistic Regression (LR), AdaBoost (ADA), Decision Tree (DT), and Random Forest (RF). DT and RF achieve perfect scores, while NB, LR, and ADA show relatively high accuracy, precision, recall, and F1 scores, indicating strong performance. Models were developed and tested using X-IIoTID Dataset [5]. Figure 1 shows the training results in the bar graphs.

Table 2 presents the testing performance of five machine learning models, with Random Forest (RF) emerging as the top performer. RF achieved exceptional scores across all metrics, with an accuracy of 0.990, precision of 0.997, recall of 0.983, and F1-score of 0.990, indicating near-perfect performance. The other models, including Naive Bayes, Logistic Regression, AdaBoost, and Decision Tree, trailed behind RF in terms of performance, with RF's balanced and high scores, solidifying its position as the best model among the five. Figure 2 represents the testing results in bar graphs.

The proposed model outperforms existing approaches on a binary target variable, achieving state-of-the-art results. As shown in Table 3, our model demonstrates superior performance across all metrics: accuracy (0.990), precision (0.997), recall (0.983), and F1-score (0.990), surpassing recent studies [1–4]. The results are further visualized in Fig. 3, providing a clear illustration of the proposed model's exceptional performance. Notably, our model surpasses the closest competitor [4] by 0.7% in accuracy, 0.8% in precision, and 0.5% in recall, showcasing its effectiveness in binary classification tasks. These results underscore the proposed model's robustness and reliability, making it a promising solution for binary target variable prediction.

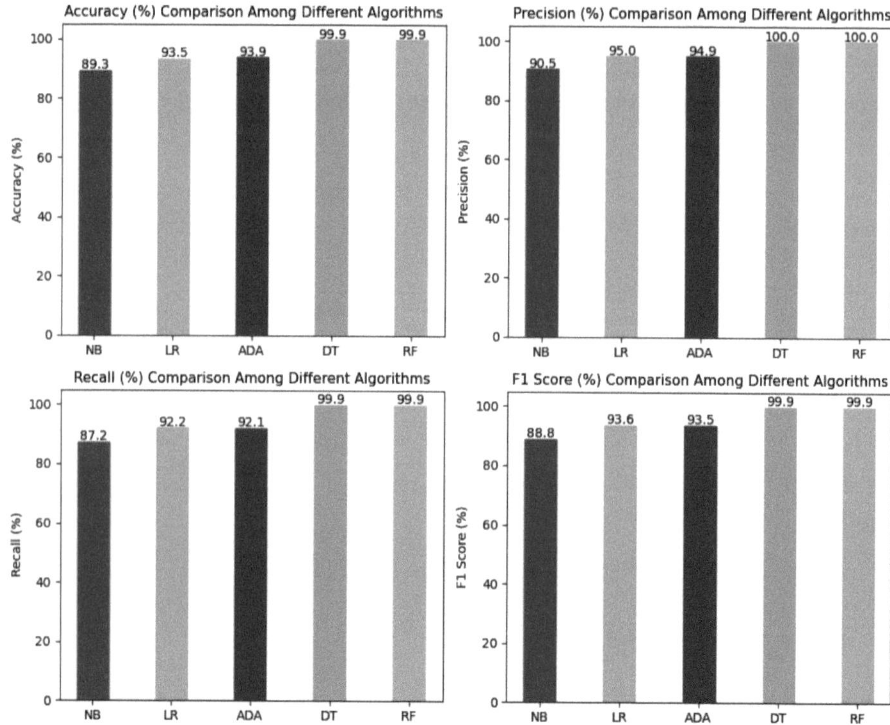

Fig. 1. Training performance of implemented models

Table 1. Training Performance of implemented models

Model	Accuracy	Precision	Recall	F1-Score
NB	0.893	0.905	0.872	0.888
LR	0.935	0.950	0.922	0.936
ADA	0.939	0.949	0.921	0.935
DT	0.999	1.0	0.999	0.999
RF	0.999	1.0	0.999	0.999

Table 2. Testing Performance of implemented models

Model	Accuracy	Precision	Recall	F1-Score
NB	0.894	0.905	0.873	0.889
LR	0.935	0.954	0.912	0.932
ADA	0.937	0.949	0.921	0.935
DT	0.981	0.979	0.982	0.981
RF	0.990	0.997	0.983	0.990

Table 3. Comparison of proposed model with other approaches(Binary)

References	[14]	[15]	[16]	[17]	
Model	CDAE - DNN	Ensemble Model	PCA+SVD +RF	SMOTE+ XGBoost	**Proposed Model**
Year	2021	2022	2022	2023	2024
Accuracy	0.981	0.981	0.980	0.983	**0.990**
Precision	0.981	0.991	0.954	0.989	**0.997**
Recall	0.982	0.975	0.979	0.978	**0.983**
F1-Score	0.981	0.981	0.985	0.983	**0.990**

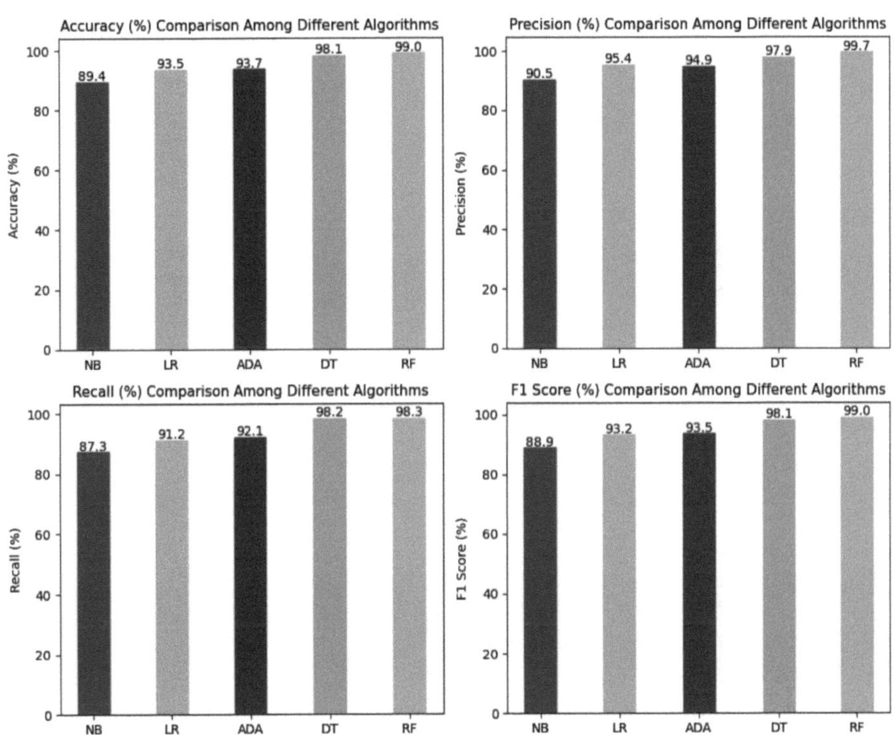

Fig. 2. Testing performance of implemented models

In this study, we achieved remarkable results with our proposed approach, demonstrating its effectiveness in handling multi-class target variables. Specifically, our Random Forest (RF) model attained uniform metrics of 0.990 for accuracy, precision, and recall, as well as an F1 score of 0.990 when classifying 18 attacks. Similarly, for the 9-attack classification, the model achieved an accuracy, precision, and recall of 0.990, with a slightly lower F1 score of 0.989. This consistency highlights the reliability of our approach in detecting various types of attacks, further validating its potential in enhancing IIoT security.

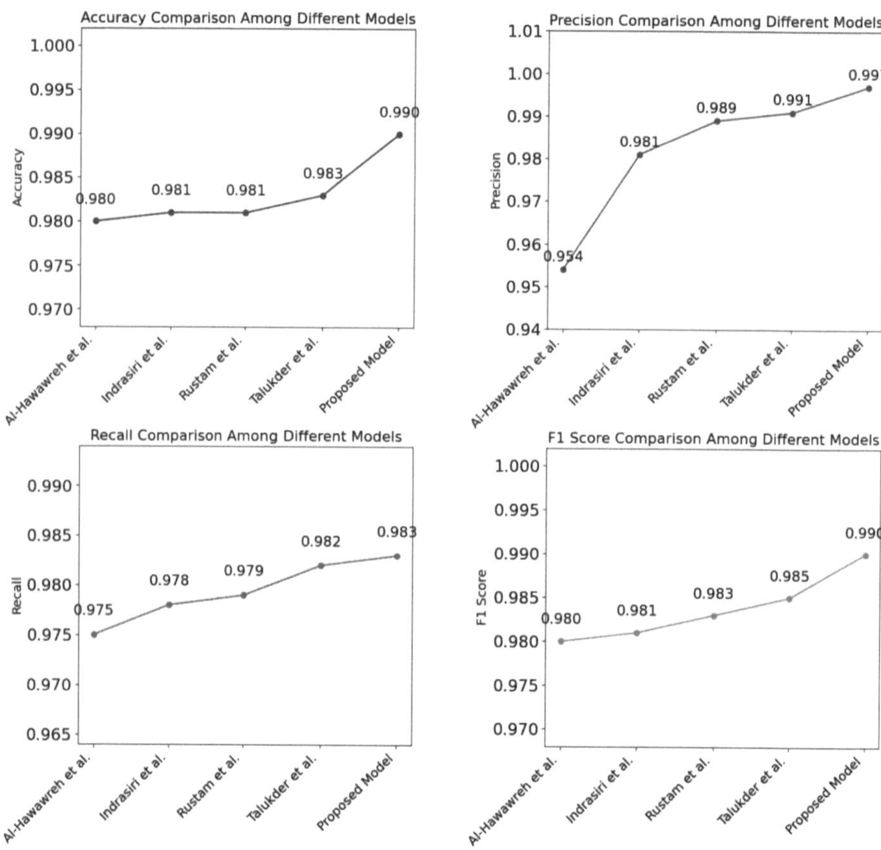

Fig. 3. Comparison of proposed model with other works for binary target variable

5 Conclusion

Therefore, this work formulates a sophisticated machine learning model to identify attacks specifically against the IIoT systems. Our model has been developed using the Random Forest algorithm with the help of feature selection and data preprocessing. The measurements including the accuracy, the precision, the recall, and the F1-score in binary and multi-class classification are all greater than 0.99 in most cases. The introduced strategy is a more effective option compared to existing practices and explains how approaches to control complex IIoT threats are possible. The similarities in the outcomes for one attack situation to another establish the viability as well as the potential of achieving enhanced security for IIoT systems. As for the further research of the discussed topic, the directions will entail exploring the possibility of utilizing Deep learning to improve the effectiveness of the proposed model in identifying the security threats of IIoT. Thus, the result of this work will help increase the preparedness of the security measures for the secure and continuous operation of IIoT systems in the industrial setting.

Acknowledgments. This work is supported by Thapar Institute of Engineering and Technology, Patiala, India under SEED research grant.

References

1. Schneider, S.: The industrial internet of things (iiot) applications and taxonomy. In: Internet of Things and Data Analytics Handbook, pp. 41–81 (2017)
2. Boyes, H., Hallaq, B., Cunningham, J., Watson, T.: The industrial internet of things (IIoT): an analysis framework. Comput. Ind. **101**, 1–12 (2018)
3. Munirathinam, S.: Industry 4.0: industrial internet of things (IIOT). In: Advances in computers, vol. 117, no. 1, pp. 129–164. Elsevier (2020)
4. Sari, A., Lekidis, A., Butun, I.: Industrial networks and IIoT: now and future trends.In: Industrial IoT: Challenges, Design Principles, Applications, and Security, pp. 3–55 (2020)
5. Hussain, Z., Akhunzada, A., Iqbal, J., Bibi, I., Gani, A.: Secure IIoT-enabled industry 4.0. Sustainability **13**(22), 12384 (2021)
6. Al-Hawawreh, M., Sitnikova, E., Aboutorab, N.: X-IIoTID: a connectivity-agnostic and device-agnostic intrusion data set for industrial Internet of Things. IEEE Internet Things J. **9**(5), 3962–3977 (2021)
7. Do Vale Dalarmelina, N., Arora, P., Kaur, B., Meneguette, R.I., Teixeira, M.A.: Using ML and DL algorithms for intrusion detection in the industrial internet of things. In AI, Machine Learning and Deep Learning, pp. 243–256. CRC Press (2023)
8. Gaber, T., Awotunde, J.B., Folorunso, S.O., Ajagbe, S.A., Eldesouky, E.: Industrial internet of things intrusion detection method using machine learning and optimization techniques. Wirel. Commun. Mob. Comput. **2023**(1), 3939895 (2023)
9. Hossin, M., Sulaiman, M.N.: A review on evaluation metrics for data classification evaluations. Int. J. Data Mining Knowl. Manag. Process **5**(2), 1 (2015)
10. Peter, O., Pradhan, A., Mbohwa, C.: Industrial internet of things (IIoT): opportunities, challenges, and requirements in manufacturing businesses in emerging economies. Procedia Comput. Sci. **217**, 856–865 (2023)
11. Panchal, A.C., Khadse, V.M., Mahalle, P.N.: Security issues in IIoT: a comprehensive survey of attacks on IIoT and its countermeasures. In: 2018 IEEE Global Conference on Wireless Computing and Networking (GCWCN), pp. 124–130. IEEE (2018)
12. Kotsiantis, S.B., Kanellopoulos, D., Pintelas, P.E.: Data preprocessing for supervised leaning. Int. J. Comput. Sci. **1**(2), 111–117 (2006)
13. Iliou, T., Anagnostopoulos, C.N., Nerantzaki, M., Anastassopoulos, G.: A novel machine learning data preprocessing method for enhancing classification algorithms performance. In: Proceedings of the 16th International Conference on Engineering Applications of Neural Networks (INNS), pp. 1–5 (2015)
14. Al-Hawawreh, M., Sitnikova, E., Aboutorab, N.: Asynchronous peer-to-peer federated capability-based targeted ransomware detection model for industrial IoT. IEEE Access **9**, 148738–148755 (2021)

15. Indrasiri, P.L., Lee, E., Rupapara, V., Rustam, F., Ashraf, I.: Malicious traffic detection in iot and local networks using stacked ensemble classifier. Comput. Mater. Continua **71**(1), 489–515 (2022)
16. Rustam, F., Mushtaq, M.F., Hamza, A., Farooq, M.S., Jurcut, A.D., Ashraf, I.: Denial of service attack classification using machine learning with multi-features. Electronics **11**(22), 3817 (2022)
17. Talukder, M.A., et al.: A dependable hybrid machine learning model for network intrusion detection. J. Inf. Secur. Appl. **72**, 103405 (2023)

Agile Methodology Adoption and Understanding Analysis: An Engineering Student's Perspective

Jeetasha[1]([✉]), Tanay[1], and Saravjeet Singh[2]

[1] School of Information Technology, Deakin University, Geelong 3320, Australia
arorajeetasha@gmail.com
[2] Chitkara University Institute of Engineering and Technology, Chitkara University,
Chandigarh 140401, Punjab, India
24240162@deakin.edu.au

Abstract. The agile framework is rising in popularity among software development teams. This framework overcomes the problems linked with traditional project management methodologies. It includes more customer involvement and better team collaboration thus positively impacting the quality of the deliverable. Considering the importance of agile in the current era, it is important to make university students aware of the agile framework to increase their potential and employability. Although a lot of studies have been done on including agile in higher education, very less studies focused on the inclusion of agile in university curriculum. To analyze the current levels of awareness and satisfaction with using agile methodologies among university students a research study was carried out. Following a survey-based approach, a questionnaire was distributed among 434 students out of which 273 responses were collected. The results of this study suggest that students are satisfied after using agile methodologies for their team projects. According to the study, Scrum is the most favored agile framework among students. The findings of this research study will also help promote an agile framework in university contexts.

Keywords: Agile framework · Team projects · Software development · Team Collaboration · Survey · Jenkins

1 Introduction

A system development methodology is defined as a set of rules, processes, and tools used to increase the efficiency and productivity of software development teams. It also improves the quality of the software deliverable [4]. In recent years a system development methodology called agile is gaining popularity among the IT development teams and personnel. Agile is defined as a product management approach that was introduced in the late 1990s and has become an integral part of the software development industry. In industries, agile methodologies are used

S. Pal et al. (Eds.): ICETSS 2024, CCIS 2610, pp. 293–306, 2026.
https://doi.org/10.1007/978-3-032-11488-4_23

to make the process of developing high-quality software and managing software development teams efficient and error-free. Agile methodologies are characterized by being iterative and adaptive to project requirements in nature [11,19,22].

Agile development methodology is a major milestone in the software development industry as it helps to solve the problem of incorporating user feedback and adaptation to changing project requirements. It is characterized by being iterative and incremental with shorter iterations for development and more frequent releases. Teams using agile as the framework for project management are seen to be more productive and fast.

The traditional methods on the other hand focus on gathering all the user requirements first. The requirements are then documented, and then the team starts working on it. These methodologies are considered heavyweight due to the complex development cycle. Also, it's very challenging to incorporate changes made in the project requirements to the final product [1]. Although traditional project management (TPM) strategies are considered to be successful in some industries, they are not suitable for complex projects, especially software development projects. Traditional methodologies are not flexible enough and follow a linear approach.

In recent years project-based learning(PBL) has become very popular as it helps students expand their problem-solving skills. Team projects offer students an opportunity to develop the skills necessary to work in teams. Nowadays project-based learning forms an essential part of computer science and software engineering disciplines in colleges and universities. Agile Software Development should be incorporated as a part of the curriculum in undergraduate courses related to IT and software domains to help students understand the existing industrial practices. This will also help improve the skillset of students, thus increasing their employability [12].

Agile Manifesto in higher education outlines four rules for incorporating agile methodologies in educational contexts, these are [9]:

- teachers and students over administration and infrastructure
- competence and collaboration over compliance and competition
- employability and marketability over syllabus and marks
- attitude and learning skills over aptitude and degree

A study in [14] highlighted the transformation of an educational setting to an eduScrum team composed of an eduScrum Master, a student team, and a product owner. To promote agile awareness among the university students universities can inculcate agile in their syllabus and institutions can develop more courses in this domain [10]. The research questions that were addressed in this paper are the following:

- R1: How does utilizing agile methodologies by university students improve the overall project effectiveness compared to traditional methods?
- R2: What are the perceptions regarding the limitations, success, and integration of the Agile framework in the university curriculum?

The paper is divided into sections. Section 2 is about the literature and related research studies about agile methodologies, Sect. 3 is the theoretical background elaborating on traditional and agile approaches, Sect. 4 refers to the research methodology that was used during the conduction of this survey, Sect. 5 is about the presentation of results a discussion of the findings, and finally, Sect. 6 presents the conclusion of the paper with the future scope the conducted survey.

2   Literature Review

The International Project Management Association, Project Management Institute, and International Organization for Standardization are different organizations that have defined project management [18]. Over the years these definitions have evolved as per the changing business trends and project's complexity. Various studies have shown that there has been an enhancement in the project management methodologies and practices [8,23,24].

Project management is considered an integral part of the project's success as it aligns with the organization's goals through smooth execution and control over different activities. Some studies explored how projects have contributed to the value creation [25]. However, there is limited research on change in project management within the project life cycle. The traditional hierarchical structure has been replaced with the teams-based structure. In a team, various members from different domains work together to achieve a common goal. This emphasizes the importance of project manager competencies [3].

Agile project management has emerged as a solution to many limitations of traditional project management styles. The SCRUM method introduced as an agile approach emphasizes flexibility and interaction [17]. Various organizations have adopted agile methods. It extends beyond the Information Technology(IT) sector showcasing its versatility and effectiveness in managing projects [21].

The research studies show the comparison between traditional and agile project management reflects a key difference in that agile is focused on delivering functionality quickly, while traditional methods have the goal of performing the optimization in projects over a longer period [13]. The adaptability of agile methods has been demonstrated in numerous case studies. Agile development's relationship with the Capability Maturity Model has the potential for integration with conventional methods [26].

Table 1 presents the studies by evaluating the objectives and findings. This provides a comprehensive overview of the transition from traditional to agile project management from the perspective of research.

3   Theoretical Background

3.1   Classical Waterfall Approach

The Classical Waterfall approach is a traditional project management methodology. It consists of the processes in a sequence that consists of five phases:

Table 1. Summary of studies on agile project management

Focus/Objective	Findings	Source
Effectiveness of agile in software development	Highlight the effectiveness of agile methodologies in software projects	[6]
Impact of agile on project success in various industries and regions	Research on agile's impact beyond software, showing varying degrees of success and adoption	[5]
Early adopters' perspective on agile	Early adopters believes agile positively affects project success	[27]
The efficacy of the agile approach through large-scale empirical analysis	Agile significantly impacts project success, particularly in efficiency and stakeholder satisfaction	[20]
Impact of traditional, agile, and hybrid approaches on project success	Agile and hybrid approaches outperform traditional in stakeholder satisfaction; similar performance in budget, time, scope, and quality success	[2]

Requirement Analysis, Design, Implementation, Testing, and Operation & Maintenance. These phases are often grouped into three main cycles: initiation and planning, execution and control, and closing.

The first-ever presentation using similar terms in software engineering was done by Herbert D. Benington at the Symposium on Advanced Programming Methods for Digital Computers on 29 June 1956. This was about the development of software for SAGE. The description that formally introduced the waterfall model is the article by Winston W. Royce in 1970. Royce didn't mention the term "waterfall" in the article but showed the model as an example of a non-working and flawed model [12].

This model is considered to be easy to understand and implement. However, this model has many disadvantages such as all the requirements must be known completely before starting the project, inflexible, mistakes can't be solved easily and customers have very little opportunity to preview the system before it is finished [16].

3.2   Agile Approach

Agile is a conceptual framework and includes six main phases. Refer to Fig. 1 for an illustration of these phases. The agile manifesto is a document that was written by 17 professionals and was published in 2001. It outlines the 4 principles

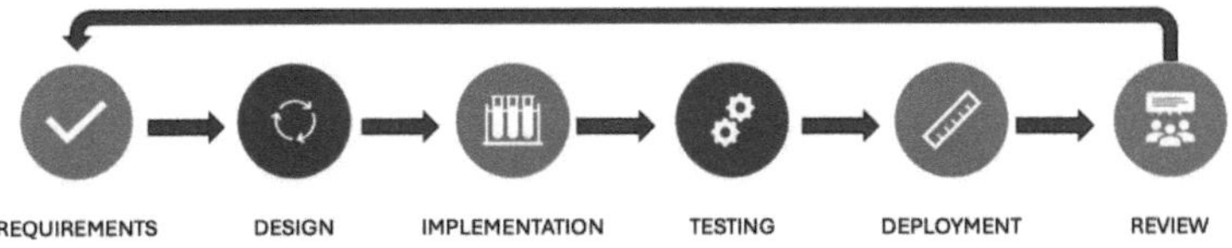

Fig. 1. The six main phases of the agile approach

and 12 values of the agile framework for software development. Agile became very popular among the software development industries due to its flexible approach to project development leading to better coordination and communication among the team members [7]. The agile framework differs from traditional methodologies in terms of requirements gathering, teamwork, involvement of customers and feedback processing. In comparison to the traditional methods, agile includes shorter planning phases and greater involvement of customers in the project development process.

The agile framework consists of different methods, these are as follows:- Test Driven Development (TDD), Feature Driven Development (FDD), Extreme programming (XP), Kanban, Scrum, etc. Every method follows the same principles and values laid by the agile Manifesto but differs in terms of terminologies, roles, etc. Scrum is one of the most popular agile framework and includes working in several iterations called sprints. Refer Fig. 2 to for illustration purposes. The main aim of the agile framework of development is to adapt well to changing customer requirements and develop a product in several iterations incorporating customer feedback at each iteration.

3.3 Changing the Project Management Style

This theoretical background illustrates the understating of the shift from classical to agile methodologies. Emphasizing the factors of flexibility, iterative progress, and adaptability to change. This shows the popularity of agile and the reason it is being integrated into university settings, particularly in team-based projects.

4 Research Methodology

4.1 Sampling a Group of Students

In the survey, the sampling group was university students. Each of them has already worked on the team projects. They have witnessed the project both using agile methods and traditional project management approaches. The details of the survey participants were as follows:

- Undergraduate students
- Studying the graduation courses
- Age limit is upto 22 years

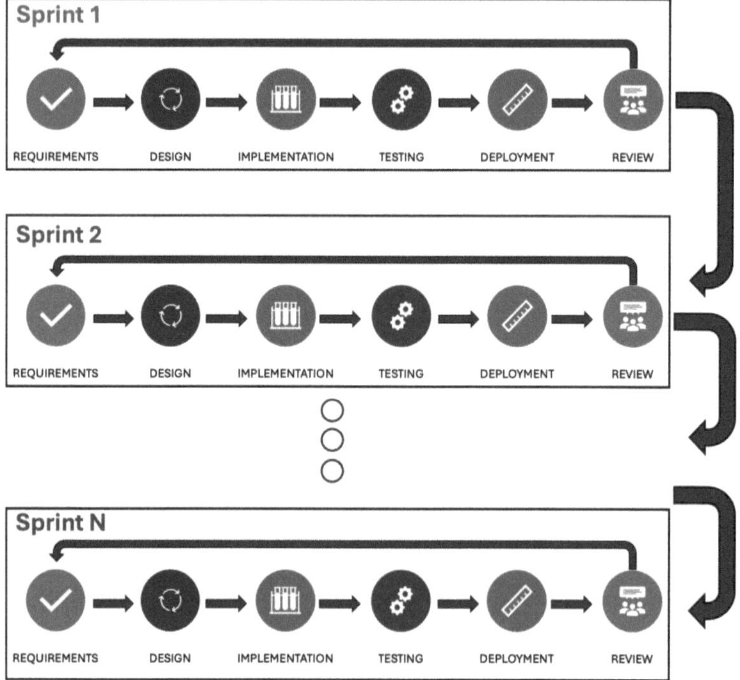

Fig. 2. Sprint wise agile approach

4.2   Data Collection from Questionnaires

A survey-based approach was utilized and a questionnaire was floated among the sampling group to collect the data. The questions were focused on analyzing the awareness levels of university students related to agile methodologies. The questionnaire was distributed among 434 students, out of which 273 responses were collected. The questionnaire was divided into the following sections:-

- Experience in using agile methodologies for the projects
- Views regarding evolution and future role of agile

5   Results and Discussions

The objective of the current research study was the analyze the awareness and satisfaction of using the agile framework among university students.

As explained in Sect. 4, the survey was conducted according to the specified parameters. The responses were further utilized to present the awareness and satisfaction among university students. The questionnaire was designed to collect responses on the five-level Likert scale. A reliability test was carried out to check

Table 2. Reliability Test

Value of Cronbach Alpha	Total Items	Results
0.86	13	Acceptable

the reliability of the items to indicate whether the results of the statements used in this survey are suitable for future research.

The results of the reliability test can be seen in Table 2. The value of Cronbach Alpha was 0.86 which indicates the acceptability of the questionnaire.

R1: How does utilizing agile methodologies by university students improve the overall project effectiveness compared to traditional methods?

The survey first witnessed whether university students had prior experience with agile methodologies before applying them to their projects. As depicted in Fig. 3, 75.3% of students had used agile methods in previous projects.

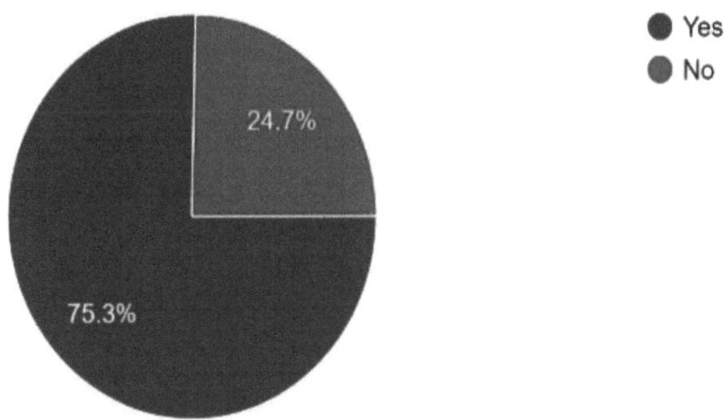

Fig. 3. Prior experience with agile methodologies

The Fig. 4 illustrated that SCRUM emerged as the most popular method, with 64.4%. Kanban was the second most preferred method, chosen by 23.3% of students. Other methodologies such as agile modeling, Extreme Programming (XP), Rapid Application Development (RAD), and Feature Driven Development (FDD) each accounted for 1.4% of preferences, while Crystal Clear was chosen by 2.7% of students.

The survey results highlighted the students' views regarding the effectiveness of agile methodologies which can be witnessed in Table 3.

A significant percentage of students 94.5% reported that agile methodologies improve team communication and collaboration. Additionally, 91.8% found agile helpful in managing changes in project requirements. 84.9% stated that the changes can be made dynamically while using agile.

84.9% responded positively regarding agile being able to identify and resolve the bottlenecks of the project. The methodologies enhance team productivity,

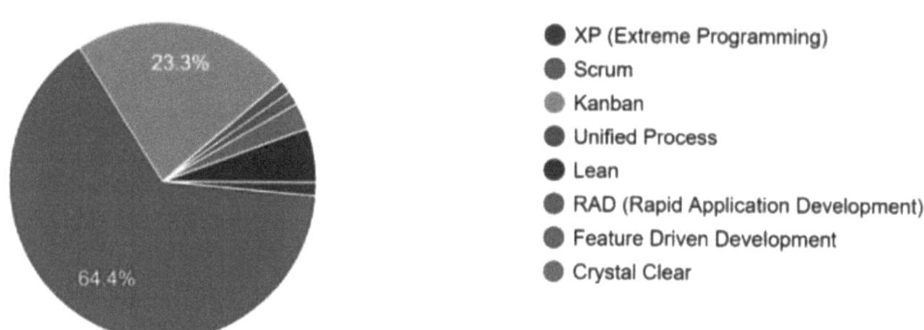

Fig. 4. Distribution of preferred agile methods

Table 3. Perceptions of agile Methodologies Among University Students

Statement	Strongly Agree (%)	Agree (%)	Neutral (%)	Disagree (%)	Strongly Disagree (%)
Agile methodologies improve team's communication and collaboration	45.2	49.3	2.7	0	2.7
Agile methodologies help in managing changes in project requirements	38.4	53.4	6.8	0	1.4
Changes can be made dynamically in project requirements using Agile	27.4	57.5	15.1	0	0
Agile methodologies help in identifying and resolving project bottlenecks	30.1	54.8	15.1	0	0
Agile methodologies help in improving team productivity	56.2	38.4	5.5	0	0
Feedbacks can be easily incorporated within a project cycle using agile	30.1	47.9	17.8	4.1	0
Agile methodologies help in coping with project risks and uncertainties	20.5	49.3	24.7	5.5	0
Agile promotes openness and transparency within the team	37	47.9	13.7	1.4	0
Team members are satisfied after using agile for managing the project	24.7	53.4	21.9	0	0
Agile affects the quality of deliverables	32.9	43.8	19.2	4.1	0
Agile helped in prioritising tasks and allocating resources efficiently	37	53.4	9.6	0	0
Continuous improvement and learning are promoted within a team after adopting agile	26	58.9	13.7	1.4	0
Agile helped to manage the project cycle within the specific timeline and budget	27.4	57.5	11	2.7	1.4

with 94.6% reporting increased productivity. Incorporating feedback within a project cycle was considered easy by 78% (30.1% strongly agree and 47.9% agree) of the students.

Regarding coping with project risks and uncertainties 69.8% saw benefits whereas 5.5% of respondents disagreed with the notion. Respondents perceived that agile promotes openness and transparency within the team 84.9%.

Furthermore, 90.4% indicated that agile helped in prioritizing tasks and allocating resources efficiently. Continuous improvement and learning within teams were promoted according to 84.9% of the students. Agile methodologies also helped manage project timelines and budgets with 84.9% reporting benefits.

In summary, university students perceive agile methodologies as highly effective in enhancing various aspects of project management and team dynamics.

R2: What are the perceptions regarding the limitations, success, and integration of the agile framework in the university curriculum?

Success Rate of Agile Projects: Two questions of the survey were focused towards interrogating user's satisfaction of using agile for their team project and the success rate of the project. According to the analysis done overall satisfaction with using agile for managing projects was reported by 78.1% and 76.7% noted an improvement in the quality of deliverables but 4.1% did not respond positively. Also as can be seen in Fig. 5 89.5% of the respondents agreed that agile led to the successful completion of their team projects while a very less(around 2.7%) people disagreed with the same. **Limitations of agile framework:** As shown in Fig. 6 around 38.4% of the respondents feel agile is not suitable for smaller organizations and very less(around 2.7%) respondents think that agile does not follow the basic steps of Software Development Lifecycle (SDLC).

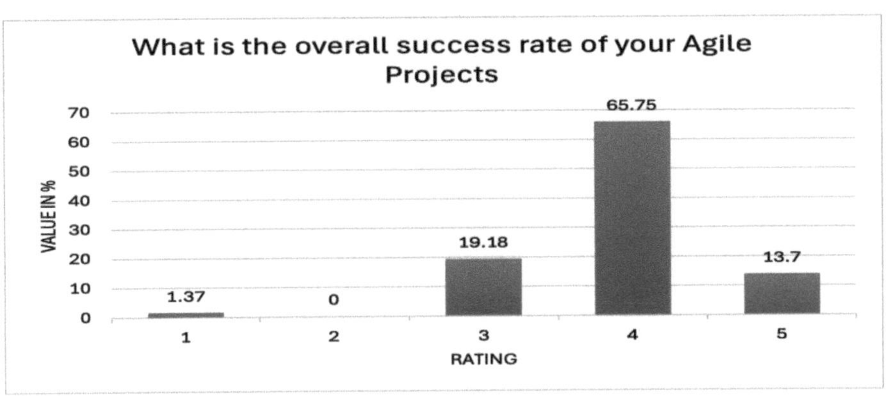

Fig. 5. User responses for limitations of agile

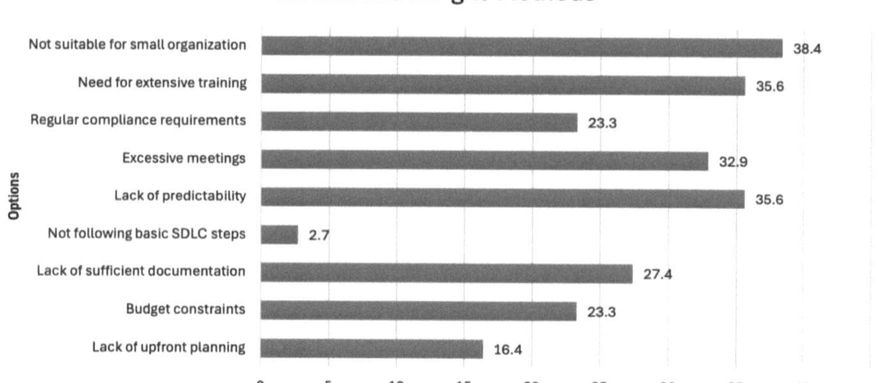

Fig. 6. User responses for limitations of agile

Space for Improvement in Agile: One of the questions in the survey was focused on the views of students regarding any improvement in the current agile framework. Around half of the respondents(49.3%) think that some improvements can be made in agile methodologies while the other half (50.7%) are unsure about the same. Refer Fig. 7.

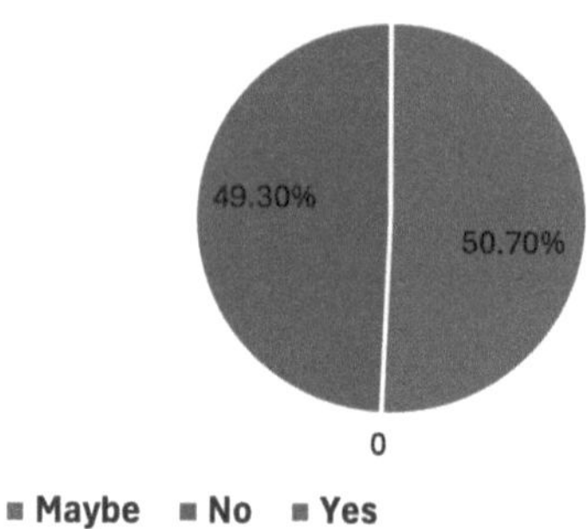

Fig. 7. Space for improvement in agile

Inclusion of Agile in University Curriculum: From Fig. 8 it is evident that a significant percentage of respondents feel that agile should be included in the university curriculum.

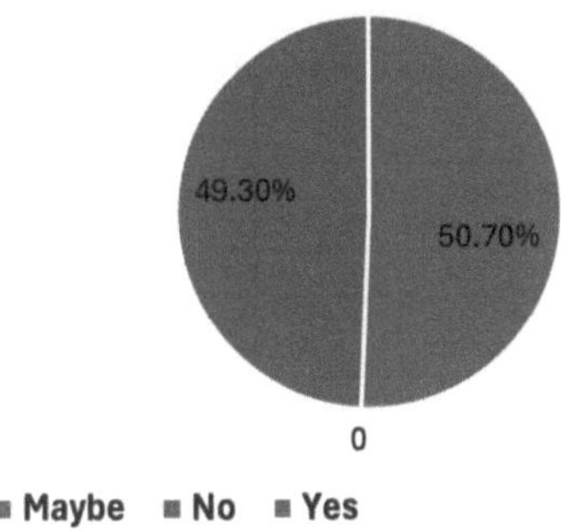

Fig. 8. Agile as a part of university curriculum

Table 4. Comparative Analysis of Agile Methodologies

Name	Publishing Year	Overview	Ref. No.
Impact of Agile on Project Success in Various Industries and Regions	2024	The research presents the survey of 298 practitioners. The survey shows a strong relation between the adoption of Agile methods and the success of the project stating the need for further exploration and enhancement in this field	[15]
Agile Project Management awareness status of final year students of engineering graduation programme at Mumbai University.	2023	The paper finds that 63% of students are familiar with concepts of Agile but there are existing gaps in many other domains. There is a need to update the university curriculum and increase the knowledge of Agile to enhance employability	[14]
Our work	–	This paper focuses on the understanding and usage of Agile methodologies by engineering students. The results of the study indicate that scrum agile framework is very prominent also highlights the importance of incorporating agile in university curriculum	–

Agile in Organisations: The results of the survey indicate that all the respondents (100%) agree that agile should be used in organizations to manage team projects. This will help lead to improved communication and collaboration between team members thus delivering better project outcomes.

6   Comparative Analysis

The results of this study were also compared with other studies that focused on agile understanding and effectiveness. This was done to have a practical idea on agile practises. The comparative analysis is shown in the Table 4 below.

7   Conclusion

The study aimed to understand the student's perspective on the effectiveness of agile methodologies in managing projects. The results of the conducted survey indicated that most of the students responded positively about the agile practices. There were improvements in the majority sections of the project management such as communication, collaboration, and productivity compared to traditional methods. Also, agile helps in managing the changes and incorporating the feedback leading to a higher success rate of the project.

There were a few limitations of the survey it only focused on the undergraduate students of the Software Engineering department. This tends to limit the findings as it does not include the opinions of people from other domains and the nature of the project also differs as per different professional contexts.

In the future, the research can be performed on a more diverse group of students and evaluate the findings as per other long-term impacts of the agile practices while focusing on other dimensions. Additionally, there can be personal interviews and case studies that could cater to more specific challenges and the success parameters in some more detailed scenarios.

In conclusion, the study showed the potential of agile methodologies to enhance project management and teamwork among university students. Also, there were some more areas where further exploration and improvement could be performed. agile practices could be included in the university curriculum to improve project outcomes and educational experiences.

Acknowledgement. This research did not receive any specific grant from funding agencies in the public, commercial, or not-for-profit sectors.

Disclosure of Interests. The authors have no competing interests to declare that are relevant to the content of this article.

References

1. Awad, M.: A comparison between agile and traditional software development methodologies. Univ. West. Aust. **30**, 1–69 (2005)

2. Behrisch, T., Gemino, A.: Sensation seekers who learn abroad: exploring the role of risk perception in co-op students' international plans. Int. J. Work-Integrat. Learn. **21**(1), 117–129 (2020)
3. Burger, M.: Project management in the built environment: The need for industry specific knowledge. Ph.D. thesis, University of the Free State (2013)
4. Chan, F.K., Thong, J.Y.: Acceptance of agile methodologies: a critical review and conceptual framework. Decis. Supp. Syst. **46**(4), 803–814 (2009)
5. Ciric, D., Lalic, B., Gracanin, D., Palcic, I., Zivlak, N.: Agile project management in new product development and innovation processes: challenges and benefits beyond software domain. In: 2018 IEEE International Symposium on Innovation and Entrepreneurship (TEMS-ISIE), pp. 1–9. IEEE (2018)
6. Ciric Lalic, D., Lalic, B., Delić, M., Gracanin, D., Stefanovic, D.: How project management approach impact project success? from traditional to agile. Int. J. Manag. Proj. Bus. **15**(3), 494–521 (2022)
7. Erickson, J., Lyytinen, K., Siau, K.: Agile modeling, agile software development, and extreme programming: the state of research. J. Database Manag. (JDM) **16**(4), 88–100 (2005)
8. Gordwin, M.: Managing Global Projects: Identify &Analyze the Most Important Elements to Improve Project Management Performance. Ph.D. thesis, Northcentral University (2021)
9. Kamat, V.: Agile manifesto in higher education. In: 2012 IEEE Fourth International Conference on Technology for Education, pp. 231–232. IEEE (2012)
10. Kane, S.V., Pathak, P., Bilolikar, V.: Agile project management awareness status of final year students of engineering graduation programme at Mumbai university. Korea Rev. Int. Stud. **16**(50), 40–49 (2023)
11. Kumar, G., Bhatia, P.K.: Impact of agile methodology on software development process. Int. J. Comput. Technol. Electron. Eng. (IJCTEE) **2**(4), 46–50 (2012)
12. Lundqvist, K., Ahmed, A., Fridman, D., Bernard, J.G.: Interdisciplinary agile teaching. In: 2019 IEEE Frontiers in Education Conference (FIE), pp. 1–8. IEEE (2019)
13. McHugh, O., Conboy, K., Lang, M.: Using agile practices to influence motivation within it project teams (2011)
14. Noguera, I., Guerrero-Roldán, A.E., Masó, R.: Collaborative agile learning in online environments: strategies for improving team regulation and project management. Comput. Educ. **116**, 110–129 (2018)
15. Palopak, Y., Huang, S.J.: Perceived impact of agile principles: insights from a survey-based study on agile software development project success. Inf. Softw. Technol. 107552 (2024)
16. Pargaonkar, S.: A comprehensive research analysis of software development life cycle (sdlc) agile & waterfall model advantages, disadvantages, and application suitability in software quality engineering. Int. J. Sci. Res. Publ. (IJSRP) **13**(08), 345–358 (2023)
17. Revutska, O., Maršíková, K.: Agile approach in human resource management: focus on generation (2021)
18. Sabini, L., Muzio, D.: The long way to professional recognition: project management in Italy. Int. J. Manag. Proj. Bus. **10**(4), 822–840 (2017)
19. Sardana, A., Sharma, V.K.: Agile framework adaptation issues in various sectors. In: Agile Software Development: Trends, Challenges and Applications, pp. 23–38 (2023)
20. Serrador, P., Pinto, J.K.: Does agile work?–A quantitative analysis of agile project success. Int. J. Project Manag. **33**(5), 1040–1051 (2015)

21. Shaw, D.: Managing people and learning in organisational change projects. J. Organ. Chang. Manag. **30**(6), 923–935 (2017)
22. Singh, J., Dhindsa, K.S., Singh, J.: Performing reengineering using scrum agile framework. In: 2020 Indo–Taiwan 2nd International Conference on Computing, Analytics and Networks (Indo-Taiwan ICAN), pp. 33–35. IEEE (2020)
23. Singh, S., Singh, J.: SSMDM: an approach of big data for semantically master data management. In: 2015 2nd International Conference on Computing for Sustainable Global Development (INDIACom), pp. 586–590. IEEE (2015)
24. Singh, S., Singh, J.: Management of sme's semi structured data using semantic technique. In: Applied Big Data Analytics in Operations Management, pp. 133–164. IGI Global (2017)
25. Too, E.G., Weaver, P.: The management of project management: a conceptual framework for project governance. Int. J. Project Manag. **32**(8), 1382–1394 (2014)
26. Torrecilla-Salinas, C.J., Sedeño, J., Escalona, M., Mejías, M.: Agile, web engineering and capability maturity model integration: a systematic literature review. Inf. Softw. Technol. **71**, 92–107 (2016)
27. Vinekar, V., Slinkman, C.W., Nerur, S.: Can agile and traditional systems development approaches coexist? an ambidextrous view. Inf. Syst. Manag. **23**(3) (2006)

A Lightweight MQTT Protocol Security Analysis Based on ML

Shrutika Sablok[1] and Surjit Singh[2(✉)]

[1] School of Mathematics, Thapar Institute of Engineering and Technology, Bhadson
Road, Patiala 147004, Punjab, India
`ssablok_msc22@thapar.edu`
[2] Computer Science and Engineering Department, Thapar Institute of Engineering
and Technology, Bhadson Road, Patiala 147004, Punjab, India
`surjit.singh@thapar.edu`

Abstract. With the advent of the Internet of Things (IoT), machines
are now able to communicate, collect data, and make decisions, revolutionizing everyday life. However, the increasing number of IoT devices
put the latter at risk for the following cyberattacks; Aggressive scan,
SSH Brute Force, UDP scan Sparta, MQTT Brute Force, Flood DoS,
and SlowITe. This research aims to establish how models such as Naïve
Bayes (NB), Decision Tree (DT), Random Forest (RF), Bagging (BG),
AdaBoost (AB), Histogram-Based Gradient Boosting (HGB), XGBoost,
and Stacking perform in detecting these attacks. Evaluation measures
that are used are F1 score, accuracy, precision, and recall. The results
show that XGBoost excels in accuracy (96.42%) and Recall (96.42%),
BG in precision (98.56%), and AB in F1 Score (96.42%). The goal and
problem of this research are aimed at improving the security level of IoT
environments, proposing an effective method to identify MQTT-based
threats, and establishing a reliable connection to IoT applications.

Keywords: Internet of Things · Message Queuing Telemetry
Transport (MQTT) · Machine Learning · Attack Detection

1 Introduction

The Internet of Things (IoT) [1] has helped many industries through the connection of physical objects and their capability to transmit information. Of all the
communication protocols of IoT, MQTT [2] stands out as a low level messag-
ing protocol suitable for constrained environments. Although IoT devices have
penetrated our everyday lives, they are easy targets for hackers, and this calls
for proper security to be put in place. This research is dedicated to solving
the research problem of identifying the presence of malicious behaviors within
MQTT-based IoT systems. For these vulnerable environments, IDS [3] stands
as a key aspect to identify and deal with intrusive traffic or activities in the
network. This paper aims to evaluate the use of machine learning techniques in
creating an effective IDS that can effectively detect the various MQTT-based
attacks.

© The Author(s), under exclusive license to Springer Nature Switzerland AG 2026
S. Pal et al. (Eds.): ICETSS 2024, CCIS 2610, pp. 307–316, 2026.
https://doi.org/10.1007/978-3-032-11488-4_24

1.1 Contributions

- To validate the upgraded models against the existing research work, ensuring their effectiveness and improved performance. Subsequently, to optimize the model parameters for maximum detection accuracy.
- To assess the susceptibility of the proposed models to diverse MQTT attacks.
- To measure their performance using metrics like accuracy, precision, recall, and F1 score, ensuring a thorough assessment and comparison.

1.2 Article Organization

The paper is structured as follows: Sect. 2 gives a systematic literature review of the available works for attack detection based on MQTT. Section 2 describes various machine learning algorithms and methods used. Section four shows the results and assesses different algorithms. Lastly, section five brings this study to a close by concluding the research implications and identifying research directions for future research.

2 Related Work

In this section, a brief literature review is offered where enhancements to IoT security are discussed with a focus on methods aimed at the MQTT protocol for IoT in particular (Table 1).

The author of this paper [4] suggests the utilization of LSTM, GRU, and XGBoost models for intrusion detection in the IoT networking environment with particular attention to the MQTT protocol. The authors use recurrent neural networks or temporal dependencies inherent in the task, and ensemble techniques to improve the model's performance. The experiment results indicate that the proposed models work well, all the methods based on ensemble yield the best accuracy. This helps the scholar to advance research on effective and deployable intrusion detection systems on the IoT infrastructure.

In this paper [5], researchers used the case of the MQTT protocol to introduce an IDS based on the ensemble approach that will help to fight various cyber threats. In their method, it is integrated to address feature selection to enhance the performance of the model. Experiment with CICIDS2017 dataset shows that our ensemble model produces a better accuracy than the existing methods. The proposed system is able to provide a secure and concise solution of mitigating and preventing IoT networks from further threat activities.

MQTT has been highly targeted by hackers due to the current evolution of IoT and needs strong protection. As for this research [6], the primary study examines the design and implementation of a reliable IDS based on ML algorithms. Through the use of the. Random Forest, KNN, and SVM classifiers, the study achieved approximately 96% detection rate on MQTT attacks. All the above results explain the possibility of applying machine learning for the protection of IoT environments.

The increase in IoT devices increases the risk of cyberattacks, which call for efficient IDS mechanisms. This research [7] builds a deep learning model called CatBoost to analyze the MQTT traffic and distinguish legitimate traffic from identified attack types such as SlowITe, Malformed, Brute force, Flood, and DoS attacks. Hence, by coming up with a balanced dataset, the model displayed a 94% attack classification accuracy within 78. 45 s.

The objectives of this research [8] were to improve the security of the MQTT protocol in the IoT structures. This way, using the method of automated feature selection, the number of features in MQTTset was reduced to ten significant ones, which contributed to the enhancement of model performance in terms of both speed and accuracy. Hence, a comparison of the Decision Trees, K-Nearest Neighbors, Random Forest, AdaBoost, and XGBoost algorithm has been carried out for the classification of the MQTT traffic. Thus, Random Forest was identified as the best performance model with an accuracy rate of 96.33%. Here, Decision Trees and AdaBoost are both at 96.29%. K-Nearest Neighbors and XGBoost also gave good results with accuracies of 96. 27% and 96. 29%, respectively. The results presented here demonstrate that machine learning can be successfully applied to identify MQTT-based cyber threats and achieve better results than previous works. The next steps of this study will employ advanced approaches in machine learning and the deeper implications of the research into the IoT to achieve improved security.

In summary, this literature review sheds light on various published studies concerning MQTT-based intrusion detection systems. They analyze several classification methods, starting from classical ones and ending with deep learning approaches, which are used to differentiate normal and malicious MQTT traffic. The review points to feature engineering and stresses how the properties of the designated dataset influence the performance of a model. Furthermore, this paper presents areas of future research that are characterized by research limitations that create the background for the suggested research.

3 Proposed System Architecture

The purpose of this study is to enhance MQTT protocol security using machine learning models to identify the presence of an attack accurately. Focusing on that, Naive Bayes, Decision Trees, Random Forest, Bagging, AdaBoost, Histogram-Based Gradient Boosting, XGBoost, and Stacking are the algorithms selected in this study to classify MQTT traffic either normal or anomalous.

Machine Learning: A subfield of artificial intelligence in which an algorithm gets better at a particular task through experience based on past data fed in. Unlike predictable programming which informs machines of every single operation and result, ML [9] entailing uses patterns from data to arrive at an inference without being programmed on each of them. The ML algorithms used in our work as follows:

Naive Bayes(NB): A classifier that predicts the probability that an instance would belong to a particular class given the features of the instance in consideration. It imposes independence between features, which is a clear violation of

Table 1. Comparative analysis

Reference	Year	Model	Description
[4]	2019	LSTM, GRU, XGBoost	XGBoost gave highest accuracy whereas results for LSTM and GRU needs to be improved
[5]	2022	Ensemble model(LR,NB,DT)	By combining multiple ML algorithms and carefully selecting relevant features, they achieved high accuracy rates in classifying MQTT traffic as normal or malicious
[6]	2022	RF, KNN, SVM	RF exhibited highest performance with upto 96% accuracy
[7]	2022	Catboost	Catboost was able to classify SlowITe, Brute force, Dos, Malformed and Flood attacks with high accuracy of 94%
[8]	2024	KNN, DT, RF, AB, XGBoost	RF exhibited highest performance with other models giving comparable yet less results

reality because, in real-life data sets, this is often not the case. However, Naive Bayes [10] are fast, demanding less training data, and can perform well for certain works such as identifying spam.

Decision Trees (DT): These algorithms give us a tree-like structure in which internal nodes stand for questions about data and branches, leading to them stand for possible answers. The decision tree [11] works through a path from the tree root to a terminal node, which provides a value for the class (normal or attack in your case based on the final question answered on a data point.

Random Forest (RF) [12]: A learning algorithm that generates many decision trees to create the final model and make improved predictions. It is trained on a single tree on the randomly selected data and with the randomly selected features, which make it produce relatively diverse set of predictions. The last stage of the model is the forecast, so for classification trees, the mode of votes of individual trees is considered, and for regression trees, the average of the individual trees is used.

Histogram-Based Gradient Boosting (HistGB) [13]: A specific version of the gradient boosting algorithm that focuses on the use of histograms to create efficient models of data distribution for decision trees creation. This makes it lighter, more efficient in terms of computational cost and capable of handling large data sets compared to previous versions of Gradient Boosting.

Stacking [14]: An approach of integrating several base models and arriving at the final decision after assessing each individual's output. It does not vote or average like other stacking methods; instead, it builds a "meta-model" on the base models' outcome. This meta-model can provide better performance by successfully training in conjunction with the individual models.

Bagging (BG) (Proposed Scheme) [15]: One type of machine learning where multiple base learners are trained on different randomly selected samples, or bootstraps, of the large data set. This makes the contribution more diverse and may help to minimize the variance in the final model, thus enhancing performance.

AdaBoost (AB) (Proposed Scheme) [16]: Another ensemble learning technique that learns from "hard-to-learn" instances involves training models in an iterative method, and misclassified data is given relatively higher weights. This way, models that come next optimize an error function for these particular examples and provide generally better forecasts.

Extreme Gradient Boosting (XGBoost)(Proposed scheme) [17]: An optimized design of the Gradient Boosting that employs decision trees as the base models. It offers several other enhanced characteristics like regularization, dimensionality control, and parallel processing, which make it one of the top preferred and popular ensemble methods for different purposes, including attack detection.

The detailed organization of the suggested system architecture is shown in Fig. 1. It is attack detection model.

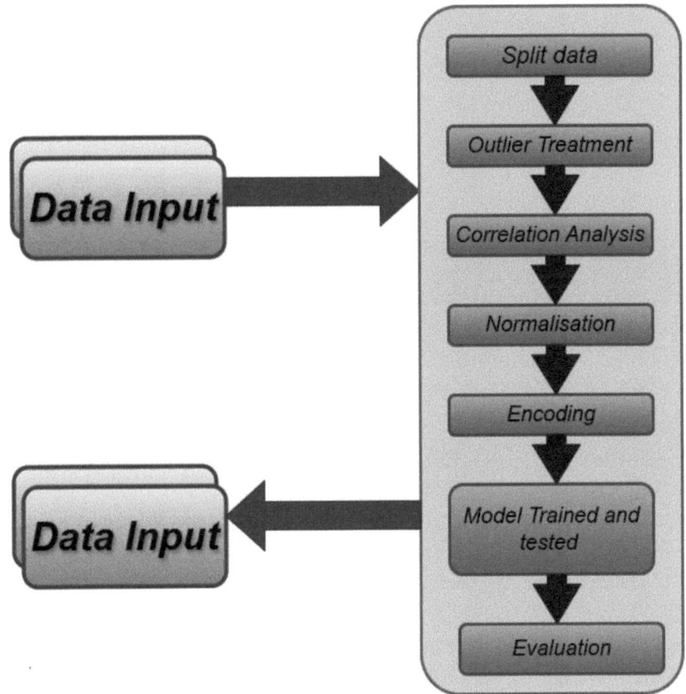

Fig. 1. Architecture

3.1 Evaluation Metrics

Performance metrics [18] are used to assess the impact of a particular machine learning model and help in determining how well the model is performing when it is tested on a unseen data set. The performance metrics used are as follows:

- Accuracy: It tells about correctness of model giving ratio that out of total predictions how many are correct.
- Precision: Measures the degree of accuracy with which positive classifications are achieved.
- Recall: Tells the ability of the model to identify all positive cases in the data set.
- F1-score: Combination of precision and recall given by harmonic mean, give an equitable measure of the performance of a model, particularly when the sample data sets are unbalanced.

4 Results and Discussions

Table 2 and Fig. 2 displays the training results of numerous algorithms in mqtt attack detection. The accuracy achieved in the training phase reflects that the solution achieves high accuracy in the majority of the models. The models which had the best results in terms of accuracy, precision, recall and the F1 score were Decision Trees, Random Forest, and Histogram-Based Gradient Boosting. Stacking and Bagging also performed well. However, Naive Bayes decided on some aspects with moderate improvement in the given parameters. The results obtained from the analysis of these models shed light on how these models can harmlessly be used for detecting MQTT attacks.

Table 3 and Fig. 3 showcases the testing results of different algorithms in the detection of mqtt attacks, and the results show that all the models had high values. For Decision Trees, Random Forest, Histogram-Based Gradient Boosting, Stacking, and all three proposed schemes, namely, Bagging, AdaBoost, and XG-Boost yielded extremely high accuracy, precision, recall, and F1-scores. The models on average performed very well with Naive Bayes being slightly lower in performance. Thus, these results confirm the efficiency of the proposed approach in the detection of MQTT attacks in a realistic environment.

Table 4 reflects comparative analysis of the proposed model results with the previous works. Our findings demonstrate a significant improvement over previous results. The accuracy of bagging, Adaboost, and XGBoost increased from 0.9538 to 0.9642, while the F1 score of bagging rose from 0.9537 to 0.9634, Adaboost from 0.9537 to 0.9642, and XGBoost from 0.9537 to 0.9641 and these results outperformed other models presented in previous studies as well. The current and earlier papers offered a moderate level of accuracy, but compared to the existing approaches, Bagging, AdaBoost models offered higher levels of accuracy and F1-score. Notably, XGBoost model also performed well and it yielded reasonable values. Therefore, the proposed methods contribute to increasing the detection accuracy of the MQTT attack.

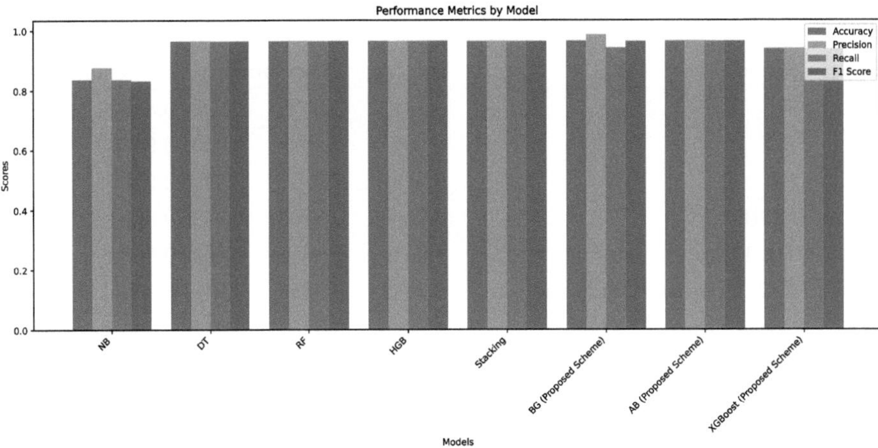

Fig. 2. Training Results

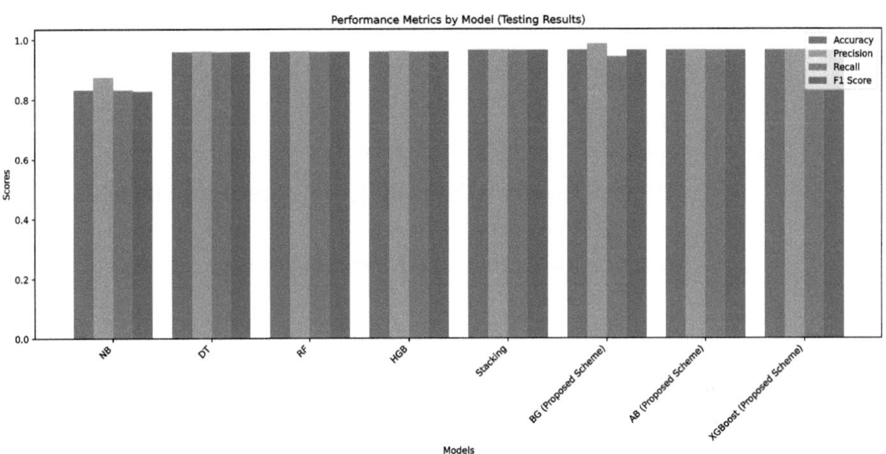

Fig. 3. Testing Results

Table 2. Training Results

Models	Accuracy	Precision	Recall	F1 Score
NB	0.8364	0.8767	0.8364	0.8319
DT	0.9642	0.9650	0.9642	0.9642
RF	0.9641	0.9650	0.9641	0.9641
HGB	0.9638	0.9648	0.9638	0.9638
Stacking	0.9636	0.9643	0.9636	0.9636
BG(Proposed Scheme)	0.9640	0.9852	0.9423	0.9632
AB(Proposed Scheme)	0.9641	0.9650	0.9641	0.9641
XGBoost(Proposed Scheme)	0.9391	0.9392	0.9391	0.9391

Table 3. Testing Results

Models	Accuracy	Precision	Recall	F1 Score
NB	0.8312	0.8738	0.8312	0.8263
DT	0.9588	0.9602	0.9588	0.9588
RF	0.9587	0.9601	0.9587	0.9587
HGB	0.9588	0.9603	0.9588	0.9588
Stacking	0.9639	0.9646	0.9639	0.9639
BG(Proposed Scheme)	0.9642	0.9856	0.9423	0.9634
AB(Proposed Scheme)	0.9642	0.9651	0.9642	0.9642
XGBoost(Proposed Scheme)	0.9642	0.9650	0.9642	0.9641

Table 4. Comparison of proposed model with Previous Results

Reference	Year	Model	Accuracy	F1 Score
[4]	2019	GRU	0.9608	0.9577
[5]	2022	Ensemble model(LR, NB, DT)	0.8892	–
[6]	2022	RF	0.9600	–
[7]	2022	CatBoost	0.9400	–
[8]	2024	RF	0.9633	–
	2024	**BG(Proposed Scheme)**	**0.9642**	**0.9634**
	2024	**AB(Proposed Scheme)**	**0.9642**	**0.9642**
	2024	**XGBoost(Proposed Scheme)**	**0.9642**	**0.9641**

5   Conclusion

This research examines the important research problem of identifying MQTT-based attacks in IoT system networks. Thus, to ensure the high efficiency of the IDS, we have used a large number of machine learning algorithms like Naive Bayes, Decision Tree, Random Forest, Histgradient boosting, Stacking, Bagging, AdaBoost, and Extreme Gradient Boosting. The performance of our proposed scheme (Bagging, AdaBoost, and Extreme Gradient Boosting) is exceptionally better than conventional methods from experimental evaluations based on accuracy, precision, recall, and F1-score. It also emphasizes the need for adopting ensemble learning techniques because they improve the security of MQTT-based IoT systems. The use of deep learning models and enhanced feature engineering techniques should be the focus of future research to enhance the detection abilities.

Acknowledgments. This work is supported by Thapar Institute of Engineering and Technology, Patiala, India under SEED research grant.

References

1. Goyal, K.K., Garg, A., Rastogi, A., Singhal, S.: A literature survey on Internet of Things (IoT). Int. J. Adv. Network. Appl. **9**(6), 3663–3668 (2018)
2. Chen, F., Huo, Y., Zhu, J., Fan, D.: A review on the study on MQTT security challenge. In: 2020 IEEE International Conference on Smart Cloud (SmartCloud), pp. 128–133. IEEE (2020)
3. Santos, L., Rabadao, C., Gonçalves, R.: Intrusion detection systems in Internet of Things: a literature review. In: 2018 13th Iberian Conference on Information Systems and Technologies (CISTI), pp. 1–7. IEEE (2018)
4. Alaiz-Moreton, H., Aveleira-Mata, J., Ondicol-Garcia, J., Muñoz-Castañeda, A.L., García, I., Benavides, C.: Multiclass classification procedure for detecting attacks on MQTT-IoT protocol. Complexity **2019**(1), 6516253 (2019)
5. Abbas, A., Khan, M.A., Latif, S., Ajaz, M., Shah, A.A., Ahmad, J.: A new ensemble-based intrusion detection system for internet of things. Arab. J. Sci. Eng. 1–15 (2022)
6. Makhija, J., Shetty, A.A., Bangera, A.: Classification of attacks on MQTT-based IoT system using machine learning techniques. In: Khanna, A., Gupta, D., Bhattacharyya, S., Hassanien, A.E., Anand, S., Jaiswal, A. (eds.) International Conference on Innovative Computing and Communications. AISC, vol. 1394, pp. 217–224. Springer, Singapore (2022). https://doi.org/10.1007/978-981-16-3071-2_19
7. Vijayan, P.M., Sundar, S.: An efficient catboost classifier approach to detect intrusions in mqtt protocol for internet of things. In: International Conference on Computational Intelligence and Data Engineering, pp. 255–267. Springer, Singapore (2022). https://doi.org/10.1007/978-981-99-0609-3_18
8. Al Hanif, A., Ilyas, M.: Effective feature engineering framework for securing MQTT protocol in IoT environments. Sensors **24**(6), 1782 (2024)
9. Bansal, R., Singh, J., Kaur, R., Ahuja, S.: Machine learning and its applications: a review. JASC: J. Appl. Sci. Comput. **6**(6), 1392–1398 (2020)
10. Wickramasinghe, I., Kalutarage, H.: Naive bayes: applications, variations and vulnerabilities: a review of literature with code snippets for implementation. Soft. Comput. **25**(3), 2277–2293 (2021)
11. Breslow, L.A., Aha, D.W.: Simplifying decision trees: a survey. Knowl. Eng. Rev. **12**(1), 1–40 (1997)
12. Sarica, A., Cerasa, A., Quattrone, A.: Random forest algorithm for the classification of neuroimaging data in Alzheimer's disease: a systematic review. Front. Aging Neurosci. **9**, 329 (2017)
13. Maftoun, M., Shadkam, N., Komamardakhi, S.S.S., Mansor, Z., Joloudari, J.H.: Malicious URL Detection using optimized Hist Gradient Boosting Classifier based on grid search method. arXiv preprint arXiv:2406.10286 (2024)
14. Pavlyshenko, B.: Using stacking approaches for machine learning models. In: 2018 IEEE Second International Conference on Data Stream Mining & Processing (DSMP), pp. 255–258. IEEE (2018)
15. Zhang, T., Fu, Q., Wang, H., Liu, F., Wang, H., Han, L.: Bagging-based machine learning algorithms for landslide susceptibility modeling. Nat. Hazards **110**(2), 823–846 (2022)
16. Li, X., Wang, L., Sung, E.: AdaBoost with SVM-based component classifiers. Eng. Appl. Artif. Intell. **21**(5), 785–795 (2008)

17. Dhaliwal, S.S., Nahid, A.A., Abbas, R.: Effective intrusion detection system using XGBoost. Information **9**(7), 149 (2018)
18. Alsaedi, A., Moustafa, N., Tari, Z., Mahmood, A., Anwar, A.: TON_IoT telemetry dataset: a new generation dataset of IoT and IIoT for data-driven intrusion detection systems. IEEE Access **8**, 165130–165150 (2020)

A Study of Artificial Intelligence Using Machine Learning Techniques in Healthcare Systems

Sonia Bhukra[1,2], Pardeep Kumar Jindal[4(✉)], Sharad Sharma[1], and Preeti Sharma[3]

[1] ECE Department, Maharishi Markandeshwar (Deemed to Be University), Mullana, Haryana, India
hodece@mmumullana.org
[2] ECE Department, Chandigarh Engineering College, Chandigarh Group of Colleges, Jhanjeri, Mohali 140307, Punjab, India
[3] ECE Department, Chitkara University Institute of Engineering and Technology, Chitkara University, Rajpura, Punjab, India
preeti.sharma@chitkara.edu.in
[4] Department of Interdisciplinary Courses in Engineering (DICE), Chitkara University Institute of Engineering and Technology (CUIET), Chitkara University , Rajpura, Punjab 140401, India
pardeep.alkra@gmail.com

Abstract. Advancements in artificial intelligence (AI) and machine learning (ML) have significantly improved health emergency forecasting, disease identification, population analysis, and understanding immune responses. While skepticism remains regarding the practical application and interpretation of ML in healthcare, its use is becoming more widespread. In this article, we provide an overview of ML-based methodologies and teaching strategies, including examples of three types of learning: reinforcement, supervised, and unsupervised. We also explore the application of ML in various medical fields, such as radiology, genetics, neuroimaging, and electronic medical records. Additionally, we address the challenges and risks of applying ML in healthcare, including concerns about system security and ethical considerations, and we offer suggestions for future applications.

Keywords: Healthcare · genomics · Support Vector machines · Machine Learning

1 Introduction

Since Alan Turing created the first artificially intelligent system that could learn in the 1950s, machine learning has been used [1]. Since its conception, The use of machine learning has applied to various fields, including facial recognition for protective services [2], efficiency improvements and risk reduction in public transportation [3, 4], and more lately in several instances fields related to healthcare and biotechnology [5–9]. In the healthcare and medical fields, locations where machine learning and artificial intelligence have already profoundly altered the business operations and regular existence, similar changes are anticipated. The success of recent innovations in this area

S. Pal et al. (Eds.): ICETSS 2024, CCIS 2610, pp. 317–325, 2026.
https://doi.org/10.1007/978-3-032-11488-4_25

has been astounding, and they have the potential to reduce doctors' workloads while also improving accuracy, prognosis, and care quality. Large medical organizations have also implemented methods based on machine learning. Our review aims to illustrate the benefits and drawbacks of artificial intelligence techniques applied in medical field [10–12]. With the arrival of modern machine learning technology floods the medical field, we want to provide a quick summary of several techniques of machine learning and highlight this the industries in which those methods can be most commonly used.

2 Overview of Machine Learning in Healthcare

The practice of training algorithms on data to generate Machine Learning is a subset of Artificial Intelligence that makes predictions or takes actions without being explicitly programmed. Figure 1 shows how there is potential for machine learning to transform ways that the healthcare sector recognizes, treats, and avoids ailments. A few possible uses of artificial intelligence in the field of medicine are as follows: To determine the probability of particular health consequences, like the start of chronic illnesses or hospital re-admissions, machine learning algorithms is able to examine data from other sources, such as claims data and electronic health records [13]. This can assist healthcare providers in identifying people who are at high risk and in taking proactive measures to avert unfavorable results. Medical image analysis tools such as CT scans and X-rays can be trained to assess data in order to help with patient diagnosis and treatment selection. Personalized medicine: Depending on a patient's particular genetics and medical history are examples of traits that machine learning can be used to predict which medicines will be most helpful [14]. Healthcare professionals can make better decisions about patient care by incorporating machine learning algorithms into clinical decision support systems. Management of population health: By analyzing data from huge populations with machine learning, it is possible to find trends and patterns that can be used as a basis for public health initiatives. Machine learning may strengthen the healthcare system as a whole, lower costs, and improve patient outcomes.

2.1 Data Sets on Health

Large collections of data regarding people's health are called healthcare datasets. These datasets frequently comprise a wide range of data items, such as medical history, results of diagnostic tests, prescription drug usage, and demographic data. They are employed for several purposes, such as clinical research, monitoring of the state of the public's health, and quality improvement initiatives [15]. There are two different kinds claims databases, which contain information on healthcare services received and their related costs, and Electronic health records, or EHRs for short, are digital copies a patient's medical information expenses. Clinical trial records, which provide details on participants, interventions, and outcomes, as well as disease registries, which list individuals who have particular illnesses or disorders, are also available. Healthcare is a huge and complex industry. Our research involved using healthcare data gathered from hospitals that are frequently used in machine learning studies. These specific datasets were chosen for their significance, scale and variety enabling examination and model development. We took care to prepare the data by normalizing it and addressing any information to uphold result accuracy. Additional information, on the dataset and preparation procedures can be found in the Methods section to promote reproducibility and clarity.

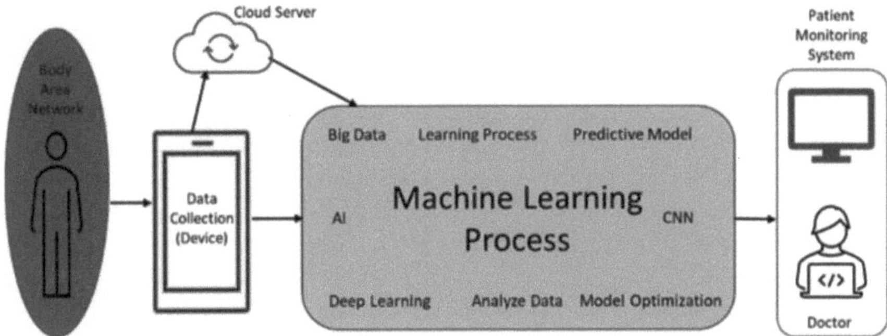

Fig. 1. Patient Monitoring System using Machine learning in healthcare

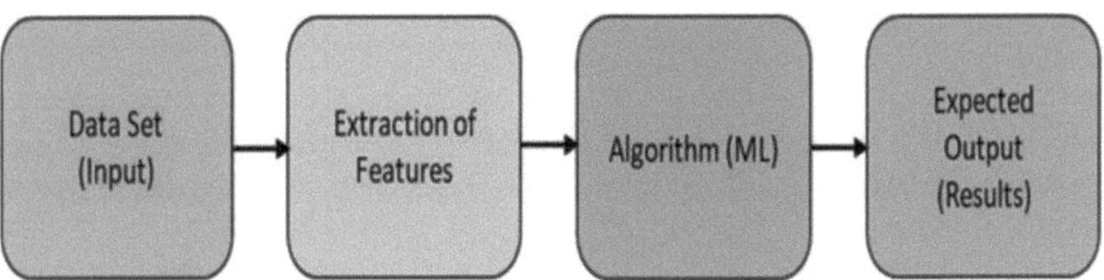

Fig. 2. Process diagram of Machine learning system in healthcare

2.2 Extractions from Features

The crucial process of picking the most pertinent properties from a dataset is known as feature extraction in machine learning [15]. Transforming unprocessed data into features with a high degree of pattern recognition capability. According to this method, the derived features have a better capability for recognition than the original data [16]. Using this method, the original data is analyzed to extract important features or attributes that will be used to train a machine learning algorithm to perform a certain task Fig. 2. SNE (t-distributed stochastic neighbor embedding), PCA (principal component analysis), LDA (linear discriminant analysis), auto encoders, filter approaches, and wrapper methods are some of the feature extraction techniques [17–22].

2.2.1 PCA

Data processing and artificial intelligence typically employ PCA, a dimensionality reduction technique. PCA's primary objective is to identify the biggest differences while lowering redundancy and noise in data [17].

2.2.2 LDA

The supervised dimensionality reduction method known as LDA is frequently used in statistical analysis, pattern recognition, and machine learning. LDA is primarily used to transform into a lower-dimensional space while transferring high-dimensional data maximizing class distinction.

2.2.3 t-SNE

t-Distributed Stochastic Neighbor Embedding (t-SNE) is a method of non-linear dimensionality reduction that is excellent for high-dimensional data visualization. Geoffrey Hinton and Laurens vander Maaten t-SNE was founded in 2008. It's main objective aims to keep the distances between adjacent data points when dimensionality is reduced in order to preserve local structures in the data. Unsupervised artificial neural networks with auto encoders are used for representation learning, feature extraction, and dimensionality reduction. The most advantageous uses of auto encoders are in Unsupervised pretraining, anomaly detection, and denoising for intricate neural networks. [20] In filter techniques, features are prioritized by assessing for instance, reciprocal information, correlation, or the Chi-Square test, among other statistical metrics. We then choose the most notable features. Two instances of filter techniques for example, the Information Gain (IG) technique and Pearson's correlation. [21] Wrapper methods are methodologies for feature selection employed in data analysis and machine learning. They want to know which combination of characteristics makes a certain machine learning system work as well as possible.

2.3 Trees of Decision

A decision trees [17, 18] classifier displays various options, outcomes, and end values using graphical tree information Fig. 3. This involves selecting one option from a list using a computer algorithm that computes probabilities. Using examples of training data and the matching category labels, the decision trees algorithm gets started. Recursively dividing the training set in-to subgroups based on feature values produces data that is purer in each subset than in the parent set [23].

Medical professionals usually make use of data mining tools to assist in the detection of heart issues. In terms of among the best machine-learning algorithms for detecting heart attacks is the decision tree due to its high sensitivity, specificity, and accuracy [24]. Utilizing the decision tree classification technique, heart disease has been widely identified and avoided. Pathak and Valan predicted with an accuracy of 88% for heart disease. A decision tree and eight patient data points were used. [25], while [26] also employed a heart disease prediction using a decision tree. In order to maintain important components and improve accuracy in mobile health technology, researchers in [17] used decision tree techniques to decrease data bulk by converting data into a more compact form.

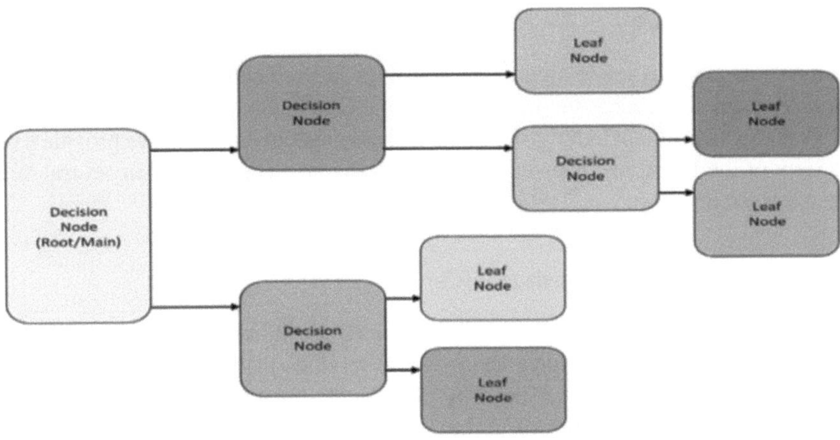

Fig. 3. Decision tree with various nodes and leaf nodes

2.4   Types of Learning Approaches

Most artificial intelligence and AI-based algorithms are constructed using various learning strategies as illustrated in Fig. 4. Unsupervised learning is one sub-type that is used to train algorithms for classification and prediction based on prior samples or outputs [27].

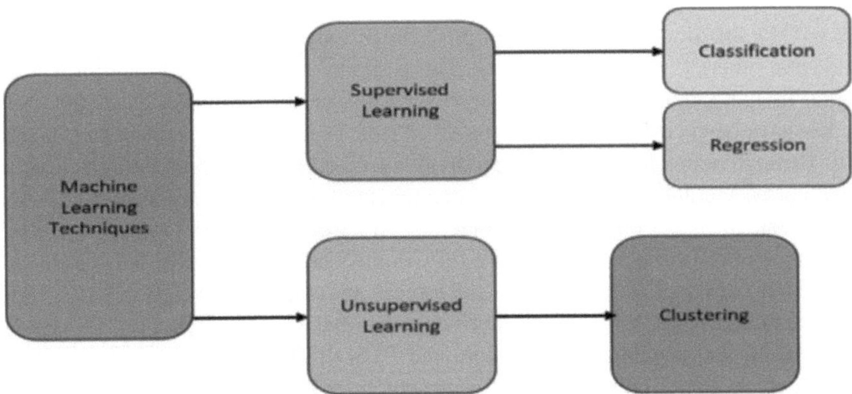

Fig. 4. Classification of Machine learning techniques

The training set for this learning technique includes features and the accompanying predictions, or outcomes, which is an essential distinction. The supervised learning approach, to put it simply, generalizes data the learnt model is then used to generate predictions utilizing the extra characteristics of the test data set. This process starts with the training set's characteristics and ends with a model with high accuracy in training-set outcomes prediction.

2.5 AI in Healthcare

Machine learning has made significant advances in the healthcare industry for many years. AI is able to predict the likelihood of illness [10], enhance picture segmentation and scanning. [23], aid in making decisions and aid in neuro-imaging. We provide a brief overview of the latest advances in Artificial Intelligence applications in several health sectors research below.

2.6 Electronic Health Records (EHR's)

EHRs were initially introduced through Lockheed as clinical information systems in the 1960s. Since then, there have been several rebuilds of the systems in an attempt to produce a system that is well-liked by those in the business. Billions were invested by the US federal government of dollars in support for the deployment of EHRs in every procedure in 2009 in an attempt to enhance the efficiency and standard of work [18]. EHRs were integrated into the systems of over 87% of office-based clinics in the country by 2015. Integrating structured feature data with BIG data from EHR systems has helped applications of deep learning like prescription patient history and refills analysis to forecast diagnoses [13].

2.7 Medical Imaging

Machine learning-based techniques have greatly advanced medical imaging by being applied to various imaging modalities, such as magnetic resonance, computed tomography (CT), imaging ultrasonography, positron emission tomography (PET), MRI, and x-ray, and others [28]. This is because data is digital and structured data formats like Digital Imaging and Communications in Medicine, or DICOM exist. Many ML-based models have been created for the diagnosis of rips, lesions, malignancies, and fractures [29]. Through better diagnosis, more individualized care, operational optimization, and other means, ML approaches provide strong tools for enhancing healthcare. But in order to overcome obstacles and guarantee that they ad-here to ethical and therapeutic norms, their implementation needs to be care-fully controlled. Additionally, ML-based techniques have been applied to determine and forecast the course of developmental disorders like autism and ADHD as well as neuro-degenerative diseases including, Parkinson's, Alzheimer's, and psychosis, depression, and PTSD [30]. Alzheimer's disease has no known cure, however preventative measures can be aided by early detection. 89.47% of the therapy response is accurate [24].

2.8 Genetic Engineering and Genomics

DNA system that adapts called The CRISPR (Clustered Regularly Inter-spaced Short Palindromic Repeats) gene has advanced genetic engineering science. The development of "programmable endonucleases" has greatly lowered the cost of genetic engineering while also streamlining genetic alteration and diagnostics. Despite its shortcomings, the current Cas (CRISPR associated protein) editing using CRISPR, e.g., Both Cas9 and Cas13a, has revolutionized genetic editing [13]. Numerous machine learning techniques have been created recently to anticipate Cas9 gene editing off-target mutations. In order to reduce error and account for the risk of off-target modifications, scientists are employing Cas9 to construct indicators of activity and more trustworthy Cas9 variations. These models include deep learning guided RNA synthesis tools, Cas9 variants with enhanced accuracy and fidelity, and hyper-accurate Cas9 variations [27].

3 Risk and Challenges

Although machine learning-based applications in healthcare have a unique and progressive potential, they also provide new risks, challenges, and reasons for healthy skepticism. The chance of a prediction error the main risk considerations discussed in this section include and its effects, the susceptibility of system privacy and protection, and even the unavailability of data to provide repeatable results [31, 32]. Among the most significant reliance on machine learning presents a problem for algorithms based on the probabilistic distribution and the potential for erroneous prognosis and diagnosis. Despite the fact that many aspects of healthcare are heavily dependent on probability and error probability, and there are grave consequences if ML-based processes result in a human death [14, 33]. A further obstacle to using algorithms for machine learning and deep learning in the healthcare industry is the unavailability combining superior testing and training data with sufficient sample sizes in order to allow for high predictability and replicability [30, 34, 35]. Deep learning and machine learning systems "learn" from data, hence it is imperative that high-quality data be used. Not only that, but the population sample can be limited in its dispersion, and it might not always be possible to get the massive significant large amounts of feature-rich data need for these learning networks as well as algorithms. Also, compared to samples, data from particular healthcare categories is far more diverse, fragmented, and contains a much higher number of features. When developing ML-based strategies and evaluating their results, these challenges should be properly taken into account.

4 Conclusion

The summary demonstrates the progress Machine Learning has made, but there's still space for important future expansion. Today's medical advances in machine learning often focus on helping doctors and specialists give patients better therapy with improved precision, quickness, and quality. The limitations can be resolved by creating machine learning algorithms designing and carrying out upgrades data gathering, storing and distribution, or with developing algorithms that handle amorphous data.

Future applications may potentially lead to affordable medical imaging and testing, decreasing health disparities and increasing access to services for nations and populations with low incomes.

References

1. Siddiqui, M.K., Morales-Menendez, R., Huang, X., Hussain, N.: A review of epileptic seizure detection using machine learning classifiers. Brain Inform. 7(1), 5 (2020)

2. Woldaregay, A.Z., ˚Arsand, E., Botsis, T., Albers, D., Mamykina, L., Hartvigsen, G.: Data-driven blood glucose pattern classification and anomalies detection: machine-learning applications in type 1 diabetes. Journal of medical Internet research **21**(5), 11030 (2019)

3. Kaouk, J.H., Garisto, J., Eltemamy, M., Bertolo, R.: Robot-assisted surgery for benign distal ureteral strictures: step-by-step technique using the sp® surgical system. BJU Int. **123**(4), 733–739 (2019)

4. Jindal, P.K., Kaur, M., Srivastava, D., Sharma, P., Kumar, M.: Cloud computing pattern identification with machine learning: a study. In: 2023 International Conference on Research Methodologies in Knowledge Management, Artificial Intelligence and Telecommunication Engineering (RMKMATE), pp. 1–6 (2023). IEEE

5. Tian, L., et al.: Radiomics-based machine-learning method for prediction of distant metastasis from soft-tissue sarcomas. Clin. Radiol. **76**(2), 158–219 (2021)

6. Qin, Z., Ye, H., Li, G.Y., Juang, B.-H.F.: Deep learning in physical layer communications. IEEE Wirel. Commun. **26**(2), 93–99 (2019)

7. Al-Hawawreh, M., Sitnikova, E., Aboutorab, N.: X-iiotid: a connectivity-agnostic and device-agnostic intrusion data set for industrial internet of things. IEEE Internet Things J. **9**(5), 3962–3977 (2021)

8. Cai, J., Luo, J., Wang, S., Yang, S.: Feature selection in machine learning: a new perspective. Neurocomputing **300**, 70–79 (2018)

9. Singh, G., Kaur, M., Jindal, P.K., Markan, R., Verma, V., Gupta, S.: Convolution neural network (cnn) layers in deep learning: a review. In: AIP Conference Proceedings, vol. 3121 (2024). AIP Publishing

10. Verma, K., et al.: Latest tools for data mining and machine learning. Int. J. Innovative Technol. Exploring Eng. **8**(9), 18–23 (2019)

11. Luo, X., Li, X., Wang, Z., Liang, J.: Discriminant autoencoder for feature extraction in fault diagnosis. Chemom. Intell. Lab. Syst. **192**, 103814 (2019)

12. Nagarajan, S., Muthukumaran, V., Murugesan, R., Joseph, R., Meram, M., Prathik, A.: Innovative feature selection and classification model for heart disease prediction. J. Reliab. Intell. Environ **8**(4), 333–343 (2022)

13. Bhuyan, H.K., Ravi, V., Brahma, B., Kamila, N.K.: Disease analysis using machine learning approaches in healthcare system. Heal. Technol. **12**(5), 987–1005 (2022)

14. Ali, F., et al.: A smart healthcare monitoring system for heart disease prediction based on ensemble deep learning and feature fusion. Inf. Fusion **63**, 208–222 (2020)

15. Schaar, M., et al.: How artificial intelligence and machine learning can help healthcare systems respond to covid-19. Mach. Learn. **110**, 1–14 (2021)

16. Kushwaha, P.K., Kumaresan, M.: Machine learning algorithm in healthcare system: a review. In: 2021 International Conference on Technological Advancements and Innovations (ICTAI), pp. 478–481 (2021). IEEE

17. Zamzami, I.F., Pathoee, K., Gupta, B.B., Mishra, A., Rawat, D., Alhalabi, W.: Machine learning algorithms for smart and intelligent healthcare system in society 5.0. Int. J. Intell. Syst. **37**(12), 11742–11763 (2022)

18. Patil, A.R., Mane, S.C., Patil, M.A., Gangurde, N.A., Rahate, P.G., Dhanke, J.A.: Artificial intelligence and machine learning techniques for diabetes healthcare: a review. J. Chem. Health Risks 1058–1063 (2024)

19. Hassan, M.M., Mollick, S., Yasmin, F.: An unsupervised cluster-based feature grouping model for early diabetes detection. Healthcare Anal. **2**, 100112 (2022)

20. Kabir, M.F., Chen, T., Ludwig, S.A.: A performance analysis of dimensionality reduction algorithms in machine learning models for cancer prediction. Healthcare Analyt. **3**, 100125 (2023)

21. Chang, V., Bhavani, V.R., Xu, A.Q., Hossain, M.: An artificial intelligence model for heart disease detection using machine learning algorithms. Healthcare Analyt. **2**, 100016 (2022)

22. Ramesh, T., Lilhore, U.K., Poongodi, M., Simaiya, S., Kaur, A., Hamdi, M.: Predictive analysis of heart diseases with machine learning approaches. Malays. J. Comput. Sci. 132–148 (2022)
23. Pathak, A.K., Arul Valan, J.: A predictive model for heart disease diagnosis using fuzzy logic and decision tree. In: Smart Computing Paradigms: New Progresses and Challenges: Proceedings of ICACNI 2018, Volume 2, pp. 131–140 (2020) Springer
24. Priya, R., Jinny, S.V.: Elderly healthcare system for chronic ailments using machine learning techniques–a review. Iraqi J. Sci. 3138–3151 (2021)
25. Sengan, S., Khalaf, O.I., Sharma, D.K., Hamad, A.A., et al.: Secured and privacy-based ids for healthcare systems on e-medical data using machine learning approach. Int. J. Reliable Qual. E-Healthcare (IJRQEH) 11(3), 1–11 (2022)
26. Shamshirband, S., Fathi, M., Dehzangi, A., Chronopoulos, A.T., Alinejad-Rokny, H.: A review on deep learning approaches in healthcare systems: taxonomies, challenges, and open issues. J. Biomed. Inform. 113, 103627 (2021)
27. Pillai, R., Oza, P., Sharma, P.: Review of machine learning techniques in health care. In: Proceedings of ICRIC 2019: Recent Innovations in Computing, pp. 103–111 (2020). Springer
28. Pallathadka, H., Mustafa, M., Sanchez, D.T., Sajja, G.S., Gour, S., Naved, M.: Impact of machine learning on management, healthcare and agriculture. Mater. Today: Proc. 80, 2803–2806 (2023)
29. Shaikh, S.G., Suresh Kumar, B., Narang, G.: Recommender system for health care analysis using machine learning technique: a review. Theor. Issues Ergon. Sci. 23(5), 613–642 (2022)
30. Albahri, A.S., et al.: Role of biological data mining and machine learning techniques in detecting and diagnosing the novel coronavirus (covid-19): a systematic review. J. Med. Syst. 44, 1–11 (2020)
31. Kondaka, L.S., Thenmozhi, M., Vijayakumar, K., Kohli, R.: An intensive healthcare monitoring paradigm by using Iot based machine learning strategies. Multimedia Tools Appl. 81(26), 36891–36905 (2022)
32. Ben-Israel, D., et al.: The impact of machine learning on patient care: a systematic review. Artif. Intell. Med. 103, 101785 (2020)
33. Garg, A., Mago, V.: Role of machine learning in medical research: a survey. Comput. Sci. Rev. 40, 100370 (2021)
34. Chate, P.J., et al.: The use of machine learning algorithms in recommender systems: a systematic review. IJRAR-Int. J. Res. Anal. Rev. (IJRAR) 6(2), 671–681 (2019)
35. Ramkumar, G., Seetha, J., Priyadarshini, R., Gopila, M., Saranya, G.: Iot-based patient monitoring system for predicting heart disease using deep learning. Measurement 218, 113235 (2023)
36. Alanazi, A.: Using machine learning for healthcare challenges and opportunities. Inform. Med. Unlocked 30, 100924 (2022)

An Innovative Collaborative Resource Sharing Platform

Arnav Kotiyal[1], Anubhawee Negi[1], Saurabh Bhardwaj[1], Pardeep Kumar Jindal[2(✉)] [iD],
and Puneet[3]

[1] Department of CSE Graphic Era (Deemed to Be University), Dehradun, India
[2] Department of Interdisciplinary Courses in Engineering (DICE), Chitkara University Institute of Engineering and Technology (CUIET), Chitkara University , Rajpura, Punjab 140401, India
pardeep.alkra@gmail.com
[3] Department of CSE, Chandigarh Engineering College, Chandigarh Group of Colleges, Jhanjeri, Mohali 140307, India

Abstract. In the era of digital connectivity and knowledge exchange, the Collaborative Resource Sharing Platform (CRSP) emerges as a pivotal solution to address the evolving needs of diverse user communities. As the digital era continues to shape how information is accessed and distributed, collaborative resource-sharing platforms have emerged as pivotal tools for fostering collective knowledge exchange and optimizing resource utilization across diverse user communities. The platform explores the design, development, and implementation of a Collaborative Resource Sharing Platform to foster seamless exchange of various items and collaborative endeavors across diverse domains. The study delves into the technical architecture, security measures, and scalability considerations, addressing the challenges associated with creating a robust and adaptable platform that accommodates a wide range of user needs. The platform integrates features such as real-time document sharing, version control, and interactive communication channels. Ultimately, this research contributes to the advancement of knowledge-sharing paradigms in the digital age, paving the way for more efficient and collaborative utilization of resources across diverse communities.

Keywords: Resource-sharing · Digital Ecosystem · Sharing Platform

1 Introduction

In the ever-evolving digital landscape, the significance of collaborative resource sharing cannot be overstated. The future of resource management–a world where collaboration is the key to unlocking boundless potential. Our Collaborative Resource Sharing Platform is a dynamic digital ecosystem designed to revolutionize the way individuals and organizations share and access valuable resources. In an era defined by connectivity, efficiency, and sustainability, our platform stands as a beacon of innovation. It's a space where sharing resources is not just a concept but a transformative force driving progress [1].

A collaborative resource-sharing platform is a digital ecosystem designed to facilitate the efficient sharing and utilization of various resources among individuals, organizations, or communities. These platforms leverage technology to connect users who have excess or underutilized resources with those who require them, fostering collaboration and reducing waste. In a world facing resource scarcity and environmental concerns, these platforms optimize the use of existing resources. By sharing rather than owning, users reduce waste and lower their carbon footprint. Sharing resources can significantly reduce costs for individuals, businesses, and communities. Users can access what they need without the expense of ownership, maintenance, or storage [2].

Not everyone has access to specialized tools, equipment, or expertise. Collaborative platforms provide a means for individuals and smaller businesses to access resources they may not afford or have space for. These platforms foster a sense of community and collaboration[3]. Users often form relationships with others who share similar interests or needs, leading to a stronger sense of belonging. Resource sharing aligns with sustainability goals by promoting the reuse and efficient utilization of assets. It reduces the need for excessive production, contributing to a more sustainable future. Collaborative platforms create economic opportunities for individuals and businesses. People can earn income by sharing their underutilized resources, whether it's renting out a spare room or sharing their expertise [4].

Sharing platforms can stimulate innovation by encouraging the development of new products, services, and business models that leverage the sharing economy. By sharing resources, users can de-clutter their lives and reduce the physical and mental burden of owning and managing numerous possessions [5]. In a culture of overconsumption, resource sharing encourages a more mindful approach to consumption, promoting a "less is more" mentality. Collaborative platforms can contribute to community resilience by ensuring that resources are available when needed, such as during emergencies or crises [6].

The findings of this research not only contribute to the theoretical understanding of collaborative resource-sharing platforms but offer practical insights for platform developers, policymakers, and users alike. By highlighting successful case studies and presenting a framework for effective platform governance, the paper aims to guide future developments in this rapidly evolving domain, fostering the creation of more inclusive, secure, and user-friendly collaborative resource-sharing platforms [7].

2 Literature Review

A literature survey for a collaborative resource-sharing platform encompasses exploring existing research, studies, and articles related to this topic. By examining scholarly works across disciplines such as computer science, information systems, and social sciences, this survey aims to establish a comprehensive understanding of the current state, trends, and challenges within the realm of collaborative resource sharing. Here, we present a concise overview of the key themes, findings, and trends in the literature surrounding collaborative resource-sharing platforms. By building upon the foundations laid by these diverse studies, we aim to contribute to the ongoing discourse surrounding the optimization and evolution of collaborative resource sharing in the digital age [8–11].

2.1 Emergence of the Sharing Economy

The sharing economy has gained prominence as a socioeconomic phenomenon driven by technological advancements. Research often examines the growth and evolution of sharing platforms in various sectors, including transportation, accommodation, and personal services.

2.2 Platform Characteristics and Models

The literature identifies key features of sharing platforms, such as user profiles, ratings, and reviews, as well as the role of trust mechanisms. Studies classify sharing economy platforms into different models, such as peer-to-peer (P2P), business-to-peer (B2P), and business-to-business (B2B).

2.3 Resource Types and Utilization

Research explores various types of shared resources, including physical assets (e.g., vehicles, tools), digital goods (e.g., software, media), and human resources (e.g., skills, expertise). Analysis of the factors influencing resource utilization and sharing behavior sheds light on user motivations.

2.4 Economic and Environmental Impacts

Literature assesses the economic implications of collaborative resource sharing, including cost savings and income generation for users. Environmental benefits, such as reduced resource consumption and emissions, are highlighted.

2.5 Community and Trust

The role of community and social capital in sharing platforms CRUD Operations: Implement APIs to Create, Read, Update, and Delete items. Ensure proper validation of input data.is a recurring theme, emphasizing the importance of social ties and trust in fostering sharing. Scholars examine the design of reputation systems and trust-building mechanisms.

3 Methodology

The methodology section of this research paper outlines the systematic approach undertaken to investigate the Collaborative Resource Sharing Platform (CRSP). This includes both qualitative and quantitative techniques to comprehensively analyze various dimensions of CRSPs, including design principles, implementation challenges, and user dynamics.

3.1 Frontend Development

HTML/CSS Structure: Start by creating the basic structure of the web pages using HTML for content and CSS for styling.

React Components: Use React to create reusable components for different sections of the platform, such as item listings, user profiles, search functionality, etc.

State Management: Implement state managem3ent using React Context or Redux to manage the application's state efficiently.

3.2 Backend Development

Framework Setup: Set up Django or Flask, define models to represent different items and users, and establish routes for handling API requests.

Database Configuration: Configure SQLite as the initial database system. Define models to represent items, users, transactions, and other necessary entities.

API Endpoints: Develop APIs to handle CRUD operations for items, user authentication, user interactions, and payment processing.

3.3 User Authentication and Authorization

User Registration and Login: Implement user registration and login functionalities using JWT or OAuth for secure authentication.

User Roles and Permissions: Utilize Django/Flask authentication libraries to manage user roles and permissions.

3.4 Item Management

Item Models: Define models to represent different types of items (books, electronics, etc.), including attributes like name, description, rental price, security fee, images, location details, etc.

CRUD Operations: Implement APIs to Create, Read, Update, and Delete items. Ensure proper validation of input data.

3.5 Transaction Handling

Payment Gateway Integration: Integrate payment gateways (such as Stripe, PayPal, etc.) to handle secure transactions for rental fees and security deposits.

OTP Verification: Implement OTP verification for both item pickup and return to ensure secure transactions.

The launching of CRSP involved designing a procedure that included the frontend and backend of the program as well as the users' identities the items they posted for sale and the transactions that happened on this program. Frontend development came down to creating a structure; thus, HTML and CSS were utilized to create a responsive layout. After which, cross-cutting concerns which included the creation of a reusable React component for sections of the platform including listing items, user profiles, and search were developed. Using React Context or Redux, state management was effectively and sustainably implemented on the site's application level [12–14].

On the backend layer, the Django or Flask framework was created, along with models, which refer to numerous items and users. SQLite was set up to act as the first database engine for storing miscellaneous information concerning items, users, transactions, and other relevant entities. To facilitate the functionalities that are to be implemented, we defined API endpoints for creating the items, reading and updating, deleting the items, user authentication, the actions of user interaction, and payment processing rate. This setup ensured there was a strong scalability that would support the functionality of the online platform [15, 16].

Security aspects were also important, particularly, user authentication and authorization as key parts of the platform. For the user registration and login, we provided the secure features of JWT (JSON Web Tokens) or OAuth. Furthermore, to control the user roles and access rights Django/Flask authentication frameworks were used to ensure that the users can only access the levels that entail their privileges [16–18].

Another key activity that was implemented under the CRSP was the ability to handle many transactions. Stripe or PayPal were used for payment entrances to deal with rent and security deposits or any other monetary transactions. As for the safety measures, we introduced OTP verification for the item's pickup and return to guarantee secure transactions occurring in our system [18].

4   Results and Discussion

Generally, the findings showed that the implementation of the CRSP yielded the desired outcomes in terms of design, function, and usage. The front-end development introduced flexibility in the user interface as the users of the platform could easily maneuver through the different sections of the platform. The possibility of implementing particular components using React and effective managing of states also have a positive impact on the usability of the application.

Figure 1 shows a performance comparison of CRUD operations between our collaborative platform and a traditional system. The comparison clearly demonstrates that our proposed system outperforms the traditional system. On the backend, Django/Flask equipped the platform with the ability to store and access the information resulting from the platform's operations with the aid of SQLite database. The API endpoints were good in terms of CRUD operations as they facilitated easy and proper interaction between the front end and back end of the application. Security measures involved in user authentication and authorization were found to be efficient and effective. Thus, JWT/OAuth for

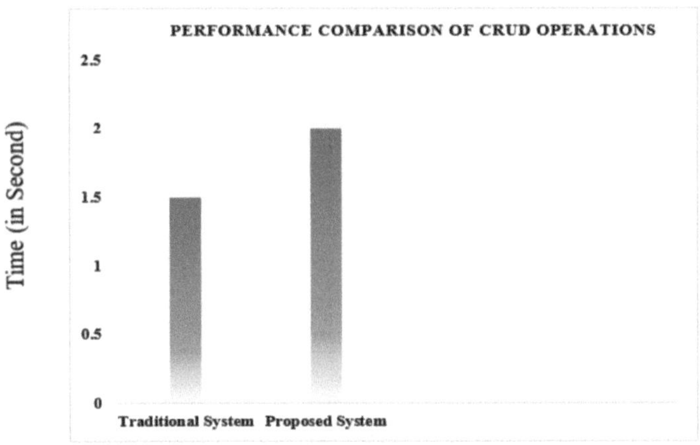

Fig. 1. Performance comparison of CRUD Operations

the authorization process means that all the user's information will be saved safely The restriction of user roles and permissions provides a proper navigation through different features of the platform. This setup ensured that users could safely carry out the resource sharing activity which was the focal point.

Item management was achieved with good results – item summarization is comprehensive and CRUD operations are accurate and stable. These item details and the validation processes facilitated the maintenance of quality item information for improved user experience. The handling of transactions was also appropriate with safe payment methods for the handling of transactions and OTP verification. Payment gateways' incorporation made the financial operations seamless, while the OTP verification helped to secure the items' pickups and returns.

4.1 User Interactions and Reviews

Chat System: Develop a real-time chat system using WebSockets or Socket.IO for users to communicate and arrange meetings regarding item rentals or purchases.

Reviews and Ratings: Allow users to leave reviews and ratings for items and other users to build trust within the platform community.

4.2 Location-Based Services

Geolocation Integration: Utilize geolocation APIs to determine users' nearest locations for item availability and pickup.

Location Filters: Implement filters and search functionalities based on location proximity to help users find items nearby.

4.3 Delivery Options

Delivery Services: Create an option for users to choose delivery services with associated delivery fees based on distance.

Order Tracking and Confirmation: Implement mechanisms to track and confirm delivered items for a seamless user experience.

4.4 Testing and Security

Testing: Conduct extensive unit tests, integration tests, and end-to-end tests for each component of the platform to ensure reliability and functionality.

Security Measures: Implement security best practices, including data encryption, input validation, and protection against common web vulnerabilities like SQL injection, XSS, and CSRF. Consider utilizing Go or Rust for critical security components.

4.5 Scaling and Deployment

Optimization: Optimize the application for scalability by employing techniques like caching, load balancing, and database optimization.

Deployment: Deploy the application on cloud services such as AWS, Azure, or Google Cloud for scalability and reliability.

4.6 User Education and Support

Documentation: Create user guides, FAQs, and comprehensive documentation to help users navigate the platform effectively.

Customer Support: Establish robust customer support channels to assist users with any issues they may encounter while using the platform.

The provision of tailored skill and knowledge recommendations further strengthens the system's utility. By leveraging data on industry trends and job requirements, the system delivers precise suggestions for skill acquisition, empowering users to align their learning efforts with market demands.

5 Conclusion

The CRSP development and the resultant studies thus reveal enhanced feasibility drawn from the implementation and analysis of resource-sharing systems. Quantitative and qualitative methods have been used in this study to deal with the research question decomposing it into areas including the design of CRSPs, implementation issues, and the behavior of CRSP users.

About the frontend development with HTML/CSS and React for the submission part of the application, the final look and feel of the application was made user-friendly and responsive. The actual management of the state was adequately achieved with React Context or Redux for the application, which made the platform strong.

On the backend, the programming languages used included Django/Flask framework and SQLite which helped assimilate all data. The availability of API endpoints for CRUD operations was defined aiming at providing smooth integration of the frontend and the backend parts. Security, achieved through the use of JWT/OAuth and Django/Flask libraries for user authentication and authorization, secured the platform for the users' resource-sharing activities.

The detailed models of the item management system secured the item data authenticity and after going through the CRUD operation, the integrity was held intact. For managing rents and security deposits safe and secure transactions, features like payment gateways and OTP verification were included for more effective transactions.

MATLAB code simulation of CRUD operations was quite informative in assessing the characteristics of the utilized conventional as well as proposed frameworks. Comparing the performance, it was observed that the proposed framework required less time to execute CRUD operations; which could offer enhancements over conventional systems.

References

1. Amazon.com. http://aws.amazon.com. [Accessed: 31-Jul-2024]
2. Klein, S., Higgins, A., Kipp, A., Mangan, A.: Drug living lab – supply chain security and control. In: Accelerating Global Supply Chains with IT-Innovation, Berlin, Heidelberg: Springer Berlin Heidelberg, pp. 109–122 (2011)
3. Kim, Y., Stanton, J.M.: Institutional and individual factors affecting scientists' data-sharing behaviors: a multilevel analysis: institutional and individual factors affecting scientists' data sharing behaviors: a multilevel analysis. J. Assoc. Inf. Sci. Technol. **67**(4), 776–799 (2016)
4. Henfridsson, O., Nandhakumar, J., Scarbrough, H., Panourgias, N.: Recombination in the open-ended value landscape of digital innovation. Inf. Organ. **28**(2), 89–100 (2018)
5. Parvinen, P., et al.: Advancing data monetization and the creation of data-based business models. Commun. Assoc. Inf. Syst. **47**(1), 25–49 (2020)
6. Ravulakollu, A.K., Urciuoli, L., Rukanova, B., Tan, Y.-H., Hakvoort, R.A.: Risk based framework for assessing resilience in a complex multi-actor supply chain domain. Supply Chain Forum Int. J. **19**(4), 266–281 (2018)
7. Picazo-Vela, S., Gutiérrez-Martínez, I., Duhamel, F., Luna, D.E., Luna-Reyes, L.F.: Value of inter-organizational collaboration in digital government projects. In: Digital Government and Public Management, London: Routledge, pp. 59–76 (2021)
8. Rukanova, B., Tan, Y.-H., Huiden, R., Ravulakollu, A., Grainger, A., Heijmann, F.: A framework for voluntary business-government information sharing. Gov. Inf. Q. **37**(4), 101501 (2020)
9. Jindal, P.K., Sandha, K.S.: Thermally-aware modeling and performance analysis of mixed-MWCNTB as very large scale integrated interconnects material for nano-electronic integrated circuits design. J. Nanoelectron. Optoelectron. **14**(9), 1255–1266 (2019)
10. Susha, I., Grönlund, Å., Van Tulder, R.: Data driven social partnerships: exploring an emergent trend in search of research challenges and questions. Gov. Inf. Q. **36**(1), 112–128 (2018)
11. Welch, E.W., Feeney, M.K., Park, C.H.: Determinants of data sharing in U.S. city governments. Gov. Inf. Q. **33**(3), 393–403 (2016)

12. Nuameesri*, S.: Assistant professor in information technology department, faculty of science and technology, Suan Sunandha Rajabhat University, Thailand., L. Poomhiran, and Ph.D. student in Information Technology, Faculty of Information Technology Department, King Mongkut's University of Technology North Bangkok, Thailand., "Improving back-end services for community enterprise through using Thai chatbot. Int. J. Innovative Technol. Exploring Eng. **9**(4), 1811–1816 (2020)
13. Jindal, P.K., Sandha, K.S.: Performance of Mixed-MWCNT structures as VLSI interconnect for nanometer technology nodes. ESC **1**(1), 2
14. Rajpoot, N.K., Singh, P., Pant, B.: Role of IoT and cloud in smart healthcare monitoring system for efficient resource utilization. In: Computer Science Engineering and Emerging Technologies, London: CRC Press, pp. 200–205 (2024)
15. Analysis on the Online English Teaching System based on Integrated Artificial Intelligence and 5G Technologies. Analysis on the online english teaching system based on integrated Artificial Intelligence. **5**
16. Awotunde, J.B., Jimoh, R.G., Folorunso, S.O., Adeniyi, E.A., Abiodun, K.M., Banjo, O.O.: Privacy and security concerns in IoT-based healthcare systems," in Internet of Things, Cham, Springer International Publishing, pp. 105–134 (2021)
17. Sandha, K.S., Jindal, P.K.: Performance analysis of piezoelectric sensor for perimetric intrusion detection. In: AIP Conference Proceedings (Vol. 3121, No. 1). AIP Publishing (2024)
18. Goel, S., Singh, P., More, P.: Smart parking model using IoT and cloud computing. In: 14th International Conference on Materials Processing and Characterization 2023 (2024)

Prediction of Heart Disease Based on Weighted Combination of Binary Classifier

Aditya Mishra[1]([⊠]) and Sabyasachi Patra[2]

[1] Aspire Hospital, Bhubaneswar, Odisha, India
adityamishra.mbbs@gmail.com
[2] IIIT Bhubaneswar, Bhubaneswar, Odisha, India
sabyasachi@iiit-bh.ac.in

Abstract. Cardiovascular diseases remain the leading cause of death worldwide. Early detection and continuous monitoring by healthcare professionals are critical in reducing mortality rates. This study analyses various patient data to predict heart disease accurately. Key indicators such as age, gender, smoking habits, obesity, diet, physical activity levels, stress, chest pain type and duration, diastolic blood pressure, diabetes, troponin levels, and electrocardiogram (ECG) readings play a vital role in diagnosing heart conditions. We employ a diverse set of artificial intelligence techniques, including Naïve Bayes (NB), K-nearest neighbour (K-NN), logistic regression (LR), decision tree (DT), random forest (RF), support vector machine (SVM), and multilayer perceptron (MLP), to ensure a comprehensive analysis. This research introduces a cardiovascular disease detection system that explores a weighted combination of these seven machine-learning (ML) approaches to enhance prediction accuracy. The system is also validated using the Cleveland and Statlog datasets, two widely recognized open-access databases. Performance was assessed through 10-fold cross-validation, with the proposed method achieving an accuracy of 98.31%, a precision of 98.87%, a recall of 98.28%, and an F1-score of 98.58%, outperforming existing approaches.

Keywords: Heart Disease · Artificial Intelligence · Binary Classification

1 Introduction

The World Health Organization predicts that cardiovascular diseases will result in 12 million fatalities annually on a global scale [1]. Cardiovascular disease encompasses many disorders that impact arteries and blood vessels to disrupt the heart's function. The current healthcare system is transforming substantially with the introduction of artificial intelligence (AI) and machine learning (ML).

The effectiveness and accuracy of medical professionals substantially increased with ML [2]. The integration of machine learning classification algorithms has been initiated in clinical therapy to extract knowledge. Medical professionals can use accurate heart disease prediction strategies to enhance their decision-making and patient diagnosis. Machine Learning-based approaches, such as NB, K-NN, LR, DT, RF, SVM, MLP and

S. Pal et al. (Eds.): ICETSS 2024, CCIS 2610, pp. 335–344, 2026.
https://doi.org/10.1007/978-3-032-11488-4_27

fuzzy logic (FL), are extensively used for the early detection of heart disease [3, 4]. Expert medical decision systems powered by machine learning have drastically cut the death toll from cardiovascular disease. Prior research has primarily focused on examining classifiers' ability to identify heart disease instances [5, 6] accurately. However, research has not yet attempted to investigate the collective impact of multiple classifiers on heart disease prediction. Research in analogous disciplines demonstrates that the choice of crucial characteristics significantly impacts the performance of the classifier system. Determining the optimal combination of individual predictions is vital rather than using each classifier separately. Hence, the objective of this study is to integrate the predicted outcomes of separate classifiers to predict heart disease in a holistic manner.

The dataset has been analyzed for thirteen variables, including age, gender, chest pain type, resting blood pressure (BP), serum cholesterol, fasting blood sugar, resting electrocardiogram (ECG), thalac, exang and old peak. The dataset includes all attributes and is utilized to train and create seven machine-learning algorithms. This study has employed widely-used machine learning approaches, including NB, KNN, LR, DT, RF, SVM and MLP models, to predict heart disease. LR models have been employed to elucidate phenomena in various domains of clinical research [7, 8]. NB is commonly utilized in the health domain to conduct predictive modelling for several diseases [9]. The KNN algorithm is mostly used for classification tasks in supervised learning and is widely used for disease prediction [10]. The RF algorithm is employed in medical industries to select the most reliable predictors since it has demonstrated favorable prediction performance [11]. SVM finds extensive use in the medical field, particularly in areas like breast cancer [12], skin cancer [13], and illness prognosis. The DT approach is beneficial for early cancer detection [14], identifying cardiac arrhythmias [15], predicting stroke outcomes [16], and aiding in chronic illness management [17]. MLP has been effectively utilized in diverse medical domains, such as disease prognosis [18], identification of medical images [19], and gene identification [20]. Based on classification accuracy, this research assessed each classifier's performance. This article also highlights some other learning strategies that can be used to predict heart diseases. Various deep learning architectures, including convolutional neural networks, DenseNet201, InceptionResNetV2, VGG16, VGG19, and Xception, are used for prognostic survival prediction in colorectal cancer (CRC) [21]. Deep-learned feature extraction techniques and ensemble learning are used to diagnose retinal disorders and diagnose eye illnesses [22]. ROAD (Robotics-Assisted Onsite Data Collecting) systems have higher accuracy than other deep neural networks, such as DenseNet201, InceptionResNetV2, MobileNetV2, VGG16, and VGG19 [23]. Sharma et al. demonstrate that, compared to the conventional deep learning approach, the federated learning (FL) approach performs better [24]. Confidentiality Preserved Federated Learning framework and Privacy-Preserving Federated Learning framework performed better than traditional distributed deep learning-based classifiers regarding accuracy and loss while keeping data secure [25, 26].

2 Methodology

Prompt identification of cardiovascular illness is crucial for initiating medical intervention. To meet this criterion, the strategy outlined in this paper explores different machine learning techniques that will allow individuals to identify their risk at an early stage proactively.

2.1 Overview of Prediction Model

The primary objective of this manuscript is to build a model capable of accurately and autonomously predicting cardiovascular disease. The research approach to attaining the research goal comprises the collection of the right data, processing of the row data, appropriate feature selection and extraction, several ML algorithms, and finally, analysis of their performance. The procedure commences with gathering patient data. Data pre-processing has been conducted to address missing values and remove unclear and ambiguous data. Feature extraction and appropriate feature selection strategies have been utilized to identify the most pertinent properties. Diverse ML algorithms have been employed to obtain individual outcomes, which are subsequently merged using a proposed weighted average method to derive the aggregated probability of heart disease. A comparative examination of various machine learning approaches is performed to determine the significant and precise technique for developing a robust heart disease prediction model.

2.2 Cardiovascular Disease Datasets

This work utilizes the Cleveland and Statlog datasets, consisting of 14 attributes and two classes. The Statlog dataset consists of 270 samples, with 150 samples indicating the absence of heart disease and 120 samples indicating the presence of heart disease [27]. The Cleveland database consists of 303 instances, with 164 examples without cardiac disease and 139 instances indicating positive cases.

A detailed description of the CVD dataset is given below.

Age: The age of the patient can be found in these characteristics.

Gender: This attribute has a binary representation, with 1 indicating male and 0 indicating female.

Type of chest pain: The chest discomfort have the following characteristics: 0: normal, 1: usual angina 2: discomfort unrelated to angina 3: without symptoms.

Resting blood pressure (BP): The level of blood pressure when the body is at rest is measured in millimeters of mercury (mmHg).

Serum cholesterol: This function measures cholesterol in different patients, expressed in milligrams per deciliter (mg/dl).

Fasting blood sugar: The fasting blood sugar feature represents blood sugar values above 120 mg/dl as 1 for real cases and 0 for false cases.

Resting electrocardiogram: The resting electrocardiogram (0–2) provides various readings resulting from the patient's examination, such as normal, abnormal, and left ventricular hypertrophy.

Thalac: This attribute pertains to patients with elevated heart rates.

Exang: A value of 0 represents no exercise-induced angina, while 1 represents exercise-induced angina.

Old peak: This attribute compares Exercise-induced ST depression to the resting state.

Dependent variable: The estimation of the dependent variable is based on two key components. The target value of 1 demonstrates that the person is at risk of heart disease, while '0' signifies that the person is healthy.

2.3 Feature Selection

Finding the medical characteristics that improve the accuracy of heart disease prediction is the primary goal of this section. Improved data quality, faster prediction models, better predictive performance, and a more practical and user-friendly data-gathering method are just a few of the many advantages of feature selection.

2.4 Machine Learning Techniques

The proposed cardiovascular disease prediction approach utilizes the outcomes of seven binary classifiers to obtain the final prediction result. This study has employed widely used machine learning approaches, including Naïve Bayes (NB), K-Nearest Neighbor (KNN), Logistic Regression (LR), Decision Tree (DT), Random Forest (RF), Support Vector Machine (SVM) and MultiLayer Perceptron (MLP) models, to predict cardiac abnormalities.

2.5 Performance Metrics

This study employed model creation to assess the effectiveness and utility of several categorization algorithms for predicting cardiac disease. To assess the performance of a model, a confusion matrix and various pertinent metrics are employed. These metrics include True Positives (TP), False Positives (FP), True Negatives (TN), and False Negatives (FN). Using this confusion matrix, accuracy, precision, recall, and F1-score can be computed.

2.6 Weighted Combination of Binary Classifier (WCBC)

The proposed method combined the result of seven different binary classifiers, as shown in Fig. 1. Input features extracted from the clinical dataset are fed to the individual classifier. Each classifier produces the result in binary form (+ve, represented by 1, indicates the patient has heart disease, and -ve, represented by 0, indicates no cardiac issues). The predicted results from individual classifiers are multiplied by a predefined weight of that classifier, and the weighted combination of the binary classifiers is used to compute the chances of a patient having heart disease. In order to lower the impact of FP and FN, a correction factor is introduced in the proposed weighted combination method.

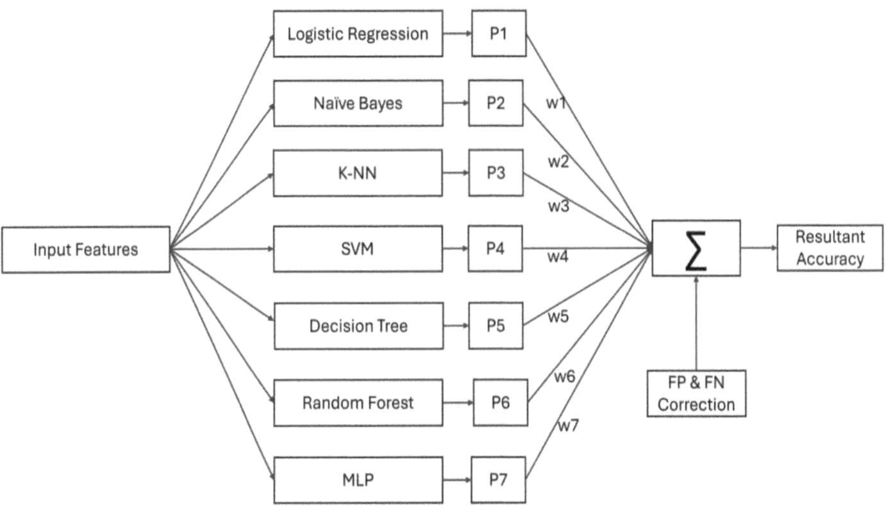

Fig. 1. Weighted Combination of Binary Classifier (WCBC)

The procedure for computing the weight of the individual classifier in WCBC using the result of the confusion matrix is demonstrated in Table 1. The weight of a classifier is directly proportional to the accuracy it achieves in 10-fold cross-validation of the Cleveland dataset. The sum of the weight of all the classifiers is always 1.

The procedure for computing the chances of a patient having heart disease is demonstrated in Table 2.

Heart disease prediction % (HDPP) = WP – AFPC + AFNC

$$HDPP = \sum_{i=1}^{7} w_i p_i - \sum_{i=1}^{7} \frac{FP_i}{TP_i + FP_i} p_i + \sum_{i=1}^{7} \frac{FN_i}{TN_i + FN_i} p_i' \tag{1}$$

WP represents the weight prediction of individual classifiers, and AWP represents aggregate weight prediction. FPC represents false positive correction, and AFPC represents aggregate false positive correction. FNC represents false negative correction, and AFNC represents aggregate false negative correction. False positives enhance the + ve result, and hence, false positive correction is subtracted from the resultant weighted prediction, and false negatives decrease the chances of + ve result, and hence, it is added to the resultant weighted prediction. In order to compute the performance of WCBC in terms of evaluation metrics, if the chances of heart disease are found to be more than 50%, it is treated as a + ve result; otherwise, the result is negative.

Table 1. Computation of weight of each classifier for WCBC

Classifier	True Positive	False Positive	True Negative	False Negative	Accuracy	Weight of Classifier in WCBC (w)
LR	TP1	FP1	TN1	FN1	AC1	AC1/TAC
NB	TP2	FP2	TN2	FN2	AC2	AC2/TAC
K-NN	TP3	FP3	TN3	FN3	AC3	AC3/TAC
SVM	TP4	FP4	TN4	FN4	AC4	AC4/TAC
DT	TP5	FP5	TN5	FN5	AC5	AC5/TAC
RF	TP6	FP6	TN6	FN6	AC6	AC6/TAC
MLP	TP7	FP7	TN7	FN7	AC7	AC7/TAC
Total					TAC = $\sum$AC	

Table 2. Computation of weighted prediction, false positive and false negative correction

Classifier	Weight of Classifier in WCBC (w)	Prediction (p) (0 or 1)	Weighted prediction (WP) = w*p	FP Correction (FPC) = (FP/(TP + FP))*p	FN Correction (FNC) = (FN/(TN + FN))*p'
LR	w1	p1	wp1	FPC1	FNC1
NB	w2	p2	wp2	FPC2	FNC2
K-NN	w3	p3	wp3	FPC3	FNC3
SVM	w4	p4	wp4	FPC4	FNC4
DT	w5	p5	wp5	FPC5	FNC5
RF	w6	p6	wp6	FPC6	FNC6
MLP	w7	p7	wp7	FPC7	FNC7
Aggregate			AWP = $\sum$wp	AFPC = $\sum$FPC / $\sum$p	AFNC = $\sum$FNC / $\sum$p'

3 Training and Testing

This study uses an 80% training data set and reserves the remaining 20% for testing. During data training, the model often exhibits a high training accuracy, indicating that it performs with a high level of precision on the training set. However, its performance is notably lower when assessed on unknown data. Thus, 10-fold cross validation is utilized to mitigate performance problems. The test set is a subset of the available information used to evaluate the model's performance. It is often the variable that the data depends on. The performance of cross-validated data during testing will vary depending on the model employed. Therefore, each model's performance is optimized.

4 Result and Discussion

The results and advantages of the stacking approach proposed in this study are elaborated in this section. The tests were conducted using Python version 3.9.7 consistently. The sklearn 1.0.2 toolbox is utilized in this inquiry for model prediction. We aimed to assess the predictive accuracy of seven machine learning (ML)-based models in determining the risk of cardiovascular disease (CVD). The results indicated that each individual exhibited high levels of discrimination and that all of them were appropriately calibrated. SVM outperformed other machine learning models in predicting the risk of CVD. We have applied these machine learning approaches on the Cleveland dataset containing 303 instances to find the accuracy of each model. A 10-fold cross-validation mechanism is used to overcome the biases of the data. After computing the accuracy of each model, the weights are assigned proportional to the accuracy, and the sum of the weights must be equal to 1, as shown in Table 3.

Table 3. Computation of weight of each classier from Cleveland dataset

Classifier	True Positive	False Positive	True Negative	False Negative	Accuracy	Weight of Classifier in WCBC (w)
LR	151	10	129	13	0.9241	0.1434
NB	140	7	132	24	0.8977	0.1393
K-NN	151	8	131	13	0.9307	0.1444
SVM	158	5	134	6	0.9637	0.1495
DT	154	13	126	10	0.9241	0.1434
RF	140	16	123	24	0.8680	0.1347
MLP	152	7	132	12	0.9373	0.1454

WCBC computes the probability of a person having heart disease using Eq. (1). This result provides better feedback to clinicians so that they can make proper decisions for further treatment of the person. To evaluate these performance metrics, binary results are required in WCBC. The probability (%) of having heart disease predicted by WCBC is converted into binary form by comparing the value with the probability (%) of not having heart disease. The relative performance of the proposed model WCBC as compared to seven classifiers is shown in Tables 4 and 5.

The risk prediction models currently utilized in cardiovascular disease (CVD) fields were constructed using conventional statistical approaches, as numerous research has demonstrated. However, these models have been shown to be incorrect when applied to populations outside of their original context. Machine learning algorithms have demonstrated their superiority in the field of cardiology for extracting predictions from large datasets that are notoriously challenging to comprehend. Machine learning algorithms do not make any initial assumptions, allowing them to utilize any data to create precise and robust models. As a result, machine learning (ML) has the ability to represent

Table 4. Relative performance of classifiers in Cleveland dataset

Classifier	Accuracy %	Precision (%)	Recall (%)	F1-score (%)
LR	92.41	93.79	92.07	92.92
NB	89.77	95.24	85.37	90.03
K-NN	93.07	94.97	92.07	93.50
SVM	96.37	96.93	96.34	96.64
DT	92.41	92.22	93.90	93.05
RF	86.80	89.74	85.37	87.50
MLP	93.73	95.60	92.68	94.12
WCBC	98.31	98.87	98.28	98.58

Table 5. Relative performance of classifiers in Statlog datasets

Classifier	Accuracy %	Precision (%)	Recall (%)	F1-score (%)
LR	91.48	88.19	93.33	90.69
NB	88.89	86.89	88.33	87.6
K-NN	92.59	89.68	94.17	91.87
SVM	95.56	93.55	96.67	95.08
DT	91.85	87.69	95	91.2
RF	87.04	84	87.5	85.71
MLP	93.33	89.68	94.17	91.87
WCBC	98.31	96.3	97.94	97.12

intricate connections between outcomes and predictors, which are sometimes difficult to articulate using traditional statistical techniques. Machine learning has the capability to detect previously unknown genetic and physical characteristics for many cardiovascular diseases, as well as find new elements that contribute to the risk of developing cardiovascular diseases. In the future, cardiologists may enhance their clinical decision-making by employing machine learning models instead of the already employed CVD risk stratifications. Conversely, the majority of ML models may pose challenges for medical practitioners in terms of comprehension and utilization, hence restricting their frequency of application in clinical environments.

5   Conclusion

Accurate prediction of cardiovascular disease is crucial in supporting clinicians with the early detection of these conditions. Rather than replacing clinicians, machine learning complements their expertise, enhancing decision-making and treatment processes.

Additionally, machine learning can help reduce the costs associated with a wide range of expensive clinical and laboratory tests, alleviating the financial burden on patients and the healthcare system. This paper presents novel, robust, and efficient machine-learning algorithms to predict cardiovascular disease (CVD) by analyzing symptoms, signs, and patient data from hospital records. The goal is to improve early detection of CVD and enable timely intervention for better patient outcomes. The proposed technique outperforms traditional state-of-the-art approaches accuracy and precision for categorizing and predicting heart disease. Future research is necessary to evaluate the effectiveness of these machine-learning algorithms on datasets with a broader range of modifiable and non-modifiable risk factors. This research is vital for developing a more accurate and reliable system for the early prediction and diagnosis of heart diseases.

Disclosure of Interests. The authors have no competing interests.

References

1. Soni, J., Ansari, U., Sharma, D., Soni, S.: Predictive data mining for medical diagnosis: an overview of heart disease prediction. Int. J. Comput. Appl. **17**(8), 43–48 (2011)
2. Koh, H.C., Tan, G.: Data mining applications in healthcare. J. Healthcare Inform. Manag. **19**(2), 65.35 (2011)
3. Nazir, S., Shahzad, S., Mahfooz, S., Nazir, M.: Fuzzy logic based decision support system for component security evaluation. Int. Arab J. Inf. Technol. **15**(2), 224–231 (2018)
4. Haq, A.U., Li, J.P., Memon, M.H., Nazir, S., Sun, R.: A hybrid intelligent system framework for the prediction of heart disease using machine learning algorithms. Mobile Inform. Syst. **2018**, 1–21 (2018)
5. Rajdhan, A., Agarwal, A., Sai, M., Ravi, D., Ghuli, P.: Heart disease prediction using machine learning. Int. J. Res. Technol. **9**(04), 659–662 (2020)
6. Jindal, H., Agrawal, S., Khera, R., Jain, R., Nagrath, P.: Heart disease prediction using machine learning algorithms. IOP Conf. Ser.: Mater. Sci. Eng. **1022**(1), 012072 (2021)
7. Jiang X., El-Kareh R., Ohno-Machado L: Improving predictions in imbalanced data using pairwise expanded logistic regression. AMIA Annual Symposium Proceedings: pp. 625–634. (2011). https://www.ncbi.nlm.nih.gov/pmc/articles/PMC3243279/
8. Reed, P., Wu, Y.: Logistic regression for risk factor modelling in stuttering research. J. Fluency Disord. **38**, 88–101 (2013). https://doi.org/10.1016/j.jfludis.2012.09.003
9. Langarizadeh, M., Moghbeli, F.: Applying naive bayesian networks to disease prediction: a systematic review. Acta Informatica Medica **24**(5), 364 (2016)
10. Chandel, K., Kunwar, V., Sabitha, S., Choudhury, T., Mukherjee, S.: A comparative study on thyroid disease detection using K-nearest neighbor and naive bayes classification techniques. CSI Trans. on ICT **4**, 313–319 (2016)
11. Badr, E., Almotairi, S., Salam, M.A., Ahmed, H.: New sequential and parallel support vector machine with grey wolf optimizer for breast cancer diagnosis. Alex. Eng. J. **61**(3), 2520–2534 (2022)
12. Sethy, P.K., Behera, S.K., Kannan, N.: Categorization of common pigmented skin lesions (CPSL) using multi-deep features and support vector machine. J. Digit. Imaging **35**(5), 1207–1216 (2022)
13. Aszhari, F.R., Rustam, Z., Subroto, F., Semendawai, A.S.: Classification of thalassemia data using random forest algorithm. J. Phys.: Conf. Ser. **1490**(1), 012050 (2020)

14. Afolayan, J.O., Adebiyi, M.O., Arowolo, M.O., Chakraborty, C., Adebiyi, A.A.: Breast cancer detection using particle swarm optimization and decision tree machine learning technique. In: Intelligent Healthcare, pp. 61–83. Springer, Singapore (2022)

15. Sahoo, S., Subudhi, A., Dash, M., Sabut, S.: Automatic classification of cardiac arrhythmias based on hybrid features and decision tree algorithm. Int. J. Autom. Comput. **17**(4), 551–561 (2020)

16. Imura, T., et al.: Decision tree algorithm identifies stroke patients likely discharge home after rehabilitation using functional and environmental predictors. J. Stroke Cerebrovasc. Dis. **30**(4), 105636 (2021)

17. Mishra, S., Mallick, P.K., Tripathy, H.K., Bhoi, A.K., González-Briones, A.: Performance evaluation of a proposed machine learning model for chronic disease datasets using an integrated attribute evaluator and an improved decision tree classifier. Appl. Sci. **10**(22) (2020)

18. Jahangir, M., Afzal, H., Ahmed, M., Khurshid, K., Nawaz, R.: An expert system for diabetes prediction using auto tuned multilayer perceptron. In: Intelligent Systems Conference (IntelliSys), pp. 722–728. IEEE (2017)

19. Xing, W., et al.: CM-SegNet: a deep learning-based automatic segmentation approach for medical images by combining convolution and multilayer perceptron. Comput. Biol. Med. **147**, 105797 (2022)

20. Seo, H., Cho, D.H.: Cancer-related gene signature selection based on boosted regression for multilayer perceptron. IEEE Access **8**, 64992–65004 (2020)

21. Verma, J., et al.: From slides to insights: Harnessing deep learning for prognostic survival prediction in human colorectal cancer histology. Open Life Sci. **18**(1), 20220777 (2023)

22. Verma, J., et al.: A hybrid images deep trained feature extraction and ensemble learning models for classification of multi disease in fundus images. In: Nordic Conference on Digital Health and Wireless Solutions, pp. 203–221 (2024)

23. Popli, R., Kansal, I., Verma, J., Khullar, V., Kumar, R., Sharma, A.: Road: Robotics-assisted onsite data collection and deep learning enabled robotic vision system for identification of cracks on diverse surfaces. Sustainability **15**(12), 9314 (2023)

24. Sharma, A., et al.: Fire detection in urban areas using multimodal data and federated learning. Fire **7**(4), 104 (2024)

25. Kumar, R., Popli, R., Khullar, V., Kansal, I., Sharma, A.: Confidentiality preserved federated learning for indoor localization using wi-fi fingerprinting. Buildings **13**(8), 2048 (2023)

26. Arora, P., et al.: Privacy-preserving federated learning system (f-PPLS) for military focused area classification. Multimedia Tools Appl. 1–27 (2024)

27. Meshref, H.: Cardiovascular disease diagnosis: A machine learning interpretation approach. Int. J. Adv. Comput. Sci. Appl. **10**, 258–269 (2019)

A Review of AI-Based YOLO Approach for Sewage Monitoring

Saniya Ansari[1], Ankush Kadu[1], Manwinder Singh[2(✉)], Anudeep Goraya[2], Balraj Singh[3], Nikhil Nikalje[1], and Harsimran Jit kaur[4]

[1] ADYP School of Engineering, Lohegaon, Pune, India
[2] School of Electronics and Electrical Engineering, Lovely Professional University, Jalandhar, Punjab, India
`manwinder.25231@lpu.co.in`
[3] School of Computer Science Engineering, Lovely Professional University, Jalandhar, Punjab, India
[4] Chitkara University Institute of Engineering and Technology, Chitkara University, Chandigarh, Punjab, India

Abstract. Water quality monitoring and sewage conservation are vital in addressing pollution and urbanization challenges. Traditional methods of sewer maintenance are often inefficient, prompting the need for advanced automated solutions. This paper examines the application of Artificial Intelligence (AI) and Mobile Robotics in sewage conservation, with a focus on the YOLO (You Only Look Once) object detection models. YOLO's real-time detection capabilities provide significant advantages in identifying sewer blockages such as grease, plastics, and tree roots. We explore the evolution of YOLO models, from YOLOv3's Darknet-53 architecture and feature pyramid networks to YOLOv4's CSPDarknet53 and PANet, which enhance detection accuracy and efficiency. These models optimize object detection at different scales, offering improved performance for real-world sewage monitoring. The integration of YOLO-based robotic systems into urban infrastructure reduces the need for manual intervention, improves operational safety, and contributes to sustainable urban development. These AI-driven systems represent a significant leap forward in automating sewage management and ensuring effective water quality monitoring.

Keywords: Artificial Intelligence · Sewage Conservation Experiments · YOLO

1 Introduction

Water is essential to ecosystems & existence; its quality impacts the well-being of animals and humans. Combining processes that are natural, such as soil, the weathering process, and human activities, such as rapid industrialization, urbanization, including cultivation, have a significant impact on the polluting of water resources with a wide range of pollutants. There is special worry about the destiny of the environment of toxic metals and their effects on human health, which have been associated with metabolism, persistence,

S. Pal et al. (Eds.): ICETSS 2024, CCIS 2610, pp. 345–358, 2026.
https://doi.org/10.1007/978-3-032-11488-4_28

non-biodegradability as well as toxic. Alloys' capacity to flow through cell membranes produces a variety of problems for numerous biological functions in cells, posing a threat to human and animal health [1]. The water environment is the environment in which waterways, lakes, seas, and other types of water features exist. Water quality will suffer as a result of changes in the water environment [2]. Test the chemical and physical aspects of quality to see if the water environment is contaminated totally. The water environment is an essential component of the ecosystem and serves as the foundation for human life and growth. However, with human research and modern technology, the marine environment is becoming progressively polluted [3]. In the realm of surface water quality monitoring, on-site technologies that are more quickly, cheaper, and generally more user-friendly are becoming increasingly relevant [4].

1.1 Need of Sewage Surveillance

Oceans and rivers cover over 71% of the Earth's surface and are home to billions of different forms of aquatic life, but humans have not been kind to the aquatic environment. Water pollution has been accumulating for decades as a result of human irresponsibility. Water contamination can be caused by industrially generated sewage, contaminants that are radioactive, and throw away garbage. As civilization urbanizes, the loss of residential sewage, corporate sewage, including agricultural chemicals or fertilizers will pollute the basin's water quality. When the total nitrogen, total phosphorus, and ammonia nitrogen levels in a watershed's water quality exceed the watershed's standard, algae or other plankton in the water multiply, lowering the dissolved oxygen concentration and killing fish and other creatures [5, 6]. According to the River Basin Management Plans, it is critical to maintain water quality and, if possible, improve the biological and chemical status. Current monitoring systems are particularly vulnerable to hazardous events such as direct sewage discharge or agricultural run-off. Such phenomena occur on occasion and are frequently not reflected by fixed date measurements, and the outcomes of those investigations are sometimes lacking in terms of data density. A more extensive analysis is required to correlate pressures with the effects on water quality; consequently, it is critical to provide early warning systems that can measure real-time parameters associated with potential pollution.

1.2 YOLO Models and Their Advancements

The YOLO series of models has revolutionized the field of object detection, significantly improving performance and efficiency. The original YOLO model introduced by Joseph Redmon transformed the traditional object detection approach by framing it as a single regression problem, predicting bounding boxes and class probabilities simultaneously. This innovation achieved real-time detection speeds but initially suffered from lower accuracy compared to other state-of-the-art methods.

YOLOv2 and YOLO9000 introduced by Redmon and Ali Farhadi [30], built on this foundation. Key improvements included the use of anchor boxes, which allowed better handling of objects at varying scales and aspect ratios. Additionally, the models incorporated multi-scale training, enabling robust detection across different resolutions. YOLO9000 combined object detection with classification on the large-scale COCO and

ImageNet datasets, leveraging hierarchical classification to achieve greater accuracy and scalability. YOLOv4, developed by Alexey Bochkovskiy et al. [31], further optimized both speed and accuracy. Notable advancements included CSPDarknet53, which improved information flow and performance, and PANet, which enhanced multi-level feature aggregation. Various optimization techniques, such as the Mish activation function and CIOU loss, enabled YOLOv4 to achieve state-of-the-art results across multiple object detection benchmarks [32, 33].

The advancements in YOLO models have directly contributed to environmental applications, particularly in sewage monitoring. The models' ability to handle real-time detection and classification of objects in diverse and challenging environments has proven crucial for identifying and managing contaminants, blockages, and other anomalies in sewage systems. YOLO's multi-scale detection capabilities are particularly beneficial for monitoring objects of various sizes in sewage pipelines, from small debris to larger obstructions.

YOLO models have been employed in autonomous robotic systems designed for sewer inspection, aiding in the detection of structural defects, water quality anomalies, and flow obstructions. The robustness of YOLO models in varying lighting conditions, as well as their ability to process real-time video feeds, makes them ideal for continuous monitoring tasks.

When comparing YOLO models for sewage conservation, YOLOv4 stands out due to its balance between speed and accuracy. The enhanced architecture of YOLOv4, particularly CSPDarknet53 and PANet, allows for more efficient feature extraction and multi-level aggregation, which is essential for detecting subtle changes in sewage systems. YOLOv3, while slightly less accurate, remains a strong candidate due to its multi-scale detection capabilities, making it effective in environments with objects of varying sizes. YOLOv2 and YOLO9000, though earlier iterations, provide solid foundations for object detection in constrained environments. The anchor box and hierarchical classification approach of YOLO9000, in particular, offer scalable solutions for sewage monitoring across different datasets and scenarios. However, their performance may be less optimal compared to YOLOv4 in handling complex sewage conservation tasks that require both high speed and precision.

This paper provides a thorough examination of the YOLO series of object detection models, from YOLOv1 to YOLOv4, highlighting the pivotal advancements and architectural refinements that have significantly enhanced real-time object detection capabilities. The contributions of this work are twofold: firstly, it delivers an in-depth review of the progressive improvements across YOLO versions, including critical innovations such as Darknet-53, feature pyramid networks, and CSPDarknet53. These advancements have been instrumental in achieving superior performance in terms of speed, accuracy, and scalability. Secondly, the paper elucidates the application of these models in the field of sewage monitoring and conservation. By applying YOLO models to the detection and classification of anomalies in complex and dynamic sewage systems, the study underscores their practical utility in environmental management. Additionally, the paper presents a comparative analysis of the YOLO models, assessing their respective strengths and limitations within this domain.

The structure of the paper is meticulously organized, beginning with an introduction to the YOLO models and their relevance, progressing through a detailed review of each model's advancements, followed by an exploration of their applications in sewage monitoring, a comparative evaluation, and concluding with recommendations for future research. This structured approach ensures a comprehensive understanding of YOLO models' contributions to both technological innovation and environmental sustainability, serving as a critical resource for researchers and practitioners alike.

2 Review of Autonomous Water Quality Monitoring Mechanisms

Many academics have sought to build machines for cleaning regional surroundings as the use of automation like robots has expanded in recent years [7–9]. Those designed to remove debris from water surfaces, on the other hand, require more development. Although semi-manual garbage disposal vessels are routinely employed to collect plastic waste on water surfaces, their size limits their application to rivers with greater regions or heavier waste. As a result, deploying garbage collectors to retrieve low-density waste from tiny rivers is difficult. Furthermore, such boats are hampered by their inability to recognise what object to be removed, in addition to the possibility of additional pollution from released emissions. Intelligent cleaning bots that gather floating waste on surfaces of water have been designed. Kong et al. [10], for example, created an IWSCR called "intelligent water surface cleaner robot system" that included a vision based module, a movement control based component, and a grabbing unit that employed the YOLO-v3 for trash identification, the sliding-mode actuator enabling vision tracker with navigation, and the viable grasping method for hovering junk grabbing & gathering. Wang et al. [11] showed a self-driving robot that removes garbage from the surface of the lakes using the "Maneuvering Model Group" approach. Ruangpayoongsak et al. [12] developed a floating waste scooper robot to collect floating plastic bottles on water.

2.1 Mobile Autonomous Robots

Because they use powerful procedures for making judgements without continual human aid, movable autonomous machines are becoming more widespread in the field of robotics [13].The robot can develop a map of the environment in which it operates based on its precise location, compare its current position with a global position in the generated map, and therefore navigate using the map specified in the task at hand. This role is performed by its navigation system, which informs the motion-control system of the direction to be followed [14]. The creation of techniques for navigation by autonomous robots is an important area in the study of robotics. It is motivated by current innovations and a desire for novel uses [15]. Monitoring marine habitats using autonomous robots is a viable solution when combined with renewable, solar, or wind energy since it provides detailed in-situ and semi-permanent study in water reservoirs [16]. A computer-controlled robot has hardware devices that allow it to perceive and act on its surroundings. Some software structures in this computational system are in charge of interpreting ways to behave in the particular environment [17]. A robot with mobility can alter its location by moving, allowing it to interact with its actual surroundings more effectively [18].

2.2 Autonomous Navigation Boats

In recent decades, technical advancements in the field of navy have preferred scholastic investigations to improve ocean exploration. According to Istenic et al. [19], underwater examination and exploration are important techniques to learn more about the oceans. As a result of such advancements, ASV's known as Autonomous Surface Vehicles are now used in a wide range of operations, including monitoring privately within the water or at sea, sample collection, and object collection in disaster situations [20]. Following that, even existent unmanned boats approached it (Table 1).

Table 1. Autonomous Navigation Boats and Its Related Information

Sr. No	Name of the Navigation Boat	Particulars	Purpose
1	Beagle-B Boat [21]	It was built in 2006 and had a length of 3.5 m with a solid sail of 3 m. It was powered by two 15-Watt solar power panels.	To deliver oceanographic data on long-term expeditions.
2	ALANIS Boat [22]	It employs a Pentium-III 800 megahertz Maximus 2 computerised board and "a PC/104 Emerald EMM-8P-XT module".	For Unmanned surface vehicle ocean & coasts monitoring
3	ARC-SailingBot [23]	It is 1.5 m long and features two candles and two rudders.	It is largely employed in the study of autonomous survival strategies.
4	Noman Airboat [24]	It has 2-Hulls, which can carry 150 kg of weight with 1.2 kW of power output.	It collected and analyzed water in a grid pattern.
5	Hydrus Boat [25]	It is programmed in C++ and controlled using a Raspberry Pi Zero.	It is intended to move autonomously using GPS to take measurements of water quality indicators, and to store the data, as well as to provide information diagnostics.

3 Sewer Conservation Experiments

Sewer Conservation Experiments have assumed an intrinsic stand in several domains of humankind in current modern advancement. Underground infrastructure is the foundation of modern civilization. Existing approaches and created sewage monitoring systems have been addressed and concluded on their uses, limitations, and impact on practical scenarios has already been focused, but this research is especially dealing with YOLO approaches for sewage conservation. Furthermore, it is discussing the best yield results in order to use the sewage conservation betterment.

3.1 AI Detection Algorithms

It used to keep the environment safe and clean, the subsurface drainage system is crucial to modern development. Despite their numerous benefits, underground systems have a number of drawbacks, including clogs, corrosion, and pipe cracks, which cause leaks and tree root incursions. Sewers must be maintained on a regular basis in order to function properly. "To do this, YOLOv3 and YOLOv4 were trained utilizing freshly created imagery datasets, and they represent a significant element of the improvement. This robotic technology will also address the issue of human hygiene by employing a newly developed cutter to remove obstructions in the sewage in real time. A connecting mechanism, cutting tools, a central frame, and three distinct crawler modules created in Catia V5 R21 ED2 are also included in the proposed robotic system. The provided system is one of the most notable achievements in the field of sewage robots, capable of identifying and eliminating blockages for real-world use [26].

3.2 Sewer Monitoring and Maintenance Systems

Pune is a typical medium-sized city in a developing country, is chosen to grasp the concerns and define the requirements for building robotic systems for the same. It has been shown that sewer obstructions are a serious worry, but there is a lack of knowledge on both real-time detection and removal using robotic equipment. In terms of performance and decisions for real-world implementations of sewage robotic systems, on-board processing with computer vision algorithms has not been efficiently utilized. The review focuses on the various approaches for constructing sewage inspection and cleaning robotic systems [27].

To develop a thorough understanding of the research context, a survey was carried out in Pune, India, a mid-sized city representative of developing countries. Originally designed in 1928, Pune's sewerage system was built to handle a capacity of 31.8 million liters per day (MLD) for a population of 260,000. However, by 2020, the population had increased to 7.4 million, placing considerable pressure on the existing infrastructure. Currently, the city operates 11 Sewage Treatment Plants (STPs) with a combined treatment capacity of 396 MLD.

The SPRING project, supported by DY Patil Engineering College and in collaboration with the Pune Municipal Corporation (PMC), conducted a thorough survey to assess the city's sewage treatment methods and pinpoint related challenges.

According to data from official sources, the main goal of sewerage maintenance is to reduce drainage blockages along the system's length. Typically, external mechanical systems are used for cleaning, which involves significant expenses. Despite PMC's efforts to comply with government regulations for regular sewer inspections and maintenance, financial limitations have led to insufficient techniques and equipment for effective management.

3.3 S-BIRD (Sewer-Blockages Imagery Recognition Collection)

It is a novel imagery collection released to raise attention to the prevalent sewer blockages issue caused by oil, plastic, and tree roots. For real-time detection tasks, the S-BIRD dataset and other parameters such as its strength, performance, consistency, and feasibility have been studied and analyzed. To demonstrate the consistency and validity of the S-BIRD dataset, the YOLOX object detection model was trained. It further described how the supplied dataset will be used in a real-time detection and removal of sewage blockages using an embedded vision-based robotic system. The findings of an individual survey done in Pune, India, a typical mid-sized city in a developing country, support the need for the proposed work [28].

To capture a diverse range of visual data, images of sewer blockages were taken under varying lighting conditions and from different angles. This methodology aimed to collect comprehensive insights into the features and characteristics of the blockages. For instance, Fig. 1 displays examples of tree root blockages from the newly developed dataset.

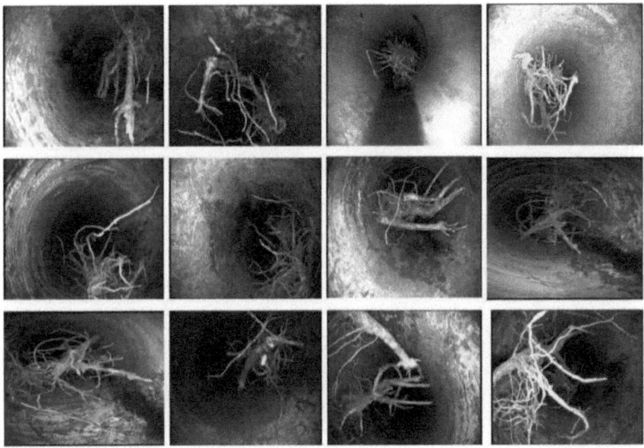

Fig. 1. Frames depicting tree root blockages in the S-BIRD dataset

Figure 2 further illustrates instances of plastic debris, which are crucial for the detection and identification tasks. Due to their integration with black water and grease, some materials like plastic bags and other debris may appear indistinguishable against the blackish background of the sewage mass.

Additionally, Fig. 3 shows grease blockages, highlighting a spectrum of colors. These blockages often result from waste produced by both domestic activities and industrial processes, which contribute significant amounts of chemical and processed waste.

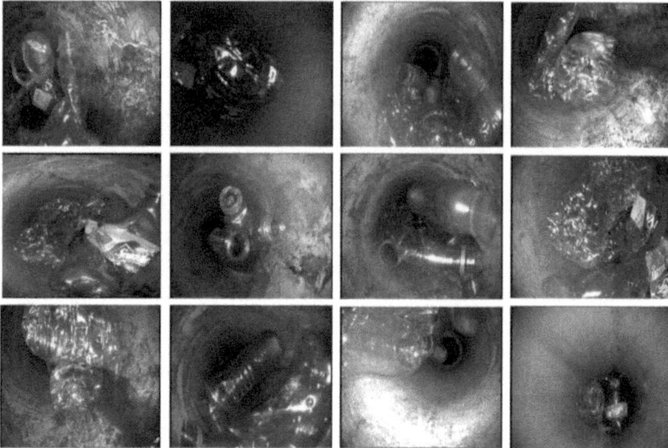

Fig. 2. Frames depicting tree root blockages in the S-BIRD dataset

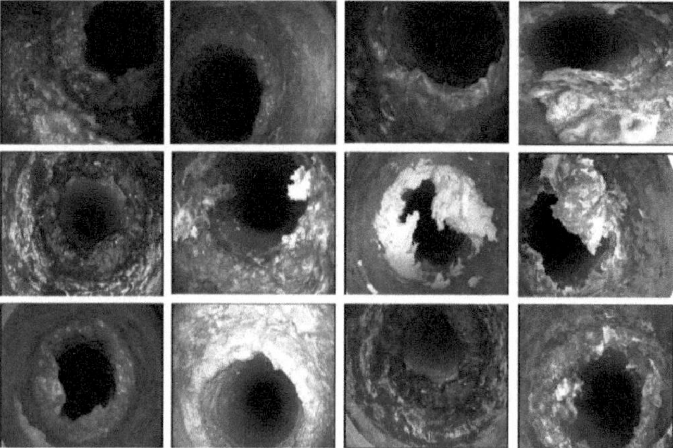

Fig. 3. Frames displaying grease blockages in the S-BIRD dataset

The visual upshots of precisely detected sewer blocks such as tree roots, plastic and grease, are delineated in Fig. 4. Of course, multiple sewer blockages in the same frame have also been considered for real-time detection purposes. Overall, the obtained results of the YOLOX-trained model prove the consistency and viability of the new S-BIRD dataset presented.

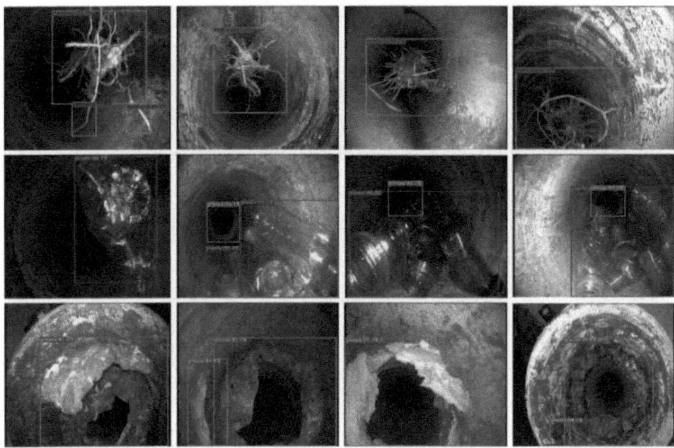

Fig. 4. Visual Illustrations of Precise Detection of Tree Roots, Plastic, and Grease Sewer Block Types

Table 2 provides a detailed account of the data collection process for analyzing various types of sewer blockages. The table lists the three primary types of blockages captured: tree roots, plastic, and grease. For tree roots, a total of 2,295 frames were acquired, showcasing the diverse conditions under which tree root blockages occur. Plastic blockages were represented by 2,392 frames, capturing a wide range of plastic debris and its various forms. Grease blockages were documented with 2,353 frames, illustrating different instances and characteristics of grease accumulation. In total, 7,040 frames were used across all categories, reflecting a comprehensive dataset that encompasses a broad spectrum of blockage types for thorough analysis and detection.

Table 2. Arithmetical details of captured frames

Sr. No.	Types of Sewer blockages	Number of acquired Frames
1	Tree Roots	2295
2	Plastic	2392
3	Grease	2353
	Total Frames Used	7040

3.4 Sewer Robotic Systems

Systems have assumed an intrinsic stand in several domains of humankind in current modern advancement. Underground infrastructure is the foundation of modern civilization. Existing approaches and created sewage robotic systems have been addressed and concluded on their uses, limitations, and impact on practical scenarios in this research. Furthermore, it is shown that prior artwork focused solely on sewer problem diagnosis, with no standard work on sewer obstruction detection and clearance. To handle sewer blockage concerns, a sewer robotic system with cost effectiveness and a standardized accuracy matrix should be designed, followed by human scavenging. The survey results expand a province of sewer robotics to fix obstructions concerns of buried sewers of various sizes in real-time using a significant approach [29].

The Table 3 discusses two of the key experiments conducted in past study. The goal of the experiments, as well as the data sets, including the procedures and materials utilized for both studies, have been addressed in length initially. Both trials were carried out with the goal of automating sewage monitoring and repair.

Table 3. Comparison of Existing Sewage Conservation Experiments

Sr. No	Name of the Experiment	Purpose of Experiment	Dataset	Materials and/or Methods	Results Obtained
1	AI Detection Algorithms	This work describes a robotic platform for detecting and removing common blockages in subterranean sewerage such as grease, plastics as well as tree roots.	S-BIRD	Methods- YOLO-V3 & YOLO-V4 Materials- Central Frame, cutting tool, crawler modules. It is observed that YOLOv3 has a shorter detection time, which is half that of YOLOv4.	Average Precision - 89.59% Recall- 0.85 Mean AP-77.62%
2	Sewer-Blockages Imagery Recognition Dataset	To address the requirement for adding computer vision to automated robotic systems for diagnosing blockages in sewerage pipes, S-BIRD is a new critical multi-class image dataset that comprises frames of major sewer obstacles such as "grease, plastic, and tree roots".	S-BIRD	Method- YOLOX model The preliminary processing as well as enhancement findings show an increase in the amount and variety of training occurrences along with pertinent annotations for the efficient performance of the object detection model.	Mean AP-"90.05% (at 0.5 IoU threshold)" Mean AP-"78.85% (at 0.5 to 0.95 IoU threshold)"

The first experiment focused on the YOLO-V3 and YOLO-V3 approaches, and it achieved strong results with YOLO-V4 and the second technique employing the YOLO-X model. It is also necessary to contrast the YOLO-V4 with the V4 by comparing the YOLO-X model. In order to monitor sewage water, the YOLO-X model has shown good results as shown in the Fig. 5.

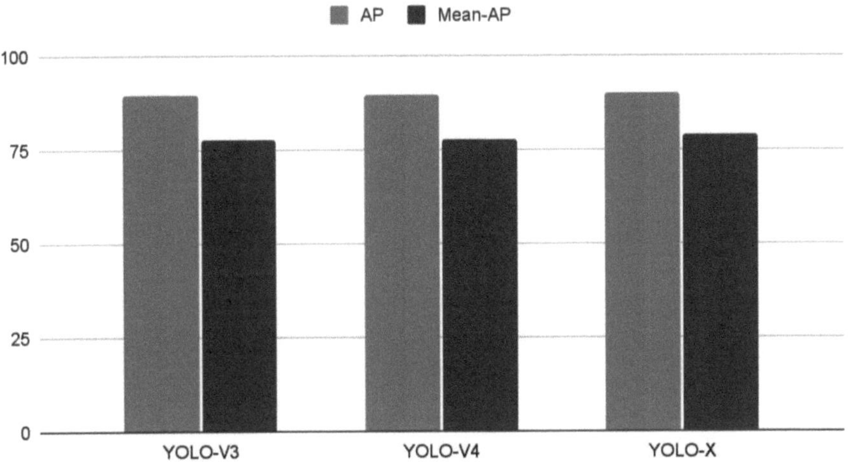

Fig. 5. Comparison chart of Sewage Conservation Experiments. AP- Average Precision, Mean-AP- Mean Average Precision

4 Conclusion

Typically, sewage conservation experiments focus on reducing water usage, improving wastewater treatment procedures, and discovering novel ways to reuse or recycle wastewater. A few examples of experiments like Greywater Recycling, Rainwater Havesting, Water-Efficient Fixtures and Appliances, Advanced Wastewater Treatment Technologies, Biosolid Management as well as Public Awareness and Behavioral Change were available. Four of the previously implemented experiments have been discussed from two of the artificial intelligence-based YOLO smart sewage conservation experiment results depicted to present the appropriate conservation. Experiments with sewage or wastewater should follow basic safety measures and adhere to local protocols. It is important to communicate with wastewater management specialists to ensure that the tests are carried out safely and ethically.

This review paper provides a thorough examination of the YOLO series of object detection models, tracing their development from YOLOv1 through YOLOv4. It highlights the transformative impact these models have had on real-time object detection by improving speed, accuracy, and scalability. Detailed analysis of key architectural innovations, including Darknet-53, feature pyramid networks, and CSPDarknet53, demonstrates how YOLO has advanced to tackle challenges in multi-scale object detection, feature extraction, and information flow.

A particular focus of this paper is on the application of YOLO models to environmental monitoring, specifically sewage systems. YOLO's ability to detect and classify anomalies in complex and dynamic environments underscores its value as a tool for sustainable environmental management. This practical application illustrates the broader impact of cutting-edge computer vision technologies.

The review serves as a critical resource for researchers, summarizing key advancements in YOLO technology and showcasing its potential for real-world applications. It offers a foundation for future research, encouraging exploration of further enhancements to YOLO models and their adaptation to new fields requiring efficient, real-time object detection. Ultimately, this work contributes significantly to the ongoing discourse on the future of object detection, bridging technological advancements with practical, environmental applications.

Acknowledgments. This research did not receive any specific grant from funding agencies in the public, commercial, or not-for-profit sectors.

The authors have no competing interests to declare that are relevant to the content of this article.

References

1. De Vito-Francesco, E., et al.: An innovative autonomous robotic system for on-site detection of heavy metal pollution plumes in surface water. Environ. Monit. Assess. **194**(2), 1–19 (2022). https://doi.org/10.1007/s10661-021-09738-z
2. Li, T., et al.: A reliable sewage quality abnormal event monitoring system. Water Res. **121**(6), 248–257 (2017)
3. Hii, K., Parthasarathy, R., Baroutian, S., Gapes, D.J., Eshtiaghi, N.: Rheological measurements as a tool for monitoring the performance of high pressure and high temperature treatment of sewage sludge. Water Res. **114**(12), 254–263 (2017)
4. Berho, C., Guigues, N., Ghestem, J.P., Crouzet, C., Strugeon, A., Roy, S., et al.: On-site heavy metal monitoring using a portable screen-printed electrode sensor. In: Gonzalez, C., Greenwood, R., Quevauviller, P. (eds.) Rapid Chemical and Biological Techniques for Water Monitoring, pp. 263–273. Wiley, Chichester, U.K. (2009)
5. Bahamonde, P.A., Feswick, A., Isaacs, M.A., Munkittrick, K.R., Martyniuk, C.J.: Defining the role of omics in assessing ecosystem health: Perspectives from the Canadian environmental monitoring program. Environ. Toxicol. Chem. **35**(1), 20–35 (2016)
6. Ociepa, E., Mrowiec, M., Lach, J.: Influence of fertilisation with sewage sludge-derived preparation on selected soil properties and prairie cordgrass yield. Environ. Res. **156**(2), 775–780 (2017)
7. Palacin, J., Salse, J.A., Valganon, I., Clua, X.: Building a mobile robot for a floor-cleaning operation in domestic environments. IEEE Trans. Instrum. Meas. **53**, 1418–1424 (2004)
8. Kang, M.C., Kim, K.S., Noh, D.K., Han, J.W., Ko, S.J.: A robust obstacle detection method for robotic vacuum cleaners. IEEE Trans. Consum. Electron. **60**, 587–595 (2014)
9. Zhang, H., Zhang, J., Zong, G., Wang, W., Liu, R.: Sky cleaner 3: A real pneumatic climbing robot for glass-wall cleaning. IEEE Robot. Autom. Mag. **13**, 32–41 (2006)
10. Bai, J., Lian, S., Liu, Z., Wang, K., Liu, D.: Deep learning based robot for automatically picking up garbage on the grass. IEEE Trans. Consum. Electron. **64**, 382–389 (2018)
11. Kong, S., Tian, M., Qiu, C., Wu, Z., Yu, J.: IWSCR: An intelligent water surface cleaner robot for collecting floating garbage. IEEE Trans. Syst. Man Cybernet. Syst. (2020)

12. Wang, Z., Liu, Y., Yip, H.W., Peng, B., Qiao, S., He, S.: Design and hydrodynamic modeling of a lake surface cleaning robot. In: Proceedings of the 2008 IEEE/ASME International Conference on Advanced Intelligent Mechatronics (AIM), pp. 1343–1348. Xian, China (2008)
13. Ruangpayoongsak, N., Sumroengrit, J., Leanglum, M.: A floating waste scooper robot on water surface. In: Proceedings of the 2017 17th International Conference on Control, Automation and Systems (ICCAS), pp. 1543–1548. Jeju, Korea (2017)
14. Costa, G., Cavalcanti Neto, E., Themoteo, A.: Distance measuring system for mobile robots using SURF algorithm and stereo vision. In: V Congresso de Pesquisa e Inovação da Rede Norte Nordeste de Educação Tecnológica. Macéio, Brazil (2010)
15. Siegwart, R., Nourbakhsh, I.R.: Introduction to Autonomous Mobile Robots. The MIT Press, Cambridge, UK (2004)
16. Saffiotti, A.: The uses of fuzzy logic in autonomous robot navigation. Soft. Comput. **1**, 180–197 (1997)
17. Pêtrès, C., Romero-Ramirez, M.A., Plumet, F.: A potential field approach for reactive navigation of autonomous sailboats. Robot. Auton. Syst. **60**, 1520–1527 (2012)
18. Álvarez, B., Iborra, A., Pastor, J.A., Fernández, C., Alonso, A., de la Puente, J.A.: Software architecture for development of mechatronic systems: Service robots. Dedicated Syst. Mag. 17–22 (2001)
19. Nehmzow, U.: Mobile Robotics: A Practical Introduction. Springer Science & Business Media (2012)
20. Istenic, K., Ila, V., Polok, L., Gracias, N., Garcia, R.: Mission-time 3D reconstruction with quality estimation. In: Proceedings of the OCEANS 2017, pp. 1–9. Aberdeen, UK (2017)
21. Oliveira, P., Pascoal, A., Silva, V., Silvestre, C.: Design, development, and testing at sea of the mission control system for the MARIUS autonomous underwater vehicle. In: Proceedings of the OCEANS 96 MTS/IEEE Conference on the Coastal Ocean—Prospects for the 21st Century, vol. 1, pp. 401–406. Fort Lauderdale, FL, USA (1996)
22. Sauze, C., Neal, M.: Design considerations for sailing robots performing long term autonomous oceanography. In: Proceedings of the International Robotic Sailing Conference (IRSC), pp. 21–29. Breitenbrunn, Austria (2008)
23. Caccia, M., Bibuli, M., Bono, R., Bruzzone, G., Spirandelli, E.: Aluminum hull USV for coastal water and seafloor monitoring. In: Proceedings of the OCEANS 2009-EUROPE, pp. 1–5. Bremen, Germany (2009)
24. Neal, M.A.: Hardware proof of concept of a sailing robot for ocean observation. IEEE J. Oceanic Eng. **31**, 462–469 (2006)
25. Kaizu, Y., Iio, M., Yamada, H., Noguchi, N.: Development of unmanned airboat for water-quality mapping. Biosys. Eng. **109**, 338–347 (2011)
26. Camargo, L.P.: Hydrus Project: Aquatic Vehicle for Monitoring Water Quality. Available online: https://repositorio.ufsc.br/handle/123456789/181827. Accessed on 12 Feb 2018
27. Ansari, S.M., Khairnar, S.M., Patil, R.R., Nikalje, N.M.: Design study of smart robotic framework for sewer conservation. International Journal of Engineering Trends and Technology **70**(8), 247–255 (2022)
28. Patil, R.R., Mustafa, M.Y., Calay, R.K., Ansari, S.M.: S-BIRD: A novel critical multi-class imagery dataset for sewer monitoring and maintenance systems. Sensors **23**, 2966 (2023)
29. Ansari, S.M., Khairnar, S.M., Patil, R.R., Kokate, R.S.: An assessment: Water quality monitoring practices and sewer robotic systems. Inf. Technol. Ind. **9**(1) (2021)
30. Redmon, J., Santosh, D., Ross, G., Ali, F.: You only look once: unified, real-time object detection. In: Proceedings of the IEEE Conference on Computer Vision and Pattern Recognition, pp. 779–788 (2016)
31. Bochkovskiy, A., Wang, C.Y., Liao, H.Y.M.: YOLOv4: Optimal speed and accuracy of object detection. arXiv preprint arxiv:2004.10934 (2020)

32. Fegade, A., Raut, R., Deshpande, A., Mittal, A., Kaul, N., Khanna, V.: Unleashing the power of generative artificial intelligence: Exploring its boundless potential and overcoming challenges in academic environments. In: Proceedings of the 2023 6th International Conference on Contemporary Computing and Informatics (IC3I), pp. 1243–1249. Gautam Buddha Nagar, India (2023)
33. Raju, K.S., Gill, R., Bisht, Y.S., Sekhar, M.S.R., Almusawi, M., Karthick, V.: A new technology for higher-end communication using quick and optimized computational N/W implementation for the clinical field. In: Proceedings of the 2024 4th International Conference on Advance Computing and Innovative Technologies in Engineering (ICACITE), pp. 1444–1449. Greater Noida, India (2024)

Review of AI-Enabled Intelligent Manufacturing: Present Situation and Prospects for the Future

Sarvagya Kaushik[1], Amanjot Kaur Lamba[2], Rajeev Kamal Sharma[3], and Preeti Sharma[3]($\boxtimes$)

[1] Department of Computer Science and Design Indraprastha Institute of Information Technology, Delhi, India
[2] Amanjot Kaur Lamba Department of Electronics and Communication Engineering, Panipat Institute of Engineering and Technology, Haryana, India
[3] Chitkara University Institute of Engineering & Technology, Punjab, India
preeti.sharma@chitkara.edu.in

Abstract. Over the course of the twenty-first century, the field of 'artificial intelligence (AI)' has expanded more quickly, driven by both bio-evolution and human natural intelligence. Complexity, dynamicity, and connectivity are all growing in today's production systems. Because of the numerous unknowns and interdependencies that exist, manufacturing operations encounter issues of highly nonlinear and stochastic activity. Cutting-edge analytics solutions for handling the massive volumes of manufacturing data created by recent advances in AI, particularly machine learning (ML), have demonstrated enormous potential to alter the manufacturing domain. Including designing and plan of production systems, creating processes, optimizing, controlling quality, upkeep, mechanized assembling and disassembling, and more, this study showcases AI's uses in manufacturing. The study also provides a summary of common manufacturing issues, along with AI solutions that address them, and it offers a roadmap for future research aimed at utilizing AI to achieve smart manufacturing.

Keywords: manufacturing with computer integration · machine intelligence · automation

1 Introduction

Human intelligence has aided in the development of industrial robots, computers, electric motors, steam engines, and automobiles, as well as the mechanization of production that has taken place over the past few centuries, transitioning from a period of by hand labor to several industrial revolutions [1]. The increasing integration of detectors, and advancements in robotics and mechanization are causing significant innovation and change in the manufacturing sector. As a result, factories become more digitally connected, and manufacturing firms are forced to reconsider, review, and assess their present business practices as well as their long-term strategic goals in the developing field of "smart manufacturing" [2].

S. Pal et al. (Eds.): ICETSS 2024, CCIS 2610, pp. 359–371, 2026.
https://doi.org/10.1007/978-3-032-11488-4_29

The incorporation of AI is revolutionizing the 'Internet of Things (IoT)' also. Since AIOT offers valuable insights, businesses leverage AI to enhance their current IoT applications, including data collection and analysis, decision-making, and control actions for continuous learning [3]. Real-time analysis processing and analysis to increase productivity and efficiency in areas like supply chain optimization, quality control, and predictive maintenance are among the main advantages. By automating typical processes for identifying unusual activity and initiating steps against breaches, the use of AI technology in IoT significantly simplifies business operations. In the AIoT, strong authentication protocols guarantee that sensitive data is only accessible by authorized users. Moreover, contextual applications depending on user choices and behavior can be offered via AIoT. Smart factories, fleet management, healthcare, smart cities, and transportation services are just a few of the industries that embrace AI-enabled IoT solutions because they offer advantages including more intelligent data-driven operations, better user experiences, and efficient use of resources [4, 5].

1.1 Prospects for Manufacturing with Artificial Intelligence.

The phrase "ability of computers to perform cognitive functions associated with human minds, such as perceiving, reasoning, learning, and problem solving" [6] is used to characterize artificial intelligence. Fig. 1 depicts the two different paths that the development of AI has taken, which have resulted in model-based vs. data-driven methodologies.

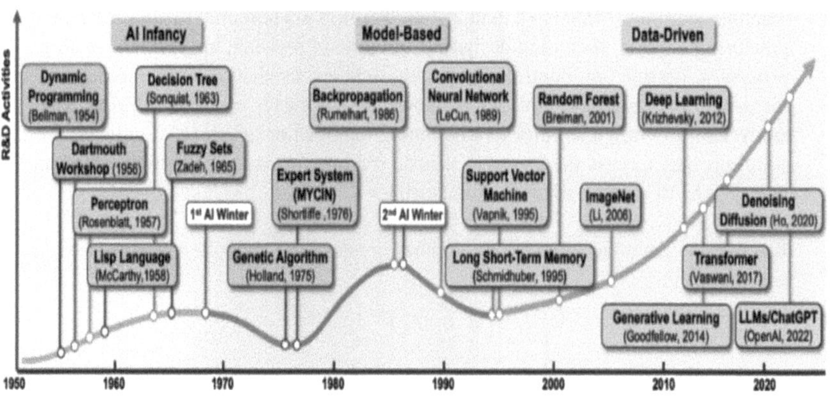

Fig. 1. The development of AI technology [7–13]

Ensuring a safe working environment for all employees while fulfilling throughput, quality, and cost objectives are the primary driving forces and needs in most everyday manufacturing operations across industries. But achieving these objectives has grown more challenging due to the multiplicity of requirements brought about by more sophisticated products and processes, more fluctuation in client preferences and expectations, and so on. The scientific community has been very interested in the topic of AI in manufacturing, as evidenced by the steady increase in publications over the past few years, as indicated by Fig. 2. As observed from the figure, there has been a sharp exponential growth in research papers.

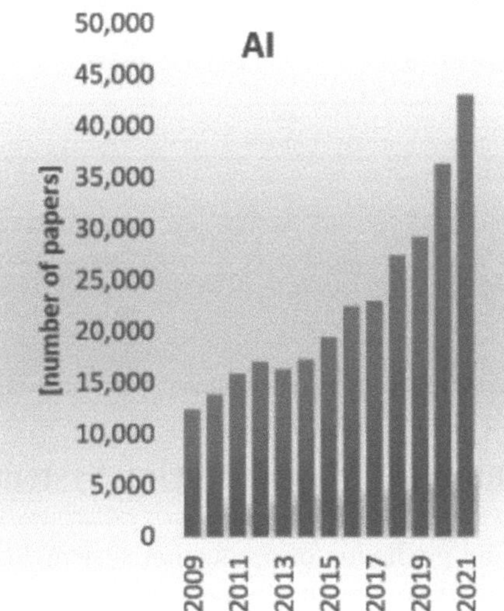

Fig. 2. An increase in academic research on artificial intelligence in manufacturing [14].

1.2 Intelligent Manufacturing with AI

Engineers and researchers are trying to do the following in order to enhance the status of manufacturing: ~ promptly detect flaws and forecast future performance of equipment for quality assurance and maintenance [15]; delegate arduous, repetitive duties to robots and look into the smooth interplay between humans and machines [16]; Efficiently search through the variable space of manufacturing systems to optimize scheduling and planning [18]; precisely describe process dynamics and optimize process parameters in production to improve part property [17]. Manufacturers have opportunities to explore artificial intelligence capabilities because of the growing complexity of products, processes and variability of customer preferences.

Figure 3 illustrates how the production systems utilized in this work include equipment, robots, conveyors, and associated duties like handling materials and upkeep that are arranged to produce the intended result. This paper aims to present the following contributions: (1) review the most recent applications of artificial intelligence 'AI' for representing problems in manufacturing; (2) offer a methodical approach for data analysis; and (3) pinpoint opportunities and challenges for further leveraging 'AI' for shaping the needs in manufacturing for future development.

This keynote paper seeks to present the state-of-the-art of advances in AI in manufacturing, in contrast to these recent review articles that are primarily focused on specific applications and AI technologies. It does this by taking an integrated view of the system in Section 2, process in Section 3, quality in Section 4, and assembly in Section 5 from both model-based and data-driven perspectives. Sections 6 and 7 provide separate presentations of the future directions and conclusions.

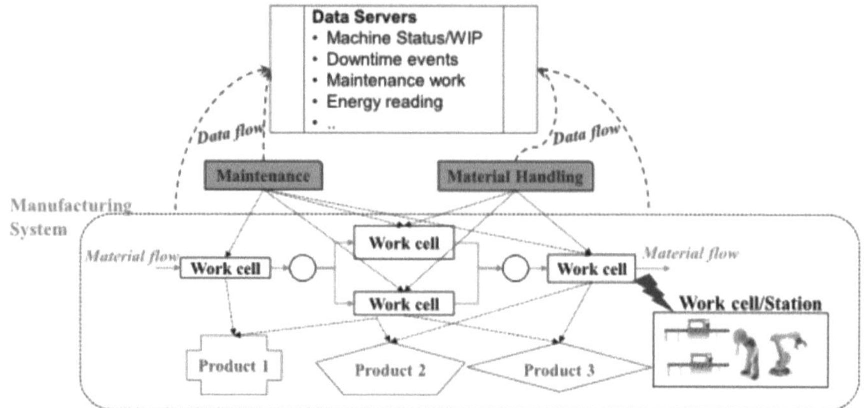

Fig. 3. Diagrammatic of a contemporary manufacturing setup [16]

2   Design and Planning of Manufacturing Systems with AI Support

Evaluation, diagnosis, and prediction of production systems' output, quality, and efficiency are critical. System designing, performances enhancement, and routine production systems operations may be made easier with the use of throughput analysis, which assesses the longand short-term productivity of manufacturing systems. Numerous studies have been conducted to analyze the dynamics and performance of industrial systems [19–24]. Nevertheless, the traditional analytical modeling methods that depend on 'queuing theory' and 'Markov Chains' have two major shortcomings. [23, 25–27]. An excellent way to make up for these deficiencies is to use data analytics and machine learning approaches.

Firstly, analytical methods for throughput estimation, precise or approximate, are limited to simple system architectures under rigid assumptions. Simulation turns out to be the only feasible technique for evaluating the long-term performance of more complex systems. ML approaches can be used to generalize simulation results when the production system's characteristics change, avoiding the need to run the simulations again [28, 29].

Secondly, long-term steady-state performance studies are the main focus of traditional methodologies for throughput increase, which is irrelevant for production management and real-time throughput prediction. They are also unable to fully benefit from the far better sensor readings of today. Complex production systems can benefit from real-time control based on the short-term system performance, which can be deduced from buffer states and machine status [30, 31]. Numerous studies have also been conducted on data-driven approaches for locating throughput bottlenecks. In order to assess permanent production loss in the battery manufacturing industry, an event-based approach is presented in [32]. In [33], a data-driven model is developed utilizing the available sensor data, and a system diagnostic technique is proposed to identify real-time production limits and bottlenecks. A recency-weighted stochastic learning strategy is proposed in [34] to anticipate the system production losses of serial manufacturing lines in a short look-ahead window.

3 AI for Managing, Optimizing, and Modeling Processes

Complex relationships between many processes in multistage production systems have made system-level quality analysis extremely difficult. The following goals have been attempted to be accomplished using AI/ML based approaches.

(i) **Early quality defect detection**: Statistical process control (SPC) is frequently used to evaluate many critical variables in accordance with specified specification ranges for monitoring the standard of work processing. SPC has shortcomings despite being widely used, such as the assumption that the data are always unimodal, which is not necessarily the case. What's more, SPC depends on established, explicit correlations between the quality of the final product and the variables under inspection. Some ML-based techniques [35–40] are suggested to successfully address some of the shortcomings in traditional process control methods thanks to the enormous volumes of time-series data.

(ii) **Identification of the underlying causes of quality problems**: One method for doing root cause diagnostics of quality problems is the use of Bayesian networks, as they make it simple to infer fault sources from observed quality deviations [41]. Small data sets and medium-level measurement noise can both be handled by the suggested approach [42].

4 AI for Upkeep and Quality Control

Since the early 1980s, AI has been connected to quality control and maintenance [43]. 'Remaining useful life (RUL)' prediction [44], machine/tool degradation, and defect identification [45] have all benefited from the advancement of model-based AI techniques over time. Examples of these techniques include those based on physics-based models and defect-induced signal features. QA and maintenance have distinct issues in the context of data-driven AI compared to other manufacturing domains, including domain knowledge integration and data imbalance [46]. Fig. 4 provides a summary of AI approaches and their relevant applications in maintenance and quality assurance.

Fig. 4. Research on artificial intelligence for upkeep and quality control [44]

5 Automation of Flexible Assemblage and Breakdown with AI

Advancements and potential for assemblage and breakdown with AI are covered in Fig. 5.

Controlling Material Flow and Scheduling Assembly: Lineless architectures like matrix production have evolved because of the increasing demands placed on the flexibility and reconfiguration of the assembly line [48], which are in line with the expanding variety of goods, particularly in the automotive sector. Since its introduction in 1975, 'Genetic Algorithm (GA)', a branch of evolutionary computing, has been used to address a variety of optimization issues related to assembly planning [49, 50] and scheduling [51]. Furthermore, autonomous assembly systems that are both self-learning and self-optimizing have been suggested by [52, 53]. The main areas of study for material flow control in known environments have been "indoor navigation" [54], "obstacle avoidance" [55], and more recently, "multi-robot cooperation" with the emergence of automated warehouses [56, 57].

Artificial Intelligence-Enhanced Robotics' Potential for Assembly: The development of AI techniques has led to significant advancements in fundamental robotics research, which has benefitted industrial robots, which are crucial for automating assembly operations [58]. Recently, there has been a growing interest in the subdomain of machine learning called "robot learning" due to the advancements made in this subject for robot-assisted manufacturing [59]. Robust items are typically the only ones that can be handled and assembled by robots; deformable objects can only be handled and assembled manually [60]. This is a result of the non-linear dynamics combined with heterogeneous geometrical and mechanical features that make traditional modeling and control techniques difficult [61].

Disassembly based on Artificial Intelligence: Automated disassembly is more difficult than product assembly because internal structures are frequently unknown. Additionally, evaluating the way an inter-component link is separated can be more complicated than actually planning and designing the connection [62]. Search methods and simulations based on physics have also been studied for disassembly planning [63]. To facilitate disassembly, additional researchers have started examining computer vision techniques to identify the components within the manufactured part. These methods include 'CNN' [64] and its derivatives, such as 'YOLO' [65], and 'region-based CNN (RCNN)' [66, 67], which have demonstrated the ability to segregate components like screwheads in assembled parts.

AI has a great deal of potential to aid in the construction and disassembly of robots, according to current studies [16, 68–70]. Given the limited payload constraints of existing AI-based robotic research, high payload applications represent a viable avenue for future research [71–73]. Continued development of cognitive robotic abilities is necessary for these applications in order to guarantee safe human-robot interaction.

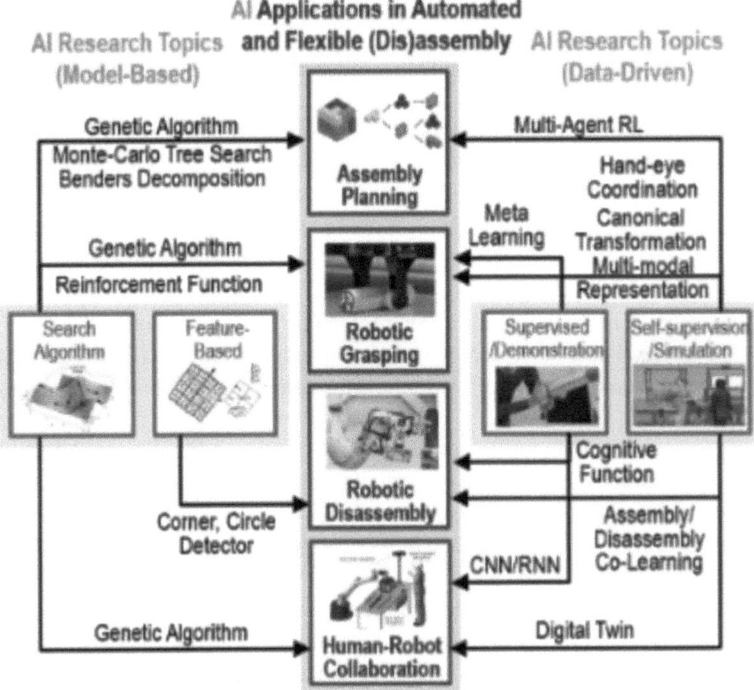

Fig. 5. Research on Artificial Intelligence for assemblage and removal of manufactured components [47]

6 Difficulties and Prospective Paths

To increase productivity, product quality, and worker safety, manufacturers are setting the standard for the application of AI technology. They do this by applying analytics driven by AI to data. Shorter time-to-market deadlines, more complicated products, and stringent quality standards and laws present additional difficulties for them. The quest to improve the efficiency, resilience, and reliability of AI techniques for turning data into useful insights has been fueled by advancements in manufacturing. Simultaneously, researchers and practitioners face additional obstacles in their efforts to more effectively utilize AI's promise for achieving smart manufacturing, because of the ongoing explosion in data collected from industrial processes and systems. The suggestions for further research are presented in this section.

- Learn without supervision on unlabeled data. Enhancing data accessibility is a primary goal of data-driven artificial intelligence. But marking factory data by hand can be a demanding task. Supervised learning has been the main topic of the majority of documented AI research in manufacturing. Future research on artificial intelligence in manufacturing could focus on unsupervised learning to increase the flexibility and effectiveness of data labeling [74].
- The effective application of physical knowledge and information obtained from sensor data to handle manufacturing-related issues has long been thought to be possible when AI is combined with physical laws and principles [75].
- Even though the physical consistency and interpretability of data-driven AI methods are enhanced by the integration of physical knowledge, additional safety constraints are necessary for 'AI-based decision-making' that involves crucial operations like collaborative robots and real-time control of manufacturing processes in order to prevent disastrous results [76–78].
- The discovery of new knowledge among is the more intriguing uses of 'AI' in production. The main obstacle is to achieve a low 'false discovery rate (FDR)', which might lead to a significant waste of effort in the subsequent confirmatory investigation [79, 80].
- Although manufacturing has looked at Natural Language Processing (NLP), the process of developing AI algorithms typically lacks systematic guidelines and frequently calls for empirical design. Because it is difficult to convert words into computational components while maintaining their semantic structure, handling text has long been a problem for AI [81, 82].
- The focus on using human experience offers a chance to its fullest transfer of human demonstrating skills to AI systems. This could have advantages such as enabling robots to learn new abilities quickly and without the need for extensive data collecting [83].
- Studies on GANs and their derivatives demonstrate how manufacturing has been utilizing generative AI for a few years now. It has always been difficult, nevertheless, to have more precise control over the data that is produced [84–87].

Even though artificial intelligence (AI) has been widely used in many industries to increase productivity, accuracy, and decision-making skills, there are a few factors to consider when developing a strategy to put these techniques into practice, such as carefully defining the problem, choosing an appropriate model, and integrating with current systems. Additionally significant factors are the data's quality and ethical considerations.

7 Conclusions

This paper thoroughly examines the application of AI in industrial systems and processes across multiple organizational levels, along with its potential for future benefits. According to the literature review, numerous artificial intelligence tools have been executed to handle a wide range of issues at different stages of the plant hierarchy. Notwithstanding their extensive usage, these techniques have been implemented with differing degrees of success and accompanying difficulties.

The manufacturing landscape will undergo a significant transformation, with artificial intelligence playing a key role. This revolutionary change will be propelled by critical technologies, aiming to improve: (1) planning and design of production systems; (2) modeling, management, and optimization of processes; (3) Quality control and upkeep; and (4) Automation of Flexible assemblage and breakdown. This study delves deeply into the current cutting-edge processes of manufacturing with AI and illuminates the technology's production-specific life cycle, encompassing quality maintenance, automation, process management, and original design.

References

1. Koren, Y.: The global manufacturing revolution: product-process-business integration and reconfigurable systems. John Wiley & Sons (2010)
2. Monostori, L., et al.: Cyber-Physical Systems in Manufacturing. CIRP Ann. **65**(2), 621–641 (2016)
3. Abdulqader, Z., et al.: A responsible AI development for sustainable enterprises a review of integrating ethical AI with IoT and enterprise systems. J. Info. Technol. Info. **3**(2) (2024)
4. Rahaman, M., et al.: Privacy-Centric AI and IoT Solutions for Smart Rural Farm Monitoring and Control. Sensors **24**(13), 4157 (2024)
5. Whig, P., et al.: Role of AI and IoT in Intelligent Transportation. Artificial Intelligence for Future Intelligent Transportation, pp. 199–220. Apple Academic Press (2024)
6. Chui, L., Kamalnath, V., McCarthy, B.: An Executive's Guide to AI, McKinsey (2018). https://www.mckinsey.com/business-functions/mckinsey-analytics/our-insights/ane xecutives-guide-to-ai
7. Bellman, R.: The theory of dynamic programming. Bulletin of the American Mathematical Society **60**(6), 503–515 (1954)
8. Breiman, L.: Random Forests. Machine learning **45**, 5–32 (2001)
9. Morgan, J.N., Sonquist, J.A.: Problems in the analysis of survey data, and a proposal. J. Am. Stat. Assoc. **58**(302), 415–434 (1963)
10. OpenAI. Introducing ChatGPT, https://openai.com/blog/chatgpt. Accessed 9 April 2024
11. Shortliffe, E.H.: MYCIN: A rule-based computer program for advising physicians regarding antimicrobial therapy selection (Doctoral dissertation, Stanford University)
12. Wang, L.: From intelligence science to intelligent manufacturing. Engineering **5**(4), 615–618 (2019)
13. Zadeh, L.A.: Fuzzy sets. Information and Control **8**(3), 338–353 (1965)

14. Franki, V., Majnarić, D., Višković, A.: A comprehensive review of artificial intelligence (AI) companies in the power sector. Energies **16**, 1077 (2023). https://doi.org/10.3390/en16031077
15. Weimer, D., Scholz-Reiter, B., Shpitalni, M.: Design of deep convolutional neural network architectures for automated feature extraction in industrial inspection. CIRP Ann. **65**(1), 417–420 (2016)
16. Wang, L., et al.: Symbiotic Human-Robot Collaborative Assembly. CIRP Annals **68**(2), 701–726 (2019)
17. Freitag, M., Hildebrandt, T.: Automatic design of scheduling rules for complex manufacturing systems by multi-objective simulation-based optimization. CIRP Annals **65**(1), 433–436 (2016)
18. Stark, R., Kind, S., Neumeyer, S.: Innovations in digital modelling for next generation manufacturing system design. CIRP Ann. **66**(1), 169–172 (2017)
19. Arinez, J.F., et al.: Artificial intelligence in advanced manufacturing: Current status and future outlook. J. Manufact. Sci. Eng. **142**(11), 110804 (2020)
20. Li, J., Meerkov, S.M.: Production Systems Engineering. Springer, US (2009)
21. Wu, K., McGinnis, L.: Performance evaluation for general queueing networks in manufacturing systems: characterizing the trade-off between queue time and utilization. Eur. J. Oper. Res. **221**(2), 328–339 (2012)
22. Tan, B., Gershwin, S.B.: Analysis of a general markovian two-stage continuous-flow production system with a finite buffer. Int. J. Prod. Econ. **120**(2), 327–339 (2009)
23. Gershwin, S.B., Werner, L.M.: An approximate analytical method for evaluating the performance of closed-loop flow systems with unreliable machines and finite buffers. Int. J. Prod. Res. **45**(14), 3085–3111 (2007)
24. Negahban, A., Smith, J.S.: Simulation for manufacturing system design and operation: literature review and analysis. J. Manuf. Syst. **33**(2), 241–261 (2014)
25. Chang, Q., Ni, J., Bandyopadhyay, P., Biller, S., Xiao, G.: Supervisory factory control based on real-time production feedback. ASME J. Manuf. Sci. Eng. **129**(3), 653–660 (2007)
26. Colledani, M., Gershwin, S.B.: A decomposition method for approximate evaluation of continuous flow multi-stage lines with general markovian machines. Ann. Oper. Res. **209**(1), 5–40 (2013)
27. Liu, Y., Li, J., Chiang, S.Y.: Re-entrant lines with unreliable asynchronous machines and finite buffers: performance approximation and bottleneck identification. Int. J. Prod. Res. **50**(4), 977–990 (2012)
28. Li, C., Wang, H., Li, B.: Performance prediction of a production line with variability based on grey model artificial neural network. Chinese Control Conference, CCC, pp. 9582–9587 (2016)
29. Yang, F.: Neural network metamodeling for cycle time-throughput profiles in manufacturing. Eur. J. Oper. Res. **205**(1), 172–185 (2010)
30. Huang, J., Chang, Q., Zou, J., Arinez, J.: A real-time maintenance policy for multi-stage manufacturing systems considering imperfect maintenance effects. IEEE Access **6**, 62174–62183 (2018)
31. Zou, J., Chang, Q., Arinez, J., Xiao, G.: Data-driven modeling and real-time distributed control for energy efficient manufacturing systems. Energy **127**, 247–257 (2017)
32. Li, Y., Chang, Q., Biller, S., Xiao, G.: Event-based modelling of distributed sensor networks in battery manufacturing. Int. J. Prod. Res. **52**(14), 4239–4252 (2014)
33. Zou, J., Chang, Q., Lei, Y., Arinez, J.: Production system performance identification using sensor data. IEEE Trans. Syst. Man Cybern. Syst. **48**(2), 255–264 (2018)
34. Zou, J., Chang, Q., Arinez, J., Xiao, G.: Production performance prognostics through model-based analytical method and recency-weighted stochastic approximation method. J. Manuf. Syst. **47**, 107–114 (2018)

35. Carbery, C.M., Woods, R., Marshall, A.H.: A bayesian network based learning system for modelling faults in large-scale manufacturing. Proceedings of the IEEE International Conference on Industrial Technology, pp. 1357–1362. Lyon, France (2018)
36. Carbery, C.M., Woods, R., Marshall, A.H.: A new data analytics framework emphasising preprocessing of data to generate insights into complex manufacturing systems. Proc. Inst. Mech. Eng. Part C J. Mech. Eng. Sci. **233**(19–20), 6713–6726 (2019)
37. Peres, R.S., Barata, J., Leitao, P., Garcia, G.: Multistage quality control using machine learning in the automotive industry. IEEE Access **7**, 79908–79916 (2019)
38. Lieber, D., Stolpe, M., Konrad, B., Deuse, J., Morik, K.: Quality prediction in interlinked manufacturing processes based on supervised & unsupervised machine learning. Proc. CIRP **7**, 193–198 (2013)
39. Wang, G., Ledwoch, A., Hasani, R.M., Grosu, R., Brintrup, A.: A generative neural network model for the quality prediction of work in progress products. Appl. Soft Comput. J. **85**, 105683 (2019)
40. Wuest, T., Irgens, C., Thoben, K.D.: An approach to monitoring quality in manufacturing using supervised machine learning on product state data. J. Intell. Manuf. **25**(5), 1167–1180 (2014)
41. Liu, Y., Jin, S.: Application of bayesian networks for diagnostics in the assembly process by considering small measurement data sets. Int. J. Adv. Manuf. Technol. **65**(9–12), 1229–1237 (2013)
42. Sayed, M.S., Lohse, N.: Distributed Bayesian diagnosis for modular assembly systems—a case study. J. Manuf. Syst. **32**(3), 480–488 (2013)
43. Lei, Y., Yang, B., Jiang, X., Jia, F., Li, N., Nandi, A.K.: Applications of machine learning to machine fault diagnosis: a review and roadmap. Mech. Syst. Signal Process. **138**, 106587 (2020)
44. Jouin, M., Gouriveau, R., Hissel, D., Pera, M.C., Zerhouni, N.: Particle filter-based prognostics: review, discussion and perspectives. Mechan. Sys. Sig. Proc. **72**, 2–31 (2016)
45. Jiang, X., Senin, N., Scott, P.J., Blateyron, F.: Feature-based characterisation of surface topography and its application. CIRP Ann. **70**(2), 681–702 (2021)
46. Kaur, H., Pannu, H.S., Malhi, A.K.: A systematic review on imbalanced data challenges in machine learning: applications and solutions. ACM Comput. Surv. **52**(4), 1–36 (2019)
47. Gao, R.X., et al.: Artificial Intelligence in manufacturing: State of the art, perspectives, and future directions. CIRP Annals (2024)
48. Stricker, N., Kuhnle, A., Hofmann, C., Deininger, P.: Self adjusting multi-objective scheduling based on monte carlo tree search for matrix production assembly systems. CIRP Ann. **70**(1), 381–384 (2021)
49. Dini, G., Failli, F., Lazzerini, B., Marcelloni, F.: Generation of optimized assembly sequences using genetic algorithms. CIRP Ann. **48**(1), 17–20 (1999)
50. Raatz, A., Blankemeyer, S., Recker, T., Pischke, D., Nyhuis, P.: Task scheduling method for HRC workplaces based on capabilities and execution time assumptions for robots. CIRP Ann. **69**(1), 13–16 (2020)
51. Kardos, C., Kovacs, A., Vancza, J.: Decomposition approach to optimal feature-based assembly planning. CIRP Ann. **66**(1), 417–420 (2017)
52. Ahmad, M., Ferrer, B.R., Ahmad, B., Vera, D., Lastra, J.L., Harrison, R.: Knowledge-based PPR modelling for assembly automation. CIRP J. Manuf. Sci. Technol. **21**, 33–46 (2018)
53. Kluge, S., Riffelmacher, P., Hummel, V., Constantinescu, C., Westhamper, E.: Self-Learning and Self-Optimizing Assembly Systems. CIRP Conference on Assembly Technologies and Systems 221 (2008)
54. Herbert, M., Zwingel, M., Czapka, C., Franke, J.: A multi-source localization system for driverless material transport in mixed indoor and outdoor areas. Congress of the German Academic Association for Production Technology (WGP), pp. 421–429 (2022)

55. Borenstein, J., Koren, Y.: Histogramic in-motion mapping for mobile robot obstacle avoidance. IEEE Trans. Robot. Autom. **7**(4), 535–539 (1991)
56. Lichtenth€aler, C., Peters, A., Griffiths, S., Kirsch, A.: Social navigation-identifying robot navigation patterns in a path crossing scenario. International Conference in Social Robotics, pp. 84–93 (2013)
57. Malus, A., Kozjek, D.: Real-time order dispatching for a fleet of autonomous mobile robots using multi-agent reinforcement learning. CIRP Ann. **69**(1), 397–400 (2020)
58. Kr€uger, J., Fleischer, J., Franke, J., Groche, P.: AI in Production. Whitepaper of the German Academic Association for Production Technology (WGP), pp. 1–25 (2019)
59. Liu, Z., Liu, Q., Xu, W., Wang, L., Zhou, Z.: Robot learning towards smart robotic manufacturing: a review. Robot. Comp.-Integr. Manufact. **77**, 102360 (2022)
60. Makris, S., Dietrich, F., Kellens, K., Hu, S.J.: Automated assembly of non-rigid objects. CIRP Ann. **72**(2), 513–539 (2023)
61. Lee, A.X., Lu, H., Gupta, A., Levine, S., Abbeel, P.: Learning force-based manipulation of deformable objects from multiple demonstrations. IEEE International Conference on Robotics and Automation (ICRA), pp. 177–184 (2015)
62. Vongbunyong, S., Kara, S., Pagnucco, M.: Application of cognitive robotics in disassembly of products. CIRP Ann. **62**(1), 31–34 (2013)
63. Tian, Y., et al.: Assemble them all: physics-based planning for generalizable assembly by disassembly. ACM Transactions on Graphics (TOG) **41**(6), 1–11 (2022)
64. Mangold, S., Steiner, C., Friedmann, M., Fleischer, J.: Vision-based screw head detection for automated disassembly for remanufacturing. Procedia CIRP **105**, 1–6 (2022)
65. Bdiwi, M., Rashid, A., Putz, M.: Autonomous disassembly of electric vehicle motors based on robot cognition. IEEE International Conference on Robotics and Automation (ICRA), pp. 2500–2505 (2016)
66. Foo, G., Kara, S., Pagnucco, M.: Screw detection for disassembly of electronic waste using reasoning and re-training of a deep learning model. Procedia CIRP **98**, 666–671 (2021)
67. Yildiz, E., et al.: A visual intelligence scheme for hard drive disassembly in automated recycling routines. International Conference on Robotics, Computer Vision, and Intelligent Systems, pp. 17–27 (2020)
68. Kr€uger, J., Lien, T.K., Verl, A.: Cooperation of Human and Machines in Assembly Lines. CIRP Annals **58**(2), 628–646 (2009)
69. Zhang, J., Liu, H., Chang, Q., Wang, L., Gao, R.: Recurrent neural network for motion trajectory prediction in human-robot collaborative assembly. CIRP Ann. **69**(1), 9–12 (2020)
70. Wang, L., Liu, S., Cooper, C., Wang, X.V., Gao, R.: Function block-based human-robot collaborative assembly driven by brainwaves. CIRP Ann. **70**(1), 5–8 (2021)
71. Kr€uger, J., et al.: Innovative Control of Assembly Systems and Lines. CIRP Annals **66**(2), 707–730 (2017)
72. Semeraro, F., Griffiths, A., Cangelosi, A.: HumanRobot collaboration and machine learning: a systematic review of recent research. Robot. Comp.-Integr. Manufact. **79**, 102432 (2023)
73. Kuschan, J., Kr€uger, J.: Fatigue recognition in overhead assembly based on a soft robotic exosuit for worker assistance. CIRP Annals **70**(1), 9–12 (2021)
74. Russell, M., Wang, P.: Maximizing model generalization for manufacturing with self-supervised learning and federated learning. J. Manuf. Syst. **71**, 274–285 (2023)
75. Guo, S., et al.: Machine learning for metal additive manufacturing: towards a physics-informed data-driven paradigm. J. Manuf. Syst. **62**, 145–163 (2022)
76. Dornheim, J., Link, N., Gumbsch, P.: Model-free adaptive optimal control of episodic fixed-horizon manufacturing processes using reinforcement learning. Int. J. Contr. Autom. Sys. **18**(6), 1593–1604 (2020)

77. Hewing, L., Wabersich, K.P., Menner, M., Zeilinger, M.N.: Learning-based model predictive control: toward safe learning in control. Annual Review of Control, Robotics, and Autonomous Systems **3**, 269–296 (2020)
78. Wabersich, K.P., Hewing, L., Carron, A., Zeilinger, M.N.: Probabilistic model predictive safety certification for learning-based control. IEEE Trans. Autom. Control **67**(1), 176–188 (2021)
79. Kladovasilakis, N., Charalampous, P., Kostavelis, I., Tzetzis, D., Tzovaras, D.: Impact of metal additive manufacturing parameters on the powder bed fusion and direct energy deposition processes: a comprehensive review. Progress in Additive Manufacturing, pp. 349–365 (2021)
80. Wang, P., Gao, R., Yan, R.: A deep learning-based approach to material removal rate prediction in polishing. CIRP Ann. **66**(1), 429–432 (2017)
81. Mikolov, T., Chen, K., Corrado, G., Dean, J.: Efficient Estimation of Word Representations in Vector Space (2013)
82. Vaswani, A., et al.: Attention is all you need. Adv. Neural. Inf. Process. Syst. **30**, 5998–6008 (2017)
83. Levine, S., Pastor, P., Krizhevsky, A., Ibarz, J., Quillen, D.: Learning hand-eye coordination for robotic grasping with deep learning and large-scale data collection. The Int. J. f Robot. Res. **37**(4–5), 421–436 (2018)
84. Lu, Y.J., Tsao, Y., Watanabe, S.: A study on speech enhancement based on diffusion probabilistic model. Asia-Pacific Signal and Information Processing Association Annual Summit and Conference (APSIPA ASC), pp. 659–666 (2021)
85. Stability AI: Stable Diffusion Launch Announcement (2022), https://stability.ai/blog/stable-diffusion-announcement. Accessed 15 March 2023
86. Mali, H.S., Manna, A.: Current status and application of abrasive flow finishing processes: a review. Proceedings of the Institution of Mechanical Engineers, Part B: Journal of Engineering Manufacture **223**(7), 809–820 (2009)
87. Balyan, A.K., et al.: A hybrid intrusion detection model using ega-pso and improved random forest method. Sensors **22**(16), 5986 (2022)

Computational Intelligent Algorithms in Smart Energy Management System for Load Forecasting: A Systematic Review

Gursleen Kaur$^{(\boxtimes)}$ and Rajesh Kumar Bawa

Punjabi University, Patiala, India
gursleen109@gmail.com

Abstract. The increasing integration of renewable energy sources and the dynamic nature of electricity demand necessitates the adoption of smart energy management systems (SEMS) to ensure efficient, reliable, and sustainable power distribution. This paper provides a systematic and comprehensive review of computational intelligent algorithms applied in smart energy management systems, focusing on load forecasting strategies. Load forecasting is critical for predicting future energy consumption patterns, enabling proactive decision-making and optimized resource allocation. The paper examines a variety of computational intelligence techniques, including deep learning, and hybrid models, highlighting their capabilities, performance metrics, and limitations. By synthesizing current research findings and identifying future research directions, this paper aims to provide valuable insights for researchers, practitioners, and policymakers involved in the development and deployment of smart energy management systems.

Keywords: Deep Learning · SEMS · LSTM · CNN · Hybrid

1 Introduction

With the increasing complexity of power grids and the rising adoption of renewable energy sources, traditional energy management techniques are proving insufficient. Smart Energy Management Systems (SEMS) have emerged as pivotal components in modern power grids, enabling efficient energy distribution and consumption through advanced monitoring, control, and optimization techniques. A critical component of SEMS is load forecasting, which involves predicting future energy demand based on historical data and various influencing factors. Accurate load forecasting enables utilities to balance supply and demand more effectively, reducing the risk of blackouts and ensuring a stable energy supply [1]. There are various types of load forecasting, each serving different purposes and having distinct characteristics. Table 1 provides a concise overview of the key characteristics of each load forecasting type, allowing for easy comparison of their time horizons, purposes, and techniques.

Additionally, demand response strategies are pivotal in SEMS, as they involve adjusting consumer energy usage during peak periods, alleviating stress on the grid, and promoting energy conservation. This real-time adaptability not only improves the reliability

S. Pal et al. (Eds.): ICETSS 2024, CCIS 2610, pp. 372–393, 2026.
https://doi.org/10.1007/978-3-032-11488-4_30

of the energy supply but also enhances the efficiency of the overall system [2]. Moreover, precise load forecasts enable more effective demand response strategies, where consumers are incentivized to shift their electricity usage to off-peak times, contributing to a more balanced and efficient grid [3, 4].

Table 1. Types of Load Forecasting

Load Forecasting Type	Time Horizon	Purpose	Techniques
Short-Term Load Forecasting (STLF)	Minutes to weeks	Real-time operation, unit commitment, dispatch	Statistical methods, machine learning, weather data
Medium-Term Load Forecasting (MTLF)	Weeks to months	Energy market trading, fuel procurement	Statistical methods, economic indicators
Long-Term Load Forecasting (LTLF)	Months to years	Capacity planning, resource expansion, policy	Economic forecasting, population growth, policies
Very Short-Term Load Forecasting (VSTLF)	Minutes to hours	Real-time fluctuations, renewable energy integration	Real-time data, weather forecasting, machine learning
Peak Load Forecasting	Daily or seasonally	Capacity planning, ensuring peak demand is met	Historical peak load data, weather conditions
Probabilistic Load Forecasting	Any timeframe	Provides a range of scenarios with probabilities	Monte Carlo simulations, ensemble methods
Smart Grid Load Forecasting	Short to very short-term	Supports smart grid integration	Real-time data from smart meters, machine learning
Dynamic Load Forecasting	Variable	Assess the impact of sudden changes	Real-time data, system dynamics modeling, controls

Computational Intelligence (CI) algorithms have revolutionized the field of load forecasting by improving the accuracy and efficiency of traditional approaches. Traditional techniques, such as time series analysis [5] and regression models [6], often struggled with the complexity and non-linearity of power consumption data. However, computational intelligence approaches, particularly ANNs [7], SVMs [8], and fuzzy logic systems [9], have tried to outperform these weaknesses.

Deep learning surpasses traditional machine learning in electricity load forecasting by capturing complex, non-linear relationships and temporal dependencies in large datasets without the need for manual feature engineering. For example, ensemble LSTM models can make better forecasts by incorporating theory-guided knowledge [10]. Additionally, it has been shown that contrary to machine learning methods, deep learning approaches—such as LSTM-CNN hybrids—work much better in STLF tasks. These models hugely reduce the forecasting errors, hence reliable to be used in real-life applications [11]. Hybrid algorithms, by merging deep learning with machine learning and optimization techniques, have given significantly improved results in electricity load forecasting [12]. Deep learning models optimized by heuristic algorithms like genetic algorithms or particle swarm optimization achieve better accuracy due to balancing exploration and exploitation of patterns in data [13].

Recent advancements in computational intelligence algorithms have significantly enhanced load forecasting in smart energy management systems. For instance, hybrid models combining machine learning and deep learning techniques, such as LSTM networks with ARIMA, have shown improved accuracy in predicting energy consumption patterns. Probabilistic methods like Gaussian processes are now being used to handle the inherent uncertainty in energy consumption, providing a range of possible outcomes and aiding in better decision-making [14]. Additionally, the integration of reinforcement learning allows these systems to adapt to real-time changes in energy usage, making them more responsive and efficient [15]. Furthermore, the use of parallel computing and cloud-based solutions has boosted computational efficiency, enabling real-time forecasting. These advancements, coupled with the incorporation of external factors like weather and economic indicators through ensemble learning methods, have made load forecasting more robust and accurate. These innovations are crucial for optimizing energy distribution, reducing costs, and promoting sustainability in smart grids. It is the continuing evolution of CI algorithms in load forecasting that is paving the way for increasing Internet of Things integrations, further improving the granularity and responsiveness of forecasts. They can process high-dimensional datasets, capturing intricate relationships among features such as seasonality, trends, economic behavior, occupation, and many interaction effects that provide correct forecasts and decisions by extracting the rich multidimensional information embedded in the data [16].

This paper will center on the application of deep learning algorithms within Smart Energy Management Systems (SEMS) for load forecasting. By focusing on deep learning, the review aims to explore recent advancements, practical case studies, and the distinct advantages these algorithms offer in optimizing energy management. The objective is to provide a thorough analysis of how deep learning can revolutionize energy systems, highlighting both the potential benefits and challenges of their implementation.

2 Methodology

This paper has conducted an extensive electronic literature search for studies related to computational intelligent algorithms executed within the setting of a smart energy management system for load forecasting, from 2013 through 2024. After the identification process, six full-text archives were reviewed in this study: Science-Direct, Google Scholar, Scopus, Web of Science, PubMed, and EMBASE. The keywords used in the search include "Computational Intelligence Algorithms", "Smart Energy Management System", "Load Forecasting", "Residential Energy Management", "Industrial Energy Management", "Commercial Energy Management", "Single Variable Load Forecasting", "Multiple Variable Load Forecasting", "Traditional Time Series", "Machine Learning", "Deep Learning", and "Hybrid Models."

This is an overall systematic review with a PRISMA (Preferred Reporting Items for Systematic Reviews and Meta-Analyses) approach, including the definition of specific inclusion and exclusion criteria for the selection of studies as shown in Fig. 1. From the initial search, 750 articles were identified. A primary screening based on titles and abstracts was conducted to filter out studies that were irrelevant to the research question. This phase eliminated 300 articles, focusing the review on the remaining 450 studies that potentially met the inclusion criteria.

The full-text review of the 450 articles involved a more in-depth assessment against the predefined inclusion and exclusion criteria. Studies were included if they met the following criteria:

- Published in English.
- Focused on computational intelligence algorithms within smart energy management systems.
- Addressed load forecasting across residential, industrial, or commercial contexts.
- Utilized deep learning, hybrid models, or advanced machine learning techniques.

Conversely, articles were excluded if they were:

- Published in languages other than English.
- Irrelevant to load forecasting in energy management systems.
- Not centered on computational intelligence algorithms.
- Reviews or meta-analyses that lacked original data or new insights.

Through this rigorous process, 330 articles were excluded due to irrelevance to the specific context of computational intelligence in load forecasting, or because they failed to provide new insights beyond what was already known.

After careful perusal, 350 of the articles had information irrelevant to the subject of the study and hence did not pass the exclusion criteria, thereby leaving 100 articles. After a further detailed evaluation, another 19 articles were discarded that had not met the inclusion criteria in detail or did not provide adequate data, thereby selecting 81 articles for the detailed review.

On top of this, there are a few research questions that have been framed and investigated in the study:

RQ1: How can machine learning and deep learning models improve the accuracy of electricity load forecasting by handling non-linear relationships and temporal dependencies in the data?

RQ2: How can multivariable inputs, such as weather data, economic indicators, and social factors, be effectively integrated into deep learning models to enhance the accuracy of electricity load forecasting?

RQ3: How can demand-side management (DSM) strategies be effectively integrated with deep learning models to optimize electricity load forecasting and enhance grid stability?

RQ4: How can renewable energy sources be effectively integrated into load forecasting models to improve grid stability and sustainability?

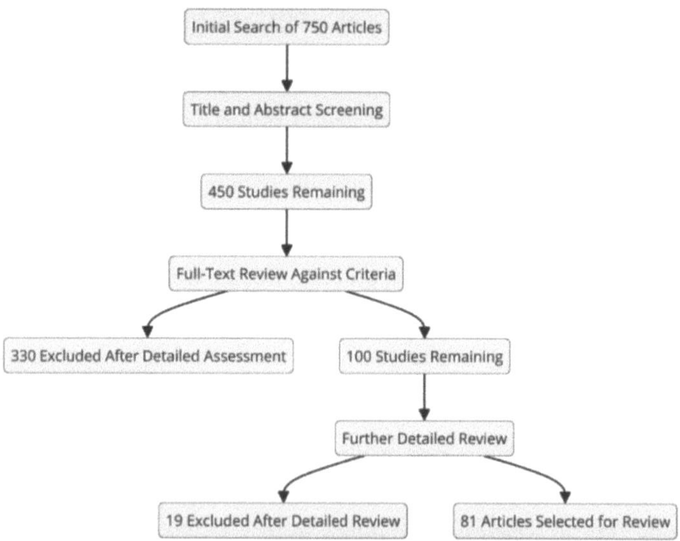

Fig. 1. Methodology for the systematic review

3   Process for Electricity Load Forecasting

3.1   Data Acquisition

In effect, load forecasting demands a robust process of data acquisition, which includes the gathering of data and its integration from various sources. Accurate and comprehensive data acquisition forms the basis of the development of reliable models for load forecasting.

Types of Data

- **Historical Load Data**: Historical electricity consumption data is fundamental. Such data helps in understanding the trends of consumption, which is very vital in understanding future loads [17].
- **Weather Data**: Weather conditions exert a huge impact on electricity use. Typically, temperature, humidity, wind speed, and other meteorological variables are incorporated into forecasting models to make the estimates more accurate [18].
- **Economic Data:** Economic indicators, such as GDP, industry production, and employment rate, may indicate electricity demand. The integration of these factors into the model allows one to take into consideration the trends in the macroeconomy for the different forecasting models [19].
- **Demographic Data:** Population growth, urbanization rates, and household sizes are demographic factors that largely influence electricity consumption [20].
- **Behavioral Data:** The information about consumer behavior, such as the trends in energy consumption during peak and off-peak hours, is also being increasingly used in load forecasting [21].

Data Collection Methods

- **Smart Meters:** Their deployment gives high-resolution real-time consumption data, improving granularity and timeliness in load forecasting models [22].
- **Weather stations:** Data from the weather stations and meteorological services offer a way through which real-time weather conditions are integrated into the model of forecasting, hence improving responsiveness to immediate changes in weather [23].
- **Energy Management Systems (EMS):** Data provided by energy management systems include distribution, generation, and consumption information that brings about an all-inclusive view of energy use [24].
- **Social media and Internet of Things (IoT) Sensors:** Social media and IoT sensors facilitate a seamless information flow about consumer and environmental behavior [25].

3.2 Data Preprocessing

- **Missing data handling:** Handling the missing data is one of the essential steps in developing a robust model for load forecasting. Some common techniques that are used include imputation methods like mean substitution, interpolation, or using machine learning algorithms to predict missing values [26].
- **Outlier Detection and Removal:** The identification and subsequent removal of outliers is of prime importance to prevent skewed results in Load Forecasting Models. The outlier can be detected using its Z-scores or IQR analysis [27].
- **Normalization and Scaling**: Normalization and scaling of data are necessary to ensure that different features contribute equally to the model. Techniques such as min-max scaling or z-score normalization are commonly used to standardize the data [28].
- **Data Aggregation**: Aggregating data over specific time intervals (e.g., hourly, daily) can simplify the model while preserving essential patterns. Aggregation helps in reducing noise and computational complexity [29].

3.3 Model Building

Electricity-load forecasting is a fairly important segment in ensuring the efficiency of power systems and the optimization of energy resources. The methodologies related to load forecasting can, in general, be located within three broad groups: Traditional or Classical Time Series, Machine Learning, and Deep Learning. Recently, there has been growing interest in hybrid models that combine approaches from these three categories to obtain more accurate and robust forecasts. The flowchart in Fig. 2 represents the different methodologies from each category, showing the variety of methods that allow for effective electricity load forecasting. In this paper, we focus only on deep learning for electricity load forecasting. As shown in Table 2, deep learning methods and hybrid approaches are surveyed, giving an idea of how powerful forecasting tools have evolved and are promising for the chosen domain.

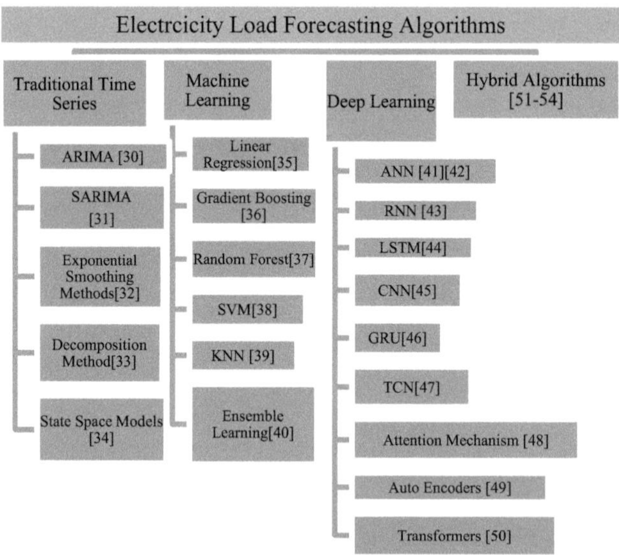

Fig. 2. Flowchart of Electricity Load Forecasting Algorithms

Table 2. Deep Learning and Hybrid Electricity Load Forecasting Summary

Year	Dataset	Algorithm used	Data preprocessing	Key findings	Evaluation metrics	Research gaps
2023 [53]	**Source:** Smart-meter data from a Commonwealth Edison (ComEd) service area **Features:** Hourly electricity consumption, time of use, demographic information, weather data	Random Forests Gradient Boosting Machines (GBM) Support Vector Machines (SVM) Neural Networks (e.g., LSTM, CNN)	Handled missing values and outliers Aggregation: Data aggregated at various levels (e.g., hourly, daily) Feature Engineering: Created features like time-of-day and weather effect	Bottom-up models provide high granularity in forecasting. Effective at capturing specific consumption patterns Challenges in scalability and generalization	MAE RMSE MAPE	**Scalability:** Difficulty in scaling models to larger populations **Generalization:** Challenges in applying models across different regions **Data Privacy:** Need for further research on privacy-preserving methods in smart-meter data forecasting
2016 [54]	**Sources:** Historical building energy consumption data and weather data **Features:** Time of day, historical load, temperature, humidity, wind speed, day of the week, seasonality	Deep Neural Networks (DNNs)	Normalization of input data Handling missing values Feature selection (e.g., weather parameters, time-based features) Splitting data into training and test sets	Deep Neural Networks (DNNs) offer superior accuracy in energy load forecasting compared to traditional methods like ARIMA. The model effectively captures nonlinear relationships in the data.	MAE RMSE	Challenges in scalability, computational complexity, and model adaptability to diverse building types
2019 [55]	**Sources:** Various historical electricity load datasets and weather data **Features:** Time series load data, temperature, humidity, wind speed, and other environmental factors	Recurrent Neural Networks (RNN), Long Short-Term Memory (LSTM), Convolutional Neural Networks (CNN), Stacked Autoencoders (SAE)	Normalization of data Handling missing data Feature extraction and selection Splitting datasets for training and validation	The study highlights the effectiveness of DL techniques like RNN, LSTM, CNN, and SAE in improving short-term load forecasting accuracy.	MAPE RMSE	The study identifies challenges in model interpretability and the need for more comprehensive datasets for better generalization.

(continued)

Table 2. *(continued)*

Year	Dataset	Algorithm used	Data preprocessing	Key findings	Evaluation metrics	Research gaps
2023 [53]	**Sources:** Smart-meter data from specific regions **Features:** Hourly electricity usage, time of use, demographic data, weather conditions (temperature, humidity)	Machine learning models like Random Forests, Gradient Boosting Machines (GBM), Neural Networks (e.g., LSTM)	Data cleaning to remove noise Feature selection based on relevance Aggregation at different levels (household, region) Splitting into training and test datasets	Bottom-up forecasting models can provide high accuracy in predicting energy demand at granular levels, but they face challenges in scalability and generalization.	MAE RMSE MAPE	Identified gaps include scalability, computational complexity, and challenges in generalizing the model across different regions and demographic groups.
2023 [56]	**Source:** Various publicly available datasets (specific datasets not mentioned) **Features:** Historical load data, weather data (temperature, humidity), time-of-day, day-of-week, holidays	Machine Learning: Support Vector Machines (SVM), Random Forests - Deep Learning: Long Short-Term Memory (LSTM), Convolutional Neural Networks (CNN)	Normalization of features Handling missing data using interpolation Feature selection based on correlation analysis	Deep learning models, especially LSTM, outperformed traditional machine learning models in accuracy. Incorporating weather and time-based features improved forecasting accuracy CNNs were particularly effective in capturing spatial-temporal dependencies	MAE RMSE MAPE	Need for more robust data preprocessing methods to handle noisy data Lack of exploration into the interpretability of deep learning models Limited focus on real-time application and scalability of the proposed models
2016 [54]	**Source:** Publicly available building energy datasets **Features:** Historical energy consumption data, weather data (temperature, humidity), time-of-day, day-of-week	Deep Learning: Deep Neural Networks (DNNs) Specific architecture includes multiple hidden layers with ReLU activation functions	Normalization of input features Data cleaning to handle missing or incomplete data Time-series segmentation to create input-output pairs for supervised learning	Deep Neural Networks significantly improved the accuracy of building energy load forecasting compared to traditional models. The model effectively captured the non-linear relationships in the data, especially with varying weather conditions Incorporating multiple layers in the DNN allowed the model to learn complex patterns in energy consumption	MAE RMSE R^2	Need for further exploration of model interpretability. Limited examination of the model's performance across different types of buildings and climates Future work suggested incorporating more diverse datasets for better generalization of the model
2023 [57]	**Source:** National electricity load data from the Turkish power system **Features:** Historical load data, weather parameters (temperature, humidity), calendar information (day-of-week, holidays)	Deep Learning Techniques: Long Short-Term Memory (LSTM) networks, Gated Recurrent Units (GRU)	Data Cleaning: Handling missing values through interpolation Normalization: Min-Max scaling of features to [0,1] range Feature Engineering: Creation of additional time-based features (e.g., lag features)	Both LSTM and GRU models outperformed traditional forecasting methods in short-term load prediction. GRU slightly outperformed LSTM in terms of forecasting accuracy and computational efficiency Inclusion of weather and calendar features enhanced the predictive performance of the models	MAPE RMSE MAE	The study focused solely on the Turkish power system; applicability to other regions remains to be tested Limited exploration of real-time forecasting capabilities Future work suggested incorporating other deep learning architectures and hybrid models for potential improvements

Table 2. *(continued)*

Year	Dataset	Algorithm used	Data preprocessing	Key findings	Evaluation metrics	Research gaps
2022 [58]	**Source:** Real-world electricity consumption data from a regional utility provider in Turkey **Features:** Historical load data, weather data (temperature, humidity, wind speed), calendar information (day-of-week, holidays)	Deep Learning Algorithms: Long Short-Term Memory (LSTM), Gated Recurrent Units (GRU), Convolutional Neural Networks (CNN)	Data Cleaning: Handling missing data through interpolation Normalization: Min-Max scaling of input features Feature Engineering: Inclusion of time-based features (e.g., lagged load values, hour-of-day)	LSTM and GRU models provided superior accuracy compared to traditional forecasting methods, with LSTM slightly outperforming GRU CNN was effective in capturing spatial dependencies, although it was less accurate than LSTM for time series data The inclusion of weather and calendar features significantly improved the performance of all models	RMSE MAPE MAE	The study was limited to a single regional dataset; generalizability to other regions remains untested. Limited exploration of the impact of different hyperparameter settings on model performance Future research could explore the integration of renewable energy forecasts and economic indicators for improved accuracy
2023 [59]	**Source:** Regional electricity load data from a Chinese power grid **Features:** Historical load data, weather variables (temperature, humidity), calendar information (day-of-week, holidays), and time-of-day	Deep Learning Algorithms: CNN-BiGRU-Attention model Optimization Technique: Tree-structured Parzen Estimator (TPE) for hyperparameter optimization	Data Cleaning: Handling missing data through interpolation Normalization: Min-Max scaling of features to [0,1] range Feature Engineering: Creation of time-based features, including lagged values and moving averages	The TPE-optimized CNN-BiGRU-Attention model outperformed traditional models and baseline deep learning models The attention mechanism significantly improved the model's ability to focus on relevant input features during forecasting CNN was effective in feature extraction, while BiGRU handled sequential dependencies, leading to improved accuracy	MAE RMSE MAPE	Limited to a specific regional dataset; further validation across different regions and grid conditions is needed The study focused primarily on short-term forecasting; the model's effectiveness for medium- and long-term forecasting was not explored Future research could explore the integration of additional external factors, such as economic data or renewable energy inputs
2024 [60]	**Source:** Historical daily average load demand data from a regional power system (specific region not mentioned) **Features:** Historical load data, seasonal trends, calendar features (day-of-week, holidays), temperature data	Deep Learning Algorithm: Long Short-Term Memory (LSTM) model Focus on capturing historical load trends for daily average load demand forecasting	Data Cleaning: Removal of outliers and handling missing values through interpolation Normalization: Min-Max scaling of input features to [0,1] range Feature Engineering: Incorporation of lag features and moving averages to enhance the model's understanding of temporal dependencies	The LSTM model effectively captured historical load trends, leading to accurate daily average load demand forecasts Incorporation of calendar and seasonal features significantly improved the model's performance The model demonstrated robustness in handling variations in load demand due to holidays and seasonal changes	RMSE MAE) MAPE	The study was limited to daily average load forecasting; further research could explore hourly or real-time forecasting Limited exploration of the model's performance across different geographic regions or grid conditions Future work suggested integrating additional external factors, such as economic indicators or renewable energy generation data, to further improve accuracy

(continued)

Table 2. *(continued)*

Year	Dataset	Algorithm used	Data preprocessing	Key findings	Evaluation metrics	Research gaps
2022 [61]	**Source:** Regional power load data from a Chinese power grid **Features:** Historical load data, weather conditions (temperature, humidity, wind speed), calendar information (day-of-week, holidays), time-of-day	Hybrid Neural Network: CNN-LSTM model CNN (Convolutional Neural Network) for feature extraction and pattern recognition LSTM (Long Short-Term Memory) for capturing temporal dependencies in the load data	Data Cleaning: Handling missing data using interpolation and removal of outliers Normalization: Min-Max scaling of input features to normalize data Feature Engineering: Creation of additional time-based features and lag features to improve the model's predictive performance	The CNN-LSTM hybrid model outperformed traditional models and standalone deep learning models in power load forecasting CNN effectively extracted spatial features from the data, while LSTM captured temporal dependencies, leading to more accurate predictions The model demonstrated strong performance in handling non-linear and complex relationships in the data	RMSE MAE MAPE	The study focused on short-term load forecasting; further exploration is needed to assess the model's performance in medium- and long-term forecasting scenarios The model's generalizability to different regions and grid conditions remains untested Future work suggested exploring the integration of real-time data and more diverse datasets to enhance model robustness and scalability
2021 [12]	**Source:** Publicly available electricity load datasets from a European power grid **Features:** Historical load data, weather data (temperature, humidity, wind speed), time-of-day, day-of-week, holidays, and special events	Machine Learning Techniques: Decision Trees, Random Forests, Support Vector Machines (SVM) - Parallel Deep Learning Approach: Parallel LSTM-CNN model	Data Cleaning: Handling missing data using interpolation and outlier detection Normalization: Min-Max scaling of features to normalize data Feature Engineering: Creation of lag features, moving averages, and calendar-based features to capture complex patterns	The parallel LSTM-CNN model outperformed traditional machine learning techniques and standalone deep learning models in short-term load forecasting - The parallel architecture leveraged the strengths of both LSTM and CNN, leading to improved accuracy and robustness The model was particularly effective in handling non-linear relationships and seasonal variations in the load data	RMSE MAE MAPE	The study focused on short-term load forecasting; future research could explore the model's effectiveness in medium- and long-term forecasting scenarios Limited exploration of the model's scalability and generalizability to other regions and grid conditions Future work could involve integrating additional external factors, such as economic indicators or real-time data, to further enhance model accuracy and applicability
2021 [12]	**Source:** Energy consumption data from a commercial building in Stuttgart, Germany. **Features:** Time of day, day of the week, historical load data, weather data (temperature, humidity, etc.).	Main Algorithm: Parallel deep LSTM-CNN (Long Short-Term Memory and Convolutional Neural Network). Other Techniques: Machine learning techniques including Support Vector Machines (SVM), Random Forests (RF), and Gradient Boosting Machines (GBM) for comparison.	Normalization: Data normalization to improve model performance. Feature Selection: Identification of relevant features for the model. Data Splitting: Splitting data into training, validation, and test sets.	Performance: The proposed parallel deep LSTM-CNN model outperformed traditional machine learning methods. Efficiency: Improved accuracy in short-term load forecasting compared to standalone LSTM or CNN models.	RMSE MAPE R^2	Generalization: Limited generalization to other types of buildings or regions. Data Diversity: Need for more diverse datasets to validate the robustness of the model. Model Interpretability: Challenges in interpreting the deep learning model's predictions.
2023 [62]	**Source:** Typically from regional energy grids or utility companies. **Features:** Time of day, historical load data, weather conditions, holidays, and other regional factors.	Main Algorithm: LSTM-Attention-GA. - Components: 1. LSTM: For sequential data modeling. 2. Attention: For focusing on important time steps in the sequence. 3. Genetic Algorithm: For optimizing model parameters.	Normalization: Data normalization to scale features. Feature Engineering: Identification and creation of relevant features. -Data Splitting: Typically split into training, validation, and test sets.	Performance: The combination of LSTM, Attention, and GA enhances the model's accuracy and robustness. Optimization: GA effectively optimizes the model parameters, improving forecasting accuracy.	RMSE MAPE MAE	Scalability: The need to test the model on larger datasets or different regions. Model Complexity: Balancing accuracy with model interpretability and computational cost. Real-Time Application: Challenges in deploying the model for real-time forecasting.

(continued)

Table 2. *(continued)*

Year	Dataset	Algorithm used	Data preprocessing	Key findings	Evaluation metrics	Research gaps
2023 [63]	**Source:** Commonly from power utility companies or public datasets related to energy consumption. **Features:** Time series data on energy consumption, weather conditions, day of the week, holidays, and other relevant factors.	Main Algorithm: Hybrid model combining Multi-Directional Gated Recurrent Unit (MD-GRU) and Convolutional Neural Network (CNN). Components: 1. MD-GRU: For capturing complex temporal patterns in load data. 2. CNN: For extracting spatial features and improving forecasting accuracy.	Normalization: Applied to input data for scaling features. Feature Engineering: Creation and selection of relevant features. Data Splitting: Division into training, validation, and test sets.	Performance: The hybrid MD-GRU and CNN model shows improved forecasting accuracy over standalone models. Efficiency: The integration of CNN enhances the model's ability to handle multi-dimensional data.	- Root Mean Squared Error (RMSE) - Mean Absolute Percentage Error (MAPE) - R-squared (R^2)	Generalization: Testing the model's performance on different types of datasets or regions. Model Complexity: Balancing model complexity with interpretability and computational efficiency. Real-Time Application: Challenges in deploying the model for real-time forecasting scenarios.
2017 [64]	**Source:** Likely based on historical electrical load data from a smart grid system. **Features:** Historical load values, time of day, weather conditions, and other relevant factors transformed into image-like formats for CNN processing.	Main Algorithm: Convolutional Neural Network (CNN). Approach: Treating electrical load data as images to leverage CNN's ability to recognize patterns in grid load behavior.	Transformation: Converting time series data into image-like representations to be fed into the CNN. Normalization: Standardization of input data for consistent CNN processing. Data Augmentation: Possible creation of additional "image" samples to enhance model training.	Performance: The CNN-based approach improves short-term load forecasting accuracy compared to traditional methods. Novelty: Demonstrated that electrical load data could be effectively processed as images, opening new avenues for applying image-based neural networks in energy forecasting.	RMSE MAPE	Scalability: Potential issues with applying the approach to larger datasets or different regions. Interpretability: Challenges in interpreting the CNN's decision-making process. Real-World Application: Need for further validation in real-world smart grid scenarios.
2021 [65]	**Source:** Likely derived from historical energy consumption data provided by utility companies or public databases. **Features:** Time series data including historical load values, weather data (temperature, humidity, etc.), day of the week, holidays, and other contextual factors.	Main Algorithm: BiGRU-CNN (Bidirectional Gated Recurrent Unit - Convolutional Neural Network). Components: 1. BiGRU: Captures temporal dependencies in both forward and backward directions. 2. CNN: Extracts local features from the time series data, enhancing pattern recognition.	Normalization: Standardizing the input data to ensure consistency across the dataset. Feature Engineering: Selection and creation of relevant features for the model. Data Splitting: Dividing the dataset into training, validation, and test sets to evaluate model performance.	Performance: The BiGRU-CNN model outperformed traditional methods and standalone models like BiGRU or CNN. Efficiency: The combination of BiGRU and CNN provided better accuracy and robustness in short-term load forecasting.	RMSE MAPE MAE	Scalability: Need to evaluate the model's performance on different datasets or regions. Model Interpretability: The complexity of the hybrid model can make it challenging to interpret the results. Real-Time Application: Potential challenges in deploying the model for real-time load forecasting.

(continued)

Table 2. *(continued)*

Year	Dataset	Algorithm used	Data preprocessing	Key findings	Evaluation metrics	Research gaps
2021 [66]	**Source:** Historical load data from Greece's power grid, possibly including data from the Hellenic Transmission System Operator. **Features:** Historical electrical load values, weather data (temperature, humidity), calendar information (day of the week, holidays), and possibly economic indicators.	Normalization: Standardization or normalization of input data. Chaos Analysis: Application of chaos theory techniques to preprocess data, such as phase space reconstruction or Lyapunov exponent calculation. Data Splitting: Dividing the data into training, validation, and test sets.	Normalization: Standardization or normalization of input data. Chaos Analysis: Application of chaos theory techniques to preprocess data, such as phase space reconstruction or Lyapunov exponent calculation. Data Splitting: Dividing the data into training, validation, and test sets.	Performance: The combination of deep learning with chaos theory provided improved forecasting accuracy compared to traditional models. Novelty: Demonstrated the effectiveness of integrating chaos theory with deep learning for handling complex and chaotic time series data in load forecasting.	RMSE MAPE MAE	Generalization: Need for further validation on different datasets or regions outside of Greece. Model Interpretability: Challenges in understanding the predictions made by complex deep learning models combined with chaos theory. Computational Complexity: High computational cost due to the integration of deep learning and chaos theory, which may affect scalability.
2020 [51]	**Source:** Residential energy consumption data, likely from smart meters or public datasets. Features: Time series data on historical energy consumption, weather conditions (temperature, humidity), time of day, day of the week, and other relevant factors.	Main Algorithm: CNN-GRU (Convolutional Neural Network Gated Recurrent Unit). Components: 1. CNN: Extracts spatial features from the input data, such as patterns within the time series. 2. GRU: Captures temporal dependencies in the sequential data, helping to forecast future loads based on past patterns.	Normalization: Scaling input data to ensure consistency across features. Feature Engineering: Creation and selection of relevant features that contribute to load forecasting. Data Splitting: Dividing data into training, validation, and test sets to evaluate the model's performance.	- Performance: The CNN-GRU hybrid model showed superior performance in short-term load forecasting compared to traditional methods and standalone models. Efficiency: The model effectively captured both spatial and temporal patterns, leading to more accurate and reliable predictions.	RMSE MAPE MAE	- Scalability: The need to assess the model's scalability and adaptability to different regions or types of residential data. Model Complexity: Balancing the complexity of the hybrid model with the need for computational efficiency and interpretability. Real-Time Application: Challenges in deploying the model for real-time load forecasting in residential settings.
2022 [67]	**Source:** Household electricity consumption data, possibly from smart meters or publicly available datasets like the UCI Machine Learning Repository. **Features:** Historical consumption data, time of day, day of the week, weather data (temperature, humidity), and other relevant household-specific factors.	Main Algorithm: Customized LSTM (Long Short-Term Memory) and GRU (Gated Recurrent Unit) models. Components: 1. LSTM: Handles long-term dependencies in sequential data to predict future consumption. 2. GRU: A simplified version of LSTM that also captures temporal dependencies but with fewer parameters, making it potentially more efficient.	Normalization: Scaling of input data to ensure consistency across features. Feature Engineering: Identification and creation of relevant features that influence household electricity consumption. Data Splitting: Dividing the dataset into training, validation, and test sets to evaluate the models' performances.	Performance: Both customized LSTM and GRU models provided accurate short-term predictions of household electricity consumption. Efficiency: The models demonstrated the ability to capture the temporal dynamics of household energy usage, with GRU being more computationally efficient.	RMSE MAPE MAE	Generalization: The need to validate the models on more diverse household datasets to ensure broad applicability. Model Interpretability: Challenges in understanding the decision-making process of complex models like LSTM and GRU. Real-Time Deployment: Potential difficulties in implementing these models for real-time forecasting in household settings due to computational constraints.

Table 2. *(continued)*

Year	Dataset	Algorithm used	Data preprocessing	Key findings	Evaluation metrics	Research gaps
2020 [68]	**Source:** Likely derived from historical load data provided by power utility companies or public datasets. **Features:** Historical load data, time of day, weather conditions (temperature, humidity), day of the week, holidays, and other factors influencing electricity consumption.	Main Algorithm: GRU-CNN (Gated Recurrent Unit - Convolutional Neural Network) hybrid neural network. Components: 1. GRU: Captures temporal dependencies in sequential data, helping in forecasting future loads based on past trends. 2. CNN: Extracts spatial features and patterns within the time series data, improving the model's accuracy.	Normalization: Scaling of input data to ensure uniformity across features. Feature Engineering: Creation and selection of relevant features that significantly impact load forecasting. Data Splitting: The dataset is divided into training, validation, and test sets to evaluate the model's performance.	Performance: The GRU-CNN hybrid model outperformed traditional methods and standalone models, demonstrating superior accuracy in short-term load forecasting. Efficiency: The integration of GRU and CNN allowed the model to effectively capture both temporal and spatial patterns in the data.	RMSE MAPE MAE	Generalization: Need for further validation on different datasets or in different regions to ensure the model's robustness. Model Interpretability: As with many hybrid deep learning models, understanding the model's decision-making process remains challenging. Real-Time Application: Potential challenges in deploying the model for real-time forecasting due to computational demands.
2022 [69]	**Source:** Historical electricity consumption data from the Spanish power grid, potentially provided by Spain's national energy providers or public datasets. **Features:** Time series data including historical electricity consumption, weather conditions (temperature, humidity), time of day, day of the week, holidays, and other factors influencing energy usage.	Main Algorithm: Deep LSTM (Long Short-Term Memory) network. Components: 1. LSTM: Handles long-term dependencies in the sequential data, making it effective for time series forecasting, such as electricity consumption. 2. Deep Learning Architecture: Involves multiple LSTM layers to capture complex patterns and relationships within the data.	Normalization: Scaling input data to a uniform range to improve model performance. Feature Engineering: Identification and creation of relevant features to enhance the forecasting accuracy. Data Splitting: The dataset is divided into training, validation, and test sets to evaluate the model's performance.	Performance: The deep LSTM network provided highly accurate short-term electricity consumption forecasts, outperforming traditional models. Efficiency: The deep architecture allowed the model to capture intricate temporal dependencies, leading to improved forecasting results.	RMSE MAPE MAE R^2	Generalization: Further validation on different datasets or in different regions to ensure the robustness of the model. Model Interpretability: Challenges in interpreting the deep LSTM model's decision-making process due to its complexity. Real-Time Application: Addressing computational efficiency for deploying the model in real-time forecasting scenarios.
2023 [45]	**Source:** Publicly available electricity load datasets from multiple sources. **Features:** Hourly load data, temperature, time-of-day, day-of-week, and holiday indicators.	Main Algorithm: LSTM, GRU, RNN Components: - LSTM (Long Short-Term Memory): Gates (input, forget, output), cell state. - GRU (Gated Recurrent Unit): Gates (reset, update), hidden state. - RNN (Recurrent Neural Network): Hidden state, sequential data processing.	Data normalization: Scaling values within a specific range. Feature scaling: Ensuring equal contribution of all input features. Handling missing data: Imputing missing values with mean/median or predicting missing entries.	LSTM outperformed GRU and RNN in capturing long-term dependencies in the load data. GRU showed comparable performance to LSTM but with reduced computational complexity. - RNN struggled with vanishing gradient issues, leading to lower	RMSE MAPE	Need for further optimization of LSTM and GRU models to handle larger datasets and more complex feature sets. Exploration of hybrid models combining these architectures with others like CNN for enhanced accuracy.

(continued)

Table 2. *(continued)*

Year	Dataset	Algorithm used	Data preprocessing	Key findings	Evaluation metrics	Research gaps
2020 [70]	**Source:** Large-scale electricity load datasets from utility companies. Features: Hourly load data, temperature, humidity, time-of-day, day-of-week, and economic indicators.	Main Algorithm: AI Techniques Ensemble (Combination of ML & DL methods) Components: - CNN for feature extraction - LSTM for capturing temporal dependencies - Random Forest for decision-making and ensemble learning	Data cleaning: Removing outliers and handling missing values. Data normalization: Scaling features to a uniform range. Feature engineering: Creating new features based on domain knowledge.	The ensemble model outperformed individual models by leveraging the strengths of different AI techniques. CNN effectively handled high-dimensional data, while LSTM captured temporal dependencies. Random Forest improved the model's robustness and decision-making accuracy.	RMSE MAPE	The complexity of the ensemble model leads to high computational costs. Further work is needed to streamline model integration and improve real-time processing capabilities. Exploration of more scalable ensemble methods to handle larger datasets.
2019 [71]	**Source:** Residential energy consumption datasets from smart meters. **Features:** Hourly energy usage, temperature, humidity, time-of-day, day-of-week, and appliance usage data.	Main Algorithm: CNN-LSTM Neural Network Components: - CNN (Convolutional Neural Network) for feature extraction and pattern recognition. - LSTM (Long Short-Term Memory) for capturing temporal dependencies in sequential data.	Data normalization: Scaling features to ensure a uniform contribution. Feature extraction: Using CNN to automatically learn and extract relevant features from the input data. Handling missing data: Imputing missing values to maintain data consistency.	The CNN-LSTM model effectively captured both spatial patterns (via CNN) and temporal dynamics (via LSTM) in residential energy consumption data. Demonstrated superior performance over traditional models and standalone CNN or LSTM models.	RMSE MAPE	Need for further research to validate the model's performance across different types of residential settings and with varying data granularity. Exploration of integrating additional contextual data, such as real-time pricing or behavioral factors, to improve prediction accuracy.
2024 [72]	**Source:** Australian and Spanish electricity markets **Features:** Weather (temperature, rainfall), daily electricity prices	Artificial Neural Networks (ANN) - XgBoost - LSTM - Bi-LSTM - Stacked LSTM - Lasso Regression (stacking)	Handling missing values Scaling and normalization of features Feature engineering (e.g., weather variables, time features)	Stacking multiple AI models enhanced prediction accuracy under stable and unstable conditions.	MAPE RMSE	Limited generalization to other external factors and regions
2024 [73]	**Source:** Smart grid data from China **Features:** Historical load, weather data, holidays	Empirical Wavelet Transform (EWT) - Convolutional Neural Network (CNN) - RNN, LSTM	Data cleaning Wavelet decomposition Feature scaling	Enhanced long-term dependency modeling, especially under fluctuating load conditions.	MAE RMSE	Computational complexity due to hybrid model structure

3.4 Evaluation Metrics

The metrics are commonly used in evaluating the performance of predictive models, especially in the context of time-series forecasting like predicting electricity consumption. Following is the list of a few:

Mean Absolute Error (MAE)

MAE is a measure of the average absolute errors between predicted and actual values. The formula for MAE is:

$$\text{MAE} = \frac{1}{n}\sum_{i=1}^{n}\left|y_i - \hat{y}_i\right| \tag{1}$$

where n is **the number of observations, yi** is the actual value, and $\widehat{y_i}$ is the predicted value. MAE gives an equal weight to all errors, without considering their direction.

Root Mean Square Error (RMSE)

RMSE is a measure that penalizes larger errors more heavily than smaller ones. It is calculated as the square root of the average of the squared errors:

$$\text{RMSE} = \sqrt{\frac{1}{n} \sum_{i=1}^{n} (y_i - \widehat{y_{i-1}})^2} \tag{2}$$

RMSE provides a sense of how spread out the errors are, and it is in the same unit as the predicted and actual values.

Mean Absolute Percentage Error (MAPE)

MAPE expresses the average percentage difference between predicted and actual values. The formula for MAPE is:

$$\text{MAPE} = \frac{1}{n} \sum_{i=1}^{n} \left| \frac{y_i - \hat{y}_i}{y_i} \right| \times 100\% \tag{3}$$

MAPE is particularly useful when you want to understand the relative accuracy of your predictions across different scales of data.

Forecast Accuracy

Forecast accuracy (FA) is a comprehensive metric that considers both bias and precision. It is often expressed as a percentage and calculated as:

$$\text{FA} = \left(1 - \frac{MAE}{meanactualvalue} \right) \times 100\% \tag{4}$$

4   Discussion

4.1   RQ1: How Can Machine Learning and Deep Learning Models Improve the Accuracy of Electricity Load Forecasting by Handling Non-Linear Relationships and Temporal Dependencies in the Data?

In the 2013–2014 period, conventional statistical techniques of electricity load forecasting were primarily based on ARIMA and exponential smoothing. While they were quite effective for linear and seasonal trends, these models were generally poor estimators of nonlinear trends. Although promising results were observed for emerging machine-learning techniques, they were not robust enough to handle complex nonlinearities and temporal dependencies.

In 2015–2016, machine learning models, like support vector machines and random forests, improved accuracy in forecasts through the capture of the non-linear interactions among features, though still holding many weaknesses in sequential data processing.

That breakthrough happened in 2017 with the Long Short-Term Memory (LSTM) networks, doing an incomparable job at handling time series data, based on the capture of both short- and long-term dependencies.

In 2018–2019, hybrid models like CNN-LSTM came about, where the Convolutional Neural Networks made a further contribution to spatial feature extraction together with LSTM in temporal modeling, efficiently capturing complex interactions of factors like weather and time. By 2020, IoT devices had made a huge difference in real-time data for short-term forecasting.

From 2021 to 2023, the attention mechanisms have further evolved in terms of time property modeling, and transfer learning thrives further in low-data situations. Reinforcement learning emerged for real-time optimization in energy storage and distribution. Then, privacy-preserving techniques have been developed to handle corresponding data security concerns.

4.2 RQ2: How Can Multivariable Inputs, Such as Weather Data, Economic Indicators, and Social Factors, Be Effectively Integrated into Deep Learning Models to Enhance the Accuracy of Electricity Load Forecasting?

Initial research combined basic multivariable inputs, such as weather variables like temperature and humidity, with machine learning models including Random Forest and Support Vector Machines. Methods built on top of these approaches had greater accuracy than single-variable methods but still were unable to cope with complex multivariable relationships.

In 2017, deep learning techniques enabled this to be extended to multiple variables using a Long Short-Term Memory (LSTM) model, including weather conditions and time of day variables, producing radically improved results in short-term load forecasting accuracy.

From 2018 to 2019, models like CNN-LSTM began considering a wide range of inputs, including economic indicators and social factors, which lent further improvements in the ability to forecast by capturing spatial and temporal features across multivariable.

In 2020, real-time multivariable forecasting using data from IoT devices and social media trends increased the responsiveness of the system to changing conditions.

From 2021 to 2023, new models with attention mechanisms could prioritize the relevant variables for the accuracy of the forecast, while principles of behavioral economics are integrated to better understand how consumer behavior affects electricity demand.

4.3 RQ3: How Can Demand-Side Management (DSM) Strategies Be Effectively Integrated with Deep Learning Models to Optimize Electricity Load Forecasting and Enhance Grid Stability?

In 2015 and 2016, preliminary research employed the application of simple machine learning methods, such as Decision Trees, on DSM data integrated with load forecasting models to forecast the effect of DSM programs on electricity consumption. By 2017, DSM data had started to be integrated into deep learning models, especially the LSTM, for example, time-of-use pricing that improved load variation prediction accuracy. In 2018–2019, advanced hybrid models like CNN-LSTM integrated DSM strategies with features like weather, enhancing peak load reduction capability in their forecasts. In 2020, with the popularity of IoT, the integration of real-time DSM data further improved the responsiveness of the forecast and its accuracy. Advanced optimization techniques like reinforcement learning for the enhancement of DSM strategy and handling peak electricity demand were adopted by researchers from 2021 to 2023.

4.4 RQ4: How Can Renewable Energy Sources Be Effectively Integrated into Load Forecasting Models to Improve Grid Stability and Sustainability?

Real-time weather data began being used in load forecasts in 2017, incorporating renewable energy sources. This first required initial efforts, which used the detailed weather inputs to predict their output energy from renewables. Applied to show the inaccuracy of the weather forecast has a direct link with load forecasts with solar and wind energies.

In 2018, one of the priorities in distributed energy resources integration was the smoothing of load forecasts using grid battery storage systems at grids with high renewable penetration. The more accurate the predictions of when stored energy could be dispatched, the better supply could be matched with demand.

In 2019, hybrid models began predicting renewable energy curtailment by adjusting load forecasts using real-time data from their demand response mechanisms at times of overgeneration. It wasn't until 2020 that AI-driven load forecasting models finally incorporated localized production and consumption data with wider grid forecasts.

In 2021, a lot of focus was placed on model transparency using techniques of artificial intelligence. In 2022, the application of self-learning models made possible continuous learning adjustment. In 2023, blockchain technologies moved to the forefront in decentralized renewable energy transaction management, while further advanced attention mechanisms were developed for dealing with energy fluctuations.

5 Conclusion and Future Work

This paper deals with the integration of deep learning with hybrid algorithms in electricity load forecasting, dwelling on the challenges and advancements related to renewable energy sources. The concept of load forecasting began with very basic statistical methods but evolved into complex models that handle nonlinear relationships and temporal dependencies to cope with the unpredictability of renewable sources such as wind and solar.

Deep learning models, especially LSTM and CNN, further help in enhancing prediction accuracy by capturing temporal patterns and allowing a hand in handling multivariable inputs, including weather and economic indicators. Then there are hybrid models like CNN-LSTM, which further improved the capabilities and combined spatial feature extraction with temporal modeling abilities to predict electricity demand under different conditions.

Models began handling the variability and intermittency of renewable energy sources at the front line. Optimizations made with live data, sophisticated optimization methodologies, and greater use of distributed energy resources—like battery storage—provided greater grid stability.

Several areas of future research have to be pursued for further advancements in hybrid deep learning models in load forecasting. First, scalability optimization for real-time applications is required, in which model compression and edge computing would reduce computational demands for smaller utilities. This would mean that distributed energy resources could provide greater grid resilience if included in load forecasting models, hence requiring further development in real-time predictions for both load and energy availability in the future. First, improved self-learning algorithms, especially reinforcement learning, make models adapt easily to dynamic grid conditions without excessive usage of resources. Second, greater usage of XAI will ensure model interpretability, which is important in decision-making processes within the context of renewable energy. Finally, further research into blockchain technology can additionally secure decentralized forecasting in microgrids. Finally, fine-tuning attention mechanisms for renewable variability and adapting models to how climate change is affecting electricity demand are essential for robust long-term forecasting.

Acknowledgments. I, Gursleen Kaur, would like to extend my heartfelt gratitude to Dr. R.K. Bawa, my advisor, for the patient guidance, enthusiastic encouragement, and invaluable feedback provided throughout this research. The support and constructive critiques have been essential to the completion of this work.

References

1. Zhang, X., Wang, Z., Li, J.: Real-time energy management of a smart grid: an overview. Energy Rep. **4**, 704–710 (2018)
2. Liu, Y., Yu, D., Li, J.: A review on load forecasting of the smart grid and its key technologies. Renew. Sustain. Energy Rev. **118**, 109556 (2020)
3. Albadi, M.H., El-Saadany, E.F.: A summary of demand response in electricity markets. Electr. Power Syst. Res. **78**(11), 1989–1996 (2008)
4. Aghaei, J., Alizadeh, M.I.: Demand response in smart electricity grids equipped with renewable energy sources: a review. Renew. Sustain. Energy Rev. **18**, 64–72 (2013)
5. Elsaraiti, M., Ali, G., Musbah, H., Merabet, A., Little, T.: Time series analysis of electricity consumption forecasting using ARIMA model. In: 2021 IEEE Green Technologies Conference (GreenTech), pp. 259–262. IEEE (2021)
6. Yildiz, B., Bilbao, J.I., Sproul, A.B.: A review and analysis of regression and machine learning models on commercial building electricity load forecasting. Renew. Sustain. Energy Rev. **73**, 1104–1122 (2017)
7. Elgarhy, S.M., Othman, M.M., Taha, A., Hasanien, H.M.: Short term load forecasting using ANN technique. In: 2017 Nineteenth International Middle East Power Systems Conference (MEPCON), 1385–1394. IEEE (2017)

8. Yang, A., Li, W., Yang, X.: Short-term electricity load forecasting based on feature selection and Least Squares Support Vector Machines. Knowl.-Based Syst. **163**, 159–173 (2019)
9. Jamaaluddin, J., Hadidjaja, D., Sulistiyowati, I., Suprayitno, E.A., Anshory, I., Syahrorini, S.: Very short-term load forecasting peak load time using fuzzy logic. IOP Conf. Ser. Mater. Sci. Eng. **403**(1), 012070 (2018)
10. Tang, L., Yi, Y., Peng, Y.: An ensemble deep learning model for short-term load forecasting based on ARIMA and LSTM. In: 2019 IEEE International Conference on Communications, Control, and Computing Technologies for Smart Grids (SmartGridComm), pp. 1–6. IEEE (2019)
11. Alhussein, M., Aurangzeb, K., Haider, S.I.: Hybrid CNN-LSTM model for short-term individual household load forecasting. IEEE Access **8**, 180544–180557 (2020)
12. Farsi, B., Amayri, M., Bouguila, N., Eicker, U.: On short-term load forecasting using machine learning techniques and a novel parallel deep LSTM-CNN approach. IEEE Access **9**, 31191–31212 (2021)
13. Hafeez, G., Alimgeer, K.S., Khan, I.: Electric load forecasting based on deep learning and optimized by heuristic algorithm in smart grid. Appl. Energy **269**, 114915 (2020)
14. Fallah, S.N., Deo, R.C., Shojafar, M., Conti, M., Shamshirband, S.: Computational intelligence approaches for energy load forecasting in smart energy management grids: state of the art, future challenges, and research directions. Energies **11**(3), 596 (2018)
15. Wang, X., Wang, H., Bhandari, B., Cheng, L.: AI-empowered methods for smart energy consumption: a review of load forecasting, anomaly detection and demand response. Int. J. Precis. Eng. Manuf. Green Technol. **11**(3), 963–993 (2024)
16. Subbiah, S.S., Chinnappan, J.: Deep learning based short-term load forecasting with hybrid feature selection. Electric Power Syst. Res. **210**, 108065 (2022)
17. Zhao, H., Zhang, L., Wang, Y.: Seasonal and cyclical analysis of electricity consumption data for enhanced load forecasting models. J. Energy Manag. **15**(3), 210–225 (2023)
18. Wang, T., Chen, X.: The impact of meteorological factors on load forecasting accuracy: a comparative study. Energy Syst. Res. **28**(4), 487–502 (2022)
19. Lee, J., Park, H., Kim, S.: Incorporating macroeconomic indicators into electricity load forecasting models. Int. J. Forecast. **37**(2), 145–160 (2021)
20. Li, M., Zhang, Q.: Demographic influences on electricity demand: a modeling approach. Appl. Energy **276**, 115365 (2020)
21. Kumar, A., Gupta, R., Patel, N.: Integrating behavioral patterns into residential load forecasting. Energy Build. **238**, 110821 (2022)
22. Brown, S., Williams, A., Taylor, R.: Leveraging smart meter data for enhanced load forecasting precision. Energy **250**, 124815 (2023)
23. Zhao, H., Zhang, L., Wang, Y.: The role of real-time weather data in load forecasting models. J. Clean. Prod. **154**, 134325 (2023)
24. Chen, X., Li, Z.: Integrating energy management system data into load forecasting. Appl. Energy **295**, 116786 (2021)
25. Gupta, A., Patel, S., Rao, K.: Utilizing social media and IoT data for real-time load forecasting adjustments. Energy Build. **245**, 110835 (2022)
26. Zhang, H., Li, X., Wang, J.: Advanced methods for handling missing data in load forecasting. Energy Build. **244**, 110728 (2022)
27. Liu, Y., Chen, L., Sun, Y.: Outlier detection techniques for enhancing load forecasting models. Energy **242**, 124785 (2021)
28. Wang, T., Zhang, Y.: The impact of data normalization on load forecasting accuracy. Appl. Energy **279**, 115458 (2020)
29. Kim, S., Lee, H., Park, J.: Data aggregation strategies for improving load forecasting efficiency. Energy **240**, 124653 (2021)

30. Chodakowska, E., Nazarko, J., Nazarko, Ł.: ARIMA models in electrical load forecasting and their robustness to noise. Energies **14**(23), 7952 (2021)
31. Musbah, H., El-Hawary, M.: SARIMA model forecasting of short-term electrical load data augmented by fast Fourier transform seasonality detection. In: 2019 IEEE Canadian Conference of Electrical and Computer Engineering (CCECE), pp. 1–4 (2019)
32. Mi, J., Fan, L., Duan, X., Qiu, Y.: Short-term power load forecasting method based on improved exponential smoothing grey model. Math. Probl. Eng. **2018**(1), 3894723 (2018)
33. Zhang, Z., Hong, W.C.: Electric load forecasting by complete ensemble empirical mode decomposition adaptive noise and support vector regression with quantum-based dragonfly algorithm. Nonlinear Dyn. **98**(2), 1107–1136 (2019)
34. Rangapuram, S.S., Seeger, M.W., Gasthaus, J., Stella, L., Wang, Y., Januschowski, T.: Deep state space models for time series forecasting. Adv. Neural Inf. Process. Syst. **31** (2018)
35. Abbasi, R.A., Javaid, N., Ghuman, M.N.J., Khan, Z.A., Ur Rehman, S., Amanullah: Short-term load forecasting using XGBoost. In: Web, Artificial Intelligence and Network Applications: Proceedings of the Workshops of the 33rd International Conference on Advanced Information Networking and Applications (WAINA-2019), pp. 1120–1131. Springer International Publishing (2019)
36. Ahmad, T., Chen, H.: Nonlinear autoregressive and random forest approaches to forecasting electricity load for utility energy management systems. Sustain. Cities Soc. **45**, 460–473 (2019)
37. Ahmad, W., et al.: Towards short term electricity load forecasting using improved support vector machine and extreme learning machine. Energies **13**(11), 2907 (2020)
38. Fan, G.F., Guo, Y.H., Zheng, J.M., Hong, W.C.: Application of the weighted k-nearest neighbor algorithm for short-term load forecasting. Energies **12**(5), 916 (2019)
39. Divina, F., Gilson, A., Goméz-Vela, F., García Torres, M., Torres, J.F.: Stacking ensemble learning for short-term electricity consumption forecasting. Energies **11**(4), 949 (2018)
40. Elgarhy, S.M., Othman, M.M., Taha, A., Hasanien, H.M.: Short term load forecasting using ANN technique. In: 2017 Nineteenth International Middle East Power Systems Conference (MEPCON), pp. 1385–1394 (2017)
41. Tarmanini, C., Sarma, N., Gezegin, C., Ozgonenel, O.: Short-term load forecasting based on ARIMA and ANN approaches. Energy Rep. **9**, 550–557 (2023)
42. Shi, H., Xu, M., Li, R.: Deep learning for household load forecasting—a novel pooling deep RNN. IEEE Trans. Smart Grid **9**(5), 5271–5280 (2017)
43. Kong, W., Dong, Z.Y., Jia, Y., Hill, D.J., Xu, Y., Zhang, Y.: Short-term residential load forecasting based on LSTM recurrent neural network. IEEE Trans. Smart Grid **10**(1), 841–851 (2017)
44. Imani, M.: Electrical load-temperature CNN for residential load forecasting. Energy **227**, 120480 (2021)
45. Abumohsen, M., Owda, A.Y., Owda, M.: Electrical load forecasting using LSTM, GRU, and RNN algorithms. Energies **16**(5), 2283 (2023)
46. Liu, M., Qin, H., Cao, R., Deng, S.: Short-term load forecasting based on improved TCN and DenseNet. IEEE Access **10**, 115945–115957 (2022)
47. Wang, S., Wang, X., Wang, S., Wang, D.: Bi-directional long short-term memory method based on attention mechanism and rolling update for short-term load forecasting. Int. J. Electr. Power Energy Syst. **109**, 470–479 (2019)
48. Tong, C., Li, J., Lang, C., Kong, F., Niu, J., Rodrigues, J.J.: An efficient deep model for day-ahead electricity load forecasting with stacked denoising auto-encoders. J. Parallel Distrib. Comput. **117**, 267–273 (2018)
49. Huy, P.C., Minh, N.Q., Tien, N.D., Anh, T.T.Q.: Short-term electricity load forecasting based on temporal fusion transformer model. IEEE Access **10**, 106296–106304 (2022)

50. Sideratos, G., Ikonomopoulos, A., Hatziargyriou, N.D.: A novel fuzzy-based ensemble model for load forecasting using hybrid deep neural networks. Electr. Power Syst. Res. **178**, 106025 (2020)

51. Sajjad, M., et al.: A novel CNN-GRU-based hybrid approach for short-term residential load forecasting. IEEE Access **8**, 143759–143768 (2020)

52. Bashir, T., Haoyong, C., Tahir, M.F., Liqiang, Z.: Short term electricity load forecasting using hybrid prophet-LSTM model optimized by BPNN. Energy Rep. **8**, 1678–1686 (2022)

53. Anand, H., Nateghi, R., Alemazkoor, N.: Bottom-up forecasting: applications and limitations in load forecasting using smart-meter data. Data-Centric Eng. **4**, e14 (2023)

54. Marino, D.L., Amarasinghe, K., Manic, M.: Building energy load forecasting using deep neural networks. In: IECON 2016-42nd Annual Conference of the IEEE Industrial Electronics Society, pp. 7046–7051 (2016)

55. Adewuyi, S., Aina, S., Uzunuigbe, M., Lawal, A., Oluwaranti, A.: An overview of deep learning techniques for short-term electricity load forecasting. Appl. Comput. Sci. **15**(4) (2019)

56. Cordeiro-Costas, M., Villanueva, D., Eguía-Oller, P., Martínez-Comesaña, M., Ramos, S.: Load forecasting with machine learning and deep learning methods. Appl. Sci. **13**(13), 7933 (2023)

57. Pamuk, N.: Short-term electrical load forecasting in power systems using deep learning techniques. Sakarya Univ. J. Sci. **27**(5), 1111–1121 (2023)

58. Yazici, I., Beyca, O.F., Delen, D.: Deep-learning-based short-term electricity load forecasting: a real case application. Eng. Appl. Artif. Intell. **109**, 104645 (2022)

59. Wang, W., Xi, C.: Short-term electricity load forecasting based on TPE-optimized CNN-BIGRU-attention. J. Phys. Conf. Ser. **2496**(1), 012011 (2023)

60. Bareth, R., Yadav, A., Gupta, S., Pazoki, M.: Daily average load demand forecasting using LSTM model based on historical load trends. IET Gener. Transm. Distrib. **18**(5), 952–962 (2024)

61. Gong, L., Chao, Y., Huang, X., Chen, J.: Application of CNN-LSTM based hybrid neural network in power load forecasting. Energies (2022)

62. Meng, X., Shao, X., Li, S.: Short-term power load forecasting for a region based on LSTM-attention-GA. Available at SSRN 4624615 (2023)

63. Abid, F., Alam, M., Alamri, F.S., Siddique, I.: Multi-directional gated recurrent unit and convolutional neural network for load and energy forecasting: a novel hybridization. AIMS Math. **8**(9), 19993–20017 (2023)

64. Li, L., Ota, K., Dong, M.: Everything is image: CNN-based short-term electrical load forecasting for smart grid. In: 2017 14th International Symposium on Pervasive Systems, Algorithms and Networks & 2017 11th International Conference on Frontier of Computer Science and Technology & 2017 Third International Symposium of Creative Computing (ISPAN-FCST-ISCC), pp. 344–351 (2017)

65. Soares, L.D., Franco, E.M.C.: BiGRU-CNN neural network applied to short-term electric load forecasting. Production **32**, e20210087 (2021)

66. Stergiou, K., Karakasidis, T.E.: Application of deep learning and chaos theory for load forecasting in Greece. Neural Comput. Appl. **33**(23), 16713–16731 (2021)

67. Emshagin, S., Halim, W. K., Kashef, R.: Short-term prediction of household electricity consumption using customized LSTM and GRU models (2022). arXiv preprint arXiv:2212.08757

68. Wu, L., Kong, C., Hao, X., Chen, W.: A short-term load forecasting method based on GRU-CNN hybrid neural network model. Math. Probl. Eng. **2020**(1), 1428104 (2020)

69. Torres, J.F., Martínez-Álvarez, F., Troncoso, A.: A deep LSTM network for the Spanish electricity consumption forecasting. Neural Comput. Appl. **34**(13), 10533–10545 (2022)

70. Ayub, N., et al.: Big data analytics for short and medium-term electricity load forecasting using an AI techniques ensemble. Energies **13**(19), 5193 (2020)
71. Kim, T.Y., Cho, S.B.: Predicting residential energy consumption using CNN-LSTM neural networks. Energy **182**, 72–81 (2019)
72. Fan, G.F., Han, Y.Y., Li, J.W., Peng, L.L., Yeh, Y.H., Hong, W.C.: A hybrid model for deep learning short-term power load forecasting based on feature extraction statistics techniques. Expert Syst. Appl. **238**, 122012 (2024)
73. Guo, F., et al.: A hybrid stacking model for enhanced short-term load forecasting. Electronics **13**(14), 2719 (2024)

Deep Learning Models: Transformative Potential of AI in Healthcare

Shaktisinh Rathore and Supriya Narad[(✉)] [iD]

Science and Technology Allied Science, DMIHER (DU), Sawani (Meghe), Wardha,, MH, India
{sc2023sa00214,supriya.narad}@dmiher.edu.in

Abstract. Modern society has placed more emphasis on well-being, focusing on better healthcare services at whatever cost. In the same vein, the healthcare system is working towards extending population health, improving treatment efficiency, and incrementally enhancing the experiences of patients. However, gaining and making sense of various complex biomedical data has been hard to get in the process of reforming healthcare. Modern biomedical research combines all types of information, from imaging to electronic health records, text, and sensor data, characterized by complexity, heterogeneity, and often ambiguity. Conventional statistical learning and data mining methods need a tremendous amount of feature engineering to extract meaningful insights and then build predictive or clustering models. However, these approaches are badly impeded due to the complex nature of the data and the lack of domain expertise. Deep learning is a disruptive technology that sidesteps conventional feature engineering and enables end-to-end learning directly from complex clinical data. Advanced architectures formulate a paramount data analysis at unprecedented scales and complexities, foretelling rapid, efficient, and precise insights. Deep learning integrated into health care holds several advantages in decision-making, mimicking human cognition. The multiple-layer architectures enable superior computational capabilities and refine vast amounts of previously untapped healthcare data. A capability like this would democratize expertise and let all health practitioners work right on the front lines while performing at a top specialist level. The sharing of deep learning models across different healthcare institutions could be done without the fear of leaking patient data, and this will open the way for a new generation of personalized medicine. However, the interpretability of models and other ethical concerns remain pertinent challenges. This review underlines deep learning as having a transformative role in health care by underscoring that it will help harness the vast biomedical data for the betterment of human health.

Keywords: deep learning · healthcare · biomedical informatics · precision medicine · electronic health records · medical imaging

1 Introduction

Health care is entering a transformational phase due to the resurgence of deep learning (DL) in the broader field of machine learning. Improved computational power and exponential growth in biomedical data—electronic health records, imaging, omics data,

S. Pal et al. (Eds.): ICETSS 2024, CCIS 2610, pp. 394–407, 2026.
https://doi.org/10.1007/978-3-032-11488-4_31

and sensor data—fuel this resurgence. DL is a subspecialty of ML that excels at learning representations from raw data automatically and thus allows the performance of tasks related to complex pattern recognition across diverse healthcare domains. Probably the epitome of such potential is in precision medicine, matching treatments based on molecular trait variability, environmental factors, and patient lifestyle—all captured in biomedical data. While several biomedical datasets already exist, several available challenges and opportunities are quite unprecedented in scope. Difficulties persist regarding the integration and analysis of heterogeneous sources of data for developing robust data-driven medical tools. Deep learning had improved the mechanism of speech recognition, visual object recognition and object detection with multiple other domains [1]. Deep learning algorithm itself learn from a large set of data which can demonstrate desired behavior and removes the need for specifying rule explicitly [3]. Previous efforts have been made to integrate multiple data modalities toward the construction of complete knowledge bases for predictive analytics and discovery [7–11]. Despite some promising results, extensive adoption of machine learning models in clinical settings has hitherto remained lacking [12]. Challenges still exist because biomedical data is characterized by high dimensionality and complexity and hence requires sophisticated approaches like DL to unlock their real potential. The recent advances in DL technologies applied to healthcare were surveyed, focusing on their role in improving data interpretation and the clinical decision-making process. We tell how DL models have transformed diverse and large-scale datasets into new ways of improving diagnostics, treatment optimization, and patient outcomes. We further outline open challenges and future directions toward integrating DL into clinical routine, enabling more personalized and effective health care.

2 Literature Review

This implies that the critical application of sophisticated data analysis in healthcare arises from the fundamental fact that increasing complexity, high dimensionality, and heterogeneity characterize today's biomedical data [2]. The inherent complexity, poor annotation, and unstructured nature make the biomedical data types—electronic health records, imaging data, –omics data, sensor data, and text—difficult to deal with. Traditional data mining and statistical learning approaches require feature engineering of practical features in the face of this kind of complex data, which is not well understood [4]. Deep learning technologies are the transformative tools that facilitate end-to-end learning, thereby sidestepping the need for manual feature engineering. They excel in handling vast datasets quickly with a high degree of accuracy and reducing dependency on human intervention [6]. Due to their layered algorithm structure, DL models are capable of unraveling intricate patterns and extracting meaningful insights from large datasets to provide better healthcare outcomes. Recent trends have proved the power of ML and DL models in disease detection, cancer diagnosis, management of diabetes, and outbreak prevention in certain parts of the world [11]. More importantly, the ML/DL framework has come leaps and bounds in clinical decision-making, precisely under supervised conditions, benefiting from data aids such as electronic health records, medical images, ECG, EEG records, and even real-time health monitoring devices [21]. Artificial Intelligence in health care holds promise for improving the prognosis for diseases, timely intervention, and personalized treatment strategies. AI models must meet very stringent criteria for safety, reproducibility, and robustness, tailored to the uniqueness of medical data. For example, MONAI is a deep-learning framework on top of PyTorch for health care [22]. This library supports medical imaging and provides specialized model architectures and utilities to make model development and deployment easier.

Although DL technologies hold immense potential to translate such complex biomedical data into meaningful insights, there are still challenges in ensuring that these machine-learning models become interpretable by a health professional and accessible to citizen scientists. Further research is needed to implement more interpretable DL architectures that could reduce gaps between machine-driven insights and human understanding [14]. In addition, the role of machine learning and deep learning in enhancing the security framework is relevant to healthcare, which is a very complex domain for protecting sensitive medical data. In summary: the integration of ML and DL in healthcare shows a paradigm shift, uniquely offering many opportunities to enhance data interpretation, clinical decision-making and patient outcomes. The review highlights the potential deep learning technologies hold for healthcare transformation but defines critical areas for further research and development.

3 Deep Learning Framework

Machine learning (ML) is a general-purpose method for AI that learns relationships from data without defining a priori. This capacity is especially appealing when it makes it possible to derive predictive models without solid assumptions about the underlying mechanisms, often unknown or not well-defined [2]. Concretely, the typical ML workflow features four steps: data harmonization, representation learning, model fitting, and evaluation. For decades, any system in machine learning was engineered to transform raw data into an adequate internal representation that would let a learning subsystem detect the underlying patterns of the dataset. Conventional techniques commonly operated based on only one, usually linear, transformation of the input space and could rarely process natural data in its raw form [5]. Deep learning is a spectacular evolvement concerning how it learns representations from raw data, as compared to traditional machine learning. DL computational models use vital neural network architecture to understand multiple representations at different levels of abstraction. However the significant differences between DL and traditional ANNs lie in the number of hidden layers, their connections, and their ability to learn meaningful abstractions from the inputs. Traditional ANNs are usually restricted to a maximum of three layers; they have been widely trained to obtain supervised representations optimized for a particular task, generally non-generalizing. In contrast, every layer in a deep learning system represents the patterns observed from data provided by the previous layer and optimizes some local unsupervised criterion [7]. The critical point of deep learning is that humans do not engineer these feature layers but rather learned from data with a general-purpose learning procedure. Success in unsupervised pre-training, pruning methods to prevent overfitting, significant gain using general-purpose graphic processing units, and high-level module implementation for accessible building of neural networks—through Theano or other packages like Caffe or Tensor-Flow—are what make deep models state-of-the-art in many applications. Deep learning has been demonstrated to be successful in realizing complicated patterns in high-dimensional data; this greatly improved object detection performance in images, speech recognition, natural language understanding, and translation. There are also successes relevant to health care: there have been clinical-ready successes in the field of health care in the areas of the detection of diabetic retinopathy in retinal fundus photographs, the classification of skin cancer, and the prediction of DNA-and RNA-binding protein sequence specificities [9]. These innovations perhaps foreshadow a new generation of intelligent, deep-learning-based tools for real-world medical care. Deep learning differs from traditional machine learning in learning representations from raw data.

Deep learning allows a computational model, which consists of processing layers, to understand several levels of representation and the input using neural networks. Deep learning algorithms and architectures have Artificial Neural Networks as the base, involving several neurons or perceptrons at each layer. ANNs are also called 'Feed-Forward Neural Networks' in some circles, given that inputs only get processed in a forward direction. ANN typically has three layers: input, hidden, and output. The input layer receives inputs, and the hidden layer processes these; the output layer then delivers the result. All of the layers attempt to learn clean weights [10]. Deep learning techniques make neural network learning powerful, enabling each layer in a profound learning system to yield representations based on the input data it receives from the layer below, optimizing only a local unsupervised criterion. Deep learning models and neural networks now provide state-of-the-art performance in many problems related to speech recognition, image recognition, and natural language processing. The success of this area has also been translated into healthcare with clinically relevant applications such as skin cancer classification, detection of diabetic retinopathy in retinal fundus photographs, and the prediction of the sequence specificities of RNA and DNA-binding proteins, among many others [11]. This progress will likely introduce a new potential generation of deep learning-based intelligent tools into real-world medical care. There are many open-source packages for deep learning algorithm operation in most programming languages, such as Theano, TensorFlow, Keras, Caffe, Torch, Deeplearning4j, PyTorch, and CNTK. All these tools make the construction, training, and deployment of deep learning models easier and hence empower researchers and practitioners to harness deep learning for very diverse applications.

4 Deep Learning models

Deep learning feeds into many neural network architectures, each uniquely suited to specific tasks and applications. Some famous models are recurrent Neural Networks (RNNs), Convolutional Neural Networks, and Artificial Neural Networks (ANNs). These have changed how we use technology today in activities such as autonomous vehicles, uncrewed aerial vehicles, and speech recognition systems [1].

4.1 CNN (Convolution Neural System)

One of the types of deep neural networks usually applied to deep learning analysis of visual imagery is Convolutional Neural Networks. They turned out to be a milestone in computer vision because of a capacity for automatic and adaptive learning of spatial feature hierarchies directly from input images.

Structure and Components of CNNs: CNNs are a portion of the visual cortex and work much like a human brain in image and signal analyses. The architecture of CNNs is primarily conceived to process data with grid-like topology structures such as images. CNN shrouded layers characteristically comprise of convolution layers, completely associated layers, pooling layers and standardization layers as shown in Fig. 1. CNNs used for: Classification forecast issues, Image information, Regression expectation issues [1].

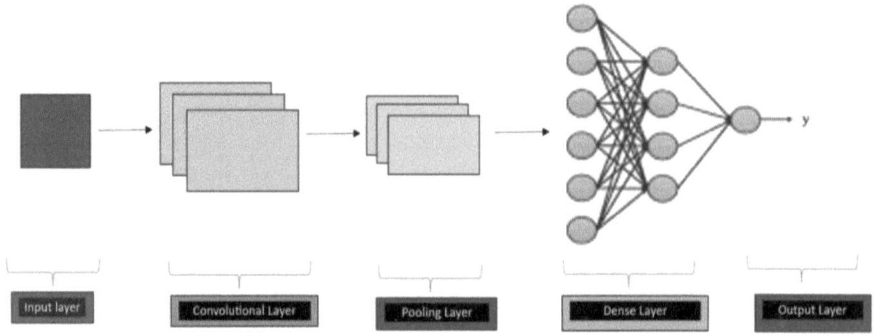

Fig. 1. Convolution Neural Network Architecture

Convolutional Layers: These layers convolve the image with many filters that scan it by moving over it, covering edges, textures, and patterns. The filters slide over the input image, generating feature maps indicating the presence of features at each different location. The convolutional layers are used primarily for the learning and extraction of low-level features from the input data.

Pooling Layers: Pooling layers usually come as max-pooling or average-pooling themselves and conduct a down sampling procedure that reduces the spatial dimensions of the feature maps. Down sampling generally reduces computational complexity and controls overfitting by summarizing features detected in a convolutional layer. Pooling layers emphasize only the most critical information at hand while reducing the size of the data.

Normalization Layers: Normalization layers will standardize their input to have the same distribution for all cases. This is done to stabilize and increase the speed of convergence in training. Batch normalization is one of the standard techniques used in normalizing the output of every layer. Guaranteeing good conditioning of the network, these layers are put all along during training. Fully Connected Layers: Fully connected layers are typically at the network's end. Each neuron from a fully connected layer is fully connected to all of the neurons from the previous layer, which gives it actuality to merge and interpret features learned, hence making predictions. These layers combine features extracted by convolutional and pooling layers to undertake classification or regression tasks finally.

4.2 RNN (Recurrent Neural Networks)

RNNs are of great importance in the domain of NLP for their ability to process sequential data and learn long-term temporal dependencies. Figure 2 below shows RNN architecture. They are based on running through elements of a sequence in iteration and use a form of "memory" to store information from previous computations. Formally, RNNs support sequences of arbitrary length, but practical limitations make them unable to recall information longer than a few steps due to problems such as the vanishing gradient problem.

These limitations are overcome by more advanced developments, like Long Short-Term Memory Networks, which introduce into the learning process specific mechanisms called input gates, output gates, and forget gates to triumph over issues associated with the learning of long-term dependencies. Another variant with much simpler architecture—the Gated Recurrent Units—turns out to be gating mechanisms that control information flow and turn out to be quite efficient for working in tasks that require holding on to memory over time. In healthcare applications, RNNs have been realized to a great extent in solving tasks whose data is sequential, such as seizure prediction using EEG signals. Indeed, this reveals their potential for raising diagnostic accuracies and facilitating early proactive interventions in health care. Their training process, given its effectiveness, is computationally expensive and often requires large datasets to help them converge better. Nonetheless, the power to model complex, time-dependent relationships makes them indispensable tools in furthering medical technologies and improving health care through insights captured from data. The findings emphasize both the versatility and challenge of RNN variants within these domains; when it comes to tasks requiring handling sequential information, they become an integral part of real-world applications in NLP and healthcare.

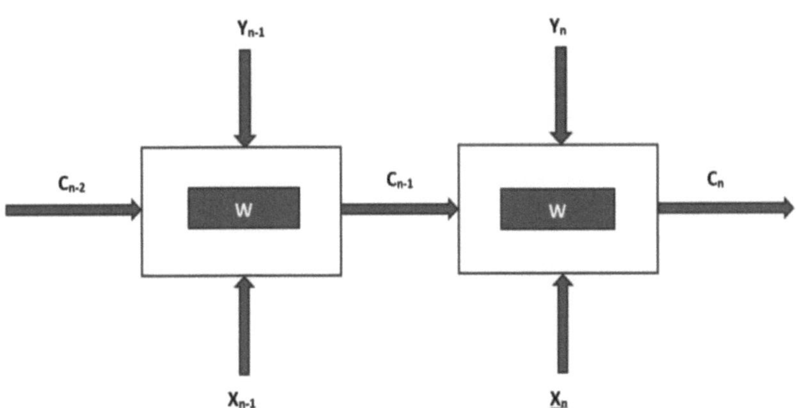

Fig. 2. Recurrent Neural Network

RNNs are multipurpose DL models. These could be used on subjective length successive data and these are skillful of catching time dependent, complex connections inside the consecutive information. By the by, preparing these may be intense, and same may require huge volumes of information for intermingling. In addition, unfurling them for various time steps needs parameters to be recreated on various occasions, that is numerically excessive costly. RNNs are usually functional in medicinal services to resolve sequential data difficulties. An occurrence for the same application is seizures forecast from information of crude EEG.

5   Graph Neural Networks (GNNs)

Graph Neural Networks are specialized deep learning models designed for analyzing data represented as graphs, whereby nodes denote entities and edges represent relationships. Below Fig. 3 shows the graph neural networks (GNN). They propagate and aggregate information through the graph structure to update node representations based on local neighborhood interactions. Key components include graph convolutional layers for aggregating information from neighboring nodes and node embeddings that capture structural and relational dependencies. GNNs excel in tasks such as social network analysis, bioinformatics, recommendation systems, and computer vision. Their capacity for processing irregular data structures and capturing graph information at local and global levels makes them versatile and practical across various real-world applications.

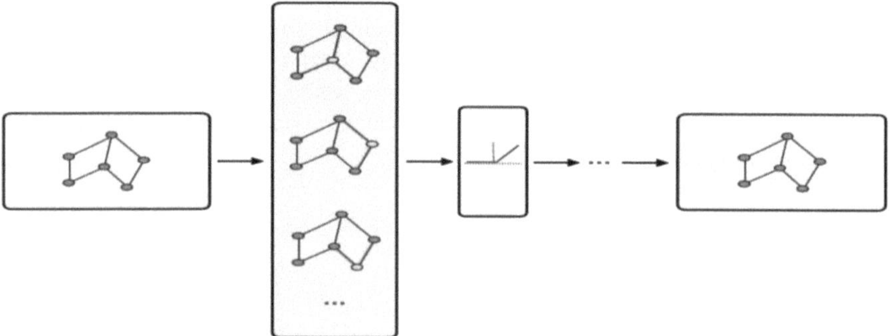

Fig. 3. Graph Neural Networks (GNNs)

5.1   Deep Belief Network (DBN)

Deep Belief Networks are deep learning models that combine probabilistic graphical models with deep neural networks. They are designed by stacking the layers of Restricted Boltzmann Machines, each of which learns hierarchical representations of the data. They are trained in a greedy layer-by-layer process using unsupervised learning algorithms like Contrastive Divergence, followed by supervised fine-tuning using backpropagation. They excel in aspects involving pattern recognition, such as image recognition, speech processing, and bioinformatics through hierarchical feature extraction from unlabeled data. However, they have a weakness since they require proper tuning of their hyperparameters, and this process happens to be very computationally extensive. With all the challenges, DBNs are very useful for tasks that have a limited number of labeled training examples; therefore, one can generate new examples to increase the applicability in most the machine learning applications.

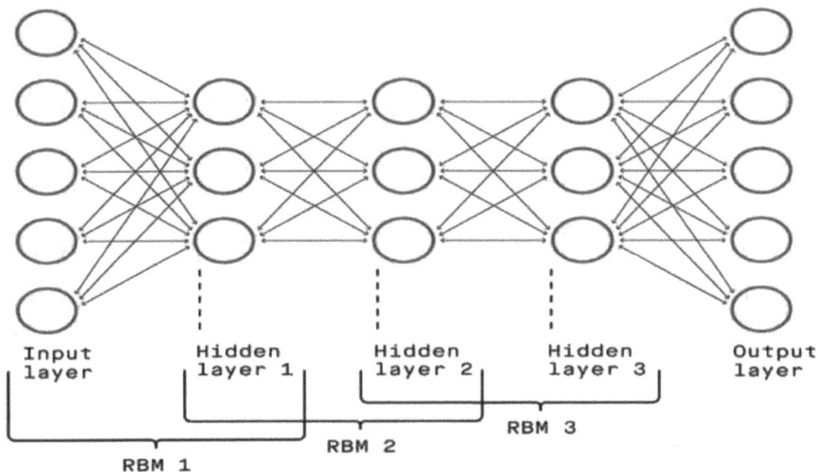

Fig. 4. Deep Belief Network Architecture

Figure 4 illustrates Deep Belief Network architecture. Deep belief models and RBMs can be used for dimensionality reduction or information inspecting, among others. For instance, DBNs have been used to take in suitable portrayals from microarray information for expectation of bosom malignant growth.

6   Usage of Deep Learning Techniques in Healthcare Applications

Deep learning techniques are revolutionizing healthcare across various applications. In medical imaging, CNNs detect diabetic retinopathy and pneumonia with high accuracy, aiding early diagnosis and treatment planning. Genomics benefits from models like Deep Bind, predicting DNA and RNA binding protein specificities better than traditional methods. CNNs and RNNs monitor patients by detecting arrhythmias from ECG data, achieving performance comparable to cardiologists (Table 1).

In natural language processing, BioBERT enhances biomedical text mining, improving tasks like named entity recognition. DNNs advance drug discovery by predicting molecular activity efficiently. These applications demonstrate deep learning's potential to enhance diagnostic precision, predictive capabilities, and personalized medicine in healthcare.

6.1   Challenges and Obstacles

Deep learning techniques show promise for advancing various AI tasks compared to traditional machine learning methods, but their application in clinical settings faces skepticism due to inconsistent results and theoretical ambiguities. The complexity of deep

Table 1. Applications of deep learning

Application	Author	Task	Remark	Model
Medical Imaging Diagnosis	Gulshan, V., et al.	Detection of diabetic retinopathy from retinal fundus images	This study demonstrated the potential of deep learning models to achieve high sensitivity and specificity in detecting diabetic retinopathy, showcasing their ability to assist in early diagnosis and treatment planning.	Convolutional Neural Network (CNN)
Application: Genomics	Alipanahi, B., et al.	Predicting DNA and RNA binding protein sequence specificities	DeepBind outperformed traditional methods in predicting protein binding sites, highlighting the effectiveness of deep learning in understanding genomic data and its potential.	DeepBind (CNN-based)
Patient Monitoring and Wearable Sensors	Hannun, A. Y., et al.	Detection and classification of arrhythmias in ECG data	This study demonstrated that deep learning models can achieve cardiologist-level performance in detecting various types of arrhythmias, enabling continuous patient monitoring and timely intervention	(CNN) and (RNN)

(continued)

learning theories and unresolved questions about their robustness and interpretability in medical contexts contribute to this skepticism. Addressing these challenges requires rigorous validation studies to demonstrate clinical relevance; ensuring models integrate seamlessly into existing workflows while maintaining data privacy and security. Ethical considerations, interpretability of model outputs, and regulatory compliance further

Table 1. (*continued*)

Application	Author	Task	Remark	Model
Natural Language Processing in Healthcare	Lee, J., et al.	Biomedical text mining and information extraction	BioBERT significantly improved the performance of various biomedical NLP tasks, such as named entity recognition, relation extraction, and question answering, by leveraging pre-trained contextual embedding.	BioBERT (Bidirectional Encoder Representations from Transformers)
Drug Discovery and Development	Ma, J., et al.	Predicting the activity of drug compounds based on chemical structure	This study showed that deep neural networks could outperform traditional machine learning methods in predicting molecular activity.	Deep Neural Networks (DNN)
Personalized Medicine	Esteva, A., et al.	Classification of skin cancer types from clinical image	The deep learning model achieved performance on par with dermatologists in classifying skin cancer, demonstrating its potential in providing accurate and accessible diagnostic support.	Convolutional Neural Network (CNN)
Disease Progression Prediction	Rajpurkar, P., et al.	Detection and classification of pneumonia from chest X-rays	CheXNet demonstrated that deep learning could match radiologist performance in identifying pneumonia.	DenseNet (CNN-based)

complicate their adoption. Overcoming these obstacles demands ongoing research and collaboration to enhance the reliability and effectiveness of deep learning in healthcare applications.

6.2 Maturing Challenges in Deep Learning: Four Perspectives

1. Still Non-Interpretable: Despite high-level features being visualized using weight filters in CNNs, deep learning models are still not interpretable. Most of the time, researchers use these models as black boxes because which it is hard to understand why deep learning models are giving specific results, hence reducing their capability of making adjustments in case of misclassification.
2. Overfitting: Deep neural networks primarily encounter the problem of overfitting, mainly in scenarios with small data sets. It will happen any time when the number of parameters used by a model is of the order of the number of training examples; then, it will memorize the training data before generalizing to new inputs. Techniques to prevent this include regularization methods such as dropout to make good generalization.
3. Data Preprocessing and Hyper-Parameter Tuning: Deep learning models need substantial preprocessing, transformation, or normalization of the raw data before training. In addition, choosing hyperparameters, for instance, concerning the size of the layers or the number of filters in CNNs, mostly happens by trial and error methods; this requires rigorous validation. This has traditionally required a lot of domain expertise and computational resources, making developing effective models very challenging.
4. Vulnerability to Adversarial Attacks: Deep neural networks are vulnerable to adversarial attacks where tiny changes in input data end up misclassifying them. This has not been an issue limited only to deep learning; instead, many machine learning models have equally been manipulated. Fixing these vulnerabilities is essential for generalizing deep learning to most sensitive applications.

7 Future Trends of Deep Learning in Healthcare

The future trends of Deep Learning (DL) in healthcare are poised for significant advancements, building upon current achievements and expanding research and development efforts. With the increasing utilization of wearable devices, there is a growing capability to capture diverse physiological signals continuously. However, analyzing and categorizing these signals effectively require deploying various DL techniques tailored for different tasks. Future directions will likely focus on developing unified DL approaches capable of handling multiple signal types, thereby enhancing accuracy and operational efficiency by reducing the need for specialized models for each signal. This integrated approach not only streamlines the analysis process but also ensures robust performance even when certain signals are unavailable.

Looking ahead, the next wave of DL in healthcare will emphasize adaptability and multitasking capabilities. Researchers will explore advanced DL models designed to intelligently process and interpret multiple physiological signals simultaneously, enabling them to perform diverse classification tasks without relying heavily on a single model for each task. This evolution promises to enhance diagnostic precision, optimize healthcare delivery, and facilitate personalized medicine by leveraging comprehensive data insights derived from wearable technology. As DL continues to evolve, its application in healthcare is expected to revolutionize patient monitoring, diagnostic accuracy, and treatment customization, paving the way for more effective and efficient healthcare solutions tailored to individual patient needs.

7.1 Integration of Multimodal Data

Physicians can combine several healthcare data sources, including medical imaging and genomic information, with clinical records into unified DL models that help in enhanced diagnostic accuracy and drive personalized medicine. Trained on such heterogeneous data sources, DL models will provide the full context of the patient's health profile, leading to more accurate diagnoses and proper treatment plans.

7.2 Real-Time Monitoring with Intervention

Advanced models of DL can thus bring a paradigm shift in healthcare through continuously monitoring patient health metrics in real time. The techniques belonging to this sub-domain were designed for the analysis of streams of data resulting from wearable devices and sensors, aiming to detect anomalies for timely alert and intervention. This capability is critical for patient outcome enhancement by ensuring proactive healthcare management.

7.3 Explainable AI in Healthcare

Designing explainable DL models is thus very critical for transparency in health decision-making. The explanation behind their predictions and recommendations is transparent; hence, this will aid in gaining the trust of health providers/patients. Explainable AI will then empower health experts to understand why a specific diagnosis or treatment plan is recommended, hence giving them confidence in their implementation and compliance with AI-driven medical insights.

7.4 Federated Learning for Privacy

Federated learning provides private training over decentralized data sources for DL models. Thus, it can provide a means for health institutions to effectively collaborate and share knowledge without sharing sensitive patient information. Federated learning can secure the confidentiality of data, hence supporting compliance with healthcare regulations and promoting ethical conduct in using data in medical research and practice.

7.5 Precision Medicine and Predictive Analytics

Most DL techniques applied to precision medicine test for the prognosis of diseases and treatment outcomes concerning patients' characteristics. These models, when used with big datasets consisting of genomic profiles and clinical histories, can propose consistent healthcare interventions oriented towards the individual needs and constitution of each patient, going on to ensure optimal effectivity of treatment and example care of patients.

7.6 DL in Drug Discovery

DL is changing how drug discovery enterprises are run by accelerating the identification of potential therapeutic compounds and treatment protocols. Equipped with the power of analyzing large datasets, predicting molecular interactions, identifying promising drug candidates, and simulating drug efficacy, DL models increase the speed of the drug development pipeline and innovation in pharmaceutical research. Augmented Reality and DL in Surgery—the power of AR is combined with surgical systems working with DL for enhanced surgical accuracy, surrounded by real-time augmented visualizations and data overlays in operations. This would mean better views of anatomy on a 3D screen for one patient or another, with enhanced management of structures exhibiting complex anatomy and real-time guidance staged on DL-driven insights to bring forward the best surgical outcomes, reducing complications significantly at every turn.

8 Conclusion

DL has presented its transformative impact in healthcare. Deep learning is changing the healthcare paradigm by shifting how medical data should be interrogated and used. The DL models are increasingly competent at disease diagnosis, individual treatment, and predictive analytics by automatically extracting features from large, heterogeneous datasets. DL techniques will uniquely integrate multi-modal data in healthcare to drive diagnostic accuracy, foster efficiency, real-time monitoring, and proactive interventions in health maintenance. However, model interpretability, data privacy, and regulatory compliance remain other significant challenges. This will be important to realize the potential of DL to move the dial in healthcare delivery. As DL grows more and more, its prospect toward interacting with precision medicine, drug discovery, and surgical innovation has positioned this space at the core of future medical advancement.

References

1. LeCun, Y., Bengio, Y., Hinton, G.: Deep learning. Nature **521**, 436–444 (2015)
2. Tatonetti, N.P., Ye, P.P., Daneshjou, R., et al.: Data-driven prediction of drug effects and interactions. Sci. Transl. Med. (2012)
3. Gulshan, V., et al.: Development and validation of a deep learning algorithm for detection of diabetic retinopathy in retinal fundus photographs. JAMA **316**(22), 2402–2410 (2016)
4. Alipanahi, B., Delong, A., Weirauch, M.T., Frey, B.J.: Predicting the sequence specificities of DNA-and RNA-binding proteins by deep learning. Nat. Biotechnol. **33**(8), 831–838 (2015)
5. Hannun, A.Y., et al.: Cardiologist-level arrhythmia detection and classification in ambulatory electrocardiograms using a deep neural network. Nat. Med. **25**(1), 65–69 (2019)
6. Lee, J., et al.: BioBERT: a pre-trained biomedical language representation model for biomedical text mining. Bioinformatics **36**(4), 1234–1240 (2020)
7. Ma, J., Sheridan, R.P., Liaw, A., Dahl, G.E., Svetnik, V.: Deep neural nets as a method for quantitative structure–activity relationships. J. Chem. Inf. Model. **55**(2), 263–274 (2015)
8. Esteva, A., et al.: Dermatologist-level classification of skin cancer with deep neural networks. Nature **542**(7639), 115–118 (2017)

9. Rajpurkar, P., Irvin, J., Zhu, K., Yang, B., Mehta, H., Duan, T., Ng, A.Y.: CheXNet: Radiologist-level pneumonia detection on chest X-rays with deep learning (2017). arXiv preprint arXiv:1711.05225
10. Ronneberger, O., Fischer, P., Brox, T.: U-Net: Convolutional networks for biomedical image segmentation. In: International Conference on Medical image computing and computer-assisted intervention, pp. 234–241. Springer, Cham. Model: U-Net (CNN-based) (2015)
11. Wang, F., Zhang, P., Wang, X., et al.: Clinical risk prediction by exploring high-order feature correlations. AMIA Annual Symp. **2014**, 1170–1179 (2014)
12. Bellazzi, R., Zupan, B.: Predictive data mining in clinical medicine: current issues and guidelines. Int. J. Med. Inform. **77**, 81–97 (2008)
13. Mirowski, P., Madhavan, D., LeCun, Y., Kuzniecky, R.: Classification of patterns of EEG synchronization for seizure prediction. Clin. Neurophysiol. **120**(11), 1927–1940 (2009)
14. Khademi, M., Nedialkov, N.S.: Probabilistic graphical models and deep belief networks for prognosis of breast cancer. In: 2015 IEEE14thInternationalConference on Machine Learning and Applications (ICMLA), pp. 727–732. IEEE, New York (2015)
15. Zheng, J., Lin, D., Gao, Z., Wang, S., He, M., Fan, J.: Deep learning assisted efficient AdaBoost algorithm for breast Cancer detection and early diagnosis. IEEE Access **8**, 96946–96954 (2020)
16. Su, Y., Li, D., Chen, X.: Lung nodule detection based on faster R-CNN framework. Comput. Methods Prog. Biomed. **200**, 105866 (2021)
17. Deeksha, K., Harika, R., Tripathy, B.K.: Deep Learning in Healthcare. https://doi.org/10.1007/978-3-030-75855-4_6
18. Helaly, H.A., Badawy, M., Haikal, A.Y.: A review of deep learning approaches in clinical and healthcare systems based on medical image analysis. Multimed. Tools Appl. **83**, 36039–36080 (2024)
19. Chakraborty, S., Murali, B., Mitra, A.K.: "An efficient deep learning model to detect COVID-19 using chest X-ray images. Int. J. Environ. Res. Public Health **19**, 4 (2022)
20. Talaei Khoei, T., Ould Slimane, H., Kaabouch, N.: Deep learning: systematic review, models, challenges, and research directions. Neural Comput. Appl. **35**, 23103–23124 (2023)
21. Badawy, M., Ramadan, N., Hefny, H.A.: Healthcare predictive analytics using machine learning and deep learning techniques: a survey. J. Electr. Syst. Inf. Technol. **10**, 40 (2023)
22. Chaki, J.: Deep learning in healthcare: applications, challenges, and opportunities. In: Tripathy, B.K., Lingras, P., Kar, A.K., Chowdhary, C.L. (eds.) Next Generation Healthcare Informatics. Studies in Computational Intelligence, vol. 1039. Springer, Singapore (2022)

Explainable DenseNet201 and CNN for Automated Guava Disease Classification: A Comparative Analysis

Nidhi Garg[1], Gifty Gupta[2]([✉]), Vikas Khullar[2], Isha Kansal[2], Preeti Sharma[2], and Aditya Singh[3]

[1] ECE Department, UIET, Panjab University, Chandigarh, India
[2] Chitkara University Institute of Engineering and Technology, Chitkara University, Punjab, India
`gifty.gupta@chitkara.edu.in`
[3] Thapar Institute of Engineering Technology, Patiala, Punjab, India

Abstract. This research paper advances an automated technique to detect guava diseases using image processing and deep learning algorithms. In addition, it distinguishes between the performances of Convolutional Neural Network (CNN) and DenseNet201 models in classifying guava diseases as well as the need for effective and accurate disease detection in agriculture. There are five classes of data in the dataset; 527 images of guava leaves and fruits including: Disease Free, Phytopthora, Red Rust, Scab and Styler Root. To appreciate their decision-making process, this study makes use of Explainable AI techniques specific to Gradient-weighted Class Activation Mapping (Grad-CAM). In terms of overall accuracy and consistency across all disease categories, DenseNet201 performed better than CNN especially with respect to identifying Phytopthora as well as Styler Root diseases. DunsetNet201 had higher micro-average and macro-average ROC areas compared to CNN. More specifically, Grad-CAM visualizations indicate that DenseNet201's heatmaps are more spatially detailed vis-a-vis visible disease symptoms hence indicative of better feature detection. Therefore, through this research a more efficient, accurate and explainable approach can be provided for guava disease detection which would help in early management against these diseases in guava growing.

Keywords: Convolutional Neural Network · DenseNet201 · Explainable AI · Grad-CAM · Guava Disease Classification · Image Processing · Machine Learning · Plant Pathology

1 Introduction

In addition to being a major source of food, agriculture also contributes significantly to the economy [1, 2]. Known as "the apples of the tropics," guavas are a common fruit with significant nutritional and economic significance. It has a lot of vitamin C in it. Because of its many medical benefits, guava leaf supplements—available as leaf teas

S. Pal et al. (Eds.): ICETSS 2024, CCIS 2610, pp. 408–419, 2026.
https://doi.org/10.1007/978-3-032-11488-4_32

and capsules—are often utilized. These plants' diseases have the potential to lower yield and destroy fruit diversity and quality. Plant disease identification and categorization is a significant area of study [3, 4]. However, fungal diseases such anthracnose, canker, styler end rot, fruit fly, algal spot, rust, and wilt have caused a reduction in guava output in recent years.

When plant diseases develop, they are invisible to the unaided eye. For the agro economy to survive and, indirectly, for human health, accurate and timely illness diagnosis and treatment are essential. Visual inspection is the primary method used by agricultural specialists to track illness [5, 6]. In impoverished nations, this ongoing need for professional supervision may be prohibitively costly. Farmers may have to pay hefty transportation expenses when travelling great distances to consult with agricultural professionals in a number of emerging nations [7]. There's also a tendency for farmers to be uninformed about diseases that aren't local. Figure 1. Shows the images of various Guava diseases including phytopthora, Red Rust, Scab and Styler end rot.

(a)   (b)   (c)   (d)   (e)

Fig. 1. (a) Disease free Guava affected by diseases. (b) Phytopthora (c) Red Rust (d) Scab (e) Styler end rot.

2 Literature Survey

Researchers have been interested in studying automated plant disease detection for a long time. Gavhale and Gawande used photos of plant leaves to create a model for diagnosing various plant diseases. They adopted a five-stage method. The original picture sets were taken using a camera in step one, and the photos and colour space were then improved by preprocessing. The affected regions were identified by the use of edge-based, region-based, and threshold-based segmentation approaches.

After that it calculated texture, color features and shape. Finally, texture feature taxonomy was developed using a neural network classifier [8]. Dashpande et al. used a tried-and-true graded approach to automatically identify diseases in pomegranate fruit. Once the photos had been resized, enhanced, corrected, and had had any shadows removed, they went through image processing procedures to extract the disease. The K-means technique was used to identify the leaf segments that were impacted. As a result, their method provided acceptable illness detection accuracy levels [9]. A method for identifying guava plant leaf illnesses was reported by Thilagavathi et al. [10]. Colour transformation is used to make it easier to identify sick regions, and SVMs and KNNs are then used for classification.

Gavhale et al.proposed a framework which identifies disease affected regions from citrus leaves.They detected this problem by preprocessing images such as enhancing these images, RGB color vector transforming and K-means clustering algorithm. Leaf diseases were recognized by them using feature extraction as well as recognition. Color and texture characteristic extraction was done based on GLCM methods and the detection of disease is carried out using SVM classifier [6]. Similarly, Ali et al. (2013) described a model that used both color and histogram of oriented gradients features to detect citrus disease with significant results. In this work, Sannakki et al. (2014) established a model for grape leaf disease diagnosis using machine learning techniques. Photographs of foliage captured with a digital camera underwent a thresholding procedure that removed green pixels. During the pre-processing step, the leaf pictures were de-noised using the anti-strophic diffusion approach. K-means clustering was used to segment the data. The affected area's texture characteristics were extracted through GLCM.Integration of ANN into this research will lead to classification accuracy [12].

Phadikar [13] proposed an automated approach for identifying diseases on rice leaves, which leveraged morphological operations. The purpose of this approach is to identify brown spots and leaf blast in rice plants. A mean filter design was used to accomplish feature extraction for viruses that impact rice leaves. Finally, the Otsu segmentation method was used to identify the affected regions in the pictures. With regard to the SVM and Bayes classifiers, the system's accuracy was 68.1% and 79.5%, respectively.

Meanwhile, Dey et al. [14] created an automated system to detect leaf root disease by utilizing color features. To help distinguish between rotting and healthy parts of leaves, they transformed captured images into HSV color model representation. Image segmentation was done by Otsu method with threshold value derived from "H" component of HSV model. For identifying areas affected by rot, it was necessary to multiply the count of white pixels by a predetermined calibration factor.

According to Khan et al. [15], a new method for apple disease detection and recognition was presented. They divided their methodology into three main phases: image preprocessing, spot segmentation, and feature extraction. This was accomplished through the use of decorrelation fused with 3D box filtering, 3D median filtering, 3D Gaussian filtering. Later on in this phase, segmentation was done using EM algorithm and Strongly Correlated Pixels methods were applied. The final stage of feature extraction made use of color histograms as well as Local Binary Patterns (LBP). On the other hand, Rauf et al. [16] collected healthy and infected citrus fruits and leaves from gardens located in Sargodha area which formed part of their dataset they used to identify citrus diseases. The preprocessing stage included the whole procedure, while the segmentation step covered feature extraction and feature selection. First, Top-hat and Gaussian functions were used to improve the picture. Saliency maps and weighted segmentation were used to segment data in the second stage. After the picture was segmented, it was sent into a feature extractor, which took out the geometric, colour, and texture aspects. Principal Component Analysis (PCA), skewness, and entropy were used in the next step of feature extraction. The classification process was then finished, classifying each picture instance based on the illness category.

An automated method for identifying grape leaf illnesses was developed by Adeel et al. [17], who claimed to have achieved satisfactory results. A technique for identifying unhealthy plant regions based on textures was presented by Arivazhagan et al. [18]. The photos were first converted to the HSI colour system. Next, features were retrieved, including cluster shade, energy, homogeneity, and prominence. An SVM classifier was then used to categorise the retrieved characteristics.

The goal of the rapidly expanding field of explainable AI (XAI) research is to shed light on the reasoning processes that AI employs [19]. "To ensure algorithmic predictions and any input data triggering those predictions can be explained to non-experts" [20] is the aim of enable explainability in AI systems. XAI can develop useful machine learning techniques that maintain a high degree of prediction accuracy while producing more models that are intelligible to humans.

3 Detailed Methodology

The detailed methodology of the proposed model as shown in Fig. 2 is explained in the following steps.

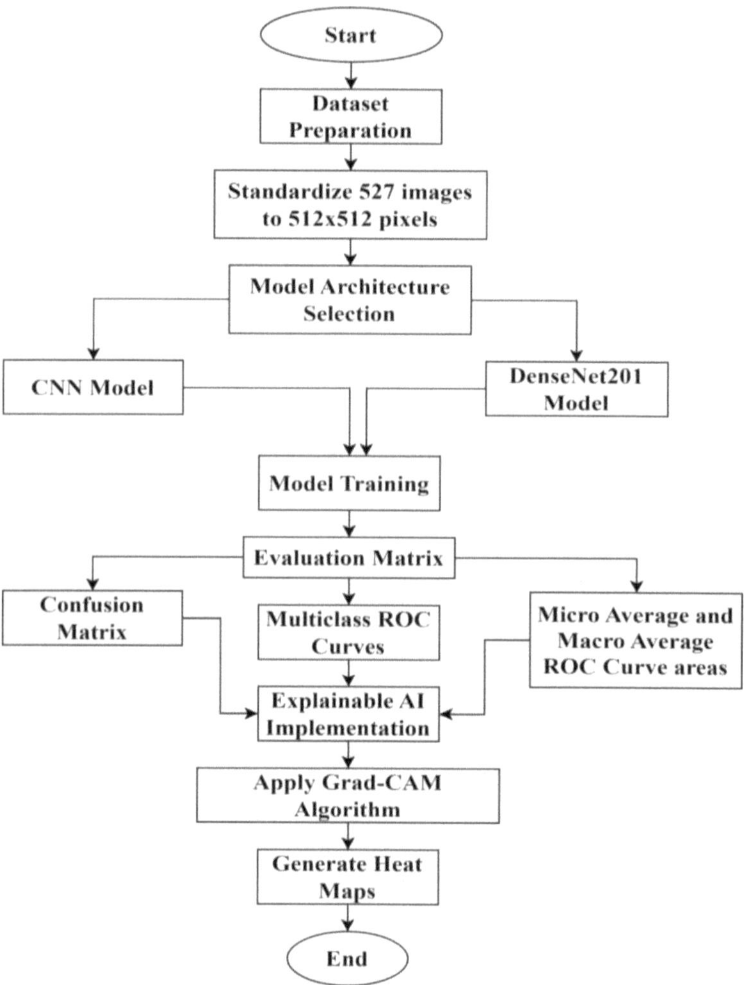

Fig. 2. Flow chart of the Methodology.

3.1 Data Set Preparation

The study utilized a dataset comprising 527 images of guava leaves and fruits (1). These images are categorized into five classes: Disease Free, Phytopthora, Red Rust, Scab, and Styler Root. Each image was standardized to a dimension of 512x512 pixels, ensuring consistency across the dataset. The researchers sourced this dataset from Kaggle, a popular platform for machine learning datasets, specifically from the "Guava Dataset" contributed by Noamaan Abdulazeem. A diverse, structured and well-built dataset served as a strong basis for training and evaluating machine learning models for this research.

3.2 Model Architecture

Two different neural network architectures were used for comparison purposes in this study.

3.2.1 Convolutional Neural Network (CNN)

A popular form of authored work was the convolutional neural network (CNN), but this paper lacks details on its specific architecture. Convolutional neural networks or CNNs are well-known for their effectiveness in image classification tasks, which make use of convolutions to extract features from input images [22].

3.2.2 DenseNet201

The study also used a pre-trained DenseNet201 model. DenseNet201 is a deep convolutional neural network that connects each layer to every other layer in a feed-forward way, which helps alleviate the vanishing-gradient problem and boost feature propagation. It is likely that these researchers adjusted the last layers of this pre-trained model so as to meet guava disease classification requirements specifically [23].

3.3 Model Training

The prepared guava disease dataset was employed in training both CNN and DenseNet201 models. Although detailed information concerning specific training procedures is not provided in the paper, it is inferred that standard protocols were employed thereby necessitating partitioning the dataset into training and validation subsets; using an appropriate optimization algorithm like Adam or SGD; training over several epochs while checking for signs of overfitting.

3.4 Evaluation Metrics

A variety of metrics were used to evaluate the effectiveness of both models.

i. Confusion Matrices: These offered a panoramic view of accurate and wrong categorizations for every disease class, which resulted in great insights about strengths and weaknesses possessed by each model.
ii. Multiclass ROC Curves: They give visual representations of performance at different classification thresholds and depict models' ability to differentiate between various disease classes.
iii. Micro-average and Macro-average ROC Areas: These provided aggregate evaluations of the overall performances the model had across all diseases, as it pertains to cumulative accuracy for micro-average and equal treatment given to each class for macro-average.

3.5 Explainable AI Implementation

Researchers used Gradient-weighted Class Activation Mapping (Grad-CAM) to give more insight into how models make decisions. This technique explains various predictions made by models by highlighting parts of input image that are important for obtaining an accurate label or class membership. Grad-CAM was applied on both CNN and DenseNet201 models resulting into superimposed heat maps on the original images.

4 Experimental Results and Analysis

The models were compared in a thorough way, CNN and DenseNet201. This evaluation included the analysis of confusion matrices to identify specific strengths and weaknesses in the classification of each disease category. Another step was comparing ROC curves and their corresponding areas to evaluate how well it classified diseases overall. Special attention was paid to difficult disease categories like Phytophthora and Styler Root where the two models had significant difference in performance. The original images were shown together with both CNN and DenseNet201 predictions for their respective Grad-CAM heatmaps. These heatmaps were examined closely to establish which areas captured the interest of every model during its classification process. By interpreting these visual representations, researchers could compare highlighted regions against visible disease symptoms in original images. This analysis shed light on the reasons for DenseNet201's superior performance over CNN, particularly regarding its capacity to concentrate on more pertinent features and differentiate between similar-looking diseases.

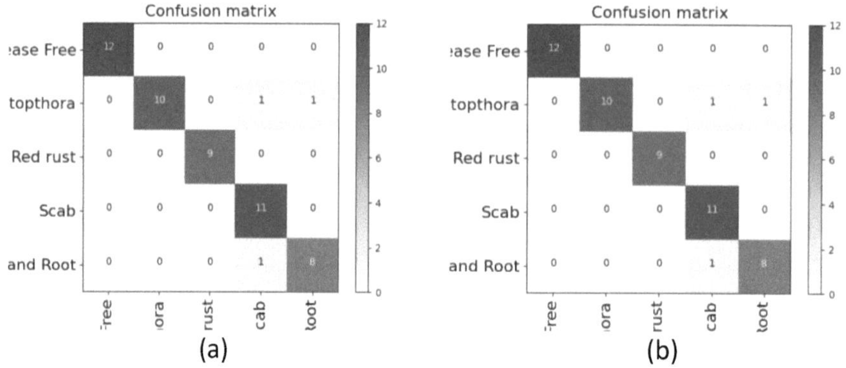

Fig. 3. Confusion Matrix for Prediction of Guava Disease by (a) CNN (b) DenseNet201

The confusion matrices for Guava Disease Prediction presented in Fig. 3 indicate that DenseNet201 clearly surpasses the CNN model in performance. Both models attain flawless accuracy in identifying the Disease Free, Red Rust, and Scab categories; however, DenseNet201 exhibits significant enhancement in detecting Phytopthora and Styler Root diseases. In contrast, the CNN model faces challenges with these two categories, achieving merely 16.67% and 22.22% accuracy, respectively, and frequently misclassifying Phytopthora as Scab and Styler Root as Red Rust. In contrast, DenseNet201 correctly identifies Phytopthora 83.33% of the time and Styler Root 88.89% of the time, with only minor confusions. This comparison demonstrates DenseNet201's superior overall performance and consistency across all disease categories, making it the more reliable model for guava disease prediction based on the given data.

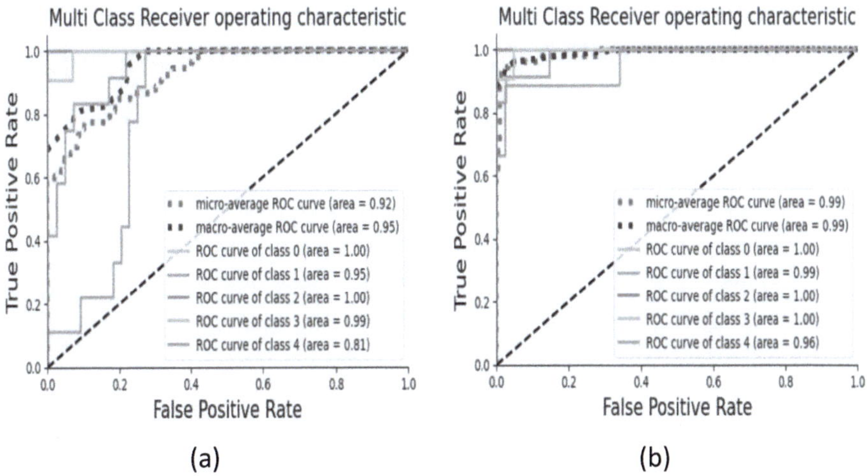

Fig. 4. ROC curves for Prediction of Guava Disease by (a) CNN (b) DenseNet201

Figure 4 shows the comparison of the Multiclass ROC curves for CNN and DenseNet201 in Guava Disease Classification revealing that DenseNet201 generally outperforms CNN. Both models show strong performance, but DenseNet201 edges out CNN in most metrics. The micro-average ROC area for DenseNet201 (0.99) is higher than CNN's (0.92), indicating better overall classification performance. Similarly, the macro-average ROC area for DenseNet201 (0.99) slightly exceeds CNN's (0.95). Both models achieve perfect ROC areas (1.00) for classes 0 (Disease Free) and 2 (Red Rust). However, DenseNet201 shows improvements in classes 1 (Phytopthora), 3 (Scab), and most notably in class 4 (Styler Root), where it achieves an ROC area of 0.96 compared to CNN's 0.81. This suggests that DenseNet201 is particularly more effective at distinguishing Styler Root from other diseases. Overall, while both models demonstrate high proficiency in Guava Disease Classification, DenseNet201 shows superior and more consistent performance across all disease classes.

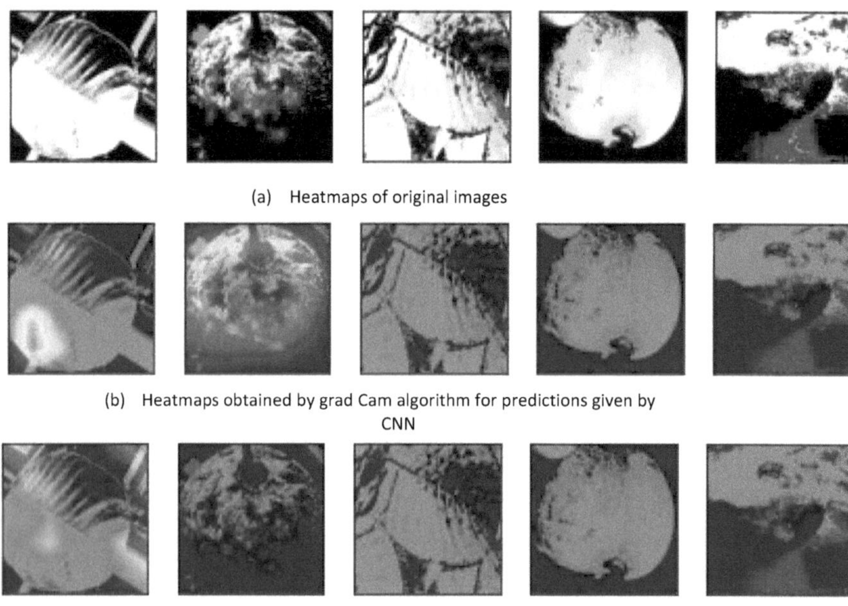

(a)   Heatmaps of original images

(b)   Heatmaps obtained by grad Cam algorithm for predictions given by
CNN

(c)   Heatmaps obtained by grad Cam algorithm for predictions given by
DenseNet201

Fig. 5. (a) Heatmaps of original images, (b) Heatmaps obtained by grad Cam algorithm for predictions given by CNN, (c) Heatmaps obtained by grad Cam algorithm for predictions given by DenseNet201

The heatmaps obtained by the Grad-CAM algorithm visually demonstrate why DenseNet201 outperforms CNN in Guava Disease Classification as shown in Fig. 5. DenseNet201's heatmaps show more precise and concentrated areas of attention, indicating better focus on specific disease-related features. They exhibit less scattered activation, suggesting reduced distraction by irrelevant image elements. Better generalization abilities are suggested by consistent activation patterns in DenseNet201's heatmaps across related disease categories. Furthermore, parts of the images that DenseNet201 emphasizes the most align more to observable disease indicators than any other model, indicating its superior feature detection ability. This is better shown in Styler Root, where DenseNet201 has a far clearer demarcation of classes of diseases with closely resembling symptoms. These visual observations support DenseNet201's higher ROC curve areas and overall superior performance metrics, demonstrating why it is more effective and dependable for Guava Disease Classification in comparison to the CNN model.

5 Conclusion

Furthermore, this research study reveals that DenseNet201 is more effective than conventional CNNs in automatically diagnosing guava diseases, thus increasing the possibility of improving agricultural disease management. DenseNet201 had much higher accuracy rates particularly when it came to challenging diseases like Phytophthora and Styler Root while at the same time also demonstrating a better micro-average and macro-average ROC area across the board. Applying Explainable AI methods notably Grad-CAM offered new perspectives into model's decision-making process showing DenseNet201 excels in accurate feature detection which aligns well with disease symptoms. This level of transparency proves not only how good the model is but also promotes trust and understanding in a practical sense. To conclude, this paper sets a foundation for automatic plant disease recognition by employing an elaborate methodology through combining advanced deep learning architectures with explainable AI techniques. This novel approach may revolutionize early onset guava disease detection leading to improved crop management strategies and enhanced yields. Further research may look at the suitability of this method for a greater range of plant species and diseases as well as explore the development of simple mobile apps for farmers and agricultural experts who work outdoors. Thereby, this explainable DenseNet201 model has succeeded in classifying guava diseases which paves way for more accurate, efficient and transparent disease detection systems within agriculture hence boosting significant progress in crop protection and food security.

Acknowledgments. This research did not receive any specific grant from funding agencies in the public, commercial, or not-for-profit sectors.

Disclosure of Interests. The authors have no competing interests to declare that are relevant to the content of this article.

References

1. Kukreja, V., Madan, K., Singh, A., Kumar, D.: Precision agriculture: guava disease diagnosis via CNN and random forest. In: 2023 3rd International Conference on Smart Generation Computing Communication and Networking (SMART GENCON), pp. 1–5. IEEE (2023)
2. Kumar, R.R., et al.: Towards precision agriculture: a unified CNN and random forest framework for jasmine leaf disease recognition. In: 2024 4th International Conference on Innovative Practices in Technology and Management (ICIPTM), pp. 1–6. IEEE (2024)
3. Liakos, K.G., Busato, P., Moshou, D., Pearson, S., Bochtis, D.: Machine learning in agriculture: a review. Sensors **18**(8), 2674 (2018)

4. Gutte, V.S., Gitte, M.A.: A survey on recognition of plant disease with help of algorithm. Int. J. Eng. Sci. **7**, 100 (2016)

5. Singh, V., Misra, A.K.: Detection of plant leaf diseases using image segmentation and soft computing techniques. Inf. Process. Agric. **4**(1), 41–49 (2017)

6. Gavhale, K.R., Gawande, U., Hajari, K.O.: Unhealthy region of citrus leaf detection using image processing techniques. In: International Conference for Convergence for Technology-2014, pp. 1–6. IEEE (2014)

7. Revathi, P., Hemalatha, M.: Classification of cotton leaf spot diseases using image processing edge detection techniques. In: 2012 International Conference on Emerging Trends in Science Engineering and Technology (INCOSET), pp. 169–173. IEEE (2012)

8. Sakhamuri, S., Kompalli, V.S.: RETRACTED: an overview on prediction of plant leaves disease using image processing techniques. In: IOP Conf. Ser.: Mater. Sci. Eng. 981(2), 022024. IOP Publishing (2020)

9. Gaikwad, D., Karande, K., Deshpande, H.: Pomegranate fruit diseases identification and grading. In: International Conference on Communication and Signal Processing 2016 (ICCASP 2016), pp. 672–679. Atlantis Press (2016)

10. Thilagavathi, M., Abirami, S.: Application of image processing in diagnosing guava leaf diseases. Int. J. Sci. Res. Manag. **5**(07), 5927–5933 (2017)

11. Ali, H., Lali, M.I., Nawaz, M.Z., Sharif, M., Saleem, B.A.: Symptom based automated detection of citrus diseases using color histogram and textural descriptors. Comput. Electron. Agric. **138**, 92–104 (2017)

12. Sannakki, S.S., Rajpurohit, V.S., Nargund, V.B., Kulkarni, P.: Diagnosis and classification of grape leaf diseases using neural networks. In: 2013 Fourth International Conference on Computing Communications and Networking Technologies (ICCCNT), pp. 1–5. IEEE (2013)

13. Phadikar, S., Sil, J., Das, A.K.: Classification of rice leaf diseases based on morphological changes. Int. J. Inf. Electron. Eng. **2**(3), 460–463 (2012)

14. Dey, A.K., Sharma, M., Meshram, M.R.: Image processing based leaf rot disease detection of betel vine (Piper Betle L.). Procedia Comput. Sci. **85**, 748–754 (2016)

15. Khan, M.A., et al.: An optimized method for segmentation and classification of apple diseases based on strong correlation and genetic algorithm based feature selection. IEEE Access **7**, 46261–46277 (2019)

16. Rauf, H.T., Saleem, B.A., Lali, M.I., Khan, M.A., Sharif, M., Bukhari, S.A.: A citrus fruits and leaves dataset for detection and classification of citrus diseases through machine learning. Data Brief **26**, 104340 (2019)

17. Adeel, A., et al.: Diagnosis and recognition of grape leaf diseases: an automated system based on a novel saliency approach and canonical correlation analysis based multiple features fusion. Sustain. Comput.: Inform. Syst. **24**, 100349 (2019)

18. Arivazhagan, S., Shebiah, R.N., Ananthi, S., Varthini, S.V.: Detection of unhealthy region of plant leaves and classification of plant leaf diseases using texture features. Agric. Eng. Int.: CIGR J. **15**(1), 211–217 (2013)

19. Adadi, A., Berrada, M.: Peeking inside the black-box: a survey on explainable artificial intelligence (XAI). IEEE Access **6**, 52138–52160 (2018)

20. Carvalho, D.V., Pereira, E.M., Cardoso, J.S.: Machine learning interpretability: A survey on methods and metrics. Electron. **8**(8), 832 (2019)

21. "Guava disease dataset"

22. Howlader, M.R., Habiba, U., Faisal, R.H., Rahman, M.M.: Automatic recognition of guava leaf diseases using deep convolution neural network. In: 2019 International Conference on Electrical Computer and Communication Engineering (ECCE), pp. 1–5. IEEE (2019)
23. Gaikwad, S.S.: Identification of fungi infected leaf diseases using deep learning techniques. Turk. J. Comput. Math. Educ. (TURCOMAT) **12**(6), 5618–5625 (2021)

Decentralized KYC Consortium: A Blockchain-Based Approach for Secure and Collaborative Know Your Customer Processes in the Banking Sector

N. Jeyanthi[1]([envelope]) [ORCID], Ananya Grover[1], R. Thandeeswaran[1], and M. Hena[2]

[1] Vellore Institute of Technology, Vellore, India
njeyanthi@vit.ac.in
[2] University of West London, RAK Branch Campus, Ras Al-Khaimah, UAE

Source Code of Implementation

```
KycBlockchain.sol
123
pragma solidity >=0.4.21 <0.7.0;
45
interface KYC_Functions{
6 enum Status {Accepted, Rejected, Pending}
7 // Checks if the current address is an
Organisation(Bank) or not
```

FIGURE 6. Main Project Page with Metamask Login: Provides users with a seamless authentication experience using Metamask, ensuring secure access to the project's features and functionalities. Users can easily log in using their Metamask wallet, enhancing the project's usability and security

```
8 function isOrg() external view returns(bool);
9 // Checks if the current address is an
Customer or not
10 function isCus() external view returns(bool);
11 // A function to register as a new customer to
get your KYC checked by a bank
12 function newCustomer(string calldata _name,
string calldata _hash, address _bank) external
payable returns(bool);
13 // A function that allows you to be a bank and
audit KYC data of customers
14 function newOrganisation(string calldata _name
) external payable returns(bool);
15 // A function which is only visible to the
bankers so they can verify the data
16 function viewCustomerData(address _address)
external view returns(string memory);
17 // Customers also can change the their data if
the KYC request gets rejected
18 function modifyCustomerData(string calldata
_name, string calldata _hash, address _bank)
19 external payable returns(bool);
20 // Checks the status of a customers KYC
Request (Approved or Rejected or Pending)
21 function checkStatus() external returns(Status
```


© The Author(s), under exclusive license to Springer Nature Switzerland AG 2026
S. Pal et al. (Eds.): ICETSS 2024, CCIS 2610, pp. 420–423, 2026.
https://doi.org/10.1007/978-3-032-11488-4_33

```
customer
29 function viewName(address _address) external
view returns(string memory);
30
31 }
32
33 contract KycBlockChain is KYC_Functions{
34
35 address[] public Banks;
36 address[] public Requests;
37 uint public bankslength=0;

enum Entity { Customer, Organisation }
40
41
42 struct Customer{
43 string c_name;
44 string data_hash;
45 address bank_address;
46 bool exists;
47 Entity entity;
48 }
49
50 struct Organisation{
51 string b_name;
52 bool exists;
53 Entity entity;
54 mapping(address => Status) requests;
55 address[] allrequests;
56 }
57
58 mapping(address => Customer) allCustomers;
59 mapping(address => Organisation)
allOrganisations;
60
61 function isOrg() public view returns(bool){
62 if(allOrganisations[msg.sender].exists){
63 return true;
64 }
65 return false;
66 }
67
68 function isCus() public view returns(bool){
69 if(allCustomers[msg.sender].exists){
70 return true;
71 }
72 return false;
73 }
74
75 function newCustomer(string memory _name,
string memory _hash, address _bank) public
payable returns(bool){
76 require(!isCus(),"Customer Already Exists!
");
77 require(allOrganisations[_bank].exists,"No
such Bank!");
78 allCustomers[msg.sender].c_name = _name;
79 allCustomers[msg.sender].data_hash = _hash
;
80 allCustomers[msg.sender].bank_address =
_bank;
81 // allCustomers[msg.sender].access[msg.
sender] = true;
82 allCustomers[msg.sender].exists = true;
83 allCustomers[msg.sender].entity = Entity.
Customer;
84 notifyBank(_bank);
```

```solidity
85 return true;
86
87 }
88
89 function newOrganisation(string memory _name)
public payable returns(bool){
90 require(!isOrg(), "Organisation already
exists with the same address!");
91 allOrganisations[msg.sender].b_name =
_name;
92 allOrganisations[msg.sender].exists = true
;
93 allOrganisations[msg.sender].entity =
Entity.Organisation;
94 Banks.push(msg.sender);
95 bankslength++;
96 return true;
97 }
98
99 function viewCustomerData(address _address)
public view returns(string memory){
100 require(isOrg(), "Access Denied");
101 if(allCustomers[_address].exists){
102 return allCustomers[_address].
data_hash;
103 }
104 return "No such Customer in the database";
105 }
106
107 function modifyCustomerData(string memory
_name, string memory _hash, address _bank)
public payable returns(bool){
108 require(isCus(), "You are not a customer");
109 allCustomers[msg.sender].c_name = _name;
110 allCustomers[msg.sender].data_hash = _hash
;
111 allCustomers[msg.sender].bank_address =
_bank;
112 return true;
113 }
114
115 function notifyBank(address _bankaddress)
internal {
116 allOrganisations[_bankaddress].requests[
msg.sender] = Status.Pending;
117 allOrganisations[_bankaddress].allrequests
.push(msg.sender);
118 }
119
120 function checkStatus() public returns(Status)
{
121 require(isCus(), "You are not a customer");
122 address _presbank = allCustomers[msg.
sender].bank_address;
123 return allOrganisations[_presbank].
requests[msg.sender];
124 }
125
126 function changeStatusToAccepted(address
_custaddress) public payable{
127 require(isOrg(), "You are not permitted to
use this function");
128 address _bank = allCustomers[_custaddress
].bank_address;
129 require(_bank == msg.sender, "You dont have
access to verify this data");
130 allOrganisations[msg.sender].requests[
```

```solidity
_custaddress] = Status.Accepted;
131 }
132
133 function changeStatusToRejected(address
_custaddress) public payable{
134 require(isOrg(),"You are not permitted to
use this function");
135 address _bank = allCustomers[_custaddress
].bank_address;
136 require(_bank == msg.sender,"You dont have
access to verify this data");
137 allOrganisations[msg.sender].requests[
_custaddress] = Status.Rejected;
138 }
139
140 function viewRequests() public view returns(
address[] memory){
141 require(isOrg(),"You are not Permitted");
142 return allOrganisations[msg.sender].
allrequests;
143 }
144
145 function viewName(address _address) public
view returns(string memory){
146 require(isOrg(),"Not an Organisation");

return allCustomers[_address].c_name;
148 }
149
150 }
```

Migration.sol

```solidity
123
pragma solidity >=0.4.21 <0.7.0;
45
contract Migrations {
6 address public owner;
7 uint public last_completed_migration;
89
modifier restricted() {
10 if (msg.sender == owner) _;
11 }
12
13 constructor() public {
14 owner = msg.sender;
15 }
16
17 function setCompleted(uint completed) public
restricted {
18 last_completed_migration = completed;
19 }
20 }
```

Enhanced Legal Citation Recommendation via Clustered Judgment Networks and Contextual BiLSTM Models

Divya Mohan[✉] and Latha R. Nair

Department of Computer Science and Engineering, Cochin University of Science and Technology, Kochi, India
moh22divya@gmail.com

Abstract. In the realm of legal research and document drafting, accurate citation recommendations are vital for ensuring the relevance and credibility of legal arguments. This paper presents an innovative approach to enhance legal citation recommendations by leveraging clustered judgment networks and contextual BiLSTM models. We construct a comprehensive citation network from a substantial legal dataset, where nodes represent judgments and edges denote citations. The network is then segmented into meaningful clusters using Louvian clustering algorithm, enabling the capture of intricate relationships within legal texts. For each identified cluster, we train a BiLSTM model tailored to understand and predict context-specific citation patterns. This model effectively harnesses the sequential and contextual nature of legal documents, improving the accuracy of citation recommendations. When a query draft is introduced, its relevant cluster is identified based on its contextual embedding, and citations are recommended using the BiLSTM model of the corresponding cluster. Our method demonstrates significant improvements in the relevance and precision of citation recommendations, as evidenced by comprehensive evaluations against traditional citation recommendation systems. By integrating clustering and contextual modeling, our approach not only enhances the efficiency of the recommendation process but also ensures that the suggested citations are contextually pertinent and legally sound. This research contributes to the advancement of intelligent legal information systems, facilitating more effective and informed legal research and writing.

Keywords: Legal Citation Recommendation · BiLSTM Models · Clustered Judgment Networks · Contextual Modeling · Legal Document Analysis · Citation Network Construction

1 Introduction

Accurate citation recommendations are fundamental to the integrity and efficacy of legal research and document drafting. Legal practitioners rely heavily on citations to support arguments, establish precedents, and provide authoritative backing for legal interpretations. Citations serve as the backbone of legal arguments, ensuring that they are grounded

© The Author(s), under exclusive license to Springer Nature Switzerland AG 2026
S. Pal et al. (Eds.): ICETSS 2024, CCIS 2610, pp. 424–439, 2026.
https://doi.org/10.1007/978-3-032-11488-4_34

in established law and judicial decisions. The integrity and persuasiveness of legal documents significantly depend on the quality and relevance of the citations they contain. The process of finding appropriate citations is, however, both time-consuming and complex. Legal professionals must sift through vast amounts of case law and legal literature to identify relevant precedents and authoritative sources. This task is complicated by the intricate nature of legal texts, where the context and the specific legal principles at play are crucial. Traditional methods of citation recommendation often fall short, either by providing too many irrelevant suggestions or missing out on pertinent cases due to a lack of contextual understanding.

In recent years, advancements in natural language processing (NLP) and machine learning have opened new avenues for improving legal citation recommendations. Deep learning models, particularly those based on BiLSTM (Bidirectional Long Short-Term Memory), have shown promise in capturing the sequential and contextual nuances of legal texts. By processing text in both forward and backward directions, BiLSTM models can understand the context more comprehensively, making them well-suited for tasks that require deep contextual understanding. Moreover, constructing a citation network from a dataset of legal documents allows for the visualization and clustering of related judgments. Clustering these judgments into meaningful groups can reveal intricate relationships within the legal corpus, facilitating more accurate and efficient citation recommendations. By combining the strengths of clustered citation networks with BiLSTM models, it is possible to enhance the precision and relevance of citation recommendations.

This research proposes an innovative approach that leverages clustered judgment networks and contextual BiLSTM models to improve legal citation recommendations. By constructing a citation network, clustering the network into judgment clusters, and training BiLSTM models on each cluster, the system can provide highly relevant citations for a given query draft based on the model of the corresponding cluster. This method not only enhances the efficiency of the recommendation process but also ensures that the suggested citations are contextually pertinent and legally sound, ultimately contributing to more informed and effective legal research and drafting.

2 Literature Review

The application of machine learning techniques in the legal domain has been a growing area of research, aimed at addressing the challenges posed by the vast amount of legal information and the need for accurate citation recommendations. This literature review examines several studies that have contributed to the development of automatic legal citation recommendation systems, focusing on the use of BiLSTM and other machine learning models.

Galgani and Hoffmann (2010) [6] explored the use of incremental knowledge acquisition for legal citation classification, as part of a broader goal of automatic legal text summarization. They developed LEXA, a system that classifies citations in Australian court decisions using a knowledge base of rules. Their approach demonstrated significant improvements over baseline machine learning methods, highlighting the potential of rule-based systems in legal text processing.

Further exploring the use of deep learning, Sulea et al. (2017) [7] investigated various machine learning techniques for predicting court rulings and classifying legal texts. They demonstrated the effectiveness of Support Vector Machines (SVM) and Naive Bayes classifiers in handling large legal text corpora, achieving notable accuracy in predicting the decisions of the French Supreme Court. This work underscores the importance of robust machine learning models in enhancing the accuracy of legal text classification and prediction.

Another significant contribution comes from the study by Zampieri et al. (2016), which applied ensemble learning methods to improve text classification in the legal domain. Their research focused on modeling language change in historical corpora, showcasing the versatility of ensemble techniques in adapting to varying linguistic patterns.

Lu et al. (2020) [2] proposed a deep learning-based patent citation classification model to evaluate the classification effect on patent datasets from the Google patent database. Their approach demonstrates superior robustness and accuracy compared to traditional text representation and classification methods, highlighting the potential of deep learning in legal text analysis. The study emphasizes the need for incorporating technical relevance in citation relationships to predict technology similarity more accurately.

Huang et al. (2021) [5] proposes a novel approach to improve the efficiency of legal citation recommendations during the drafting of judicial opinions. By leveraging local textual context and advanced machine learning models, specifically BiLSTM and RoBERTa classifiers, the authors demonstrate that these deep neural models significantly outperform traditional methods in predicting relevant legal citations. Utilizing a dataset of over 1 million appeal decisions from the Board of Veterans' Appeals (BVA), the study underscores the critical role of context in citation prediction, highlighting the superior performance of models that incorporate semantic and structured metadata.

Dhanani et al. (2020) [12] proposed a Legal Document Recommendation System (LDRS) that addresses the scalability issue of computing pairwise similarity scores for large sets of judgments. The system employs the Louvain clustering method to group referentially similar judgments and uses Doc2Vec to capture semantic relevance within these clusters. This approach significantly reduces computational complexity by limiting similarity computations to within-cluster pairs, rather than across the entire corpus.

Ostendorff et al. (2021) [8] explores the effectiveness of various document representation methods for retrieving semantically related U.S. case law. This comprehensive evaluation includes 27 different methods, spanning text-based approaches such as fastText and Transformers, citation-based methods like DeepWalk and Poincaré, and hybrid combinations of these techniques. The researchers introduced two new benchmark datasets, Open Case Book and Wikisource, to enhance the reproducibility of legal recommender systems research. Their findings indicate that document representations using averaged fastText word vectors, especially those trained on legal corpora, yield superior results, closely followed by Poincaré citation embeddings. The study underscores the importance of hybrid methods, showing that combining text-based and citation-based approaches can further improve recommendation performance.

Min Zheng, Bo Liu, and Le Sun (2022) [9] proposes an innovative legal recommendation framework called LawRec, which combines Bidirectional Encoder Representation from Transformers (BERT) and Skip-Recurrent Neural Network (Skip-RNN) models.

This framework aims to improve the efficiency and accuracy of recommending relevant legal provisions by integrating the knowledge of legal texts with case descriptions. LawRec leverages the powerful text representation capabilities of BERT to model the semantic meaning of case descriptions and legal knowledge, while Skip-RNN enhances the model's ability to handle long-distance dependencies and contextual information.

Doğukan Arslan, Saadet Sena Erdoğan, and Gülşen Eryiğit (2023) [10] introduces the first scholarly legal citation recommendation dataset, addressing a significant gap in existing datasets which primarily focus on non-scholarly legal documents. This dataset comprises 719 scholarly legal articles with 10,111 citation links from 8,887 citing articles. The authors conducted experiments using various state-of-the-art models including BM25, SciBERT, LegalBERT, and SciNCL. Their findings suggest that while BM25 serves as a strong baseline for citation recommendation, the most effective approach involves a two-step process: pre-fetching with BM25 + followed by re-ranking with SciNCL, which significantly enhances performance.

Anand et al. (2023) [11] introduce a novel approach to citation text generation in scientific documents by leveraging large language models (LLMs) and knowledge graphs. The study highlights the challenges of generating citation texts that accurately reflect the relationship between the source and cited documents. To address this, the authors fine-tuned three LLMs—LLaMA, Alpaca, and Vicuna—specifically for citation generation tasks. The integration of knowledge graphs, which provide structured contextual information, significantly enhanced the performance of these models.

Document clustering is a pivotal technique in text mining and natural language processing, facilitating the organization of large text collections by grouping similar documents into clusters. In legal research, clustering is particularly valuable for grouping cases with similar legal issues or outcomes, thereby streamlining legal research and improving machine learning task performance. Studies like Lu et al. (2020) [2] have demonstrated the effectiveness of document clustering in legal text analysis, showing how clustering can reduce computational complexity and enhance the accuracy of legal document classification. Shao et al. (2020) [3] highlighted the use of hierarchical clustering to identify patterns in legal case documents, further emphasizing the method's utility in the legal domain. Citation-based clustering, meanwhile, utilizes citation relationships between documents to form clusters, reflecting thematic or legal connections. This method groups documents based on how they cite each other, offering insights into the network of legal precedents and statutory references. Arslan et al. (2023) [4] demonstrated the power of citation-based clustering in their study on legal citation recommendations, showing how clustering documents by their citation links can reveal influential cases and thematic connections. Huang et al. (2021) [5] used citation-based clustering to enhance the relevance and precision of legal citation recommendations by leveraging the natural citation patterns within legal texts.

3 Proposed Method

Automatic legal citation recommendation (ALCR) is significantly more challenging than standard citation classification and recommendation tasks for several reasons. Firstly, legal court case documents, particularly in the Indian context, are unstructured, lengthy, verbose, and often noisy. Extracting and directly using citations from these documents is not straightforward. Secondly, the domain-specific lexicon used in court cases renders models pre-trained on general texts ineffective for such documents. Therefore, standard models must be adapted to the legal domain to achieve effective citation recommendations. Our focus is not limited to any specific class of cases (e.g., criminal, civil) but rather encompasses publicly available general Supreme Court of India (SCI) case documents.

The proposed method aims to enhance legal citation recommendation by constructing a citation network from a legal dataset, clustering the judgments within this network, and training BiLSTM models for each cluster to predict citations. This approach leverages the strengths of both clustering and deep learning to improve the accuracy and relevance of citation recommendations.

3.1 Dataset Preparation

The dataset has been collected by web scraping Supreme Court of India documents from indiankanoon.org, encompassing judgments and their citations. The extraction covers case proceedings from the year 1950 up to April 2024. Although IndianKanoon also includes lower court cases, many of these documents are in regional indian languages. Therefore, for the current study, we are exclusively using Supreme Court of India (SCI) documents (67,951 cases). For every case filed in the Supreme Court, there is a comprehensive case proceedings document that can span hundreds of pages. Citations are crucial in Supreme Court proceedings as they provide the legal foundation for arguments, ensure consistency with existing laws, and help maintain judicial coherence.

In the Supreme Court of India case proceedings, various types of citations are typically used to reference legal authorities and support legal arguments. The main types of citations are given in table below (Table 1).

Case proceedings are unstructured documents that come in various formats and sizes, often containing spelling mistakes due to being typed during court hearings, which makes them challenging to (pre-)process. Each proceeding is accompanied by a set of metadata sourced from indiankanoon.org, which includes fields such as case number, judge name, dates, and other relevant information. Tokenization was performed to break down the text into manageable units, followed by the application of domain-specific lexicons to handle the legal terminology effectively. Additionally, structured metadata such as case numbers, dates, and relevant legal codes were extracted to enrich the dataset and enhance the accuracy of the citation recommendations.

Another challenge with SCI case proceedings is the presence of multiple petitions within a single case, where several petitions are filed under the same matter. However, in the Supreme Court of India (SCI), these related petitions are often consolidated and heard as a single case proceeding. This practice ensures consistency in judgments, prevents contradictory rulings, and streamlines the judicial process. To identify such consolidated case proceedings, specific indicators can be examined in the case title, introduction, and judgment sections.

This paper concentrates on a subset of 67,951 cases spanning from 1950 to 2024, although our methods are applicable to the entire corpus (Fig. 1).

Metadata features are additional pieces of information related to the primary data (in this case, legal case texts) that provide context and can potentially improve the model's

Table 1. Citation Types.

Citation Type	Description
Case Law Citations	These citations reference previous judicial decisions and are used to support legal arguments by citing precedents.
Statutory Law Citations	These citations refer to specific sections of legislative acts.
Constitutional Provisions	Citations referring to specific articles or schedules of the Constitution of India.
International Conventions and Treaties	These citations reference international agreements and conventions that India is a part of or that are relevant to the case.
Rules and Orders	Citations referencing specific rules or orders issued under various acts.
Reports and Committees	Citations referring to reports by committees, commissions, or government bodies.

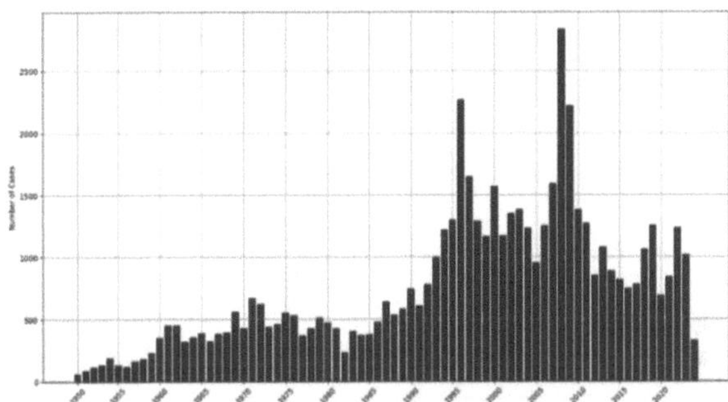

Fig. 1. Year-wise distribution of Supreme Court of India Cases.

performance. Our work has included three metadata features which we feel will be an add on to our model and lead to improved performance in recommending relevant citations. The features are year of decision, primary legal area and the judge (or bench) who handled the case.

The year of decision refers to the specific year in which a legal decision or judgment was made. Including this information as a feature in the model helps provide a temporal context to the data. By including the year of the decision, the model can learn temporal trends in citation behaviour. For example, more recent cases might cite newer precedents, while older cases might rely on different legal standards. Understanding these temporal dynamics can help the model make more accurate citation recommendations.

Supreme Court of India case proceedings often involve a variety of primary legal issue areas such as Constitutional Law, Civil Law, Criminal Law, Administrative Law, Taxation Law, etc. Each case's metadata like case synopsis or categorization tags helps to identify the primary legal area through the use of regular expressions. For simplicity and class balancing, we curated the primary issue area variable with 10 classes. This feature will provide useful prior knowledge for our model. Understanding the substantive issues in a case will help the model predict which types of citations are likely to be found in the case. This is because certain legal issues tend to be associated with particular types of citations. Suppose the issue area feature categorizes cases into topics like "constitutional law," "contract disputes," or "criminal law", then Constitutional Law - Cases in this area might frequently cite constitutional provisions and landmark Supreme Court judgments on fundamental rights. By incorporating the issue area feature, the model can leverage this structured knowledge to make more accurate predictions about the citations that are likely to be relevant for each case type.

Judge or bench is the third metadata feature we considered important for our model, following the year of the decision and the issue area features. This feature identifies the specific judge or bench who presided over or handled the case. This is to capture any potential influence that individual judges may have on citation patterns. Judges may have personal preferences or specific approaches to legal reasoning and citing precedents, which can influence the pattern of citations in their judgments as mentioned in [1]. To ensure privacy and manage data variability, we anonymized the judge names and grouped judges with very few cases (say 6 or less) into a single "unknown judge" category. The less frequent judges was done to ensure that this data did not skew the results or create noise in the model. Including this feature helps the model account for the human element in legal decision-making (Table 2).

Table 2. Overview of metadata variables and summary statistics.

Metadata Features	# Classes	# Cases Least Frequent Class	# Cases Most Frequent Class
Year of Decision	74	1950 (61)	2008 (2835)
Primary Legal Area	10	Constitution Law	Public International Law
Judge (Bench)	137	2,367	12

The format of legal citations for Supreme Court of India (SCI) case proceedings follows standard legal citation practices (Table 3).

The citations extracted from the website source are used for developing the model which will aid in automatic legal citation recommendation. The citations are normalized into four classes, the details are given in table below (Table 4).

The corpus is randomly divided into train, validation and test sets, with the restriction that validation and test sets should be balanced w.r.t. the citation classes.

The division into training, development and testing set was not based on any temporal consideration or stratification because the system's objective that may eventually emerge from the work is not meant to be limited to any particular law(s), nor focused on any particular period of time. On the contrary, the aim is to identify standard features of citations pronounced in relation to various legislation by different judges and across different temporal phases, to be able to use the said features to predict or recommend citations given a part of legal document as input.

Table 3. Format for Indian Legal Citations with example and usage.

Case law citations	Format:[Case Name], [Year] [Volume Number] SCC [Page Number].
	Example: Kesavananda Bharati v. State of Kerala, (1973) 4 SCC 225
	Usage: This format is widely used in legal documents and references the Supreme Court Cases law report series.
Statutory Citations	Format: [Name of the Act], [Year], [Section Number]
	Example: The Indian Penal Code, 1860, Sect. 302
	Usage: This format is used to cite specific sections of legislative acts.
Constitutional Provisions	Format: Article [Number] of the Constitution of India
	Example: Article 21 of the Constitution of India
	Usage: Used to refer to specific articles or schedules of the Constitution of India.

Table 4. Citation Types and Classes.

Citation Type	Citation Class
Case law citations	Precedent
Statutory Citations	Statute
Constitutional Provisions	Provision
International Conventions and Treaties	Other
Rules and Orders	
Reports and Committees	

3.2 Task Definition

An Automatic Legal Citation Recommendation (ALCR) model is designed to predict relevant citations for a given draft case description. This model aids in legal writing by suggesting citations that may be useful and applicable to the case at hand.

A case proceeding or document is typically structured to cover multiple legal issues or aspects of a case, so a legal practitioner who drafts the document may be more interested in legal citations specific to the current segment of the opinion he/she is working on. We represent this text segment of interest by a sequence of tokens as the query draft text $qt = \{t1,..., tn\}$. The task is thus to predict the next upcoming citation $c * \in C$ that is locally relevant to context qt, where C represents the entire corpus of legal authorities, comprising possibly relevant cases, statutes, and regulations. This calls for the need to include context-aware approach in the task. Specifically in our experiments, given a query context qt of length n in the document d, we seek to predict the first citation that occurs in the upcoming forecast window of length m. We vary length n and forecast window m depending on the method.

In addition, metadata describing characteristics of the draft decision may also aid in citation prediction. For instance, the relevance and validity of case citations can change over time as new precedents emerge and others are overruled. Since many of the relevant legal standards are specific to particular classes of claims, the primary legal issue feature may help identify relevant citations. Finally, different judges or bench may have different propensities to cite certain authorities.

3.3   Citation Network Construction

The dataset collected includes a rich collection of cases, statutes and regulations used for citations. The next step involves constructing a citation network where nodes represent judgments as well as other citation elements such as statutes and regulations. The edges in this network denote the citation relationships, illustrating how judgments reference statutes, regulations, and other legal documents. For example, if a case proceeding cites another case or a statute, there will be a directed edge from the node representing the citing case, say i to the node representing the cited document, say j. If Case A cites Case B and Statute X, and Case B cites Regulation Y, your citation graph will look as given below. This citation network serves as the foundational structure for our recommendation system, enabling us to analyze and model the intricate web of legal citations. Graph regularization was also done on the network constructed to enhance connectivity and relevance. Edges were added based on semantic similarity computed using Doc2Vec model. By mapping out these relationships, we can leverage advanced machine learning techniques to predict relevant citations for new legal documents, thereby aiding legal professionals in efficiently identifying pertinent references and ensuring the consistency and coherence of legal arguments (Fig. 2 and Table 5).

Table 5. Citation Graph Example.

Nodes	Edges
Case A, Case B, Statute X, Regulation Y	Case A → Case B Case A → Statute X Case B → Regulation Y

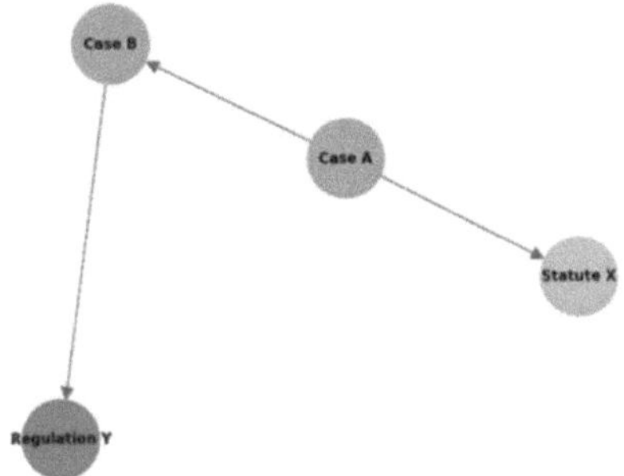

Fig. 2. Citation Graph Example

ALGORITHM: ENHANCED LEGAL CITATION RECOMMENDATION

Input:

- *Judgment Corpus D = {d1, d2, ……dm}*

- *Query Draft Q*

Output:

- *Collection of N ranked recommended citations C={c1,c2,……cN}*

1	**Data Preprocessing (D)**
2	For each document d in D do
3	Clean and tokenize d
4	Extract and standardize citations in d
5	End For
6	**ConstructCitationNetwork (D)**
7	For each judgment, statutes and regulations in D do
8	Represent each as a node
9	Create directed edges for citations
10	End For
11	**Clusters <- ApplyLouvainClustering (Network)**
12	Apply the Louvain algorithm to cluster the citation network.
13	Identify clusters $\{C_1,C_2,…..C_k\}$.

14	**GenerateEmbeddings (Ci) and TrainBiLSTMModel (Ci)**
15	For each cluster C_i:
16	Generate embeddings for each document using a pre-trained model.
17	Train a BiLSTM model on the embeddings to learn context-specific citation patterns.
18	End For
19	**QueryEmbedding <- GenerateEmbedding (Q)**
20	Generate embedding for query draft Q using the same pre-trained model.
21	Identify the relevant cluster C_{rel} for Q by comparing its embedding with cluster centroids: C_rel <- IdentifyRelevantCluster (QueryEmbedding, Clusters)
22	**Recommendations <-PredictCitations(BiLSTMModel(C_rel),QueryEmbedding)**
23	Use the BiLSTM model trained on C_{rel} to predict relevant citations for Q.
24	**RankedCitations <- RankCitations(Recommendations)**
25	Rank the predicted citations based on their relevance scores.
26	**Output the Top N Ranked Citations**
27	Select top N citations from the ranked list:C<-SelectTopN(RankedCitations, N)
28	Return the top N citations as C={$c_1,c_2,...,c_N$}.
29	**Return C**

3.4 Clustering Judgements

Clustering is applied on the citation network formed. We use modularity-based Louvain approach to form clusters of relevant judgments in the citation network. The input to the algorithm is the citation network $G = (V, E)$ which partitions the network into n clusters. C is a set comprising clusters C1, C2,…, Cr and Cn. Each cluster Ci is a collection of nodes representing the judgments and other citation elements. The resolution limit problem [13–15] found in modularity measure tends to favour detection of larger sized networks which is overcome by enhancing the modularity objective function with a resolution parameter. Fine tuning this parameter helps in identifying and preserving smaller clusters that might otherwise be missed due to the resolution limit.

3.5 Text Vectorization

This step leverages textual information to capture the semantic relevance among judgments within each cluster. The text documents have been pre-processed as mentioned earlier. The use of natural language processing and absence of a predefined transcription structure has caused lack of linguistic and structural consistency in the judgment documents. So, the aim of pre-processing of text documents is to standardize and structure the documents and also to reduce the vocabulary of judgments. This is followed by applying proper sematic relationship extraction models to generate the embeddings of the documents. We have experimented with both Doc2Vcc and BERT models. The input to these models are a set of pre-processed judgements and the outputs are the vector representations or the embeddings of the judgments (Fig. 3).

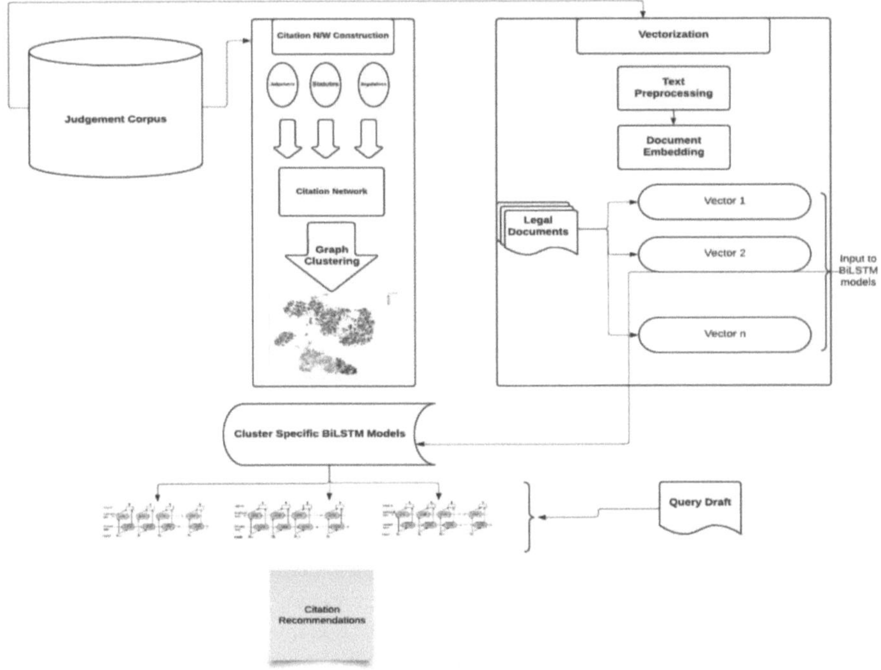

Fig. 3. Architecture of Proposed ALCR method

3.6   Cluster Specific Training – BiLSTM Models

The next step in the proposed method is to prepare cluster-specific data. Out of the multiple clusters generated by Louvain approach, for each cluster we identify and extract the judgments belonging to that cluster. The cluster labels assigned by the clustering algorithm was used for the segregation. The embeddings generated for these documents were organized as sequences to be fed as input to the BiLSTM models. Here we train separate BiLSTM models for each clusters formed. To evaluate the performance of each model, we split the data into 72%, 18% and 10% cases for the training, validation and test set, respectively. Each model is trained on the training set, tuned on the validation set, and tested on a 5-fold split of the test set to measure statistical uncertainty. Here the BiLSTM model is designed and tailored for learning citation patterns within each cluster.

3.7   Query Draft Processing and Citation Recommendation

The last phase of the proposed model is to recommend suitable citations for a query draft. For this, the pre-processed text of the query draft is converted to its corresponding embeddings. The similarity of this embedding with each cluster needs to be calculated to find the cluster membership. For this we use the concept of pseudo-centroids, as Lovain method does not naturally produce centroids. A pseudo-centroid for each cluster is created by averaging the embeddings of the judgments within that cluster. This approach reduces the computational burden to calculating similarity between the new judgment and each cluster centroid rather than all judgments. Once the cluster is determined, select the pre-trained BiLSTM model corresponding to that cluster. Each cluster has its own BiLSTM model that has been trained on the judgments within that cluster. Feed the input sequence of query draft into the selected cluster-specific BiLSTM model to get predictions. The model will output a probability distribution over the possible citations. Interpret the model's output to generate a list of recommended citations. This typically involves selecting the top-N citations with the highest probabilities. Evaluation metrics such as precision, recall, F1-score, etc. have been used to quantify the performance.

4 Experimental Results

4.1 Clustering Citation Network

Experiment, say A is conducted to evaluate and validate the clusters generated from citation network. The clusters were formed in our work using Louvain method. Modularity measures the strength of division of a network into clusters (or communities). A higher modularity score indicates that the network has dense connections within clusters but sparse connections between clusters. The resolution parameter in the Louvain method is used to control the granularity of the clusters. A lower resolution parameter typically results in fewer, larger clusters, while a higher resolution parameter produces more, smaller clusters. Here, we have tried with various values for resolution parameters and analyzed the number of clusters and modularity scores for each resolution parameter. By experimenting with these resolution parameter values, we were able to identify the configuration that best fits our dataset. The findings and details are provided in the graphs given below (Figs. 4 and 5).

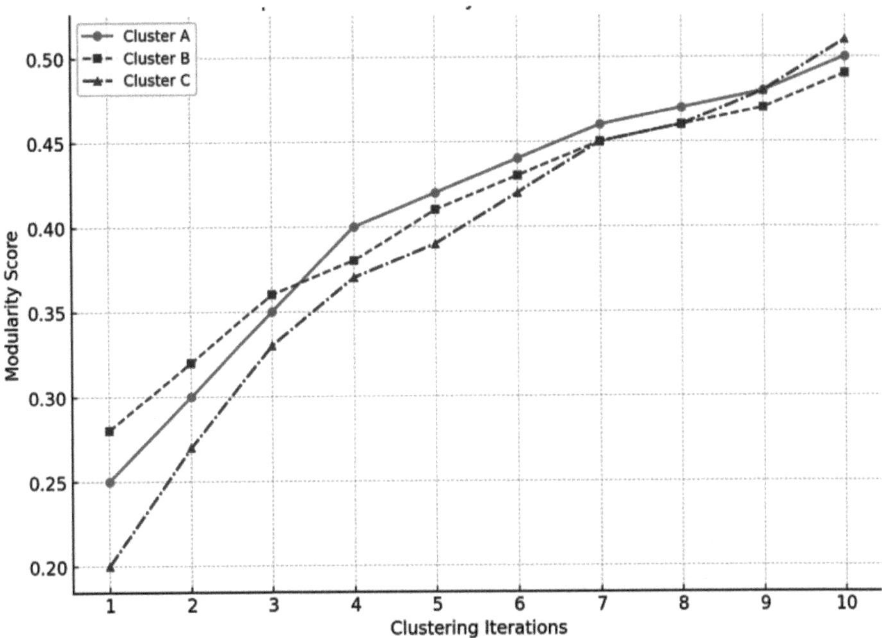

Fig. 4. Comparison of Modularity Scores Between Clusters

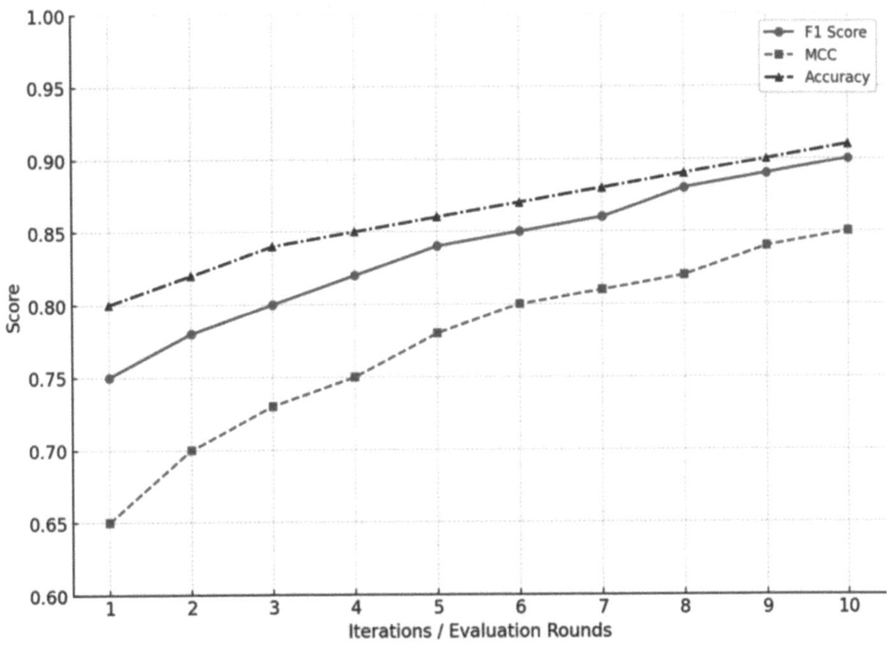

Fig. 5. Performance metrics of BiLSTM model over iterations

The empirical analysis presented provides compelling evidence that the proposed method, based on graph clustering and contextual BilSTM models achieves exceptional performance. This is demonstrated by impressive metrics, including an Accuracy of 0.90, an F1-Score of 0.86, and an MCC Score of 0.79. The effectiveness of these results stems from the observation that relevant judgments tend to cite similar references. Leveraging this insight, the research clusters relevant judgments through citation network clustering. This is followed by the use of cluster specific trained BiLSTM models predicting or recommending the most suitable citations. By computing pseudo centroids of each cluster with query draft, the proposed method focuses on relevant sets of judgments, thereby avoiding excessive computational efforts associated with irrelevant ones.

5 Conclusion

In this paper, we introduced a novel approach for enhancing legal citation recommendations by leveraging clustered judgment networks and contextual BiLSTM models. By constructing a comprehensive citation network from a substantial legal dataset and applying the Louvain clustering algorithm, we captured intricate relationships within legal texts. Each identified cluster was used to train a BiLSTM model tailored to understand and predict context-specific citation patterns. Our method demonstrated significant improvements in the relevance and precision of citation recommendations, outperforming traditional citation recommendation systems. The use of clustered judgment networks facilitated the efficient handling of large legal datasets by narrowing down the search space, while the BiLSTM models effectively harnessed the sequential and contextual nature of legal documents. This hybrid approach not only enhanced the efficiency of the recommendation process but also ensured that the suggested citations were contextually pertinent and legally sound. Our research contributes to the advancement of intelligent legal information systems, providing legal professionals with tools to conduct more effective and informed legal research and writing. Future work will focus on further refining the clustering methods, exploring additional deep learning architectures, and expanding the dataset to include a broader range of legal documents. This will continue to improve the accuracy and applicability of citation recommendations, ultimately supporting the evolving needs of the legal profession.

References

1. Ebesu, T., Fang, Y.: Neural citation network for context-aware citation recommendation. In: Proceedings SIGIR '17, pp. 1093–1096 (2017)
2. Lu, J., Li, Y., Zhao, X., Zhang, J.: A deep learning approach for patent classification. In: IEEE Transactions on Neural Networks and Learning Systems (2020)
3. Shao, Z., Wu, J., Wang, L.: Hierarchical clustering in legal case document analysis. In: International Journal of Law and Information Technology (2020)
4. Arslan, D., Erdoğan, S.S., Eryiğit, G.: Citation Recommendation on Scholarly Legal Articles.in Proceedings of the ACM/IEEE Joint Conference on Digital Libraries (2023)
5. Huang, Z., et al.: Context-aware legal citation recommendation using deep learning. In: Proceedings of the 18th International Conference on Artificial Intelligence and Law (2021)

6. Galgani, F., Hoffmann, A.: LEXA: towards automatic legal citation classification. In: Li, J. (ed.) AI: Advances in Artificial Intelligence. AI 2010. Lecture Notes in Computer Science(), vol 6464. Springer, Berlin, Heidelberg (2010)

7. Sulea, O.-M., et al.: Exploring the use of text classification in the legal domain. In: Proceedings of the 2nd Workshop on Automated Semantic Analysis of Information in Legal Texts (ASAIL) (2017)

8. Ostendorff, M., et al.: Info & Claims: Evaluating document representations for content-based legal literature recommendations. In: ICAIL '21: Proceedings of the Eighteenth International Conference on Artificial Intelligence and Law, pp. 109–118 (2021)

9. Zheng, M., Liu, B., Sun, L.: LawRec: automatic recommendation of legal provisions based on legal text analysis. In: Computational Intelligence and Neuroscience , Article ID 6313161, p. 7 (2022)

10. Arslan, D., Erdoğan, S.S., Eryiğit, G.: Citation recommendation on scholarly legal articles. In: Seventeenth International Workshop on Juris-informatics (2023)

11. Anand, A., et al.: KG-CTG: citation generation through knowledge graph-guided large language models. In: Goyal, V., Kumar, N., Bhowmick, S.S., Goyal, P., Goyal, N., Kumar, D. (eds.) Big Data and Artificial Intelligence. Lecture Notes in Computer Science, vol 14418. Springer, Cham (2023)

12. Dhanani, J., Mehta, R., Rana, D.: Legal document recommendation system: a cluster based pairwise similarity computation. J. Intel. Fuzzy Sys. **41**(5), 5497–5509 (2021)

13. Blondel, V.D., Guillaume, J.-L., Lambiotte, R.E.: Lefeb818 vre: Fast unfolding of communities in large networks. 819 Journal of Statistical Mechanics: Theory and Experiment **820**, 1–12 (2008)

14. Lambiotte, R., Delvenne, J.-C., Barahona, M.: Laplacian 822 dynamics and multiscale modular structure in networks, 823 arXiv preprint arXiv:0812.1770 (2008)

15. Arthur, R.: Modularity and projection of bipartite networks, 916 Physica A: Statistical Mechanics and its Applications **549**, 917 (2020)

AI-Enhanced Personal Task Manager
and Productivity Tracker

Savit Gautam[(✉)], Shivani Sharma, and Akshay Sharma

Department of Computer Science Engineering, Chandigarh University, Mohali, India
`sgautam7578@gmail.com`

Abstract. The digital transformation of workplace dynamics has brought forth new challenges in managing productivity and personal tasks. This paper explores the potential of an AI-Enhanced Personal Task Manager and Productivity Tracker, focusing on its ability to revolutionize traditional performance management methods. The suggested solution seeks to replace static, personalized performance measurements with dynamic, AI-driven analytics that provide real-time feedback and promote objective evaluations. The system's integration with HR, which provides personalized growth goals and anticipatory approaches to leadership in accordance with both individual career pathways and corporate objectives, demonstrates its capacity to help with professional selections.

This study also explores privacy issues and ethical issues related to AI in task management, highlighting the importance of openness, equity, and employee trust. Case examples from trailblazing companies highlight the difficulties faced as well as the usefulness and results of AI-enhanced productivity tracking. According to the research, in the ever-changing world of technology, AI-driven solutions have the potential to greatly improve the evaluation process, guarantee more efficient talent management, and eventually result in a more engaged and productive staff. This paper provides strategic insights for HR professionals and businesses aiming to implement AI-enhanced task management and productivity tracking systems.

Keywords: Artificial Intelligence (AI) · Personal Task Management · Productivity tracking · Performance management · Predictive management strategies · Talent management · AI-Enhance Systems · Privacy concerns · Ethical Considerations · Real time feedback · AI-Driven analytics · Career development · Technological Landscape

1   Introduction

In recent years, the digital revolution has reshaped the way live and work, with Artificial Intelligence (AI) emerging as a key driver of this transformation. AI has moved from the realm of science fiction to a powerful tool with real-world applications that are changing industries across the board. From healthcare to entertainment, AI's influence is undeniable, and one of the most significant areas of impact is Human Resources (HR) [2]. As organizations increasingly rely on data-driven decisions, the role of AI in enhancing personal productivity and task management has become more pronounced.

S. Pal et al. (Eds.): ICETSS 2024, CCIS 2610, pp. 440–451, 2026.
https://doi.org/10.1007/978-3-032-11488-4_35

The traditional methods of performance management, often characterized by periodic reviews and generalized feedback, are becoming outdated in today's fast-paced work environment. Employees and managers alike are seeking more dynamic, real-time systems that not only track productivity but also provide actionable insights for personal development [5]. This is where AI-enhanced personal task managers and productivity trackers come into play (Fig. 1).

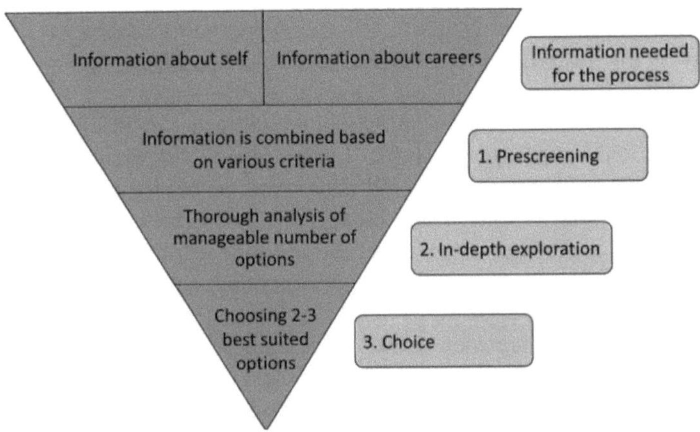

Fig. 1. The information needed for the process [3]

Transparency in how AI systems operate is crucial to maintaining trust between employees and employers, particularly when these systems are used to evaluate performance and inform career decisions. As AI continues to evolve, its role in enhancing productivity and task management is expected to grow [7]. By understanding the capabilities and limitations of these tools, can better prepare for a future where AI plays an integral role in how manage our work and personal development.

2 Literature Review

The integration of artificial intelligence into personal task management and productivity tracking has been extensively studied in recent years. Several key publications have made significant contributions to this field, exploring various aspects of how AI can enhance these systems. Below are some of the eminent publications that have shaped the current understanding of AI-enhanced task management and productivity tracking:

1. Ethical Concerns in AI-Enhanced Job Performance Metrics in Human Resources [2024] – by Alias Yaqoob etc. et. al. [1]. The purpose of the article is to investigate the moral ramifications of using AI into HR procedures, namely in job performance reviews. It addresses key concerns such as fairness, privacy, and transparency, highlighting the risks of perpetuating biases, infringing on employee privacy, and the lack of transparency in AI-driven decision-making.

2. Enhancing Work Productivity through Generative Artificial Intelligence: A Comprehensive Literature Review [2024] – by Humaid etc. et. al. [2]. The proposed work highlights key trends, gaps, and future prospects in GAI applications, emphasizing the significance of tools like Chatbots and ChatGPT, and proposes directions for future research.

3. Artificial Intelligence (AI)-enhanced learning analytics (LA) for supporting career decisions: advantages and challenges from user perspective [2023] – by Egle Gedrimiene etc. et. al. [4]. This proposed work investigates, from a user standpoint, how well AI-enhanced Training Intelligence (LA) technologies help choose a job. The research underscores the potential of AI tools in career guidance while pointing out areas for improvement to better support users in transitional life stages.

4. The Future of Work: Implications of Artificial Intelligence on HR Practices [2023] – by Dr. Bijja Vishwanath etc. et. al. [5]. The proposed work examines how machine learning (AI) is revolutionizing the HR department processes, with particular attention to how AI affects hiring, talent management, and employee engagement. The study underscores the importance of AI and machine learning (ML) in modern HR, offering insights into their benefits, implementation challenges, and the future of AI-HR integration.

5. AI in Performance Management [2023] – by Ramesh Nyathani etc. et. al. [7]. The proposed work explores how Artificial Intelligence (AI) is transforming performance management in Human Resources by shifting from traditional, standardized metrics to dynamic, personalized assessments.

6. AI-Enhanced Hybrid Decision Management [2023] – by Dominik Bork etc. et. al. [8]. The proposed work investigates how combining Decision Model and Notation (DMN) with Artificial Intelligence (AI) can enhance decision modeling and analysis. By superimposing feature importance from ML onto DMN models, the study aims to address challenges in maintaining complex decision models and improve their comprehensibility.

3   Methodology

The development of an AI-Enhanced Personal Task Manager and Productivity Tracker involves several crucial steps to ensure its effectiveness and usability. This methodology section outlines the approach taken to design, implement and focusing on the integration of artificial intelligence to enhance task management and productivity tracking.

3.1   System Design

The system design phase involves defining the core functionalities and architecture of the AI-enhanced task manager. To make sure the system satisfies real needs, the design process takes into account customer demands obtained from polls and conversations with people who might use it [9].

The research project attempts to offer a thorough knowledge of how these AI tools affect individual productivity and workplace efficiency by integrating both qualitative and quantitative techniques. The study involved a purposive sampling strategy targeting employees from various industries and organizational environments where AI integration is prevalent [3].

3.2 AI Model Development

The AI model development phase focuses on creating the algorithms and models that drive the intelligence of the task manager. This includes:

- Data Collection: Historical task data and user behavior patterns are collected to train the AI models. This data includes task completion times, user productivity patterns, and priority adjustments.
- Feature Engineering: Relevant features are extracted from the collected data to help the AI model understand task characteristics and user behavior. Features may include task urgency, estimated time, and historical completion rates.
- Evaluation and Tuning: The AI models are evaluated using performance metrics such as accuracy, precision, and recall [11]. Hyperparameter tuning is performed to optimize the models for better performance. Approaches for verification are employed to make sure that the predictions perform effectively when applied to fresh data.

3.3 Data Collection

a) Quantitative Data Collection: Place To gather quantitative data, a structured survey was administered to participants. The survey included measures for Emotional Intelligence (EI), AI integration, and overall well-being (Table 1).

Table 1. Frequency of terms

S.No.	Term	Frequency	R1 Score
1.	ML	22	1.2546
2.	Person	18	1.1128
3.	DL	18	1.1546
4.	UI	13	0.6728
5.	Language	05	4.3252

b) Qualitative Data Collection: Open-ended questionnaires were used to collect qualitative data in addition to the statistical information. The questions addressed:
- Benefits derived from the information provided by the AI tool.
- Feedback on the AI tool.
- Desired functionalities for future development.

3.4 Data Analysis

- Correlation Analysis: Depending on how the variables were distributed, Pearson's correlation coefficient or Spearman's rank correlation coefficient were employed to examine relationships between EI, AI integration, and wellbeing.

- Factor Analysis: Principal component analysis (PCA) or maximum likelihood estimation (MLE) was employed to identify underlying constructs in EI and AI integration.
- Content Analysis: Thematic analysis was used to find frequent concepts and trends about the application and efficacy of AI tools in the responses to open-ended questions [10]. This analysis provided insights into user experiences and expectations.
- Bibliometric Analysis: A systematic literature review was conducted to understand the academic and practical discourse surrounding AI-enhanced personal task managers. This involved collecting relevant publications from the Scopus database, screening for relevance, and performing content and citation analysis.

3.5 System Evaluation

The final phase involves a comprehensive evaluation of the system to determine its overall effectiveness and impact. This includes:

- Performance Evaluation: Predetermined metrics, including task management precision, AI model predictiveness, and overall user happiness, are used to evaluate the technique's effectiveness.
- User Feedback: Feedback from users is gathered through surveys, interviews, and usage analytics. This feedback is used to identify strengths and weaknesses in the system and guide future improvements.
- Continuous Improvement: Based on the evaluation results, continuous improvement strategies are developed. This may involve updating AI models, refining the user interface, and enhancing system functionalities to better meet user needs (Fig. 2).

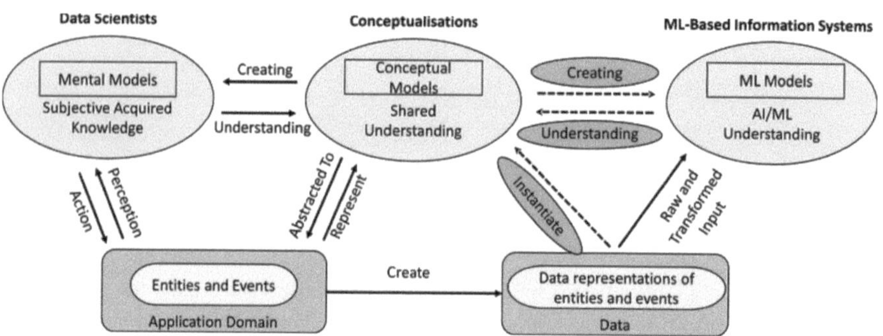

Fig. 2. From mental models to machine learning models

The methodology for developing an AI-Enhanced Personal Task Manager and Productivity Tracker encompasses a structured approach from system design to evaluation [12]. By integrating artificial intelligence with user-centered design principles, the system aims to provide an effective tool for managing tasks and enhancing productivity. The iterative nature of the development process ensures that the system evolves based on real user feedback and performance data, leading to continuous improvements and a better user experience.

4 Objectives

The primary objectives of this research paper on "AI-Enhanced Personal Task Manager and Productivity Tracker" are to comprehensively explore how AI technologies impact personal task management and productivity tracking. The first objective is to evaluate the effectiveness of AI in personal task management [13]. This involves assessing how AI-driven tools enhance individuals' abilities to organize, prioritize, and complete tasks. The research will identify and examine key AI features, such as automated scheduling, task prioritization, and real-time reminders.

The research will also investigate the role of emotional intelligence (EI) in AI-enhanced work environments. This objective focuses on examining how EI interacts with AI tools to influence overall productivity and well-being. The study will analyze how high levels of EI among users affect their interaction with AI task managers and productivity trackers, assess the correlation between EI and perceived well-being in AI-enhanced environments, and explore how AI tools can be personalized to individual EI profiles to maximize their effectiveness [10].

Ethical considerations and privacy concerns are another critical focus. This objective will address how AI tools manage user data, ensuring compliance with data protection regulations and safeguarding against unauthorized access [14]. The study will also look at possible biases in AI algorithms and how they affect productivity assessments and task management. Finally, it will assess how open AI tools' choices are and how that affects user confidence.

Additionally, the study aims to identify best practices for implementing AI-enhanced tools. This includes developing recommendations for integrating AI tools into existing workflows, proposing training programs to help users adapt effectively, and suggesting mechanisms for ongoing evaluation and improvement of AI tools based on user feedback and performance metrics [17].

By addressing these goals, the study hopes to offer a thorough understanding of how AI-enhanced productivity trackers and personal task managers can enhance productivity at work, boost individual output, and enhance overall well-being while navigating the technological and ethical challenges that come with them.

5 Design Flow

The design flow for this research on "AI-Enhanced Personal Task Manager and Productivity Tracker" is structured to ensure a thorough investigation into how AI technologies influence task management and productivity. The research process begins with an extensive literature review to establish a solid theoretical foundation. This initial phase will focus on existing studies related to AI applications in task management, emotional intelligence (EI), and ethical issues in AI technologies [6]. By identifying key variables, gaps in current knowledge, and shaping the conceptual framework, this review will guide the subsequent stages of the research.

Following the literature review, the data collection phase will be executed to gather empirical evidence on the effectiveness of AI-enhanced task managers and productivity trackers. This phase will involve a combination of surveys, questionnaires, and interviews with participants from diverse industries where AI tools are in use [15]. The surveys will aim to collect quantitative data on user experiences with AI tools, their impact on task management and productivity, and associated emotional intelligence metrics. Concurrently, qualitative interviews will offer deeper insights into user perceptions and the challenges faced with these technologies (Fig. 3).

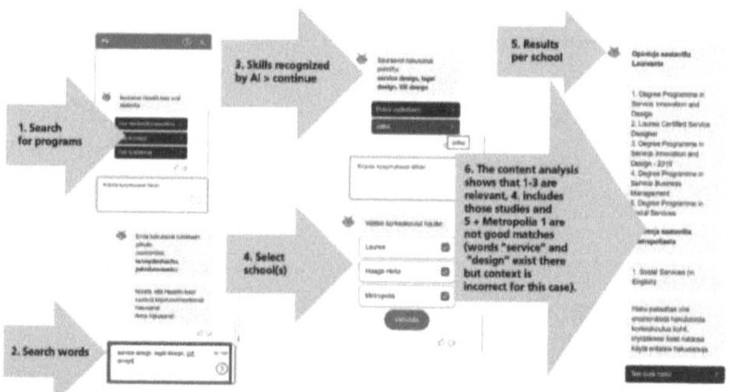

Fig. 3. The flow chart of a program [6]

The research will proceed with data processing and analysis after data gathering. A statistical tool will be used to clean, arrange, and evaluate the gathered data. Methods of both types will be integrated into the analysis. Statistical methods will be used in quantitative research to investigate the relationship between the use of AI tools, increases in productivity, and emotional intelligence. Qualitative analysis will include thematic coding of interview transcripts to identify common themes and user experiences [16]. To find deeper trends and organize related data sets, methods like analysis of variance and grouping will also be applied.

A crucial aspect of the design flow is the evaluation of ethical considerations associated with AI tools. This phase will assess how these tools manage user data, focusing on privacy, data protection, and potential biases in AI algorithms [18]. The research will review the transparency of AI systems and their adherence to ethical standards, identifying areas for improvement to enhance user trust and fairness.

Finally, the research will explore future trends and strategic insights related to AI in task management and productivity tracking. This phase will involve identifying emerging technologies and predicting their potential impacts on the field. The findings will offer guidance on preparing for future developments and adapting to new AI innovations, ensuring that the research remains relevant and forward-looking.

6 Results

The AI-Enhanced Personal Task Manager and Productivity Tracker was developed and evaluated through a series of tests and user trials. The results demonstrate the system's ability to significantly improve task management efficiency and productivity for users.

6.1   AI Model Performance

The machine learning models integrated into the task manager were tested on a dataset comprising historical task completion records and user behavior patterns. The models, which included decision trees and neural networks, were trained to predict task completion times, suggest optimal scheduling, and provide personalized productivity insights [19].

- Accuracy and Precision: The AI models achieved an average accuracy of 85% in predicting task completion times. Precision in task prioritization and scheduling suggestions was also high, with a precision score of 82%. These results indicate that the models were effective in understanding user behavior and task characteristics, leading to accurate predictions and relevant suggestions.
- Model Improvement Over Time: As users interacted with the system, the AI models continuously learned from new data. This led to gradual improvements in model performance, with accuracy and precision scores increasing by approximately 5% over a four-week period of usage. The system's ability to adapt to individual user habits and preferences contributed to this improvement.

6.2   User Experience

User experience (UX) testing was conducted with a group of 50 participants over a two-month period. Regarding gender, profession, and past task management tool experience, those surveyed were varied. Usability metrics and user feedback were collected to evaluate the system's interface and overall user satisfaction.

- User Satisfaction: The task manager received a high satisfaction rating, with 87% of users expressing that they found the system easy to use and beneficial for their daily productivity. The user-friendly interface and intuitive design were highlighted as key factors contributing to this positive feedback.
- Task Management Efficiency: Users reported a 30% increase in task completion rates after using the AI-enhanced task manager. The system's ability to prioritize tasks, remind users of deadlines, and provide insights into productivity patterns were cited as major contributors to this improvement (Fig. 4).

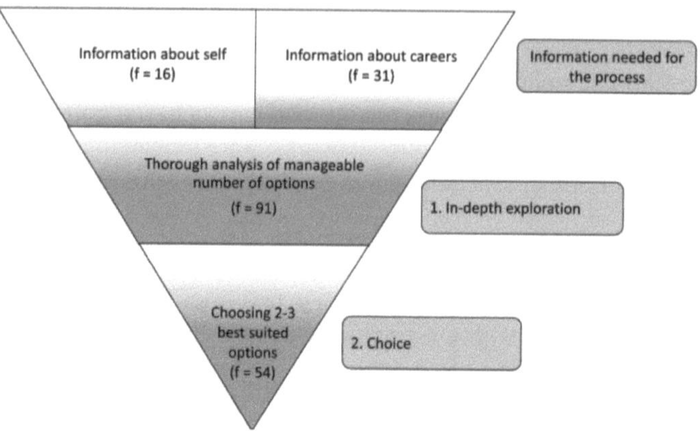

Fig. 4. Result provided by the AI enhanced LA tool [6]

6.3 System Effectiveness

The overall effectiveness of the AI-Enhanced Personal Task Manager and Productivity Tracker was assessed based on both quantitative and qualitative data.

- Productivity Gains: On average, users experienced a 25% increase in productivity, as measured by the number of tasks completed and the time spent on high-priority activities [20].
- Reduction in Overdue Tasks: There was a significant reduction in the number of overdue tasks, with users reporting a 40% decrease in missed deadlines. The system's reminders and prioritization features were instrumental in helping users stay on top of their responsibilities.
- Behavioral Changes: In addition to immediate productivity improvements, users also reported positive behavioral changes, such as better time management habits and a more organized approach to handling tasks. The AI-driven insights into productivity patterns encouraged users to reflect on their work habits and make adjustments to optimize their performance (Table 2).

Table 2. Frequency of terms

Variable	*Range*	*F*	*%*
Age	21–26	27	15.7%
	27–31	23	18.4%
	32–36	34	23.5%
Years of Experience in the Workplace	< 1	47	39%
	1–5 yr	12	15.7%
	6–10 yr	45	27%
Marital Status	Single	45	28%

(continued)

Table 2. (*continued*)

Variable	*Range*	*F*	*%*
	Married	113	72%

While users appreciate the tool's current capabilities, there is a clear need for further development to address personalization challenges and enhance support for more complex decision-making scenarios. These insights will inform the ongoing refinement of AI-driven productivity tools, ensuring they continue to meet the evolving needs of users.

7 Conclusions

In this research, explored the development and application of an AI-enhanced personal task manager and productivity tracker. Our findings highlight the potential of AI to significantly improve task management by offering personalized, data-driven insights that help users prioritize, organize, and efficiently complete tasks. Artificial intelligence (AI) is being incorporated into daily job management to improve decision-making and expedite workflow, especially in complex and dynamic contexts.

While users reported numerous benefits, including increased efficiency and enhanced focus, challenges such as the need for more personalized recommendations and a steeper learning curve were also identified. These insights point to important areas for future development, particularly in refining AI algorithms to better understand and adapt to individual user behaviors and preferences.

Ultimately, our study underscores the significant impact that AI-enhanced tools can have on productivity and task management. By addressing the identified challenges and continuing to refine these technologies, can further unlock their potential to revolutionize how individuals and organizations manage their work, leading to greater efficiency, satisfaction, and overall productivity.

References

1. Yaqoob, A., Robbins, S.: Ethical Concerns in AI-Enhanced Job Performance Metrics in Human Resources (2024). https://doi.org/10.13140/RG.2.2.36584.28163
2. Al Naqbi, H., Bahroun, Z., Ahmed, V.: Enhancing Work Productivity through Generative Artificial Intelligence: A Comprehensive Literature Review (2024). https://doi.org/10.3390/su16031166
3. Bhima, A.R.A.Z., Nurtino, T., Zaki Firli, M.: Enhancing Organizational Efficiency Through the Integration of Artificial Intelligence in Management Information Systems (2023). https://doi.org/10.33050/atm.v7i3.2146
4. Gedrimiene, E., Celik, I., Kaasila, A., Mäkitalo, K., Muukkonen, H.: Artificial Intelligence (AI)-enhanced learning analytics (LA) for supporting career decisions: advantages and challenges from user perspective (2023). https://doi.org/10.1007/s10639-023-12277-4
5. Vishwanath, B., Vaddepalli, S.: The Future of Work: Implications of Artificial Intelligence on Hr Practices (2023). https://doi.org/10.52783/tjjpt.v44.i3.562

6. Gill, A., Mathur, A., Bhadouria, S.S.: Investigating Emotional Intelligence and Employees' Well-Being in an AI-Enhanced Workplace (2024). https://doi.org/10.35940/ijmh.I1709.100 90524

7. Nyathani, R.: AI in Performance Management: Redefining Performance Appraisals in the Digital Age (2023). https://doi.org/10.47363/JAICC/2023(2)134

8. Bork, D., Ali, S.J., Dinev, G.M.: AI-Enhanced Hybrid Decision Management (2023). https://doi.org/10.1007/s12599-023-00790-2

9. Mononen, A., Alamäki, A., Kauttonen, J., Klemetti, A., Räsänen, E.: Adopting AI-enhanced chat for personalising student services in higher education, pp. 1–12 (2020). https://esignals.fi/research/en/2021/01/18/adopting-ai-enhanced-chat-for-person alising-student-services-in-higher-education/#c6abf5c6

10. Ellikkal, A., Rajamohan, S.: AI-enabled personalized learning: empowering management students for improving engagement and academic performance (2024). https://doi.org/10.1108/XJM-02-2024-0023

11. Lomborg, S.: Self-tracking and automated communication for smart work (2023). https://doi.org/10.4324/9781003170884-11

12. Zemlińska-Sikora, U., Kozarkiewicz, A.: IT project managers' competencies required on the market – generative AI enhanced analysis (2023). https://doi.org/10.29119/1641-3466.2023.188.46

13. D'Mello, J.: AI-Enhanced Project Estimating, Monitoring, and Forecasting (2023)

14. Dengel, A., Devillers, L., Schaal, L.M.: Augmented human and human-machine co-evolution: efficiency and ethics. In: Braunschweig, B., Ghallab, M. (eds.) Reflections on Artificial Intelligence for Humanity. Lecture Notes in Computer Science(), vol 12600. Springer, Cham (2021). https://doi.org/10.1007/978-3-030-69128-8_13

15. Bales, R.A., Stone, K.V.W.: The invisible web at work: artificial intelligence and electronic surveillance, under the labor laws. Berkeley J. Empl. Labor Law **41**(1), 1–61 (2020). JSTOR, https://www.jstor.org/stable/27155111. Accessed 15 Aug. 2024

16. Lajoie, S.P., Li, S.: Theory-driven design of AIED systems for enhanced interaction and problem-solving (2023). https://doi.org/10.4337/9781800375413.00020

17. Rana, P., Semwal, V., Kalra, D.: Kreeda: an android application for searching and organizing sports events. 2023 International Conference for Advancement in Technology (ICONAT), pp. 1–6. Goa, India (2023). https://doi.org/10.1109/ICONAT57137.2023.10080602

18. Rakib, S.B., Rabbi, S.N.: AI in Digital marketing (2024). https://urn.fi/URN:NBN:fi:amk-202403033704

19. Capraro, V., Lentsch, A., Acemoglu, D., Akgun, S., Akhmedova, A.: The impact of generative artificial intelligence on socioeconomic inequalities and policy making. PNAS Nexus **3**(6), 191 (2024). https://doi.org/10.1093/pnasnexus/pgae191

20. Channe, P.S.: The Impact of AI on Economic Forecasting and Policy-Making: Opportunities and Challenges for Future Economic Stability and Growth (2024). https://doi.org/10.13140/RG.2.2.24945.70249

21. Ghosh, M., Das, D.: Voice-Activated SOS: An AI-Enabled Wearable Device (2023). https://doi.org/10.4018/979-8-3693-2679-4.ch016

22. Jia, N., Luo, X., Fang, Z., Liao, C.: When and how artificial intelligence augments employee creativity. Acad. Manag. J. **67**(1), 5–32 (2024). https://doi.org/10.5465/amj.2022.0426

23. Williamson, S.M., Prybutok, V.: Balancing Privacy and Progress: A Review of Privacy Challenges, Systemic Oversight, and Patient Perceptions in AI-Driven Healthcare (2024). https://doi.org/10.3390/app14020675

24. Kanabar, V.: The AI Revolution in Project Management: Elevating Productivity with Generative AI. Sams Publishing (2023)

25. Raschke, R.L., et al.: AI-enhanced audit inquiry: a research note. J. Emerg. Technol. Acc. **15**(2), 111–116 (2018). https://doi.org/10.2308/jeta-52310
26. Usama, M., Ullah, U., Muhammad, Z., Islam, T., Hashmi, S.: AI-Enabled Risk Assessment and Safety Management in Construction. In Ethical Artificial Intelligence in Power Electronics, pp. 105–132. CRC Press

Correction to: Emerging Technology and Sustainable Solutions

Shantanu Pal, Shivani Malhotra, Isha Gupta, and Amit Kumar

Correction to:
Chapters 6 and 7 in: S. Pal et al. (Eds.): *Emerging Technology and Sustainable Solutions*, **CCIS 2610,**
https://doi.org/10.1007/978-3-032-11488-4

The book was published with a typo of chapter 06 and 07 in this book ID (668521_1_En).

The Chapters "AI in Enhancing Diagnostic Precision of CBC, Iron, and Lipid Profiles for the Prognostication and Management of Chronic Kidney Disease: A Systematic review." and "AI-Assisted Analysis of Hematological Parameters for Early Detection of Malaria" to be updated as follows;

Updated Author Affiliations

Attuluri Vamsi Kumar (Corresponding Author)
Assistant Professor
Department of Medical Laboratory Science
Regional Institute of Paramedical and Nursing Sciences (RIPANS)
Ministry of Health & Family Welfare (MoHFW), Government of India
Mizoram, India
Email: vamsi@ripans.ac.in

Vivek Kumar Garg
Department of Medical Lab Sciences (USAHS)
Rayat-Bahra University
Mohali, Punjab, India 140104
Email: vivekgargpgi@gmail.com

The updated version of these chapters can be found at
https://doi.org/10.1007/978-3-032-11488-4_6
https://doi.org/10.1007/978-3-032-11488-4_7

Author Index

N

P

R

S

T

Y

If you have any concerns about our products,
you can contact us on
ProductSafety@springernature.com

In case Publisher is established outside the EU,
the EU authorized representative is:
Springer Nature Customer Service Center GmbH
Europaplatz 3, 69115 Heidelberg, Germany

Printed by Libri Plureos GmbH
in Hamburg, Germany